Philip
Ma
C000278306

OXFORD MEDICAL PUBLICATIONS

Contemporary Approaches to the Study of Hysteria

Oxford University Press makes no representation, express or implied, that the drug dosages in this book are correct. Readers must therefore always check the product information and clinical procedures with the most up to date published product information and data sheets provided by the manufacturers and the most recent codes of conduct and safety regulations. The authors and the publishers do not accept responsibility or legal liability for any errors in the text or for the misuse or misapplication of material in this work.

Contemporary Approaches to the Study of Hysteria

Edited by Peter W. Halligan, Christopher Bass, and John C. Marshall

OXFORD
UNIVERSITY PRESS

OXFORD
UNIVERSITY PRESS

Great Clarendon Street, Oxford OX2 6DP

Oxford University Press is a department of the University of Oxford.
It furthers the University's objective of excellence in research, scholarship,
and education by publishing worldwide in
Oxford New York

Athens Auckland Bangkok Bogotá Buenos Aires Cape Town
Chennai Dar es Salaam Delhi Florence Hong Kong Istanbul Karachi
Kolkata Kuala Lumpur Madrid Melbourne Mexico City Mumbai Nairobi
Paris São Paulo Shanghai Singapore Taipei Tokyo Toronto Warsaw
with associated companies in
Berlin Ibadan

Oxford is a registered trade mark of Oxford University Press
in the UK and in certain other countries

Published in the United States
by Oxford University Press Inc., New York

© Oxford University Press 2001

The moral rights of the authors have been asserted
Database right Oxford University Press (maker)

First Published 2001

All rights reserved. No part of this publication may be reproduced,
stored in a retrieval system, or transmitted, in any form or by any means,
without the prior permission in writing of Oxford University Press,
or as expressly permitted by law, or under terms agreed with the appropriate
reprographic rights organization. Enquiries concerning reproduction
outside the scope of the above should be sent to the Rights Department,
Oxford University Press, at the address above

You must not circulate this book in any other binding or cover
and you must impose this same condition on any acquirer

A catalogue record for this title is available from the British Library

Library of Congress Cataloging in Publication Data
Contemporary approaches to the science of hysteria : clinical and theoretical
perspectives / edited by Peter W. Halligan, Christopher Bass, John C. Marshall.
Includes bibliographical references and index.
ISBN 0 19 263254 X (Hbk : alk. paper)
1. Hysteria. I. Halligan, Peter W. II. Bass, Christopher M.
III. Marshall, John C.
[DNLM: 1. Conversion Disorder. 2. Hysteria. WM 173.5 C761 2001]
RC532 .C66 2001   616.85'24–dc21   00-050204

ISBN 0 19 263254 X (Hbk)

Typeset by Bibliocraft Ltd, Dundee
Printed in Great Britain on acid-free paper by
T. J. International Ltd, Padstow, Cornwall

Contents

List of contributors   vii

Acknowledgements   ix

Introduction   x

Part I: HISTORY

1 All in the mind? the history of hysterical conversion as a clinical
  concept   1

2 War based hysteria — the military perspective   12

3 Recovering hysteria from history: Herodotus and
  'the first case of shell-shock'   36

Part II: CLASSIFICATION AND EPIDEMIOLOGY

4 The origins of DSM and ICD — criteria for conversion and
  somatization disorders   49

5 Discrepancies between diagnostic criteria and clinical
  practice   63

6 The epidemiology of hysterical conversion   73

Part III: AETEOLOGICAL, CLINICAL AND LEGAL PERSPECTIVES

7 Life events: meanings and precursors   88

8 Hysterical conversion — a view from clinical
  neurology   102

9 Factitious disorders and malingering   126

10 Non-epileptic seizures   143

11 Conversion hysteria: a legal diagnosis   155

Part IV: THEORETICAL PERSPECTIVES

12 Conversion, dissociation, or doxomorphic disorder   171

13 Psychodynamic theories in conversion hysteria   184

14 Conversion hysteria: the relevance of attentional
   awareness   192

15 Hysteria and hypnosis: cognitive and social influences   203

16 Imaging hysterical paralysis   216

17 Disorders of willed action   235

18 The anthropology of hysteria   251

Part V: PROGNOSIS AND MANAGEMENT

19 The prognosis of hysteria/somatization disorder   271

20 Psychodynamic psychotherapy in the treatment of conversion
   hysteria   283

21 Cognitive behavioural therapy as a treatment for conversion
   disorders   298

22 Hypnosis and suggestion in the treatment of hysteria   312

23 Rehabilitation for hysterical conversion   330

Index   347

Contributors

Hiroko Akagi, Specialist Registrar in Psychiatry, Academic Unit of Psychiatry, University of Leeds, Leeds.

Bal S. Athwal, Senior Research Fellow, Wellcome Department of Cognitive Neurology, Institute of Neurology, London.

Christopher Bass, Consultant Liaison Psychiatrist, Department of Psychological Medicine (Barnes Unit), John Radcliffe Hospital,Oxford.

German E. Berrios, Senior Lecturer, Department of Psychiatry, University of Cambridge, Addenbrooke's Hospital, Cambridge.

Trudie Chalder, Academic Department of Psychological Medicine, Guy's, King's, and St Thomas' School of Medicine, London.

C. Robert Cloninger, Departments of Psychiatry, Genetics, and Psychology, Washington University, St Louis.

Tom Craig, Professor of Community Psychiatry, Guy's, King's and St Thomas' School of Medicine, London.

Gereon R. Fink, Institut für Medizin, Forschungszentrum Jülich, Germany and Department of Neurology, RWTH Aachen, Aachen, Germany.

Richard S.J. Frackowiak, Wellcome Department of Cognitive Neurology, Institute of Neurology, London.

Peter W. Halligan, MRC Senior Research Fellow, Department of Psychology, Cardiff University, Cardiff.

Allan House, Professor of Liaison Psychiatry, Academic Unit of Psychiatry and Behavioural Sciences, University of Leeds, Leeds.

Michael A. Jones, Professor of Common Law, Faculty of Law, University of Liverpool, Liverpool.

Helen King, Departments of Classics and History, Faculty of Letters and Social Sciences, University of Reading, Whiteknights, Reading.

Laurence J. Kirmayer, Institute of Community and Family Psychiatry, Montreal, Quebec.

Chris Mace, Senior Lecturer in Psychotherapy, University of Warwick, Coventry and Consultant Psychotherapist, South Warwickshire Combined Care NHS Trust.

John C. Marshall, Neuropsychology Unit, University Department of Clinical Neurology, Radcliffe Infirmary, Oxford.

Kevin M. McConkey, School of Psychology, University of New South Wales, Sydney.

Harold Merskey, Professor Emeritus of Psychiatry, University of Western Ontario, London Health Sciences Centre, University Campus, London, Ontario.

David A. Oakley, Hypnosis Unit, Department of Psychology, University College London, London.

Ian P. Palmer, Tri-Service Professor of Defence Psychiatry, Royal Defence Medical College, Fort Blockhouse, Gosport, Hampshire.

Maria A. Ron, Professor of Neuropsychiatry, University Department of Clinical Neurology, Institute of Neurology, London; National Hospital for Neurology and Neurosurgery, London.

Radhika Santhanam, Institute of Community and Family Psychiatry, Sir Mortimer B. Davis-Jewish General Hospital, Montreal, Quebec.

Peter Shoenberg, Consultant Psychotherapist, Department of Psychological Medicine, University College Hospital, London.

Mauricio Sierra, Clinical Researcher, Institute of Psychiatry, King's College London.

Sean A. Spence, Senior Lecturer in Psychiatry, University of Sheffield, Academic Department of Psychiatry, Northern General Hospital, Sheffield.

Alan Sprince, Lecturer in Law, Faculty of Law, University of Liverpool, Liverpool.

Jon Stone, Research Fellow in Neurology, Department of Clinical Neurosciences, University of Edinburgh, Western General Hospital, Edinburgh.

Nick Temple, Consultant Psychiatrist in Psychotherapy, Adult Department, Tavistock Clinic, London; Psychoanalyst; Chairman, Tavistock Clinic, London.

Michael R. Trimble, Professor of Behavioural Neurology, Institute of Neurology, National Hospitals for Neurology and Neurosurgery, London.

Derick T. Wade, Consultant and Professor in Neurological Disability, Rivermead Rehabilitation Centre, Oxford.

Simon Wessely, Professor of Epidemiological and Liaison Psychiatry, Guy's, King's and St Thomas' Hospital Medical School and the Institute of Psychiatry, London.

Adam Zeman, Consultant Neurologist and Senior Lecturer, Department of Clinical Neurosciences, University of Edinburgh, Western General Hospital, Edinburgh.

Acknowledgements

The editors gratefully acknowledge the considerable help provided by Collette Keane and Meriel Patrick. We would also like to thank all those contributors at the Woodstock meeting who provided constructive comments and feedback on the presentations: Professor Anthony David, Dr Morgan O'Connell, Professor Lewis Wolport, Dr Michael Sharpe, Dr John Sharpley and Professor Edgar Miller. The meeting and this book would not have been possible had it not been for the generous support of the Mary Kinross Trust (Mrs Elizabeth Shields) and the Wellcome Trust.

A calming introduction to hysteria

Marshall, J.C., Bass, C. and Halligan, P.W.

The sense of hysteria with which we are primarily concerned in this volume is not, for the most part, that of hysterical personality, demonic possession, or wandering womb (Goldstein, 1987). Rather, we seek to understand why some patients show neurological signs and symptoms seemingly without having suffered neurological trauma or disease. This paradoxical (indeed contradictory) way of phrasing the problem is intended to reflect the mysterious nature of our topic. To put the central issue in a rather more banal fashion: There are a very substantial proportion of 'patients' in neurology wards and outpatient clinics for whom no convincing explanation of their symptoms can be found.

This fact holds even after one has excluded the most notorious conditions such as headache, back pain, sexual malfunctions, and general malaise. We are dealing, that is, with 'straightforward' impairments that include paralysis, sensory loss, aphonia, and memory disorder — the bread and butter of neurological practise. And we emphasize that a high incidence of these unexplained symptoms is found even in hospital departments staffed by expert consultant neurologists with access to structural neuroimaging, electrophysiology and the full range of relevant laboratory investigations. 'Hysterical conversion' is one name for the condition that gives rise to such symptoms, although the meaning of the term has often changed since it was first coined by Ferriar (1795). What, then, could in principle, account for these *functional* (or hysterical) phenomena (and do so without recourse to dualism)?

Two fairly obvious stratagems come into play at this point. First, one could claim that these supposedly hysterical conditions are consequent upon an orthodox underlying neurological disease or structural lesion, but the investigations carried out to date on the particular patient in question have not been sufficiently rigorous, detailed, and prolonged to reveal the true cause of the symptoms. In some instances, no doubt, inadequate examination of the patient will have resulted in the postulation of an occult cause when a perfectly ordinary one would have sufficed. Yet if there is *prima facie* evidence that the examination has been conducted according to best clinical practice including appropriate technical back-up with regard to neuroanatomy, neurophysiology, and biochemistry, it seems a little perverse to continue to insist that a recognized (organic) disease process must nonetheless be at work.

Of course, it *could* be the case that the patient has, for example, a very small tumour that is transparent to CT and MRI, an incredibly rare viral infection, or a hitherto unknown genetic disorder. But unless *evidence* can be provided to support such claims, their postulation is little more than hand-waving. It is particularly dangerous to claim that hysterical patients will *eventually* show signs of a conventional neurological disease that might explain the current symptoms. Sooner or later we are all going to die of something or other, but how (for example) Alzheimer's disease at age seventy might explain bizarre gait or loss of cutaneous sensibility at age thirty is somewhat opaque.

We accordingly turn to the other chief way of explaining away inexplicable symptoms. The patient is faking it. It is best to begin with the most artless version of this hypothesis. 'Faking it' means that the patient is consciously, deliberately, voluntarily choosing not to move the left arm or not to speak; likewise the patient is consciously lying when he or she says that the pinprick is not felt, or the scene not seen.

No doubt, there will be some apparently hysterical patients who *are* faking it in this sense. All normal human beings have the capacity to lie and most, if not all, of us do so on suitable occasions. Such feigning of organic symptoms might be based in part upon the observation of patients who are suffering from 'the real thing'. For some of us, the opportunity to collect substantial damages might be sufficient to feign a bad back (or at least to exaggerate how severe a genuine injury was). To subvert the terminology of DSM IV, the primary gain of money and secondary gain of even more money, for example, could result in seeming disability without underlying structural pathology.

The issue, then, is not 'can this happen?' Rather, it is how can we discover if someone is indeed faking it. (We use ordinary language here, rather than more obviously psychiatric terms such as factitious disorder or malingering: clarity and logic are initially best served by calling a spade a spade.) The simple, but totally impractical, solution would be 24-hour surveillance on audio- and video-tape *unbeknownst to the putative patient*. Anyone who behaved perfectly normally when alone but who invariably developed the 'disability' when in company might plausibly be thought to be feigning. Short of this Big Brother solution, investigators have tried to devise catch-trials and catch-tests to detect the cheater. For example, it is sometimes assumed that a patient who 'guesses' a randomized stimulus sequence (touch, touch, no touch....) significantly *below chance* must be faking it. But the existence of such phenomena as blindsight, unfeeling touch, unconscious perception in visuo-spatial neglect, and priming in amnesia show how misleading it can be to assume that odd relationships between behaviour and verbal report necessarily constitute evidence of cheating. We do not impugn the honesty of patients who perform visual discriminations at an *above chance* level while claiming to have seen nothing. Why should we perforce distrust those who score *below chance*? In short, the detection of lying in the neurology clinic is at least as difficult as it is in a court of law.

Nonetheless, once we have ruled out, insofar as is humanly possible, both neurological misdiagnosis and cheating, there remains a (non-null) set of patients for whom the diagnoses-by-exclusion of hysterical paralysis, hysterical aphonia, hysterical blindness, hysterical anosmia, hysterical anesthesia (and so on) seem at least half-way appropriate.

So far, for the sake of perspicuity, we have attempted to describe the differential diagnosis of hysteria in black and white: The patient either has or does not have an organic disease; the patient either is or is not lying. But the clinical world is usually somewhat more nuanced than these simplistic dichotomies might suggest. How are we to interpret the patient who does indeed have visible lesions or abnormal biochemistry but in whom we nonetheless suspect that the full range and intensity of the symptoms is not plausibly accounted for by these organic factors alone? Is it appropriate (sometimes) to claim that the overt impairment is a hysterical overlay on the symptoms of a genuine neurological disease? Is such an overlay any different from normal exaggeration?

Likewise, the distinction between veracity and mendacity is not always as sharp as we might wish it to be. Most people have very fluctuating insight into their own motives, feelings, and actions. And thus we enter the slippery slope that leads from bad faith to 'lying to oneself'. With respect to hysteria, some scholars have entertained the notion that the patients are dissemblers who do not know they are dissembling. This strand of unintended duplicity ranges from the Socratic injunction to 'Know thyself' to the Freudian claim that we cannot know ourselves without spending long hours on the couch. Hysteria, and related conditions such as psychogenic fugue, multiple personality, and depersonalization disorder, raise in the most acute form the issue of how to make clinically pertinent distinctions in the shady regions between being myself and acting a part. When Joseph Babinsky (1901) claimed that the symptoms of hysteria were merely the result of 'suggestion' (and could be cured by 'countersuggestion'), it was not entirely clear how much insight into his or her suggestibility Babinsky was prepared to credit the patient with; he was, however, convinced that individuals differed greatly in their susceptibility to suggestion and countersuggestion.

And however one attempts to square these hermeneutic circles, there will always remain the question of mechanism. DSM-III-R (1987) and subsequent editions take a strictly 'psychological' line on the mechanism of conversion disorder (= hysterical neurosis): The patient derives *primary gain* from 'keeping an internal conflict or need out of awareness', and *secondary gain*' by avoiding a particular activity that is noxious to him or her and getting support from the environment that otherwise might not be forthcoming.' Conflicts and needs are converted into physical symptoms, and then the symptoms are what in turn allow the achievement of primary and secondary gain. One difficulty with this approach is that one can always find primary and secondary gain if one is looking hard enough post-hoc (that is, after the patient has developed hysterical blindness, for example). The account, in brief, will be impossible to falsify (just as all patients may too easily be conjectured to have hysterical personality *after* the inexplicable neurological signs have been made manifest).

But irrespective of such Popperian considerations, these psychic factors were *not* (or at least not entirely) what Jean-Martin Charcot (1889), or Sigmund Freud (1893) meant by mechanism. For there still remains the question of how *physiologically* conflict is converted into blindness, paralysis, anosmia, and so forth (even assuming that 'conversion' is the appropriate psychological device). Thus Charcot (1889), for example, conjectured that hysterical hemiparesis was caused by '*dynamic* or *functional*' lesion in the relevant cortical motor zone opposite the paralysis. These functional lesions were regarded as akin to localized oedema, anaemia, or active hyperaemia, 'of which no trace is found after death' (Freud, 1893). It was only with the advent of functional neuroimaging techniques that such hypotheses could be put to the test (Tiihonen et al., 1995; Marshall et al., 1997). Although one may say (as it were, psychodynamically) that shame can cause blushing, or terror cause involuntary freezing, Freud, as a good student of 'Master Brucke himself' — 'a positivist by temperament and conviction' (Gay, 1988), was never in any doubt that explicit *pathophysiologic* mechanisms must translate thoughts and feelings into motor, sensory, or cognitive loss and derangement. Freud's claim that 'hysteria behaves as though anatomy did not exist' (Freud, 1893) was intended to *describe* how the nature and distribution of hysterical symptoms differed from those produced by organic lesions; there was never any intention to deny that 'functional' disorders (including paralysis and language loss) had pathophysiological correlates (Marshall, 1974). Although, for example, Sigmund Freud and Pierre Janet agreed that fixed subconscious ideas were at the core of (conversion) hysteria, Janet (1893) argued that 'a narrowing of the field of consciousness' was responsible for negative symptoms. Consciousness is withdrawn from a body part which then, depending upon the particular part in question, develops blindness, paralysis, somatosensory loss and so on. By contrast, Breuer and Freud (1893) conjectured that 'control over the whole of the somatic innervation passes over to the hypnoid consciousness.'

It is important to stress mechanisms in the plural here because there is no reason to assume any less variability in hysterical pathophysiologies that in ordinary neurological pathologies (see Halligan and David (1999)). We do not expect the lesions that cause acquired (organic) blindness to have the same locus as those that cause hemiparesis. Indeed, even for (approximately) the same organic symptom, lesions will be found in different patients at different points in the responsible neuronal circuit. It is possible but very unlikely that there is only one functional lesion underlying the hysterical phenomena that mimic structural neurologic disease.

These, then, are just a few of the highly contentious issues on which we hope to provoke discussion (and, eventually, much more empirical research). The current volume represents the start of that enquiry into the scientific understanding of hysteria, that most protean of diseases.

References

Babinsky, J. (1901). Définition de l'hystérie. *Revue Neurologique, 9,* 1074–1080.

Breuer, J. and Freud, S. (1893). Über den psychischen Mechanismus hysticher Phänomene (Vorläufige Mitteilung). *Neurologisches Centralblatt, 12,* 4–10 and 43–47.

Charcot, J.M. (1889). *Clinical lectures on diseases of the nervous system.* London: New Sydenham Society.

Ferriar, J. (1795). *Medical histories and reflections, Volume 2.* London: Cadell and Davies.

Freud, S. (1893). Quelques considerations pour une étude comparative des paralysies motrices et hystériques. *Archives de Neurologie, 26,* 29–43.

Gay, P. (1988). *Freud: A life for our time.* London: Dent.

Goldstein, J. (1987). *Console and classify: The French psychiatric profession in the nineteenth century.* Cambridge: Cambridge University Press.

Halligan, P. W. and David, A. S. (1999) Eds *Hysterical Conversion: Toward a Cognitive Neuropsychology Account.* Lawrence Erlbaum Associates, Hove, East Sussex.

Janet, P. (1893). Quelques définitions récentes de l'hystérie. *Archives de Neurologie, 25,* 417–438.

Marshall, J.C. (1974). Freud's psychology of language. In R. Wollheim (ed.), *Freud: A collection of critical essays.* New York: Doubleday.

Marshall, J. C., Halligan, P. W., Fink, G. R., Wade, D. T. and Frackowiak, R. S. J. (1997). The functional anatomy of a hysterical paralysis. *Cognition, 64* B1–B8.

Tiihonen, J., Fuikka, J., Viinamäki, H., Lehtonen, J. and Partanen, J. (1995). Altered cerebral blood flow during hysterical paraesthesia. *Biological Psychiatry, 37,* 134–135.

1 All in the mind? The history of hysterical conversion as a clinical concept

Chris Mace

Before becoming part of the diagnostic nomenclature, 'conversion' was associated with hysteria by Freud to designate a psychological mechanism he believed led to the symptoms. A century before Freud, John Ferriar had also used 'hysterical conversion' to refer to a chameleon-like condition that had no clear pathogenesis, mental or otherwise. Ferriar's concept might be an inevitable artefact of a highly formalized diagnostic system. Some of those psychological accounts of hysterical conversion, before and after Freud, are summarized. Although the modern concept of hysterical conversion presumes psychological causation, it is no longer linked to a clear psychological process. Instead, it is an elastic concept having as much in common with Ferriar's concept as Freud's. As modern conceptions of somatization disorder have even more in common with this pre-Freudian view, diagnostic divisions between conversion disorder and somatization syndromes appear increasingly difficult to justify.

Introduction: medical history and method

'Hysteria' became 'conversion hysteria' almost a century ago. Despite many changes in nomenclature, the underlying concept has been surprisingly resilient. Any worthwhile history needs to account for this. The present account will do so by considering significant factors within clinical thinking over the last two centuries or so. In an era when social histories are all pervasive, this is an unpopular, even disparaged, approach. Improperly used, it will produce only myopic revisionism — a projection of present prejudice of the kind Butterfield abhorred as the 'whig interpretation' of history (Butterfield, 1931). However, it can also stimulate reconstruction of the kind commended by the Oxford historian, R. G. Collingwood. Collingwood (1939) proposed a key test of validity of historical accounts — that they should unearth the (often hidden) questions to which the seeming chaos of actions and artefacts met by the historian represent answers. These historical questions would not be the questions that motivate us now, but, once discovered, would reorganize and bring coherence to previously inexplicable coincidences. (Interested readers will find a more philosophical treatment of the implications of this approach for psychiatric diagnosis in general, and hysterical disorders in particular, in Mace, 2000.)

I shall be proposing that this kind of account leads to a number of conclusions. First, if the term 'conversion hysteria', or something similar, had not been coined, then the relationship between psychiatry and neurology would be significantly different from what it is today. Second, that the diagnostic association of 'conversion' with 'hysteria' arose and was maintained for largely extraneous reasons. A corollary of this view, in contrast to 'social' accounts such as those of Showalter (1985) or Shorter (1992), is that there is no evidence that, beyond vicissitudes in medical construction, a group of explanation-resistant disabilities (most commonly taking the form of seizures, weakness, and sensory loss and therefore appearing to mimic neurological disease) have occurred less often over the last 200 years. Conversely, historical parallels between present diagnostic practice and those prevalent 200 years ago can remind us that much of what is being practised now is regressive rather than progressive. To demonstrate this, it is necessary to begin with the biggest single myth surrounding the history of hysterical conversion — that it was invented by Sigmund Freud.

Two phases of conversion: (1) Ferriar's conversion

Although 'hysterical conversion' is indelibly linked with Freud's use of the term a century ago, it has had not one but two clinical incarnations. The first came a century before, when the English physician, John Ferriar, introduced it in his *Medical Histories and Reflections:*

> In hysterical conversion the body possesses a power of representing the most hazardous disorders, without incurring danger; of counterfeiting the greatest derangement in the circulating system, without materially altering the movements; of producing madness, conscious of its extravagances, and of increasing the acuteness of sensation, by oppressing the common sensorium . . . Nature as if in ridicule of the attempts to unmask her, has in this class of diseases, reconciled contradictions, and realised improbabilities with a mysterious versatility which inspires the true philosopher with diffidence, and reduces the systematist to despair. (Ferriar, 1794, p. 12)

The idea of hysteria as the great imitator was not new, being presaged in Cullen's identification of hysteria with the quality of mobility (Cullen, 1797) and likened to a chameleon by Sydenham (1848). However, its harmlessness in Ferriar's description contrasts with the dangerousness and mortality that Sydenham attributed to it. Two further distinctions are that whereas Sydenham had recognized hysteria as having some characteristic and recurrent features alongside its changeability (for instance, collections of fluid and head pains), Ferriar denies that any individual symptom could be characteristic. In contast to Sydenham's elaborate vision of the pathogenesis of hysteria, attributing it to the action of the 'animal spirits', Ferriar is agnostic concerning its origins and mechanism. One possible explanation for this was an increasing emphasis through the preceding decades on formal taxonomic completeness at the expense of clinical explanation across the whole of medicine (cf. Mace, 1992a). This raised expectations concerning the extent to which illness was amenable to diagnosis, while keeping labels to the status of ciphers designating a condition's affinities rather than its cause. In such an atmosphere, the natural response to anomaly is to diagnose it rather than admit defeat, even if this requires a beast like Ferriar's hysterical conversion that is a different kind of concept altogether. (Logically, it constitutes what Ryle (1949) termed a 'category mistake'.) By allowing inconsistency and resistance to diagnosis as evidence of another diagnosis in themselves, 'hysterical conversion' affirmed diagnostic completeness.

Two phases of conversion: (2) Freud's conversion

The formalism of this taxonomic world was to be devalued as anatomico-clinical thinking superseded it. As histopathology and then germ theory permitted classification on the basis of reliable relationships between morbid changes and symptomatology, individual diagnoses were established and consolidated according to these criteria with less reference to their interrelationships. The diagnostic landscape was very different by the time Freud reapplied the term 'conversion' to hysteria a century later, with no reference (or apparent awareness) of its earlier use. Freud's language (following Strachey's translation) as he introduces it in his *Neuropsychoses of Defence* is very different too:

> In hysteria, the incompatible idea is rendered innocuous by its sum of excitation being transformed into something somatic. For this I would like to propose the name of conversion. (Freud, 1894, p. 49)

Curiously, here too hysteria is not identified with any specific symptoms, beyond an understanding that these are somatic and the consequence of nervous action. His use of the language of electrophysiology conveys the presumption of simple, direct correspondences between neural and psychological events. However, hysteria is not only seen as an induced reaction, and one that is psychologically induced, but also as one that involves conflict between mental contents and attempts to selectively suppress some of these from conscious awareness.

Freud elaborated this concept through his clinical histories of hysteria, while adding some characteristic features. Key among these was his equation of the conflict involved with passive sexual experience prior to puberty (Freud, 1896), and his subsequent switch of focus from the impact of actual sexual trauma to early sexual fantasy as the key pathogenic factor in all cases of conversion (Freud, 1906).

The background to Freud's conversion

To understand how such a different and complex model arose and gained wide interest and admiration within medical (as opposed to purely psychoanalytic) circles, it is necessary to describe a number of currents that he effectively brought to a confluence. Essentially, there were four themes in medical accounts of the pathogenesis of hysteria that he united: the neurological; the gynaecological; the erotogenic; and the psychogenic. These were often not mutually exclusive, with neurologists such as Briquet (1859) being sensitive to synergism between neurological predisposition and psychological precipitation (Mai and Merskey, 1980), but can be separated for convenience here.

Neurological accounts grew in sophistication throughout the nineteenth century in proportion to increasingly differentiated understanding of the relationships between neurological structure, function, and disease. Thus, from vague notions of hysteria being associated with greater 'excitability' of the nervous system, attempts were made to generalize from the theory of reflex action as this became elaborated. Laycock (1840) emphasized spinal reflexes, while Brodie's 'local hysteria' implicated the joints as a source of reflex irritation precipitating hysterical symptoms (Brodie, 1837). However, as the correlations between neural structures and function, and underlying changes associated with neurological disease became better understood, the resistant nature of hysterical symptoms to this more straightforward explanation become more apparent. To maintain faith in their neurological origin, it was necessary to appeal to central rather than peripheral mechanisms. There were at least three distinct paradigms as a result — appeals to a local lesion, to 'dissolution', and of a purely physiological, 'functional' disorder.

This central tendency was especially clear in Charcot's work. Accepting that the chronic stigmata of 'minor hysteria' and the seizures of 'major hysteria' were distinct from similar features arising in the course of other diseases, he attributed them to central lesions in the motor cortex that, being invisible, were 'functional' rather than structural (Charcot, 1889). The second principal paradigm of the central nervous basis of hysteria was its attribution to a release of 'lower' centres in the nervous system from central control — a pathology coterminous with that of disorders such as epilepsy. The determining role of 'dissolution' in such explanations was promoted by Hughlings Jackson, who refused to use the term 'functional' (Dewhurst, 1982). The concept of 'functional' disorder was nevertheless elaborated into a distinct sub-category of neurological disorder by Gowers (1886), incorporating disorders that were lesionless and transient. Gowers proposed that there was a change in function, separate from any presumption as to localization.

While gynaecological accounts of hysteria represent the oldest strand (Veith, 1965), they remained popular through to the end of the century, revealing many interesting adaptations to the shifting basis of medical explanation. It should be remembered that a major attraction of gynaecological explanations was that they offered a hope of specific treatment, from surgery or manipulative treatments like ovarian compression. Interest in associations between hysterical illness and reproductive organs extended beyond the womb to the ovaries and external genitalia. Theories of their influence were a popular extension of reflex theory, while the most extraordinary claims were made, true to the time, of associations with lesions in these organs (e.g. Lee, 1871).

Sexual assocations of hysteria were as old as the gynaecological, with lack rather than excess of sexual activity being seen as a predisposing cause, and marriage as a cure. In the nineteenth century, increasingly sophisticated ideas concerning the somatization and psychologization of sexual instincts were developed. Among the former, the idea of libido had been coined by Benedikt (1868) to posit how spinal action allowed sexual energy to have psychological form.

Like the erotogenic explanations, psychological accounts were individual inventions, none achieving widespread currency. It is interesting to quickly review some highlights. (Those familiar with them may wonder, with some justification, whether twentieth-century ideas have really offered an advance.) The oldest link between hysteria and mental events was emotion. Emotions associated with hysterical symptoms were usually strong, and in some sense inadmissible. A psychologically sophisticated understanding of the place of feeling was offered by Brudenell Carter (1853), who distinguished between primary, secondary, and tertiary hysteria by reference to the emotional processes that triggered attacks. Primary hysteria was involuntary, the automatic consequence of strong emotions of fear, passion, or jealousy being unintentionally aroused. In secondary hysteria, seizures could be precipitated involuntarily by circumstances associated with these emotions, but without the emotions being felt. In the last to develop, and the greatest therapeutic challenge, tertiary hysteria could be induced at will by a patient who had gained some control over his or her reactions. Patients could then initiate seizures voluntarily by exploiting these mental associations. Such patients were observed to manipulate others in their immediate environment. Carter offered an ambitious recipe for treatment based upon separation, ignoring attacks, and reinforcement of desired behaviours — in effect, he proposed behaviour modification nearly a century before James Watson.

In a completely independent development, similar precipitants were noted by Benedikt who, observing the inadmissability of the emotions concerned and the often curative effect of disclosure, felt the key psychopathogenic feature was what he termed a secret 'second life' (cf. Ellenberger, 1970, p. 301). Personal secrets represented one way in which ideas could be pathogenic; others implicated ideas that were further removed from past personal experience. For example, Janet described the 'fixed idea' as an unconscious residuum that was common to hysterics (Janet, 1907), while J. Russell Reynolds (1869) proposed a direct correspondence between an idea of the form of illness in a patient's mind and the symptoms a patient actually experienced. This provided a direct way of explaining discrepancies between the symptoms a patient reported and presentations that were typical of neurological disease. This perception was the basis of Freud's first clinical studies of hysteria, and his description, as a neurologist, of how 'hysteria behaves as though anatomy did not exist' (Freud, 1888).

In the light of this background, Freud's real achievement as a psychopathologist of hysteria is an ingenious synthesis. It might be argued that the key elements (including some recognition of unconscious factors and, according to Freud at least, erotogenesis) were accepted by Charcot. However, the maitre never brought them together into a single coherent model, emphasizing one insight at the expense of another as he continued to add sub-types of hysteria to the repertoire (such as the essentially masculine traumatic hysteria) whenever he recognized a distinct new aetiology.

It was in building upon Charcot's perceptions of the importance of trauma in the pathogenesis of hysteria that Freud attempted to make it the basis of a unicausal model of the disorder. This was the job that the concept of conversion was originally intended to assist — denoting a common mechanism by which psychologically traumatic experiences brought about their symptomatic consequences. This project was, however, doomed. Freud could not maintain the effort, and he accepted that some cases of hysteria would be, in effect, 'organic' (Freud, 1909). Even among those where psychogenesis was sufficient explanation he also accepted that more than one mechanism was at play. In abandoning the assumption of unicausality, he also stopped referring to conversion as a psychological process. Instead, he continued to refer to a syndrome of 'conversion hysteria' that could be contrasted to other sub-types such as 'anxiety hysteria'.

For completeness, we might mention one other enduring contribution to the psychological understanding of hysteria dating back to Freud — the notion of secondary gain. A shrewd clinician, Freud recognized that many neurotic patients' failure to recover needed to be explained in terms of an unresolved need to be ill. While he used 'secondary gain' in a similar fashion to later writers, i.e. for factors in the current environment that maintained the reporting of symptoms (Freud, 1909), he emphasized that it could only be of secondary importance in explaining the symptoms' persistence. There would always be a primary, unconscious and intrapsychic basis to a patient's failure to recover.

The legacy of Freud's conversion: medicine

Hysteria ceased to play a central part in Freud's explorations of the mind and psycho-pathology as his work became identified with the emerging discipline of psychoanalysis. The legacy of his work on hysterical conversion can be understood by separate reference to medicine and psychoanalysis.

While medicine had little use for his theory of conversion, the term 'conversion hysteria' was widely adopted to refer to hysterical illnesses in which the signs were somatic rather than psychological ('dissociation hysteria' being used to describe hysterical amnesias and fugues) — see Merskey's chapter in this volume, p. 171. But even though the terms 'hysteria' and 'neurosis' have found disfavour, subsequent changes in nomenclature have all retained the qualifier 'conversion'. They are summarized in Table 1.1.

These fashions should not disguise the broader diagnostic implications of hysteria's transmutation to conversion hysteria. It was not only a key export from psychoanalysis, but entered the lexicon as psychiatry was establishing itself as a broad-based clinical

Table 1.1 Uses of 'conversion' in the official classification of hysteria. (In each case, first and subsequent references are quoted.)

Standard Classified Nomenclature (US)	
5th revision (AMA, 1935)	Conversion hysteria.
6th revision (AMA, 1948)	Conversion hysteria.
7th revision (AMA, 1957)	Conversion hysteria.
8th revision (AMA, 1970)	Hysteria with localized somatic dysfunction.
Diagnostic and Statistical Manuals (US)	
DSM–I (APA, 1952)	Conversion reaction.
DSM–II (APA, 1968)	Hysterical neurosis, conversion type.
DSM–III (APA, 1980) *(and DSM–III–R)*	Conversion disorder.
DSM–IV (APA, 1994)	Conversion disorder (sub-types: with motor symptom or deficit; with sensory symptom or deficit; with seizures or convulsions; with mixed presentation).
Nomenclature of Disease (UK)	
7th edition (Royal College of Physicians, 1948)	Conversion hysteria.
International Classification of Diseases	
ICD–6 (WHO, 1948)	311 Hysterical reaction without mention of anxiety reaction (includes 'hysterical conversion').
ICD–7 (WHO, 1955)	311 Hysterical reaction without mention of anxiety reaction (includes 'hysterical conversion').
ICD–8 (WHO, 1965)	300.1 Hysterical neurosis (includes 'conversion hysteria', 'conversion reaction').
ICD–9 (WHO, 1975)	300.1 Hysteria (includes 'conversion hysteria').
ICD–10 (WHO, 1992)	F44 Dissociative [conversion] disorders. (These include: dissociative motor disorders; dissociative convulsions; dissociative anesthesia and sensory loss; and mixed dissociative [conversion] disorders.)

specialty. As a neurological disorder, hysteria had been a 'neurosis'; as a psychological one, it became, at least for a transitional period, a 'psychoneurosis'. I have argued that by facilitating its transfer from neurology to psychiatry, the concept of hysterical conversion assisted diagnosis within both of these disciplines (Mace, 1992b). The fundamental point is that conversion's widespread adoption owed more to it being the psychological formulation of hysteria than any other. This occurred at a time when, for largely extrinsic reasons, the medical world was much more receptive to psychological formulations of hysteria than it had previously been. (Major developments like the ideas of Brudenell Carter had faded in obscurity; conversely, those that were subsequently enormously influential, like those of Russell Reynolds, had not been presented as a theory of 'hysteria'.) In effect, 'conversion hysteria' neatly fitted a niche that was being created, rather than being accepted as an independent contribution to clinical science (cf. Mace, 2000). However, the resulting state of psychiatric diagnosis was problematic, particularly for the nosographers who found themselves with a category to define that had been invented in psychoanalysis and whose users continued to be neurologists (cf. Wessely's chapter in this volume).

The problems refer to the recognition of conversion hysteria and explanation of individual cases. Psychoanalytic theory informed a number of assumptions as to how hysterical patients might be recognized as well as feeding the expectation that the onset of a patient's symptoms could be explained in psychological terms. These included ideas that symptoms would somehow symbolize patients' hidden conflicts, as well as those of secondary gain and the (Janetian) expectation of affective 'belle indifference'. While these enjoyed a considerable longevity on the basis of clinical prejudice, it was evident that research was failing to corroborate their unique association with this diagnosis (cf. Lewis *et al.*, 1965; Cloninger's chapter in this volume). At the same time, the whole idea of a syndrome being defined with reference to its presumed cause, rather than consistent features, became increasingly out of step as attempts to establish greater consistency in psychiatric diagnosis favoured phenomenological definition (see Craig's chapter in this volume, p. 88).

Freudian theories of the psychogenesis of conversion hysteria were quickly succeeded by other contenders from medical authors. Examples included Babinski's identification of hysteria with the effects of suggestion, coining the neologism 'pithiatism' for symptoms induced in this way (Babinski and Froment, 1918). Janet (1907) emphasized the role of dissociation between parts of the personality, while Kretschmer (1926) postulated hysteria as an atavistic return to primitive but universal reflex responses under extreme stress. Talking of 'organic repression', Paul Schilder (1935) conceived hysteria as a complex interplay of organic and unconscious factors. Within neurology, others such as Symonds (1970) suggested hysterical illness was largely artefactual and explicable as dissimulation. Interesting as these ideas remain, none was any more successful in influencing diagnostic habits than the succession of ideas that had been their nineteenth-century forbears.

The legacy of Freud's conversion: psychoanalysis

Psychoanalysis inherited the concept of conversion while having little to do with hysteria in the consulting room. Within the relative orthodoxy of North American psychoanalysis in particular, the term was used instead in accounting for all kinds of characterological problems, while its psychodynamic associations drifted considerably from its oedipal origins. Psychoanalysts from Karl Abraham (1921) to Leo Rangell (1959), continuing to interpret hysteria in terms of psychosexual fixations, referred back to pre-genital (i.e. anal or oral) origins. A shift of paradigms within psychoanalysis in favour of object relations theory allowed the hysteric's primary gains to be recast in terms of object fixations (Fairbairn, 1954). Later still, interest in psychoanalysis as a theory of meaning and communication rather than causal sequences led to a resurgence of interest in hysterical conversion as the paradigm of the symptom as symbol, metaphor, or communication (Rycroft 1966; Szasz, 1972).

Conversion and psychiatric diagnosis

In brief, there was little further to be extracted from psychoanalytic developments that could inform diagnosis, although as a 'neurosis', 'reaction', or 'disorder', conversion still needed some content. Apart from the constant name changes, the diagnostic career of conversion in the second half of the twentieth century was characterized by loss of aetiological specificity, subdivision, and competition. The tangential relationship of the theory of conversion to introduction of the term for diagnostic use, and the lack of specific criteria for a diagnosis of conversion symptoms have already been discussed. However, across the field of psychiatry, diagnostic conventions have become increasingly explicit and manualized. It is evident from the way in which conversion syndromes were coded in these manuals that the criteria for psychogenesis — the part of the definition which made it a psychiatric disorder — were being increasingly diluted (see Craig's chapter in this volume, p. 88). If the definitions given in the American Psychiatric Association's manuals are taken as an example, a list of criteria, as late as 1987, still included, in addition to a temporal association between its onset or exacerbation and psychological conflict or need, features such as 'the symptom enables the individual to avoid some activity that is noxious to him or her' and 'the symptom enables the individual to get support from the environment that otherwise might not be forthcoming' (APA, 1987). In DSM–IV one criterion only remains: 'the initiation or exacerbation of the symptom or deficit is preceded by conflicts or other stressors' (APA, 1994).

Subdivision within the ambit of conversion hysteria has involved the splitting off of pain syndromes, leaving four symptomatic groups — motor, sensory, seizures, and mixed presentations. As a consequence, the syndrome has become more directly identified with specific symptoms than aetiological factors. Competition has occurred with the development, via 'Briquet's syndrome', of 'somatization disorder' as a polysymptomatic, multi-system hysteria (cf. Cloninger's chapter in this volume). While the diagnostic criteria allow separation of somatization disorder from conversion disorder, conceptually and diagnostically, the admission of a category of 'undifferentiated somatization disorder' in which essentially any symptom that is judged not to result from physical disorder and has persisted for longer than six months qualifies for this designation. The case for singling out symptoms resembling those of neurological disorder (as conversion disorder) from those resembling any other form of recognized medical disorder (as undifferentiated somatoform disorder) appears to require further justification.

Conclusion: history and contemporary concepts of conversion

One conclusion is that these developments in the field of psychiatric diagnosis — where a formal diagnostic system in which the boundaries between many categories are not based on any stronger reason than convention — will always be suspect. The authors of DSM–III (APA, 1980) had claimed (inaccurately) that 'conversion disorder' was unique within the classification because it was based upon aetiology. As has already been summarized here, this is supported neither by the history of analytic investigation (from Freud onwards) nor empirical investigation of conversion patients. 'Conversion disorder' is unique in the classification because its arrival never depended on the strength of such claims, while its intrinsic flexibility has allowed the definitions of other disorders, both in neurology and in the psychiatry of neurosis, to develop relatively rationally.

Within the history that has been presented here, one is reminded of Ferriar's concept of hysterical conversion as an entity with an endless variety of presentations, and no clear cause. On the latter score especially, modern conversion diagnoses are closer in spirit to Ferriar's concept of hysterical conversion than to Freud's. It is curious that the current formalism in today's diagnostic conventions is also highly reminiscent of the broader situation in which Ferriar was practising. This parallel supports the argument that the survival of conversion in the twentieth century owes more to the broader needs of the diagnostic process than its intrinsic merits, as diagnostic convenience appears to have been the *raison d'être* of Ferriar's concept.

Although 'conversion disorder' is no longer reserved for the most changeable conditions, patients attract the diagnosis by their capacity for imitation of neurological disorders. But the diagnostic distinctions drawn between these pseudoneurological symptoms and others suggestive of physical disease in other body systems (currently attributed to USD) seem increasingly tenuous. Once many somatic symptoms — pseudoneurological or otherwise — have been present, the diagnosis is more likely to be that of somatization disorder. (As Maria Ron's chapter in this volume relates, SD and conversion disorder can co-occur.) However, the greater symptomatic range of SD is even more in accord with Ferriar's clinical description of hysterical conversion than was the case for conversion disorder. The historical irony of this transposition increases when one considers that somatization disorder had been eponymously named after the nineteenth-century French neurologist, Paul Briquet (Guze, 1970). Briquet (1859) had always insisted that hysteria, despite the variety of symptoms with which it presented, was a neurological disorder (cf. Mai and Merskey, 1980). When one looks at the range of the symptoms Briquet described, all referrable to the nervous system, they in turn resemble contemporary criteria for conversion disorder even more than those for somatization disorder. Indeed, contemporary diagnoses of conversion disorder, lacking aetiological specificity and shading into the spectrum of somatization disorder, appear to have more in common with syndromes included within the group of 'somatoform' disorders than those of 'dissociative' disorders.

References

Abraham, K. (1921). Contribution to a discussion on tic, in *Selected Papers of Karl Abraham* (1927), pp. 323–5. London: Hogarth.

American Medical Association (5th revision, 1935; 6th revision, 1948; 7th revision, 1957; 8th revision, 1970). *A Standard Classified Nomenclature of Disease*. New York: Commonwealth Fund.

American Psychiatric Association (1st edn, 1952; 2nd edn, 1968; 3rd edn, 1980; revised 3rd edn, 1987; 4th edn, 1994). *Diagnostic and Statistical Manual of Mental Disorders*. New York: APA.

Babinski, J. and Froment, J. (1918). *Hysteria or Pithiatism*. London: University of London Press.

Benedikt, M. (1868). *Elektrotherapie*. Vienna: Tendler.

Briquet, P. (1859). *Traite de l'Hysterie*. Paris: Bailliere.

Brodie, B. C. (1837) *Lectures Illustrative of Certain Nervous Affections*. London: Longman.

Butterfield, H. (1931). *The Whig Interpretation of History*. London: Bell.

Carter, R. B. (1853). *On the Pathology and Treatment of Hysteria*. London: Churchill.

Charcot, J. M (1889). *Clinical Lectures on the Diseases of the Nervous System, Volume III*. London: New Sydenham Society.

Charcot, J. M. and Marie, P. (1892). Hysteria mainly hystero-epilepsy. In *A Dictionary of Psychological Medicine* (ed. Tuke, H.). London: J. & A. Churchill.

Collingwood, R. G. (1939). *An Autobiography*. Harmondsworth: Penguin.

Cullen, W. (1797). *Clinical Lectures Delivered in the Years 1765 and 1766*. London: Lee & Hunt.

Dewhurst, K. (1982). *Hughlings Jackson on Psychiatry* Oxford: Sandford Publications.

Ellenberger, H. (1970). *The Discovery of the Unconscious*. New York: Basic Books.

Faber, K. (1923). *Nosography in Modern Internal Medicine*. New York: Hoeber.

Fairbairn, W. R. D. (1954). Observations on the nature of hysterical states. *British Journal of Medical Psychology* **27**, 105–25.

Ferriar, J. (1795). *Medical Histories and Reflections, Vol. II*. London: Cadell and Davies.

Freud, S. (1888). Hysteria. In *The Complete Psychological Works, Vol. I* (standard edn (1966), ed. Strachey, J.) pp. 39–59. London: Hogarth.

Freud, S. (1894). The neuro-psychoses of defence. In *The Complete Psychological Works, Vol. III* (standard edn (1962), ed. Strachey, J.) pp. 45–61. London: Hogarth.

Freud, S. (1896). Further remarks on the neuro-psychoses of defence. In *The Complete Psychological Works, Vol. III* (standard edn (1962), ed. Strachey, J.) pp. 162–85. London: Hogarth.

Freud, S. (1906). My views on the part played by sexuality in the aetiology of the neuroses. In *The Complete Psychological Works, Vol. VII* (standard edn (1953), ed. Strachey, J.) pp. 271–82. London: Hogarth.

Freud, S. (1909). Some general remarks on hysterical attacks. In *The Complete Psychological Works, Vol. IX* (standard edn (1959), ed. Strachey, J.) pp. 229–34. London: Hogarth.

Gowers, W. R. (1886). *Manual of the Diseases of the Nervous System*.

Gowers, W. R. (1887). *Lectures on the Diagnosis of Diseases of the Brain*.

Guze, S. B. (1970). The role of follow-up studies: their contribution to diagnostic classification as applied to hysteria. *Seminars in Psychiatry*, **2**, 392–402.

Janet, P. (1907). *The Major Symptoms of Hysteria*. New York: Macmillan.

Kretschmer, E. (1926). *Hysteria, Reflex and Instinct* (trans. Baskin, V. and Baskin, W.). New York: Philosophical Library (1960).

Laycock, T. (1840). *A Treatise on the Nervous Diseases of Women*. London: Longman.

Lee, R. (1871). *A Treatise on Hysteria*. London: Churchill.

Lewis, W.C., Berman, M. and Madison, W.I. (1965). Studies of conversion hysteria: I Operational study of diagnosis. Archives of General Psychiatry, **13**, 275–82.

Mace, C. J. (1992*a*). Hysterical conversion I: a history. *British Journal of Psychiatry*, **161**, 369–77.

Mace, C. J. (1992*b*). Hysterical conversion II: a critique. *British Journal of Psychiatry*, **161**, 378–89.

Mace, C. J. (2000). Survival of the fittest? Conceptual selection and psychiatric classification. In *Values and Psychiatric Classification* (ed. Sadler, J.). Baltimore: Johns Hopkins Press.

Mai, F. M. and Merskey, H. (1980). Briquet's treatise on hysteria. *Archives of General Psychiatry*, **37**, 1401–3.

Rangell, L. (1959). The nature of conversion. *Journal of the American Psychoanalytic Association*, **7**, 632–62.

Reynolds, J. Russell (1869). Paralysis, and other disorders of motion and sensation, dependent on idea. *British Medical Journal* 483–5.

Royal College of Physicians (1st edn, 1869; 2nd edn, 1884; 4th edn, 1906; 5th edn, 1918; 6th edn, 1931; 7th edn, 1948). *Nomenclature of Disease*. London: Royal College of Physicians.

Rycroft, C. (1966). Introduction: causes and meaning. In *Psychoanalysis Observed* (ed. Rycroft, C.), pp. 7–22. London: Constable.

Ryle, G. (1949). *The Concept of Mind*. London: Hutchinson.

Schilder, P. (1935). *The Image and Appearance of the Human Body*. New York: International Universities Press.

Shorter, E. (1992). *From Paralysis to Fatigue*. New York: Free Press.

Showalter, E. (1985). *The Female Malady*. New York: Pantheon.

Sydenham, T. (1848). Epistolary dissertation. In *The Works of Thomas Syndenham, M. D.* (trans. Latham, R. G.). London: Sydenham Society.

Symonds, C. (1970). Hysteria. In *The Analysis of Hysteria* (2nd edn, 1995) (ed. Merskey, H.) pp. 407–13. London: Gaskell.

Szasz, T. (1972). *The Myth of Mental Illness*. London: Paladin.

Veith, I. (1965). *Hysteria: The History of a Disease*. Chicago: University of Chicago Press.

World Health Organisation (6th revision, 1948; 7th revision, 1955; 8th revision, 1965; 9th revision, 1975; 10th revision, 1992). *Manual of International Classification of Diseases, Injuries and Causes of Death*. Geneva: WHO.

2 War-based hysteria — the military perspective

Ian P. Palmer

Although psychological reactions to combat have been recognized as far back as ancient Greece, it is only in the past one hundred years that they have been studied to any degree. From the literature, it is difficult to separate hysteria from the multitude of other psychological reactions to combat, as diagnostic criteria are seldom applied uniformly during war, and the battlefield is not conducive to controlled research. The variety of physical, psychiatric, and physiological symptoms seen in soldiers causes diagnostic confusion and raises issues concerning mental illness, stigma, cowardice, malingering, and other social constructs which shape the delineation of psychological reactions to combat. In addition, the practice of military psychiatry during combat has the 'organization' rather than the individual as its 'patient', which may present the military physician with moral, and at times ethical, dilemmas.

Introduction

> Were it not for the stigma attaching to the word, one would not hesitate to class them as hysterical. (Adrian and Yealland 1917)

Military interest in any medical subject is proportional to the effect the condition has on the fighting efficiency of that force. This chapter must be viewed in the context of armies existing to fight, not to go to hospital. Medical research on a battlefield is of low priority and difficult: researchers may die, records lost, and vagaries and variations in diagnostic practice and nomenclature are legion. Account must therefore be taken not only of hysteria but also its bedfellows — malingering, somatization, war syndromes, and anxiety reactions — for 'medical disorders create complex problems, ones that have extended beyond questions of medical diagnosis and therapy to issues of social attitudes and policy' (Feudtner 1993) and military societies are not exempt in this matter.

War is a group endeavour where 'the individual is of small account' (Lord Gort's evidence to the 1922 Shell-shock Committee (War Office 1922). Yet the individual serviceman is important in the same way that a machine part is vital to the smooth functioning of a larger machine. Although 'mental' cases were occurring from the outset of the First World War, it was not until 1916 that the manpower costs of psychiatric casualties were addressed seriously (Shepard 1996).

Most of the information in this chapter is based on research and observation of conscript armies. Today's armed forces are volunteers, have much widened roles, and as a consequence are more highly selected and trained. How they will fare during or after future conflicts only time will tell. Space only allows me to focus on the army in this chapter.

Military psychiatry

War is a social event and armed forces a distinct social–psychological system. During war, military psychiatry has to view the organization as its patient rather than the individual if the group is to achieve its stated mission. This mission is guided by the government of the day and therefore reflects the nation's wishes.

> It would be well to bear in mind constantly that while the task of the civilian psychiatrist is often to help a patient satisfy himself and to function satisfactorily and contentedly, the goal of the Army psychiatrist must be the efficient functioning of the individual as a soldier, without primary regard to satisfaction or contentment . . . Many people suffer in war. The criterion of one's ability to perform military duty should not necessarily include happiness at the task. (Quoted in L'Etang 1951)

Military psychiatry maintains the strength of the force by ensuring that commanders and their medical officers (MO) are trained to recognize and manage uncomplicated stress reactions and return their men to duty as rapidly as possible. It explains and adjudicates on inappropriate or deviant (military) behaviour, detects malingerers, undertakes diagnoses, and not infrequently becomes involved in aspects of man management and psychological support for unit commanders. Military doctors have a duty to both the organization and to their patients, which may pose ethical and moral dilemmas for them.

Military psychiatry is not without its detractors and mental breakdowns have long been ascribed to failure in morale, which in turn is seen as a failure of leadership. Commanders therefore have opinions about the subject which may be at variance with the medical profession. Sir Winston Churchill disliked psychiatrists (Ahrenfeldt 1958). General Patton apparently advised his officers and men to deride and ridicule soldiers with neurotic symptoms as if cowards and malingerers. And as recently as 1963, Admiral Rickover of the US Navy stated:

> I view with horror the day the Navy is induced to place psychiatrists on board our nuclear submarines. We are doing very well without them because the men don't know they have problems. But once a psychiatrist is assigned, they will learn that they have lots of problems. (Quoted in Ninnow 1963)

It would be wrong to assume that medical personnel were any less antipathetic to matters psychiatric. One medical officer considered that psychiatrists discharged individuals perfectly capable of performing some form of duty and that 'psychiatric methods and policies resulted in inaccurate assessment, diagnosis and disposal of so-called psychiatric cases' (L'Etang 1951).

A soldier's lot

On a battlefield, a soldier is faced with the moral dilemma of saving himself by deserting, surrendering, malingering, or perhaps through real illness or injury. He may also risk death, wounding, or capture by remaining with his comrades to fight. There is nothing in the human condition that provides such a dramatic conflict.

A battlefield is a dangerous place to break down, and combat involves exposure to sudden and violent death. Survivor's relief at escaping death often turns to ambivalence, especially following the loss of a close friend: this is often described as 'he died for me' or 'instead of me'. Such ambivalence can lead to anger, shame, and guilt. There is a loss of innocence and the sense of invulnerability, a loss of humanity (of having to kill or be killed), and there may be the loss of group support through death or injury. Loss of an officer can be particularly distressing — a form of parental abandonment (Garb *et al.* 1987). It is hardly surprising that there are psychological costs to combat, perhaps the largest of which are loss and grief — the connecting thread throughout all disorders, secondary to combat. So why fight?

The existential omnipotence of youth and the group experience are important. Denial and suppression are to my mind a prerequisite for functioning as a soldier. Denial must also exist at a societal level if too early an expression or acceptance of the loss and pain which war brings is not to undermine the national 'will' to fight (Mangelsdorff 1985). War is the most ambivalent of human experiences and the most human of all disasters, where victims and perpetrators within the tragedy suffer. The threat of imminent death can however accentuate the sweetness of life, as may the camaraderie which may never be experienced again. Some societies and individuals see war as the ultimate male experience and a rite of passage (see King's chapter in this volume, p. 36). Veterans often talk warmly of the feelings of belonging, achievement, closeness, and shared goals and experiences during service. War represents an experience where individuality is subsumed and personal resources mobilized altruistically for the benefit of the group.

After enlistment, recruits join a clear hierarchy. From the outset they know their place within it and that there is always someone senior who is responsible for them — a sort of 'facultative regression'. The biological family is replaced by the new (military) family wherein rules, structures, and boundaries are obvious and lead to the forging of close peer-group relationships. Survival on the battlefield is dependent on these relationships; reciprocal responsibility and the bonds created in training become forged in the heat of combat. As such, they rival familial bonds in intensity and importance. Some may idealize or even idolize these relationships, but this carries with it the increased risk of demoralization and disillusionment should things go wrong (Garb *et al.* 1987).

Regard for comrades, respect for leaders, and the urge to contribute are the major elements of resilience in combat. Thus, well-trained soldiers arrive at the action with a psychosocial mind-set which is both their strength and resolution in battle but harbours within it a vulnerability to bereavement from the loss of close bonds forged under the stress of battle. Support of the group is vital for survival; it offers unity and strength as opposed to isolation and insecurity. It has rituals and rules and gives the individual help with the emotional experience that is combat. From the outset, recruits are subject to military law and, despite individual and group psychological strengths, military discipline is required to keep some individuals in the 'firing line'. In the First World War, the ultimate sanction for British 'Tommies' was execution.

In addition to the individual there are other players in the drama of breakdown in combat. In order to maintain morale, the military has to invest in all aspects of man management to minimize the loss of effective manpower. Military society is based on ideals of courage and self-sacrifice as well as being built around group strengths. It is important to note that for every case evacuated there is a cost to be borne by those remaining in the field, as the same amount of work has to be carried out by fewer personnel. Other members of the group will be aware of those who have or cause problems within the group. In such circumstances those who 'do their best' and fail are often looked upon sympathetically but those who do not 'cut the mustard' will be given short shrift by their comrades. There will always be a tension between the 'good guys' who stay and the 'bad guys' who 'escape' the realities of the battlefield — a sort of reverse Darwinism.

Most breakdowns will be managed by MOs, who are usually the least experienced and youngest doctors. If it becomes widely known that the MO is 'soft' then his sick parades burgeon and malingerers will be seen to 'get away with it'. By contrast, if he or she is too severe and fails to recognize the 'deserving' case, the doctor's stock will fall within the whole unit, among both officers and men.

The individual responsible for the health of servicemen and women is however their commanding officer (CO), **not** the MO. The CO has responsibility for those in his charge, whilst at the same time answering to his superiors who direct him to undertake specific tasks. In turn, the Chiefs of Defence answer to Ministers who are answerable to the Treasury, Parliament, and the people (including veterans, families, and widows). All these parties will have opinions about the mental health of servicemen and women. Ultimately, it is society that decides how to view those who break down, how to manage them, and how to reconcile this with those who remain fit. The diagnosis of any mental condition during combat is therefore the result of a complex interplay between both medical and non-medical personnel as well as the military culture.

Estimation of psychiatric casualties is difficult for many reasons, including the sensitivity of the subject (which was, and still is, considered to reflect leadership qualities) and the desire not to hand a propaganda coup to the other side. Whilst offering a natural theatre in which to study how stress can effect or produce psychopathology, war is not conducive to such research and as a result, much of the research on psychiatric casualties is incomplete because it concentrates on the more static units and, by inference, the study of 'more severe' cases.

Although psychiatric classifications have existed for years, they are seldom rigorously used during combat. Hysterical conversion is comparatively easy to diagnose in the calm of a hospital ward but it is often misdiagnosed by MOs in the field. As a consequence, these disorders have often been mismanaged in wartime. Diagnostic boundaries blur and a process of normalization is negotiated in which the stigma of psychiatric labels is removed by terms such as 'shell-shock' and 'battle exhaustion' — neither of which imply 'weakness'. Rather, they refer to individuals who have given their all. Hence the popularity of these terms among the ranks and civilians, and the begrudging acceptance by the authorities (Mangelsdorff 1985)

Cowardice and fear

The First World War was the turning point for understanding the psychological reactions to combat. But even today, the concepts of fear and cowardice occupy military thinking and remain fundamental to the management of 'mental cases' in war. All military authorities consider cowardice to be a deviant (military) behaviour and hence deal with it seriously. One way in which military psychiatry seeks to explain aberrant behaviour under fire and to avoid stigma is to 'normalize' psychological reactions to combat. Although acute psychological breakdown is inevitable in certain circumstances, there will always be opprobrium from some military quarters for behaviour deemed cowardly. During the First World War, the term 'shell-shock' offered an organic and therefore acceptable explanation for breakdown. By contrast, cowardice was a moral and social construct of 'bad' or unacceptable behaviour and therefore punishable.

Distinguishing between shell-shock and cowardice was, from the outset, fraught with problems. Despite this, most of the witnesses to the Southborough Committee of 1922 agreed that cowardice was a military crime and should be punishable by death. The death penalty in the British Army was abolished in 1930.

> I know that every man has his limit; but just as some men are taller and heavier, some men can go longer and take more. Bravery is a fickle thing. It runs in some kind of cycle: it comes and it goes. One day a man is a lion in a fight: the next day a mouse . . . I have seen men who were brave when their feet were dry, cowards when they were wet; brave when they were warm, cowards when they were cold; brave when they were full, cowards when they were hungry; brave as long as they got their sleep, but cowards when they didn't. We often contrast bravery and cowardice. We think there is nothing between the two, but most men who know war know that there is. (Davis 1988)

It is easily forgotten that individuals who developed shell-shock or combat neuroses under fire had often been 'in the line' for 12 or more months, and some had even been decorated for bravery. An American study comparing 75 neuropsychiatric patients with 75 patients having plastic surgery revealed that the 'psychoneurotic' group received more medals, awards, and decorations than the surgical group. Furthermore, they had served outside the USA for an average of 12.5 months compared with 8.4 months for the surgical cases (Pratt and Neustadter 1947). One of the patients in the Northfield Experiments had even received the Victoria Cross (Harrison and Clarke 1992). [Northfield was a military hospital in the UK where novel treatments were used].

Combat psychiatry

There have always been avenues of escape from the field of battle. Physical illness, injury, and latterly psychiatric disturbance, as reflected in behavioural abnormalities, all offer a legitimate exit from combat. It is the role of all military medical services to ensure that, in order for the military objective to be achieved, such exits are as few as possible.

The experiences of soldiers in wars have been instrumental in not only advancing our understanding of mental processes but also influencing psychoanalytical ideas, which have in turn found their way into public consciousness (Stone 1985). When reading sources, it is clear that diagnostic categories were imprecise, and it is difficult to distinguish hysteria, heterogeneous war syndromes — effort syndrome (ES), disordered action of the heart (DAH), neurocirculatory asthenia (NCA), and anxiety states from one another (Mott 1918). An overview is provided in Table 2.1

Nostalgia

Nostalgia was the first war-related psychological syndrome to be studied. The term was coined by Johannes Hofer in 1678 to describe an affliction seen in Swiss soldiers serving with the French, who termed it 'maladie du pays'. A similar condition had been

Table 2.1 Summary of war-related psychiatric conditions

War	Acute mental reaction	Somatic syndrome	Post-conflict mental illness
American Civil War	'Psychoses' Nostalgia	Nostalgia Soldier's / irritable heart — Da Costa's syndrome	'Psychoses' Depressive and anxiety states Neurasthenia Hysteria
Boer War		Neurasthenia DAH Psychogenic rheumatism	
First World War	Hysteria Shell-shock Neurasthenia	DAH Effort syndrome Neurocirculatory asthenia	Anxiety disorders Depressive disorders Alcoholism Neurasthenia
Second World War	Combat exhaustion or fatigue Combat neuroses	Effort syndrome Non-ulcer dyspepsia	Anxiety neuroses Depressive neuroses Alcoholism Neurasthenia
Korea	Combat exhaustion	Cold injury	Anxiety neuroses Depressive neuroses Substance misuse
Vietnam	Combat exhaustion	'Agent Orange' syndrome	Anxiety disorders Depressive disorders Substance misuse Post-traumatic stress disorder
Yom Kippur	Combat stress reaction Battle-shock		Post-traumatic stress disorder
Current	Battle-shock Acute stress reactions Combat stress reactions	Post-conflict, medically unexplained symptoms or war syndromes	Post-traumatic (conflict) mental illness

recognized in the Spanish Army in Flanders during the Thirty Years' War and was termed 'el mal de corazon' or 'estar roto' (Rosen 1975). In 1761, Auenbrugger described symptoms of intense homesickness, over-tiredness, poor concentration, and poor appetite occurring in mercenaries from Switzerland and Scotland.

Napoleon's surgeon, Dominique Jean Larrey, described nostalgia as a condition with three phases:

> . . . soldier's minds become preoccupied with ruminations on idealised thoughts of home, family and friends. Such thoughts are associated with a raised temperature, tachycardia, conjunctival injection, unusual movements and rapid and incoherent utterances. After which individuals feel oppressed and weary and sigh and stretch frequently. The individual

is constipated and has various and variable aches and pains. This is followed by an increase in fever with anorexia, gastrointestinal symptoms and dysfunction after which there is 'great prostration' and mental depression as evidenced by 'weeping and groaning'. Food may be refused and individuals may commit suicide or simply 'surrender to death'. (Quoted in Rosen 1975)

The term nostalgia was fading from usage when it was resurrected during the American Civil War by Surgeon-General William Hammond (Hammond 1883) who noted that the numbers of such cases rose as the war progressed. Between 1862 and 1863, the number of cases had risen from 572 to 2016.

Nostalgia gradually became subsumed within melancholia, which was thought to lead to gastrointestinal dysfunction and fevers. Some of the symptoms could be caused by infections, although these disorders were said to occur more commonly in young conscripts and in prisoners of war (Peters 1863). Anecdotal evidence suggests that the symptoms could be reversed by a period of leave at home or discharge from service.

Evacuation syndromes

One of the fundamental principles of military psychiatry is the attempt to keep the soldier in their social role as a soldier and to avoid him or her assuming or being given the role (label) of patient. The Russians demonstrated the importance of this during the Russo–Japanese War (1904–5). Because it took 30 to 40 days to return casualties to Moscow, military hospitals held casualties locally until they were fit to travel. Two fundamental psychiatric truths were discovered as a consequence of this practice. Firstly, some soldiers recovered and could be returned to duty; and second, psychiatric symptoms became 'fixed' in those evacuated to Moscow – the so-called 'evacuation syndrome' (Awtokratow 1907).

Regrettably, this information was ignored from the outset in the First World War. The French initially sent their psychological casualties directly home, where the sight of damaged young men caused an outcry. Accordingly, such cases were kept nearer the Front, where the French discovered, like the Russians before them, that some recovered and could be returned to duty. The British also made the same mistake by sending their casualties back to the UK, until they learnt from the French experience.

Mental breakdown — shell-shock, hysteria, neurasthenia, and anxiety states

From the outset of the First World War, reports of mental illness — mainly hysterical paralyses, gait disturbances, amnesias, aphonias — were being reported and evacuated to the UK, where they stimulated a search among physicians for a physical cause (Ritchie 1968). There had never been a war like it, with slaughter on a vast scale and exposure to high explosives. Not unreasonably, it was proposed that subsequent physical (hysterical) and psychological symptoms were the result of the physical effects of explosives whose concussive blast somehow damaged the nervous system (Mott 1919).

To be a man is to retain your self-control at all times and not to break down, especially within the military environment (Ritchie 1968, p. 173 et seq.). This view was particularly prevalent when the British Empire was at its height and 'Imperial Man' reigned the known world and his emotions. Loss of control meant lack of will-power and moral fibre, and was considered to be more common in 'other ranks' (OR). Furthermore, within these ranks it was deemed more likely in the weakling recruits from cities (Ritchie 1968, p. 121).

Myers described an officer's neurasthenic breakdowns as the result of a process of 'wearing down', whereas the other ranks' hysterical symptoms represented a sudden 'breaking down'. During combat, officers had to busy themselves with orders and were protected by their upbringing and 'traditions', whereas the other ranks had simply to wait patiently for either death or command to action (Myers 1940). Rivers (1918) related these observations to differences in character, schooling, and the effects of military training and duty. Hysteria solves the conflict between instinct and duty instantly, as the soldier becomes a patient and is absolved from duty. Officers were deemed less likely to have such conflicts because of their (public) schooling; they were however more vulnerable to being 'worn down' by the burden of leadership, responsibility, and decision making. Hence, hysteria was seen less often in officers. In addition, fewer officers were returned to duty at the Front (Ritchie 1968, p. 211).

Thus breakdowns *without* an inherited constitutional cause were perceived, within military and imperial frames of reference, as characterological weakness manifest as socially deviant behaviour. As a consequence, they were punishable under military law. Of over 3000 recommendations for the death penalty during the First World War, 346 British soldiers were actually executed — 18 for cowardice and 266 for desertion (Ahrenfeldt 1958, p. 271). In the Second World War, it is estimated that over 15 000 Germans soldiers were executed for desertion, mainly in the latter stages of the conflict (Binneveld 1997). The number of Russian troops executed is not known.

Odd or bad behaviour on the battlefield was likely to be punished however. By 1916, the scale of psychiatric breakdowns was such that distinctions between normal and abnormal, mad or bad (cowardly) had broken down. Military authorities were unsure how to deal with this situation; mass executions would not stem the flow and only add to losses. It therefore fell to the medical officers of the Royal Army Medical Corps (RAMC) to act as moral arbiters for the military. But whilst their stock rose within the non-medical departments of the armed forces, so did their moral dilemmas (Ritchie 1968, p. 172).

Shell-shock

The term 'shell-shock' was first used in a medical journal by Captain Myers in 1915 (Myers 1915). Like no other word before or since, shell-shock encapsulated the psychological cost of war and its use rapidly became widespread among soldiers, their medical officers, and civilians. It soon lost any coherence as a diagnosis, however, as it was applied to nearly everything; even individuals who had never been to the Front (or even left the UK) were being assigned the diagnosis. It had become 'a most desirable' psychiatric label and a 'ticket' out of active service (Ritchie 1968, p. 247 et seq.).

Myers (1940, p. 75) described the psychopathology of shell-shock as follows:

(a) Emotional 'trauma'
Conscious, due to extreme fright, horror or other intolerable distress
Unconscious, after physical violence
Producing:

(b) Mental 'shock', ranging from slight dizziness or 'cloudiness' to profound stupor,

Leading to:

(c) Disordered personality, characterised by amnesia, fission of personality, suggestibility etc.

Accompanied perhaps by:

(d) Hysteric ('functional') symptoms, and/or by neurasthenic ('exhaustive') symptoms, in the emotional, cognitive, volitional and autonomic systems.

Given the diagnostic uncertainty relating to psychological disorders during the First World War and the subsequent large pension bill, attempts were made to tighten definitions (Myers 1940, p. 88). Abuse of the term shell-shock led to British General Routine Order No. 2384 (June 1917), in which MOs were ordered to record *no* diagnosis on cases transferred to 'special hospitals'. Instead, they were encouraged to append 'NYDN' (not yet diagnosed, nervous). In addition:

> In no circumstances whatever will the expression 'shell shock' be used verbally or be recorded in regimental or other casualty report, or in any hospital or other medical document. (Quoted in Binneveld 1997, p. 142)

Hysteria

Both hysteria and neurasthenia were seen from the outset of the First World War and were 'difficult to separate' (Mott 1918). They were recognizable to the psychologically minded but caused minimally trained MOs many diagnostic headaches. Only later in the course of the War did RAMC MOs receive instruction in the management of mental cases (Shephard 1991). Early in the War there were, therefore, many inappropriate evacuations, where kindly and well-meaning nursing staff and volunteers ensured 'fixation' of hysterical symptoms. By contrast, hysteria was much less common during the Second World War, whereas anxiety neuroses were diagnosed more frequently (Hadfield 1942; Ahrenfeldt 1958, p. 23).

The main problem with hysteria was the diagnostic dilemma for the clinician — was the patient feigning illness and if so, why? Hysteria occurred mostly in the other ranks, and during both World Wars symptoms were often occupationally determined. These included gross gait abnormalities, hand pareses, or more subtle symptoms that, whilst not incapacitating, limited employability (for example, symptoms such as reduced visual acuity, hearing difficulties, and impaired depth perception in air crew). Rivers postulated that the rapid induction and training of conscripts worked to enhance their suggestibility, and therefore 'predisposed' individuals to hysteria (Rivers 1918).

Episodes of dissociation, derealization, or depersonalization also occurred and led to acts of great valour and self-sacrifice for others:

> A feature of collective bravery is the ecstatic surrender, equivalent to a suicidal impulse, of the self. I have known soldiers to whom it seemed that only through their deaths could their ideals be obtained. They constituted themselves the human sacrifice for the good of the community. This feeling was generally accompanied by a melancholy, a detachment from life, which acted as a stimulus to sacrifice. A man must have lost much that makes life

worth living before he reaches this stage. I have met boys who, having lost friends or family, no longer valued life, and were ready to face danger for the sake of their country. (Meerloo 1944)

Neurasthenia

In the second half of the nineteenth century, there was heated debate about the existence of neurasthenia as a distinct medical entity. It was viewed either as a 'catch-all' label for symptoms of differing aetiology or as a specific condition of nervous fatigue accompanied by a multitude of symptoms. An American physician called Beard named the condition in 1868 and described its core symptoms as a combination of undue and excessive fatigue with gastrointestinal symptoms and headache. Tanzi succinctly described it as 'a state of habitual valetudinarianism with no characteristic organic lesion' (Cobb 1920). In the UK and the USA it was a condition of the upper classes, thought to be caused by the fatigue that decent, hard-working, and upstanding individuals 'suffered' from their endeavours. Hence the tendency to equate it with heroic endeavour.

Thus from the outset of the First World War there was a class-specific label, with minimal stigma, for breakdown in the 'officer class'. It not only avoided the moral taints of Freud's theories, but also the prospect of treatment in an asylum. Furthermore, it was socially acceptable (Ritchie 1968, p. 120). But, as with other classifications, it lost its validity through indiscriminate usage:

> . . . this term (neurasthenia) for years has meant little, but in the army nomenclature it has absolutely lost any scientific value it ever had, since any functional syndrome seems thus officially designated. Any nerve disorder short of insanity that is not patently hysterical is thus connoted. (Read 1920)

Anxiety neuroses

Anxiety neuroses became the most common psychiatric diagnosis during the Second World War and subsequently. Disorders previously diagnosed as shell-shock, hysteria, and neurasthenia were now conceptualized as anxiety, dissociative, or mixed states (Palmer 1945). The Command Psychiatrist to British Middle East Forces, Brigadier Rees, saw 'minor mental disorders' as occurring in two main groups:

> **I: Battle Neurotics**. Battle incidents may precipitate the sudden onset of acute symptoms . . . the symptoms produced may vary from a shivering stuporous state to hysterical manifestations like deaf mutism, a paraplegia or blindness. It is these patients that provide the dramatic element in war neuroses. **II: Neurotic Sick** . . . are much less obvious and consist of patients whose symptoms are suggestive of physical illness, and who complain of indigestion, palpitation, headache, pains in the chest etc. Investigation reveals no 'organic' explanation of the symptoms, but it will always be found on enquiry that such cases have many 'nervous' accompaniments of their illness, such as loss of sleep . . . nightmare(s) . . . and fears of many kinds. (Rees 1941)

He pointed out the 'contagion' of such presentations; the added difficulty of dealing with individuals carrying deadly weapons; and the role of the MO in excluding organic causes.

He noted that the incidence of battle neuroses was directly linked to the severity of combat as measured by numbers of physical casualties sustained (see also Swank 1949).

Seldom did combat precipitate anxiety states in isolation; other factors — for example, climatic stresses, insects and flies, lack of leave, lack of feminine company, lack of sleep, irregular feeding and fluids, poor hygiene, and exhaustion — needed to be present. Fear that led to flight ended with court martial, and fear with symptoms led to the suspicion of malingering; an MO was not encouraged to allow his sympathy to colour his judgement. The hysterical symptoms most commonly seen were amnesia, blackouts, fugue states, and 'hospital hysteria' (where symptoms from real injuries or illnesses are prolonged and/or exaggerated). These disorders had also been described in the First World War.

A psychiatrist with extensive 'field' experience (Palmer 1945) considered that two thirds of psychological battle casualties were a result of 'impaired or broken morale'. He observed that the most common precipitant was the death of a close friend or platoon officer and that 'more often than not we are studying a reaction to handling as much as a primary reaction to danger and stress'. He went on to describe 'four low-morale subgroups, classified as panic reactions, and four good-morale subgroups, classified as anguish reactions'. In these situations responses could be either anxious or dissociative in nature.

His so-called 'primary symptoms' of these panic and anguish reactions were reported as:

Lack of concentration	Visceral disturbances
Amnesia	Disturbance of special senses
Torpor	Motor disturbances
Pseudo-torpor	Sensory disturbances
Stammer	Lassitude
Tics	Emotional instability
Diffuse anxiety and/or depression	Feelings of unreality
Insomnia	Irritability
Battle dreams	Hypersensitivity
Headache	Fatigability
Dizziness	

Medically unexplained syndromes and post-conflict combat or war syndromes

Medically unexplained syndromes

The presentation of physical symptoms during war is influenced by the health concerns of the day. During the American Civil War, for example, the concerns about rheumatic heart disease were reflected in the appearance of symptoms attributed to the heart. Da Costa described the syndrome of 'irritable heart' or 'soldier's heart', and the symptoms of dyspnoea, palpitations, chest pain, and dizziness attracted a label of organic cardiac disorder (Da Costa 1871). Similar cases were seen in the Boer War and the First World War, where they were termed DAH (disordered action of the heart). Close examination revealed however that fewer than 10 per cent of cases had any cardiac abnormality (Lewis 1918). These patients were difficult to treat and said to deteriorate when informed that a murmur had been detected.

During the First World War, the term 'effort syndrome' was used to describe patients with these disorders, who presented with the following symptoms:

> . . . breathlessness, consciousness of the heart beat, giddiness, faintness, fatigue, aching of the limbs with tremulousness and exhaustion following exercise followed by stiffness of the muscles, feelings of lassitude, actual malaise and . . . pain in the precordial region (Lewis 1918, p. 3).

There is clearly considerable overlap between this disorder and that described by Da Costa, yet it was another 20 years before Paul Wood conclusively showed no relevant organic cause for the symptoms (Wood 1941).

Examination of Public Record Office archives reveals that many of the individuals receiving pensions following gassing in the First World War, but who had no physical or objective signs of such exposure, were diagnosed as having DAH (Jones 2000).

Medically unexplained disorders were common in both World Wars, and particularly increased in frequency as the Second World War become more protracted.

> Late recognition of somatization reactions meant the costly and dangerous practices of over-examination and numerous diagnostic procedures, with the making of diagnoses by exclusion, excessive treatment programs, unnecessary hospitalisations, or too long bed rest and prolongation of convalescence. Soldiers hospitalised too quickly or for trivial reasons were found to get the hospital habit . . . Bed rest was abused in such disorders as neurocirculatory asthenia; that unrecognised personality disturbances and conversion syndromes complicated and retarded convalescences from infections and trauma . . . a symptom found to predominate in all functional disorders was that of general fatigue . . . four main groups of disorders: dyspeptic, rheumatic, cardio-circulatory and headaches. (Lewis and Engle 1954)

In the Second World War it was said that German solders had no or little neurotic breakdown, which was attributed to their intimate fighting groups and the zero or low tolerance of such breakdowns (Binneveld 1997, p. 91). An additional deterrence was the creation of 'Magenbattalionen' — battalions of those who had gone sick (with physical illnesses such as dyspepsia, debility, and so on). In the latter stages of the Second World War however, the number of breakdowns in German forces increased (Binneveld 1997, p. 93).

Post-conflict combat or war syndromes

Following both World Wars, interest in functional conditions such as soldier's heart, DAH, effort syndrome, and neurocirculatory asthenia (NCA) seemed to wane, despite the numbers of individuals receiving pensions for such conditions. More recently, interest has been rekindled in medically unexplained symptoms from veterans said to have been exposed to Agent Orange in Southeast Asia in the late 1960s and illnesses following the Persian Gulf War in 1991 (Hyams *et al.* 1996).

Despite a massive research investment in the USA into Gulf War illness, no simple explanation has been forthcoming. The only British study to date has found no evidence for a specific Gulf War syndrome (Ismail *et al.* 1999), but did report a definite increase in non-specific symptomatology following active service in the Gulf (Unwin *et al.* 1999).

Table 2.2 Comparison of the symptoms of war-related syndromes

Symptoms	Soldier's Heart (1)	DAH (2)	NCA (3)	Effort syndrome (4)	Neurasthenia (5)	Shell-shock (6)	Acute combat stress reaction (6)	Agent Orange Exposure (6)	PTSD (6)	GWS (6)
Palpitations	+	+	+	+	+	+	+		+	
Chest pain	+	+	+	+		+			+	+
Tachycardia	+		+				+			
Dyspnoea	+	+	+	+			+		+	+
Headache	+		+		+	+	+	+	+	+
Dizziness	+	+	+	+	+			+		+
Sleep disturbance	+	+	+	+	+	+	+	+	+	+
Bad dreams	+				+	+			+	
Indigestion	+				+					
Diarrhoea	+		+	+	+	+	+	+	+	+
Anxiety	+	+	+	+	+	+	+	+	+	+
Trembling	+	+	+	+	+	+	+		+	
Fatigue	+	+	+	+	+	+	+	+	+	
Fainting	+	+	+	+		+			+	
Irritability					+		+	+	+	+
Memory problems						+	+	+	+	+
Joint pains						+		+	+	+
Hysterical symptoms					+	+	+	+	+	

1 Da Costa, J. M. (1871). On irritable heart; a clinical study of a form of functional cardiac disorder and its consequences. *American Journal of Medical Science*. **61**: 17–52.

2 Hume, W. E. (1918). A study of the cardiac disabilities of soldiers in France (VDH and DAH). *Lancet*, **1**: 529–34.

3 Cohen, M. E. and White, P. D. (1972). Neurocirculatory asthenia: 1972 concept. *Military Medicine*, **April**: 142–4.

4 Army Directorate of Psychiatry Directive 1918. RDMC Library.

5 Forsyth, D. (1915). Functional nerve disease and shock of battle. *Lancet*, **December**: 1399–403.

6 Hyams, K. C., Wignall, S., and Roswell, R. (1996). War syndromes and their evaluation; from the US Civil War to the Persian Gulf War. *Annals of Internal Medicine*. **125(5)**: 398–405.

Conflicts from 1945

Korea

Against the backdrop of the Cold War media attention focussed on brainwashing, torture, and propaganda — a situation which highlighted to the public the role of the subconscious mind. Initially, the main psychological problems were seen in those recalled to the colours (soldiers who had seen action in the Second World War).

It was 14 months before there was a British psychiatrist in Korea. Before this casualties were evacuated to Japan (Jones and Palmer 2000). Of the 564 casualties seen by the British psychiatrists, 10 were officers (5 with conditions related to combat). Of the 554 other ranks interviewed, 365 were returned to duty and 69 evacuated to the UK. Anxiety reactions predominated, but a handful of cases of hysteria were treated and with more success than the anxiety states (Flood 1954). Hysterical disorders were more common in situations when troops were exposed to mortar and artillery fire. At one stage of the war there was an epidemic of frostbite which came to be seen as a good indicator of morale, some men removing their boots in order to develop the disorder. Treatments were much the same as in the Second World War and included narcosis, abreaction (especially for hysterical patients), reassurance, suggestion, and appeals to the sense of duty in the individual and their unit.

Vietnam

Although there were few acute combat-related psychiatric casualties during the campaign (Neel 1973), a rear echelon hospital found the following unexplained symptoms in wounded and non-wounded casualties in 1966:

- Wounded — persistent pain, anaesthesia, weakness and hyperaesthesia.
- Non-wounded — syncope, pseudoseizures, locomotor symptoms, amnesias, blurred vision, aphonia, stuttering, gastric complaints, headaches, narcolepsy-like symptoms, somnambulism, anxiety dreams, and shouting.

Such symptoms were most likely to occur when the individual was about to be returned to duty.

Yom Kippur, 1973

In this war, acute combat breakdown was found to occur within hours of fighting (War Psychiatry 1995). Yom Kippur provided a timely reminder that combat breakdowns were not a thing of the past, can occur with frightening rapidity (Abraham 1982), and need to be anticipated and catered for (Dasberg *et al.* 1987).

Falklands, 1982

No more than 2–4 per cent of acute psychiatric casualties were encountered, despite difficult fighting many miles from home in poor weather conditions. Morale was high throughout despite a number of losses. Psychiatric support was provided by the Royal

Navy, on-board ship (not on land), where therapeutic groups and individual work was undertaken (Price 1984). Some individuals have suffered long-term mental health problems following their involvement in the campaign.

Gulf War, 1991

There were few psychiatric casualties in this war and there is little or no mention of hysterical casualties in the forces in the Gulf. Most cases seen were anxiety reactions. The fear of gas attack by Iraq was an ever-present and frightening aspect of the deployment that led to high levels of anxiety for prolonged periods (Martin *et al.* 1996). Both during the preparation and the war itself, troops were well supported by numerous psychiatrists and psychiatric nurses. Luckily for the allies little resistance was encountered and the war was over in 100 hours. Despite this, a number of service personnel subsequently developed multi-system symptoms — the putative 'Gulf War syndrome' — on their return from the Persian Gulf. No satisfactory explanation for this phenomenon has yet been proposed (Ismail *et al.* 1999).

Malingering

Malingering, the purposeful development of symptoms to avoid duty, is more than loss of manpower for the military — it goes against the military code of honour. Why should the best soldiers, sailors, and airmen face danger and the malingerer escape? Doctors in both World Wars suggested that malingering was rare, a fact not necessarily believed by military commanders! The reported low incidence of malingering may relate to the overt and covert selection processes that occur at all levels from recruitment to deployment and combat.

Most published authors from 1914 to 1945 state that malingering was rare and relatively easily detected (Hadfield 1942). 'Scrimshanking' on the other hand was not uncommon and a distinction can be drawn between this characteristically group activity and malingering (when the individual's body becomes the focus of the doctor–patient discourse). Bourke (1996) divides the motives for malingering into the following groups:

1. to avoid service altogether
2. to get sent home from combat
3. to prolong symptoms, both physical and psychological.

She describes a number of devious practices, such as the use of picric acid to cause jaundice, cordite from .303 cartridges to produce pyrexia and cardiac arrhythmias, and the rubbing of horse dung into the gums to simulate scurvy (Bourke 1996, p. 84 et seq.). Soldiers' terms for malingering included 'sodgering', 'stuffing the doctor', 'funking', 'scrimshanking', 'gold baring', and 'becoming a 'hospital bird'.

It has been suggested that malingering is the spur for medicine to develop objective medical tests for conditions rather than rely on the reports of patients (see Bass' chapter in this volume, p. 126). The relationship between doctor and patient is changed in war: some doctors feel acutely uncomfortable accusing individuals of malingering, a punishable offence, whereas others take a more military and less psychological stance. But gradually, even malingering was brought under the psychological umbrella as an almost 'unconscious' mental process, or certainly occurring in an individual with character flaws (psychopathy) (Cooter 1998). Although civilian doctors could assuage their consciences using this paradigm, military authorities remained unimpressed. Thus by the outset of the Second World War, malingering, in medical circles at least, was seen as a manifestation of 'psychopathy' (Good 1942), and 'badness' had been transformed into 'sickness' (Cooter 1998, p. 135).

All military doctors are expected to become experts at spotting the malingerer, which is not an easy task on a battlefield. It should also be remembered that any unnecessary evacuation from combat puts the lives of others at risk and there has always been a core of military men who feel that psychiatrists 'let malingerers off'. This debate will continue as long as armies exist.

Prevention

Could these conditions be prevented? Following the experiences of the First World War and influenced by the theory that those who broke down had an inherited or environmental predisposition, the Southborough Committee (War Office 1922, p. 50) suggested that selection should be used to screen out undesirable recruits. Psychoanalytical theories, many emanating from the USA, drove the search for ways of screening out those vulnerable to breakdowns. Despite these however 'psychiatric disabilities were by far the largest cause of medical discharge among military personnel (other ranks) during the Second World War' (Ahrenfeldt 1958, p. 211). Furthermore, there was little to separate those who broke down early from those who endured long periods of combat and service before breaking down. The experience of the First World War had demonstrated that breakdown was the result of the complex interplay of many factors which are unlikely to be identified by abbreviated selection processes or the opinion of psychiatrists.

The importance of rest in protecting against breakdown was noted to be vital: 'unless an infantryman is motivated to look forward to a "break", he has nothing to look forward to but "death, mutilation or psychiatric breakdown"' (Surgeon General US Army 1944). And such breakdowns were more likely to occur in the following circumstances: when taking heavy casualties; loosing; being under indirect fire; and when immobile and unable to fight back. Certain groups were considered particularly vulnerable: for example, new recruits; unit misfits; those new to a unit; and badly led, fed, and supplied troops. These latter factors are related to issues of leadership and morale. The soldier's buddies are the first to note changes in behaviour and character that signify impending breakdown. They may be able to help the individual pull through; if not, they will turn to the MO for advice. 'Personal pride and the group loyalty of the soldier seemed to be the most conscious sustaining factors' (Ludwig 1947). Brigadier Rees felt that the average well-trained (British) solder was likely to show signs of stress after four or five days of intense day and night fighting and after two years of active service overseas.

As with all psychiatric conditions, the aetiology of combat-related mental illness is multifactorial. Whilst good training, group cohesion, and morale are essential for psychological protection during combat, it is inevitable that some individuals will be effected by their experiences. Secondary prevention — the early recognition of those in difficulties — is important if such individuals are not to deteriorate.

Treatment

At the front

All military interventions in the field are simple and applied using the principles enunciated by Salmon in 1917 (Salmon 1917). That is, *proximity* — as close to the front as possible; *immediacy* — as soon as possible; *expectancy* — with the expectation of return to duty, and *simplicity* — as simple an intervention as possible; otherwise known as 'PIES'. Such interventions involve *recognition* — of the reaction; *respite* — from the fight; *rest* — and sleep; *recall* — talk it out with 'mates'; *reassurance* — their reactions are normal; *rehabilitation* — staying in uniform undertaking military duties; and *return* — to duty. These are the so-called 'seven Rs'.

It is important to maintain a positive therapeutic expectation that the soldier will return to duty. This is more likely to occur if the treatment is delivered quickly and as close as possible to the front. Whilst this is in the interests of the unit, it may also serve to protect the individual from post-conflict psychological disturbances. Many acute reactions will have been self-limiting and managed by comrades and NCOs and officers in the field. It is possible to return 40–80 per cent of soldiers back to duty in this way.

In war, normalization of 'symptoms and syndromes' is an important part of therapy. The terms battle or combat fatigue or exhaustion came to be used in the Second World War in the same way that shell-shock was coined to describe the psychological casualties of the First World War. All these terms have face validity and, to a degree, diminished the stigma of a psychiatric label such as 'psychoneurosis' which, within the ranks, became transformed to 'psycho': a term which remains in common usage today. Fatigue or exhaustion described what was being seen and experienced and 'normalized' the experience. It demonstrated that even the best of men could only take so much. The Americans worked out that any soldier was practically useless after 240 days of active service and fighting. Even so, they did not rotate their men as frequently as the British (or Germans), who felt you could get 400 days out of a 'Tommy' before he became a liability to himself and the group (Ahrenfeldt 1958, p. 172).

Behind the front

Treatment behind the lines occurs as near to the front as possible, in aid stations or field and base hospitals. The treatment is still based on 'PIES' and the 'seven Rs', and it is estimated that at each echelon it should be possible to return 40–80 per cent to their units after 48 hours. They are kept with 'their own group' and encouraged to help each other. Throughout this and subsequent phases there is an expectancy that they *will* return to their units.

If they do not respond then they are evacuated further back, but kept in a military setting, where they are given more rest and have organic causes excluded and treated. The emphasis is on respite, recollection, and then rehabilitation and return. Individuals are encouraged to recall their experiences in groups where the normality of their experiences is impressed upon them. This follows the experience in both World Wars that suggested that abreaction and catharsis of unpleasant events and sharing of experiences is therapeutic (Sargant and Slater 1972).

Rather cynically one could say that whatever the diagnosis, the treatments on offer were generally similar; many were used at different times on the same patient. Simplistically, therapy could be directed at the symptoms ('coverers') or their causes ('uncoverers').

The 'uncoverers' derived from the theories of Janet, Freud, and Breuer, who believed that retrieval of the traumatic memories with their attached affects (so-called 'abreaction') was therapeutic (Rivers 1916). The 'coverers' emerged from the work of Babinski and Froment (1918), who believed that hysterical symptoms were caused by suggestion and could therefore be removed by counter-suggestion. In both World Wars the coverers had the upper hand, as therapy directed at them gave quicker results — although it is difficult to know how effective these treatments were in the long term.

Types of treatment: 'coverers'

Rest, baths, massage, and isolation. It was felt that the tranquillity of isolation from stimulation, a healthy diet, and rest would restore shattered nerves. First enunciated for the treatment of neurasthenia by Wier Mitchell, this treatment was not a success (Salmon 1917). The expectation that a return to beauty and tranquillity would be beneficial was unfounded and unrealized (Ahrenfeldt 1958, p. 247 et seq.).

Physical rehabilitation. Special hospitals such as Colchester (in the First World War) and Mill Hill (in the Second World War) were established to deal with cases of effort syndrome and functional cardiac syndromes. In these places, graded exercise programmes, re-education, and re-attribution were undertaken (Wood 1941).

Discipline. Treatment was undertaken in a setting of military discipline. It was noted that individuals were more likely to recover, whatever their symptoms, in such environments.

Work therapy. Distraction in the form of work, especially agricultural work, was found to be helpful for some. Occupational therapy flourished, especially for those wounded both physically as well as psychologically.

Suggestion. This was akin to implanting an idea in such a way as to secure its acceptance (Cobb 1920, p. 289). Suggestion could be accomplished either when awake or under hypnosis.

Persuasion. This was felt to be different from suggestion. It involved reasoning with the individual about the cause, nature, and mechanism of their symptoms — with no attempt to address any underlying cause (Cobb 1920, p. 292). Persuasion and suggestion could be augmented by electrical stimulation.

Re-education. Cobb (1920, p. 297) described two types of re-education: (1) following an ether or hypnotic analysis, and (2) mental training following a full history (a way of helping the individual to perceive past events in a different way). This may progress to exploration of unconscious memories at a later stage. The aim was to assimilate unpleasant memories to prevent them from causing future difficulties.

Desperate times called for desperate measures, and there was a need to restore individuals to 'health and usefulness' as a matter of urgency: psychotherapy took too long (Yealland 1918). At times, therapy developed an air of combat and struggle for supremacy, and such 'disciplinary' therapies (Binneveld 1997, p. 107 et seq.) lent themselves to use in cases of hysteria (which were more commonly reported by other ranks and seldom used on officers).

Electrotherapy — faradism, torpillage. Electricity had been used in medicine for some time before 1914, especially in the treatment of neurasthenia. It was hardly surprising that with the number and range of gross hysterical symptoms reported that it would be used extensively in cases of hysteria during the First World War (Hurst and Symns 1918). The French called it 'torpillage' and its main exponent in France was Dejerine. In Germany, Kaufmann was its main advocate, and in the UK it was promoted by L. R. Yealland (Yealland 1918). In both these latter countries, severe shocks were administered which unfortunately led to deaths in Austria and Germany. In France, it came to be associated with torture (Myers 1940, p. 103).

Electricity provided a powerful counter-suggestion and disincentive to retain any symptoms. It was used a little in the Second World War (Binneveld 1997, p. 128).

Psychotropic drugs in combat. In Vietnam, tranquillisers were sometimes used before combat (Colbach 1985).

Types of treatment: 'uncoverers'

Abreaction. Abreaction was used from the First World War onwards, as it was found that allowing the individual to revisit their trauma might free them from it (Culpin 1920). This found even more support in the Second World War, by which time Freud's ideas had spread widely within psychiatry. But in situations of national emergencies there was no time for protracted talking therapies. As a result, physical aids to abreaction were used, such as sodium pentothal, ether, as well as hypnosis. Treatment even occurred in groups.

Narcosis and hypno-analysis. The aim of this was synergistic with abreaction, but more attention was paid to the patient's mental 'content' or processes. Narcosis was attempted by many drugs including sodium amytal, cocaine, hashish, mescaline, alcohol, and paraldehyde (Horsley 1936). Its efficacy was variable and it was indicated for anxiety states, hysteria, post head injury, malingering or simulation, and diagnostic uncertainty. Hypno-analysis was popular in the First World War and still used in the Second (Hadfield 1920).

Individual psychotherapy. This was rapidly discarded as too time-consuming, but it was accepted that some required this treatment (Rivers 1916).

Group psychotherapy. The Second World War saw a growing understanding and interest in group therapy. Given the large numbers of individuals requiring help and the lack of psychiatrists, groups offered a way of providing psychotherapy to many (James 1945). Bold initiatives were started in Birmingham (Ahrenfeldt 1958, p. 120) and have ever after been known as the 'Northfield Experiments' (Harrison and Clarke 1992). These formed the basis of therapeutic communities after the War.

Since a number of psychiatrists served in both World Wars, many of the treatments from the First World War were also used in the Second. But in the Second World War the focus moved towards the increasing use of physical treatments, and in the UK William Sargant was their most active proponent. The two aims of interventions were firstly, to secure rest and, secondly, to undertake therapy following physical restoration (Sargant 1942).

Heavy sedation — 'first aid treatment'. This has been used — with drugs such as paraldehyde, sodium amytal, and alcohol — to treat panic and hysteria. Intravenous barbiturates were said to restore memory in hysterical amnesia and aid diagnosis. Conversely, benzedrine would be used at times to alleviate fatigue.

Continuous sleep treatment. For anxiety and hysterical states of over one week's duration, this treatment aimed to put the patient to sleep for 20 out of 24 hours using paraldehyde, sodium amytal, or hyoscine.

Modified insulin treatment. This was used for mixed presentations with weight loss (Sargant and Crask 1941).

Convulsive therapy — ECT. Unmodified ECT (possibly with insulin treatment) was used for depression, especially when accompanied by obsessional symptoms.

Hypnosis. Hypnosis never went completely out of fashion and was used to establish the diagnosis, especially when the patient was amnesic.

Current practice

Other than prescribing ECT for severe depression, no physical therapies are currently used. Therapy is aimed at giving individuals control of their symptoms, followed by brief psychotherapeutic interventions to address the underlying causes of the problem. Drugs (including antidepressants, tranquillisers, and hypnotics) are likely to be used, but therapies involving alteration of consciousness are no longer popular. A number of psychotherapies are used and include cognitive behavioural therapy, exposure therapy (in vivo, imaginal, audio, eye movement desensitization), and psychodynamic therapy.

Conclusion

War is seldom a place for research. The meaning of war is different for all involved, and subject to recall bias. Without doubt, conflict can create mental reactions and illnesses, although understanding and acceptance of this fact has been slow and is still questioned by some areas of society. The First World War taught us about breakdown during combat; the Second World War about the importance of group processes in the genesis and prevention of such breakdowns; and Vietnam that there is a psychological legacy to involvement in war.

The symptoms exhibited in combat are legion and variable in their presentation and it is difficult to disentangle all but the grossest hysterical reactions from other psychiatric reactions. There is no reason to think this will change in future conflicts.

Primary prevention is not possible unless soldiers no longer deploy to areas of conflict. Secondary prevention is therefore of great importance. Its aim is to enhance the early

Table 2.3 Summary of treatments for war-related psychological symptoms and conditions

	Front line	**Rear areas**
1914–18	PIES and 7Rs	Rest, isolation, diet, massage. Suggestion, persuasion, re-education, ECT. Abreaction — hypnotic and drug-induced. Psychotherapy — individual. Occupational therapy. Physical rehabilitation. Discipline.
1939–80	PIES and 7Rs	Rest — narcosis and insulin therapy. Abreaction. Group therapy. Suggestion, persuasion, re-education. ECT.
Vietnam	PIES and 7Rs	Psychotropic drugs before combat.
1980 et seq.	PIES and 7Rs	Control of symptoms with medication and mixture of psychotherapies — individual or group. Avoidance of altered consciousness to effect treatment.

recognition of those individuals experiencing difficulties, as there are now effective psychological interventions. Education for all ranks and commanders is of special relevance to diminish the malign effects of avoiding talking and seeking help, which is so often seen in combat veterans.

Front-line treatment of psychiatric casualties has not changed since first enunciated by Salmon in the First World War. The aim is to keep the soldier with his comrades, whilst attending to his pastoral care and rehabilitation back into his unit, which is important for both the individual and the group. Treatment behind the lines has not changed in principle but therapies using alteration of consciousness are no longer in vogue. Brief psychotherapies and more effective drugs are available, but the key dilemma remains that of returning an individual, who has assumed the role of the patient and relinquished that of the soldier, to his unit.

Armies exist to fight, not go to hospital. During war, the needs of the group outweigh the rights of the individual, so the moral dilemmas facing the military medical officer and psychiatrist are likely to continue.

Disclaimer

The views expressed in this chapter are my own and are not to be construed as either the policy or views of the Ministry of Defence. The term 'he' has been used throughout for simplicity and as most of the published work relates to men in combat; 'he' may be read as 'she' throughout.

References

Abraham, P. (1982). Training for battleshock. *Journal of the Royal Army Medical Corps*, **128**, 1827.

Adrian, E. D. and Yealland, L. R. (1917). The treatment of some common war neuroses. *The Lancet*, **9 June**, 86772.

Ahrenfeldt, R. H. (1958). *Psychiatry in the British Army in the Second World War*, p. 26. Routledge & Kegan Paul, London.

Awtokratow, P. M. (1907). Die geisteskranken in Russischen heere wahrend des Japanischen krieges. *Allgemeine Zeitschrift fur Psychiatrie*.

Babinski, J. and Froment, J. (1918). Hysteria or Pithiatism (ed. Farquhar Buzzard, E.). London: University of London Press.

Binneveld, H. (1997). *From Shellshock to Combat Stress. A Comparative History of Military Psychiatry*, p. 93. Amsterdam University Press, Amsterdam.

Bourke, J. (1996). *Dismembering the Male*, Chapter 2. Reaktion Books, London.

Cobb, I. G. (1920). *A Manual of Neurasthenia (Nervous Exhaustion)*, p. 20. Balliere, Tindall & Cox, London.

Colbach, E. M. (1985). Ethical issues in combat psychiatry. *Military Medicine:* 256–65.

Cooter, R. (1998). Malingering in modernity. Psychological scripts and adversarial encounters during the First World War, p. 136 et seq. In *War, Medicine and Modernity* (ed. Cooter, R., Harrison, M., and Sturdy, S.) Sutton Publishing Ltd., Stroud.

Culpin, M. (1920). *Psychoneuroses of War and Peace*. Cambridge University Press, Cambridge.

Da Costa, J. M. (1871). On irritable heart. A clinical study of a form of functional cardiac disorder and its consequences. *American Journal of Medical Sciences*, **61**, 17–52.

Dasberg, H., Davidson, S., Durlacher, G. L., Filet, B. C., and de Winde. (1987). *Society and Trauma of War*. Assen.

Davis, R. (1988). *Marine at War*, p. 9. Bantam Books, New York.

Editorial. (1915). Nerves and war: the Mental Treatment Bill. *The Lancet*, **1 May**, 919.

Feudtner, C. (1993). Shellshock and the ecology of disease systems. *History of Science*, **31(4)**, 377–420.

Flood, J. J. (1954). Psychiatric casualties in the UK. Elements of the Korean force December 1950 November 1951. *Journal of the Royal Army Medical Corps*, **190**, 407.

Garb, B., Beich, A., and Lerer, B. (1987). Bereavement in combat. *Psychiatric Clinics of North America*, **10(3)**, 421–36.

Good, R. (1942). Malingering. *British Medical Journal*, **26 Sept**, 359–62.

Hadfield, J. A. (1920). Hypno-analysis. In *Functional Nerve Disease*. Crighton Miller, London.

Hadfield, J. A. (1942). War neurosis: a year in a neuropathic hospital. *British Medical Journal*, **28 Feb**, 281–5.

Hammond, W. A. (1883). *A Treatise on Insanity in its Medical Relations*. H. K. Lewis, London.

Harrison, T. and Clarke, D. (1992). The Northfield Experiments. *British Journal of Psychiatry*, **160**, 698–708.

Horsley, J. S. (1936). Narcoanalysis. *Journal of Mental Science*, **82**, 416.

Hurst, A. F. and Symns, J. L. M. (1918). The rapid cure of hysterical symptoms in soldiers. *Lancet*, **3 Aug**, 139–41.

Hyams, K. C., Wignall S., and Roswell, R. (1996). War syndromes and their evaluation: from the US Civil War to the Persian Gulf War. *Annals of Internal Medicine*, **125(5)**, 398–405.

Ismail, K. *et al.* (1999). Is there a Gulf War syndrome? *The Lancet*, **353**, 179–82.

James, G. W. B. (1945). Psychiatric lessons from active service. *The Lancet*, **22 Dec**, 801–5.

Jones, E. and Palmer, I. P. (in press). Army psychiatry in the Korean War: the experience of one Commonwealth Division. *Military Medicine*.

Jones, E. (2000). Personal communication, January.

L'Etang (1951). A criticism of military psychiatry in the Second World War. *Journal of the Royal Army Medical Corps.* **97**, 316–27.

Lewis, N. D. C. and Engle, B. (1954). *Wartime Psychiatry*, p. 139. Oxford University Press, New York.

Lewis, T. (1918). *The Soldier's Heart and the Effort Syndrome*, p. 2. Shaw & Sons, London.

Ludwig, A. O. (1947). Neuroses occurring in soldiers after prolonged combat exposure. *Bulletin of the Menninger Clinic*, **11**, 15–23.

Mangelsdorff, A. D. (1985). Lessons learned and forgotten: the need for prevention and mental health interventions in disaster preparedness. *Journal of Community Psychology*, **13**, 239–57.

Martin, J. A., Sparacino, L. R., and Belenky, G. (ed). (1996). *The Gulf War and Mental Health — A Comprehensive Guide*. Prager Publishers, Westport, CT.

Meerloo, A. M. (1944). *Total War and the Human Mind*, p. 59. George Allen & Unwin Ltd., London.

Mott F. W. (1918). War psycho-neuroses (I) Neurasthenia: the disorders and disabilities of fear. *The Lancet*, **26 Jan**, 127–9.

Mott, F. W. (1919). *War Neuroses and Shell Shock*. Oxford Medical Publications, London.

Myers, C. S. (1915). A contribution to the study of shell shock. *The Lancet*, **1**, 316–20.

Myers, C. S. (1940). *Shell Shock in France 191418*, p. 40. Cambridge University Press, Cambridge.

Neel, S. (ed). (1973). *Vietnam Studies. Medical Support of the US Army in Vietnam 19651970*. US Government Printing Office, Washington DC.

Ninnow, E. H. (1963). Submarine psychiatry. *Archives of Environmental Medicine*, **6**, 57988.

Palmer, H. (1945). Military psychiatric casualties — experience with 12,000 cases. *The Lancet*, **13 Oct**, 45–47.

Peters, D. W. C. (1863). Remarks on the evils of youthful enlistments and nostalgia. *American Medical Times*, **6**, 75–6.

Pratt, D. and Neustadter, A. (1947). Combat record of psychoneurotic patients. *Bulletin of the US Army Medical Dept.*, **7**, 809–911.

Price, B. H. (1984). The Falklands: rate of British psychiatric combat casualties compared to recent American wars. *Journal of the Royal Army Medical Corps*, **130**, 109–113.

Read, S. C. (1920). *Military Psychiatry in Peace and War*, p. 144. H. K. Lewis & Co Ltd., London.

Rees, G. W. B. (1941). *Psychiatric Casualties. Hints to Medical Officers in the Army of the Middle East*, p. 3. GHQ, ME Cairo, March 613/PMEC/40004/41. Middle East Campaigns, 1940–1943, RAMC Library.

Ritchie, R. D. (1968). *One History of Shellshock*, p. 190. PhD Thesis, University of California (San Diego).

Rivers, W. H. R. (1916). The repression of war experience. *The Lancet*, **2 Feb**, 173–77.

Rivers, W. H. R. (1918). War neurosis and military training. *Mental Hygiene* **2(4)**, 513–33.

Rosen, G. (1975). Nostalgia: a 'forgotten' psychological disorder. *Psychological Medicine*, **5**, 340–5.

Salmon, T. W. (1917). The care and treatment of mental diseases and war neuroses ('shell shock') in the British Army. *Mental Hygiene*, **1(4)**, 509–47.

Sargant, W. (1942). Physical treatment of acute war neuroses. Some clinical observations. *British Medical Journal*, 574–76.

Sargant, W. and Craske, E. (1941). Modified insulin therapy. *The Lancet*, **2**, 212–14.

Sargant, W. and Slater, E. (1972). *An Introduction to Physical Methods of Treatment in Psychiatry* (5th edition). Churchill Livingstone: London.

Shephard, B. (1991). The early treatment of mental disorders: R. G. Rows and Maghull 1914–1918. In *150 Years of Psychiatry 1841–1991* (ed. Berrios, G. E. and Freeman, H. L.), p. 434–464. Gaskell, London.

Shephard, B. (1996). Shell-shock on the Somme. *Royal United Services Institute Journal*, **June**, 51–56.

Stone, M. (1985). Shellshock and the psychologists. In *The Anatomy of Madness, Vol. II* (ed. Bynum *et al.*), p. 242–71. Tavistock Publications, London.

Surgeon General US Army Monthly Progress Report (1944). Army Service Forces, War Department. 31 August, Section 7, Health.

Swank, R. L. (1949). Combat exhaustion: a descriptive and statistical analysis of cases, symptoms and signs. *Journal of Nervous and Mental Disease*, **109**, 475–508.

Unwin, C. *et al.* (1999). Health of UK servicemen who served in Persian Gulf War. *The Lancet*, **353**, 169–78.

War Office (1922). *Report of the Committee of Enquiry into 'Shell Shock'.* HMSO, London.

War Psychiatry (1995). *Textbook of Military Medicine. Warfare, Weaponry and the Casualty: Part I*, p. 21. Office of the Surgeon General, US Army.

Wood P. (1941). Aetiology of Da Costa's syndrome. *British Medical Journal*, **7 June**, 845–51.

Yealland, L. R. (1918). *Hysterical Disorders of Warfare*. Macmillan and Co. Ltd., London.

3 Recovering hysteria from history: Herodotus and the first case of 'shell-shock'

Helen King

In the construction of medical history, ancient Greek materials have long held a privileged position. Taken out of their own historical context, however, this may be deceptive. In 1919, the fifth-century BC Greek historian's description of the blinding of the warrior, Epizelos, at the battle of Marathon, was labelled 'the first account of "shell-shock"'. Herodotus' story allows us to reassess the appearance of hysterical symptoms on the battlefield. Comparisons between ancient Greek warfare and the conditions of the Great War demonstrate not continuity, but rather the importance of the individual and cultural meanings that a sufferer may attribute to his symptoms. Far from being mocked for cowardice, Epizelos' blindness led to him acquiring heroic status, possibly within his own lifetime. Such comparisons also suggest that in order to be effective a 'cure' must make sense in terms of the patient's illness narrative.

Introduction

Hysteria is a condition for which a very long history has been constructed, going back to the earliest written medical texts from Egyptian and Greek antiquity (e.g. Veith 1965; Merskey 1985; Merskey and Potter 1989). How can the construction and uses of this history not only draw on, but also inform, current clinical debates?

In my own work on hysteria, I have previously concentrated on the hysterical convulsive fit in women, showing that the alleged textual origin for this phenomenon — the ancient Greek medical writings now known as the Hippocratic corpus — neither used the term 'hysteria' nor contained any description which even approximates to the powerful image of Blanche Wittmann performing to her medical audience at the Salpêtrière (King 1993, 1995, 1998). However, to focus on women with hysterical seizures can only give limited insight into the many issues raised by the history of conversion hysteria, both because it privileges women as the 'problem' and also because it concentrates only on the most dramatic of the challenges to our understanding of the mind and the body posed by this group of conditions. By the late eighteenth century, indeed — as Risse (1988) showed in his study of the Edinburgh Infirmary — only a minority of women given the diagnostic label of 'hysteria' had such fits and, in the nineteenth century, the seizure of the *grande paroxysme* was not seen as an essential part of the diagnosis even in the writings of Charcot (Micale 1990, pp. 82–3).

In this paper I therefore want to move away from the named nineteenth-century female hysterics — whom Roy Porter (1993, p. 229) has called the 'immortals' — to consider less dramatic areas of conversion hysteria, including visual abnormality and paralysis of a limb. In particular, I will be using the example of hysterical symptoms in war not only as a way of understanding the gendering of hysteria, but also to illustrate the deceptive prestige of ancient Greek materials in the construction of a history for the medical present.

Conversion hysteria is a disorder in which the boundaries between deceit and self-deceit, and between malingering and illness, appear to be particularly confused, above all for those who issue the diagnosis. In the history of hysteria, the imagery of war has been used to express the frustration which characterizes the doctor–patient relationship in this condition (King 1993, p. 11). Mark Micale (1990, pp. 78–9) has described the relationships of doctors with their hysterical female patients as having followed a number of possible models: as a form of conversation or scientific collaboration; as a love story; or as war, characterized by Robert Brudenell Carter's *On the Pathology and Treatment of Hysteria* (1853). Carter discusses 'the rules for the detection of malingerers' and describes the patient's resistance to treatment in terms of a 'siege' (1853, p. 117). Only doubt on her part will lead to her 'admitting the enemy . . . also rendering inefficient the weapons of defence'. Applying this imagery more broadly, Roy Porter has asked whether, for the medical profession as a whole, hysteria was 'to be their finest hour or their Waterloo' (1993, p. 230).

But war, or more specifically the Great War, was also the context in which the medical profession needed to confront the difficulties of using the 'hysteria' label, with its gynaecological overtones arising from its etymological basis in the Greek *hystera* (uterus), for conditions in men. It was not the first time that the label was applied to men; indeed, from 1850 onwards, 'recognition of the neuroses in men came into its own' (Micale 1990, p. 95). The American Civil War (1861–5) and its 'battle fatigue' influenced Silas Weir Mitchell's 'rest cure' in the 1870s (Ellis 1984, pp. 170 and 172). But, as Martin Stone has argued, for psychologists and psychoanalysts at the beginning of the twentieth century, it was the experience of what came to be called not 'male hysteria' but 'shell-shock' which provided them with a way into mainstream medical practice (1985, pp. 242–3). (See Palmer's chapter in this volume, p. 12.)

This new and less feminine label, with its 'simplicity, alliteration, and military sound' (Showalter 1993, p. 321) was created in early 1915 by the English military doctor Charles Myers — a pupil of W. H. R. Rivers, one of the first British followers of Freud. The term was quickly taken up by the soldiers themselves as an appropriate tag (Stone 1985, p. 257), even though many were suffering the symptoms without the proximity to an exploding shell which Myers initially thought to be the precipitating cause (Showalter 1987a, p. 168). The nineteenth-century theory that a passing cannon-ball could have an effect on those who were close to it, but who had not been hit, led to the proposal of the 'wind of a ball' theory (Ellis 1984, p. 169). By 1916, 40 per cent of casualties in the combat zones were being diagnosed as suffering from shell-shock (Showalter 1987b, p. 63). War neurosis was soon found to be four times more common in the officer class than in enlisted men (Showalter 1987b, p. 63; 1997, p. 73). While reactions to enlisted men exhibiting the symptoms ranged from hostility — including the risk of execution for cowardice — to electric shock treatment, officers such as Siegfried Sassoon were more likely to be labelled as having 'neurasthenia' and to be given psychotherapy; in Sassoon's case, from Rivers himself (Showalter 1987b ; 1993, pp. 322–3).

The blinding of Epizelos

In his recent book, *Shell-Shock. A History of the Changing Attitudes to War Neurosis* (1997), Anthony Babington refers to an incident from ancient Greek history which has become a well-known *exemplum* in twentieth-century studies of battle neurosis. This is the blinding of a certain Epizelos, son of Cyphagoras, who — fighting valiantly on the side of the heavily-outnumbered Athenians at the battle of Marathon (490 BC) — saw a giant warrior, with a beard that covered his shield, pass in front of him and kill the man beside him. Epizelos then lost his sight, and remained blind for the rest of his life (1997, p. 7). The full account in our earliest Greek literary source for this incident, the historian Herodotus (c. 484–425 BC), runs as follows:

> During the action a very strange thing happened: Epizelos, the son of Cyphagoras, an Athenian soldier, was fighting bravely when he suddenly lost the sight of both eyes, though nothing had touched him anywhere — neither sword, spear, nor missile. From that moment he continued blind as long as he lived. I am told that in speaking about what happened to him he used to say that he fancied he was opposed by a man of great stature in heavy armour, whose beard overshadowed his shield; but the phantom passed him by, and killed the man at his side (*The Histories* 6.117; translation by de Sélincourt 1972, p. 430).

Herodotus describes the event as 'a strange/marvellous/amazing thing'; in Greek, a *thôma* (6.117). It was standard practice for nineteenth-century commentators on Herodotus to concentrate on the apparition of the phantom rather than the battlefield as the precipitating factor in Epizelos' blindness; for example, on this passage, Reginald Walter Macan's commentary of 1895 stated, 'There is nothing wildly improbable in the story of Epizelos. Authentic cases are on record of total or partial blindness, consequent on visions (cp. *Acta App.* 9.1–9). It is for the biographer to record such cases, and for the psychologist to explain them' (1895, p. 373). Epizelos' vision is here elided with St Paul's experience on the road to Damascus; however, St Paul's experience was temporary, lasting only three days, whereas Herodotus tells us that Epizelos 'continued blind as long as he lived'. St Paul's recovery was attributed to the laying on of hands by Ananias (*Acts* 9.17–18): in this chapter, I will argue that Epizelos' recovery was not possible because of the status he received from his experience at Marathon. Epizelos' case thus becomes a way of understanding the problems of treating hysterical conversion within different cultural contexts. It also allows us to reflect historically on a number of other issues in conversion hysteria today. How is the condition most effectively treated? What role should the specialist treating the condition assume? How can we appreciate the specific individual and cultural meanings a sufferer may attribute to what we want to interpret as a traumatic life event?

For medical writers after the First World War, the story of Epizelos was not linked to a religious context, but instead became an early example of war neurosis, or conversion hysteria in the context of a battlefield (e.g. Fenton 1926, p. 18). This retrospective diagnosis has been supported by Herodotus' own comment that there was no physical cause for the blindness: Epizelos lost his sight 'though nothing had touched him anywhere — neither sword, spear, nor missile'. This sounds very much like the 'near-miss shock' of the Great War (Ellis 1984, p. 173). Modern references to Epizelos as a case of war neurosis trace the origin of this connection to the journal *Mental Hygiene* in 1919, where the

'Notes and Comments' section included an anonymous section headed 'War neurosis in the battle of Marathon' which quoted a letter by Dean A. Worcester to *Science* (e.g. Ellis 1984, p. 168; Babington 1997, p. 7). The original letter in fact appeared in the 5 September 1919 issue of *Science*. After beginning 'Herodotus, describing the battle of Marathon, 490 BC (Book VI, section 117) says:' Worcester simply quoted the relevant section, and then ended, 'Is this, perchance, the first account of "shell-shock"?' The connection was not pursued in subsequent issues: the phenomenon had been given its origin in myth, and that myth has remained undisputed. Yet, according to Yealland (1918, pp. 52–3), in the Great War disorders of vision were the 'least common of hysterical manifestations'; indeed, he argued, patients who claimed to be able to see nothing at all were probably malingering.

Herodotus and the Battle of Marathon

What is the status of this event in Herodotus' *Histories*? The historian N. G. L. Hammond argued that, when writing his account in around 455–445 BC, Herodotus 'must have consulted many veterans of the battle such as Epizelus, from whose lips he heard the story of his vision' (1973, p. 194). But this is debatable. Subsequently known both as 'Father of History' and 'Father of Lies', Herodotus uses a number of stylistic devices to indicate the nature and reliability of his sources. In the story of Epizelos, he distances himself from the vision of the giant hoplite by framing it within a double repetition of the verb 'to say', *legein*. But he also uses *êkousa*, literally 'I heard', in the phrase 'I am told/I heard that . . . he used to say', making this — according to Detlev Fehling — one of the passages where 'a miraculous event is recounted by a named informant but Herodotus does not claim to have spoken with him' (Fehling 1989, p. 117; cf. Gould 1989, p. 35). For Fehling, this makes the passage more likely to be entirely fictional, part of 'the almost indispensable props in the build-up before a great event'. This position has not been universally accepted among classical scholars; W. Kendrick Pritchett, for example, finds it perfectly possible that the vision and subsequent blindness really occurred, asserting that 'Fehling has not explored the non-rational factors in human experience' (Pritchett 1993, p. 106).

The Battle of Marathon certainly rapidly became a 'great event' to the Athenians; one, indeed, of mythic status. What precisely did it mean to them? The Persian Wars saw the small, independent Greek city-states uniting with their traditional rivals against the greater enemy of the Persian empire. At Marathon, the Athenians won despite being dramatically outnumbered by the Persians, with claimed losses to the Persians of 6400 men against Athenian losses of only 192 (Herodotus, *The Histories*, 6.117). John Boardman has argued that the Parthenon frieze should be understood as a monument to Marathon, as 'the number of males in the whole cavalcade hovers around 192' (Boardman 1985, p. 250). Furthermore, their allies from Sparta failed to arrive in time. The Athenian victory was thus not just one against overwhelming odds, but was also a reminder that they did not need the Spartans. Marathon became a doubly powerful statement of defeating the 'barbarians' while standing without one's main competitors within the Greek world: it came to be seen as 'a purely Athenian victory' (Loraux 1986, p. 155).

Herodotus was writing probably forty or fifty years after Marathon; it is therefore possible that his account was influenced by paintings of the battle such as those in the Stoa Poikile, the painted colonnade surrounding the Athenian *agora*, which were executed about thirty years after the battle (Gould 1989, pp. 35–6). Now lost, these are known to us from the descriptions of tourists from the period of the Roman empire who visited such sites (Francis and Vickers 1985, p. 109). Pausanias, traditionally thought to have been a retired doctor, who wrote a *Guide to Greece* in around 150–170 AD, gives the most detailed description, from which it is clear that, at the time the paintings were executed, Marathon was already being linked to the heroic battles of the mythic past; the scenes alongside this painting showed Athens fighting Sparta at Oinoê, the Athenian mythical hero Theseus protecting Athens from the Amazons, and the Greek army taking Troy (*Guide to Greece* 1.15.1–4). Pausanias does not mention Epizelos in the painting of Marathon, saying only that it showed 'those who fought at Marathon'; however, another reference to the paintings of the Stoa Poikile, this time from the late second-century AD work by Aelian, *On Animals* 7.38, mentions specifically that the representation of Marathon included Epizelos.

The appearance of the gods at battles contributed to their subsequent identification as events of mythic status (Garbrah 1986). Perhaps the most famous such epiphany was also at Marathon, where the god Pan appeared to the runner Pheidippides (Herodotus, *The Histories*, 6.105); Pan was a god honoured by soldiers because of his power to produce panic (Greek *paneion*) in the enemy. Other epiphanies which apparently occurred at Marathon are preserved in later literary sources for the battle: for example, the hero Theseus was seen fighting on the Athenian side (Plutarch, *Life of Theseus*, 35.5). Pausanias also tells us that the people of Marathon saw a man of rustic appearance killing Persians with a ploughshare; after the battle, he too was identified as a mythic hero. Even in his own day, Pausanias claims, the sounds of horses whinnying and men fighting could still be heard at Marathon (*Guide to Greece*, 1.32.4). The giant warrior seen by Epizelos may therefore have been interpreted as another mythic hero.

It may seem odd that Herodotus' account excludes these stories about the presence of various named mythic heroes at Marathon, yet includes the blinding of Epizelos by the anonymous apparition. Garland (1992, p. 55) suggests that Herodotus, despite his lack of personal belief in such supernatural interventions, felt obliged to include Epizelos 'because no other explanation could be found for his blindness'. A further possibility is that, because of the Stoa Poikile painting, within a few decades of his blinding Epizelos had become a fixed feature of any literary or artistic representation of this battle.

There is one other example in Herodotus of eye problems in the context of war, this time on the eve of battle. Although this example has not been used in the construction of a history for shell-shock, it is worth examining. Before another great battle of the Persian Wars, in which 300 Spartans were massacred at Thermopylae (480 BC), two Spartan soldiers, Eurytos and Aristodemos, were suffering badly from ophthalmia (*The Histories*, 7.229). Their general, Leonidas, sent them away to recover, and they discussed whether to return home to Sparta or to go and fight in a battle in which they knew they would die. They could not agree on the best policy; so Eurytos called for his armour and was led to the battle, where he was killed. Herodotus' statement that he had to be led indicates how badly his sight was affected. Aristodemos remained in safety and then returned to Sparta in disgrace; he was known afterwards as 'The Trembler' (*The Histories*, 7.231). He tried to redeem himself in the Battle of Plataea (479 BC), where he deliberately courted death, but even his bravery on this occasion was interpreted as an inferior form because his motive was to retrieve his personal reputation (*The Histories*, 9.71).

Beyond Marathon

Herodotus' narrative provides one example among many of the strong connection made in ancient Greek thought between bravery and male identity. It refers explicitly to Epizelos' bravery in the field of battle, and the vocabulary used, based on *andreia* (meaning 'manliness' or 'courage') is itself derived from the Greek word for a mature male, *anêr*. As Nicole Loraux has demonstrated in her study of the funeral orations delivered at the state funerals of the Athenian war dead, 'andreia is the essential property of the aner: therefore, to be truly an aner one certainly runs the risk of being dead! . . . in the funeral oration one is a *man* only after death' (Loraux 1986, p. 385 n.104; cf. King 1986, pp. 66–7). To show courage is thus to show oneself a man: the supreme form of manhood is death in battle.

In 1917 Albert Buck published a history of medicine in which his interpretation of a passage of the first-century AD encyclopaedist, Pliny the Elder, reveals how a close causal relationship between war and healthy manhood could be envisaged in the period of the Great War, and how classical sources could be used to support such a relationship. In his account of the early history of Roman medicine, Pliny stated that the Roman people had lived without doctors for over six hundred years (*Natural History*, 29.5.11). This surprising claim has been interpreted by historians in a variety of ways; for example, it is possible that by 'doctor' (Latin *medicus*) he is designating a particular type of healer based on the model of the Greek Hippocratic practitioner. However, in *The Growth of Medicine from the Earliest Times to About 1800*, Buck took Pliny entirely at face value. Pliny said there were no doctors, so there were no doctors. In his discussion of Roman medicine, it was easy for him to elide this statement with more general attitudes to the manly vigour of the Romans:

> There were, at this period, no regularly established physicians and no such thing as a medical practice. For several hundred years the Romans were almost constantly at war with the neighbouring tribes and nations, and this life of outdoor exposure and active exercise kept them free from the numerous and very varied bodily ills of the later generations (Buck 1917, pp. 117–18).

He thus appears to be arguing that the Romans were simply too busy to be ill; war is good for men. Yet 1917 is precisely when the experience of 'shell-shock' challenged the image of the 'benefits' of war for male health.

Stone argues that the ideals of patriotism and courage, and of war as the ultimate test of the self (Showalter 1987*a*, p. 169), continued to be present on the field of battle in 1914–18. The nature of the fighting, however, based on obedience to orders and repetitive drill, made the received notion of 'masculine values' no longer appropriate, or even dangerous to the new form of warfare (Stone 1985, pp. 260–1). In the context of Marathon, however, where the Athenians fought in long lines of infantry where each man's life depended on the overlapping shield of his neighbouring hoplite to protect him, discipline was just as important, even if the fighting was hand to hand rather than at an impersonal distance, and battles lasted for a single day rather than months (cf. Stone 1985, p. 248).

But 'masculine values' were also problematic in early fifth-century BC Athens. The disciplined hoplite line of the emerging democracy, in which each soldier depended on his neighbour for protection, existed alongside older values — now negatively labelled as 'aristocratic' or 'oligarchic' — in which the individual gained a reputation through personal display in one-to-one combat and where war became an opportunity to achieve the 'beautiful death', the *kalos thanatos* (Loraux 1986). These older values were enshrined in the poetry of Homer: to die fighting for the fatherland is described as being a far from dishonourable death (*Iliad* 15. 496–7). A generation later, the poet Tyrtaeus stated that 'it is beautiful (*kalos*) for a good man fallen among those fighting in the front line to die, fighting on behalf of the fatherland' (10.1–2). Poems such as this, upholding martial and civic values, were read at the aristocratic male drinking parties (*symposia*). But, at the time of Marathon, aristocratic images of masculinity as displayed in activities such as athletic competitions, open only to the rich, met democratic ideals in which the means to demonstrate 'manhood' should be available to all free-born men of the community. Although death in battle was still the 'beautiful death' and remained a way to show one's masculinity (Osborne 1998, pp. 26–30), it is possible that a death based on the inadequate protection provided by the man whose shield was supposed to cover your body was not considered as impressive as a death resulting from your own brave and impulsive actions. Provided, of course, that those actions were carried out for motives other than salvaging a lost personal reputation, as in the attempted heroics of Aristodemos at Plataea.

Stone (1985, pp. 242–3 and 255–6) notes that many British medical writers of the First World War felt that shell-shock disproved Freud's theories of the sexual aetiology of hysteria, as there could be no repressed sexual experiences behind a man's response to the pressures of the battlefield. However, from an ancient Greek perspective, war is a highly gendered and sexualized field, since it is through performance in war that a man demonstrates his masculinity to himself and to his peers (cf. Showalter 1987*a*, p. 169). Furthermore, city-states such as Thebes and Sparta regarded sexual relationships between soldiers as a positive asset contributing to fighting spirit. In Homeric and classical Greece, the imagery of war in a man's life and childbirth in that of a woman are connected, with each experience completing the transition between immaturity and a mature social identity (Loraux 1981). In the First World War, initial reactions to shell-shock saw it as a sign of cowardice, with sufferers ceasing to be 'real men' (Stone 1985, p. 253). This attitude was a continuation of Victorian horror at the idea that men could be overcome by their emotions in a way which had previously been gendered as female (Micale 1991; Showalter 1997, pp. 64–5).

In contrast, it is precisely as Epizelos demonstrates his true *andreia* that he is struck blind: he does not lose status by his loss of sight but, instead, his blindness appears somehow to confirm his masculinity. Why is this? What did blindness signify in a classical Greek context? In Greek myth, it is associated with poets and with prophets (Buxton 1980, p. 27) — two groups whose powerful inner sight allows them to speak about the past, the present, and the future in a way which brings them closer to the realm of the gods. For example, in the poetry of Hesiod and Homer, the poet or seer has the power to reveal that synthesis of past, present, and future which constitutes 'the truth' (*alêtheia*) (Detienne 1967, p. 130 n.101). This privileged access to time is also, ideally, an attribute of the ancient Greek doctor; the Hippocratic treatise *Prognostics* opens with the statement, 'It seems to me that the best doctor is one with foreknowledge (*pronoia*)' (1), and goes on to say that, at the patient's bedside, the doctor will know in advance (*progignôskô*) and speak in advance (*prolegô*) the present, the past, and the future. There is a similar passage in *Epidemics* (1.11), in which the doctor must 'speak (*legô*) the past, know (*gignôskô*) the present and predict (*prolegô*) the future'. This sort of knowledge, in myth and poetry, is normally the preserve of the gods, so to claim it for the art of medicine is a deliberate challenge to traditional sources of authority over human life.

Blindness also features as a punishment for those who overstep the limits of mortal activity by, for example, observing a goddess bathing or telling a god what he does not want to hear. Blinding is therefore a particularly common reaction to visual transgressions, in which a mortal sees a god (Buxton 1980, p. 27). Epizelos saw an apparition which was in some sense divine, but there is no suggestion that this was a transgressive act. So, although Buxton (1980, p. 30) includes Epizelos in his category of 'visual infringements against divinities', I would not follow this classification; instead, Epizelos — commemorated in literature and art, known for his bravery, telling his amazing story to anyone who will listen — seems to be closer to those favoured with blindness than those punished by it. However, Buxton also argues that, because the gods have both sight and insight which are superior to those of mortals, 'blindness is a powerful verbal and visual *metaphor* for the limits of humanity' (1980, p. 25). In the euphoria of the Athenian victory over the Persians at Marathon, therefore, Epizelos can become a reminder, for the community as a whole, of the true source of their success — the gods.

How does this reading of 'the first account of "shell-shock"' affect our understanding of conversion hysteria in the Great War? Showalter (1987*a*, p. 172) argues that breakdowns on the battlefield were 'a disguised male protest not only against the war but against the concept of "manliness" itself' (cited in Micale 1990, p. 100). In contrast, in the very different cultural context of classical Athenian warfare, Epizelos' blindness is not a protest but a reinforcement of what it is to be human and what it is to be courageous, to have *andreia*. The symptoms through which men rejected their society's definition of masculinity may be interpreted as having symbolic significance in the context of the horrors of trench warfare. As 'soldiers lost their voices and spoke through their bodies' (Showalter 1987*b*, p. 64), they reacted against views that the female sex is 'body' and that the male sex is somehow able to rise above the constraints of the body. One could argue that a hysterical paralysis of the arm is a refusal to pull the trigger; a hysterical paralysis of the leg, a refusal to go 'over the top'; or hysterical blindness, a refusal to see the mutilated bodies of one's friends.

But Showalter also demonstrates that, once the label of shell-shock had been issued, it proved hard to escape, particularly when it became a guarantee of a war pension. She notes that 'by 1929, about 114 600 ex-servicemen had applied for pensions for "shell-shock-related" disorders' (Showalter 1997, pp. 73–4). For the mid-fourth century BC, we know that the Athenians gave a small daily maintenance allowance to poor citizens 'who are physically maimed so as to be incapable of work' (Aristotle, *Athenian Constitution* 49.4); Hands (1968, p. 100) suggests that this provision was originally aimed at those disabled by war. The situation in 490 BC is not known but, even without financial considerations, I would argue that Epizelos' blindness was so saturated with positive meaning that it would have been difficult to relinquish.

Getting better: curing conversion hysteria

In response to Sir Charles Symonds' address to the National Hospital on 27 February 1970, Harold Merskey noted that 'one of the difficulties encountered by the hysteric is that of a graceful recovery' (1979, p. 263). It is not clear how soon after the event Epizelos would have achieved heroic status —in his lifetime, or only after his death? But, even in the latter case, the knowledge that heroic status was impending would have affected him and the reactions of others to him. If your hysterical conversion makes you a hero, then how can the possibility of cure remain an option?

This question in turn depends on theories of causation. In the decades before the First World War, hysterical conversion had come to be explained by the notion of the idea, or the 'perverted condition of the will' (Russell 1869, p. 632). In the words of Sir James Paget: 'They say "I cannot"; it looks like "I will not"; but it is "I cannot will"' (1873: cited in Merskey 1979, p. 20). Commenting on an earlier discussion by John Russell Reynolds, James Russell suggested that this condition was 'produced through the influence of the imagination, or by an abnormal development of the emotional element of the mind'. Reynolds had cited 'the well known case of the butcher, who was agonised almost past endurance by the fact that a flesh-hook had caught itself, not in his skin, but only in his sleeve' (Reynolds 1869, p. 483). If the cause was an idea, could what Reynolds described as the removal of 'the erroneous idea' act as a cure? (See Mace's chapter in this volume, p. 1.)

Micale locates Reynolds' work within a British tradition of using the presence or absence of structural pathology as a guide to differentiate between organic and functional disorders, suggesting that this tradition 'conduced less to psychoanalytic theory than to late twentieth-century neuropsychiatry' (Micale 1995, pp. 126–8). Reynolds regarded what he called 'morbid ideation' as lying somewhere between the extremes of 'distinct nervous injury' and 'malingering and sham'. He insisted that there was no deception on the part of the patients: 'They believe, and they believe utterly, in the reality of their symptoms; they are anxious to be cured' (Reynolds 1869, p. 484).

But, after the experiences of the trenches, it was acknowledged that events rather than an abnormal emotion could cause hysterical symptoms. Writing in 1917, G. Elliot Smith and T. H. Pear suggested that modern warfare was far removed from what they called 'natural fighting', in which the combatant could see immediately the effects of his efforts, so that excitement could block out fear (1917, p. 9). They also argued that the long period of time spent in the trenches, and the impossibility of suppressing fear long-term, made shell-shock more likely in the context of modern warfare (1917, p. 8). By 1926, Norman Fenton could argue that 'it is possible that the neuroses have been present in all the wars of history, but certainly never before in such overwhelming numbers as in the World War' (1926, p. 18). (See Palmer's chapter in this volume, p. 12.)

However, Reynolds' suggestion — evoking modern cognitive therapy — that the removal of 'the erroneous idea' could produce a cure was retained, as was his insistence on promoting a positive attitude in the patient. Reynolds described the case of 'a young lady' whose father was in financial difficulties after becoming paralysed. Forced to seek work as a governess, the young woman's fear of paralysis eventually led to her developing hysterical paralysis. In Reynolds' account, two aspects stand out. The first is the role played by the patient's expectation of cure; Reynolds writes:

> Her expression is anxious, but with some hopefulness. She thinks that, having come to the hospital — a great mental struggle for some who have, in former days, enjoyed every luxury at home — *she may get better* (1869, p. 483).

The second is the creation of a positive atmosphere in which those caring for the patient act to reinforce her hopefulness:

She was told, and the nurses, and those about her, were all told, most confidently, that she would soon walk quite well (1869, p. 483).

The patient recovered in a fortnight, after being treated with a tonic, the application of electric currents to her legs, massage of the back and limbs, and being made to walk with the assistance of two nurses. In the discussion of Reynolds' paper at the Leeds meeting of the British Medical Association, Dr Banks of Dublin described a woman of thirty-eight whom he cured by telling her that 'if she followed simple rules and regulations, she would perfectly recover' (Reynolds 1869, p. 378). However, he added an interesting aside which shows that the patient felt she needed a pharmaceutical explanation for her eventual recovery:

It was to some aperient that she gave the credit of her recovery: this was simply a rhubarb pill with a small quantity of the extract of nux vomica (1869, p. 378).

Like Sir Charles Symonds' description of the patient with hysterical paralysis whose cure could only be confirmed by a service of thanksgiving for her recovery (Merskey 1979, p. 263), this suggests that, even if the patient is convinced by the confidence of his or her carers, some additional action appropriate to the everyday world of the individual patient may be necessary.

In the *longue durée*, physical cures have played as large a role in the treatment of hysteria as in other psychiatric disorders (Scull 1994, p. 4). From the mid-nineteenth century into the early twentieth century, electricity provided the dominant physical mechanism for treatment. It was warmly recommended in the discussion of Reynolds' paper in 1869, but its best-known exponent was Lewis Yealland, who combined electric shocks of increasing strength with a strong paternal or even punitive presence. Showalter describes his 'blatant use of power and authority' and places him 'at the most punitive end of the treatment spectrum' (1987a, pp. 176–7). But, as the examples from Reynolds show, suggestion was in fact a traditional cure (Ellis 1985, p. 36), and Yealland's insistence to the patient that his disorder could be quickly and easily cured (1918, p. 53) also replicated Reynolds' methods. Yealland's assertion that the doctor should retain control over all aspects of treatment rather than delegating to other carers reinforced his authority (Merskey 1979, p. 40) and recalls the ancient Hippocratic healer's decree that all tasks, including those we would now classify as 'nursing', should be kept within his jurisdiction to ensure that he receives the credit for a successful treatment (King 1998, p. 165). (See Palmer's chapter in this volume, p. 12.)

In treating conversion hysteria today, clinical studies have shown that the prognosis is good if the condition is of recent onset (Couprie *et al.* 1995), unless there is an underlying independent psychiatric condition (Binzer *et al.* 1997). But such studies have also noted that some patients do not want to be cured. Singh and Lee (1997, p. 429) mention a woman who refused help because she was worried that a cure would not only deprive her of financial support but would also adversely affect her relationship by removing her dependency.

One of the main difficulties in the treatment of conversion hysteria appears to be the mind–body division. Patients with conversion hysteria are convinced that they have an organic condition, rather than a disorder of the mind; Binzer (1998, p. 664) found that they have more 'disease conviction' i.e. they are convinced that they have a physical illness which accounts for their symptoms. They therefore continue 'doctor shopping' in the hope that the next round of tests will confirm their belief, even though recent clinical studies have shown that unexplained motor symptoms for which no organic basis can be found after thorough investigation do not subsequently turn out to have an organic explanation (Crimlisk *et al.* 1998). This is not new; Reynolds remarked that 'it has often occurred to me to see cases which have gone the round of many theories with their therapeutic applications' (1869, p. 484).

If the cause is believed by the patient to be physical, located in the body, this would suggest the need for at least some physical treatment. Scull (1994, p. 7) would date the shift away from physical explanations and cures in psychiatric medicine to around 1900, arguing for a 'crisis in confidence' which 'led to a break with somaticism', although Merskey (1994, p. 388) argued that Scull had 'grossly misinterpreted the nature of major advances and the reasons for their decline'. St Paul was cured of his blindness by the laying on of hands, an intervention which made sense to him and in the construction of events he had created around the incident on the road to Damascus.

Although the 'origin myth' of shell-shock, the story of Epizelos, is linguistically marked by Herodotus in a way that makes it difficult to judge its authenticity, the blinding of an uninjured man on the battlefield at Marathon seems to have quickly become part of Athenian tradition. I would suggest that Epizelos' blindness shows how conversion hysteria can be a response to situations of gender-specific anxiety. He is not protesting against the Greek concept of manliness; rather, he is supporting it by adding to the atmosphere of divine significance surrounding the battle.

I have argued here that the conflicting 'masculine values' of the period, the exceptional status of the battle, and the cultural valuations of blindness suggest that the story Epizelos told was one which made him a hero, so that his illness narrative could never end in cure. Heroic status cannot be withdrawn: if a god had cured his blindness, this would have represented a loss of status. His blindness not only elevates him to heroic status but, for the wider community, it acts as a reminder of mortal ignorance in comparison with divine knowledge. His lesson for the later history of shell-shock, and indeed of conversion hysteria in general, therefore extends beyond his claims to be 'the first case of shell-shock'. Rather, Epizelos demonstrates the importance of the patient's core beliefs and attribution of cause in the development and maintenance of physical symptoms.

Note
All references in the text to classical literature can be found in the Loeb Classical Library editions.

References

Anon. (1919). 'War neurosis in the battle of Marathon', *Mental Hygiene*, **3**, 676.

Babington, A. (1997). *Shell-Shock. A History of the Changing Attitudes to War Neurosis*. Leo Cooper, London.

Binzer, M. *et al.* (1997). Clinical characteristics of patients with motor disability due to conversion disorder: a prospective control group study. *Journal of Neurology, Neurosurgery, and Psychiatry*, **63**, 83–8.

Binzer, M. *et al.* (1998). Illness behaviour in the acute phase of motor disability in neurological disease and in conversion disorder: a comparative study. *Journal of Psychosomatic Research*, **44**, 657–66.

Boardman, J. (1985). *The Parthenon and its Sculptures*. Thames and Hudson, London.

Buck, A. H. (1917). *The Growth of Medicine from the Earliest Times to About 1800*. Yale University Press, New Haven and Oxford University Press.

Buxton, R. G. A. (1980). Blindness and limits: Sophokles and the logic of myth. *Journal of Hellenic Studies*, **100**, 22–37.

Carter, R. Brudenell (1853). *On the Pathology and Treatment of Hysteria*. J. Churchill, London.

Couprie, W. *et al.* (1995). Outcome in conversion hysteria: a follow up study. *Journal of Neurology, Neurosurgery, and Psychiatry*, **58**, 750–2.

Crimlisk, H. *et al.* (1998). Slater revisited: 6 year follow up study of patients with medically unexplained motor symptoms. *British Medical Journal*, **316**, 582–6.

De Sélincourt, A. (1972). (trans.) Herodotus, *The Histories*. Penguin Books, Harmondsworth, Middlesex.

Detienne, M. (1967). *Les maîtres de verité dans la grèce archaïque*. Maspero, Paris. (English translation by Lloyd, J. (1996). *The Masters of Truth in Ancient Greece*. Zone Books, New York.).

Ellis, P. S. (1984). The origins of the war neuroses. Part 1. *Journal of the Royal Naval Medical Service*, **70**, 168–77.

Ellis, P. S. (1985). The origins of the war neuroses. Part 2. *Journal of the Royal Naval Medical Service*, **71**, 32–44.

Fehling, D. (1989). *Herodotus and his 'Sources': Citation, Invention and Narrative Art* (German original 1971; trans. Howie, J. G.). Francis Cairns, Leeds.

Fenton, N. (1926). *Shell Shock and its Aftermath*. Henry Kimpton, London.

Francis, E. D. and M. Vickers (1985). The Oenoe paintings in the Stoa Poikile, and Herodotus' account of Marathon. *Annual of the British School at Athens*, **80**, 109–15.

Garbrah, K. (1986). On the *theophania* in Chios and the epiphany of gods in war. *Zeitschrift für Papyrologie und Epigraphik*, **65**, 207–10.

Garland, R. (1992). *Introducing New Gods: The Politics of Athenian Religion*. Duckworth, London.

Gould, J. P. (1989). *Herodotus*. Weidenfeld and Nicolson, London.

Hammond, N. G. L. (1973). *Studies in Greek History*. Clarendon Press, Oxford.

Hands, A.R. (1968). Charities and Social Aid in Greece and Rome. Thames and Hudson, London.

King, H. (1986). Agnodike and the profession of medicine. *Proceedings of the Cambridge Philological Society*, **32**, 53–77.

King, H. (1993). Once upon a text: the Hippocratic origins of hysteria. In *Hysteria Beyond Freud* (ed. Gilman, S. *et al.*), pp. 3–90. University of California Press, Berkeley and London.

King, H. (1995). Conversion disorder and hysteria: social section. In *History of Clinical Psychiatry* (ed. Berrios, G. and Porter, R.), pp. 442–50. Athlone Press, London.

King, H. (1998). *Hippocrates' Woman: Reading the Female Body in Ancient Greece*. Routledge, London and New York.

Loraux, N. (1981). Le lit, la guerre. *L'Homme*, **21**, 37–67.

Loraux, N. (1986). *The invention of Athens: The Funeral Oration in the Classical City* (French original 1981; trans. Sheridan, A.). Harvard University Press, Cambridge, Mass.

Macan, R. W. (1895). *Herotodus: The Fourth, Fifth, and Sixth Books*. Macmillan, London.

Merskey, H. (1979). *The Analysis of Hysteria*. Bailliere Tindall, London.

Merskey, H. (1985). Hysteria: the history of a disease: Ilza Veith. *British Journal of Psychiatry*, **147**, 576–9.

Merskey, H. and Potter, P. (1989). The womb lay still in ancient Egypt. *British Journal of Psychiatry*, **154**, 751–3.

Merskey, H. and Potter, P. (1994). Somatic treatments, ignorance, and the historiography of psychiatry. *History of Psychiatry*, **5**, 387–91.

Micale, M. (1990). Hysteria and its historiography: the future perspective. *History of Psychiatry*, **1**, 33–124.

Micale, M. (1991). Hysteria male/hysteria female. In *Science and Sensibility: Essays on Gender and Scientific Inquiry* (ed. Benjamin, M.), pp. 200–39. Basil Blackwell, London.

Micale, M. (1995). *Approaching Hysteria: Disease and its Interpretations*. Princeton University Press, Princeton, NJ. .

Osborne, R. (1998). Sculpted men of Athens: masculinity and power in the field of vision. In *Thinking Men: Masculinity and its Self-Representation in the Classical Tradition* (ed. Foxhall, L. and Salmon, J.), pp. 23–42. Routledge, London and New York.

Paget, J. (1873). Nervous mimicry of organic diseases, Lecture I. *The Lancet*, **(2)**, 511–13.

Porter, R. (1993). The body and the mind, the doctor and the patient: negotiating hysteria. In *Hysteria Beyond Freud* (ed. Gilman, S. *et al.*), pp. 225–85. University of California Press, Berkeley and London.

Pritchett, W. Kendrick (1993). *The Liar School of Herodotos*. J. C. Gieben, Amsterdam.

Reynolds, J. Russell (1869). Remarks on paralysis, and other disorders of motion and sensation dependent on idea (paper read at 37th Annual Meeting of the British Medical Association, Leeds, July 1869). *British Medical Journal*, **(2)**, 6 November, 483–5; discussion of original paper, *British Medical Journal*, **(2)**, 2 October, 378–9.

Risse, G. B. (1988). Hysteria at the Edinburgh Infirmary: the construction and treatment of a disease, 1770–1800. *Medical History*, **32**, 1–22.

Russell, J. (1869). A fatal case of hysterical paraplegia under the care of Dr James Russell. *British Medical Journal*, **(2)**, 11 December, 632–3.

Scull, A. (1994). Somatic treatments and the historiography of psychiatry. *History of Psychiatry*, **5**, 1–12.

Showalter, E. (1987*a*). *The Female Malady: Women, Madness and English Culture 1830–1980*. Virago, London. (First publication, Pantheon Books, New York, 1985).

Showalter, E. (1987*b*). Rivers and Sassoon: the inscription of male gender anxieties. In *Behind the Lines: Gender and the Two World Wars* (ed. Higonnet, M. R. *et al.*), pp. 61–9. Yale University Press, New Haven and London.

Showalter, E. (1993). Hysteria, feminism, and gender. In *Hysteria Beyond Freud* (ed. Gilman, S. *et al.*), pp. 286–344. University of California Press, Berkeley and London.

Showalter, E. (1997). *Hystories: Hysterical Epidemics and Modern Culture*. Columbia University Press, New York.

Singh, S. P. and Lee, A. S. (1997). Conversion disorders in Nottingham: alive, but not kicking. *Journal of Psychosomatic Research*, **43**, 425–30.

Smith, G. Elliot and Pear, T. H. (1917). *Shell Shock and its Lessons*. Manchester University Press, Manchester.

Stone, M. (1985). Shellshock and the psychiatrists. In *The Anatomy of Madness: Essays in the History of Psychiatry II* (ed. Bynum, W., Porter, R., and Shepherd, M.), pp. 242–71. Tavistock Publications, London and New York.

Veith, I. (1965). *Hysteria: The History of a Disease*. University of Chicago Press, Chicago and London.

Worcester, D. A. (1919). Letter to the Editor of *Science*. *Science*, **50, no.1288**, 230.

Yealland, L. R. (1918). *Hysterical Disorders of Warfare*. Macmillan, London.

4 The origins of DSM and ICD criteria for conversion and somatization disorders

C. Robert Cloninger

The origins of modern diagnostic criteria for conversion and somatization disorders in DSM and ICD are described. Guze's criteria for Briquet's syndrome have been simplified for clinical use on the basis of practical experience in consultation psychiatry, as well as research on the distribution and inheritance of somatoform disorders, comorbid personality disorders, and prospective prediction of outcome. The derivation and testing of specific DSM and ICD criteria for somatoform disorders is described. Individual differences in personality are described as a way of understanding patterns of adaptation to life experience, underlying psychobiological predisposition to somatoform disorders, and planning of treatment.

Introduction

The first major practical problem facing a clinician evaluating a patient with unexplained neurological or other somatic complaints is diagnosis. Before initiating a responsible treatment plan a clinician must know how to recognize cases of hysterical conversion or somatization disorder in a way that is valid and reliable, so that any other physical and psychiatric disorder requiring treatment will not go unrecognized and untreated. If such cases can be reliably diagnosed — and they can (Guze, 1967; Yutzy et al., 1995; Crimlisk et al., 1998) — then the features that permit reliable differential diagnosis from other mental and physical disorders are the chief clues for understanding their underlying psychobiology and planning treatment. In this chapter, I will review the research and thinking that has led to the construction of modern diagnostic criteria for conversion and somatization disorders, and show how this provides a useful — in my opinion, essential — basis for diagnosis, aetiological research, and treatment planning.

Available psychobiological findings indicate that conversion and somatization syndromes are most likely to emerge when individuals with particular multidimensional personality configurations are under stress. Accordingly, the assessment of the conversion and somatization syndromes, together with associated personality traits, provides a crucial approach to quantifying reliably the intuitive judgements that experienced clinicians make. Personality refers to individual differences in adaptation to experience, so it offers a way of measuring the emotional significance of the social context and life events.

Furthermore, in this chapter I will review ongoing psychobiological and genetic research that demonstrates the complex interactions of body, mind, and spirit in the development of conversion and somatization disorders (Cloninger and Svrakic, 1997). Efforts to reduce psychiatry to a form of molecular determinism are contradicted by such mental mechanisms as conversion and transference. Accordingly, molecular psychiatrists tend to regard all conversion as intentional malingering and to deny the existence of unconscious influences, symbolism, and other psychodynamic phenomena. The early Freudian account of these symptoms did not allow for reliable, quick diagnosis or a clear set of quantifiable hypotheses that could be tested regarding their psychobiology. However, over the last few decades systematic diagnosis has given a firm basis for both reliable diagnosis and rigorous psychobiological research regarding aetiology and treatment, which preserve the richness of the original clinical observations of Freud and his contemporaries and provide a systematic account of the pathway from genes to psychobiology and then to emotions, thoughts, and behaviour.

Differential diagnosis of hysterical disorders

When somatic complaints are unexplained by routine physical and neurological examinations and laboratory tests, they are often described as unexplained. According to studies by Slater (1965), such individual, unexplained somatic complaints — formerly called hysteria — have a highly variable prognosis, often turning out to be early or atypical presentations of a physical or neurological disorder that is diagnosed later, after other features emerge or additional examinations. Even when the symptom involves the nervous system, such as abnormal movement or sensation, and a diagnosis of conversion disorder is made by the examining neurologist, the prognosis of unexplained individual symptoms is highly variable (Gatfield and Guze, 1962). Consequently, diagnosis of hysterical conversion on the basis of apparent exclusion of physical disorder is notoriously unreliable. However, recent follow-up studies of unexplained neurological symptoms using modern diagnostic criteria show that the differential diagnosis of neurological and psychiatric disorders can be reliably made in most cases (Binzer and Kullgren, 1998; Crimlisk *et al.*, 1998).

A wide variety of clinical criteria have been suggested as inclusion criteria for distinguishing hysterical conversion from other physical and mental disorders when the presenting symptoms are unexplained by routine physical examination and testing. The chief features used in routine practice are summarized in Table 4.1. Follow-up studies show that many features that are characteristically attributed to hysterical disorders are insufficient for reliable differential diagnosis. These include onset after stressful life events, comorbidity with anxiety or depression, indifference or overdramatization, secondary gain (i.e. derivation of personal benefits from the sick role), or improvement with suggestion or sedation. Some features are predictive of the symptom remaining unexplained: these include a previous history of other conversions (particularly remitting after resolution of the precipitating conflict), a previous history of a wide variety of recurrent somatic complaints, and exposure to a model for the symptoms. Such observations are replicable and support the basic concept that conversion disorders are induced by stress in vulnerable individuals who unconsciously mimic an illness to reduce anxiety about the conflict.

These findings that useful discriminators could be identified prompted efforts to make the diagnosis of hysterical disorders more reliable by establishing explicit decision rules. Guze and colleagues developed criteria for *chronic hysteria*, later called Briquet's

Table 4.1 Psychiatric criteria for distinguishing conversions and physical disorders

Possible diagnostic criteria	Predicts no physical disorder	References*
Prior history		
Prior conversions	Yes	1–4, 6–8
Recurrent somatic complaints	Yes	1–4, 6–8
Model for symptoms	Yes	4
Prior remission with conflict resolution	Yes	4
Emotional stress prior to onset		
(1) Any	No	4, 5
(2) With symbolism	No	4, 8
Current symptoms and context		
Anxiety or dysphoria	No	5
La belle indifference	No	4, 8
Overdramatization	No	1, 4, 8
Secondary gain	No	4
Treatment		
Improved by suggestion	No	1
Improved by sedation	No	1

* Reference numbers: 1 (Gatfield and Guze, 1962); 2 (Slater, 1965); 3 (Perley and Guze, 1962); 4 (Raskin *et al.*, 1966); 5 (Watson and Buranen, 1979); 6 (Purtell *et al.*, 1951); 7 (Guze *et al.*, 1971a,b); 8 (Bishop and Torch, 1979)

syndrome and now somatization disorder (Guze, 1967; Perley and Guze, 1962; Guze *et al.*, 1971*a, b*). Guze's work formed the basis for the diagnosis of somatization disorder in DSM–III. His goal was to identify a subgroup of individuals with conversion disorders who had a chronic course of multiple, unexplained somatic symptoms throughout their body. He distinguished between earlier concepts of hysteria involving a small number of unexplained symptoms (acute hysteria) and dramatic personality traits (hysterical or histrionic personality), and avoided using psychodynamic concepts in favour of direct behavioural observations. The history of this approach is described in detail elsewhere (Guze, 1967).

Guze's original criteria required 20 or more medically unexplained symptoms from a checklist of 59 symptoms, distributed across at least 9 of 10 possible groups of symptoms, along with onset of at least one of these prior to the age of 30. So defined, the disorder was highly reliable cross-sectionally by different raters. Follow-up after five or more years showed few changes in diagnosis to other mental or physical disorders, and there was an increased proportion of family members with the same diagnosis. The disorder nearly always occurred in young women (Guze 1975), whereas their male relatives often had an excess of antisocial personality disorder and substance dependence. This gender difference was not simply a rating bias; when the number of symptoms required to diagnosis the disorder was tentatively reduced in men to eliminate the gender difference, the somatizing men and their relatives had anxiety and mood disorders but no excess of somatizing female relatives (Cloninger *et al.*, 1986).

Despite the reliability and validity of the diagnosis of Briquet's syndrome, this approach to diagnosis was rarely applied in consultation psychiatry because of the complexity of the criteria and their apparently arbitrary grouping of symptoms. When DSM–III was introduced in 1980, the checklist was simplified somewhat to require at least 14 complaints in women and 12 in men from a shorter list of 37 symptoms, excluding depressive and panic symptoms that had been included in Guze's original checklist. These alternative criteria were tested empirically in clinical data sets in which the original Guze criteria had been fully assessed by Lee Robins, Sam Guze, and Robert Cloninger (Cloninger, 1987). The DSM–III criteria were still regarded as overly complex in practice and they were little used except by psychiatrists trained by Guze. This showed that diagnostic reliability and validity do not guarantee acceptance in clinical practice, especially when treatment implications are largely limited by a prediction of chronicity.

Swedish adoption studies of somatization

My Swedish collaborators felt the diagnostic criteria for somatization disorder were too complex. They invited me to examine a large panel of adopted Swedish residents for whom lifetime medical records and registrations for sick leave (i.e. absence from work due to illness), kept by the National Health Insurance Board, were available.

Eight hundred and fifty-nine adopted women were compared with non-adopted controls who were individually matched for social and demographic variables (Sigvardsson et al, 1984; Cloninger et al., 1984; Bohman et al., 1984). We identified a somatization syndrome that is consistently associated with psychiatric impairment and repeated brief periods of disability with chief complaints of multiple bodily pains (such as headache and backache) and gastrointestinal disturbance (such as dyspepsia or irritable bowel symptoms). A method based on discriminant analysis was derived to detect somatizers and was shown to have a classification accuracy of 97 per cent in a replication sample. Somatizers accounted for 36 per cent of all cases of psychiatric disability and 48 per cent of all instances of sick leave.

Next, two sub-types of somatizers were identified. High-frequency somatizers resembled patients with somatization disorder, and were characterized by their high frequency of recurrent bodily pains, gastrointestinal symptoms, and psychiatric impairment (Cloninger et al., 1984). In addition, the biological fathers of women with high-frequency somatization disorder who had been adopted often had a history of recurrent convictions for violent crimes since adolescence, confirming the results of family studies of somatization disorder in the USA. A milder pattern of somatization was associated with anxiety disorders in the adopted women. These adopted women had biological parents with alcoholism but not criminality.

Similar analyses were carried out in a sample of 807 adopted men in Sweden (Sigvardsson et al., 1986; Cloninger et al., 1986). Adopted men with prominent somatization were usually described as 'asthenic' with frequent complaints of fatigue, weakness, and slow recovery from minor ailments.

The genetic and enviromental antecedents of somatization were compared in male and female adoptees. The female somatizers, but not the male somatizers, had an excess of alcoholic biological fathers compared to controls. They had a lower incidence of criminality in their biological parents than in the biological parents of non-somatizers of either gender.

In summary, male somatizers usually have anxiety disorders that are negatively correlated with predisposition to criminality and alcoholism, whereas female somatizers usually have somatization disorder which is positively correlated with criminality and alcoholism in biological relatives, despite being adopted at an early age. This showed clearly that somatization disorder was associated with heritable personality traits such as a predisposition to antisocial behaviour and substance abuse. It also showed the importance of the differential diagnosis of somatization disorder and anxiety disorders associated with chronic fatigue and asthenia.

Development of the DSM–IV criteria

Because of the unacceptable complexity of the DSM–III and DSM–IIIR criteria for somatization disorder, I was asked to simplify them for DSM–IV (American Psychiatric Association, 1994). Based on my experience with the Swedish adoption studies, I decided to group the possible diagnostic features — bodily pains, gastrointestinal symptoms, anxiety symptoms, pseudoneurological symptoms, and sexual or menstrual symptoms — into domains that were familiar and easy for clinicians to remember. These features were used in multiple logistic regression to predict patients with Guze's original Briquet's disorder in a sample of 500 psychiatric out-patients. From this emerged the current diagnostic criteria for somatization disorder in DSM–IV: the diagnosis requires each of the following four features:

1. Four or more unexplained bodily pains.

2. Two or more unexplained gastrointestinal symptoms.

3. One or more pseudoneurological symptom.

4. One or more sexual or menstrual symptom.

These criteria showed excellent concordance with the original decision rule of Guze.

These criteria were tested in a field trial at multiple sites, including with psychiatric patients and primary medical care patients (Yutzy *et al.*, 1995); they showed good reliability at all sites and were consequently adopted for use in DSM–IV.

Unfortunately, the criteria proposed by the ICD for somatization disorder were never empirically tested and show poor agreement with the DSM criteria (Yutzy *et al.*, 1995). The same general concepts as in DSM–IV were adopted, but the numbers and types of symptoms were modified on the basis of impressions by international committees of what is characteristic in various cultures throughout the world. However, this means that the diagnosis is highly dependent on culture-specific sick-role behaviour which, in turn, involves an interaction between the patient seeking help and clinical judgements by the physician as to what is medically explainable (Jablensky, 1999; Cooper, 1999). Given the extensive evidence of the reliability and validity of the diagnosis of Briquet's syndrome and the high concordance of the DSM with those criteria, it is strongly recommended that the DSM criteria be used in clinical practice in industrialized Western countries similar to the USA.

In other countries it will be necessary for psychiatrists to define and test suitable criteria appropriate for their culture, perhaps using as a cross-cultural bridge findings about the relationships between personality and psychology, because the structure of personality is remarkably uniform across cultures (Cloninger *et al.*, 1994). This recommendation has been further supported by progress that relates diagnosis, aetiology, and treatment of somatization disorder to personality variables. Personality assessment provides a way of reliably measuring vulnerability to specific forms of stress and of understanding the psychosocial context of psychiatric complaints and sick-role behaviour. Personality is measured in terms of individual differences in learning or adaptation to experience (Cloninger, 1987). Thus it reflects the patient characteristics that give emotional significance to life events, social context, and familial interactions.

Personality as diathesis to somatization and conversion

Given the importance of personality as a way of understanding individual vulnerability to life events, social context, and other aspects of adaptation to experience, I next developed a model of personality to characterize the differences in vulnerability to somatization and anxiety disorders (Cloninger, 1986). In a long series of investigations in many countries over the subsequent decade, my colleagues and I built up a comprehensive general model of personality that includes four dimensions of tempera-ment and three dimensions of character. These quantify individual differences in all seven dimensions of variation in personality observed in comprehensive studies in English-speaking countries. The structure of the four dimensions of temperament corresponds to individual differences in basic stimulus-response characteristics to pain and pleasure as defined by behavioural conditioning and genetic studies in human twins and adoptees (Cloninger, 1987). The structure of the three dimensions of character correspond to the three possible sets of propositions rising from self–object differentia-tion (Cloninger *et al.*, 1993).

Reliable quantitative measures of each dimension were developed and evaluated in samples from the general population and from psychiatric patients with various diagnoses. These dimensions are summarized in Table 4.2 for the four temperaments and in Table 4.3 for the three character dimensions. The Temperament and Character Inventory (TCI) measures these with strong test–retest reliability (retest correlations over 0.8 after one year) and strong concordance with independent ratings by spouses or clinical raters (Cloninger *et al.*, 1993, 1994). The four temperament dimensions are: harm avoidance (anxious vs. risk-taking); novelty seeking (impulsive vs. reflective); reward dependence (sympathetic vs. aloof); and persistence (tenacious vs. irresolute). The three character dimensions are: self-directedness (resourceful vs. irresponsible); co-operativeness (agreeable vs. hostile); and self-transcendence (intuitive vs. materi-alistic). The TCI has been translated and studied in many languages on five continents, and the structure is highly reproducible regardless of cultural background, gender, or age.

Studies of the TCI in clinical samples showed that all individuals with personality disorder are low in self-directedness and co-operativeness (Cloninger *et al.*, 1993; Svrakic *et al.*, 1993). Individuals with cluster A personality disorders are low in reward

Table 4.2 Descriptors of individuals who score high and low on the four temperament dimensions

Temperament dimension	Descriptors of extreme variants	
	High	Low
Harm avoidance	Pessimistic	Optimistic
	Fearful	Daring
	Shy	Outgoing
	Fatigable	Energetic
Novelty seeking	Exploratory	Reserved
	Impulsive	Rigid
	Extravagant	Frgual
	Irritable	Stoical
Reward dependence	Sentimental	Critical
	Open	Aloof
	Warm	Detached
	Sympathetic	Independent
Persistence	Industrious	Lazy
	Determined	Spoiled
	Ambitious	Underachiever
	Perfectionist	Pragmatist

Table 4.3 Descriptors of individuals who score high and low on the three character dimensions

Character dimension	Descriptors of extreme variants	
	High	Low
Self-directedness	Responsible	Blaming
	Purposeful	Aimless
	Resourceful	Inept
	Self-accepting	Vain
	Disciplined	Undisciplined
Co-operative	Tender-hearted	Intolerant
	Empathic	Insensitive
	Helpful	Hostile
	Compassionate	Revengeful
	Principled	Opportunistic
Self-transcendent	Self-forgetful	Unimaginative
	Transpersonal	Controlling
	Spiritual	Materialistic
	Enlightened	Possessive
	Idealistic	Practical

dependence (aloof), those with cluster B are high in novelty seeking (impulsive), and those with cluster C are high in harm avoidance (anxious). In psychodynamic terms, individuals who are low in TCI self-directedness use immature defences, the type of which depends on temperament (Mulder and Joyce, 1997). For examples relevant to hysteria, high novelty seeking is associated with use of conversion, dissociation, and splitting. Likewise, high harm avoidance is associated with somatization when immature defences are used i.e. when self-directedness is low and the person feels threatened.

Studies of patients with conversion disorder and somatization disorder reveal that these syndromes depend on the multidimensional structure of personality. When somatization is measured in terms of the number of bodily pains and irritable bowel complaints, somatization is correlated with the combination of high harm avoidance and low self-directedness; that is, it depends on both immaturity of character and anxiety proneness in response to the threat of pain, punishment, or frustrative non-reward. Conversion or dissociative reactions are associated with high novelty seeking, as in cluster B personality disorders, including borderline, passive–aggressive, histrionic, and antisocial personality disorder. Thus, the patients with the full syndrome of DSM–IV somatization disorder (which combines multiple bodily pains, irritable bowel symptoms, conversions, and menstrual and sexual dysfunction) are those patients who are high in both harm avoidance and novelty seeking and low in self-directedness (Battaglia et al., 1998; Hudziak et al., 1996). Such patients also are likely to have eating and mood disorders, substance abuse, and high self-transcendence which is associated with a tendency toward hypnotic absorption and suggestibility (Cloninger et al., 1994).

Note that there is no specific personality type associated with somatization disorder. Rather there is a multidimensional set of heritable predisposing factors, as well as multiple experiential variables. Accordingly, no one factor, either a heritable personality trait or any stressful experience is necessary or sufficient to produce somatization disorder. In other words, the development of a conversion or somatization disorder occurs as part of a complex adaptive process involving non-linear interactions among multiple contributing factors (Cloninger et al., 1997).

Thus, patients with somatization disorder are most likely to have borderline personality disorder and to be high in both harm avoidance and novelty seeking (Battaglia et al., 1998; Hudziak et al., 1996). However, not all patients with borderline personality develop somatization disorder; nor do all patients with somatization disorder have a borderline personality. Occasionally, patients with avoidant or obsessional personality disorders, who are high in harm avoidance but low in novelty seeking, may also manifest the full somatization syndrome (Rost et al., 1992).

The expression of specific features like conversion and somatization can be understood therefore in terms of the level of maturity of character and specific patterns of defensive responses to the perceived threat of pain, punishment, and non-reward. These transient symptoms are stable psychobiological predispositions that can be reliably measured. Such personality analysis then is helpful in understanding vulnerability factors underlying unstable clinical symptoms that occur in a context that can be specified in terms of basic emotions, personal goals and values, and social attitudes.

Implications for neurobiological research

The application of the TCI in neuroscience research has been described in more detail elsewhere (Cloninger *et al.*, 1994). The dimensions of the TCI have already been used extensively by investigators in clinical and psychobiological research in many countries (Cloninger *et al.*, 1994). We are actively working to map specific genes that contribute to variation in each of these dimensions (Cloninger, 1998). Others have used the TCI in studies of regional brain imaging, neuropsychology, and neurochemistry. Some of the major neurobiological correlates of novelty seeking, harm avoidance, and self-directedness that have been independently replicated are summarized in Tables 4.4, 4.5, and 4.6 respectively (Cloninger, 1998). Such psychobiological findings help us to understand the clinical behaviour of patients. Much additional research is likely to be fruitful, whether done in specific patient samples or in the general population, since the TCI dimensions can be quantified reliably in anyone who is not floridly psychotic or confused.

All scientific progress requires reliable measurement as its foundation for observation. The TCI provides a set of stable personal dispositions that can be reliably quantified and used in both research and clinical practice.

Implications for treatment

Patients with hysterical conversion or prominent somatization are most likely to be high in harm avoidance (anxious, fearful) and low in self-directedness (immature, irresponsible). They are also probably high in novelty seeking (impulsive, quick-tempered) and

Table 4.4 Reported psychobiological correlates of harm avoidance

Variable	Effect
Neuroanatomy (PET)	
Medial prefrontal(L)	Increased activity (behavioural inhibition)
Anterior paralimbic (R)	Increased activity (sensitivity to threat)
Neuropsychology	
Aversive conditioning	Greater associative pairing with punishment ($r = 0.4$)
Eye-blink startle reflex	Potentiation of response to aversive stimulus (effect size 1.9)
Posner validity effect	Greater slowing of responses after invalid cues ($r = +0.3$)
Spatial delayed response	Better ability to delay responses after ingesting amphetamines ($r = +0.5$)
Neurochemistry	
Platelet 5HT2 receptor	Fewer receptors ($r = -0.6$)
Plasma GABA	Lower level ($r = -0.5$)
Neurogenetics	
5HT transporter promoter	Greater re-uptake activity

Table 4.5 Reported psychobiological correlates of novelty seeking

Variable	Effect
Neuroanatomy (PET)	
Medial prefrontal(L)	Decreased activity (behavioural disinhibition)
Cingulate	Increased activity (behavioural activation)
Caudate (L)	Increased activity (behavioural activation)
Neuropsychology	
Reaction time	Slower to respond if not reinforced (neutral stimuli, $r = -0.4$)
Stimulus intensity (N1/P2 ERP)	Augmentation of intensity of cortical responses to novel auditory stimuli ($r = 0.5$)
Sedation threshold	More easily sedated by diazepam (lower threshold, $r = -0.3$)
Rey word list memory	Deterioration of verbal memory when excited (after ingesting amphetamine, $r = 0.6$)
Neurochemistry	
Dopamine transporter	Higher density observed in striatum
Platelet MAO B	Lower activity (associated with cigarette smoking)
Neurogenetics	
Dopamine receptor D4	Association with long alleles of exon III variant
Dopamine transporter	Greater re-uptake activity

Table 4.6 Relation of character traits to psychobiological differences in event-related potentials in parietal leads of healthy adult individuals*

Character trait**	Correlation with: P300	CNV
Self-directedness	$+0.31$ ($p = 0.023$)	-0.26 (ns)
Co-operativeness	$+0.14$ (ns)	-0.34 ($p = 0.035$)
Self-transcendence	$+0.06$ (ns)	-0.32 ($p = 0.048$)

* P300 is the averaged amplitudes of P300 across parietal leads (P3, Pz, P4) in 56 subjects; CNV is early contingent negative variation across parietal leads (P3, Pz, P4) in 37 subjects.
** All correlations controlled for age; correlations of P300 were controlled for other character traits.

self-transcendence (acquiescent, intuitive). Both of these sets of temperament and character features have strong implications for treatment planning and management.

Individuals who are high in harm avoidance and low in self-directedness respond slowly and poorly both to antidepressant drugs (tricyclic or SSRI) and to cognitive–behavioural therapy (Joffe *et al.*, 1993; Joyce *et al.*, 1994; Tome *et al.*, 1996; Bulik *et al.*, 1998). More specifically, the higher the harm avoidance and the lower the self-directedness, then the slower and poorer is the response to treatment with drugs or psychotherapy. Accordingly, the combination of antidepressants and psychotherapy may be helpful (rather than either one alone), and the antidepressants are likely to require supplementation with a mood stabilizer or atypical neuroleptic. Somatization disorder is usually associated with chronic depression that is refractory to antidepressants, but many such patients respond to the combination of antidepressants with psychotherapy and adjunctive medications.

Individuals who are high in novelty seeking and self-transcendence are more likely to improve with the adjunctive use of psychostimulants, as has been shown in patients with childhood attention deficit disorder and adult somatization disorder (Wender *et al.*, 1981). The adjunctive use of pindolol with SSRIs has also been shown to be most beneficial in those patients who are high in novelty seeking (Tome *et al.*, 1996). More work on differential use of specific antidepressants in patients with somatoform disorders should be fruitful.

High self-directedness is the most important predictor of a rapid and stable response to cognitive–behavioural therapy (Bulik *et al.*, 1998; Bulik *et al.*, in press); indeed, the therapy alone may be sufficient to treat the disorder. On the other hand, if the patient is too low in self-directedness, it is unlikely that such therapy with be effective unless combined with appropriate antidepressant medications with adjunctive neuro-modulators.

Discussion and conclusions

The history of hysterical conversion and somatization has contributed greatly to psychiatry's appreciation of the complexity of human psychobiology. Recent genetic, neuropharmacological, neuropsychological, and descriptive research on these disorders, using modern methods of investigation, have extended and clarified the early and insightful observation of Freud. The syndromes of conversion and somatization do appear as emergent properties of a complex adaptive process involving the interaction of multiple predisposing personality traits in a threatening context. Although there are no simple one-to-one causal relationships between a personality type and a disorder, there are predictable non-linear relations between multidimensional temperament profiles, character profiles, and psychopathological syndromes.

This indicates that it is crucial to systematically ascertain information about the clinical syndrome in terms of the onset, number and severity of bodily pains, gastrointestinal symptoms, conversion and dissociative features, sexual and menstrual dysfunction, as is recommended in DSM–IV for somatization disorder. In addition, it is important to obtain a multidimensional personality assessment similar to that provided by the TCI, although this can be done approximately by an experienced clinician during the routine psychiatric history. These are both crucial for treatment planning and management, including the choice of psychotropic drugs and/or psychotherapy technique. Not to make such systematic assessment of personality and psychopathology would seem to be neglectful given information currently available about the importance of individual differences in psychobiology in tailoring available therapy to individual patients. This does not mean that the current diagnostic categories are truly discrete disease entities, or even that they represent optimal thresholds for treatment planning. However, the symptom domains assessed are related to multidimensional profiles of personality that make the treatment process more understandable and rewarding to both the patient and the therapist.

References

American Psychiatric Association (1994). Diagnostic and Statistical Manual of Mental Disorders (4th edn). Washington, DC: APA.

Battaglia, M., Bertella, S., Bajo, S., Politi, E. and Bellodi, L. (1998). An investigation of the co-occurrence of panic and somatization disorders through temperamental variables. *Psychosomatic Medicine*, **60**, 726–9.

Binzer, M. and Kullgren, G. (1998). Motor conversion disorder. A prospective 2- to 5-year follow-up study. *Psychosomatics*, **39**, 519–27.

Bishop, E. R. Jr. and Torch, E. M. (1979). Dividing 'Hysteria': a preliminary investigation of conversion disorder and psychalgia. *Journal of Nervous and Mental Diseases*, **167**, 348-57.

Bohman, M., Cloninger, C. R., von Knorring, A.-L. and Sigvardsson, S. (1984). An adoption study of somatoform disorders. III. Cross-fostering analysis and genetic relationship to alcoholism and criminality. *Archives of General Psychiatry*, **41**, 872–8.

Bulik, C. M., Sullivan, P. F., Joyce, P. R., Carter, F. A. and McIntosh, V. V. (1998). Predictors of 1-year treatment outcome in Bulimea Nervosa. *Comprehensive Psychiatry*, **39 (4)**, 206–14.

Bulik, C. M., Sullivan, P. F., Carter, F. A., McIntosh, V. V. and Joyce, P. R. (in press). Predictors of rapid and sustained response to cognitive-behavioral therapy for Bulimea Nervosa. *International Journal of Eating Disorders*.

Cloninger, C. R. (1986). A unified biosocial theory of personality and its role in the development of anxiety states. *Psychiatric Developments*, **4**, 167–226.

Cloninger, C. R. (1987). A systematic method for clinical description and classification of personality variants: a proposal. *Archives of General Psychiatry*, **44**, 573–88.

Cloninger, C. R. (1994). Temperament and Personality. *Current Opinion in Neurobiology*, **4**, 266–73.

Cloninger, C. R. (1998). The genetics and psychobiology of the seven-factor model of personality. In *Biology of Personality Disorders* (ed. Silk, K.R.) pp. 63–92. Washington DC, American Psychiatric Press.

Cloninger, C. R., Sigvardsson, S., von Knorring, A.-L. and Bohman, M. (1984). An adoption study of somatoform disorders. II. Identification of two discrete somatoform disorders. *Archives of General Psychiatry*, **41**, 863–71.

Cloninger, C. R., von Knorring, A.-L., Sigvardsson, S. and Bohman, M. (1986). Symptom patterns and causes of somatization in men: II. Genetic and environmental independence from somatization in women. *Genetic Epidemiology*, **3**, 171–85.

Cloninger, C. R., Svrakic, D. M. and Przybeck, T. R. (1993). A psychobiological model of temperament and character. *Archives of General Psychiatry*, **50**, 975–90.

Cloninger, C. R., Przybeck, T. R., Svrakic, D. M. and Wetzel, R. D. (1994). *The Temperament and Character Inventory (TCI): A Guide to its Development and Use*. Washington University, Center for Psychobiology of Personality.

Cloninger, C. R., Svrakic, N. M. and Svrakic, D. M. (1997). Role of personality self-organization in development of mental order and disorder. *Development and Psychopathology*, **9**, 881–906.

Cloninger, C. R. and Svrakic, D. M. (1997). Integrative psychobiological approach to psychiatric assessment andtreatment. *Psychiatry*, **60**, 120–41.

Cooper, J. (1999). The Classification of Somatoform Disorders in ICD-10. In *Somatoform Disorders. A Worldwide Perspective* (eds Ono, Y., Janca, A., Asai, N. and Sartorius, N.) pp. 11–18. Tokyo: Springer.

Crimlisk, H. L., Bhatia, K., Cope, H., David, A., Marsden, C. D. and Ron, M. A. (1998). Slater revisited: 6 year follow up study of patients with medically unexplained motor symptoms. *British Medical Journal*, **316**, 582–6.

Gatfield, P. D. and Guze, S. B. (1962). Prognosis and differential diagnosis of conversion reactions (A follow-up study). *Diseases of the Nervous System*, **23**, 1–8.

Guze, S. B. (1967). The diagnosis of hysteria: What are we trying to do? *American Journal of Psychiatry*, **124**, 491–8.

Guze, S.B. (1975). The validity and significance of the clinical diagnosis of hysteria (Briquet's syndrome). American Journal of Psychiatry **132**, 138–41.

Guze, S. B., Woodruff, R. A. Jr. and Clayton, P. J. (1971*a*). A study of conversion symptoms in psychiatric outpatients. *American Journal of Psychiatry*, **128**, 643–6.

Guze, S. B., Woodruff, R. A. Jr. and Clayton, P. J. (1971*b*). Hysteria and antisocial behavior: further evidence of an association. *American Journal of Psychiatry*, **127**, 957–60.

Hudziak, J. J., Boffeli, T. J., Kreisman, J. J., Battaglia, M. M., Stanger, C. and Guze, S. B. (1996). Clinical study of the relation of borderline personality disorder to Briquet's syndrome (hysteria), somatization disorder, antisocial personality disorder, and substance abuse disorders. *American Journal of Psychiatry*, **153**, 1598–606.

Jablensky, A. (1999). The Concept of Somatoform Disorders: A Comment on the Mind-Body Problem in Psychiatry. In *Somatoform Disorders. A Worldwide Perspective* (eds Ono, Y., Janca, A., Asai, N., Sartorius, N.) pp. 3–10. Tokyo: Springer.

Joffe, R. T., Bagby, R. M., Levitt, A. J., Regan, J. J. and Parker, J. D. A. (1993). The tridimensional personality questionnaire in major depression. *American Journal of Psychiatry*, **150 (6)**, 959–60.

Joyce, P. R., Mulder, R. T. and Cloninger, C. R. (1994). Temperament predicts clomipramine and desipramine response in major depression. *Journal of Affective Disorders*, **30**, 35–46.

Mulder, R. T. and Joyce, P. R. (1997). Temperament and the structure of personality disorder symptoms. *Psychological Medicine*, **27**, 99–106.

Mulder, R. T., Joyce, P. R., Sellman, J. D., Sullivan, P. F. and Cloninger, C. R. (1996). Towards an understanding of defense style in terms of temperament and character. *Acta Psychiatrica Scandinavica*, **93 (2)**, 99–104.

Perley, M. J. and Guze, S. B. (1962). Hysteria — the stability and usefulness of clinical criteria. *New England Journal of Medicine*, **266**, 421–6.

Purtell, J. J., Robins, E. and Cohen, M. E. (1951). Observations on the clinical aspects of hysteria. *Journal of the American Medical Association*, **146**, 901–9.

Raskin, M., Talbott, J. A. and Meyerson, A. T. (1966). Diagnosis of conversion reactions: predictive value of psychiatric criteria. *Journal of the American Medical Association*, **197**, 102–6.

Rost, K. M., Akins, R. N., Brown, F. W. and Smith, G. R. (1992). The comorbidity of DSM–III–R personality disorders in somatization disorder. *General Hospital Psychiatry*, **14**, 322–6.

Sigvardsson, S., von Knorring, A.-L., Bohman, M. and Cloninger, C. R. (1984). An adoption study of somatoform disorders. I. The relationship of somatization to psychiatric disability. *Archives of General Psychiatry*, **41**, 853–9.

Sigvardsson, S., Bohman, M., von Knorring, A.-L. and Cloninger, C. R. (1986). Symptom patterns and causes of somatization in men: I. Differentiation of two discrete disorders. *Genetic Epidemiology*, **3**, 153–69.

Slater, E. T. O. (1965). Diagnosis of hysteria. *British Medical Journal*, **1**, 1395–9.

Svrakic, D. M., Whitehead, C., Przybeck, T. R. and Cloninger, C. R. (1993). Differential diagnosis of personality disorders by the seven-factor model of temperament and character. *Archives of General Psychiatry*, **50**, 991–9.

Tome, M. B., Cloninger, C. R., Watson, J. P. and Isaac, M. T. (1997). Serotonergic autoreceptor blockade in the reduction of antidepressant latency: personality variables and response to paroxetine and pindolol. *Journal of Affective Disorders*, **44**, 101–9.

Watson, C. G. and Buranen, C. (1979). The frequency and identification of false positive conversion reactions. *Journal of Nervous and Mental Diseases*, **167**, 243–7.

Wender, P. H., Reimherr, F. W. and Wood, D. R. (1981). Attention deficit disorder (minimal brain dysfunction) in adults: a replication study of diagnosis and drug treatment. *Archives of General Psychiatry*, **38**, 449–54.

Yutzy, S. H. *et al.* (1995). DSM–IV field trial: testing a new proposal for somatization disorder. *American Journal of Psychiatry*, **152**, 97–101.

5 Discrepancies between diagnostic criteria and clinical practice

Simon Wessely

The conventional psychiatric diagnostic criteria for hysteria are unsatisfactory for many reasons. Key concepts such as secondary gain, belle indifference, psychogenic preciptiation, and so on are unreliable and lack validity and prognostic significance. Variables that appear to have clinical and prognostic importance, such as attributions, cognitions, and avoidances, are ignored. Physicians therefore rightly tend to ignore the psychiatric classifications of hysteria, and for the following reasons. First, we keep changing them. Second, they were invented by psychiatrists but used by neurologists. Third, they do not include the patients they should. And finally, the diagnosis cannot be used in front of patients anyway. Instead, doctors tend to use the term hysteria first to simply mean the absence of organic causes, and second, as a complex system of codes and euphemisms. It is now time to finally abandon the classic psychoanalytic derived criteria for conversion disorder, and instead classify hysterical symptoms in clinically relevant ways.

Introduction

In this chapter I shall discuss the problem of classifying conversion disorders, and conclude that there is a wide discrepancy between the official psychiatric classifications of conversion disorders and their use in clinical practice. This is partly a reflection of the dilemmas and ambiguities that underlie the concepts of conversion disorders, and partly because of the general problems of applying psychiatric thinking to non-psychiatric practice.

What are the current classification systems?

In DSM–IV (American Psychiatric Association, 1994) conversion disorder, which includes motor and sensory symptoms as well as non-epileptic seizures, is included under somatoform disorders, and, as many have pointed out, fugue and multiple personality under dissociative disorders. DSM–IV continues to be faithful to the analytic origins of conversion by insisting that conflicts and 'other stressors' are associated with the onset of symptoms. However, DSM–IV seems for once to lack the confidence it shows elsewhere — conversion disorder, unlike much of DSM–IV, is 'tentative and provisional' (American Psychiatric Association, 1994). The current DSM–IV criteria for conversion disorder are shown in Table 5.1.

Table 5.1 DSM–IV criteria — 'conversion disorder (F44)'

Criterion A	Symptoms or deficits affecting voluntary motor or sensory function
Criterion B	Associated with psychological factors
Criterion C	Not malingering/factitious
Criterion D	Not organic, substance induced or 'culturally sanctioned'
Criterion E	Impairment necessary
Criterion F	Not another mental disorder (including somatization disorder)

ICD–10 uses a generally similar description to DSM–IV, but the placement of conversion disorder differs between the two. ICD–10 is broader than DSM–IV, including all the neurotic, conversion, and somatoform disorders under the heading of 'neurotic, stress related, and somatoform disorders'. Conversion itself comes under 'dissociation', the preferred term being 'dissociative (conversion) disorders (F44)'. In keeping with its tradition, the glossary does not list formal criteria but gives a clinical description, and links symptoms with traumatic events and with the patient's 'idea' of illness, describing symptoms as 'an expression of emotional conflicts or needs'. F44 is subdivided, with F44.4 (dissociative motor disorders) covering the standard neurological conversion symptoms. The same code (F44) also includes trance, possession, Ganser's, and multiple personality disorder.

The chequered history of the classification of conversion disorder shows why doctors are right to be confused. Mace has usefully traced the history of the idea of conversion (Mace, 1992) through the official psychiatric classification systems. It has, as Roy Porter puts it, 'waltzed in and out of the Diagnostic and Statistical Manual' (Porter, 1995). Perhaps the authors of the DSM system were uncertain — as Micale points out in the casebook that accompanies the advice from the American Psychiatric Association. The authors re-analysed the prototypical patient 'Anna O' and concluded that no fewer than four separate diagnoses were needed to explain her illness — a sign of classificatory disillusionment (Micale, 1995).

How valid are these criteria?

The formal classifications are therefore varied, and all have a negative and positive aspect. On the negative side, all the definitions of hysteria insist that the symptoms are not explained by organic illness — in other words, hysteria is one psychiatric disorder in which we can agree that symptoms are, in the famous phase, 'all in the mind'. But are they?

There are two challenges to this view. One is the classic Slater position. This will be addressed in detail in the chapter by Maria Ron, but suffice it to say that Slater's essential argument, that sooner or later most 'hysterical' conditions turn out to be presentations of classic illnesses, physical or mental, has been overstated (Crimlisk *et al.*, 1998). The other challenge questions the concept of any illness that is 'all in the mind' within the psychosomatic or somatization disorder spectrum (White and Moorey, 1997; Sharpe and Bass, 1992) or the 'pure' conversion disorders themselves (see Spence's chapter in this volume p. 235). In this critique, no disorder can ever be purely psychogenic, and mind–body dualism is suspect in general.

It is the 'positive' features of the diagnosis of conversion disorder that pose the most problems, since these classic criteria do not distinguish satisfactorily between hysteria and organic disorders. This is a serious challenge, since these classic features of conversion disorder remain enshrined in its official definitions. As Sir Aubrey Lewis predicted, several studies have criticized classic concepts such as psychogenic precipitation, secondary gain, symbolic significance, life events, and belle indifference (Miller, 1988; Chabrol *et al.*, 1995; Gould *et al.*, 1986; see Cloninger's chapter in this volume, p. 49).

The requirement for psychogenic precipitation is certainly questionable. Early studies tended to confirm this (e.g. Raskin *et al.*, 1966), but are open to debate. Even though a patient of Raskin's reported that her right arm dystonia had been caused by a bitter argument with her father during which he had twisted her arm, what are we to make of this? Clearly patients and doctors alike can search after psychological meaning. Other studies cast considerable doubt on the specificity of psychological precipitation (Watson and Buranen, 1979). It may be, however, that psychogenic precipitation becomes more clear-cut in certain settings, such as a military one (see Palmer's chapter in this volume p. 12).

Secondary gain, although often reported as present (Raskin *et al.*, 1966; Baker and Silver, 1987), must be one of the most difficult judgements to make in clinical practice, and is anyway hard to separate from the general advantages of the sick role. For example, Raskin stated that the majority of hysterical patients 'reported using conversion reactions or other physical symptoms as a psychological defence' — but this judgement obviously depends on Raskin's own interview skills and interpretation. There are benefits to being ill, whether one has cancer or hysteria, yet that does not prove that the purpose of developing cancer is to gain extra care and attention and to avoid work.

Clinical experience suggests that patients are rarely indifferent to their symptoms (Kirmayer and Taillefer, 1997). Far from being indifferent, anxiety levels are actually high and physiological reactivity increased (Lader and Sartorius, 1968; Rice and Greenfield, 1969). Even DSM–IV concedes that 'belle indifference' can occur in other medical conditions. Finally, Gould and colleagues looked for all of the classic features of conversion disorder (history of hypochondriasis, secondary gain, la belle indifference, non-anatomical sensory loss, split of midline by pain or vibratory stimulation, changing boundaries of hypalgesia, give-away weakness) in a consecutive series of 30 acute neurological admissions. All subjects showed at least one of these findings; most presented three or four. The authors concluded that 'the presence of these "positive" findings of hysteria in patients with acute structural brain disease invalidates their use as pathognomonic evidence of hysteria' (Gould *et al.*, 1986; see also Cloninger's chapter in this volume p. 49).

Thus, the classic features of conversion disorder, as repeated in the current official classifications, are either unreliable, untrue (belle indifference), unratable (primary gain) or a non specific consequence of being sick (secondary gain).

What happens in real life?

Perhaps for the reasons already given, the current classifications leave much to be desired. In psychiatric clinics around the world, the classification has 'limited utility' (Alexander *et al.*, 1997); the diagnoses are rarely made, whilst the majority of patients for whom the doctor considers the diagnosis is appropriate do not fit into the defined sub-categories of dissociative (conversion) disorders (Das and Saxena, 1991; Alexander *et al.*, 1997). Instead, in India the two main groups were those with short-term alterations of consciousness (which they called 'brief depressive stupor') and pseudo seizures. In a Japanese psychosomatic clinic the most common DSM–III–R and DSM–IV diagnosis was 'somatoform disorders NOS' (Nakao *et al.*, 1998). Even in the USA the majority of patients with a primary diagnosis of dissociative disorder were placed in that well-known but unsatisfactory category, unspecified or atypical (Mezzich *et al.*, 1989).

There is a further irony. As noted here, DSM–IV has made a determined effort, as part of its nosological drive, to remove the word 'conversion' from hysteria and replace it with dissociative disorder. As part of 'the Second Coming' of biological psychiatry, American psychiatry has been keen to distance itself from its Freudian origins by removing hysteria from its psychiatric classifications. Thus hysteria, from being the quintessential Freudian disorder, becomes dissociative disorder.

However, few clinicians seem to have taken any notice. Why is this? One reason may be that the classic Freudian interpretations of conversion made little impact on the clinicians (non-psychiatrists) who actually treated these patients. One possible exception remained in French psychiatry, where classic interpretations of hysteria survive and prosper, but perhaps more from a sense of nationalistic pride than intellectual rigour.

What do doctors actually do?

Most doctors probably do not use the classic psychoanalytic formulations and certainly hardly ever use 'not otherwise specified' (NOS), atypical, and the like. So what do they do? In an interesting study, Mace and Trimble (1991) conducted a survey amongst British neurologists regarding their diagnostic practices. The first point to note is that when asked in what percentage of cases psychological factors were important, answers ranged from 1 per cent to 90 per cent! The second confirms one's own intuition that neurologists use terms such as 'functional', 'hysterical', and 'psychogenic' interchangeably, whilst 'conversion' is distinctly less popular. The term 'somatoform' might as well not exist as far as UK neurologists were concerned.

Instead, Mace and Trimble demonstrated that neurologists tended to make both formal and informal diagnoses. For example, 29 per cent said they never used the term 'hysteria', but another 18 per cent said they used it 'informally', by which they meant in conversation with their colleagues. Many years of hospital research and discussions at conferences have convinced me that this indeed is the case. I would argue that doctors use hysteria in two ways — the formal one being the hysterical symptom, in which the cardinal, and indeed only rule, is that the symptom cannot be explained by organic disease. At the same time doctors also use it in an informal, behavioural sense, touching on the concept of abnormal illness behaviour, and using the concept to mean a distortion of the doctor– patient relationship. 'Hysteric' is one of the many synoymns that doctors have adopted for the difficult patient, joining 'heartsink' and so many other terms — although in practice the difficult patient is more often part of the multi-symptom/somatization disorder class (Hahn *et al.*, 1996; Jackson and Kroenke, 1999).

Why don't doctors use the term 'hysteria'?

Why are doctors so reluctant to follow the strictures of psychiatric classification when confronted with a patient with unexplained loss of function? Perhaps the most obvious reason lies in the professional demarcation between neurology and psychiatry. It is psychiatrists who are most involved in the formal classification of hysterical symptoms — and anyone who reviews the rich intellectual history of psychiatric writings on hysteria might be forgiven for thinking that dealing with hysterical patients is at the heart of psychiatric practice. Not so. Indeed almost the opposite is true. Psychiatrists have increasingly little practical experience in dealing with neurosis of any kind (Wessely, 1996), let alone the complex disorders that exist in general hospitals. Of those actually diagnosed with conversion disorder in general practice in Nottingham, only one third had been referred to psychiatrists (Singh and Lee, 1997). Numerous studies have demonstrated that the patient with medically unexplained symptoms in general, and conversion disorder in particular, is rarely seen by a psychiatrist (e.g. Ewald *et al.*, 1994; Hamilton *et al.*, 1996; Anon, 1995).

We therefore have the paradoxical situation of psychiatrists deciding the diagnostic rules for patients who are largely under the care of physicians. As Mace has pointed out, during the last hundred years hysteria has become progressively more identified with the syndromes of neurology, and 'finally exclusively so' (Mace, 1992). At the same time, the psychiatric literature has become crowded with titles on the 'end of hysteria' (Slavney, 1990) and bemoaning the disappearance of 'Anna O' (see Micale, 1993).

In practice, neurologists have a rather more straightforward view of conversion — they use the term when there is loss or distortion of neurological function which cannot be explained by organic disease (Marsden, 1986). Used in this way, Marsden estimates that hysteria accounts for about 1 per cent of admissions to the National Hospital for Neurology in London, and has done so for the last 50 years. This is unlikely to change.

The problem of somatization

A rarely discussed issue is the diagnostic status of somatization disorder. In theory, these patients should be different — even if the St Louis school confused matters by widening the scope of hysteria to include multiple medically unexplained symptoms, as in Briquet's hysteria, and subsequently somatization disorder. 'Conversion is conceptual, somatization is purely descriptive' (Martin, 1999) — but in practice it is not so simple. There is no rigid distinction between the categories, despite what the nosologists have tried to convince us..

Mace and Trimble (1996) reported that although only 4 per cent of patients in their study initially received the diagnosis of somatization disorder, ten years later 64 per cent met criteria for the disorder. Likewise, among the 23 cases that GPs 'thought fulfilled the criteria' for conversion disorder, six were polysymptomatic and one fulfilled criteria for somatization disorder (Singh and Lee, 1997). In Marsden's clinical practice of conversion disorder at an in-patient neurology ward in London, perhaps one fifth would satisfy diagnostic criteria for somatization disorder (Marsden, 1986). Researchers themselves seem not to heed such distinctions (Ewald *et al.*, 1994). There are numerous other studies showing that in practice the distinction between the two is not clear-cut — instead, a more meaningful distinction might be between acute and gradual onset.

In clinical practice the two can be similar — patients can shift, both symptomatically and diagnostically, from one to the other. Conversion seems not to cover the problem of the person who gradually deteriorates, ending up in a wheelchair — yet such clinical presentations are common. In a recent report on wheelchair patients it was noticeable that the specific diagnosis of conversion or somatization disorder made little difference to what was actually done (Davison *et al.*, 1999). Other physicians seem to use similar value-laden codes — 'wheelchair' patients in gastroenterological practice are labelled 'functional' (Chiotakakou-Faliakou *et al.*, 1996). And as Trudie Chalder describes in her chapter in this volume, whether such seriously disabled patients are diagnosed with conversion disorder or somatization disorder has few implications when it comes to treatment (Powell *et al.*, 1999). Instead, what matters are people's beliefs, behaviours, attitudes, and social circumstances, none of which are covered in the classification systems.

Doctors do not therefore make a rigid distinction between somatization and hysteria, and nor do they need to when management is planned.

What is the long-term utility of the diagnostic term?

I will go further — not only do physicians avoid hysteria as a formal diagnosis, there are many practical and sensible reasons for so doing (Wessely, 1999).

A diagnosis is essentially a means of communicating — with fellow professionals, but also with patients. It is a shorthand way of communicating information about aetiology, likely treatment, and prognosis. Hysteria then is fatal to the doctor–patient relationship. Whatever we say or do or write, hysteria, hysterical, and histrionic are all used interchangeably, and all are unmistakably a term of abuse (Wessely, 1999). 'So it is all in my mind, is it doctor?' says the patient threateningly. The correct answer would of course be 'yes', followed by a plaintive 'but psychiatric disorders really are genuine illnesses' — but by that time the patient may well have left the room in disgust. Using the term will guarantee only one thing – that the patient does not return for another consultation, which may of course be the intention of the doctor anyway!

The term hysteria is therefore rarely spoken about, at least not to the patient. 'A diagnosis which cannot be made face to face with the sufferer and which condemns him to a lifetime of chronic non-recovery if only to prove the doctor wrong is both ethically and strategically wrong' (David, 1993). And the more the patient denies it, the more the doctor is certain that 'non-organic' factors are present — a therapeutic 'catch-22' (Mant, 1994).

Instead what happens is often worse. In my clinical practice I see the problems of the reluctance of physicians to use the term hysteria in two rather contradictory situations. The first is that when I assess a patient with a conversion disorder, whose medical records leave little doubt as to what is in the neurologist's mind, it is surprising how often the diagnosis has never been discussed. The patient will tell me with conviction that he or she has been informed that they have a 'loose disc', 'possible MS', and so on and so forth. Whether or not these labels are used by the doctors as euphemisms, or alternatively have been generated by the patient, is unclear, but our research in chronic pain patients suggests that doctors frequently use anatomical or pathological terms loosely and not always accurately (Kouyanou *et al.*, 1997).

The reluctance of doctors to use the term hysteria has had another unlikely side-effect: patients can suspect that it is being applied to them when that is probably not the doctors' intention. It is a rare patient in our chronic fatigue clinic who does not report that one or more doctors have implied or insinuated that their problems are hysterical (Deale and Wessely, in press). Conversion disorder is actually relatively uncommon in a chronic fatigue clinic, but all too often we have the impression that the lack of diagnostic clarity, the fear that the doctor says one thing and means another, and a simple misinterpretation of the meaning of phrases such as depression, means that the spectre of hysteria hangs over all encounters between patients with medically unexplained symptoms and their conventional doctors.

Nortin Hadler has outlined the dilemma facing patients with medically unexplained symptoms in general, and conversion in particular (Hadler, 1996). That is, to get well in these circumstances is to abandon veracity. Patients will be more inclined to get better when they have satisfactory explanations for their problems (Brody, 1994). By satisfactory I mean from the patient's point of view, from a symbolic or even metaphorical perspective — not in a narrow scientific sense (Coulehan, 1991; Kirmayer, 1993; Butler and Rollnick, 1996). Explanations that are not acceptable are not immediately discarded. Instead, the patient may embark on a mission to actively prove them false. Hysteria then, is a term used by doctors, but not shared with patients. Hysteria is, as David has remarked, the 'H' word — the diagnosis that dare not speak its name (David, 1993).

What has been proposed?

A group of international researchers experienced in this area made a laudable effort to improve the classification of psychosomatic disorders, but their efforts on conversion disorder remained trapped in history (Fava *et al.*, 1995). Symptoms and loss of function were joined, and belle indifference, histrionic personality, precipitation by stress (but of which the patient is unaware), and a history of similar symptoms 'observed in someone else or wished on someone else' were retained.

Another suggestion is to have a category of 'specific somatoform disorder' (Rief and Hiller, 1999), based on the presence of at least one symptom (but not multiple symptoms, which is included under their proposed polysymptomatic somatoform disorder), and in which the only other mandatory requirement is for disability. Within this category will appear not only conversion disorder but also 'chronic fatigue sub-type' — a proposal not likely to endear the authors to some. Others place conversion disorders firmly under the heading of somatization disorders (Martin, 1999).

However, perhaps the most persuasive solution is simply to regard conversion as a symptom, rather than a diagnosis (Ebel and Lohmann, 1995; Binzer *et al.*, 1997). It seems that that is how neurologists use it in practice (Marsden, 1986) — it is a 'descriptive neurological shorthand' (Marsden, 1986), in the same category as an hemianopia. Even DSM–IV concedes that it is 'tentative and provisional' (American Psychiatric Association, 1994).

Another reason for the difficulty in classifying conversion disorder is the ambiguity of the term. The contributors to this volume, who have carefully reviewed the issues, remain in considerable doubt as to what hysteria actually means. So what chance does the average doctor have? The term hysteria is unsuited to the diagnostic process anyway — a diagnosis is supposed to determine what a patient has, but as Slavney points out, hysteria is more what a patient is, or what a patient does (Slavney, 1990).

Conclusion

The formal diagnostic criteria for hysteria are unsatisfactory for the following reasons:

1. we keep changing them;
2. they were invented by psychiatrists but are used by neurologists;
3. they have too many categories, which are too unreliable for both clinical and research purposes;
4. they do not include the patients they should, or do so via categories such as NOS;
5. they cannot be used in front of patients;
6. they do not relate to variables that have clinical and prognostic importance, such as attributions, cognitions, and avoidances;
7. in severe cases, hysteria is indistinguishable from somatization disorder.

Instead, doctors tend to:

1. use a system of codes and euphenisms;
2. use hysteria as a symptom, not a diagnosis;
3. distinguish between symptoms and loss of function;
4. use it simply in a crude organic versus non-organic form.

So, what should we do or propose?

1. The classic psychoanalytic-derived criteria for conversion disorder should be dropped once and for all.
2. We should classify in clinically relevant ways — the suggested distinctions that appear to have some empirical and practical validation would be a diagnosis that continues to insist that either symptoms and/or loss of function be inexplicable in conventional biomedical terms, and then distinguish between symptoms and loss of function, and between acute and chronic onset of either.
3. Finally, whatever we call these conditions, we can anticipate that in time they will acquire the stigma now associated with the term hysteria. Stigma comes not from the term itself, but from the dualistic way in which doctors continue to approach medically unexplained symptoms, and the way in which the physical/psychological divide carries so much subtext of deserved/undeserved or real/unreal (Kirmayer, 1988).

References

Alexander, P., Joseph, S. and Das, A. (1997). Limited utility of ICD-10 and DSM-IV classification of dissociative and conversion disorders in India. *Acta Psychiatrica Scandinavica*, **95**, 177–82.

American Psychiatric Association. (1994). *Diagnostic and Statistical Manual of Mental Disorder (DSM-IV)* (4th edn). American Psychiatric Association: Washington DC.

Anon (1995). *The Psychological Care of Medical Patients: Recognition of Need and Service Provision*. The Royal College of Physicians and the Royal College of Psychiatrists: London.

Baker, J. and Silver, J. (1987). Hysterical paraplegia. *Journal of Neurology, Neurosurgery and Psychiatry*, **50**, 375–82.

Binzer, M., Andersen, P. and Kullgren, G. (1997). Clinical characteristics of patients with motor conversion disability due to coversion disorder: a prospective control group study. *Journal of Neurology, Neurosurgery and Psychiatry*, **63**, 83–8.

Brody, H. (1994). 'My story is broken: can you help me fix it?' Medical ethics and the joint construction of narrative. *Literature and Medicine*, **13**, 79–92.

Butler, C. and Rollnick, S. (1996). Missing the meaning and provoking resistance: a case of myalgic encephalomyelitis. *Family Practice*, **13**, 106–9.

Chabrol, H., Peresson, G. and Clanet, M. (1995). Lack of specificity of the traditional criteria for conversion disorders. *European Psychiatry*, **10**, 317–19.

Chiotakakou-Faliakou, E., Dave, U. and Forbes, A. (1996). Wheelchair use: a physical sign in gastroenterological practice. *Journal of the Royal Society of Medicine*, **89**, 490–2.

Coulehan, J. (1991). The word is an instrument of healing. *Literature and Medicine*, **10**, 111–29.

Crimlisk, H., Bhatia, K., Cope, H., David, A., Marsden, C. D. and Ron, M. (1998). Slater revisited: 6 year follow up study of patients with medically unexplained motor symptoms. British Medical Journal **316**, 582–6.

Das, P. and Saxena, S. (1991). Classification of dissociative states in DSM–III–R and ICD–10 (1989 draft). A study of Indian outpatients. *British Journal of Psychiatry*, **159**, 425–7.

David, A. (1993). Camera. lights, action for ME. *British Medical Journal*, **307**, 688.

Davison, P., Sharpe, M., Wade, D. and Bass, C. (1999). 'Wheelchair' patients with non-organic disease: a psychological inquiry. *Journal of Psychosomatic Research*, **47**, 93–103.

Deale, A. and Wessely, S. (in press) Medical interactions and symptom persistence in chronic fatigue syndrome. *Social Science Medicine*.

Ebel, H. and Lohmann, T. (1995). Clinical criteria for diagnosing conversion disorders. *Neurology Psychiatry and Brain Research*, **3**, 193–200.

Ewald, H., Rogne, T., Ewald, K.,and Fink, P. (1994). Somatization in patients newly admitted to a neurological department. *Acta Psychiatrica Scandanivica*, **89**, 174–9.

Fava, G. *et al.*(1995). Diagnostic criteria for use in psychosomatic research. *Psychotherapy and Psychosomatics*, **63**, 1–8.

Gould, R., Miller, B., Goldberg, M. and Benson, D. (1986). The validity of hysterical signs and symptoms. *Journal of Nervous and Mental Disease*, **174**, 593–7.

Hadler, N. M. (1996). If you have to prove you are ill, you can't get well. The object lesson of fibromyalgia. *Spine*, **21**, 2397–400.

Hahn, S. *et al.* (1996). The difficult patient: prevalence, psychopathology, and functional impairment. *Journal of General Internal Medicine*, **11**, 1–8.

Hamilton, J., Campos, R. and Creed, F. (1996). Anxiety, depression and management of medically unexplained symptoms in medical clinics. *Journal of the Royal College of Physicians*, **30**, 18–21.

Jackson, J. and Kroenke, K. (1999). Difficult patient encounters in the ambulatory clinic. *Archives of Internal Medicine*, **159**, 1069–75.

Kirmayer, L. (1988). Mind and body as metaphors: hidden values in biomedicine. In *Biomedicine Examined* (ed Lock, G. D.), pp. 57–92. Kluwer: Dordrecht.

Kirmayer, L. (1993). Healing and the invention of metaphor: the effectiveness of symbols revisited. *Culture, Medicine and Psychiatry*, **17**, 161–95.

Kirmayer, L. and Taillefer, S. (1997). Somatoform disorders. In *Adult Psychopathology and Diagnosis* (ed Turner, S. and Hersen, M.), pp. 333–83. John Wiley: New York.

Kouyanou, K., Pither, C. and Wessely, S. (1997). Iatrogenic factors and chronic pain. *Psychosomatic Medicine*, **59**, 597–604.

Lader, M. and Sartorius, N. (1968). Anxiety in patients with hysterical conversion symptoms. *Journal of Neurology, Neurosurgery and Psychiatry*, **31**, 490–5.

Mace, C. (1992). Hysterical conversion II: a critique. *British Journal of Psychiatry*, **161**, 378–89.

Mace, C. J. and Trimble, M. R. (1991). 'Hysteria', 'functional' or 'psychogenic'? A survey of British neurologists' preferences. *Journal of the Royal Society of Medicine*, **84**, 471–5.

Mace, C. and Trimble, M. (1996). Ten-year prognosis of conversion disorder. *British Journal of Psychiatry*, **169**, 282–8.

Mant, D. (1994). Chronic fatigue syndrome. *Lancet*, **344**, 834–5.

Marsden, C. (1986). Hysteria — a neurologist's view. *Psychological Medicine*, **16**, 277–88.

Martin, R. (1999). The somatoform conundrum: a question of nosological values. *General Hospital Psychiatry*, **21**, 177–86.

Mezzich, J., Fabrega, H., Coffman, G. and Haley, R. (1989). DSM–III disorders in a large sample of psychiatric patients: frequency and specificity of diagnoses. *American Journal of Psychiatry*, **146**, 212–19.

Micale, M. (1993). On the 'disappearance' of hysteria. *Isis*, **84**, 496–526.

Micale, M. (1995). *Approaching Hysteria: Disease and Its Interpretations*. Princeton University Press: Princeton.

Miller, E. (1988). Defining hysterical symptoms. *Psychological Medicine*, **18**, 275–7.

Nakao, M., Nomura, S., Yamanaka, G., Kumano, H. and Kuboki, T. (1998). Assesment of patients by DSM–III–R and DSM–IV in a Japanese psychosomatic clinic. *Psychotherapy and Psychosomatics*, **67**, 43–9.

Porter, R. (1995) The body and the mind, the doctor and the patient. In *Hysteria Beyond Freud*, pp. 225–85. (ed Gilman, S. *et al.*) University of California Press, Berkeley and London.

Powell, P., Edwards, R. and Bentall, R. (1999). The treatment of wheelchair-bound chronic fatigue syndrome patients: two case studies of a pragmatic rehabilitation approach. *Behavioural and Cognitive Psychotherapy*, **27**, 249–60.

Raskin, M., Talbott, J. and Myerson, A. (1966). Diagnosis of conversion reactions: predictive value of psychiatric criteria. *Journal of the American Medical Association*, **197**, 530–4.

Rice, D. and Greenfield, N. (1969). Psychophysiological correlates of la belle indifference. *Archives of General Psychiatry*, **20**, 239–45.

Rief, W. and Hiller, W. (1999). Towards empirically based criteria for the classification of somatoform disorders. *Journal of Psychosomatic Research*, **46**, 507–18.

Sharpe, M. and Bass, C. (1992). Pathophysiological mechanisms in somatisation. *International Review of Psychiatry*, **4**, 81–97.

Singh, S. and Lee, A. (1997). Conversion disorders in Nottingham: alive but not kicking. *Journal of Psychosomatic Disorders*, **43**, 425–30.

Slavney, P. (1990). *Perspectives on 'Hysteria'*. Johns Hopkins Press: Baltimore.

Watson, C. and Buranen, C. (1979). The frequency and identification of false positive conversion reactions. *Journal of Nervous and Mental Disease*, **167**, 243–7.

Wessely, S. (1996). The rise of counselling and the return of alienism. *British Medical Journal*, **313**, 158–60.

Wessely, S. (1999). To tell or not to tell: the problem of medically unexplained symptoms. In *Ethical Dilemnas in Neurology* (ed Zeman, A. and Emanuel, L.), pp. 41–53. Saunders: London.

White, P. and Moorey, S. (1997). Psychosomatic illnesses are not 'all in the mind'. *Journal of Psychosomatic Research*, **42**, 329–32.

6 The epidemiology of hysterical conversion

Hiroko Akagi and Allan House

We have conducted a literature search in which we dealt with the problem of case definition by choosing diagnostic criteria which were restricted to significant motor or sensory loss, so we can be reasonably confident about the clinical problem being described. Difficulties in case ascertainment are inherent in researching the epidemiology of hysteria, because case identification requires medical judgement; we can only note the likelihood that it will have affected the accuracy of the studies we report.

Our findings suggest that in a population of a quarter of a million people there will be between 10 and 25 new cases of hysterical conversion per year, and at least 150 prevalent cases. Psychiatric services may see only a minority. There is no good evidence that hysteria is getting rarer or that it is more common in underdeveloped countries. All case series show a predominance of women. The problem of acute and transient hysteria is neglected, with important implications for our understanding of the epidemiology and natural history of hysterical conversion.

Introduction

Clinical epidemiology is the study of illness in populations. One of its aims is to *estimate the magnitude of the problem* posed by a particular disorder — usually defined according to the disorder's frequency and severity in the population. It may also *provide clues as to the cause* by identifying the characteristics — such as age, sex, socio-economic status, or exposure to risk factors — of those who have the disorder, or by highlighting variations in occurrence over time or between places. The third value of epidemiology is that it can *assist in planning treatment trials*, successful design of which relies on accurate knowledge of rates of occurrence (to plan recruitment) and of natural history (to estimate sample size).

Epidemiologists face certain difficulties which are common to the study of all disorders, but which are particularly troublesome in the study of psychiatric disorders: these are the questions of case definition, case ascertainment, and selection of a suitable population to study (Neugebauer *et al.* 1980). Each of these problems is evident in determining the epidemiology of hysterical conversion. In this chapter, we present evidence from published epidemiological studies of hysteria and discuss the problems in their interpretation which arise predominantly from failure to resolve these three primary research difficulties.

Case definition

The dubious status of hysteria as a diagnosis stems to a considerable extent from problems of case definition — the hysteria literature often lacks clarity about what it is that is being discussed, terminology is used inconsistently, and diagnostic practice has changed over time.

In one usage, hysteria refers to an underlying disposition which may manifest, for example, as emotional instability, sexual dysfunction, relationship difficulties, or suggestibility. The problem here — apart from the looseness and lack of specificity of the terminology — is the lack of evidence for the inferred disposition, other than the behaviour from which it is inferred.

A second theme is the use of the term hysterical as an aetiological statement to describe physical illnesses which have a psychological provocation and which develop as a means of adapting to (or defending against) that provocation. One trouble with adopting psychogenesis as a diagnostic criterion is its lack of specificity, since many illnesses which are not traditionally considered hysterical may yet have a psychosocial provocation (see, for example, Brown and Harris 1989; Craig's chapter in this volume, p. 88). On the other hand it is paradoxically restrictive, since it is not always possible to establish a psychological cause for an illness which is patently not caused by organ disease.

The third — and currently most prevalent — usage is to describe as hysterical those disorders characterized by loss of physical or mental function which is not explained by organ disease. In this approach, conditions in which the only abnormality is the presence of symptoms (as opposed to signs) are not included in the definition: it is broadly the approach taken by the standardized diagnostic classifications — DSM–IV (American Psychiatric Association 1994) and ICD–10 (World Health Organisation 1992) — although they differ in where the conversion disorders are placed. DSM–IV includes them under somatoform disorders, whereas ICD–10 places them with dissociative disorders. Both classifications include disorders of voluntary movement and sensation but exclude those involving solely autonomic dysfunction and symptom states such as chronic pain or chronic fatigue syndrome and Briquet's syndrome. In both systems, the diagnosis depends on the physical syndrome, exclusion of organic cause to account for the syndrome, and some evidence of psychological factors in its cause. Malingering and factitious disorders, where the symptoms are produced or feigned intentionally, are excluded.

The distinction between symptom states and hysteria is not clear-cut in individuals: several studies have found that a proportion of patients with conversion hysteria also meet the criteria for Briquet's syndrome or somatization disorder. Among neurological patients, between a quarter and half of those with a diagnosis of conversion hysteria have characteristics of Briquet's syndrome (Marsden 1986; Perkin 1989), and in one study of liaison psychiatry referrals, 34 per cent had a primary diagnosis of somatization disorder with a conversion symptom as the primary presenting clinical feature (Folks *et al.* 1984).

For this reason, hysterical and somatoform disorders are often grouped together, on the assumption that they are two manifestations of the same pathology. However, the strength of the association may be overestimated (see later discussion) and it would be better to keep an open mind by conducting research that treats them as separate (but often coexisting) disorders.

This descriptive–syndromal approach has its critics for other reasons. It appears an oddity to base diagnosis on the absence of disease, and there is no robust test for psychological causes. The result will inevitably be diagnostic errors. But lack of reliability is not the same as lack of validity, and it seems to us that this syndromal approach to case definition is the most practical given our current state of knowledge. It not only allows us to avoid prejudgement about the status of the conditions, but it makes for ease of case definition.

Case ascertainment

In Western practice, conversion disorders rarely present to psychiatrists in the first instance, and even those diagnosed with the condition by others may not be referred to a psychiatrist. In Watts' general practice study (Watts *et al*. 1964), at least 40 per cent of the patients were not seen by a psychiatrist. Psychiatric referral from accident and emergency departments is similarly limited (Dula and DeNaples 1995; Anstee 1972a). We do not know how common it is for people with conversion disorders to escape referral to *any specialist*, but it is possible that a proportion of patients — perhaps especially those whose symptoms are transient — will not present in secondary health care. Patients from ethnic minorities may present to other non-medical healers. Therefore, comprehensive case ascertainment will require a system that is not dependent on referrals to specialisms such as neurology or psychiatry, but on a prospective search for cases.

Case ascertainment requires not just a comprehensive search strategy but an accurate case-finding instrument. The need for the exclusion of an organic cause makes a diagnosis based on questionnaire or a single interview impracticable. At the very least, a medically-informed case review is needed, even if detection of psychological factors underlying the symptoms is not considered essential to diagnosis. The complexity and expense of case ascertainment has meant that many of the major psychiatric epidemiological studies make no attempt to identify hysteria. To give some examples, the Epidemiological Catchment Area Studies (Robins *et al*. 1984), the US National Co-morbidity Survey (Kessler *et al*. 1994), and the British Psychiatric Morbidity Survey (Jenkins *et al*. 1997) do not use case finding measures which can identify conversion disorders (or indeed many other types of psychologically-caused physical presentations) and therefore do not give us any estimate of their incidence or prevalence.

Defining the target population

A standard approach to epidemiological study is to define a target population, from which a study population is chosen and then a sample taken using appropriate sampling methods. As we have just noted, large-scale population-based surveys of this sort are severely limited by the expense and difficulty inherent in making a diagnosis of conversion disorders, and they therefore rarely address the problem of hysteria.

An alternative, more informal approach is to identify cases (the sample) from a clinical (study) population and to estimate the target population rate from this administrative rate (that is, from the service contact rate). The calculation depends upon the assumption that cases all make contact with the services, and that all relevant services are surveyed for cases. Inaccuracies arise when the relation between the target population and the study (clinical) population is unclear — for example, when the service has no sharply defined catchment area — or when referral practice means that cases do not present to the surveyed clinical services. The method may hold up when a disorder all but invariably presents to local services (as, for example, in studies on the epidemiology of schizophrenia), but they are problematic when we consider hysterical conversion.

A systematic literature review

We have undertaken a systematic review of the published literature, with the aim of identifying epidemiological studies which provide information on the rates of hysteria in the general population and in clinical populations.

Method

In preparing this review, we sought published studies on the epidemiology of hysteria from a number of sources: we searched the Medline database from 1966 to September 1999, using three strategies which were then applied with modifications to the Psychlit database; we consulted textbooks on hysteria, consultation–liaison psychiatry, and psychiatric epidemiology; and we consulted colleagues, both through direct contact and by posting a request on a liaison psychiatry mailbase.

We obtained secondary references from the articles identified by these routes, and we sought other papers by entering the most widely quoted papers into a forward search using Science Citations Index. The studies reviewed were confined to English language articles which dealt with hysteria in adults.

We included all studies in which rates (incidence or prevalence) of hysteria were reported or from which they could be calculated, provided the definition of hysteria used was broadly in line with DSM or ICD criteria. Thus, loss of motor or sensory function was a necessary component. When presenting the results, we indicate whether a study:

1. explicitly used DSM or ICD criteria or;
2. used other explicitly stated criteria (which we call 'own diagnostic criteria') or;
3. did not use explicit criteria, but included cases that were clinically diagnosed as hysteria or conversion disorder (which we call 'criteria not stated').

We excluded studies which described Briquet's hysteria (somatization disorder). Because diagnosis is more than usually problematic in certain groups, we excluded studies which were solely concerned with non-epileptic attacks (pseudoseizures), disorders of special senses (blindness, deafness), and voice loss (aphonia or dysphonia). So that the results could be applied in routine clinical practice, we also excluded those studies which described hysteria in prisoners or war veterans.

We used a standard data extraction form to obtain the following information from all the identified studies: date; sample size; setting; study population; study design; case definition; case mix; rates (incidence and prevalence).

The quality of each study was assessed on three criteria: use of a standardized case definition; systematic case ascertainment; and clear definition of the population denominator.

Table 6.1 Annual incidence in a defined population

Type of study	Area	No. of cases	Calculated incidence per 100 000	Case definition	References
Case register	Monroe County, New York	1374	22*	DSM–II Hysterical neurosis, conversion type	Stefánsson et al. 1976
Case register	Iceland	200	11	DSM–II Hysterical neurosis, conversion type	Stefánsson et al. 1976
Prospective general practice survey	England & Wales Scotland	55 21	8.9 5.6	Hysteria Criteria not stated	Watts et al. 1964
Neurology referral	Sweden	30	4.6–5.0**	DSM–III–R Motor conversion Duration <3 months	Binzer et al. 1997
Neurology referral	Gloucester, UK	181	11.8**	Own diagnostic criteria	Stevens 1989
In-patient liaison psychiatry	Bronx	3	1.2**	Conversion reaction Criteria not stated	Karasu et al. 1977

* Incidence includes existing patients reported for the first time in the first year of the register
** Incidence inferred from the catchment size of the service

Results

General population rates

We identified six studies from which we could estimate an annual incidence in a defined population (see Table 6.1). None is a true community survey but figures are based on those who came to the attention of the health services.

Two incidence rates were based on case register data (Stefánsson *et al.* 1976) and two on general practice surveys (Watts *et al.* 1964). These might be expected to be closer to the true community incidence than the figures deduced from neurological practice (Binzer *et al.* 1997; Stevens 1989). The particularly low incidence deduced from psychiatric contacts (Karasu *et al.* 1977) seems to confirm the fact that psychiatrists only see a proportion of these patients. For example, in Watts' study, approximately a third of incident cases and a half of prevalent cases of hysteria were managed without a psychiatric referral (Watts *et al.* 1964).

What is perhaps surprising, given the differences between the studies, is that they yield rather similar incidence rates, with only one substantially outside the range 5–10 per 100 000 per annum. The higher rates — from Monroe County (Stefánsson *et al.* 1976) and from Stevens' study of neurology referrals in the UK (Stevens 1989) — are both based on case definition which included cases of unexplained physical symptoms without signs.

Community prevalence rates (Table 6.2) vary much more widely. One reason is that the prevalence rates are calculated for different time periods — from near lifetime prevalence

Table 6.2 Community prevalence rates

Type of study	Area	No. of cases	Prevalence per 100 000 (Type of prevalence)	Case definition	References
Birth cohort	Iceland	22	408 (To age 60–62)	Hysterical neurosis Own diagnostic criteria	Helgasson 1964
Postal general practice survey	Nottingham, UK	18	48 (Point)	Modified DSM–III–R Conversion disorder	Singh and Lee 1997
General practice survey	England and Wales	332	53	Hysteria Criteria not stated	Watts et al. 1964
	Scotland	124	33 (Point)		
Field survey in general practice	Florence, Italy	2	300 (One year)	DSM–III–R Conversion disorder	Faravelli et al. 1997
Field survey	West Bengal, India	28	691 (one year)	WHO definition of hysteria 1960	Nandi et al. 1980
Field survey	West Bengal, India	3–36	205–3230*	Dissociation Conversion Own diagnostic criteria	Nandi et al. 1992

* Two communities in two time periods, see Table 6.6

(Helgasson 1964), through period prevalences of 12–18 months, to two studies of point prevalence in general practice (Singh and Lee 1997; Watts et al. 1964). Diagnostic criteria were less clear than in the incidence studies, and undoubtedly the higher prevalence rates are obtained by including cases of somatoform disorder which would not meet our definition.

Only one study identified during our literature search met all three of our quality criteria, and that was the population-based study of Faravelli and colleagues in Florence, Italy (Faravelli et al. 1997). However, their estimate of the point prevalence of conversion disorder was based on two cases identified during interviewing of a community sample of 673.

In clinical practice, many cases of hysteria recover spontaneously, while an unknown proportion become chronically symptomatic. We do not have accurate data on the relative frequency of chronicity as an outcome because follow-up studies have not recruited true inception cohorts (see Ron's chapter in this volume, p. 271), but the lowest prevalence figures we have found suggest a rate of about 50 per 100 000 for cases of conversion disorder known to health services at any one time, with perhaps twice that number affected over a 1–2 year period. It has to be said that none of these studies is perfect, but they suggest a burden of disability associated with chronic hysteria which is far higher than a typical practising psychiatrist might suspect or than is reflected in standard textbooks of psychiatry or clinical psychology.

Rates in clinical populations

There is a larger number of studies documenting the rate of hysterical conversion in patients presenting to out-patient and in-patient hospital services. They are summarized according to the medical speciality in Tables 6.3a to 6.3e. The rates are expressed as the proportion of attenders in each clinical situation who are identified as suffering from hysteria.

Not surprisingly, rates are lowest among unselected general hospital patients (Table 6.3a) and attenders in the accident and emergency department (Table 6.3b). It is of note that in the two studies of the patients attending accident and emergency departments, only 4 out of 42 patients were referred to psychiatrists in one study (Dula and DeNaples 1995) and more than half the patients were not seen by a psychiatrist in the other (Anstee 1972*a*). As one might expect, the rate is higher among patients presenting to neurological services (Table 6.3c).

The rate reported among psychiatric referrals (Table 6.3d) — 2–7 per cent (with one exception) — appears higher than we might expect from informal discussion with colleagues in general psychiatry. Changes in diagnostic practice may be part of the reason. Many of the studies were carried out in early 1960s and it is probable that general psychiatrists really do see fewer cases now. Referral patterns to general psychiatry have changed in recent decades — under the influence of Slater's famously sceptical paper (Slater 1965) and the emergence of liaison psychiatry services in general hospitals. For example, rates among referrals to liaison psychiatry services (Table 6.3e) bear out the impression of Brownsberger that 'to a psychiatrist who sees patients on the medical and surgical services of a general hospital, it appears that hysteria remains a rather common phenomenon' (Brownsberger 1966).

Table 6.3a Prevalence among general hospital patients

Type of hospital	Area	No. of cases	Rate (%)	Case definition	References
Medical/surgical admissions	Alabama, USA	62*	0.12	DSM–III Conversion disorder	Folks *et al.* 1984
University Hospital, in- and out-patients	Iowa, USA	51**	0.02	DSM–III Conversion disorder	Tomasson *et al.* 1991

* Includes 12 not seen by liaison psychiatry service   ** 12 comorbid with somatization

Table 6.3b Prevalence among patients attending accident and emergency department

Area	No. of cases	Rate among attenders (%)	Case definition	References
PA, USA	42	0.01	Conversion disorder Criteria not stated	Dula and DeNaples 1995
London, UK	52	0.21	Hysteria Criteria not stated	Anstee 1972*a*

Table 6.3c Prevalence among neurology patients

Patient population	Area	No. of cases	Rate (%)	Case definition	References
Neurology in-patients	Sweden	30	0.09–0.85	DSM–III–R Symptoms <3months	Binzer *et al.* 1997
Neurology in-patients	Germany	405	9	Conversion Own diagnostic criteria	Lempert *et al.* 1990
Neurology in-patients	London, UK	34	1	Hysterical conversion disorder Own diagnostic criteria (20% Briquet's)	Marsden 1986
Neurology out-patients	London, UK	297	3.8	Conversion hysteria Criteria not stated (50% Briquet's)	Perkin 1989
Neurosurgery	UK	20	0.71	Own diagnostic criteria	Maurice–Williams and Marsh 1985
Spinal injuries Tertiary referral	UK	20 3	0.29 1.5	Own diagnostic criteria	Baker and Silver 1987

Because Freud's work on hysteria was based on patients from middle-class backgrounds, it has often been assumed to be an illness of affluence. However, epidemiological studies have tended to show that, if anything, it is more common in those of lower socio-economic status (Helgasson 1964; Bhushan *et al.* 1967; Bagadia *et al.* 1973; Folks *et al.* 1984). Another bias in clinic populations may therefore be the over-representation of higher social classes.

Table 6.3d Rates among psychiatric patients

Patient population	Area	No. of cases	Rate (%)	Case definition	References
In-patients	Baltimore, USA	53 / 58	1.8 / 2	Conversion reaction Dissociative reaction Own diagnostic criteria	Stephens and Kamp 1962
In-patients	London, UK	Not given	7	Hysteria Criteria not stated	Fleminger and Mallett 1962
Referrals from general practice	UK	53	4.8	Hysteria Criteria not stated	Watts *et al.* 1964
Out-patients	Athens, Greece	130–283	3–6	Hysteria Own diagnostic criteria	Stefanis 1976
Psychiatric clinic	Kur, Germany	220	0.87	Neuropsychiatric conversion symptoms Own diagnostic criteria	Krull and Schifferdedker 1990

Age, sex, and ethnic influences on rates

We were unable to find any studies which reported reliable age–sex specific rates. Hysteria has always been regarded as quintessentially a women's illness, and the epidemiological studies seem to bear this out; at least with respect to diagnostic practice, the

Table 6.3e Rates among referrals to liaison psychiatry

Patient population	Area	No. of cases	Rate among referrals (%)	Case definition	References
In-patients	London, UK	45	15	Hysteria Criteria not stated	Fleminger and Mallett 1962
Accident and emergency	London, UK	6	18.8	Hysteria Criteria not stated	Bridges et al. 1966
Out-patients		10	4.9		
In-patients		10	7.0		
General hospital	Yale, New Haven, USA	144	14	Conversion reaction Own diagnostic criteria	McKegney 1967
General hospital	New Haven, West Haven, USA	20–289	6–12	Conversion reaction Criteria not stated	Kligerman and McKegney 1971
Liaison referrals	London, UK	36	14	Hysteria Criteria not stated	Anstee 1972b
Neurology and neurosurgery	Montreal, Canada	34	8	Conversion reaction Engel's definition (Engel 1970)	Lipowski and Kiriakos 1972
General hospital	New York, USA	74	4.5	DSM–II Hysterical neurosis, conversion type	Stefánsson et al. 1976
General hospital	New Hampshire, USA	52	5	Hysterical neurosis, conversion type Criteria not stated	Shevitz et al. 1976
General hospital	New York, USA	3	2	Conversion reaction Criteria not stated	Karasu et al. 1977
General hospital	Alabama, USA	50	5*	DSM–III Somatoform conversion disorder	Folks et al. 1984
General hospital	New York, USA	11	0.61	DSM–III Conversion disorder	Snyder and Strain 1989

* Includes 1.7% with coexisting somatization and conversion symptoms
** Neurology and neurosurgery patients

Table 6.4 Sex ratios

Setting	Area	% female	References
Community / general practice	Europe	67–80	Helgasson 1964; Singh and Lee 1997; Stefánsson *et al.* 1976; Watts *et al.* 1964
	India	78–100	Nandi *et al.* 1980, 1992
Hospital patient populations	General hospital	78	Tomasson 1991
	Neurological	40–64	Baker and Silver 1987; Binzer *et al.* 1997; Lempert *et al.* 1990
	Liaison psychiatry	52–88	Folks *et al.* 1984; Lipowski and Kiriakos 1972; McKegney 1967
	Psychiatry — Europe	64–88	Krull and Schifferdedker 1990; Stefanis *et al.* 1976; Stephens and Kamp 1962
	Psychiatry — India	61–78	Bagadia *et al.* 1973; Dutta Ray and Mathur 1996; Subramanian *et al.* 1980

great majority of cases are women (Table 6.4). Interestingly, the sex differences are least striking among neurological patients. Perhaps more women seek medical help or are referred from primary care to general physicians, but fewer are referred to specialist neurology services.

Stefanis *et al.* (1976) found that the proportion of men referred to a psychiatric clinic in Athens, Greece, increased from 14 to 27 per cent in the post-war period, but such a trend was not seen in studies conducted over time in the USA (Stephens and Kamp 1962) or West Bengal (Nandi *et al.* 1992).

Population surveys (described earlier) suggest higher rates for hysteria in India than in Europe, although doubts about case definition undermine our confidence in this finding. For example, later textual references indicated that many of the patients had non-epileptic attacks or unexplained symptoms rather than loss of motor or sensory function. When we looked at published rates among referrals to psychiatric services outside the USA and Europe (Table 6.5), we found that they were similar to those reported from European and North American liaison psychiatry services.

Is hysteria disappearing?

It has been asserted that hysteria is a disease on the wane (see, for example, Walshe, 1965; Reed 1971). Veith (1965) stated that there has been a 'nearly total disappearance of the illness' and, more recently, a British Medical Journal editorial reported that hysteria was 'virtually a historical curiosity in Britain' in contrast to its frequency in Indian psychiatric hospitals (Anon. 1976). What is the evidence for these claims? We found six studies that have documented rates in one place on more than one occasion (Table 6.6). These studies generally do not support the belief that the illness is disappearing in Western countries.

Stefanis' study (Stefanis *et al.* 1976) indicated a 50 per cent drop in the proportion of psychiatric out-patients with the diagnosis, but the absolute number of cases have more than doubled in the 20 years of the study. A field study in two villages from India has

Table 6.5 Psychiatric contact rates outside USA/Europe

Country	Setting	No. of cases	Rate (%)	Case definition	References
India, New Dehli	Psychiatric clinic	330	6	Conversion including fits Dissociation Criteria not stated	Dutta Ray and Mathur 1966
India, Bombay	Psychiatric clinic	192	6.5	DSM–II hysteria (conversion + dissociation)	Bagadia *et al.* 1972
India, Chandigarh	Psychiatric clinic	214	9	ICD (1967) Hysterical neurosis	Khanna *et al.* 1974
India, Chandigarh,	Psychiatric clinic	474	8–10	ICD–8 Hysterical neurosis	Wig *et al.* 1978
India, Vellore	Psychiatric department	276	11	Conversion Dissociation Own diagnostic criteria	Subramanian *et al.* 1980
Eastern Libya	Liaison in neurology out-patients	100	8.25	Own diagnostic criteria	Pu *et al.* 1986
Sudan	Psychiatric clinic	61	10	ICD–9 Hysterical conversion	Hafeiz 1980

documented a large drop in prevalence over a relatively short time (Nandi 1992). In this study, the proportion of those with psychiatric morbidity from any cause had not dropped in the two time periods and the rate of depression had increased, indicating that the drop in the rate for hysteria was not part of an overall trend of improved mental health in the communities. The change has been attributed to the improved socio-economic status of women in these communities over the period, but perhaps changes in diagnostic practice were as important.

Summary and conclusions

We only identified one study which met all our quality criteria, and that was too small to yield an accurate estimate of the rate of hysteria. We must therefore be cautious about conclusions that we draw from the literature. Nonetheless, we can make some general observations:

1. Despite assertions about the disappearance of hysteria, the published evidence suggests that it is as common as other disabling conditions such as multiple sclerosis and schizophrenia.

2. The incidence: prevalence ratio supports an inference from clinical practice — that many cases improve spontaneously but there is a residue of chronic hysteria which may last years.

Table 6.6   Change in incidence over time

Setting	Area	Period	No. of cases	Rates (%)	Case definition	References
Psychiatry in-patients	Baltimore, USA	1913–20 1945–60	58 53	2 1.8	Conversion reaction Dissociative reaction Own diagnostic criteria	Stephens and Kamp 1962
Liaison psychiatry	London, UK	1955–60 1968–69	45 36	15 14	Hysteria Criteria not stated	Anstee 1972b
Psychiatry out-patients	Athens, Greece	1948–52 1958–60 1969–71	130 189 283	6 3 3	Hysteria Own diagnostic criteria	Stefanis et al. 1976
Neurology — tertiary referral admissions	London, UK	1951, 53, 55 1961, 63, 65 1971, 73, 75	104 82 91	1.5 0.9 0.95	Hysteria Criteria not stated	Trimble 1981
Psychiatric clinic	India	1969–70 1974 1975	214 109 151	9.2 7.8 10.1	ICD–8 hysterical neurosis	Wig et al. 1978
Field survey	West Bengal Village 1 Village 2	1972 1982 1972 1987	18 7 36 3	1.7 0.5 3.2 0.2	Dissociative conversion Own diagnostic criteria	Nandi et al. 1992

3. Great disparities in rates found in different clinical settings indicate the selection biases which can distort results in hysteria research. This is particularly true of psychiatric practice, since many cases are not referred even from specialist medical clinics. These biases are especially likely to lead to under-representation of acute or transient cases in clinical populations.

4. Hysteria is more commonly diagnosed in women — at least in the published literature. This may be a true reflection of vulnerability to the illness, or it may reflect bias in referral or diagnosis.

5. The evidence is not strong enough to allow us to say whether hysteria is becoming rarer, or whether it is rarer in Europe and North America than it is elsewhere.

A great deal of the literature on hysteria — and especially the psychiatric literature — is concerned with cases which have been identified by referral to specialist services. Acute and transient cases will be under-represented in such populations, and there may be other biases. The emphasis on chronic hysteria has problems.

We run the risk of overemphasising certain clinical associations. For example, if a cause of chronicity in hysteria (childhood sexual abuse, say) is also a risk factor for developing somatization, then we will overestimate the association between somatization and hysteria if we study only chronic cases of the latter. We may miss important causal factors by studying the reasons for failure to improve (in chronic cases) rather than the reasons for onset (in acute cases). An example would be the emphasis in much of the literature on abnormalities of character and the pursuit of secondary gains as causes of hysteria.

We still know little about the outcome of hysteria (see Maria Ron's chapter in this volume, p. 271). Prognostic studies which exclude new and transient cases will inevitably give a distorted picture of the natural history of a disorder, and yet there is no true inception cohort study in the literature. This is a particular problem for the design of clinical trials.

We conclude that, for all these reasons, there needs to be better epidemiology of hysterical conversion than is currently available.

References

American Psychiatric Association (1994). *Diagnostic and Statistical Manual of Mental Disorders* (4th edn). American Psychiatric Association, Washington DC.

Anon. (1976). The search for a psychiatric Esperanto. *British Medical Journal*, **ii**, 59–60.

Anstee, B. H. (1972*a*). Psychiatry in the casualty department. *British Journal of Psychiatry*, **120**, 625–9.

Anstee, B. H. (1972*b*). The pattern of psychiatric referrals in a general hospital. *British Journal of Psychiatry*, **120**, 631–4.

Bagadia, V. N., Shastri, P. C. and Shah, L. P. (1973). Hysteria — a prospective study of demographic factors of 192 cases. *Indian Journal of Psychiatry*, **15**, 179–86.

Baker, J. H. E. and Silver, J. R. (1987). Hysterical paraplegia. *Journal of Neurology, Neurosurgery and Psychiatry*, **50**, 375–82.

Bhushan, A., Bhaskaran, K. and Varma, L. P. (1967). Socio-economic class and neurosis. *Indian Journal of Psychiatry*, **9**, 334–8.

Binzer, M., Andersen, P. M. and Kullgren, G. (1997). Clinical characteristics of patients with motor disability due to conversion disorder: a prospective control group study. *Journal of Neurology, Neurosurgery and Psychiatry*, **63**, 83–8.

Bridges, P. K., Koller, K. M. and Wheeler, T. K. (1966). Psychiatric referrals in a general hospital. *Acta Psychiatrica Scandinavia*, **42**, 171–82.

Brown, G. and Harris, T. (1989). *Life Events and Illness*. Guilford Press, London.

Brownsberger, C. N. (1966). Hysteria — a common phenomenon? *American Journal of Psychiatry*, **123**, 110.

Dula, D. J. and DeNaples, L. (1995). Emergency department presentation of patients with conversion disorder. *Academic Emergency Medicine*, **2**, 120–3.

Dutta Ray, S. and Mathur, S. B. (1996). Patterns of hysteria observed at psychiatric clinic Irwin Hospital, New Delhi. *Indian Journal of Psychiatry*, **8**, 32–6.

Faravelli, C., Salvatori, S., Galassi, F., Aiazzi, L., Drei, C. and Cabras, P. (1997). Epidemiology of somatoform disorders: a community survey in Florence. *Social Psychiatry and Psychiatric Epidemiology*, **32**, 24–9.

Fleminger, J. J. and Mallett, B. L. (1962). Psychiatric referrals from medical and surgical wards. *Journal of Mental Sciences*, **108**, 183–90.

Folks, D. G., Ford, C. V. and Regan, W. M. (1984). Conversion symptoms in a general hospital. *Psychosomatics*, **25**, 285–95.

Hafeiz, H. B. (1980). Hysterical conversion: a prognostic study. *British Journal of Psychiatry*, **136**, 548–51.

Helgasson, T. (1964). Epidemiology of mental disorders in Iceland — a psychiatric and demographic investigation of 5395 Icelanders. *Acta Psychiatrica Scandinavia*, **Suppl. 173**.

Jenkins, R. *et al.* (1997). The national psychiatric morbidity surveys of Great Britain — strategy and methods. *Psychological Medicine*, **27**, 765–74.

Karasu, T. B., Plutchik, R., Steinmuller, R. I., Conte, H. and Siegel, B. (1977). Patterns of psychiatric consultation in a general hospital. *Hospital and Community Psychiatry*, **28**, 291–4.

Kessler, R. C. *et al.* (1994). Lifetime and 12-month prevalence of DSM–III–R psychiatric disorders in the United States. *Archives of General Psychiatry*, **51**, 8–19.

Khanna, B. C., Wig, N. N. and Varma, V. K. (1974). General psychiatric clinic — an epidemiological study. *Indian Journal of Psychiatry*, **16**, 211–20.

Kligerman, K. J. and McKegney, F. P. (1971). Patterns of psychiatric consultation in two general hospitals. *Psychiatry in Medicine*, **2**, 126–32.

Krull, F. and Schifferdedker, M. (1990). Inpatient treatment of conversion disorder: a clinical investigation of outcome. *Psychotherapy and Psychosomatics*, **53**, 161–5.

Lempert, T., Dieterich, M., Huppert, D. and Brandt, T. (1990). Psychogenic disorders in neurology: frequency and clinical spectrum. *Acta Neurologica Scandinavia*, **82**, 335–40.

Lipowski, Z. J. and Kiriakos, R. Z. (1972). Borderlands between neurology and psychiatry: observations in a neurological hospital. *Psychiatry in Medicine*, **3**, 131–47.

Marsden, C. D. (1986). Hysteria — a neurologist's view. *Psychological Medicine*, **16**, 277–88.

Maurice–Williams, R. S. and Marsh, H. (1985). Simulated paraplegia: an occasional problem for the neurosurgeon. *Journal of Neurology, Neurosurgery and Psychiatry*, **48**, 826–31.

McKegney, F. P. (1967). The incidence and characteristics of patents with conversion reactions. I: a general hospital consultation service sample. *American Journal of Psychiatry*, **124**, 542–5.

Nandi, D. N. *et al.* (1980). Socio-economic status and mental morbidity in certain tribes and castes in India — a cross-cultural study. *British Journal of Psychiatry*, **136**, 73–85.

Nandi, D. N., Banerjee, G., Nandi, S. and Nandi, P. (1992). Is hysteria on the wane? A community sruvey in West Bengal, India. *British Journal of Psychiatry*, **160**, 87–91.

Neugebauer, R., Dohrenwend, B. P. and Dohrenwend, B. S. (1980). Formulation of hypothesis about the true prevalence of functional psychiatric disorders among adults in the United States. In *Mental illness in the United States*, pp. 45–94. Praeger, New York.

Perkin, G. D. (1989). An analysis of 7836 successive new outpatient referrals. *Journal of Neurology, Neurosurgery and Psychiatry*, **52**, 447–8.

Pu, T., Mohamed, E., Imam, K. and El–Roey, A. M. (1986). One hundred cases of hysteria in Eastern Libya. A socio-demographic study. *British Journal of Psychiatry*, **148**, 606–9.

Reed, J. L. (1971). Hysteria. *British Journal of Hospital Medicine*, **5**, 237–47.

Robins, L. N. *et al.* (1984). Lifetime prevalence of specific psychiatric disorders in three sites. *Archives of General Psychiatry*, **41**, 949–58.

Shevitz, S. A., Silberfarb, P. M. and Lipowski, Z. J. (1976). Psychiatric consultations in a general hospital. A report on 1,000 referrals. *Diseases of the Nervous System*, **37**, 295–300.

Singh, S. P. and Lee, A. S. (1997). Conversion disorders in Nottingham: alive, but not kicking. *Journal of Psychosomatic Research*, **43**, 425–30.

Slater, E. (1965). Diagnosis of 'hysteria'. *British Medical Journal*, **I**, 1395.

Snyder, S. and Strain, J. J. (1989). Somatoform disorders in the general hospital inpatient setting. *General Hospital Psychiatry*, **11**, 288–93.

Stefànsson, J. G., Messina, J. A. and Meyerowitz, S. (1976). Hysterical neurosis, conversion type: clinical and epidemiological considerations. *Acta Psychiatrica Scandinavia*, **53**, 119–38.

Stefanis, C., Markidis, M. and Christodoulou, G. (1976). Observations on the evolution of the hysterical symptomatology. *British Journal of Psychiatry*, **128**, 269–75.

Stephens, J. H. and Kamp, M. (1962). On some aspects of hysteria: a clinical study. *Journal of Nervous and Mental Diseases*, **134**, 305–15.

Stevens, D. (1989). Neurology in Gloucestershire: the clinical workload of an English neurologist. *Journal of Neurology, Neurosurgery and Psychiatry*, **52**, 439–46.

Subramanian, D., Subramanian, K., Devaky, M. N. and Verghese, A. (1980). A clinical study of 276 patients diagnosed as suffering from hysteria. *Indian Journal of Psychiatry*, **22**, 63–8.

Tomasson, K., Kent, D. and Coryell, W. (1991). Somatization and conversion disorders: comorbidity and demographics at presentation. *Acta Psychiatrica Scandinavia*, **84**, 188–93.

Trimble, M. R. (1981). Liaison psychiatry with special reference to neurological units. In *Neuropsychiatry*, pp. 70–90. John Wiley and Sons, Chichester.

Veith, I. (1965). *Hysteria. The History of a Disease*. The University of Chicago Press, Chicago and London.

Walshe, F. (1965). Diagnosis of hysteria. *British Medical Journal*, **ii**, 1451–4.

Watts, C. A. H., Cawte, E. C. and Kuenssberg, E. V. (1964). Survey of mental illness in general practice. *British Medical Journal*, **2**, 1351–9.

Wig, N. N., Varma, V. K. and Khanna, B. C. (1978). Diagnostic characteristics of a general hospital psychiatric adult outpatients' clinic. *Indian Journal of Psychiatry*, **20**, 262–6.

World Health Organisation (1992). *ICD–10 Classification of Mental and Behavioural Disorders*. WHO, Geneva.

7 Life events: meanings and precursors

Tom K. J. Craig

The presumption of an aetiological role for stressful experience in the genesis of hysterical conversion can be traced to some of the earliest descriptions of these disorders. But convincing evidence to support this notion is hard to come by, not least because of the considerable methodological challenges facing studies of stressful life experiences. This chapter reviews recent developments in the measurement of stressful life events, focussing in particular on the Life Events and Difficulties Schedules developed by George Brown and colleagues and most widely used in studies of depression. The relatively few studies of functional somatic disorders to have employed these measures are also reviewed. From these studies, a consistent finding of an association with threatening experience clearly emerges. Furthermore, it appears that of the many varieties of stressful experience, it is situations involving problematical relationships and rejection which play the most significant role.

Introduction: methodological considerations

The notion that there is a causal link between traumatic life events and the onset of hysterical conversion symptoms has a long and venerable history (Janet 1907; Mai and Merskey 1980) and remains at the heart of most modern diagnostic classifications. The ICD–10, for example, states that these disorders, particularly paralyses and anaesthesia, require for a definite diagnosis the presence of a 'clear association in time with stressful events and problems, or disturbed relationships even if denied by the individual' (ICD–10 pp. 152–3).

While the observation of an apparently causal link between stressful experience and hysterical disorders is therefore both widely recognized clinically and an important component of at least one popular diagnostic system, there are several reasons why one might wish to look more carefully at the empirical evidence for the claimed association.

Separating outcome from putative causes

The first and most obvious issue concerns the definition of experiences of possibly causal relevance. For any aetiological investigation, we must decide whether we are interested in both discrete events that can be pinpointed in time (for example, a change of job, a death, the receipt of bad news) as well as chronic difficulties whose origins may be impossible to date precisely (for example, marital problems, poor quality housing, chronic ill health of a household member).

Next, our measure of such experiences must be capable of distinguishing dependent and independent variables of interest, and this is more difficult than might appear at first sight. For conversion disorders, for example, the underlying assumption is that the causal events and difficulties are distressing and that it is this distress that is 'converted'. But if we only include events that subjects report as distressing we will be unable to test the assumption that it is *only* these experiences that matter as there will, by definition, never be an event without such an outcome. Such an approach would also rule out the possibility of studying conditions where subjects are thought likely to play down or deny the emotional impact of crises.

One way of avoiding the circularity inherent in defining the qualifying life experience in terms of the effect it has on the individual is to distinguish the unit of study from its qualities. For example, we can decide to include in our study all changes of employment, regardless of whether this is a promotion or demotion, or is reported to be stressful, desirable, or undesirable. This approach has the advantage of permitting the collection of data systematically without a prior commitment to what constitutes 'stressful experience'.

While separating the definition of the unit of experience from its possible qualities takes us part of the way, there is yet another problem. Most life event studies are retrospective in nature. Patients are seen after the occurrence of their symptoms and asked to reflect upon some past time to recall the occurrence of events of interest. This raises the spectre of contamination of event and outcome by either the subject or the investigator. The most commonly discussed example of this is the so-called 'effort after meaning' (Bartlett 1932) in which the patient searches for an explanation as to why he should have become ill at this point in his life. In so doing, he recalls more events than he would were he well, or misplaces the occurrence of an event closer to onset, or preferentially recalls particular events because of his current mood. For conversion disorders, of course, there is also the possibility that recall may be suppressed or distorted in a way that minimizes causal associations — events forgotten or erroneously reported as having occurred after the onset of symptoms.

These problems of 'effort after meaning' are particularly serious threats to the validity of respondent-based checklist instruments. In such measures, a checklist of possible 'events' is given to respondents who simply check off, say, an item asking whether there has been 'a recent illness in the family', and in so doing must decide which family members to include and how serious the illness need be to count. An illness in a distant relative may only be remembered because the subject himself has recently developed similar symptoms. These checklist measures have been severely criticized for poor reliability, poor accuracy in terms of cross-respondent agreement about the same event, and the huge variability in the range of experiences reported to the same checklist prompt (Brown 1974; Dohrenwend *et al.* 1987).

A related issue concerns the need to distinguish those events which are the result of illness and therefore cannot be said to play a causal role. This determination of the 'independence' of stressful experience goes beyond simply discounting experiences which are a direct result of illness (for example, attending hospital, being off work because of symptoms). Consider three examples of loss of employment. In the first, the subject is fired for poor timekeeping; in the second, the subject leaves to take up another job; and in the third he is made redundant when the firm goes bust. Clearly, the first example reflects a direct consequence of a change in the subject's behaviour that itself heralds the first signs of illness, and such events ought to be excluded from any consideration of an aetiological role. In the second example, it is possible that the decision to change employment was influenced by incipient illness and, in the most strict test, would also be excluded from consideration. In the third example, a link to illness is unlikely as the decision was both external to the subject and has nothing to do with his performance in the job. The most robust test of a causal association would therefore concentrate only on these 'independent' events — at least as a first step.

To summarize at this point, valid measures of life event stress will include both discrete events and chronic difficulties; will employ an explicit set of rules, devised well in advance of the main study as to what experiences should and should not be included; will pay close attention to detailed assessment of time order; and will have some means of assessing the 'independence' of an event from the target disorder under consideration.

Very few measures meet these stringent criteria. Perhaps the best known and most widely used is the Life Events and Difficulties Schedule (LEDS) developed by George Brown and his colleagues (Brown and Harris 1978). This interview-based measure defines events and difficulties in terms of their likelihood to produce strong emotion (positive or negative) in most people. Such crises are largely restricted to the subject and their close ties (spouse, immediate family, confidante) and covers some 40 broad classes of event ranging from changes in role, through changes in the amount or quality of contact with close ties, to forecasts of change and fulfilments of valued goals. The inclusion criteria for each class of event is fully defined as are rules for rating their 'independence' from illness.

The measurement of meaning

Despite the initial caveat concerning problems of basing the inclusion criteria for events in terms of some specific emotional impact, it is obvious that an experience can only matter because it carries some personal meaning for the individual. But such personal meaning may be largely inaccessible to direct assessment. The subject of a crisis may not report his response accurately, either because he has forgotten the details or because a subsequent emotional disorder colours his responses or even because many of the components of 'meaning' are not fully accessible to conscious awareness. In order to bypass these problems of respondent bias, some investigators have advocated a *general* approach to the rating of meaning in which each experience is classified according to a number of broad categories such as pleasant or unpleasant, desirable or undesirable (Paykel *et al.* 1971).

Taken together with an investigator-based approach to defining the unit of experience and care over dating, such global ratings of meaning are a distinct advance over straightforward reliance on subjective report alone and can show some broad but rather non-specific associations with illness. So for example, in a recent study of motor conversion disorder (Binzer *et al.* 1997), 30 consecutive patients with an onset of the disorder were compared with 30 patients with definite organic illness. Cases were far more likely than controls to report psychiatric symptoms, to have lower educational attainment, and to have higher depression scores at interview. An interview was used to collect information on the occurrence of life events in five pre-determined broad categories. The cases had statistically significant excess of life events across all five categories, with approximately 80 per cent reporting at least one 'negative' event (compared to around 22 per cent of controls). However, no attempt was made to distinguish independent from non-independent events and the analysis of the life event data did not take into account differences in education level and concurrent psychiatric symptoms between groups. Thus, although of interest as the only recent study to have looked at life events in a prospectively gathered cohort of motor conversion hysteria, little more than a general association between onset and stressful experience can be derived.

But this general approach to meaning also does not go far enough. Consider the event of a birth. Most births are desirable and happy events. But the meaning of a birth of a longed-for third child to an affluent couple is likely to be very different than the equivalent event to a single unemployed mother who has recently been abandoned by her partner. This capacity to 'intuit' the likely responses of most individuals in a particular society once we know the wider context in which the event occurs forms the basis of a particularly important aspect of the LEDS measure. In this approach, ratings of the *contextual meaning* of events and difficulties are made by members of the research team based on detailed information about the subject's plans and goals and the wider social context at the time the event occurred. The investigator takes account not only of the immediate situation (say, a loss of a job) but also of the wider context (whether there are debts, whether other members of the household are in secure employment, the current level of employment opportunity in his trade, and so on). The contextual ratings can also be made blind to whether any disorder developed subsequent to the event. In making the contextual rating, no attention is paid to what the respondent said she or he felt about the event, thus minimizing respondent bias in reporting while also allowing later comparison of subjective and contextual ratings.

There is no theoretical limit to the number of qualitative dimensions on which events can be rated, which as we shall see opens up interesting possibilities for hysteria. The most widely investigated dimension is that of 'threat'. As used by the LEDS, threat is a rather global term, encompassing a wide range of unpleasant experiences including bereavements and other losses. It is customary to distinguish short-term threat occurring on the day of the event and its immediate aftermath from long-term threat, seen as the enduring impact of the event some 10–14 days after its occurrence (difficulties are rated on long-term threat only for obvious reasons). For depression, only long-term threatening experience focussed on the subject or his close ties plays a significant causal role. Such *severe events* and *major difficulties* (defined as markedly threatening difficulties of at least two years' duration) are found prior to onset in around 75–90 per cent of cases of depression in the general population (Paykel *et al.* 1969; Costello 1982; Campbell *et al.* 1983; Bebbington *et al.* 1984; Surtees *et al.* 1986).

Threat and 'functional' illness

There have now been several studies that have used the LEDS to explore the role of threatening experience in functional disorders. The results of two of these early studies are summarized in Fig. 7.1

In the first of these, Creed (1981) interviewed 119 patients who had an appendectomy for acute abdominal pain. Subjects were classified as 'organic' or 'functional' according to histological evidence of definite inflammation reported by an independent pathologist. The experience of life events and difficulties in the 38 weeks prior to presentation in these patient samples was compared with that of a general population sample. While the total

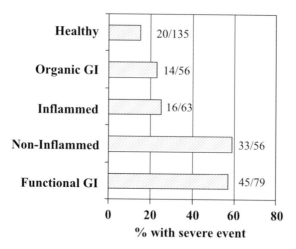

Fig. 7.1 Percentage of subjects experiencing at least one severe event prior to onset of gastrointestinal (GI) disorder. (Adapted from Creed 1981 and Craig 1989)

frequency of all events was similar between groups, 59 per cent of patients with a non-inflammed appendix compared with 25 per cent of those with an inflammed appendix and 20 per cent of the general population sample had experienced one or more severe events. Most of these events occurred within eight weeks of onset.

In a broadly comparable study, Craig (1989) interviewed 135 consecutive patients attending gastroenterology clinics who had a recent onset of abdominal pain and a similar number of healthy members of the general population. On the basis of the opinions of independent gastroenterologists after comprehensive clinical investigation, 56 patients were thought to have 'organic' pathology sufficient to account for their symptoms. No such pathology was identified amongst the remaining 79 patients who were classified as having 'functional' disorders. Approximately two thirds of functional patients, but only a quarter of organic patients and 23 per cent of the healthy comparison sample had experienced a severe event or major difficulty prior to onset of abdominal pain. Non-severe events and minor difficulties appeared to play no aetiological role in these functional disorders, nor was there convincing evidence for an additive effect. The severe events of the patients with functional complaints in this study commonly involved a break-up of a close relationship, and the overall quality of their relationships with partners and close friends was poorer than that found in the organic patients or healthy controls.

In a more recent study which is of direct relevance to hysteria, Harris *et al.* (1996) used the LEDS to investigate the role of threat in the aetiology of globus pharyngis in 50 patients referred to an ENT clinic in Edinburgh. These 50 patients were compared to 33 patients attending the same clinic but who had an organic pathology sufficient to account for their symptoms. The average elapsed time between onset of symptoms and interview was 12.4 months. The proportion of patients and controls with at least one severe event or major difficulty were compared with that reported in previous LEDS studies of depressed and healthy subjects in the general population. There was no significant difference in total numbers of life events and difficulties between cases and controls in this study. However, during the year before onset, 72 per cent (36 out of 50) of the globus patients had experienced a severe event compared to only 27 per cent (9 out of 33) of the comparison subjects. This highly significant difference in the exposure of cases and controls to stressful life crises is strikingly similar to that reported for depression in the general population and also to that found by the earlier studies of gastrointestinal disorder. The most common severe event prior to globus onset was the breakdown of a close relationship. Controls showed no strong clustering of particular life events. Finally, the globus patients also reported significantly fewer confiding relationships than did control subjects.

Deconstructing threat

Threat, however, is but one crude way to describe stressful experience and there have been continual attempts to refine and narrow the concept in the search for more specific associations between particular disorders and sub-categories of event. For example, Finlay–Jones and Brown (1981) deconstructed threat to components of 'loss' and 'danger' and explored the relevance of these dimensions to depression and anxiety. The quality of danger was defined as the degree of threat of a specific future crisis which *might* occur as a result of the present event (for example, following a knee injury, a professional dancer is told there is a possibility she may never be able to dance again). In this study, loss was found to be causally linked to the occurrence of depression, and danger to that of anxiety, with events characterized by both loss and danger being associated with the onset of mixed states of both depression and anxiety. Similar results were also found in a study in Edinburgh where severe life crises involving loss were highly predictive of depression and those concerning threat alone were predictive of anxiety (Miller and Ingham 1983). More recently these findings have been broadly confirmed in a prospective investigation of depression (Brown et al. 1987).

The role of loss and danger events have been explored in a number of studies of relevance to hysteria. In the study of globus, significantly more danger events were reported by the globus group throughout the year prior to onset. An excess of loss events was also reported, though this fell just short of statistical significance (Harris et al. 1996). Similar findings of an association between loss and danger events and the onset of functional symptoms have been reported for gastrointestinal disorders (Craig 1989), functional menorrhagia (Harris 1989), and acute somatization (Craig et al. 1994).

From these studies, it appears that functional somatic syndromes can be precipitated by events that can also lead to depression and anxiety. Indeed, in view of the well-established relationship between severe events and depression and the very high frequency of depression reported by patients suffering from these functional disorders, it is appropriate to ask whether mood disorder is an intervening variable between event and onset of somatic symptom or whether the mood disorder develops later, possibly as a response to the persistent discomfort of the somatic symptoms. On this question, the jury is still out. Some of these studies have reported a causal pathway involving mood disorders as intervening between event and disorder (Craig 1989), while others find persistent somatic symptoms relate more closely to the development of depression than to the presence of a preceding stress (Creed 1981); still others find no association at all (Harris 1989).

In his most recent work, Brown *et al.* (1995) have refined the notion of threat even further. Brown comments that the experience reported by many depressed women is, at heart, one of defeat, humiliation, and entrapment, in which an individual experiences a loss of sense of rank, attractiveness, and value. In an effort to test the relevance of these ideas, Brown and colleagues used life event material gathered in earlier studies to develop a new qualitative dimension involving the experience of humiliation and entrapment. The ratings attempted to capture the extent to which the subject could be expected to experience a sense of powerlessness or marked devaluation of the self. When the characteristics of events were rated hierarchically (that is, where an event could be rated as both 'humiliation' and 'loss', the former is given priority) it was clear that events involving humiliation or entrapment preceded the bulk of onsets of depression. If these categories are combined, the risk of depression was three times that of women who experienced only a loss (31 per cent vs. 9 per cent). Of the various residual categories of experience, only deaths appeared to have an obviously high risk of onset of depression. Severe events which did not involve either loss, humiliation, or entrapment, had the lowest rate of onset (Brown *et al.* 1995).

Beyond threat

In the study of conversion disorder, or indeed of any of the functional illnesses, such sophistication in the measurement of threat is yet to be attempted. However, studies which have looked beyond sub-categories of threat have proven interesting. In one of the earliest of these, Harris (1989) studied 163 patients who had presented to gynaecological clinics with secondary amenorrhea or menorrhagia and compared these to 224 women in the general population. The LEDS was used to gather information on the occurrence of life events and difficulties over the year prior to onset of disorder. In addition to the usual ratings of threat, loss, and danger, Harris devised a new contextual measure of 'challenge'. Events were rated as 'challenging' where they presented the subject with an opportunity to perform in a praiseworthy fashion (for example, starting a new job or accepting responsibility for making a difficult decision). The onset of menorrhagia appeared to be linked to the same kind of provoking agents (severe events and major difficulties, particularly involving loss) found in other studies of functional illness. However, a different pathway appeared to be at work with secondary amenorrhea. Here, the association was largely with the occurrence of events characterized as being of marked challenge (for example, final examinations, going abroad to take up a position as an au pair) and which typically occurred within a month of onset of disorder.

This conceptualization of challenge overlaps with several alternative constructs, notably those of personal responsibility and commitment, that have been noted in other studies in a somewhat different guise. House and Andrews (1988) examined 56 women attending a speech therapy department with a diagnosis of functional dysphonia and compared these women with healthy women drawn from a separate general population survey. In addition to conventional LEDS ratings, they explored the relevance of a new contextual measure which they called 'conflict over speaking out' (CSO). These CSO events and difficulties were defined as situations in which the subject might wish to protest or complain or to intervene verbally in some way, but where problems would arise from such forthrightness and where what they might say would only worsen the situation. An example is given of a middle-aged supervisor who suspected that her immediate manager had been embezzling company funds. Her co-workers encouraged her to take her worries to higher management but were unable or unwilling to provide any incriminating evidence themselves. The subject was very committed to her job and for personal and financial reasons needed to remain in full-time employment and therefore to do nothing that might threaten her position. The crisis rated as a CSO event was her being asked by her colleagues to tell the company director of her suspicions. At this point, if she did nothing she would be implicitly accepting a possibly corrupt situation and would lose face with her colleagues, while if she complained she ran the risk of discovering that her suspicions were unfounded and, at the very least, would find it difficult to continue working with her supervisor.

The authors were able to achieve a satisfactory level of inter-rater reliability for the new measure (Kw 0.75). Unusually, this study failed to find any association between disorder and severe events or major difficulties. However, a third of the dysphonic women had experienced at least one CSO event and 46 per cent had experienced a CSO difficulty. In contrast, only 16 per cent of healthy women had a CSO event or difficulty. The overlap of this measure with the conventional measures of threat was modest, suggesting that CSO acted independently of threat. In all instances, CSO events arose against a background of high commitment to some aspect of the situation. The event itself called for action, though in every instance subjects avoided taking the final decision. Furthermore, in all instances there was an apparent denial of the unpleasant emotions that might accompany such unpleasant crises.

Until now we have seen that with the exception of one study of functional dysphonia, the available data suggests a link between life-event stress and 'functional' somatic complaints that is similar to that observed for depression. They fall far short however of offering any explanation as to why some people respond to stress with depression while others experience mainly somatic symptoms. The most parsimonious explanation is one involving a non-specific role for stressors — that they trigger distress which in turn either produces or draws attention to bodily sensations that would otherwise pass unnoticed. An alternative, more speculative explanation relates to the themes of shame, humiliation, and support and sympathy for shameful crises from close friends and family. One of the striking features of these studies is the way that causal events seem to revolve around failed relationships, loss of face, and less than adequate support during the crisis.

Attempts to measure secondary gain

The notion of 'secondary gain' runs through much of the literature on hysteria and functional illness. Put simply, this suggests that physical illness can serve as a means of saving face, excusing failure, or achieving monetary or other compensation at a time when expressions of distress would be ineffective or even counter-productive (Pilowsky 1969; Kendell 1983; Kleinman 1986; Craig and Boardman 1990). These observations stem mostly from clinical reports of individual patients and the concept has not been widely investigated in well-designed controlled studies. In one early study for example, Raskin *et al.* (1966) judged secondary gain to have been present in 81 per cent of 26 patients with hysterical conversion compared to only 28 per cent of comparison patients with organic disease.

The relevance of secondary gain was also investigated in our study of acute somatization in general practice (Craig *et al.* 1993 and 1994). In this study, we hypothesized that somatizers would be more likely than patients suffering from organic disease or than healthy members of the general population to have experienced life events and difficulties characterized by a contextual measure of 'secondary gain potential'. The study sample comprised four groups of consecutive attenders at general practice: s*omatizers* — defined as patients presenting with bodily symptoms for which no explanation in terms of organic disease pathology could be found; *psychologizers* — who presented with 'psychological' complaints only (for example, low mood, nervous tension); *physically ill* subjects who presented with bodily symptoms of a definite organic disease; and *mixed physical–psychiatric* subjects who had symptoms of both psychiatric disorder and organic disease. These four patient groups were followed up over approximately 24 months and their experience of stressful life events was compared with that of a healthy comparison series drawn from the general population.

Each subject's experience of stressful life events and chronic difficulties was assessed using the standard LEDS measures of threat, loss, and danger. In addition, we devised a new contextual rating of the potential of stressors to produce symptoms of secondary gain. In this measure we attempted to assess the likelihood that the development of a publicly declared physical illness could reverse, prevent, or lessen the undesirable consequences of the event, either through affording an effective escape from the immediate situation or by providing a desirable change in the social circumstances of the subject which could mitigate the impact of the crisis (for example, monetary or practical compensation). It was clear that some people might respond to such events with active coping strategies that would involve both the admission that the event was intolerable and the public declaration of distress. For example, a woman who was physically assaulted by her husband might leave home and initiate divorce proceedings; someone accused of significant failure at work might strike back at her accusers in a public forum. In order to deal with these active coping strategies, events and difficulties with secondary gain potential were further classified according to the presence or absence of these *neutralizing efforts* in the 10–14 days following the occurrence of the event or presence during the course of a chronic difficulty. We argued that the presence of neutralizing efforts provides some concrete evidence that the significance of the event as a distressing experience has been recognized and a non-illness coping strategy has been adopted to deal with it. We further speculated that only non-neutralized secondary gain events would be relevant to the aetiology of somatization.

One hundred and eighty-four patients (44 somatizers, 11 psychologizers, 39 mixed, and 90 pure physical) and 123 healthy subjects recruited from the general population took part in the study. As typically reported by the majority of studies of functional somatic disorder using the LEDS, there were no significant differences between patient groups in the experience of non-severe events or difficulties. However, both the somatizers and psychologizers showed a statistically significant excess of severe events and major difficulties compared to the other patient groups. This is in keeping with the majority of those studies already described, which reported an association between functional disorder and severe threat of the kind commonly seen before the onset of depression.

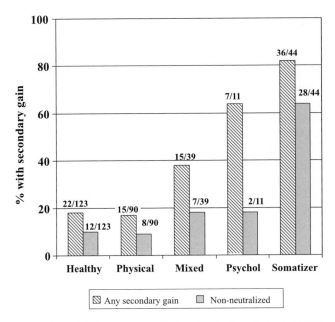

Fig. 7.2 Secondary gain crises and the impact of neutralization. (Adapted from Craig *et al.* 1994)

More specific differences between the somatizers and other subject groups emerged following an analysis of secondary gain events. Figure 7.2 shows the proportion of each subject group who experienced at least one secondary gain crisis by whether neutralization efforts had been made. The three groups with psychiatric disorder had a significant excess of secondary gain potential events compared with the physically ill or healthy subjects — 82 per cent of somatizers, 64 per cent of psychologizers, and 38 per cent of mixed subjects experienced at least one secondary gain crisis compared to fewer than a fifth of the purely physically ill and healthy comparison subjects. More importantly, however, somatizers were far more likely to have experienced a secondary gain crisis *and* to have failed to have made any effort to neutralize it, while the psychologizers, who were just as likely to have experienced secondary gain events, were far more likely to have made neutralization efforts. Overall, neutralizing efforts were far more common among non-somatizers — in over half of all crises with potential for secondary gain, compared with only one in five such crises among somatizers (see Fig. 7.2: $X^2 = 9.11$, d.f. $= 1$, P $< .0.01$). Although secondary gain potential was positively correlated with threat, when the relationship was examined among subjects without a severe event or major difficulty, the somatizers still showed a statistically significant excess of non-neutralized crises.

The impact of childhood risk factors

Somatizers were also far more likely than the other patient groups to report having suffered significant parental neglect and abuse in childhood and to have experienced a serious childhood illness themselves. These childhood factors were strongly related to the likelihood that the subject would experience events with secondary gain potential in adulthood and this excess was accompanied by a parallel failure to adopt neutralizing coping strategies. For example, the rate of non-neutralized secondary gain events in somatizers was twice that in the remaining subjects — a pattern that was not explained by a small number of subjects experiencing large numbers of events as a similar picture emerged if, instead of rates, the occurrence of a single event in the period of risk was taken. Among those with childhood risk, 60 per cent (18 out of 30) experienced a crisis which they failed to neutralize compared with only 17 per cent (27 out of 154) of remaining subjects ($X^2 = 20.562$, df $= 1$, P $< .0.001$).

The longitudinal nature of the study also allowed us to replicate these basic findings. During the follow-up period of 24 months, in addition to plotting the course of the index illness, we attempted to identify all 'new' episodes of illness. The date of the most recent somatic illness from the point of final contact was established and the LEDS again used to cover the entire follow-up period. The most recent illness was chosen in order to maximize the likelihood that we were dealing with discrete episodes of illness and to minimize the possibility that our selected episode would deal with the same life events as the original episode two years earlier. We included only those illnesses which began at least a year after the first interview. For the index episode we had access to very complete diagnostic information on which to classify subjects as suffering from 'functional' or 'organic' disorders; later episodes however were classified crudely on the basis of the diagnostic judgement of the GP. However, since this was likely to have the effect of increasing the number of organic cases erroneously classified as 'functional', and since our hypotheses specified an excess of causal events only in those suffering from functional illness, such misclassification would only tend to reduce rather than amplify any relevant associations in the data. Subjects with functional illness were three times more likely to have experienced a non-neutralized secondary gain crisis than those whose illnesses could be explained by organic factors. The role of early childhood experiences as a risk factor for non-neutralization also persisted into the follow up. Examining the entire period, and regardless of the diagnosis of the index episode, we found that subjects with childhood risk factors were much less likely to adopt neutralizing coping strategies. By the close of the follow up, 86 per cent (25 out of 29) of subjects with childhood risk had experienced at least one non-neutralized crisis compared with just a third of those without childhood risk.

This study demonstrated both general and specific associations between life event stress and acute somatization. The association between severe events, major difficulties, and the onset of emotional disorder was observed across all subjects with psychiatric symptoms regardless of their final classification. In contrast, the study also found a more specific association between somatization and a particular sub-type of event which was only thrown into sharp focus once the individual's style of coping with distressing crises was taken into account.

Conclusions

There are relatively few studies of functional disorders that have used the LEDS or other methodologically sound measures of life event stress, and none yet published that have explored these issues in relation to motor conversion disorder. However, for all the functional disorders examined to date there appears to be some agreement about the presence of stressful antecedents to disorder. The most consistent finding is of a general and rather non-specific association with severe events and major difficulties, the associations being usually of the magnitude found for depression and anxiety in the general population. It appears that experiences which are threatening only in the short term are unrelated to onset and there is no consistent evidence for an additive impact of successive events — just one severe event being enough to precipitate disorder in a susceptible individual.

Many of the apparently causal events and difficulties involve entrapment in problematical relationships and overt rejection that, surprisingly, have not been given the attention that has been paid to comparable concerns for the aetiology of depression. The five studies which have explored 'new' contextual measures all tap into this broad dimension. The notion of challenge in secondary amenorrhea, for example, included first, sexual relationships, reunions with ex-partners, and coping with public humiliations (Harris 1989); the severe events of the functional gastrointestinal patients were characterized by rejection experiences (Craig 1989); globus patients experienced more crises in relationships and poorer overall confiding with their partners (Harris *et al.* 1996); CSO events involve high levels of prior commitment and the women were 'unusually and intractably involved in their immediate social network, unable to disengage themselves from it when it was unsatisfactory yet equally unable to modify it' (Andrews and House 1989, pp. 358–9); while the events with secondary gain potential frequently involved situations where the individual was shamed or threatened by humiliation.

While there is considerable scope for the further refinement of the definition and measurement of stressful events, the findings reviewed in this chapter suggest that the next generation of studies will also need to take into account wider issues concerning the quantity and quality of personal relationships. Many individuals will experience broken relationships and rejection in the course of their lives, but only a few will go on to develop a disorder of the kind described here. It may be that those few are specially vulnerable in some way. Exposure to abusive relationships earlier in life or the experience of rejection at critical periods in development may be one such vulnerability factor. There is some evidence, for example, that adverse childhood experiences are associated with insecure attachment (Crittenden 1985) which can persist into adulthood and that such insecure attachment is in turn associated with depression (for example, Carnelley *et al.* 1994).

But while studying patterns of attachment may help to explain why some people are more sensitive to rejection than others, it is unlikely to tell us why these patients respond with physical symptoms. For this we probably need to explore other vulnerabilities including exposure to parental illness (Craig *et al.* 1993; Hotopf *et al.* 2000) or childhood ill health, particularly involving abdominal pain, which has recently been shown to be a powerful predictor of adult hospitalizations for medically unexplained symptoms (Hotopf *et al.* 2000). The findings concerning exposure to parental ill health are particularly intriguing. There is some evidence that illness behaviour is influenced by parental reactions to ill health (for example, Turkat and Noskin 1983) and that this early experience may influence later reactions to stressful circumstances.

References

Andrews, H. and House, A. (1989). Functional dysphonia. *In Life Events and Illness* (ed. Brown, G. W. and Harris, T. O.), pp. 343–60. Guilford Press, New York.

Bartlett, F. (1932). *Remembering: A Study of Experimental and Social Psychology*. Cambridge University Press, Cambridge.

Bebbington, P., Hurry, J., Tennant, C. and Sturt, E. (1984). Misfortune and resilience: a community study of women. *Psychological Medicine*, **14**, 347–63.

Binzer, M., Andersen, P. M. and Kullgren, G. (1997). Clinical characteristics of patients with motor disability due to conversion disorder: a prospective control group study. *Journal of Neurology, Neurosurgery and Psychiatry*, **63**, 83–8.

Brown, G. W. (1974). Meaning, measurement and stress of life events. In *Stressful Life Events: Their Nature and Effects* (ed. Dohrenwend, B. S. and Dohrenwend, B. P.), pp. 217–43. New York, Wiley.

Brown, G. W. and Harris, T. O. (1978). *Social Origins of Depression: A Study of Psychiatric Disorder in Women*. Tavistock Press, London.

Brown, G. W., Bifulco, A. and Harris, T. O. (1987). Life events, vulnerability and onset of depression: some refinements. *British Journal of Psychiatry*, **150**, 30–42.

Brown, G. W., Harris, T. O. and Hepworth, C. (1995). Loss, humiliation and entrapment among women developing depression: a patient and non-patient comparison. *Psychological Medicine*, **25**, 7–21.

Campbell, E., Cope, S. and Teasdale, J. (1983). Social factors and affective disorder: an investigation of Brown and Harris' model. *British Journal of Psychiatry*, **143**, 548–53.

Carnelley, K. P., Pietromonaco, P. R. and Jaffe, K (1994). Depression, working models of others, and relationship functioning. *Journal of Personality and Social Psychology*, **66**, 127–40.

Costello, C. G. (1982). Social factors associated with depression: a retrospective community study. *Psychological Medicine*, **12**, 329–39.

Craig, T. K. J. (1989). Abdominal Pain. *In Life Events and Illness*. (Eds. G. W. Brown and T. O. Harris), pp 233–259. Guilford Press, New York.

Craig, T. K. J. and Boardman, A. P. (1990). Somatization and primary care. *In Somatization: Physical Symptoms and Psychological Illness* (ed. Bass, C.). Blackwell. Oxford.

Craig, T. K. J., Boardman, A. P., Mills, K., Daly–Jones, O. and Drake, H. (1993). The South London Somatization Study: I. Longitudinal course and the influence of early life experiences. *British Journal of Psychiatry*, **163**, 579–88.

Craig, T. K. J., Drake, H., Mills, K. and Boardman, A. P. (1994). The South London Somatization Study. II: Influence of stressful life events and secondary gain. *British Journal of Psychiatry*, **165**, 248–58.

Creed, F. (1981). Life events and appendicectomy. *Lancet*, **i**, 1381–5.

Crittenden, P. (1985) Maltreated infants: vulnerability and resilience. *Journal of Child Psychology and Psychiatry*, **26**, 85–96.

Dohrenwend, B. P., Link, B. G., Kern, R., Shrout, P. E. and Markowitz, J. (1987). Measuring life events: the problem of variability within event categories. In *Psychiatric Epidemiology: Progress and Prospects* (ed. Cooper, B.), pp. 103–19. Croom Helm, London.

Finlay–Jones, R. and Brown, G. W. (1981). Types of stressful life events and the onset of anxiety and depressive disorders. *Psychological Medicine*, **11**, 803–15.

Harris, M. B., Deary, I. J. and Wilson, J. A. (1996). Life events and difficulties in relation to the onset of globus pharyngis. *Journal of Psychosomatic Research*, **40**, 603–15.

Harris, T. O. (1989). Disorders of menstruation. In *Life Events and Illness* (ed. Brown, G. W. and Harris, T. O.), pp. 261–94. Guilford Press, New York.

House, A. and Andrews, A. (1988). Life events and difficulties preceding the onset of functional dysphonia. *Journal of Psychosomatic Research*, **32**, 311–319.

Hotopf, M., Wilson–Jones, C., Mayou, R., Wadsworth, M. and Wessely, S. (2000). Childhood predictors of adult medically unexplained hospitalisations. Results from a national birth cohort study. *British Journal of Psychiatry*, **176**, 273–80.

Janet, P. J. (1907). *The Major Symptoms of Hysteria*. Macmillan, New York.

Kendell, R. (1983). Diagnosis and classification. In *Companion to Psychiatric Studies* (ed. Kendell, R. and Zeally, A.). Churchill Livingstone, Edinburgh.

Kleinman, A. (1986). *Social Origins of Distress and Disease: Depression, Neurasthenia and Pain in Modern China*. Yale University Press, New Haven.

Mai, F. M. and Merskey, H. (1980). Briquet's treatise on hysteria. *Archives of General Psychiatry*, **37**, 1401–5.

Miller, P. M. and Ingham, J. G. (1983). Dimensions of experience. *Psychological Medicine*, **13**, 417–29.

Paykel, E. S., Myers, J. K., Dienelt, M. N., Klerman, G. L., Lindenthal, J. J. and Pepper, M. P. (1969). Life events and depression: a controlled study. *Archives of General Psychiatry*, **21**, 753–60.

Paykel, E. S., Prusoff, B. A. and Uhlenhuth, E. H. (1971). Scaling of life events. *Archives of General Psychiatry*, **25**, 340–7.

Pilowsky, I. (1969). Abnormal illness behaviour. *British Journal of Medical Psychology*, **42**, 347–51.

Raskin, M., Talbott, J. A. and Myerson, A. T. (1966). Diagnosis of conversion reactions: predictive value of psychiatric criteria. *Journal of the American Medical Association*, **197**, 530–4.

Surtees, P. G., Miller, P. M., Ingham, J. G., Kreitman, N. B., Rennie, D. and Sashidharan, S. P. (1986). Life events and the onset of affective disorder: a longitudinal general population study. *Journal of Affective Disorders*, **10**, 37–50.

Turkat, I. D. and Noskin, D. E. (1983) Vicarious and operant experiences in the etiology of illness behaviour: a replication with healthy individuals. *Behaviour Research and Therapy*, **21**, 169–72.

8 Hysterical conversion — a view from clinical neurology

Jon Stone and Adam Zeman

. . . some of the most serious disorders of the nervous system, such as paralysis, spasm, pain and otherwise altered sensations, may depend upon a morbid condition of emotion, of idea and emotion, or of idea alone. (J. Russell Reynolds 1869)

One third of new patients attending neurology clinics present with medically unexplained symptoms. Some have disabling symptoms which appear to have a psychosocial basis, and acquire the label of 'conversion hysteria'. Its diagnosis has negative and positive elements. On the negative side, an explanation of the symptoms in terms of neurological disorder must be excluded by history taking, examination, and investigation. Positive historical clues include atypical character of the presenting complaint, previous unexplained symptoms, concurrent anxiety and depression, and recent life events. Positive clues on examination turn on inconsistencies, both between aspects of the examination and between the physical signs and established principles of neurology. The evidence base for both sets of positive clues is slender and should engender a cautious approach to diagnosis. Nevertheless, hysteria undoubtedly occurs, and contemporary rates of misdiagnosis are low. It creates a therapeutic opportunity for neurologists to minimize iatrogenic harm, supply explanation and reassurance, and open up necessary avenues of psychological management.

Introduction

Symptoms which prove to be medically unexplained are ubiquitous for the clinical neurologist. Although they range throughout the domain of neurology, weakness, sensory disturbance, dizziness, and blackouts are particularly common presentations. A proportion of patients satisfy the following working definition of hysteria:

- They appear initially to suffer from a neurological disease.
- There turns out, however, to be no evidence of a neurological disease.
- They do not appear to be malingering.
- A psychosocial cause for the symptoms is plausibly suspected.

In this chapter, we outline the process by which neurologists arrive at the diagnosis of hysteria so defined and examine the evidence on which our current practice rests.

Terminology

How do neurologists refer to medically unexplained symptoms? The term 'hysteria' is occasionally used, but a wide range of other descriptions, ranging from the frankly pejorative to the cautiously non-judgemental are in current use in the UK (Mace and Trimble 1991). Some describe the person ('nuts', neurotic, somatizer); others, the symptom (functional, non-organic, supratentorial, conversion, psychogenic, psychosomatic, dissociative, medically unexplained). As a general rule, we prefer to use 'medically unexplained' as the least theory-laden and pejorative term.

In this chapter, we will mainly use the adjective *neurological* to refer to symptoms and signs that we can explain in terms of orthodox neurological diagnoses, *unexplained* to those that we cannot. We will sometimes revert to the terms *hysterical* and *psychogenic* — without meaning to deny the important social and biological dimensions in the genesis of medically unexplained symptoms.

How common are unexplained symptoms in neurology?

Out-patients

Unexplained symptoms are very common in neurology, as they are in every branch of medicine. Patients suffering from unexplained symptoms probably outnumber those with any other single diagnosis in neurological practice. A recent study of 300 consecutive out-patients in our department confirmed that 11 per cent had symptoms 'not at all explained by organic disease' and 19 per cent had symptoms only 'somewhat explained' (Carson *et al.* 2000). In Hamilton *et al.*'s study (1996), 42 per cent of 149 neurological out-patients were labelled as 'functional'. A London neurologist gave a diagnosis of 'conversion disorder' to 3.8 per cent of 7836 consecutive patients and 26.5 per cent were given 'no diagnosis' (Perkin 1989). If primary care referral rates to neurologists continue to increase along current lines, these percentages are likely to increase further.

In-patients

The puzzling or disabling nature of the symptoms, combined with a need for further time to explore psychosocial factors, sometimes lead to hospital admission. Studies of unexplained neurological symptoms among neurology in-patients in Munich (Lempert *et al.* 1990) and at a London tertiary centre (Marsden 1986) found frequencies of 14 per cent and 1 per cent respectively. A study of 133 female neurology in-patients in Manchester rated 24 per cent as 'non-organic', 35 per cent as mixed, and 41 per cent as 'organic' (Creed *et al.* 1990). A similar study of 100 patients of both sexes in Denmark described 14 per cent as 'somatizers without organic disease', 26 per cent as 'mixed organic and non-organic', and 60 per cent as having an organic disease only (Ewald *et al.* 1994).

The spectrum of unexplained symptoms in neurology

The presentations of unexplained symptoms mimic the entire spectrum of neurological disease. This reflects the primary role of the central nervous system in the control of behaviour. As neurological disorders mainly manifest themselves in alterations of behaviour, and this can be disrupted at many levels, including the highest levels of voluntary

Table 8.1 Distribution of conversion symptoms in different populations. (Numbers represent percentages.)

	London: Carter (1949)	Sweden: Ljungberg (1957)	New York: Stefansson (1976)	London: Trimble (1981)	London: Roy (1977)	Munich: Lempert (1990)	Denmark: Couprie (1995)
Population sampled	M	P and N	P	NP	NP	N	N
Motor symptoms	23	10	20	25	14	12	73
Pain	–	–	69	23	–	23	–
Sensory symptoms	–	–	28	7	–	14	5
Convulsions	6	20	–	14	64	15	–
Visual	3	0.8	12.5	10	4	2	2
Dizziness	–	–	12.5	9	–	18	–
Amnesia	23	10	–	4	6	–	–
Tremor	10	10	–	4	–	1	–
Dysphonia	29	1.3	–	–	6	–	5
Astasia–abasia/gait	–	47	–	–	4	7	12
Other	6	–	24	4	2	8	2

Abbreviations: P = psychiatric; N = neurological; NP = neuropsychiatric; M = medical

command, they are natural targets for conscious or unconscious simulation. Studies have varied greatly in their inclusion criteria and the population sampled, making them hard to compare (Table 8.1). Lempert's study in a neurological population is the largest and least selected and therefore probably the most representative (Lempert *et al.*1990).

Laterality — two-thirds on the left

It has often been noted that unexplained symptoms are more likely to be experienced on the left than the right. This phenomenon has become so well-known that some clinicians use it as a diagnostic pointer. Review of the literature reveals that, indeed, around two-thirds of unexplained motor and sensory symptoms do occur on the left. Table 8.2 summarizes some of the main studies. The year of study did not appear to influence the overall trend.

The relationship between the laterality of unexplained symptoms and handedness has been examined in some studies (Crimlisk *et al.* 1998; Pascuzzi 1994; Stern 1977). A pooled analysis unexpectedly demonstrated that left-handed cases were more likely to have left-sided symptoms (20 out of 25) than right-handed cases (123 out of 203). This argues against an explanation of the preponderance of left-sided presentations in terms of the greater convenience of disability in the non-dominant limb.

The clinical approach

The diagnosis of unexplained symptoms offers one of the greatest challenges in neurological practice. It requires a simultaneous advance on several fronts: the physician must rule out neurological disorder with the usual methods of history taking, examination, and

Table 8.2 Laterality in 13 studies of unexplained unilateral motor or sensory symptoms

Study	Number with sensory symptoms	% with left-sided sensory symptoms	No. with motor symptoms	% with left- sided motor symptoms	Total no. in study	% with left-sided motor or sensory symptoms
Briquet (1859)	90	78	60	77	150	77
Magee (1962)	–	–	–	–	50	94
Fallik (1971)	–	–	33	24	33	24
Stefansson et al. (1976)	–	–	–	–	31	39
Galin et al. (1977)	11	55	41	66	52	63
Stern (1977)	114	68	81	64	195	67
Bishop, Jr. et al. (1978)	–	–	–	–	22	55
Axelrod et al. (1980)	–	–	–	–	53	79
Lempert et al. (1990)	82	46	51	45	133	46
Rothwell (1994)	35	77	25	80	60	78
Binzer et al. (1997)	–	–	21	76	21	76
Pascuzzi (1994)	29	86	26	85	55	86
Crimlisk et al. (1998)	–	–	20	50	20	50
Totals and averages	361	**68%**	358	**64%**	875	**66%**

* Summarizes earlier studies and case reports

investigation, while at the same time seeking the 'positive signs' of hysteria and establishing that there is an appropriate psychosocial background for the emergence of medically unexplained symptoms. In the following discussion we track the process of diagnosis in the order in which it occurs, through the history, examination, and investigation.

1. The history

The history will often supply important clues to the diagnosis of hysteria. The onset, tempo, and character of the presenting complaint may be atypical for neurological disorders, and a number of specific historical features should lower the threshold of diagnostic suspicion. We review these briefly. These features will sometimes only emerge after an interview with a family member or review of the hospital notes.

Previous unexplained symptoms

Evidence is accumulating that the more unexplained symptoms a patient has, the more likely the primary symptom is to be unexplained (Wessely et al. 1999). In Crimlisk et al.'s study (1998) of unexplained motor symptoms, additional unexplained symptoms included paraesthesia (65 per cent), pseudoseizures (23 per cent), and dysphonia (5 per cent). In Binzer et al.'s study (1997) of unexplained motor symptoms, 6 out of 30 subjects had a prior history of conversion symptoms, compared to none of the controls with neurological disease. A history of repeated surgical procedures, particularly without clear evidence of pathology, is common in patients with somatization disorder and may be associated with unexplained neurological symptoms.

Psychiatric comorbidity

A high frequency of anxiety and depression in patients with unexplained symptoms, neurological or otherwise, is a consistent finding. Studies of unexplained neurological symptoms sampled from neurological practice report rates of depression varying from 27–41 per cent (Binzer *et al.* 1997; Crimlisk *et al.* 1998; Lempert *et al.* 1990). In studies of unexplained motor symptoms and globus, depression and anxiety were significantly more common among cases than disease controls (Binzer *et al.* 1997; Deary *et al.* 1992). While a history of psychological distress is often readily forthcoming, a proportion of patients are exceptionally reluctant to allow discussion to wander from the physical domain; they require an especially circumspect approach.

A high frequency of personality disorder — 50 per cent (Binzer *et al.* 1997) and 59 per cent (Crimlisk *et al.* 1998) — was found in two recent studies of unexplained motor symptoms. Although these included histrionic personality disorder, other types of personality disorder such as dependent personality disorder were more common.

Recent life events or difficulties

An increased number of life events in the year preceding symptom onset have been recorded in small controlled studies of unexplained motor symptoms (Binzer *et al.* 1997), globus pharyngis (Harris *et al.* 1996), and pseudoseizures (Bowman and Markand 1999). (See also Craig's chapter in this volume p. 88.)

Secondary gain/litigation

The methodologically difficult issue of secondary gain in somatization has very rarely been tackled. Craig *et al.*'s South London Somatization Study is an exception and is discussed in Craig's chapter in this volume p. 88.

The importance of impending litigation based on the symptom in question is a vexed issue. Such litigation seems to be common: 23 per cent (Crimlisk *et al.* 1998), 39 per cent (Factor *et al.* 1995), and 12.5 per cent (Koller *et al.* 1989) in studies of unexplained motor symptoms and tremor. Sometimes, the conclusion that the symptom will only be resolved by a court of law is inescapable.

Neurological comorbidity and symptom modelling

It is often said that patients model their symptoms on their own past diseases or on those of people they know. In two older studies of 'hysterical' symptoms, neurological disease was present in over 60 per cent of cases (Merskey and Buhrich 1975; Slater 1965). In Crimlisk *et al.*'s study (1998), 42 per cent of patients with unexplained motor symptoms had a comorbid neurological disease and, interestingly, half of these had a peripheral origin. Epilepsy is thought to coexist in a significant percentage of patients with non-epileptic attacks, although there is debate about the degree of overlap (Devinsky and Thacker 1995).

There is little evidence on symptom modelling on other people's illness (for example, friends, relatives, work colleagues). Twenty-two per cent of the patients in Crimlisk *et al.*'s study (1998) had worked in medical or paramedical professions, which may have increased the scope for symptom modelling, but this association has not been subject to a controlled study. In addition to symptom modelling, there may be several other mechanisms by which neurological disorders can predispose to hysterical manifestation. These include elaboration to convince others, their secondary emotional effects, and the results of the personality change wrought by disease of the brain.

Illness beliefs

People develop a surprising variety of beliefs about their symptoms and it is always a good idea to ask the patient what he or she thinks about the cause, treatability, and prognosis of their condition. In a study of benign headache (Fitzpatrick and Hopkins 1981), 39 per cent of patients had a specific worry about a disease (such as tumour or blood clot) even though most of them had no formal psychiatric disorder. In chronic fatigue syndrome, studies suggest that a strong belief in having a physical illness cause is associated with a poor prognosis (Joyce *et al.* 1997)

History from relative/informant

A discussion with a relative or informant, preferably away from the patient, often illuminates the history. Occasionally, its main value is to point to the informant's role in fanning the flames of unexplained symptoms. This touches on the concept of tertiary gain, or the benefit to the carer of looking after someone who is ill. In a small study of carers of patients with chronic pain (Benjamin *et al.* 1992), two-thirds rejected completely any possibility of a psychological contribution to the symptoms. Ninety-four per cent had some personal previous experience of prolonged illness or caring for an invalid. When asked 'what do you think you can do to help the patient?', 53 per cent replied 'care as much as possible', in preference to 9 per cent who replied 'encourage to do more'. More work is needed here, but these observations suggest that the attitudes of carers may be an important factor in the perpetuation of medically unexplained symptoms.

2. The examination

The neurological examination has a twofold purpose in patients with suspected psychogenic disorders. Its first aim is to exclude any clear signs of neurological disorder — abnormalities of muscle tone, asymmetries of reflex, extensor plantar responses, and so forth. Its second, and much less straightforward aim is to gather 'positive' evidence for hysteria. These positive signs, which were extensively discussed by the founding fathers of neurology (Charcot 1889; Gowers 1892; Head 1922), almost all depend upon the presence of inconsistency — either inconsistency between aspects of the examination (as when a patient strides into the room wearing a heavy set of callipers, but claims to be unable to raise his leg from the examination couch), or inconsistency between the signs we elicit and what we know of anatomy, physiology, and pathophysiology (as when a patient claims absolute loss of all modalities of sensation below the shoulder with abrupt restoration of normality above). There are three important reasons for caution in interpreting these 'positive' signs of hysteria.

The first is that they can occur in patients with neurological disorders who are, for whatever reasons, 'elaborating' or exaggerating their physical impairment: indeed these positive signs are precisely signs of elaboration. Second, although some of the 'positive signs' can fairly claim to be obvious, few have had their sensitivity, specificity, or reliability rigorously tested in unselected samples containing both patients with neurological disorders and patients with unexplained symptoms. Gould *et al.*'s study (1986) sounds a warning note: 30 consecutive admissions with acute onset of neurological symptoms based on structural damage to the central nervous system (83 per cent stroke) were assessed for the presence of seven alleged features of hysteria (Fig. 8.1); 29 out of 30 patients displayed at least one of these widely cited pointers. Thirdly, even 'hard' neurological signs, such as the plantar reflex and deep tendon reflexes have only fair to moderate inter-rater reliability (Hansen *et al.* 1994) and modest sensitivity (Stam 1999) for detecting neurological disease. This is very likely to apply to the positive signs of hysteria as well.

General examination

It is uncontroversial that simple observation, as the patient enters the room, undresses, or departs down the corridor, can be an invaluable source of clues to the nature of their disorder. Several features that are supposedly common to the whole spectrum of psychogenic disorder are more dubious. Charcot's 'ovarian hyperaesthesia' is an example of how a physical sign can achieve prominence under famous patronage, despite a very shaky premise. 'La belle indifference', the apparent indifference of the sufferer to his or her predicament, continues to be cited as a tell-tale feature of

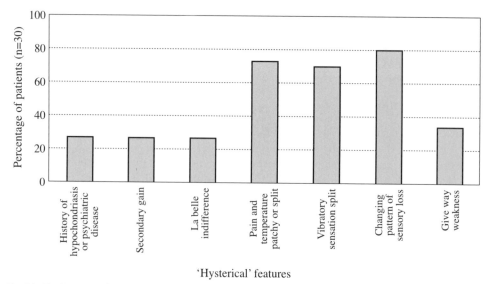

Fig. 8.1 The frequency of seven alleged clinical features of hysteria in patients with organic lesions (From Gould *et al.* 1986)

psychogenic disorder. But the evidence suggests it is an indifferent sign. It has been reported variously in 4 out of 57 (Lewis and Berman 1965), 15 out of 113 (Reed 1975), and 13 out of 32 (Raskin *et al*. 1966) patients with hysteria, and in 3 out of 7 (Raskin *et al*. 1966) and 8 out of 30 (Gould *et al*. 1986) patients with undoubted brain disease. As Lewis and Berman observed (1965), in marked contrast to their alleged indifference, many hysterical 'patients manifest a deep interest, and some a delight, in describing their ailments'.

Weakness or paralysis

Hysterical weakness ranges from one of the most dramatic presentations in neurology to a subtle intermittency of effort revealed on formal testing. Brief observation sometimes brings major inconsistencies to light. Consider, for example, the patient who walks into the examination room but is unable to raise his leg from the bed, or who wobbles unsteadily on two feet but can stand on one leg to put on a pair of trousers. One of us encountered a patient with an apparent hemiparesis whose paretic arm was lifted passively by the visiting consultant only to become 'stranded' in space, unsupported, under the neurologist's withering gaze. A commonly used, if somewhat unkind manoeuvre in suspected hysterical hemiparesis is to raise the flaccid arm above the patient's head and let it fall: consistent failure of the arm to strike the face is taken to suggest psychogenic weakness (and may also be useful in psychogenic disorders of consciousness). So far as we know, none of these signs has been systematically examined, but they can claim the support of commonsense.

Some alleged features of hysterical weakness have been examined more closely. Figure 8.1 suggested that 'give-way weakness' is an unreliable sign as it was present in 10 out of 30 of Gould's neurological patients, but an interesting paper by Knutsson and Martensson (1985) supports the view that power is unusually variable in patients with hysterical paresis. Using quantitative methods they showed that the variability of the strength of knee movements on the 'healthy' side was 'usually less than 10 per cent', while in 22 out of 25 psychogenic 'paretic' limbs, the variability was 20 per cent or more. This observation merits further exploration with more varied controls and more rigorous statistics.

The most impressive quantitative discrimination to date between hysterical and neurological weakness is reported in a study of Hoover's sign — the involuntary extension of a hysterically paralysed leg when the 'good leg' is flexing against resistance. Ziv and colleagues (1998) studied this, using computerized myometry, in 9 patients with unilateral leg weakness, compared to 10 healthy controls and 7 patients with psychogenic leg weakness. They demonstrated a clear difference in the pattern of response between neurological and psychogenic groups. Figure 8.2 shows the ratio between involuntary extension of the limb (when the contralateral limb was being tested) and voluntary extension (when the ipsilateral limb was being tested).

The absence of expected signs is sometimes an important clue to hysterical weakness. Thus, a patient with a flexed arm, extended leg, and hemiplegic gait following a 'stroke', who proves to have entirely normal tone and reflex responses, may well have a hysterical hemiparesis. It is important to be aware that reflexes are sometimes rendered 'exceptionally' brisk by anxiety, that 'pseudoclonus' may occur due to semi-voluntary

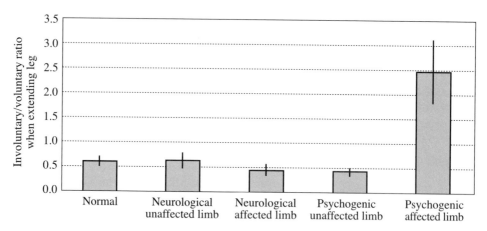

Fig. 8.2 Hoover's Sign. Lower limbs: involuntary/voluntary force ratio IVVR (mean). A unique pattern is observed in the affected weak limbs of patients with psychogenic weakness, in contrast to their unaffected limb, normal controls, and patients with neurological weakness. (From Ziv et al. 1998) (Error bars represent standard error of mean.)

contraction in the calf muscles, and that in patients with longstanding hysterical weakness, disuse atrophy, trophic change, and even contractures (Marsden 1986) may all complicate the picture.

Finally, there is a suggestion that monoparesis may be over-represented among cases of unexplained motor weakness. In Binzer et al.'s controlled study (1997), 9 out of 30 cases had a monoparesis against none of the 30 controls with organic cause for weakness. Raskin et al.'s sample (1966) contained 4 out of 23 cases versus none of the 6 controls. In Lempert et al.'s large consecutive series (1990) there were 31 cases of monoparesis against 20 of hemiparesis, 18 of tetraparesis, 10 of paraparesis, and 2 of bibrachial weakness.

Movement disorder

Eight case series (Factor et al. 1995; Kim et al. 1999; Koller et al. 1989; Lang 1995; Lang et al. 1995; Monday and Jankovic 1993; Deuschl et al. 1998; Fahn and Williams 1988) have examined psychogenic movement disorder over the past decade; five are summarized in a recent review (Gálvez–Jiménez and Lang 1997). Psychogenic movement disorder may account for only 2–3 per cent of cases seen in specialist movement disorders clinics (Factor et al. 1995; Fahn 1994).

Several common features of psychogenic movement disorders emerge from these studies: distractibility, variability (in frequency, amplitude, and distribution), and the response to placebo or psychological treatments. However, almost all of these studies are vulnerable to the criticism that the practical usefulness of these features in diagnosis has not yet been demonstrated by testing them in a mixed population of patients with both neurological and psychogenic disorders. The everyday observations that neurological movement disorders are markedly influenced by emotion (like the tremor of Parkinson's disease), and often under some degree of voluntary control (like the tics of Gilles de La Tourette syndrome), underline the difficulty in drawing sharp distinctions between psychogenic and neurological conditions.

Table 8.3 Comparison of four case series of 'psychogenic' tremor. (Numbers are percentages.)

Feature	Koller *et al.* (1989) n = 24	Factor *et al.* (1995) n = 15*	Deuschl *et al.* (1998) n = 25	Kim *et al.* (1999) n = 70
Distractibility	96	93	86	80
Variability of frequency and characteristic	92		Not assessed	88
Abrupt onset	88	40	92	73
Rest tremor	96	Not assessed	0	63
Selective disability	Not assessed	53		34
Entrainment				49
Other 'psychogenic' neurological features	96 (other 'functional' symptoms)	80	32	56 (symptoms) 60 (signs)
Compensation or litigation pending	12.5	40	Not assessed	30

*Extracted from published data

Tremor

Table 8.3 compares the features noted in four recent series. Distractibility and variability were very common; abrupt onset and the presence of other unexplained symptoms and signs were often observed. Two particular features found in psychogenic tremor — selective disability (the interference of the tremor with certain activities but not others) and entrainment (the change of original tremor frequency to match the frequency of a task in another limb) — may also be useful diagnostic features for psychogenic movement disorders in general.

Deuschl *et al.* (1998) studied the 'coactivation sign of psychogenic tremor' — the presence of a tremor and rigidity within a limited range which can be gradually enlarged and then broken down completely by the examiner. Once the rigidity is gone the tremor also disappears. This sign, analogous to synergistic co-contraction in psychogenic weakness, was present in all 25 of Deuschl's patients and is supported by neurophysiological data. Deuschl also performed quantitative accelerometry (measuring tremor amplitude with 500g and 1000g weights on the hands) in his psychogenic group and in controls with essential tremor and Parkinson's disease. Among the neurological controls the amplitude of the tremor decreased with increasing load, but in 11 out of 16 cases of psychogenic tremor it increased. These are interesting and clinically applicable findings which merit a further, fully controlled study.

Dystonia

The competing claims of neurology and psychiatry over dystonia in the past century tell a cautionary tale. Neurologists are now incredulous of symbolic explanations of dystonia

— for example, the interpretation of torticollis as a turning away from responsibility — yet psychogenic dystonia does occur. Fahn and William's description of 21 cases (1988) suggested that incongruity or inconsistency of movement (85 per cent), lower limb onset (67 per cent), onset of dystonia at rest (52 per cent), pain (43 per cent), bizarre nature of the movements (33 per cent), excessive slowness (24 per cent), and startle-induced 'elaborate' movements (10 per cent) are useful diagnostic features. Lang (1995), in his 18 cases, found pain (88 per cent), abrupt onset (50 per cent), onset of dystonia at rest (66 per cent), and known precipitating injury (78 per cent) to be important.

Both series emphasize the presence of 'give-way weakness', multiple somatization, and non-anatomic sensory changes. As ever, the lack of adequate control groups bedevils these conclusions. *Neurological* dystonia, as the authors stress, often has features which might give rise to suspicions of a psychological cause — variability, spontaneous remission, task specificity, and the relief of dystonia by 'gestes antagonistes' (for example, touching the chin to relieve cervical dystonia).

Myoclonus

There are two case series of psychogenic myoclonus. Monday and Jankovic (1993) found that it accounted for one fifth of their psychogenic movement disorders and almost 10 per cent of cases of myoclonus. The clinical features in their 18 cases were similar to those in other psychogenic movement disorders comprising inconsistent or incongruent movements with two of the following: diminished movement with distraction, other psychogenic physical symptoms, periods of spontaneous remission, acute improvement in symptoms, response to placebo suggestion, and other psychiatric history. Terada *et al.* (1995) demonstrated a Bereitschaftspotential preceding psychogenic myoclonus using jerk-locked EEG back-averaging in five of their six patients. Since the Bereitschaftspotential broadly correlates with the voluntary intention to move, this may prove to be a useful investigation in this group.

Parkinsonism

Lang (1995) reported 14 patients from three specialist centres with a diagnosis of psychogenic parkinsonism. Besides the features already mentioned in relation to tremor, Lang found a rest tremor without the usual transient dampening on action and posture, an arm often held tightly to the side, and a lack of the decrementing amplitude of repetitive movement usually seen with bradykinesia.

Gait disorder

Two case series have analysed psychogenic gait disorder systematically (Keane 1989; Lempert *et al.* 1991). Lempert distilled six commonly occurring features of psychogenic gait disorder, at least one of which occurred in 97 per cent of the patients (see Table 8.4). Application of these criteria to an unselected group would once again be of great interest. A pseudohemiparetic gait with dragging of the affected limb is also commonly described. Some neurological disorders, particularly when paroxysmal, can give rise to bizarre gait disturbance. Paroxysmal kinesigenic and non-kinesigenic choreoathetosis, idiopathic torsion dystonia, progressive supranuclear palsy, frontal gait apraxia, and Huntingon's

Table 8.4 Lempert *et al.*'s study (1991) of psychogenic gait disturbance (n = 37)

Clinical features	Description	%
1. Fluctuation of impairment	Variability during a 5–10 min. period, either spontaneously or provoked by distraction e.g. finger nose testing while standing.	19
2. Excessive slowness of movements or hesitation	Simultaneous contraction of agonist and antagonist muscles — not related to pain in this sample. Hesitation refers to delayed or failed initiation of gait. Small forward and backward movements of the leg while the feet 'stick' to the ground. Does not improve after first step like parkinsonism.	19
3. 'Psychogenic Romberg' test	Constant falls towards or away from the observer, irrespective of his position. Fall avoided by clutching physician. Large amplitude body sway. Improvement with distraction.	12
4. 'Walking on ice' pattern	The gait pattern of a normal person walking on slippery ground: cautious, broad-based steps with decreased stride length and height, stiff knees and ankles. Arms sometimes abducted as if on a tightrope.	11
5. Uneconomic postures with waste of muscle energy	e.g. Eccentric displacement of centre of gravity. Standing and walking with flexion of hips and knees.	11
6. Sudden knee buckling	Patients usually prevent themselves from falling (8/10) before they touch the ground, requiring excellent muscle function. N.B. Knee buckling can occur in Huntington's chorea and cataplexy.	10

chorea can all appear psychogenic on casual inspection. In a follow-up study of unexplained motor symptoms (Crimlisk *et al.* 1998), the 3 patients out of 64 who did receive new organic diagnoses (myotonic dystrophy, spinocerebellar degeneration, and paroxysmal hemidystonia) all had gait disorder

Seizures

Commonly coexisting with other pseudoneurological symptoms, non-epileptic attacks or pseudoseizures are dealt with in the chapter by Trimble in this volume (p. 143).

Sensory disturbance

The clinical detection and localization of sensory dysfunction is probably one of the least reliable areas of the neurological examination (Lindley *et al.* 1993). Table 8.5 summarizes alleged features of psychogenic sensory loss. What evidence exists suggests that these signs are extremely untrustworthy. Gould *et al.* (1986) found 'psychogenic' features on sensory examination in over half his neurological patient group; Rolak (1988)

Table 8.5 Alleged features of 'non-organic' sensory dysfunction

Clinical feature	Theoretical basis
Midline splitting involving mucous membranes and genitalia	Exact midline splitting of pinprick sensation is said not to occur because contralateral segmental sensory nerves supply an area 1–2 cm lateral to the midline. Phenomenon reproducible with hyperventilation (O'Sullivan *et al.* 1992) suggesting a common central mechanism. Present in organic disease (Gould *et al.* 1986).
Mimics motor disturbance in distribution	Non-organic sensory loss may be dependent on the idea of where it ought to be (Reynolds 1869).
Midline alteration of vibration over skull and sternum	Lateralized stimulation of midline bony structures should not theoretically produce unilateral perception. Found commonly in organic disease (Rolak 1988; Gould *et al.* 1986).
Complete disappearance of light touch	Unusual in the absence of severe intracranial or spinal pathology, marked peripheral neuropathy, or presence of normal reflexes.
Discrepancy tests	e.g. 1. Ability to find nose with eyes shut using completely anaesthetic finger. e.g. 2. Absent foot proprioception on the bed but a negative Romberg test.
Vulnerability to examiner trickery	e.g. 1. 'Say "yes" when you feel it and "no" when you don't.' e.g. 2. Forced-choice method described by Miller (1986).

similarly noted diminished vibration sense over the affected part of the forehead in 69 of 80 patients with neurological disorders. This study also found that 'midline splitting' of sensory function was not helpful in determining whether there was an underlying neurological disorder. The features summarized in Table 8.5 should clearly be interpreted with circumspection.

We have often encountered a characteristic pattern of hemisensory disturbance in association with panic disorder, anxiety, or depression. There is sometimes additional ipsilateral intermittent blurring of vision (asthenopia) and occasionally decreased ipsilateral hearing. Similar hemisensory disturbance can be provoked by hyperventilation (O'Sullivan *et al.* 1992) or hypnotic suggestion (Fleminger *et al.* 1980). The clinical pattern is so consistent that it seems plausible that in the future its pathophysiology may become sufficiently understood for it no longer to be described as unexplained.

Visual disturbance

Ophthalmologists have estimated that psychogenic visual disorders account for up to 5 per cent of their practice (Kathol *et al.* 1983; Miller 1973). As with other unexplained symptoms, the history may depict an atypical onset and pattern. Simple observation of visually guided behaviour will sometimes reveal telling inconsistencies, particularly in the case of severe apparent visual loss. A number of relatively reliable optometric techniques are available to support bedside tests in the diagnosis of psychogenic visual loss, field disturbance, or gaze abnormality (summarized briefly in Table 8.6) (Bose and

Table 8.6 Some clinical features and tests which are useful in the assessment of non-organic visual symptoms

Clinical feature	Response in patients with non-organic symptoms
Complete visual loss	
Simple tests	• Good navigational vision — although this can be the case in severe optic nerve disease with poor central but good peripheral vision e.g. Leber's optic atrophy. • Unable to sign name — a truly blind person usually can. • Unable to bring fingers together in front of eyes — relies on proprioception not vision. • Failure to direct eyes towards hands during manual tasks. • Normal response to menace. • Emotional response to visually shocking material or a 'rude face'. • Flinching with increasing light intensity (emergency light reflex).
Rotating drum test	Optokinetic nystagmus with rotating drum (or pursuit movements with a mirror) is equivalent to Snellen >6/60.
Partial visual loss	
Fogging test	Plus lenses of increasing power placed in front of the 'good' eye until the patient is tricked into seeing well with their 'bad' eye.
Others	Prism shift test, polarizing lens test, stereoscopic acuity — see review by Beatty (1999).
Field loss	
Goldmann perimetry	• A patient with tubular vision who shakes your hand while fixing on your eye reveals a discrepancy. • Tubular fields, detected by testing fields at different distances (the seeing field should expand conically). • Spiral fields, detected using manual perimetry (can also be seen in fatigue). • Star-shaped field, detected using manual perimetry.
Double vision / gaze abnormality	• Monocular diplopia in the presence of a normal eye and polyopia in the absence of cortical pathology both suggest psychogenic disorder. • Convergence spasm is a common cause of initially unexplained diplopia: it disappears quickly looking side to side or up. • Nystagmus can be simulated
Ptosis	• On attempted eye opening, no compensatory overactivity of frontalis. • Affected eyebrow lower than normal side.

Kupersmith 1995). As always, the diagnosis of psychogenic visual impairment should only be made with great caution. The curious phenomena of visual agnosia, for example, with selective impairment of face, place, or object recognition might easily be misinterpreted in psychogenic terms (Beatty 1999).

Deafness

Complete psychogenic deafness is now thought to be rare, although patients with hemisensory disturbance will often complain that their hearing on that side is diminished. Despite a complaint of severe hearing loss the patient may make no attempt to listen to the examiner and fail to speak in a raised voice. Demonstrating an emotional response to shocking words and waking the patient in the middle of the night with an alarm clock are some of the cruder methods of detection described. The cochlear-orbicular and cochlear-palpebral reflex (the reaction of the orbicularis muscle and eyelid to a loud noise) should not be present in complete organic deafness. More sophisticated forced-choice tests have been described (Haughton *et al.* 1979). Testing milder hearing loss requires more specialized equipment which is usually available only to the otolaryngologist.

Dysphonia

Dysphonia, like deafness, is mainly the province of otolaryngologists. Up to 40 000 patients with dysphonia are seen each year in the UK, a substantial proportion of whom are given a diagnosis of psychogenic dysphonia (Wilson *et al.* 1995). Presentations range from simple hoarseness, through a whispering delivery seen with laryngeal hyperabduction, to the total mutism well known in World War One. Direct inspection of the vocal cords is obligatory in reaching a diagnosis. The distinction between psychogenic dysphonia and laryngeal dystonia (a form of focal dystonia affecting the vocal cords) is especially problematic, and sometimes impossible.

Globus pharyngis

Globus (the sensation of having a ball in the throat) is as old as the uterine concept of hysteria itself. Considerable debate still exists over the significance and frequency of physiological factors such as abnormalities on oesphageal manometry or subtle erythema on inspection. However, Deary and colleagues have demonstrated in community and controlled hospital populations that, in common with other unexplained symptoms, patients with globus have higher rates of severe life events in the one year prior to onset (Harris *et al.* 1996), anxiety, depression, and neuroticism (Deary *et al.* 1995).

Pain

'Hysterical pain' used to feature commonly in tables of conversion symptoms but is now no longer one of the accepted symptoms in the DSM–IV definition of conversion disorder. Nevertheless, pain frequently accompanies other medically unexplained neurological symptoms. Unexplained pain syndromes, such as fibromyalgia, are associated with similar factors to those already mentioned for unexplained neurological symptoms (Wessely *et al.* 1999). Pain is a sensory modality, and the only justification for its exclusion from the realm of 'conversion disorder' seems to be that it is particularly difficult to establish with confidence whether it does or does not have a neurological explanation. We will not expand further on this complex subject here.

Amnesia and cognitive dysfunction

Affective disorders, particularly depression, commonly give rise to a degree of cognitive impairment. Hysterical disorders of cognition occur more rarely, but both focal disorders (such as amnesia and dysphasia) and global impairment (manifesting as an apparent dementia) are encountered (Lishman 1998). Inconsistencies both within the cognitive examination and with the pattern of cognitive impairment that usually occurs in neurological disease can be useful in making the diagnosis. These are exemplified by the patient who is able to converse normally but unable to follow a three-stage instruction, and the patient with no admitted knowledge of personal identity despite an otherwise well-preserved intellect. Formal testing can help to reveal such inconsistencies and, occasionally, demonstrate 'below chance' performance on memory tests, which belies the appearance of amnesia.

3. Investigations

There is little evidence bearing on the question of how much investigation is appropriate in patients with medically unexplained symptoms. There are cogent arguments both for and against extensive testing. 'Full' investigation may be reassuring to the patient and the doctor, and meets the worry that a patient with positive signs of hysteria might be 'elaborating' the symptoms and signs of a hitherto undiagnosed neurological disorder. On the other hand, exhaustive tests may waste time and money, undermine clinical reassurance, fuel a patient's anxieties, and delay the process of psychosocial enquiry and management which is often sorely needed. The discovery of asymptomatic irrelevant pathology is particularly problematic. For example, many people over the age of 40 begin to collect asymptomatic white periventricular blobs on T2 MRI, referred to as 'unidentified bright objects' or UBOs. If a 45-year-old woman with an apparently psychogenic hemiparesis has a single, tiny, high attenuation lesion in the appropriate area is this the cause, the nidus, or irrelevant?

The authors' preference is to undertake a focussed set of investigations in most cases of disabling motor and sensory symptoms, even if a psychogenic basis is suspected, but to make it clear from the start that psychological and social avenues will also be explored. These investigations often include MRI scanning of appropriate regions, CSF examination, and neurophysiology. The availability of these tests may help to explain the drop in rates of misdiagnosis of hysteria from the alarming levels reported by Slater — who regarded the diagnosis as a 'disguise for ignorance and a fertile clinical error' — to the more tolerable levels reported in recent series. Slater (1965) claimed misdiagnosis in 32 per cent of his cases (many of whom had pain), while recent series quote rates from 4–7 per cent (Mace and Trimble 1996; Couprie et al. 1995; Crimlisk et al. 1998).

'Truth drugs' and diagnostic placebo

Interview after administration of intravenous sodium amytal was initially promoted as a method of uncovering the hidden psychic conflict causing the patient's symptom. More recently, examination under sedation, including the use of benzodiazepines (Ellis 1990) has demonstrated to the neurologist (and by means of video, to the patient) that the apparently paralysed limb can move. White et al. (1988) report positively on this technique in 11 patients with psychogenic locomotor disorders, who had been disabled for an average of 3.4 years. The use of diagnostic intravenous placebo, for example to start and stop non-epileptic attacks, may have a high sensitivity and specificity but is controversial (Slater et al. 1995) because it involves the deliberate deception of the patient. These methods merit more systematic study.

Evoked potentials, magnetic stimulation, and functional imaging

These techniques may have a role in the diagnosis of psychogenic disorder, and also hold out the promise of elucidating its neurobiology. Most of these are discussed in detail in this volume in the chapters by Spence, Sierra and Berrios, and Athwal *et al.* (p. 216).

Transcranial magnetic stimulation in hysterical conversion

In this form of evoked potential study, the stimulus is administered over the motor cortex and recorded peripherally. Seven studies, summarized in Table 8.7, have looked at this modality in patients with psychogenic weakness. They suggest that the technique may be a useful adjunct in distinguishing neurological from psychogenic weakness and that there may be some scientific benefit in further studies of subtle interside differences.

Illustrative cases

Two brief case descriptions should help to illustrate the preceding discussion. Both cases sprang surprises — of rather different kinds.

Case 1

A 41-year-old man was admitted to the neurology ward having presented himself without warning to a local private hospital, demanding to see an ophthalmologist. He was complaining of difficulty looking to the left, blurring of his vision, and unsteadiness of

Table 8.7 Studies examining transcranial magnetic stimulation (TMS) in psychogenic weakness

Study	Findings	Comments
Mullges *et al.* 1991	TMS was normal in 10 cases of acute psychogenic weakness and 2 cases of chronic psychogenic weakness. One chronic case did not have a response.	
Meyer *et al.* 1992	Normal TMS in 59/60 muscles in 15 cases of psychogenic weakness. Abnormal TMS in 98/119 muscles in 50 patients with neurological weakness.	Normal range wide. Small interside differences in latency and amplitude within normal range in cases.
Foong *et al.* 1997	Normal TMS in 2 patients with left hemiparesis; but right hemisphere less excitable than left at moderate stimulus intensities.	Asymmetry may represent cerebral dominance despite one of the cases being left-handed.
Case reports Jellinek *et al.* 1992; Pillai *et al.* 1992; Morota *et al.* 1994; Gomez *et al.* 1998	Normal TMS in 4 case reports of 'hysterical paraplegia' and 'hysterical quadriparesis'.	Jellinek *et al.* suggest that observation by the patient of his own movement during TMS aided recovery.

gait. He admitted to a substantial alcohol intake, an unstable social life, and gave an account of recent travels in 'the South Seas' which struck several doctors as implausible. Examination revealed a partial left homonymous hemianopia (which was unusually incongruous between the two eyes), a highly variable gaze palsy to the left, and collapsing weakness and ill-defined blunting of sensation affecting the left arm and leg. One of us wrote that 'most if not all of his symptoms are likely to be "functional"', but suggested that investigations should be performed nonetheless to help rule out CNS inflammation. These proved positive, with multiple high-signal abnormalities in the periventricular white matter on MRI and an oligoclonal antibody response in the cerebrospinal fluid. The final neurological diagnosis was of probable multiple sclerosis.

Case 2

A previously healthy 20-year-old female student presented with a two-day history of initial dazzling visual disturbance which moved from her left to her right visual field, followed by blurring of vision and unsteadiness. Examination revealed an unusual rapid to and fro movement of the eyes (taken to be ocular flutter), a limited range of voluntary eye movement, inability to perform rapid repetitive movements with her limbs, and severe unsteadiness. Diagnoses of migraine, demyelination, and 'dancing eyes, dancing feet syndrome' were considered by successive doctors. MRI of the brain and CSF examination were normal. Review by a neuro-ophthalmologist suggested that the eye movement disorder was a combination of convergence spasm and self-induced nystagmus (the neuro-ophthalmologist supported his argument with a successful imitation of the abnormality). A variety of psychological stresses emerged on further questioning and the patient left the ward, entirely well, three days after the onset of her symptoms.

These cases illustrate a number of the points we have discussed, in particular the danger of relying too heavily on the 'positive signs' of hysteria (case 1), the value of appropriate investigations in confirming and excluding neurological disorder (cases 1 and 2), and the importance of exploring the psychological background of a patient's presentation (case 2).

Differential diagnosis

Several alternatives to the diagnosis of hysteria should be borne in mind. Could there be a cryptic neurological disorder underlying some or all of the patient's symptoms and signs (as there was in case 1)? Could there be a cryptic psychiatric disorder (for example, delusional disorder) with the delusions driving the symptoms? Even if the diagnosis of psychogenic disorder is sound, one should ask oneself whether there might be an *associated* neurological or psychiatric disorder. We have already noted that comorbid disorders of both kinds are common.

In assessing patients with unexplained symptoms, it is particularly helpful to use an approach in which independent axes of neurological morbidity, psychological morbidity, social circumstances, and illness beliefs are formulated together. This provides a fuller picture of the problem and lessens the probability of missing cryptic or associated neurological and psychological morbidity.

Malingering/factitious disorder

Outside medico-legal settings, physicians are not as a rule on the lookout for conscious fabrication of symptoms. There is, however, no doubt whatever that this sometimes occurs. We will not consider this topic further here; it is discussed in detail in this volume in the chapter by Bass (p. 126).

What do neurologists say to their patients?

This subject is usually neglected in reviews of hysteria (Wessely 2000). Here is a sample of the explanations offered by neurologists we have worked with:

- *'The good news is that we have found nothing really bad, and there is no obstacle to you eventually making a good recovery.'*
- *'The parts of the nervous system are all there but they're not connected up right.'*
- *'There may be a tiny patch of inflammation that we can't see on the scan, causing the symptoms.'*
- *'Modern medicine lets you down with these sorts of symptoms.'*
- *'Depression can make symptoms feel ten times worse.'*
- *'Your nervous system is like a car engine that needs tuning even though nothing is broken.'*

Although most of these formulations acknowledge the patient's illness and avoid an unhelpful discussion about mind/body dualism, they illustrate the difficulty of phrasing a diagnosis which can be easily passed on by the patient to someone else. They are no competition for a short label that emphasizes damage, for example, 'cervical spondylosis' or causation, 'wheat allergy'. The search for more satisfying explanations of psychogenic illness to impart to patients, perhaps supported by information leaflets, is well worth pursuing (Thomas and Trimble 1995).

The neurologist's role in treatment

Hysteria is traditionally a disorder diagnosed by neurologists but treated by psychiatrists. This unusual division of labour may help to explain its relative neglect by science. It may also underestimate the therapeutic value of a thorough examination, good rapport, and careful explanation. Contrary to many doctors' beliefs, in a study of what patients suffering from headache want from a consultation, 'explanation' and 'neurological examination' were rated above 'medication' and 'X-rays' (Packard 1979). Other simple manoeuvres used since time immemorial, such as suggesting the symptom will resolve, considering non-specific treatment, and following the patient, may also be important (Kathol 1997). The detection and treatment of depression and anxiety can begin in a neurology consultation, and their recognition may be an important positive prognostic factor (Crimlisk *et al.* 1998). Nevertheless, the neurologist should be willing to call on the help of a liaison psychiatrist, and multidisciplinary treatment is often required. In this domain, as elsewhere, there is a clear need to gather more compelling evidence.

Treatment is discussed more fully in this volume in the chapters by Temple, Chalder, Oakley, and Wade.

Conclusion

Unexplained symptoms are common in neurological practice and exist in protean forms. Their diagnosis depends on:

- the absence of typical features of neurological disease;
- the presence of 'positive signs' of psychiatric disorder — although these should be interpreted with great caution;
- negative relevant investigations;
- the presence of a plausible psychosocial origin for the symptom.

Clinicians should always maintain a critical attitude to the diagnosis of psychiatric disorder, bearing in mind both the limitations of their own individual knowledge of neurological disease and the limitations of our current collective wisdom.

Acknowledgements

We would like to thank Dr Michael Sharpe and Professor Charles Warlow for their helpful comments.

References

Axelrod, S., Noonan, M. and Atanacio, B. (1980). On the laterality of psychogenic somatic symptoms. *Journal of Nervous and Mental Disease*, **168**, 517–25.

Beatty, S. (1999). Non-organic visual loss. *Postgraduate Medical Journal*, **75**, 201–7.

Benjamin, S., Mawer, J. and Lennon, S. (1992). The knowledge and beliefs of family care givers about chronic pain patients. *Journal of Psychosomatic Research*, **36**, 211–17.

Binzer, M., Andersen, P. M. and Kullgren, G. (1997). Clinical characteristics of patients with motor disability due to conversion disorder: a prospective control group study. *Journal of Neurology, Neurosurgery and Psychiatry*, **63**, 83–8.

Bishop, E. R. Jr., Mobley, M. C. and Farr, W. F. Jr. (1978). Lateralization of conversion symptoms. *Comprehensive Psychiatry*, **19**, 393–6.

Bose, S. and Kupersmith, M. J. (1995). Neuro-ophthalmologic presentations of functional visual disorders. *Neurological Clinics*, **13**, 321–39.

Bowman, E. S. and Markand , O. N. (1999). The contribution of life events to pseudoseizure occurrence in adults. *Bulletin of the Menninger Clinic*, **63**, 70–88.

Briquet, P. (1859). *Traité Clinique et Thérapeutique de l'Hysterie*. J. B. Ballière, Paris.

Carson, A. J., Ringbauer, B., Stone, J., McKenzie, L., Warlow, C. and Sharpe, M. (2000). Do medically unexplained symptoms matter? A prospective cohort study of 300 new referrals to neurology outpatient clinics. *Journal of Neurology, Neurosurgery and Psychiatry*, **68**, 207–10.

Carter, A. B. (1949). The prognosis of certain hysterical symptoms. *British Medical Journal*, **i**, 1076–9.

Charcot, J–M. (1889). *Lectures on the Diseases of the Nervous System*. The New Sydenham Society, Paris.

Couprie, W., Wijdicks, E. F., Rooijmans, H. G. and van Gijn, J. (1995). Outcome in conversion disorder: a follow up study. *Journal of Neurology, Neurosurgery and Psychiatry*, **58**, 750–2.

Creed, F., Firth, D., Timol, M., Metcalfe, R. and Pollock, S. (1990). Somatization and illness behaviour in a neurology ward. *Journal of Psychosomatic Research*, **34**, 427–37.

Crimlisk, H. L., Bhatia, K., Cope, H., David, A., Marsden, C. D. and Ron, M. A. (1998). Slater revisited: 6 year follow up study of patients with medically unexplained motor symptoms. *British Medical Journal*, **316**, 582–6.

Deary, I. J., Smart, A. and Wilson, J. A. (1992). Depression and 'hassles' in globus pharyngis. *British Journal of Psychiatry*, **161**, 115–17.

Deary, I. J., Wilson, J. A. and Kelly, S. W. (1995). Globus pharyngis, personality, and psychological distress in the general population. Psychosomatics, *36*:570–7.

Deuschl, G., Koster, B., Lucking, C. H. and Scheidt, C. (1998). Diagnostic and pathophysiological aspects of psychogenic tremors. *Movement Disorders*, **13**, 294–302.

Devinsky, O. and Thacker, K. (1995). Nonepileptic seizures. *Neurological Clinics*, **13**, 299–319.

Ellis, S. J. (1990). Diazepam as a truth drug. *Lancet*, **336**, 752–3.

Ewald, H., Rogne, T., Ewald, K. and Fink, P. (1994). Somatization in patients newly admitted to a neurological department. *Acta Psychiatrica Scandinavica*, **89**, 174–9.

Factor, S. A., Podskalny, G. D. and Molho, E. S. (1995). Psychogenic movement disorders: frequency, clinical profile, and characteristics. *Journal of Neurology, Neurosurgery and Psychiatry*, **59**, 406–12.

Fahn, S. (1994). Psychogenic movement disorders. In *Movement Disorders, Vol. 3* (ed. Marsden, C. D. and Fahn, S.), pp. 359–72. Butterworth–Heinemann, Oxford.

Fahn, S. and Williams, D. T. (1988). Psychogenic dystonia. *Advances in Neurology*, **50**, 431–55.

Fallik, A. and Sigal, M. (1971). Hysteria — the choice of symptom site. *Psychotherapy and Psychosomatics*, **19**, 310–18.

Fitzpatrick, R. and Hopkins, A. (1981). Referrals to neurologists for headaches not due to structural disease. *Journal of Neurology, Neurosurgery and Psychiatry*, **44**, 1061–7.

Fleminger, J. J., McClure, G. M. and Dalton, R. (1980). Lateral response to suggestion in relation to hand edness and the side of psychogenic symptoms. *British Journal of Psychiatry*, **136**, 562–6.

Foong, J., Ridding, M., Cope, H., Marsden, C. D. and Ron, M. A. (1997). Corticospinal function in conversion disorder (letter). *Journal of Neuropsychiatry and Clinical Neuroscience*, **9**, 302–3.

Galin, D., Diamond, R. and Braff, D. (1977). Lateralization of conversion symptoms: more frequent on the left. *American Journal of Psychiatry*, **134**, 578–80.

Gálvez–Jiménez, N. and Lang, A. E. (1997). Psychogenic movement disorders. In *Movement Disorders: Neurologic Principles and Practice* (ed. Watts, R. L. and Koller, W. C.), pp. 715–32. McGraw–Hill, New York.

Gomez, L., Fernand ez, A., Mustelier, R., Calzada, D., Vidal, B. and Telleria, A. (1998). [Evoked motor potentials in the diagnosis of conversion hysteria (letter)]. *Reviews in Neurology*, **26**, 839–40.

Gould, R., Miller, B L., Goldberg, M. A. and Benson, D. F. (1986). The validity of hysterical signs and symptoms. *Journal of Nervous and Mental Disease*, **174**, 593–7.

Gowers, W. R. (1892). Hysteria. In *A Manual of Diseases of the Nervous System*, pp. 903–60. Churchill, London.

Hamilton, J., Campos, R. and Creed, F. (1996). Anxiety, depression and management of medically unexplained symptoms in medical clinics. *Journal of the Royal College of Physicians of London*, **30**, 18–20.

Hansen, M., Sindrup, S. H., Christensen, P. B., Olsen, N. K., Kristensen, O. and Friis, M. L. (1994). Interobserver variation in the evaluation of neurological signs: observer dependent factors. *Acta Neurologica Scandinavica*, **90**, 145–9.

Harris, M. B., Deary, I. J. and Wilson, J. A. (1996). Life events and difficulties in relation to the onset of globus pharyngis. *Journal of Psychosomatic Research*, **40**, 603–15.

Haughton, P. M., Lewsley, A., Wilson, M. and Williams, R. G. (1979). A forced-choice procedure to detect feigned or exaggerated hearing loss. *British Journal of Audiology*, **13**, 135–8.

Head, H. (1922). The diagnosis of hysteria. *British Medical Journal*, **i**, 827–9.

Jellinek, D. A., Bradford, R., Bailey, I. and Symon, L. (1992). The role of motor evoked potentials in the management of hysterical paraplegia. *Paraplegia*, **30**, 300–2.

Joyce, J., Hotopf, M. and Wessely, S. (1997). The prognosis of chronic fatigue and chronic fatigue syndrome: a systematic review. *Quarterly Journal of Medicine*, **90**, 223–33.

Kathol, R. G. (1997). Reassurance therapy: what to say to symptomatic patients with benign or non-existent medical disease. *International Journal of Psychiatry in Medicine*, **27**, 173–80.

Kathol, R. G., Cox, T. A., Corbett, J. J., Thompson, H. S. and Clancy, J. (1983). Functional visual loss: I. A true psychiatric disorder? *Psychological Medicine*, **13**, 307–14.

Keane, J. R. (1989). Hysterical gait disorders: 60 cases. *Neurology*, **39**, 586–9.

Kim, Y. J., Pakiam, A. S. and Lang, A. E. (1999). Historical and clinical features of psychogenic tremor: a review of 70 cases. *Canadian Journal of Neurological Sciences*, **26**, 190–5.

Knutsson, E. and Martensson, A. (1985). Isokinetic measurements of muscle strength in hysterical paresis. *Electroencephalography and Clinical Neurophysiology*, **61**, 370–4.

Koller, W. *et al.* (1989). Psychogenic tremors. *Neurology*, **39**, 1094–9.

Lang, A. E. (1995). Psychogenic dystonia: a review of 18 cases. *Canadian Journal of Neurological Sciences*, **22**, 136–43.

Lang, A. E., Koller, W. C. and Fahn, S. (1995). Psychogenic parkinsonism. *Archives of Neurology*, **52**, 802–10.

Lempert, T., Brand t, T., Dieterich, M. and Huppert, D. (1991). How to identify psychogenic disorders of stance and gait. A video study in 37 patients. *Journal of Neurology*, **238**, 140–6.

Lempert, T., Dieterich, M., Huppert, D. and Brand t, T. (1990). Psychogenic disorders in neurology: frequency and clinical spectrum. *Acta Neurologica Scand inavica*, **82**, 335–40.

Lewis, W. C. and Berman, M. (1965). Studies of conversion hysteria. *Archives of General Psychiatry*, **13**, 275–82.

Lindley, R. I., Warlow, C. P., Wardlaw, J. M., Dennis, M. S., Slattery, J. and Sand ercock, P. A. (1993). Interobserver reliability of a clinical classification of acute cerebral infarction. *Stroke*, **24**, 1801–4.

Lishman, W. A. (1998). *Organic Psychiatry: The Psychological Consequences of Cerebral Disorder.* Blackwell Science, Oxford.

Ljungberg, L. (1957). Hysteria: a clinical, prognostic and genetic study. *Acta Psychiatrica Neurologica Scand inavica*, **Suppl. 112**, 1–162.

Mace, C. J. and Trimble, M. R. (1991). 'Hysteria', 'functional' or 'psychogenic'? A survey of British neurologists' preferences. *Journal of the Royal Society of Medicine*, **84**, 471–5.

Mace, C. J. and Trimble, M. R. (1996). Ten-year prognosis of conversion disorder. *British Journal of Psychiatry*, **169**, 282–8.

Magee, K. R. (1962). Hysterical hemiplegia and hemianaesthesia. *Postgraduate Medicine*, **31**, 339–45.

Marsden, C. D. (1986). Hysteria — a neurologist's view. *Psychological Medicine*, **16**, 277–88.

Merskey, H. and Buhrich, N. A. (1975). Hysteria and organic brain disease. *British Journal of Medical Psychology*, **48**, 359–66.

Meyer, B–U. *et al.* (1992). Motor response evoked by magnetic brain stimulation in psychogenic limb weakness: diagnostic value and limitations. *Journal of Neurology*, **239**, 251–5.

Miller, B. W. (1973). A review of practical tests for ocular malingering and hysteria. *Survey of Ophthalmology*, **17**, 241–6.

Miller, E. (1986). Detecting hysterical sensory symptoms: an elaboration of the forced choice technique. *British Journal of Clinical Psychology*, **25(Pt 3)**, 231–2.

Monday, K. and Jankovic, J. (1993). Psychogenic myoclonus. *Neurology*, **43**, 349–52.

Morota, N., Deletis, V., Kiprovski, K., Epstein, F. and Abbott, R. (1994). The use of motor evoked potentials in the diagnosis of psychogenic quadriparesis. A case study. *Pediatric Neurosurgery*, **20**, 203–6.

Mullges, W., Ferbert, A. and Buchner, H. (1991). [Transcranial magnetic stimulation in psychogenic paralysis.] *Nervenarzt*, **62**, 349–53.

O'Sullivan, G., Harvey, I., Bass, C., Sheehy, M., Toone, B. and Turner, S. (1992). Psychophysiological investigations of patients with unilateral symptoms in the hyperventilation syndrome. *British Journal of Psychiatry*, **160**, 664–7.

Packard, R. C. (1979). What does the headache patient want? *Headache*, **19**, 370–4.

Pascuzzi, R. M. (1994). Nonphysiological (functional) unilateral motor and sensory syndromes involve the left more often than the right body. *Journal of Nervous and Mental Disease*, **182**, 118–20.

Perkin, G. D. (1989). An analysis of 7836 successive new outpatient referrals. *Journal of Neurology, Neurosurgery and Psychiatry*, **52**, 447–8.

Pillai, J. J., Markind, S., Streletz, L. J., Field, H. L. and Herbison, G. (1992). Motor evoked potentials in psychogenic paralysis. *Neurology*, **42**, 935–6.

Raskin, M., Talbott, J. A. and Meyerson, A. T. (1966). Diagnosis of conversion reactions. Predictive value of psychiatric criteria. *Journal of the American Medical Association*, **197**, 530–4.

Reed, J. L. (1975). The diagnosis of 'hysteria'. *Psychological Medicine*, **5**, 13–17.

Reynolds, J. R. (1869). Paralysis and other disorders of motion and sensation dependent on idea. *British Medical Journal*, **i**, 483–5.

Rolak, L. A. (1988). Psychogenic sensory loss. *Journal of Nervous and Mental Disease*, **176**, 686–7.

Rothwell, P. (1994). Investigation of unilateral sensory or motor symptoms: frequency of neurological pathology depends on side of symptoms. *Journal of Neurology, Neurosurgery and Psychiatry*, **57**, 1401–2.

Roy, A. (1977). Cerebral disease and hysteria. *Comprehensive Psychiatry*, **18**, 607–9.

Slater, E. T. (1965). Diagnosis of 'hysteria'. *British Medical Journal*, **i**, 1395–9.

Slater, J. D., Brown, M. C., Jacobs, W. and Ramsay, R. E. (1995). Induction of pseudoseizures with intravenous saline placebo. *Epilepsia*, **36**, 580–5.

Stam, J. (1999). [Physical diagnostics — tendon reflexes]. *Nederlands Tijdschrift voor Geneeskunde*, **143**, 848–51.

Stefansson, J. G., Messina, J. A. and Meyerowitz, S. (1976). Hysterical neurosis, conversion type: clinical and epidemiological considerations. *Acta Psychiatrica Scandinavica*, **53**, 119–38.

Stern, D. B. (1977). Hand edness and the lateral distribution of conversion reactions. *Journal of Nervous and Mental Disease*, **164**, 122–8.

Terada, K. *et al.* (1995). Presence of Bereitschaftspotential preceding psychogenic myoclonus: clinical application of jerk-locked back averaging. *Journal of Neurology, Neurosurgery and Psychiatry*, **58**, 745–7.

Thomas, L. and Trimble, M. R. (1995). *A Patient's Guide to Non-epileptic Seizures*. Wrightson Biomedical Publishing, Petersfield.

Trimble, M. R. (1981). Liaison psychiatry with special reference to neurological units. In *Neuropsychiatry*. John Wiley & Sons, Chichester.

Wessely, S. (2000). To tell or not to tell? The problem of medically unexplained symptoms. In *Ethical Dilemmas in Neurology* (ed. Zeman, A. and Emmanuel, L.), pp. 41–53. W. B. Saunders, London.

Wessely, S., Nimnuan, C. and Sharpe, M. (1999). Functional somatic syndromes: one or many? *Lancet*, **354**, 936–9.

White, A., Corbin, D. O. and Coope, B. (1988). The use of thiopentone in the treatment of non-organic locomotor disorders. *Journal of Psychosomatic Research*, **32**, 249–53.

Wilson, J. A., Deary, I. J., Scott, S. and MacKenzie, K. (1995). Functional dysphonia. *British Medical Journal*, **311**, 1039–40.

Ziv, I., Djaldetti, R., Zoldan, Y., Avraham, M. and Melamed, E. (1998). Diagnosis of 'non-organic' limb paresis by a novel objective motor assessment: the quantitative Hoover's test. *Journal of Neurology*, **245**, 797–802.

9 Factitious disorders and malingering

Christopher Bass

In this chapter, the validity of the diagnostic criteria for factitious disorders provided by DSM–IV is questioned, and the difficulties inherent in measuring or inferring motivational drives or intentions of deceptive individuals are highlighted. Because pathological lying (pseudologia fantastica) is often a key component in factitious illness, it is argued that identification of this should be actively sought by the clinician. The characteristics of pseudologia fantastica are outlined, and its important associations (in some patients) with central nervous system dysfunction noted. Malingering in a clinical or medico-legal context is difficult to establish, and methods of clinical assessment of malingered physical complaints and cognitive deficits are described. Finally, the complex relationships between malingering, factitious illness, and hysteria are outlined, and the recent interest in accounts of self-deception are described. It is argued that patients with conversion hysteria are self-deceived, whereas those who malinger 'know' the truth and are intent on the deception of others.

Introduction

Factitious disorders

Factitious disorders are characterized by 'physical or psychological symptoms that are intentionally produced or feigned in order to assume the sick role' (American Psychiatric Association, 1994). The judgement that a particular symptom is intentionally produced is made both by direct evidence and by excluding other causes of the symptom. In factitious disorder, the motivation for producing the symptom is deemed to be a psychological need to assume the sick role, as evidenced by 'an absence of external incentives for the disorder' (American Psychiatric Association, 1994).

Factitious disorders are distinguished from acts of malingering. In malingering, although the individual also produces the symptoms intentionally, he or she is thought to have a goal that is obviously recognizable (to the clinician) when the environmental circumstances are known (American Psychiatric Association, 1994) — for example, the intentional production of symptoms to avoid jury duty or conscription into the army. In clinical practice however it is not always easy to differentiate between these disorders.

Diagnostic issues

How valid is the diagnosis of factitious disorder (FD)? Can the degree of 'intentionality' be measured, or even attributed to another on the basis of their behaviour? When does an internal goal become an external goal? What is the relevance and relationship of factitious disorder and malingering to hysterical conversion? These are key questions and I will attempt to address them in this chapter.

First, how reliable is a diagnosis of factitious disorder? It has been suggested that patients with FD consciously fabricate symptoms but are unaware of their motivation to do so. But Jonas and Pope (1985) suggested that impossible questions about voluntariness and consciousness be abandoned in favour of phenomenological research into biological factors, treatment, and outcome in dissimulating patients. More recently, Cunnien (1997) confirmed that these questions of intentionality and motivation are likely to evade any objective assessment, and he called into question the validity and reliability of the diagnostic criteria used in psychiatric glossaries. He also pointed out that much of the clinical information about these patients was based on single-case reports from deceptive patients, and was therefore likely to be unreliable. He argued that the pitfalls of diagnosing factitious disorders by DSM–IV were as follows: the clinician must determine *conscious* production of symptoms, based upon *unconscious* motives, in an *uncooperative* patient.

Rogers *et al.* (1989) have also highlighted the seemingly intractable difficulties in unravelling the motivational drives of deceptive individuals on the basis of the artificial dichotomization (to be or not to be a patient). Most individuals are unlikely to know their motivations, as in the patient with evident factitious behaviour who, following confrontation, subsequently asked, 'What if it is true?' (Spivak *et al.*, 1994). Thus, the specific motivations for 'factitious presentation' *may never be knowable*. If this is the case, then the attempt to differentiate between FD and malingering is futile.

Furthermore, the theory that intrapsychic phenomena alone would account for a complex set of interpersonal behaviours is not a sufficient explanation. In DSM–IV (American Psychiatric Association, 1994) there is a requirement for 'evidence of an *intrapsychic* need to maintain the sick role' in FD, whereas malingering is assumed to be motivated by *external* incentives, many of which have clear biological benefit, for example, avoiding prison. As a consequence, clinicians tend to lean towards assigning a label of malingering as opposed to FD or hysteria if obvious gains and incentives are apparent to them. But this latter criterion is dependent, to a large extent, on the judgement, training, and reaction of the clinician. For example, if a patient with fabricated skin lesions carries out this behaviour to remain an invalid, so that her husband will not leave her, is this an external incentive? If so, then this woman is malingering and should not be characterized as having an artefactual skin disorder (Kalivar, 1996).

It is also worth noting that the diagnosis of FD appears to be based on the assumption that such motivation for dissimulation, whether intrapsychic or not, is necessarily maladaptive. An alternative view is that such dissimulation could also be an adaptive approach to overwhelming intrapersonal or interpersonal problems. For example, a single mother with financial problems may find that her fabricated (yet undiagnosed) symptoms produce considerable welfare benefits and practical support.

Because of these methodological problems it has been argued that the rationale that underlies and informs the diagnostic criteria for FD is, at present, 'logically indefensible and empirically unfounded' (Rogers *et al.*, 1989). It is difficult not to disagree with this assertion. Neither is it possible to implement with any degree of reliability the diagnostic criteria provided by DSM–IV.

If it is not possible for the clinician to either infer or measure the motivational drives or intentions of deceptive individuals with FD, is there any more reliable way in which the diagnosis can be established? Are there any 'prototypical' or even biological features of the disorder that can be assessed with more reliability than measuring 'intrapsychic needs'?

One method that has clinical (and medico-legal) utility is to establish whether the reported symptoms are bona fide; that is, is the patient telling the truth? This may involve extensive interviews of the patient, the patient's family (if available), and any other informants and careful scrutiny of the hospital and GP notes. Because these patients often engage in pathological lying (pseudologia fantastica), establishing this fact may be more helpful than attempting to quantify the degree of 'voluntariness' or 'motivation' to attain the sick role (however the sick role is defined). The relation between FD, malingering, and hysteria will be addressed later in the section on malingering, but at this stage an account of pathological lying and its importance in establishing a diagnosis of FD will be described.

Pathological lying (pseudologia fantastica)

It is possible to identify pathological lying if the clinician has sufficient medical information at his or her disposal (most often the medical notes). If the patient reports, for example, that they have chronic renal failure or have recently recovered from leukaemia, when there is evidence that contradicts this, then this suggests dissimulation. On some occasions patients will even admit to lying, although this is very rare. When it does occur it must, by definition, be suspect.

Because pseudologia fantastica (PF) is often a key component in factitious disorders, evidence for it should be actively sought by the clinician. PF is a descriptive term of a form of behaviour that is sometimes associated with fabricated medical illness. (It is not *specifically* related to the medical setting, and can also occur in a variety of forensic settings, for example, imposture.) Pathological lies are distinguished from 'normal' lies by a number of characteristics (see Table 9.1). In general, lying becomes pathological when it is considered maladaptive or destructive to the quality of life of the person involved. A good example of the pervasive and self-destructive nature of pathological lying is demonstrated in the following fragment of a letter written by a patient to a psychiatrist colleague seeking help for her condition:

> I am very much afraid I am someone who, over the years, has invented a number of illnesses, a couple of them very serious. I don't know if this is what people call 'Munchausen's Syndrome' — but when I try to discover more about it (by trying to look up references on the internet), it sounded more like what was called 'Factitious Disorder'. But I don't go

Table 9.1 Pseudologia fantastica

- not determined by situational factors
- presumed that unconscious factors predominate
- 'kernel' of truth embedded in matrix of falsehoods
- compulsive
- fantastic (often self-aggrandizing)
- recurrent and often enduring
- destructive to the quality of life of the liar
- can be ego dystonic
- underlying motive to gain attention from others
- when confronted the patient can acknowledge falsehoods

round hospitals and try and get lots of admissions and operations, and I don't seek medical attention per se. What I have rather done is to lie on several occasions to gain attention from friends and others, and then fabricated medical letters etc., in order to get treated to support my lies. I have also harmed myself to support my lies. On at least one occasion, I invented an extremely serious illness, for which I received very dangerous treatment.

My reason for trying to find out more is not some morbid fascination but because I am *desperate* to try and get help. I despise myself for all the things I have done, and have continually tried to stop what is like an addiction.

This correspondence illustrates the compulsive quality of the lying, and hints at its motive — to gain attention from friends and medical practitioners. It also suggests that it is at times ego dystonic.

Pathological lying should be distinguished from confabulation, which has been described as 'a falsification of memory occurring in clear consciousness in association with an organically derived amnesia' (Lishman, 1998, p. 31). There is general agreement that confirmed or suspected damage to the frontal lobe and/or related structures is frequently connected with confabulation (Dalla Barba, 1993). A rare form of 'fantastic confabulation' has been described however, in which a sustained and grandiose theme is elaborated, usually describing far-fetched adventures and experiences which clearly have not taken place at any time. This kind of persistent and extraordinary confabulation has been linked to the presence of frontal lobe problems, in addition to memory problems (Stuss *et al.*, 1978). Pseudologia can be distinguished from confabulation of this type however by two factors: (1) the absence of an appreciable memory deficit in most cases; and (2) the tales that the fantastic confabulator tells are not 'durable' as are those of the pseudologue (Berlyne, 1972).

There have been very few systematic studies of patients with PF. In a review of 72 cases collected from 26 reports since 1891, King and Ford (1988) highlighted a number of characteristics, which are shown in Table 9.2. They found that 40 per cent had evidence of central nervous system dysfunction, and they suggested that it was the pseudologia, and not the factitious disorder per se, that was associated with brain dysfunction (see p. 131). Others have pointed out the overlap between PF, impostership (the assumption of a false identity), and factitious disorder (Hardie and Reed, 1998). These latter authors pointed out that PF and impostership share the common feature of an intentional goal that involves deception. They believed that deliberate *deception for psychological reasons* was the core feature of factitious illnesses, and argued for the inclusion of a 'deception syndrome' with various behavioural manifestations in psychiatric glossaries. This would overcome the current exclusion of PF and impostership with psychological origins from existing diagnostic systems.

Table 9.2 Characteristics of patients with pseudologia fantastica

- age of onset — 16 years
- 40% have CNS abnormalities
- 50% suffer pathological wandering
- 25% simulate illness
- 20% simulate illness and wander

What motivates such behaviour? The grandiose ideas and behaviours may be used to counter profound feelings of unworthiness and emptiness. They also evoke the response of a care giver in a safe and structured setting (Spivak *et al.*, 1994). A patient may be seeking an escape from stressful life situations or trying to compensate for developmental traumas. Often patients with factitious disorder enact past and present developmental disturbances within the medical setting. For example, the patient or a member of his family may have suffered at the hands of a physician.

Clinical features

Notwithstanding these nosological problems, what are the defining clinical features of patients with factitious disorders? Because the clinical presentations are diverse, attempts to sub-type patients have not always been helpful. One characteristic of the Munchausen 'sub-type' is a triad of pathological lying, pathological wandering (moving from town to town), with the presentation of dramatic complaints (Bursten, 1965). Most clinical series however do not conform to this stereotype of an antisocial, socially rootless male. The majority of patients with factitious physical disorder are socially conformist young women (often nurses) with less dramatic symptoms and relatively stable social networks (Carney, 1980; Eisendrath, 1996).

Factitious disorders typically begin before the age of 30 years (Sutherland and Rodin, 1990; Hengeveld, 1992). There are often prodromal behaviours in childhood and adolescence (see under 'aetiology'). These individuals often report an unexpectedly large number of childhood illnesses and operations, and many have some association with the health care field (Reich and Gottfried, 1983). High rates of substance abuse, mood disorder, and borderline personality disorder have been reported.

Factitious disorder in patients with physical illness

It is important to be aware that factitious illness can also occur in patients with co-existing physical diseases, and this combination can lead to dramatic medical emergencies. For example, patients with brittle diabetes are usually young females under 30 years old who deliberately interfere with their treatment, causing unstable diabetic control (Kent *et al.*, 1994). A syndrome of severely unstable asthma ('brittle asthma') which also affects young females has recently been described (Barnes and Chung, 1989). Such patients can neglect to take medication at appropriate times and then ignore adequate management of the potentially dangerous consequences. This may lead to repeated admissions to hospital with medical emergencies such as diabetic ketoacidosis, status asthmaticus, or even pseudostatus (simulated status epilepticus) (Howell *et al.*, 1989).

Epidemiology

Factitious disorders are relatively uncommon but probably under-diagnosed. Prevalence depends on clinical setting and the investigators' 'index of suspicion'. Of 1288 liaison psychiatric consecutive referrals in a US general hospital, 0.8 per cent had FD

(Sutherland and Rodin, 1990). Similar figures have been reported by Dutch investigators (Hengeveld, 1992).

The best epidemiological studies however relate to specific symptoms examined under careful conditions. For example, 3.5 per cent of patients with, respectively, fever of unknown origin and urinary calculi were shown to have symptoms that were factitious in origin (Knockaert et al., 1992; Gault et al., 1988). Of 1644 patients with chronic wounds referred to a surgical unit over a 2.5 year period, nine had a diagnosis of FD as the main aetiological factor in non-healing wounds — an incidence of 0.5 per cent (Baragwanath and Harding, 1996). A similar prevalence (0.3 per cent) was reported in a consecutive series of patients admitted to a neurological hospital with 'neurological' syndromes (Bauer and Boegner, 1996)

Aetiology

Most information on aetiology is based on a number of case series and case studies. A number of themes are however apparent (Hyler and Sussman, 1981; Lawrie et al., 1993):

Developmental:
- Parental abuse, neglect, or abandonment.
- Early experiences of chronic illness or hospitalization.

Medically related:
- A significant relationship with a physician in the past.
- Experiences of medical mismanagement leading to a grudge against doctors.
- Paramedical employment.

Physical disease:
- Organic brain disorder (see below).

Evidence of neurological abnormalities

Although there has been an emphasis on psychodynamic and behavioural issues in the literature on Munchausen's syndrome, there is increasing evidence that some patients do show evidence of brain damage (Barker, 1962; Enoch and Trethowan, 1979; Fenelon et al., 1991; Lawrie et al., 1993; Diefenbacher and Heim, 1997). However, evidence of brain damage per se cannot fully explain the behaviour. It is thought that PF, and not the factitious disorder per se, is associated with brain dysfunction — though such a distinction may be difficult to support in clinical practice.

Pankratz and Lezak (1987) described five cases who appeared intellectually intact because of excellent verbal skills but on formal neuropsychological testing showed deficits in conceptual organization, management of complex information, and judgement. In their clinical experience of some 25 patients, about one in three had evidence of serious brain dysfunction, but the authors could not identify a relationship between the onset of Munchausen's behaviour and the development of brain dysfunction.

They proposed that subtle but important neuropsychological impairment may contribute to Munchausen's syndrome and suggested that pseudologia may be the product of the illogical reasoning and verbal disinhibition known in patients with dysfunction of the non-dominant and frontal lobes. Pankratz (1981) also pointed out that patients with damage to the right hemisphere showed defects in organization, fragmented awareness, and illogicality without generally impaired verbal reasoning on pathological lying. It is worth noting that early-onset prefrontal damage is associated with defective social and moral reasoning. Anderson *et al.* (1999) recently described two patients with lesions in the prefrontal cortex occurring before 16 months: both patients displayed chronic, persistent, and motiveless lying as adolescents and adults (as well as a number of other antisocial traits).

Although brain damage is neither necessary nor sufficient to explain FD, there is evidence that a significant proportion of Munchausen patients are suffering from organic brain disorder. Indeed, the syndrome shares much in common with potential sequelae of fronto-temporal damage, particularly in the right hemisphere (Pankratz, 1981). These findings have important implications for management: if there is a past history of neuropsychiatric abnormality, such as traumatic brain injury, perinatal damage, or developmental disorder, then screening for evidence of brain dysfunction should be considered (Diefenberger and Heim, 1997). Clinicians should not be discouraged from seeking a potentially treatable disorder because of such patients' often incomprehensible utterances and behaviour (Lawrie *et al.*, 1993).

Course and prognosis

Factitious disorders may be limited to one or more brief episodes, but are usually chronic. For example, of 10 patients identified in a general hospital setting and followed up, at least one was known to have died as a result of factitious behaviour four months after the index admission (Sutherland and Rodin, 1990). Only one of the remaining nine patients accepted psychiatric treatment after discharge from hospital. Other authors have however reported a less gloomy outcome (Reich and Gottfried, 1983). Outcome may be determined by how the patients are managed, once their deceptions become manifest. Psychological support following hospital discharge may be associated with improved outcome (Reich and Gottfried, 1983). Non-wanderers with more stable social networks may have a better prognosis than wanderers (Carney, 1980).

Ethical and legal issues in factitious illness

The doctor–patient relationship becomes very difficult when it assumes that deceit is a motive of the patient. Patients with FDs create a number of unique ethical and medico-legal issues for physicians and other health care professionals. First, should the physician break confidentiality, especially if the patient's behaviour leads to risks for others? Second, if the diagnosis is incorrect the patient may sue the physician (and the hospital that employs him or her) for wrongful diagnosis. Third, if the patient is a health care worker (and more than half are) then there will be important implications for that person's employment. It is good practice therefore to convene a multidisciplinary staff meeting involving doctors, nurses, and medico-legal representatives when FD is suspected. This can help to develop a management policy and share responsibility for difficult decisions about employment and other issues (see below).

There has also been debate about carrying out room searches, diagnostic studies, and secret surveillance without informed consent. Some physicians consider that such behaviour infringes patients' rights and that none of these activities should be carried out without the patient's knowledge and consent. One way of avoiding this dilemma is to make it clear to the patient that FD is among the differential diagnoses, and then request permission for a room search or special diagnostic test. If needles or syringes are discovered during the course of treating the patient, the ethical issue of invasion of privacy does not arise.

Because the patient with FD may engage in behaviour that leads to permanent maiming or even death, it has been argued that in such cases a compulsory order may be used to protect the patient from himself or herself. This will provide time for not only a more in-depth psychiatric assessment but also the development of a more trusting relationship with a therapist. This is a contentious subject, but some case reports do indicate that extended involuntary hospitalization may result in therapeutic progress (O'Shea *et al.*, 1984).

Management

It is regrettable that by the time the diagnosis has been established the doctor–patient relationship may have become irreparably damaged: negative emotions in the doctor may need to be dealt with before any consideration can be given to 'engaging' the patient in any therapeutic endeavour. Ethical and legal issues may also intrude (see p. 132) and have an impact on management. Despite these obstacles a variety of treatment approaches have been attempted, and some of these will be described. The primary approach to treatment rests with psychological interventions. These can be divided into confrontational and non-confrontational strategies.

Confrontational approaches

The approach to the patient during confrontation and thereafter should be non-punitive and supportive, stressing continuity of care and the recognition that the patient is a sick person who needs help. Following such indirect confrontations roughly one third of patients have been shown to end their deceptions. They vigorously denied what they were doing, but if they were given face-saving explanations, the behaviour stopped — at least for a time (Reich and Gottfried, 1983). An example of such follows (29-year-old nurse in a US hospital with a self-induced septic artritis of the knee):

> 'Instead of different doctors seeing you at different times, we thought we would all see you together today. We know it's been difficult for you considering the pain and the length of your hospitalisation. It's been difficult for us also, trying to figure out how best to help you. You have been a very good patient, putting up all these tests, and we've been good doctors, examining everything we could. In any good relationship, whether it be among friends, couples, or a doctor and a patient, the most destructive thing there can be is a conspiracy of silence. That's when one partner keeps silent and doesn't talk about her

feelings to the other partner. We've had too good a relationship to let this conspiracy of silence continue. That's why we are going to tell you what we think.'

'We believe you are doing this to yourself. [Minimal protest from patient.] I don't want this to be a trial with evidence, a prosecutor, and a defense, but we must tell you how we feel. We will continue your antibiotics for the infection and the analgesics for the pain. We will continue to see you every day. We'll begin rehabilitation to strengthen your knee. When this quiets down, we will follow you as an outpatient.' Following this exchange we added, 'we'll be back a little later to see how you're feeling'. (Guziec *et al.*, 1994)

Non-confrontational strategies

These approaches, advocated by Eisendrath (1989), are less concerned with the origin of the illness and more with shaping future behaviours. The face-saving aspect of the treatment is a key element, and it is important for the patient to subsequently explain their 'recoveries' without admitting that their original problems were psychiatric.

Another face-saving approach is the use of 'inexact interpretations'. This involves suggesting to the patient a relationship between certain events or stressors (for example, being abandoned) and the emergence of the factitious symptoms. The technique involves presenting the patient with a brief formulation of the problem which stops short of overtly identifying the factitious origin. By avoiding confrontation the doctor makes it safe for the patient to relinquish the symptom with a feeling of control. Regrettably, none of these non-confrontational techniques have been evaluated in a systematic fashion.

Systemic interventions

Patients with FDs often elicit negative and hostile emotions in general hospital staff, especially after the deception has been exposed. The psychiatrist can help staff members to ventilate and reduce the anger they experience when a factitious diagnosis is confirmed and to understand the likely mechanisms underlying the factitious behaviour. These issues are often best addressed at a multidisciplinary staff meeting. The major task of this group, which should include a member of the hospital medico-legal department as well as the patient's family doctor, is to develop practical treatment guidelines and to discuss the complex legal and ethical issues raised with factitious physical disorders. Some of these issues have already been discussed.

Malingering and exaggeration

Introduction

Malingering is the deliberate simulation or exaggeration of physical or psychiatric symptoms for obvious and understandable gain such as monetary compensation, disabled status, and avoidance of criminal prosecution or conscription. The incidence of malingering cannot be assessed accurately because it overlaps with a host of everyday behaviours, for example, making excuses to avoid social functions. Malingering can co-occur with conversion disorders, personality disorders, and factitial behaviour. In this section, malingered physical symptoms will be given precedence.

Definition

Malingering is not coded as a mental disorder in either International Classification. However, DSM–IV (American Psychiatric Association, 1994) states that the:

> . . . essential feature of malingering is the intentional production of false or grossly exaggerated physical or psychological symptoms, motivated by external incentives such as avoiding military duty, avoiding work, avoiding financial compensation, evading criminal prosecution, or obtaining drugs.

But ICD–10 (World Health Organisation, 1992) and DSM–IV choose to list it under Z76.5 'person encountering health services in other circumstances' and V65.2 'additional conditions that may be a focus of clinical attention' respectively. This suggests that malingering is to be conceptualized as a behaviour (not as a diagnosis or illness) which can be manifest in any individual whether or not he is ill.

Malingered physical disease

Malingering is the feigning of disease when it does not exist at all in a particular patient. It also involves the attribution by one person of another's intention(s). Partial malingering is the exaggeration of existing symptoms or the fraudulent allegation that prior genuine symptoms are still present. Malingering is probably uncommon, whereas exaggeration of symptoms is quite common, especially in medico-legal contexts (Trimble, 1981). A common example is a patient with chronic neck or back pain, often sustained after a road traffic accident or injury at work, who is involved in litigation or seeking disability payment. Although the initial physical injury is not in doubt, the length and severity of symptoms, subsequent disability, and distress is usually out of proportion to the relevant organic findings, and may raise the possibility of malingering or simply low pain tolerance.

In patients with persistent pain or loss of function after an injury that cannot be explained by organic pathology, the differential diagnosis includes malingering, conversion disorder (CD), and persistent somatoform pain disorder. In spite of this there is no reliable method for detecting malingering in patients with chronic pain (Fishbain *et al.*, 1999). In contrast to the malingerer, the person with CD is considered to have a psychiatric disorder, and if this can be shown to be caused by a particular injury, then it is compensable (see Jones' chapter in this volume, p. 155; and Cole, 1970). For example, if a man developed hysterical paralysis of the legs (conversion disorder) after a frightening road traffic accident in which he was not physically injured, the disability would be causally linked to the accident. The key assumption here is that the paralysis is neither voluntary nor a deliberate choice for the injured victim.

There are some behavioural characteristics that may assist in the differential diagnosis between malingering and CD (Resnick, 1997). These include:

1. The malingerer often presents as sullen, suspicious, uncooperative, and resentful. By contrast, patients with CD are more likely to be co-operative and even dependent.
2. The malingerer may try to avoid examination, unless it is required as a condition for receiving some financial benefit. By contrast, the patient with CD welcomes examinations and appears anxious to be cured.

3. The malingerer is more likely than the patient with CD to refuse employment that could be handled in spite of some disability.

4. The malingerer is likely to give every detail of the accident and its sequelae; the patient with CD is more likely to give an account that contains gaps, inaccuracies, and vague generalized complaints.

Malingering and the medico-legal context

Comparatively little is known about the prevalence of malingering in patients involved in personal injury claims, apart from highly selected sub-groups of litigants (Trimble, 1981). In a recent prospective study of 96 road accident victims, Bryant *et al.* (1997) found little evidence of malingering: the vast majority had genuine psychosocial problems. There was no evidence that subjects exaggerated their losses; many preferred not to claim or to settle early. Neither was there evidence that settlement was followed by significant change in clinical state. Indeed, subjects were often more concerned with recognition of their distress and suffering than with the size of financial settlements. These findings suggest that there is a higher prevalence of dissimulation in a small number of (highly selected) patients who become involved in contested legal proceedings.

There is a perception that both physical and psychological symptoms after injury are being maintained by the thought of financial reward. But there is little evidence to support the view that such patients invariably become pain-free and resume work within months of the resolution of their claim. On the contrary, up to 75 per cent of those receiving compensation after injury may fail to return to gainful employment two years after legal settlement (Mendelson, 1995).

Continued incapacity despite apparent medical recovery after an injury may be due to several factors other than malingering. Physical injury and pain can provoke a crisis in predisposed individuals, characterized by a breakdown of the more mature coping mechanisms. Injured patients may become totally dependent on their families, doctors, and lawyers, even though they were formally quite autonomous. Injury that leads to disability can be a challenge to one's self concept as a mature person and a fundamental threat to one's sense of personal worth. One reaction to such a stress is to abandon ambition and adopt a more infantile, dependent way of life. The patient's family may become over-protective and unwittingly reinforce the development of such an invalid lifestyle (Tarsh and Royston, 1985).

In some Western countries the medico-legal process is considered to have some bearing on the evolution of medically unexplained symptoms after potentially compensable injuries. For example, in Lithuania, very few car drivers and passengers are covered by insurance and there is little awareness among the general public about the potentially disabling consequences of a whiplash neck injury following a rear-end collision. As a consequence, it has been argued that chronic neck symptoms are not usually caused by car accidents; rather, expectation of disability and attribution of pre-existing symptoms to the trauma may be more important determinants of the late whiplash syndrome (Schrader *et al.*, 1996).

Clinical assessment of malingered physical complaints

It has been suggested that there are only two situations in which a diagnosis can be confirmed with certainty:

1. When malingerers are caught in the act of moving the supposed paralysed limb when they think they are unobserved; (the most common means is by covert video surveillance used by lawyers or insurance companies).

2. When malingerers confess (although such an event should alert the clinician to the patient's motivation).

Therefore, unless the clinician has very strong evidence, it is usually best to state that a firm conclusion is not possible.

The main methods used to confirm the diagnosis are observation and inference (LoPiccolo *et al.*, 1999). The observational method involves either (1) controlled environment observation or (2) covert 'real-world' surveillance. Controlled environment observation is probably more useful because it depends on a number of sources (for example, the multidisciplinary team) and a range of patient-initiated activities, conversations, and abilities. For example, there is often a breakdown of the vigilance needed to maintain a deception under the constant observation of a multidisciplinary observation. A malingered limp might disappear when a tired, forgetful malingering in-patient goes to the bathroom at 3 a.m. — a time when one might expect an increase in such a deficit. Unlike hysterical symptoms, the complaints of malingerers can rarely be sustained continuously; for this reason, discreet and prolonged observation will usually provide useful information.

Covert, real-world surveillance is most useful when physical disabilities are claimed. It is most definitive when supported by several instances of documentation of the denied ability. It is used by insurance companies and, rarely, in specific clinical settings, for example, detection of mothers carrying out factitious illness by proxy (Southall *et al.*, 1997).

Inferential methods of confirming a suspicion of malingering require carefully detailed documentation and observations on frequent occasions. An example of this would be a patient with chronic low back pain who successfully maintains his or her household without any assistance, does laundry for several children, and lives in a three-storey house while claiming disability payments.

Malingered cognitive deficits

It has been estimated that as many as 33–60 per cent of patients seen in neuropsychology clinics in the US are feigning cognitive deficits (Greiffenstein *et al.*, 1994). If this figure is correct, then the financial costs of malingering to the health care system must be substantial.

Schmand *et al.* (1998) found that 61 per cent of litigants after whiplash neck injury had evidence of under performance on memory testing compared with 29 per cent of out-patient controls. The under-performing post-whiplash litigants scored as low on tests of memory and concentration as controls with definite evidence of closed head injury. In this study, the authors stressed that malingering was defined as not only deliberate fabrication of bad test results, but also ;a possibly unconscious tendency to perform below the actual level of competency'. They noted that 'such a tendency might be induced by factors such as the assumption of patient role, the need to achieve recognition for complaints in the face of medical scepticism, or perhaps by a strategy of self-protection against exhaustion'. The finding that under-performance was twice as frequent in litigation cases as in clinical patients suggests that financial claims may strongly influence test behaviour.

Strategies for the assessment of malingered cognitive deficits

Because of the high cost of malingering to the health care system, methods of detecting malingered cognitive deficits have been the subject of considerable research effort (Iverson and Binder, 2000). A recent area of malingering detection to be explored is the application of forced-choice methodology and the binomial theorem to assess for intentionally poor performance (Binder, 1992). In a forced-choice task (for example, identifying which of two five-digit numbers was presented previously; identifying whether one was touched once or twice), it is conceivable that someone with severe brain damage could perform at chance level. However, if a patient performs significantly worse than chance (based on the binomial distribution), the assumption is that they had to know the correct answer to perform at such an improbably poor level (Larrabee, 1997).

Differential diagnosis: malingering, factitious disorder, and hysteria

Various attempts have been made to distinguish between malingering, factitious illness, and hysteria. In clinical practice the most difficult differential diagnosis is between factitious disorder and malingering for specific physical symptoms. Modern psychiatric textbooks state that conversion disorder is an unconsciously produced disorder, whereas in malingering, the physical symptoms are intentionally or voluntarily produced. Factitious disorders are thought to occupy an intermediate position. But the difficulties in distinguishing the conscious from unconscious in a practical sense have already been referred to, and there is a need to invoke other explanatory models. Recently, it has been suggested that deception of others is a key component of malingering, whereas self-deception occurs in hysteria. These complex relationships are shown in Table 9.3.

Table 9.3 Relationships between *conversion hysteria, factitious* disorder, and malingering

	Motivations/intentions		Process: deception		Goal
	Aware	Unaware	Self	Other	
Hysterical conversion		+	+		Reduce emotional conflict
Factitious disorder	+			+	Sick role
Malingering	+			+	Personal gain

Turner (1999) has argued that only a cognitive, psychologically informed account of self-deception can cover both the range of phenomena that require explanation and make sense of the close association between malingering and hysteria. He cites Mele (1987) who states that a self-deceived individual often systematically manipulates the evidence to support his or her desired hypothesis. Mele (1997) goes on to say that a patient who employs such strategies as positive and negative misinterpretation, selective attending, and selective evidence gathering, and who is also 'primed' (that is, motivationally biased) can become self-deceived. Thus, the hysteric misinterprets evidence and selectively attends to only a certain part of the overall evidence. In doing so, the patient arrives at a mistaken conclusion about his or her own health or the nature of his or her past experiences. There is no requirement that the patient at any stage or at any level knows the truth.

Turner remarks that this approach allows the clinician to understand hysterical phenomena simply as false beliefs that are out of line with the evidence. For example, the patient believes that she cannot move her left leg because 'there is something in the brain that is causing it not to work' (despite evidence to the contrary). By contrast, the malingerer appreciates the evidence for what it is and in a sense 'knows' the truth. But as one moves in the direction of hysteria, individuals are less and less certain about the truth as they are more and more *self-deceived*. At the hysterical end of the spectrum, individuals are convinced that the false proposition is true. It is not surprising therefore that an individual's hysterical symptoms correspond to his or her ideas about what their symptoms should look like and how these should appear to the doctor (that is, the patient's symptoms are a physical manifestation of his or her ideas). This view is not new: nearly one hundred years ago Babinski and Froment (1918) suggested that conversion symptoms represented the patient's ideas about illness. (These ideas are developed further in Merskey's chapter in this volume, p. 171.)

It should by now be evident that although the psychiatric glossaries demand that clinicians attempt to estimate both intrapsychic and extrapsychic motivation in these patients, such a task is at best unreliable, and at worst fruitless and posssibly unethical. Invoking theories of dissociation also has limited explanatory power: dissociation may have more to do with the psychology of deception and self-deception than with any 'incapacity to integrate the self or personality'. Paradoxically, it has also been pointed out that the maintenance of 'unconsciously derived' hysterical symptoms seems to require '*conscious*' attention (Spence, 1999; and his chapter in this volume, p. 235).

Conclusions

Current definitions of factitious disorder and malingering are characterized by their shortcomings since it is not always possible for the clinician to know the motivations or intentions of the behaviour in an individual patient. Assessments based on assumptions of gain, whether internal or external, are similarly open to a variety of interpretations. As a consequence, the diagnostic validity of factitious disorder is called into question.

In this chapter an attempt has been made to encourage the clinician to establish whether or not the patient is habitually lying, because the core clinical feature is assumed to be a 'conscious' intention to deceive others. It is argued that this approach is more fruitful for a number of reasons:

1. It depends less on inference and the subjective judgement of the clinician.
2. If lying is established beyond reasonable doubt, then the information can be used in the management of the patient (supportively rather than in an accusatory way).
3. Because of the association between pathological lying and brain damage, it may lead to detailed neuropsychological assessment. In this way the emphasis changes from detection and confrontation to one of assessment.

Finally, the difficulties in differentiating between hysteria and malingering are described. It has recently been argued that a knowledge of deception and self-deception aids understanding of these two disorders, which in the past have been posited to lie on a 'hysteromalingering continuum'. As one moves in the direction of hysteria, the patient becomes more and more self-deceived, whereas the malingerer 'knows' the truth and is intent on deception of others. It remains to be seen whether these descriptive concepts have better clinical or theoretical utility in helping us to understand these disorders than current definitions in psychiatric glossaries which, it is claimed, have limited validity.

References

American Psychiatric Association *Diagnostic and Statistical Manual of Mental Disorders*. 4th edn. APA, 1994.

Anderson, S. W., Bechara, A., Damasio, H, Tranel, T. and Damasio, A. (1999). Impairment of social and moral behaviour related to early damage in human prefrontal cortex. *Nature Neuroscience*, **2**, 1032–7.

Babinski, J. and Froment, J. (1918). *Hysteria or Pithiatism and Reflex Nervous Disorders in the Neurology of War*. University of London Press: London.

Baragwanath, P. and Harding, K. G. (1996). Factitious disorders and the surgeon. *British Journal of Surgery* **83**, 711–12.

Barker, J. C. (1962). The syndrome of hospital addiction (Munchausen Syndrome) — a report on the investigation of seven cases. *Journal of Mental Science*, **108**, 167–82.

Barnes, P. J. and Chung, K. F. (1989). Difficult asthma. *British Medical Journal*, 1989; **299**, 695–8.

Bauer, M. and Boegner, F. (1996). Neurological syndromes in factitious disorders. *Journal of Nervous and Mental Disease*, **184**, 281–8.

Berlyne, N. (1972). Confabulation. *British Journal of Psychiatry*, **120**, 31–9.

Binder, L. M. (1992). Forced choice testing provides evidence of malingering. *Archives of Physical Medicine and Rehabilitation*, **72**, 377–80.

Bryant, B., Mayou, R. and Lloyd-Bostock, S. (1997). Compensation claims following road accidents: a six-year follow-up study. *Medicine Science and Law*, **37**, 326–36.

Bursten, B. (1965). On Munchausen's Syndrome. *Archives of General Psychiatry*, **13**, 261–8.

Carney, M. W. (1980). Artefactual illness to attract medical attention. *British Journal of Psychiatry*, **136**, 542–7.

Cole, E. S. (1970). Psychiatric aspects of compensable injury. *Medical Journal of Australia*, **1**, 93–100.

Cunnien, A. J. (1997). Psychiatric and medical syndromes associated with deception. In: Rogers, R., ed. *Clinical Assessment of Malingering and Deception*. 2nd edn. Guildford Press, New York.

Dalla Barba, G. (1993). Confabulation: knowledge and recollective experience. *Cognitive Neuropsychology*, **10**, 1–20.

Diefenbacher, A. and Heim, G. (1997). Neuropsychiatric aspects of Munchausen's syndrome. *General Hospital Psychiatry*, **19**, 281–5.

Eisendrath, S. J. (1989). Factitious physical disorders: treatment without confrontation. *Psychosomatics*, **30**, 383–7.

Eisendrath, S. J. Current overview of factitious physical disorders. (eds Feldman, M. D. and Eisendrath, S. J.). *The Spectrum of Factitious Disorders*. Washington DC: American Psychiatric Press, pp. 21–36.

Enoch, M. D. and Trethowan, W. H. (1979). *Uncommon Psychiatric Syndromes*. Bristol: John Wright.

Fenelon, G., Mahieux, F., Roullet, E. and Guillard, A. (1991). Munchausen's syndrome and abnormalities on magnetic resonance imaging of the brain. *British Medical Journal*, **302**, 996–7.

Fishbain, D. A., Cutler, R., Rosomoff, H. L. and Rosomoff, R. S. (1999). Chronic pain disability exaggeration/malingering and submaximal effort research. *Clinical Journal of Pain*, **15**, 244–74.

Gault, M. H., Campbell, N. R. and Aksa, A. E. (1998). Spurious stones. *Nephron*, **48**, 274–9.

Greiffenstein, M. F., Baker, W. J. and Gola, T. (1994). Validation of malingered amnesia measures with a large clinical sample. *Psychological Assessment*, **6**, 218–24.

Guziec, J., Lazarus, A. and Harding, J. J. (1994). Factitious disorder. The utility of psychiatric intervention on a general medical floor. *General Hospital Psychiatry*, **16**, 47–53.

Hardie, T. J. and Reed, A. (1998). Pseudologia fantastica, factitions disorder and impostership: a deception syndrome. *Medicine Science and Law*, **38**, 198–201.

Hengeveld, M. W. (1992). Factitious disorders: what can the psychiatrist do? In: Hawton K and Cowen P, eds. *Practical Problems in Clinical Psychiatry*. Oxford: Oxford University Press, pp. 118–29.

Howell, S. J., Owen, L., Chadwick, D. W. (1989). Pseudostatus epilepticus. *Quarterly Journal of Medicine*, **266**, 507–19.

Hyler, S. E. and Sussman, N. (1981). Chronic factitious disorder with physical symptoms (the Munchausen Syndrome). *Psychiatric Clinics of North America*, **4**, 365–77.

Iverson, G. L. and Binder, L. M. (2000). Detecting exaggeration and malingering in neuropsychological assessment. *Journal of Head Trauma Rehabilitation*, **15**, 829–58.

Jonas, J. M. and Pope, H. G. (1985). The dissimulating disorders: a single diagnostic entity? *Comprehensive Psychiatry*, **26**, 58–62.

Kalivar, J. (1996). Malingering versus factitious disorder. *American Journal of Psychiatry*, **153**, 1108.

Kent, L. A., Gill, G. V. and Williams, G. (1994). Mortality and outcome of patients with brittle diabetes and recurrent keto-acidosis. *Lancet*, **344**, 778–81.

King, B. H. and Ford, C. V. (1998). Pseudologia fantastica. *Acta Psychiatrica Scandinavica*, **77**, 1–6.

Knockaert, D. C. *et al.* (1992). Fever of unknown origin in the 1980s. An update of the diagnostic spectrum. *Archives of Internal Medicine*, **152**, 51–5.

Larrabee, G. J. (1997). Neuropsychological outcome, post concussion symptoms and forensic considerations in mild closed head trauma. *Seminars in Clinical Neuropsychiatry*, **2**, 196–206.

Lawrie, S. M., Goodwin, G. and Masterson, G. (1993). Munchausen's Syndrome and organic brain disorder. *British Journal of Psychiatry*, **162**, 545–9.

Lishman, W. (1998). *Organic Psychiatry. The Psychological consequences of cerebral disorder*. Oxford: Blackwell, p. 31.

LoPiccolo, C. J., Goodkin, K. and Baldewicz, T. T. (1999). Current issues in the diagnosis and management of malingering. *Annals of Medicine*, **31**, 166–74.

Mele, A. (1987). Recent work on self deception. *American Philosophical Quarterly*, **24**, 1–17.

Mele, A. (1997). Real self-deception. *Behavioural and Brain Science*, **20**, 91–102.

Mendelson, G. (1995). 'Compensation neurosis' revisited: outcome studies of the effects of litigation. *Journal of Psychosomatic Research*, **39**, 695–706.

O'Shea, B., McGennis, A., Cahill, M. and Falvey, J. (1984). Munchausen's Syndrome. *British Journal of Hospital Medicine*, **35**, 269–74.

Pankratz, L. and Lezak, M. D. (1987). Cerebral dysfunction in the Munchausen Syndrome. *Hillside Journal of Clinical Psychiatry*, **9**, 195–206.

Pankratz, L. (1981). A review of the Munchausen Syndrome. *Clinical Psychology Review*, **1**, 65–78.

Reich, P. and Gottfried, L. A. (1983). Factitious disorders in a teaching hospital. *Annals of Internal Medicine*, **99**, 240–7.

Resnick, P. J. (1997). Malingering of post-traumatic disorders. In: Rogers, R., ed. *Clinical Assessment of Malingering and Deception*. New York: Guildford.

Rogers, R., Bagby, R. and Rector, N. (1989). Diagnostic legitimacy of factitious disorder with psychological symptoms. *American Journal of Psychiatry*, **146**, 1312–14.

Schmand, B. *et al.* (1998). Cognitive complaints in patients after whiplash injury: the impact of malingering. *Journal of Neurology, Neurosurgery and Psychiatry*, **64**, 339–43.

Schrader, H., Obelieniene, D. and Bovim, G. (1996). Natural evolution of late whiplash syndrome outside the medico-legal context. *Lancet*, **347**, 1207–11.

Southall, D. P., Plunkett, M. C., Banks, M. W., Falkov, A. F. and Samuels, M. P. (1997). Covert video recordings of life threatening child abuse: lessons for child protection paediatrics. *Paedeatrics*, **100**, 735–60.

Spence, S. (1999). Hysterical paralyses as disorders of action. *Cognitive Neuropsychiatry*, **4**, 203–26.

Spivak, H., Rodin, H. and Sutherland, A. (1994). The psychology of factitious disorders: a reconsideration. *Psychosomatics*, **35**, 25–34.

Stuss, D. T., Alexander, M. P., Lieberman, A. and Levine, H. (1978). An extraordinary form of confabulation. *Neurology*, **28**, 1166–72.

Sutherland, A. J. and Rodin, G. M. (1990). Factitious disorders in a general hospital setting: clinical features and review of the literature. *Psychosomatics*, **31**, 392–9.

Tarsh, M. and Royston, C. (1985). A follow-up study of accident neurosis. *British Journal of Psychiatry*, **146**, 18–25.

Trimble, M. R. (1981). Posttraumatic Neurosis from the Railway Spine to the Whiplash. New York: Wiley.

Turner, M. (1997). Malingering. *British Journal of Psychiatry*, **171**, 409–11.

Turner, M. (1999). Malingering, hysteria and the factitious disorders. *Cognitive Neuropsychiatry* **4**, 193–201.

World Health Organisation (1992). *International Classification of Diseases*. 10th edn. Geneva: WHO.

10   Non-epileptic seizures

Michael R. Trimble

In this chapter, the presentations of non-epileptic seizures are described. The frequency with which these conditions are misdiagnosed as epilepsy is emphasized. It is estimated that more than 25 per cent of patients receiving a diagnosis of epilepsy in a chronic epilepsy clinic do not have epilepsy. Some reasons for this are outlined. These include the misleading nature of the interictal EEG and the misleading acceptance of a number of clinical fallacies, for example, that patients with non-epileptic seizures do not damage themselves or are not incontinent. The importance of good history taking is emphasized.

A differential diagnosis is given of those psychiatric disorders that are often associated with non-epileptic seizures and a brief discussion of the relevance of dissociation in this disorder is included.

It is acknowledged that these disorders have been a conundrum for neuropsychiatric practice for well over 200 years and that failure to diagnose non-epileptic seizures leads to considerable clinical morbidity.

Introduction

The motor and sensory symptoms of hysteria are amongst the most dramatic of its presentations. They have been observed since ancient times, and the hysterical anaesthetic areas were deemed witches' 'patches' in the Middle Ages. The extravagant movement disorders formed part of the dancing manias which occurred around the same time.

In the mid- to late nineteenth century it was the French physicians in particular who described the glorious clinical manifestations of a large number of patients with hysteria, and again it was the motor and sensory pictures which dominated attention. Charcot's book, *Clinical Lectures on Diseases of the Nervous System*, is illustrated with pictures of contortions, contractures, and anaesthetic areas. The latter formed some of the stigmata of hysteria, a useful guide to diagnosis, along with others, such as concentric visual fields.

One of the most dramatic motor manifestations, non-epileptic seizures (pseudoseizures), also fascinated Charcot, and his school who defined various clinical phases of the disorder. Charcot opined 'hysteria is governed, in the same way as other morbid conditions, by rules and laws, which attentive and sufficiently numerous observations always permit us to establish' (Charcot 1889).

Charcot went on to subdivide hysteria into two main groups, hysteria major and hysteria minor. Hysteria major essentially was hysteria with associated seizures. Even in Charcot's day the suggestion was that there may be some fundamental differences, particularly with regards to mechanism, between patients presenting with non-epileptic seizures and those presenting with other manifestations of conversion disorders (Charcot 1889).

Table 10.1 Types of non-epileptic attack disorders

Physical
1. Neurological e.g. cataplexy, transient ischaemic attacks
2. Cardiovascular e.g. Stokes Adams, aortic stenosis
3. Other e.g. hypoglycaemia

Psychiatric disorder
   e.g. hyperventilation/panic, derealization

Emotional attack
1. 'Swoon' — cut-off behavior
2. 'Tantrum' — frustration/rage
3. 'Abreactive' — symbolic attacks
4. Deliberate simulation — conscious or unconscious
5. Pseudo-status epilepticus — usually 'abreactive'

(Reproduced from Betts and Bowden 1991)

The widespread use of videotelemetry in the past ten years or so for the diagnosis of seizure disorders has led to a dramatic increase in the number of patients diagnosed as suffering from non-epileptic seizures. Moreover, it is clear that these patients present considerable diagnostic and management problems.

Clinical features

Non-epileptic seizures take on a complete spectrum of presentations, from partial seizures with an apparent alteration of consciousness, brief episodes of 'going blank', apparent tonic clonic movements of part of the body, to the classical, pseudo-generalized, tonic clonic seizure. In the latter the patient is writhing on the ground simulating the classic grand mal seizure, sometimes dribbling sputum from the mouth, and with associated urinary incontinence.

Betts and his colleagues (1991) classified the presentation of non-epileptic seizures into three main groups (Table 10.1). The first represented those attacks associated with underlying physical abnormalities. The second group were those associated with obvious psychiatric problems, such as hyperventilation or panic disorder. However, in the third group, his 'emotional attacks', four patterns emerged. The first — a 'swoon' — he described as showing 'cutting off behavior'. This occurred often during environmental stress — the patients closed their eyes, sank to the floor without injuring themselves, and remained flaccid and inert for variable periods of time.

In the second group of emotional attack, patients had violent disruptive behaviour. This resembled a childlike temper tantrum and was therefore referred to as 'tantrums'. Patients sometimes let out a loud scream before throwing themselves to the floor, kicking and screaming. It is often this patient who, in their history, will tell you 'it took four of them to hold me down'. Again, this attack continues for a variable length of time and self-injury is a common result.

The third type of attack they noted was so-called 'abreactive attacks'. This accounted for about one-fifth of their patients, and the attacks often occurred at night. They may be

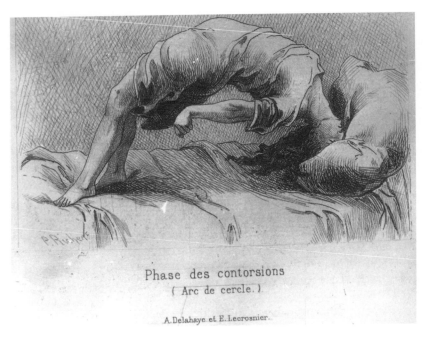

Phase des contorsions
(Arc de cercle.)

A. Delahaye et E. Lecrosnier.

Fig. 10.1 shows the classical picture of the *arc de cercle* (Charcot, 1889).

preceded by hyperventilation, followed by an increased stiffening of the body, eventually leading to arching of the back with thrashing of the limbs and characteristic pelvic thrusting (Fig. 10.1).

Finally, they referred to 'simulated' epileptic seizures, related to conscious or unconscious elaboration of an epileptic seizure. The patients' imitated what they thought an epileptic seizure should look like, for some kind of gain. They pointed out that not all patients fell into an obvious category, and that mixed forms and variants occurred.

Terminology

The term pseudoseizures itself is problematic. The *Oxford English Dictionary* gives us the definition of 'pseudo', as 'false, counterfeit, pretend, or spurious'. Thus the term pseudoseizures is misleading, in that the seizures that are being discussed are none of these: they are real and experienced by patients and observed by bystanders or physicians.

It is accepted that alternative terms, including hysterical pseudoepileptic seizures, hysteroepilepsy, and psychogenic seizures are all inadequate, as they often lead to a pejorative inference about the nature of the episodes or are frankly misleading, as is the term psychogenic seizures. This last term logically should be used to imply a form of reflex epileptic seizure induced by mental activities (Fenwick 1981).

The author's preferred term for what is discussed here is 'non-epileptic seizures'. This acknowledges that these phenomena are different from those of epilepsy, but also that the patient has had a sudden paroxysmal experience that may be interpreted as being epileptic-like.

More recently, the term 'non-epileptic attack disorder' has been popularized (Betts 1996).

Incidence

One important reason to write on this topic is the frequency with which this diagnosis is missed. There are a number of reasons for this, which are discussed further in this chapter.

Non-epileptic seizures occur most commonly in neurological settings and are frequent in patients with conversion symptoms. Ljungberg (1957) reported seizures in 25 per cent of males and 41 per cent of females in a large sample of patients with conversion disorder. Purtell *et al.* (1951) gave a figure of 12 per cent of women with Briquet's syndrome presenting 'pseudoseizures', and Trimble (1981) in reviewing the diagnosis of hysteria at the National Hospitals for Neurology and Neurosurgery throughout three decades (1950s, 1960s, and 1970s) gave figures for seizures of 11.1 per cent, 13.2 per cent, and 13.8 per cent respectively. (See the Chapter in this volume by Akagi and House, p. 73).

The incidence of non-epileptic seizures in these selected populations is undoubtedly increasing. In a later report from the same hospital (Wilson–Barnett and Trimble 1985), seizures were reported in 34 per cent of a consecutively referred sample of 79 patients with conversion symptoms. In this sample, patients were not included if an alternative neurological diagnosis was apparent — in other words, these were not patients in whom a diagnosis of both epilepsy and hysteria would be acceptable. This emphasizes the important clinical point that although patients with epilepsy may have non-epileptic seizures, the latter frequently occur in the absence of epilepsy, and it is not necessary to entertain both diagnoses in the same patient. Lesser (1985) cautioned against making a double diagnosis, noting definite epilepsy in only 12 per cent and possible epilepsy in 24 per cent of over 300 reported cases of non-epileptic seizure.

More recent estimates of the frequency of non-epileptic seizures amongst patients attending clinics with treatment-resistant seizures give estimates of prevalence at between 10 and 26 per cent (Ramani 1986; Gates 1989; Smith *et al.* 1999).

If these figures are correct many patients with non-epileptic seizures carry with them a diagnosis of epilepsy, and most of these patients take anticonvulsant drugs chronically, until such a time as the diagnostic error has been corrected-if it ever is. Clearly, at some stage in their history, a diagnostic pitfall was encountered and an inappropriate diagnosis was given.

There are a number of reasons why such failures occur. There is a pressure on all of us to make an instant diagnosis. Further, in a diagnostic setting in which symptoms, rather than a patient's history, are often given primary importance, there seems to be a need to concentrate primarily on the phenomenology of the attacks themselves. There is also often a reliance on a third-party description of the episodes.

It is clearly preferable, in cases of difficult seizure disorders, to accept that the patient is a diagnostic conundrum, to note that there are alternative diagnoses to epilepsy that might apply to the patient, and to follow the patient over time with the expectation that the appropriate diagnosis will reveal itself at a later date.

Seizure phenomenology

The presentation of patients with non-epileptic seizures is highly variable but, in general, the condition can be mistaken for epilepsy if the patterns reported are similar to those found in an epilepsy population. Thus patients are either going to present with a partial seizure type or a generalized seizure type or a mixture of the two.

One of the problems in terms of diagnosis is that, in many settings still (and certainly before the advent of videotelemetry monitoring), description of the patient's seizure is dependent upon what the patient reports or upon third-party descriptions. These are known in many cases to be highly inaccurate. A third-party description may be particularly fallacious in substantiating whether a diagnosis of epilepsy is appropriate or not. The physician fits this lay interpretation of abnormal muscular movements into his or her own preconceived idea of what a description of epileptic seizure ought to sound like!

From the psychiatric point of view however, careful attention to the patient's phenomenology is very relevant. So often, simple cases of panic disorder are missed because of failure to ask appropriate probing questions. Likewise, depressive illness may not be enquired about.

It is often forgotten by investigating physicians that 'loss of consciousness' means different things to patients and doctors, and many patients with non-epileptic seizures actually present with an alteration of consciousness rather than loss of consciousness. Nonetheless, this is reported as loss of consciousness by patients when asked as a direct question.

Patients are often amnesic for their attacks and this is often thought to be a hallmark of the epileptic seizure. However, amnesia is also a hallmark of dissociation, and to equate amnesia for the episode as an attack of epilepsy is a fundamental clinical error. Many patients with partial epileptic seizures do not have alteration of consciousness (simple partial seizures). Further, on close questioning, patients who say they are unconscious during an episode may actually report having experienced a variety of sensory impressions which are much more in keeping with dissociation than unconsciousness in the neurological sense.

Betts and Bowden (1991) related seizure phenomenology to aetiology, dividing their seizure types as noted into emotional attacks, swoons, tantrums, and abreactive types. The frequency of sexual abuse was greatest in patients with swoons and abreactive seizure types. In the latter attack, the well described *arc en cercle*, (Fig. 10.1) with arching of the back and pelvic thrusting has been related to 'the acting out of an abuse flashback' (Betts 1996).

Differential diagnoses

History

The main non-psychiatric conditions that may be mistaken for epilepsy are shown in Tables 10.2 and 10.3. In this chapter, only the psychiatric variants are described, alternative references to the other disorders being readily available (for example, Vossler 1995).

Table 10.2   Medical disorders mistaken for epilepsy

- Hypoglycaemia
- Vasovagal episodes
- Cardiac disorders (e.g. TIA)
- Migraine
- Vestibular disorders
- Narcolepsy
- Dystonias, tics, stimulus-sensitive myoclonus

Table 10.3   Sleep disorders mistaken for epilepsy

Parasomnias
 REM
- Nightmares
- Sleep behaviour disorder
 NON-REM
- Somnambulism
- Night terrors

Hypersomnias
- Cataplexy
- Narcoleptic automatic behaviour
- Sleep drunkenness

It should be emphasized that although textbooks for over a century have given advice as to how to distinguish between epileptic and non-epileptic seizures, all such listings are unreliable. Videotelemetry, where the patient's seizure can be viewed at the same time as the electro-encephalographic record, is an important method for the diagnosis of non-epileptic seizures in many patients, but it is not widely available. In fact, reliance on videotelemetry alone for diagnosis is another clinical pitfall since history taking, particularly in terms of exploring underlying potential psychopathology, is a vital component of the diagnostic process.

In patients with seizure disorders, a purely symptom-orientated approach, concentrating solely on the phenomenology of the seizures, may lead to wrong conclusions. An essential part of the investigation is to understand the history of the patient in whom the symptoms are presenting. In addition, information regarding such obvious factors as seizure-precipitating events should be sought, paying particular attention to the setting and timing of the first attack.

It is a truism that seizures occurring many times a day in the presence of a normal interictal EEG are most likely to be non-epileptic, and that talking, screaming, or displays of emotional behaviour after the attack are likely to lead to a similar conclusion.

A history of 'status epilepticus', where the patient is rushed to hospital with an attack which continues 'for hours', should always be viewed with suspicion. Status epilepticus is a medical emergency but it is estimated that perhaps 50 per cent of patients admitted to emergency care with a diagnosis of status epilepticus do not actually have this condition

(Betts 1996). A history of repeated status epilepticus, with a normal interictal EEG, is highly unlikely to represent epilepsy. Treatment in an intensive care unit with sedative medications does not reinforce the diagnosis of epilepsy. Indeed, iatrogenic damage is common in patients with non-epileptic seizures — some patients have suffered respiratory arrest and unnecessary tracheostomies following inappropriate sedation.

EEG

The electroencephalogram (EEG) can be the most misleading of investigations. Non-specific interictal EEG abnormalities are reported in up to 74 per cent of patients with non-epileptic seizures (Wilkus *et al.* 1984; Lelliot and Fenwick 1991). The presence of paroxysmal abnormalities on the EEG does not mean a diagnosis of epilepsy, and epilepsy can only be confirmed when classical discharges associated with the seizure are viewed and captured on videotelemetry.

Paroxysmal discharges, even generalized spike wave complexes, can be found in up to 3 per cent of healthy people (Fenton 1982). Certain rhythmic abnormalities on the EEG are associated with psychopathology. For example, rhythmic mid-temporal discharges (paroxysmal theta activity maximally seen in mid-temporal regions) and small, sharp spikes (which are brief duration, small amplitude spikes, again often exclusively temporal in location) have been associated with affective disorders and a tendency towards suicide (Hughes and Hermann 1984; Small 1970). Often these variants can have a sharp appearance, leading the electroencephalographer to refer to them as 'epileptiform'. Unless the clinician is experienced in understanding the nuances of EEGs, this is rapidly translated into 'epileptic' and the patient's seizure diagnosed as epilepsy.

As emphasized, one way round this trap is to place only minimal reliance on the interictal EEG and to examine, wherever possible, the ictal EEG using videotelemetry or rather less satisfactory, ambulatory monitoring. In the latter, patients are connected to a portable EEG and can therefore freely continue their daily lives. However, there is no direct viewing of the seizure. Only the EEG record is available for analysis and artefacts are readily provoked, particularly during the seizure episode itself. Again, it requires an experienced encephalographer to interpret such data.

Some more fallacies

The diagnosis can also be mistaken if a number of clinical fallacies are not heeded. One of these relates to self injury, another to incontinence. Self injury is just as likely to occur in epileptic as in non-epileptic seizures, although the site of the injury may be different. Patients with epilepsy often damage themselves under the chin or eyebrows or other bones of prominence. Patients with non-epileptic seizures, whose injuries may be quite horrific, may present, for example, with carpet burns on the cheeks or on the surface of the brow. Carpet burns are never seen in association with epilepsy and are virtually pathognomonic of non-epileptic seizures.

Patients with non-epileptic seizures may fracture bones, dislocate joints, and have head injuries which in themselves may lead to unconsciousness. Incontinence occurs frequently in non-epileptic seizures and is of no diagnostic value.

Other fallacies include the relationship of the attacks to head injury and also to a family history. The characteristics of head injury that lead to seizures are well documented (Jennett and Teasdale 1981), and the relatively minor head injuries of everyday life cannot be associated with an increased incidence of epilepsy.

There are some well-known epilepsy syndromes that have a genetic base (for example, juvenile myoclonic epilepsy), but the genetic component to most epileptic disorders is not significant and is at present poorly characterized.

Thus, a history of minor head injury or a family history of epilepsy should not allow the physician to immediately bias a diagnosis in favour of epilepsy. In fact, epilepsy in a family member may be an association by imitation, with the presentation of non-epileptic attacks.

Specific, associated psychiatric conditions

A variety of psychiatric disorders are found in patients with non-epileptic seizures and these are listed in Table 10.4. The most common are anxiety disorders, in which seizures are linked to panic attacks (with or without agoraphobia), episodes of depersonalization or derealization, and to dissociative states.

A common underlying psychopathology is a depressive illness, and more rarely one encounters schizophrenia. In the latter setting, patients with a sudden onset of catatonic behaviour are mistakenly diagnosed as epilepsy.

The condition can be malingered — a diagnostic entity of dubious validity. This has to be considered in certain settings, particularly where compensation is involved.

An underlying affective disorder, particularly major affective disorder, is important to diagnose. In some cases this is most obvious when the seizures are presenting as a new problem, and initially the affective disturbance may not be readily apparent. However, once they commence as a clinical pattern, the non-epileptic seizures may continue for some considerable time, well beyond the treatment period for the depression. Once a patient is being prescribed polytherapy with anticonvulsant drugs the situation may be compounded, since a number of these drugs themselves may provoke or exacerbate depressive symptoms (Trimble 1996).

Briquet's syndrome (somatization disorder) — a form of stable hysteria originally defined by Guze and Perley (1953) — is also an important consideration (Woodruff *et al.*

Table 10.4 Psychiatric disorders that occur in patients with non-epileptic seizures

Anxiety
• GAD (generalized anxiety disorder)
• Panic disorder (hyperventilation; depersonalization)
Depression (fugues)
Schizophrenia
Conversion disorder
Somatization disorder
Episodic dyscontrol
Malingering

1982). Patients with this condition can often present with pseudoneurological problems which include faints and convulsions. To the experienced eye, the past history of abnormal illness behaviour is usually apparent, but a purely symptom-orientated approach to history taking of seizures will miss the rich variety of complex somatization that these patients bring with them to the clinical investigation. Since by definition the condition is intractable and difficult to treat, recognition of these patients is of paramount importance to avoid unnecessary surgical and medical intervention, including the prescription of anticonvulsant drugs.

Panic attacks and rage attacks are the psychiatric symptoms most frequently confused with epileptic seizures. The former usually occur in settings of stress. Distinguishing the aura of panic in a patient with temporal lobe epilepsy can be diagnostically difficult. The clue to the epilepsy may lie in the more stereotyped, fleeting nature of the panic, with its greater paroxysmal quality. There is no build up of anxiety before the attack and no continuation of anxiety after the attack — features which tend to accompany the panic attack of anxiety.

The unpleasant, fear-like aura of temporal lobe epilepsy often initiates as a definite, epigastric feeling, rising up from abdomen along the midline of the chest into the throat, before the patient loses consciousness. In panic disorder, the feeling is often epigastric in origin, but the pattern of radiation is more diffuse, spreading through the whole body. Further, hyperventilation, tachycardia, sweating, shortness of breath, and other autonomic manifestations of anxiety are often reported by the patient.

The episodic dyscontrol syndrome (Mark and Ervin 1970) is a condition of repeated paroxysmal episodes of violence, which often seem to come out of the blue, and are relatively shortlived, for which afterwards patients feel intense remorse. This may be confused with epilepsy, particularly if it is associated with a history of head injury, and an abnormal EEG with temporal lobe abnormalities are noted.

Dissociation

Dissociative states are a heterogeneous group of psychosensory and psychomotor events in which 'a partial or complete loss of the normal integration between memories of the past, awareness of identity and immediate sensations, and control of bodily movements' occur (WHO 1992, p. 151). The categorization suggests a relationship to psychological aetiology, related to 'trauma, insoluble or intolerable problems or disturbed relationships' (WHO 1992, p. 152).

Dissociative mechanisms play a role in a variety of disorders, most notably with acute and chronic post-traumatic stress disorders, but also in affective disorder and certain personality disorders. Further, particular conditions, especially temporal lobe epilepsy, seem more linked to the reporting of dissociative phenomena (Schneck and Bear 1981).

Dissociation is noted in many patients presenting with non-epileptic seizures, and this group are readily misdiagnosed as suffering epilepsy. The two main reasons for this are the reporting of amnesia and the high incidence of EEG abnormalities in patients with dissociative episodes (Jawad et al. 1995).

Dissociative amnesia is one variant of psychogenic amnesia, and it is the reporting of the amnesia by the patient that often leads to the mistaken diagnosis of complex partial seizures. It is a clinical fallacy to assume that loss of awareness of and an amnesia for an episode leads to an automatic diagnosis of epilepsy.

Fugue states are prolonged episodes of amnesia associated with wandering. They are interlinked with a variety of psychopathologies. The amnesia lasts hours, weeks, or occasionally years, and if related to psychiatric disability such as depression, can usually be allied to an escape from difficult or intolerable circumstances. Fugue states are quite unlike briefer epileptic automatisms. In fugues the patients usually remain in contact with their environment, manipulating it successfully, often failing to draw much attention to themselves. This is also unlike episodes of transient global amnesia, which tend to be short-lived, and during which the patient often behaves inappropriately, asking repeatedly the same questions and appearing in some state of confusion.

Somnambulism implies sleepwalking; this is one of the parasomnias and usually arises out of non-REM sleep. There may be only brief wanderings or lengthier episodes, with a completion of quite complex but semi-purposeful tasks for which there is amnesia. Its onset in adulthood is usually associated with emotional trauma and is a further reflection of a patient's ability to dissociate.

Although not strictly one of the diagnostic criteria for post-traumatic stress disorder (American Psychiatric Association 1994), non-epileptic seizures may occur in this setting. The seizure may be the most dramatic aspect of the clinical presentation leading to a line of enquiry which fails to detect the other underlying criteria which would allow diagnosis of this syndrome. Obviously, the precipitating trauma is a significant criterion for entry, but in many cases this may reflect upon previous trauma, perhaps reactivated by recent events. The similarity between post-traumatic stress disorder and non-epileptic seizure disorder has been commented on by Betts (1996), and even the hyperekplexia (increased startle response) of post-traumatic stress disorder may be mistaken for myoclonic seizures.

Finally, a number of quite common psychiatric symptoms, which actually are not so common in epilepsy, may lead to a mistaken diagnosis. Derealization and the related depersonalization refer to a disturbance of feeling about the surrounding world or about the self respectively. The self is felt as unreal, dead; the world is seen as flat, two-dimensional, or alien. Some patients feel that familiar objects are new or startling and want to touch them to test their reality. These phenomena are usually distressing, associated with high levels of anxiety, and accompany states of dissociation. In autoscopy, patients report that they can stand outside of their body and look down upon it.

Déja vu is an associated state, as is jamais vu and déja vecu. These essentially represent mnestic dislocations. The most common medical association of déja vu is with an anxiety disorder, in which setting the experience fails to have the vivid, and often clearly repetitive nature, that an aura of temporal lobe epilepsy brings.

Investigations

Clinical evaluation can be enhanced by laboratory and biochemical assessments and neuroimaging.

Apart from the EEG, measurement of serum prolactin — comparing a baseline level to a postictal one — is helpful, particularly in distinguishing seizures which have a generalized, tonic-clonic expression. (Levels rise dramatically in patients with epilepsy.) This can also sometimes be helpful in diagnosing complex partial seizures, although it appears not to be useful in patients either with status epilepticus or frontal seizures (Trimble 1978, Meierkord 1992). A postictal rise to > 1000 iu per litre, in the presence of a normal baseline, is highly suggestive of an epileptic seizure.

There are a number of reasons for false positive results. These include interpreting a lesser rise as relevant, incorrect laboratory analysis, and the detection of a physiological spike of prolactin release. If in doubt, repeat the test.

High-resolution MRI scanning is also proving helpful in detecting relatively discrete lesions, particularly in medial temporal structures, which may be the site of epilepsy in many patients. Imaging with SPECT or PET may reveal areas of hypometabolism, usually concordant with the site of abnormality of any EEG focus or MRI scan abnormality. Normal findings on structural or functional brain imaging does not rule out an epileptic cause for the seizure but, taken in conjunction with other findings, may be helpful in the differential diagnoses of epileptic from non-epileptic attacks.

With the advent of more acurate neurological investigations in recent years, the differential diagnosis of many neurological conditions has become clearer. In patients with non-epileptic seizures however, diagnostic practice is still considerably at fault. That being the case, many patients with these disorders do not receive appropriate treatment until they have suffered for a considerable period of time, at which point intervention is much more difficult.

Urgent investigations are required to understand further underlying pathogenesis of these disorders, since the cost to health care services is substantial.

References

American Psychiatric Association (1994). *Diagnostic and Statistical Manual for Mental Disorders* (4th edn; DSM–IV). A. P. A. Washington.

Betts, T. (1996). Psychiatric aspects of non-epileptic seizures. In: *Epilepsy, a Comprehensive Textbook* (eds. Engel J. and Pedley T. A.), pp. 2101–16. Raven Press, New York.

Betts, T. and Bowden, S. (1991). Pseudoseizures (non-epileptic attack disorder). In: *Women and Epilepsy* (ed. Trimble, M. R.), pp. 243–58. Wiley & Sons, Chichester.

Charcot, J. M. (1889). *Clinical Lectures on Diseases of the Nervous System. Vol. 3*. New Sydenham Society, London.

Fenton, G. W. (1982). Hysterical alterations of consciousness. In: *Hysteria* (ed. Roy A.), pp. 229–46. J. Wiley & Sons, Chichester.

Fenwick, P. (1981). Precipitation and inhibition of seizures. In: *Epilepsy and Psychiatry* (eds. Reynolds, E. H. and Trimble, M. R.), pp. 306–21. Churchill Livingstone, Edinburgh.

Gates, J. R. (1989). Psychogenic seizures. In: *Nonepileptic Seizures* (ed. Rowan, J. A. and Gates, J. R.). Butterworth–Heinemann, Boston.

Guze, S. D. and Perley, M. J. (1953). Observations on the natural history of hysteria. *American Journal of Psychiatry*, **119**, 960–5.

Hughes, J. R. and Hermann, B. P. (1984). Evidence for psychopathology in patients with rhythmic midtemporal discharges. *Biological Psychiatry*, **19**, 1623–34.

Jawad, S. S. M., Jamil, N., Clark, E. J., *et al.* (1995). Psychiatric morbidity and psychodynamics of patients with convulsive pseudo-seizures. *Seizure*, **4**, 201–6.

Jennett, B. and Teasdale, G. (1981). Assessment of head injuries. In: *Management of Head Injuries*, pp. 301–16. Contemporary Neurological Series, F. A. Davis, Philadelphia.

Lelliot, P. T. and Fenwick, P. (1991). Cerebral pathology and pseudo-seizures. *Acta Neurologica Scandinavica*, **83**, 129–32.

Lesser, R. P. (1985). Psychogenic seizures, In: *Recent Advances in Epilepsy, Vol. 2* (ed. Pedley, T. and Meldrum, B. S.), pp. 273–96. Churchill Livingstone, Edinburgh.

Ljungberg, L. (1957). Hysteria: clinical, prognostic and genetic study. *Acta Psychiatrica Scandinavica*, **32** 1–162, Suppl. 112.

Mark, V. H. and Ervin, F. R. (1970). *Violence in the Brain*. Harper Rowe, London.

Meierkord, H., Shorvon, S., Lightman, S. and Trimble, M. R. (1992). Comparison of the effects of frontal and temporal lobe partial seizures on prolactin levels. *Archives of Neurology*, **49**, 225–30.

Purtell, J. J., Robins, E. and Cohen, M. E. (1951). Observation on clinical aspects of hysteria. *JAMA*, **146**, 902–10.

Ramani, S. V. (1986). Intensive monitoring of psychogenic seizures, aggression and dyscontrol syndromes. In: *Advances in Neurology* (ed. Gumnit, R. J.), pp. 203–17. Raven Press, New York.

Schneck, L. and Bear, D. (1981). Multiple personality and related dissociative phenomena in patients with temporal lobe epilepsy. *American Journal of Psychiatry*, **133**, 1311–16.

Small, J. G. (1970). Small spikes in a psychiatric population. *Archives of General Psychiatry*, **22**, 277–84.

Smith, D., Defalla, B. A. and Chadwick, D. W. (1999). The misdiagnosis of epilepsy and the management of refractory epilepsy in a specialist clinic. *Quarterly Journal of Medicine*, **92**, 15–23.

Trimble, M. R. (1978). Serum prolactin in epilepsy and hysteria. *BMJ*, **2**, 1682.

Trimble, M. R. (1981). *Neuropsychiatry*. J. Wiley & Sons, Chichester.

Trimble, M. R. (1996). *Biological Psychiatry* (2nd edn). J. Wiley & Sons, Chichester.

Vossler, D. G. (1995). Non-epileptic seizures of physiologic origin. *Journal of Epilepsy*, **8**, 1–10.

Wilkus, R. J., Thompson, P. M. and Vossler, D. G. (1990). Bizarre ictal automatisms: frontal lobe epileptic or psychogenic seizures. *Journal of Epilepsy*, **3**, 29–313.

Wilson–Barnett, J. and Trimble, M. R. (1985). An investigation of hysteria using the Illness Behaviour Questionnaire. *British Journal of Psychiatry*, **146**, 601–8.

Woodruff, R. A., Goodwin, D. W. and Guze, S. D. (1982). Hysteria (Briquet's syndrome). In: *Hysteria* (ed. Roy, A.), pp. 117–43. J. Wiley & Sons, Chichester.

World Health Organisation (10th revision, 1992). The ICD-10 Classification of Mental and Behavioural Disorders. Clinical descriptions and diagnostic guidelines. Geneva: WHO.

11 Conversion hysteria: a legal diagnosis

Michael A. Jones and Alan Sprince

Lawyers would categorize conversion hysteria as a form of psychiatric harm. Tradition-ally, the Law has taken a rather sceptical approach to claims for compensation involving such damage. It has been easier to recover compensation for physical injury than for psychiatric harm. There have been some recent judicial statements to the effect that the Law should march more in tune with medical thinking on this issue and that the two forms of harm should be treated equally. This has not yet occurred. Whereas Medicine approaches psychiatric harm as an issue for diagnosis, treatment, and prognosis, the Law deals with it in the context of actions for compensation, where legal policy can impose constraints on claiming. This chapter considers these themes in the context of conversion hysteria, focussing on the claimant's difficulties in meeting the burden of proving their case in the face of lingering judicial scepticism over the validity of psychiatric harm.

Introduction

Conversion hysteria is not a diagnosis that has featured significantly in English law, at least in terms of reported decisions. Less than two per cent of civil claims come before the courts, the remainder being settled by the parties before trial, and not all cases that go to trial are reported. There is however very little direct reference to conversion hysteria in the legal electronic databases or the Law reports. This suggests that practising lawyers are unlikely to recognize it from their typical case-loads, though they will be more familiar with phrases such as 'psychological overlay', 'functional overlay', 'illness behaviour', and 'litigation neurosis'[1]. Lawyers, particularly defence lawyers, are also very familiar with the notion of claimants who exaggerate their symptoms and those who are malingering.

Initially this tends to suggest that there is perhaps a continuum of conditions presenting themselves in a legal context which ranges from outright fraud (a claimant pretending to have suffered injury or consciously exaggerating injury with a view to obtaining financial reward through the legal system) through 'illness behaviour' to, at its extreme, conversion hysteria. The problem, from the Law's perspective, is being able to identify whether the claimant is genuine or not, and in practice lawyers will tend to take a somewhat robust, indeed some might say cynical, attitude to apparently 'unexplained' symptoms, at least in the absence of convincing medical evidence.[2]

Lawyers react to an apparently novel phenomenon by attempting to place it within an existing legal category. The question would be, not simply '*what* is hysteria?', but '*where* does it fit legally?' The process of categorizing as a means of explaining is not unique to lawyers, of course, but it can sometimes result in the rather stifling formalism that can typify legal discourse.[3] That formalism is perhaps at its most extreme in the context of damages claims involving psychiatric harm. Given the generally accepted medical features of hysteria, lawyers would attach significance to its fundamental *psychiatric* characteristic, and so would be inclined to classify it legally as 'psychiatric harm'. This, in turn, enables one to place it within a legal framework that has been erected over the last hundred years or so to address the diverse circumstances in which such damage might be in issue. The key points of that complex, controversial, and peculiarly legal taxonomy will be outlined in this chapter.

At the outset it is worth noting what, for lawyers, is an almost axiomatic feature of the legal regime governing compensation for personal injuries — namely, the sharp distinction drawn between claims in respect of *physical* injury and those for *psychiatric* injury. Put simply, it is easier to obtain compensation for physical injury than for psychiatric injury.

Key to understanding the reaction of the courts to claims for compensation in respect of psychiatric harm is the distinctly legal agenda through which a lawyer's approach will inevitably be mediated. There are essentially three features of lawyers' thinking that should be borne in mind. First, the real concern that claims for psychiatric harm could result in a rapid expansion of the scope of liability for personal injuries (the 'floodgates' argument). Secondly, an initially hostile but now merely ambivalent attitude to psychiatry as a discipline, which has left a residual impression that psychiatric harm is less tangible and therefore less real, and perhaps less worthy of protection by the law. Finally, and most crucially, is the fact that in virtually all the situations in which the courts have to rule upon the issue of psychiatric harm they do so in the context of allocating responsibility for the consequences of actions that are being subject to scrutiny.

A legal conception of hysteria as 'psychiatric harm'

Lawyers would look to the relevant medical literature in order to understand the basic phenomenon of hysteria. They would by-pass much of the detail and choose instead to meet the legal definitional challenge by latching onto the general notion of hysteria as a *psychiatric* diagnosis. To dwell on what is essentially just a broad description of hysteria might seem somewhat unsophisticated next to the medical discourse, which, it would appear, takes hysteria's emotional characterization for granted and concentrates instead on identifying precise diagnostic criteria that might account for the wealth of conflicting features and make actual findings so controversial and difficult. In practice, however, all that the lawyer needs to know for the purpose of classification is that hysteria can be placed alongside other legally recognized psychiatric phenomena.

It is one thing though to suggest an inevitable association between the accepted notion of hysteria and a causal mechanism that is distinctly emotional rather than physical. That might even amount to a relatively uncontroversial legal *or* medical conclusion. But, it is quite another thing to assume that the legal and medical conceptualization of the mechanics of emotional suffering are essentially similar or that they are rooted in compatible governing ideologies.

Generally, lawyers have always been prone to draw some kind of distinction between physical and psychiatric harm. There are, however, two important differences between the past and present legal discourses on this dichotomy. First, there is now a willingness to absorb relevant medical scientific knowledge and so to recognize the credibility and

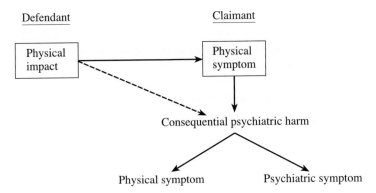

Fig. 11.1 'Consequential' psychiatric harm

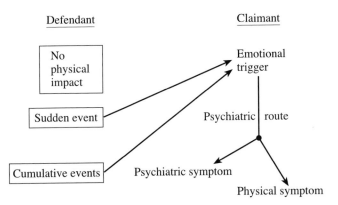

Fig. 11.2 'Pure' psychiatric harm

validity of both physical and psychiatric harm. In the past, the law seemed fixated with a unidimensional notion of tangible physical damage only[4] and determinedly set its face against permitting recovery for emotional harm. We have moved on, however, from nineteenth-century scepticism and recognition of psychiatric harm as a valid head of claim has now been factored into the traditional physical-only model.

The courts will accept claims for psychiatric harm in two broad categories:

1. where physical harm *has* been sustained, with the claimant subsequently developing psychiatric harm — a situation which we will call '*consequential psychiatric harm*' (see Fig. 11.1);

2. where there has been no tangible physical impact with the claimant — which we will call 'pure psychiatric harm' (see Fig. 11.2).

Different sets of legal rules apply to these two categories.

The second difference between the past and present approaches is that, rather than characterizing harm as 'psychiatric damage' simply by reference to the nature of its ultimate manifestation, lawyers now defer to the rudimentary medical scientific notion that the uniquely emotional characteristic in issue emanates, instead, from a supposedly distinct psychiatric aetiology — what Lord Browne–Wilkinson recently termed '*a psychiatric route*'.[5] In this way, lawyers would appreciate that the fact that hysteria could manifest physically (as conversion hysteria) would make it no less psychiatric in origin.

Thus, physical symptoms which have a physical explanation (an understandable anatomical cause) will fall into a different legal category from the same physical symptoms that do not have an organic explanation. The outcome on the question of legal liability may, as it happens, be the same, since the most basic question is whether the claimant's problems can reasonably be attributed to the defendant's faulty conduct (usually, negligence), and the fact that those problems are the product of a psychiatric causal route does not bar the claim. But the characterization of the causal mechanism as psychiatric will open up whole avenues of enquiry for defendants' lawyers attempting to resist the claim that would not be available in a straightforward case of physical impact causing anatomically understood physical harm.

The relevant underlying considerations

In this context, describing a contemporary legal acceptance of the notion of psychiatric harm is less important than identifying the influential underlying considerations from which it results. In turn, it could be said that the Law's current position on psychiatric harm is the product of an uncomfortable process of balancing three interlinking, and sometimes conflicting, forces.

1. Legal 'policy' and 'floodgates'

The law in this area has been shaped as much by so-called 'policy' considerations as by any legal or extra-legal principle. The predominant legal policy concerns have been the so-called 'floodgates' fears — initially of too many fraudulent compensation claims, and then also of too many genuine ones. Statements by judges about 'floodgates' tend not to be based upon any empirical evidence, but on the untested assumption that if a particular case is allowed to succeed it will create a precedent for numerous similar cases, possibly overwhelming the legal system itself or defendants' ability to meet the cost of claims. As a result, courts have erected what they considered to be necessary legal safeguards against a flood of civil claims in cases of psychiatric, as opposed to physical, personal injury.

Initially, the strategy was to refuse the claim altogether, unless it was on familiar physical territory through the 'consequential psychiatric harm' phenomenon. This most extreme form of legal antipathy to the notion of psychiatric harm peaked in 1888 with the Privy Council's decision in *Victorian Railway Commissioners* v *Coultas*.[6] By 1901, however, the courts were able to draw on the more reliable probative mechanisms of a then more established psychiatry discipline in order to countenance financial recoverability for emotional 'shock' that was not also the product of a tangible physical injury.[7] Even then, the underlying floodgates concern still prompted the court to limit claims to those at risk of immediate physical injury — subsequently labelled 'primary victims'. There was no duty to avoid psychiatric harm to A by negligently injuring or endangering B. Twenty-four years later this barrier was also breached, when the Court of Appeal objected to the notion that a mother who suffered a psychiatric reaction on witnessing injury to her children might not recover compensation whereas a mother who was fearful only for her own safety, rather than that of her children, would.[8] It was, perhaps, inevitable that once claims for pure psychiatric harm were admitted they would be extended to such 'secondary victims'.

The following 75 years have seen the courts attempting to establish the parameters for these claims, with a marked tension between, on the one hand, a trend towards treating pure psychiatric harm on the same basis as physical harm, and on the other, concern that to do so would leave the courts without any legal principles with which to stem the anticipated flood of claims. The underlying judicial caution that a century ago refused such claims outright is evident even in the most recent cases. In *White* v *Chief Constable of South Yorkshire*[9], in which the House of Lords rejected claims of post-traumatic stress disorder (PTSD) by police officers involved in the Hillsborough disaster emergency operation, Lord Steyn reasserted the contemporary relevance of 'floodgates' and related policy fears, even though the modern legal view had tended to be that such concerns are overstated and that, even if taken seriously, they could also apply in cases of physical harm.[10]

A curious aspect of the courts' reaction to psychiatric harm is that this struggle between seeking some consistency of approach in cases of physical and psychiatric harm and the worry about opening the 'floodgates' does not feature at all in cases of consequential psychiatric harm. For all one knows, there could be a flood of cases involving quite trivial physical harm which results in abnormal psychiatric responses, and yet the courts have not been concerned to erect doctrinal obstacles to the recovery of damages in such cases. Generally speaking, if there is a causal connection between the accident and the harm, the plaintiff will succeed. The issues in such cases tend to be the forensic problems associated with proof, essentially 'is the claimant genuine?' and 'does the medical evidence support a causal link?'.

2. The legal attitude to developments in medical science

Developments in medical science — psychiatry in particular — would, it might be assumed, be naturally absorbed into the legal analysis. Yet, until relatively recently, there was very little direct reference in the jurisprudence to medical science, other than occasional disparaging references to psychiatry in the older cases. This was neatly encapsulated in Lord Bridge's observation in 1983 in *McLoughlin* v *O'Brian* that '[f]or too long earlier generations of judges have regarded psychiatry and psychiatrists with suspicion, if not hostility'[11] and, perhaps most famously, 13 years earlier in Windeyer J.'s much-quoted reflection that, in 'nervous shock' cases, he could observe 'Law, marching with medicine, *but in the rear and limping a little*'.[12] Eminent medical commentators have also remarked that this area of the Law and psychiatry has hitherto developed without a great deal of demonstrable mutual consultation.[13]

Experience over the last decade or so has suggested that the tide might be turning. Lord Bridge's remark seemed to signal a modern era in which, generally, the weight of legal academic opinion at least would be that the courts' approach in such cases ought to evolve towards a closer association with the developing medical scientific view. The House of Lords' decision in *Page* v *Smith*[14] appeared to create a momentum for this sort of initiative. Their Lordships referred extensively to medical science and used it to prop up their decision. Indeed, Lord Lloyd observed that '[a]s medical science advances, it is important that the law should not be seen to be limping too far behind'. The Law Commission, in their report on *Liability for Psychiatric Illness*[15], proclaimed that 'any discussion of the possible future development of the law in this area should only be undertaken in the light of current medical knowledge'. Additionally, lawyers have been urged to drop the label 'nervous shock' in favour of what is considered to be the more correct term 'psychiatric damage', and, for some time, they have deferred to the medical profession's notion of a 'recognized psychiatric disorder', bringing in the well-established, classificatory mechanisms used by the psychiatric profession itself.[16]

It might, though, be a little premature to conclude that any modern legal trend for express medical correctness in this area has now gained an irresistible momentum. For, while it is possible to identify a clear direction in relevant judicial pronouncements over the last two decades, the most recent judicial 'traffic' has, significantly, not all been one way. The tone of their Lordships' speeches in *White* v *Chief Constable of South Yorkshire*, for instance, has the potential to slow down the trend towards more overt expressions of a common medical and legal understanding of psychiatric harm.

3. The 'blame' agenda

The underlying legal policy concerns mentioned before as the key influential factor in this area could, of course, partially explain this. But, it is more common for any such agenda to act as a covert force only, rarely admitted to by the judiciary, and for courts, instead, to shelter behind entrenched doctrinal principles as the express means of resisting any extra-legal insight. Psychiatric harm has certainly been no exception to this phenomenon. In fact, it might be its paradigm form. The lingering dominance of peculiarly legal doctrinal concerns in this area constitute a third force that, together with legal policy and the potential for an interdisciplinary dimension, has significant influence on the modern law on psychiatric harm.

That there is a distinctly legal agenda markedly different from that of any other discipline has been hinted at recently by the Law Lords themselves. Aside from his express references to policy, Lord Steyn in *White* also contended that there were other fundamental limitations on any practical conflation of the legal and medical discourses in any particular area. While conceding that 'courts of law must act on the best medical insight of the day', his Lordship nonetheless asserted that:

> [i]t would, however, be an altogether different proposition to say that no distinction is made *or ought to be made* between principles governing the recovery of damages in tort for physical injury and psychiatric harm. The contours of tort law are profoundly affected by distinctions between different kinds of damage or harm.

The factor most responsible for marking a practical separation between the relevant legal and medical agendas, no matter how much interdisciplinary dialogue there might be, is the 'blame agenda' by which the law has to allocate responsibility for harm suffered. While, for the medical practitioner, the nature of psychiatric damage might make diagnostic and other conclusions more tentative than in equivalent cases of physical harm, such problems are at least not compounded by having to attribute third-party responsibility. As Professor Trimble has observed: 'all this legal meandering seems odd to the practising clinician with his suffering patient'.[17]

That legal conceptions of any harm *are* conventionally wrapped up with such notions of blame allocation has, in turn, to be factored into the particular legal response to psychiatric harm. As is evident from Figs. 11.1 and 11.2, the lawyer searches for a link to a potentially responsible party, whether through proof of their direct impact with the claimant in a case of physical or consequential psychiatric harm, or in the event or events that trigger the emotional harm in the case of pure psychiatric damage.

It is at this point that the lawyer contemplating the phenomenon of hysteria might identify a significant distinction between hysteria as psychiatric harm and the other forms of psychiatric harm with which lawyers have become familiar. Though the law's task of integrating psychiatric harm into its standard blame allocation mechanisms has been fraught with the sort of underlying conflict just outlined, it has to some extent happened with PTSD in shock cases and, latterly, anxiety disorders and depression in work-stress cases. It is, broadly speaking, integral to the very notion of the harm itself in such cases that there is the possibility of a link between the claimant's damage and a third party which, in turn, lends itself to legal forensic examination for the purposes of blame allocation — the traumatic event that the third party might have caused in the case of PTSD; the cumulative occupational events that the employer might have controlled in the stress case.

Though hysteria could, in particular circumstances, be similarly event-driven and so attributed to a third party, it is, by definition, intrinsically personal to the sufferer. This contrast helps to explain why PTSD and the like have formed the basis of *claimant* allegations in cases in which it is just not possible for the claimant to allege wholly physical harm, and why it will be speculated here that, generally, hysteria might more often be seized upon by *defendants* as a means of placing the maximum possible distance between them and the claimant's harm.

A legal framework for psychiatric harm

It is not possible in this context to set out the full complexity of the rules that the courts have developed for dealing with cases of psychiatric harm. For the purposes of determining how conversion hysteria would fit within the structure of those rules, it is better to highlight four principal points as a means of cutting across the labyrinthine complexity of the current scheme. These distinctions are the rather unbalanced product of a peculiarly legal discourse and of the three forces already identified (fears about a flood of claims from the many potential witnesses to an horrific event; the Law's ambiguous relationship with Medicine; and the blame agenda — i.e. the process of attributing responsibility). They are unlikely to accord with medical reasoning and, in certain cases, may be the antithesis of it.

1. The initial focus of the legal forensic enquiry: the *defendant*

In negligence claims, the first enquiry is the determination of what the defendant did and what he should have done i.e. was the defendant's conduct blameworthy? The doctor may look to the patient's condition (their diagnosis and treatment), whereas the lawyer (in a fault-based system) looks to the defendant's fault and the causal link between the defendant's conduct and the claimant's damage. The predominant form of non-contractual civil liability is the tort of negligence. In all actions for negligence a claimant must prove that the defendant owed him a *duty* to exercise reasonable care to avoid causing him harm; there must be *breach* of that duty (carelessness) by the defendant; and that breach must *cause* the claimant's loss.

2. Consequential psychiatric harm or *pure* psychiatric harm?

Where the harm includes psychiatric damage, the important question will be *how* did that psychiatric damage occur? Did it occur as a direct consequence of physical harm also suffered by the claimant? If so, subject to acceptance of a causal link, the claimant will recover compensation for the psychiatric harm on the same basis as for the physical injuries. Consequential psychiatric harm can occur *as a result of/or along with* physical damage to the claimant. The courts do not really distinguish between these theoretically distinct causal mechanisms. Thus, if as a result of serious physical injuries the claimant subsequently develops a psychiatric condition (e.g. depression), he is entitled to damages for the depression. And if, as a result of seeing the defendant's motor car being driven towards him at speed, he suffers from post-traumatic stress disorder, he is entitled to recover for the consequences of PTSD, even if the medical evidence indicates that the causal mechanism was being placed in fear for his life rather than the fact that he was actually struck by the vehicle and suffered physical injuries. In other words, it matters not whether the psychiatric harm is a reaction to the physical harm or a reaction to a perception of the accident which caused the physical harm. The presence of physical injury operates as a 'passport' to recovery for psychiatric injury.

Consequential psychiatric harm is distinguished from pure psychiatric harm which is sustained wholly independently of physical harm to the claimant. Typically, for the lawyer, pure psychiatric harm arises where the claimant witnesses a traumatic event, usually involving physical injury or perceived physical injury to others, but sometimes involving anticipated physical injury to him or herself. As a general proposition, it is easier for a claimant who sustains consequential psychiatric harm to recover damages.

Technically, proof of breach of duty is identical whether the damage be pure or consequential psychiatric harm. In the case of *consequential* psychiatric harm, however, questions of duty are rarely in issue since a duty of care to avoid the careless infliction of physical injury is normally owed. The focus will tend to be on causation — did the accident for which the defendant is responsible cause the claimant's psychiatric harm (or would the psychiatric harm have manifested itself at some stage, in any event?) — and the credibility of the claimant (is the claimant genuine, exaggerating, malingering?). Clearly, the claimant's credibility and questions of causation overlap considerably, and there is no reason why questions of credibility should be exclusive to cases of psychiatric harm (since a physically injured claimant may be exaggerating or malingering, without any suggestion of psychiatric harm). It is simply that in cases of consequential psychiatric harm, the focus of the forensic process is more likely to be upon the veracity of the claimant's allegations (prompted of course by the defendant's case), reflecting perhaps the initial, nineteenth-century concern with the flood of fraudulent claims.

For example, in the Scottish case of *McWhinnie* v *British Coal Corporation*[18], the claimant suffered a minor injury to his back, but displayed a great deal of overt pain behaviour on examination, including guarding, bracing, grimacing, sighing, exclamations, collapsing, and hyperventilation. There were also a number of non-organic and behavioural responses to the examination with low back pain reported on axial loading and simulated rotation of the spine, widespread non-anatomical tenderness, improvement in lumbar flexion and straight leg raising with distraction, and generalized giving way of multiple muscle groups in both legs. This was characterized by an expert for the claimant as an entirely genuine and unconscious 'abnormal illness behaviour', whereas an expert for the defendant said that the claimant was grossly exaggerating his symptoms and was deliberately and consciously attempting to maximize his compensation from the case.[19] The trial judge had to resolve this conflict in the evidence, and concluded that on the particular facts the claimant's symptoms were genuine and unconsciously produced, notwithstanding that they were a grossly excessive reaction to the minor injury he had sustained.[20] Damages of approximately £150,000 were awarded.

A similar stark conflict in the medical evidence was apparent in *Burke* v *Royal Infirmary of Edinburgh NHS Trust*[21] between those medical experts who considered that the claimant's problems were genuine and those who considered him to be a malingerer. Again, the claimant had sustained a minor back injury and was demonstrating symptoms and disability completely out of proportion to the objective physical pathology in his back, and again it was concluded, in the light of the medical evidence, that this was the product of an unconsciously determined abnormal illness behaviour (although the action failed on the basis that there had been no breach of duty).[22]

It may seem unfair to require a defendant to pay thousands of pounds in compensation for what may initially have been a fairly trivial injury. The legal basis for this (assuming that breach of duty is established) lies in the proof of a causal link between the breach of duty and the damage, and a policy which states that 'a wrongdoer must take his victim as he finds him'. Thus, in the case of physical harm, if the defendant negligently injures a man with a thin skull who dies as a consequence, the defendant is liable for the death even though he could not have anticipated that the damage would have been so severe. So also, a defendant must take a claimant's psychological make-up as he finds it, so that if the claimant is vulnerable to an abnormal psychiatric reaction then that too must be compensated for.[23]

3. Sudden or gradual?

With *pure* psychiatric harm, the analysis shifts and depends upon whether the harm was the product of a sudden traumatic event (typically involving PTSD) or was a reaction to a series of events over a period of time. In the case of sudden events, the distinction between primary and secondary victims (as will be explained) is of enormous significance, being dealt with as an aspect of the defendant's duty of care. Proving breach of duty and causation are, of course, still essential, but the principal focus will be on the nature of the claimant's damage and the circumstances in which it arose (which determine the extent of the defendant's duty).

In the case of an *event,* the claimant's psychiatric damage must be caused by 'shock', defined as an assault on the nervous system through a sudden appreciation by sight or sound of a horrifying event which violently agitates the mind. It does not include psychiatric illness caused by the accumulation over a period of time of more gradual assaults on the nervous system.[24] Thus, witnessing an accident in which one's child is seriously injured, producing PTSD, falls within the parameters of compensation. Developing depression as a result of having to care for a seriously injured child over a period of time does not. Technically, the courts will say that in such circumstances the defendant did not owe a duty of care to the claimant.

On the other hand, if the claimant's psychiatric problems are the product of the work environment (e.g. occupational stress), it is conceded that employers owe a duty of care in respect of the health and safety of their employees, including their mental health. The battle lines will be drawn around breach of duty (could the employer reasonably have foreseen that conditions in the workplace would have brought on a psychiatric illness in *this* particular plaintiff?) and causation (can it be said that the psychiatric illness was the product of work rather than other possible 'stressors' such as a difficult childhood, marital or financial problems?). Thus, the approach to the claimant who has a gradual onset of psychiatric problems depends on the causal context. If it is a gradual reaction to a specific event, the claim is excluded; if it is a gradual reaction to a series of events it may be allowed, at least in the context of the employer–employee relationship.

There is little, in logic, to explain these distinctions which have been much criticized. The need to determine the presence or absence of a sufficiently 'shocking' event and, particularly, the immediacy of a claimant's response to it has proved a fertile source of arbitrary distinctions and inconsistent decisions.[25] More fundamentally, it has regularly been argued that the 'sudden shocking event' requirement is a completely inappropriate criterion to employ, in that it reflects an outmoded view of the physiological processes by which psychiatric damage might result.[26]

4. Primary or secondary victim?

A further distinction that the courts draw in pure psychiatric damage cases that are adjudged to be the result of a sufficiently sudden shocking event is between so-called 'primary' victims and 'secondary' victims. A primary victim is one who sustains psychiatric harm through direct participation in a traumatic event in which they were at risk of, but actually avoided, physical injury.[27] A secondary victim is one who, following a sudden traumatic event, sustains psychiatric harm through witnessing the suffering of others. In addition to proving that psychiatric harm was foreseeable to a person of 'normal fortitude', secondary victims have to comply with a restrictive test in order to establish a relevant *duty of care* and do not recover compensation unless:

1. there was a relationship of close love and affection between the claimant and the person(s) seen to have been injured or endangered by the defendant; and

2. the claimant was close in time and space to the event, or its immediate aftermath; and

3. the claimant witnessed the event with his own unaided senses (being told about the event is not sufficient).

In broad terms, this excludes from compensation those who witness the death of or injury to 'strangers', and relatives who were not at or very close to the scene of death or injury to a loved one.

Primary victims do not have to satisfy these criteria. They qualify for a duty of care automatically, by virtue of having established the exposure to the risk of physical harm that categorized them as primary victims in the first place. Effectively, a primary victim is treated *as if* he sustained physical injury and is then dealt with on the same basis as a claimant who suffered consequential psychiatric harm. Moreover, the primary victim is entitled to compensation for *a completely unforeseeable* psychiatric reaction provided there was even a small risk of physical harm which has not actually occurred (i.e. the claimant sustained no physical injury).[28]

Fitting hysteria into the Law's structure

Given the paucity of cases in which there is even any reference to hysteria[29], it could be misleading to make categorical statements about the legal position. Its characterization as a form of psychiatric harm allows one, theoretically at least, to superimpose the same legal framework onto conversion hysteria. Hysteria is broad enough to provide for all the permutations offered by the consequential/pure, sudden/gradual, primary/secondary dichotomies. Thus, there is no reason why, if the medical evidence supports the contention, a claimant should not be entitled to be compensated for what is diagnosed as a hysterical reaction to an apparently trivial physical injury. For example, in *Williams* v *Department of the Environment*,[30] the plaintiff sustained an 'insignificant' physical injury to his back, but developed multiple symptoms of pain in the back, legs, arms, and fingers; retention of urine; difficulty with his bowels; dizziness; vomiting; and impairment of sexual function. The medical experts were agreed that the plaintiff's symptoms were without any organic basis, but also that the claimant was 'entirely genuine' and that he was probably suffering from hysteria. It was held that this was 'a case of genuine and disabling hysteria'. The judge commented that: 'It is the defendants' misfortune that the plaintiff has reacted as he has but, in law, they must take the plaintiff as they find him'.

Of course, the courts are heavily reliant on expert medical evidence in reaching judgements about diagnosis and causation, and if there is a dispute between the experts, the judge must resolve the conflict by selecting the view that he considers the most probable. The court wants to know basically two things:

1. Does the presentation correspond to a real psychiatric condition, and if so, are the symptoms genuine rather than exaggerated?

2. Is it causally linked to conduct of the defendant for which the defendant is culpable (i.e. can responsibility for these symptoms be allocated to the defendant's negligence?).

Sometimes, the causal link between the event and the claimant's damage is obscure, and here the claim is likely to fail on the basis that the claimant has not discharged the burden of proof that the defendant is responsible for his psychiatric condition. For example, in *Schofield* v *National Coal Board*[31], the claimant developed blepharospasm some time after an accident in which a jet of muddy water struck his face. Everyone accepted that his condition was genuine — he was not malingering — but there was no clear medical explanation for what the judge termed 'Mr. Schofield's mystifying complaint'. Several theories were put forward in evidence, involving both an organic origin and a non-organic origin, but the judge was quite simply unable to accept any of the explanations on the balance of probabilities.[32] One suggestion involved a hysterical reaction, but the judge commented that it was 'unprofitable' to discuss whether the condition was 'hysterical' in origin:

> ... for the term quite plainly has more than one meaning — as witness the energy expended by Mr. Field in demolishing a thesis in terms of classical Freudian psychoanalysis, involving the working out of childhood Oedipal conflicts, which I do not believe the plaintiff's advisers were ever putting forward. It is better to begin by asking whether there is any reason to suppose that the plaintiff is unconsciously feigning the symptoms of blepharospasm.

The answer to that question was 'no'. Nonetheless, the claim failed on causation, because the only real basis for the claimant's case was that he did not have the symptoms before the accident; he did develop them shortly afterwards; and therefore the accident must have caused the symptoms. This proposition was rejected because it was a '*post hoc ergo propter hoc*' argument and, said the judge, at best an unproven hypothesis.

The potential causal disparity

It seems likely that the problems of causation and proof faced by claimants are likely to be significantly greater in the case of hysteria. With legal conceptions conventionally being wrapped up with the notion of allocation of responsibility, the lawyer would see the precise diagnosis of a sufferer's harm as merely a preliminary step in the task of establishing a causal link to a responsible party. In a case of physical or consequential psychiatric harm, that link might be established in proving the direct impact with the claimant, and in cases of no physical impact, it would be sought in a link between a defendant and the event or events that triggered the emotional harm. Though the factual link between the nature of the harm and a third party might be difficult for a claimant actually to prove in any given case of PTSD, it is at least integral to the very notion of the harm itself in such cases. By contrast, while hysteria *could* be similarly event-driven and so attributable to a third party, we cannot ignore that it is, by definition, intrinsically personal to the sufferer. On one view, this could be seen as simply a more acute problem of causation, just as in a case of occupational stress the employer may allege that the claimant's depression was not work-related.

The only major case law example of hysteria[33] supports the suspicion that it is far more likely to be introduced by the defendant than the claimant. In *Pickford* v *Imperial Chemical Industries plc,* the claimant, a secretary, alleged that cramp in her hand was a work-induced 'repetitive strain injury' ('r.s.i.').[34] The genuineness of the symptoms was not in dispute, though their aetiology was. The court heard medical evidence from the claimant that the injury was an organic condition, due to trauma or physical injury, and *from the defendant* employers that it was psychogenic, due to a conversion hysteria. Such assertions suited the parties' respective contentions on the question of causation. The claimant would, inevitably, contend that the cramp had an organic cause because, in turn, that would be most consistent with her assertion that it was work-related and, thereby, the defendant's responsibility. By contrast, the defendant would naturally assert that the cause of any cramp was psychogenic because, in the absence of a finding that the claimant was malingering, that would put the maximum possible distance between their work systems and the claimant's harm, thereby probably frustrating the claimant's task of proving causation. It also raised the hurdle for the claimant in proving breach of duty, since it is easier to demonstrate that an employer should reasonably have foreseen that a regime of unrelieved repetitive movements might cause physical injury, but significantly more difficult to prove that the employer ought reasonably to have anticipated a psychiatric reaction to such a regime. The claimant lost. The House of Lords found that, by virtue of the controversy over the origin of the claimant's injuries, she had not discharged her positive legal burden of proof. Their Lordships did not conclude that the claimant's genuine symptoms were actually a hysterical reaction, merely that she had not proved on the balance of probabilities that, *as she alleged*, they had a physical origin. The claim failed because, in effect, it fell into the legal limbo of 'not proven'.

Thus, where the claimant alleges a physical 'route' for the symptoms, he or she must prove, on the medical evidence, that there was actually a physical causal mechanism. Of course, in order to succeed in the claim, he or she would then have had to go on to prove that the physical cause was attributable to the defendant's fault.

Similarly, in *McWhinnie* v *British Coal Corporation*[35], the claimant suffered a minor back injury, but had serious symptoms of pain for which there was no organic explanation. The defendants sought to allege that he was suffering from conversion hysteria through a process of 'converting' his initial conscious and deliberate exaggeration of symptoms into a state of unconscious chronic invalidism. This argument was rejected on the medical evidence, it being accepted that although there was no organic basis for his symptoms, the claimant had developed the unconscious psychological condition of abnormal illness behaviour.[36]

The inconsistency of symptoms allowed for by DSM–IV can also make conversion hysteria a problematic diagnosis for a claimant to advance:

> Conversion symptoms are often inconsistent. A 'paralyzed' extremity will be moved inadvertently while dressing or when attention is directed elsewhere. If placed above the head and released, a 'paralyzed' arm will briefly retain its position, then fall to the side, rather than striking the head. Unacknowledged strength in antagonistic muscles, normal muscle tone, and intact reflexes may be demonstrated.

Whilst psychiatrists, as opposed to bigoted orthopaedic surgeons,[37] might be comfortable with such inconsistencies, the lay person, including the lawyer, may view with scepticism a diagnosis that with some degree of rhetorical flourish might be described as the 'malingerer's charter'. It is here that the medical and legal discourse really do part company — the medical profession may want to treat the patient's condition; the legal system wants to be convinced (on a balance of probabilities) that there are good grounds for saying that a third party, the defendant, should pay money, possibly large sums of money, to the claimant. At this point, the tension that has encapsulated the relationship between law and psychiatry over the last hundred years or so is probably at its most acute. This is not to suggest that a judge could never be persuaded by expert medical opinion that apparently inconsistent symptoms can be explained by the claimant's psychiatric condition (although it would appear that this is more likely to be diagnosed as 'abnormal illness behaviour'). Nonetheless, whatever the diagnostic niceties, it is probable that a trier of fact[38] would respond to such evidence with some caution, at least raising the possibility of conscious malingering or, more neutrally, as an indication that the claimant's condition (whatever its explanation, genuine or not) cannot be regarded as causally linked to the event(s) alleged by the claimant. It may be that this judicial caution is not necessarily the product of scepticism about the medical evidence as much as unease about a legal rule that requires a defendant to pick up the bill for all the unforeseeable psychiatric consequences that a claimant with a 'vulnerable personality' might develop.

Notes

1 A search of 'Lexis' — a database of all Court of Appeal or House of Lords decisions and many, though not all, High Court cases that have gone to trial since 1945 — found only four cases in which the term 'conversion hysteria' or 'hysteria' has been used. The term 'illness behaviour' produced nine cases; and 'functional overlay' identified 77 cases.

2 See e.g. *Scott* v *Nucrete Buildings Ltd* [1998] PIQR Q112 — no pathological cause for gross restriction of the plaintiff's back; in the absence of psychiatric evidence demonstrating a psychogenic component of the claimant's complaints, the appropriate conclusion was that there was a significant degree of conscious exaggeration of symptoms by the plaintiff.

3 Professor Dawson has memorably, but somewhat disdainfully, characterized it as 'that well-known ailment of lawyers, a hardening of the categories': Dawson, (1959) Restitution or damages. *Ohio State Law Journal*, **20**, 175 at 187.

4 Mendelson, (1998) *The Interfaces Between Law and Medicine, the History of Liability for Negligently Occasioned Psychiatric Injury (Nervous Shock)*, p. 24. Dartmouth.

5 *Page* v *Smith* [1995] 2 All ER 736, 752, emphasis added.

6 [1888] 13 AC 222. For discussion of the *medical* controversies which underlay this response see: Mendelson, (above, note 4), Chapter 2.

7 *Dulieu* v *White* [1901] 2 KB 669.

8 *Hambrook* v *Stokes Bros* [1925] 1 KB 141.

9 [1999] 1 All ER 1.

10 See Law Commission (1998) *Liability for Psychiatric Illness*, Law Com. No. 249, para. 6.5 *et seq*; McCulloch *et al.* (1995) Post traumatic stress disorder: turning the tide without opening the floodgates. *Medicine, Science and Law* **35**, 287–9; Mullany, N. (1995) Psychiatric damage in the House of Lords — fourth time unlucky: Page v Smith. *Journal of Law and Medicine*, **3**, 112; and, most forcefully, Mullany and Handford, (1993) *Tort Liability for Psychiatric Damage, The Law of 'Nervous Shock'*, The Law Book Co., Sydney; and (1998) *Law Quarterly Review*, **113**, 410 at 415.

11 [1983] 1 AC 410, 432.

12 *Mount Isa Mines Ltd* v *Pusey* [1970] 125 CLR 383, 395. For an analysis of how the modern legal approach might measure up to Windeyer J. 's concerns see Sprince, A. (1998) *Legal Studies*, **18**, 59.

13 Trimble, M. (1995) Medicine and the Law: conflict or debate. *Journal of Psychosomatic Research*, **39**, 671–4.

14 [1995] 2 All ER 736.

15 Law Commission (1998) *Liability for Psychiatric Illness*, Law Com. No. 249.

16 In particular, those contained in the *Diagnostic and Statistical Manual of Mental Disorders* and the *International Classification of Mental and Behavioural Disorders* — known, in their latest guises, as 'DSM– IV' and 'ICD–10' respectively.

17 (1995) *Journal of Psychosomatic Research*, **39**, 671 at 673.

18 1993 SLT 467.

19 A view which the claimant's expert characterized as a 'bigoted orthopaedic opinion', in the sense that there was a tendency among some orthopaedic surgeons to consider that if a problem cannot be dealt with by means of surgery, it either does not exist or the persons with the problem are malingerers. Of course, there may be both a genuine physical injury together with deliberate exaggeration of symptoms: *McFall* v *West Dunbartonshire Council* 1999 SLT 775.

20 In the final analysis, a judge's decision about whether the claimant is 'genuine' comes down to who he believes in the witness box. This is not to say that if the claimant is found to be 'genuine' an expert's opinion that the claimant is malingering will be regarded as an untruth, simply that the judge will conclude that the expert is mistaken. It is a case of assessing the evidence as a whole, including the expert evidence supporting the claimant's case that his symptoms are genuine, and the claimant's demeanour in giving evidence. 'Genuine' symptoms will be distinguished from feigned or exaggerated symptoms (the assumption being that if they are unconsciously produced, they are 'genuine'), although there remains the question of whether the symptoms are causally related to the defendant's negligent conduct. On that issue, the expert evidence will be crucial, though there may be other evidence (previous instances of similar symptoms which could not be attributed to a specific event, for example) which may undermine the claimant's case on causation.

21 1999 SLT 539. See also *Burns* v *Harper Collins Ltd* 1997 SLT 607 — another case of low back pain resulting in illness behaviour.

22 On the other hand, there are of course cases in which malingering, amounting to outright fraud, has been found: *Spence* v *Wilson* (1998) unreported, Court of Session. Note that from the perspective of establishing legal liability there is no distinction between 'abnormal illness behaviour' and 'hysteria' provided that they are both characterized by expert medical evidence as genuine psychiatric illnesses. What the court wants to know is basically two things: (1) is it genuine? (i.e. is this a real psychiatric condition, and if so are all the symptoms genuine, as opposed to exaggerated?); and (2) is it causally linked to conduct of the defendant for which the defendant is culpable (i.e. can we allocate responsibility for these symptoms to the defendant's wrong —usually, negligence?).

23 Though if there is evidence that the claimant would probably have suffered such a psychological reaction to some other event for which the defendant is not responsible, this will have the effect of reducing the award of damages, just as, for example, where the claimant loses his job as a result of a physical injury caused by the defendant but it subsequently emerges that he has a disease which would in any event have caused him to give up work, the defendant is only responsible for loss of earnings up to the point in time at which the disease would have forced the claimant to give up his employment: *Jobling* v *Associated Dairies Ltd* [1982] AC 794.

24 *Alcock* v *Chief Constable of the South Yorkshire Police* [1991] 4 All ER 907, 918. This partly explains the lawyer's use of the term 'nervous shock', despite being urged on occasions to drop the phrase from the legal lexicon.

25 See, in particular, *Sion* v *Hampstead Health Authority* [1994] 5 Med LR 170; *Taylorson* v *Shieldness Produce Ltd* [1994] PIQR P329; and *Tredget* v *Bexley Health Authority* [1994] 5 Med LR 178.

26 See, for example, Teff, H. (1996) *Tort Law Review*, **4**, 44.

27 *Page* v *Smith* [1995] 2 All ER 736, 755, *per* Lord Lloyd.

28 This is the effect of the much-criticized majority ruling of the House of Lords in *Page* v *Smith*.

29 We have found four: *Williams* v *Department of the Environment* (1981) unreported, QBD; *Schofield* v *National Coal Board* (1983) unreported, QBD; *McWhinnie* v *British Coal Corporation* 1993 SLT 467, Court of Session, Outer House; *Pickford* v *Imperial Chemical Industries plc* [1998] 3 All ER 462, HL. In only one of these cases (*Williams*) did the court conclude that the claimant had actually suffered a hysterical reaction.

30 (1981) unreported, QBD.

31 (1983) unreported QBD.

32 The balance of probabilities is the standard of proof applied in civil cases, meaning simply 'more likely than not'. This is clearly not a particularly exacting standard, at least when compared to what counts as 'proof' in scientific inquiry. Nonetheless, once a fact is 'proved' to this standard (a process that, essentially, requires the parties to convince the judge), it is assumed to be 100 per cent true. This is because the court has a duty to make a decision on the evidence presented to it. A doctor may be able to 'wait and see' before reaching a conclusion on diagnosis; a court must simply make up its mind, since at the end of the day that is its function — to give a judgement on the matters in dispute. Occasionally, the evidence is so equivocal that the judge may be unable to decide the issue one way or the other, in which case the claimant will fail to discharge the burden of proof which rests with the claimant on both the question of breach of duty and causation.

33 That is, the only example to have reached the appellate courts.

34 The term 'r.s.i' has been condemned as 'meaningless in medical terms' (in a letter to *The Times*, 4 November 1993, from Mr Campbell Semple FRCS), and in *Mughal* v *Reuters Ltd* [1993] IRLR 571 the court refused to recognize it as a diagnosis in its own right. Nowadays, 'work-related upper limb disorders' ('WRULDS') appears to be the generally accepted generic term for the group of conditions that r.s.i. has been used to label.

35 (1993) SLT 467, Court of Session, Outer House.

36 The evidence of Professor Gordon Waddell, Honorary Professor of Orthopaedic Surgery at Glasgow University, suggested that conversion hysteria was not a term commonly used and that many psychiatrists now regard it as being totally discredited. However, when it was used it involved a conversion from a psychiatric illness into physical symptoms, such as pain, not the reverse. It was a psychiatric diagnosis of a primarily psychiatric illness and that was partly why it became discredited when it was used by non-psychiatric medical practitioners. (Note that this was the evidence of a surgeon, expressing a view about a psychiatric condition.).

37 See footnote 19.

38 The trier of fact is the person or tribunal who tries or hears the case, as opposed to an appellate court who do not re-hear the case and do not make findings of primary fact. The Court of Appeal do not (except in very rare cases) decide which witness should be believed, if the judge has given reasons for believing witness A rather than witness B.

12 Conversion, dissociation, or doxomorphic disorder

Harold Merskey

Conversion and dissociation are late nineteenth-century terms used for what have been regarded as classical hysterical symptoms: conversion for bodily symptoms e.g. paralysis; dissociation for psychological symptoms such as loss of memory, fugue, or alleged alternation of personalities. Conversion is associated with Freud's views of dynamic psychiatry in which an emotional conflict, associated with repression of a problem into the unconscious mind, causes the production of a physical symptom that solves the problem. In dissociation, the Freudian view holds that a mental symptom serves a similar purpose.

Dissociation, a term favoured by Pierre Janet, was understood by Janet to be due to degeneration and weakness of the mental structure of the individual. Most recently, it has been used as a term for the equivalent of conversion in Freudian thinking. Still more recently, some have favoured using the word as a concept to justify alleged loss of memory, frequently associated with allegations of sexual abuse in recovered childhood memories.

This article briefly states the background to ideas of hysteria, and the evolution of these terms. It then considers the phenomena linked with classical hysterical symptoms of conversion disorder and emphasizes the key notion of a symptom that corresponds to the patient's idea of a disorder. Such a symptom may be called doxogenic (from the Greek *doxa* for thought or opinion, and *gennan* for causing).

Different causal relationships of hysterical symptoms are examined. Certain organically based symptoms can resemble symptoms due to patients' thoughts, particularly in the case of regional pain. Some temporary apparent conversion symptoms may also have a relevant organic aetiology. Accordingly, we should talk of doxomorphic symptoms (i.e. symptoms resembling those due to patients' thoughts) without automatically committing the description to a particular aetiology.

Introduction

I should begin by explaining or apologizing for a new word: doxomorphic. I hope the importance of the word will be evident later, but for the moment I should simply state its origins. There is an existing word *doxogenic* which comes from the Greek *doxa* (opinion) and *gennan* (to produce) (Dorland 1974). I put this old word forward a few years ago (Merskey 1994) as a step in the neutralization of pejorative descriptions of hysteria, or as an alternative to more ambitious theories of hysteria. I offer doxomorphic as a word to describe symptoms which resemble those due to patients' ideas. Doxomorphic, unlike *doxogenic*, does not state an aetiology.

The theoretical position on aetiology is that so-called hysterical symptoms resemble and are due to notions that patients have about their bodies or mental functions.

Doxogenic implies that the symptoms resemble notions that the patients entertain, and also the symptoms develop because of those ideas, whether about bodily functions or mental abilities. Doxogenic fits well with sceptical views of multiple personality disorder. However, it is imperfect with regard to some bodily complaints. For example, regional pain was commonly described in the past as hysterical. Thus, a painful complaint throughout a limb or loss of sensitivity in a limb, widely distributed, was often held to be a hysterical symptom (Hurst 1920) — which it might be.

Current neurophysiology has made it abundantly clear that a regional pain can occur as a result of noxious stimulation affecting a small area of a limb or other part of the body and generalizing to a larger area that crosses dermatomal divisions. This happens because of the plasticity of response in second order neurons of the spinal cord. Thus, receptor fields of second order neurons in the spinal cord may enlarge, giving regional effects rather than effects limited to a segmental boundary or the territory of a particular nerve. These pathophysiologically induced symptoms or signs correspond to symptoms or signs that may be induced as a result of patients' ideas. Whatever the cause, the symptoms can be described as doxomorphic since the pattern may correspond to complaints due to ideas. Thus, when we talk of doxomorphic symptoms we are not committed necessarily to a psychological aetiology for the symptoms — only that the symptoms resemble complaints that have a psychological aetiology, and this can prove handy, as I hope I shall show later.

The origins of conversion and dissociation

Whilst what is currently called conversion or dissociation has often been represented under the term hysteria, historical studies have shown that the word hysteria has had a larger scope. That scope has included some physical illness, some depressive states, some anxiety disorders, psychophysiological changes, hypochondriasis, unconscious ideas, various personality traits, allegations about motives, and patterns due to suggestion or even to self-deception. My task here is to focus on the issues of conversion and dissociation. In doing that it helps to note the historical background so that we can circumscribe the main problem and then, I hope, advance.

Notions of hysteria are typically attributed to the Greeks and linked to the unnecessary idea that the womb moved around the body. I say unnecessary because it is not clear that the Hippocratic collection ever endorsed such a notion (King 1994, Merskey and Potter 1989, Merskey and Merskey 1993, Merskey 1995a). Whatever obscurities or absurdities clouded the notion of hysteria in the long march from classical antiquity through the mediaeval era to the early modern period, the concept of hysteria or hysterical complaints achieved a certain coherence, exemplified in the works of two overlapping seventeenth-century physicians, Willis (1684) and Sydenham (1697).

For Sydenham, a hysterical symptom essentially resulted from a stressful event, caused a disturbance in the nervous system, and was liable to have varied emotional and physical expression, including organic changes in the body. This thinking about hysteria only really changed after nineteenth-century advances in neurology which enabled physicians to determine that some bodily symptoms had an organic cause while others apparently did not. The notion of hysteria as a physical complaint following from an idea was formally stated by Reynolds (1869), but in the second half of the nineteenth century, hysteria was still understood by Breuer, and even also later by Freud, as 'any general neurosis without specific localisation' (Hirschmuller 1989). This is essentially the starting point from which both Freud and Janet began their writing about conversion or dissociation. For them, hysteria was an illness affecting the brain, not restricted to any part, commonly influenced by hereditary degeneration, often linked with anxiety or even depression, and manifesting physical complaints. These two authors overlapped with Janet in their understanding both of dissociation and conversion, but differed significantly in certain respects.

Janet established his ideas about dissociation on the basis of his concept of consciousness derived from John Stuart Mill and from Herbert Spencer's book, *The Principles of Psychology* (Janet 1889). According to these theories, consciousness was a field of variable size in which sensory phenomena — and other experiences including ideas — received attention. A universal experience shifts the direction of attention and the items which remain in consciousness vary. Janet assumed or argued that consciousness could be narrowed or enlarged. The most extreme case of 'retraction' (narrowing) was attributed to catatonia. Currently, we might say that he believed that the contents of consciousness fluctuated in accordance with selective attention, monitoring first one set of sense data and then another. Sounds give way to visual items, which give way to tactile sensations, and so on; our own thoughts, or comments addressed to us, pop in and out of attention or consciousness.

The field of consciousness must vary with individuals and with their states of mind (Janet 1907, p. 307). There is a kaleidoscope of impressions or notions. According to Janet (1907, p. 304), the kaleidoscope also involves the idea of 'I see, I feel a movement'. In addition, consciousness includes the idea of personality, or the whole person of the individual, as well as all those other cognitive constituents which do not necessarily involve self-reference.

Janet held that the field of consciousness tended to diminish or become more 'retracted' (rétrécissement) while neglected sensation might become lost altogether. Thus, anaesthesia might appear in a neglected arm. The difference from normal lies in the patient's susceptibility to such retraction or narrowing or losses in consequence of 'feebleness . . . of thinking' (1907). Patients subject to this would also suffer from a loss of will or abulia.

Janet then used the concept of dissociation to explain the varied phenomena which were considered to be hysteria:

> Hysteria is a form of mental depression characterized by the retraction of the field of personal consciousness and a tendency to dissociation and emancipation of the systems of ideas and functions that constitute personality (Janet 1889, p. 322).

He was pleased to observe that Breuer and Freud had expressed a very similar opinion with respect to hysteria when they wrote, according to his translation:

> The disposition to this dissociation, and at the same time, the formation of [hypnoid] states of consciousness . . . constitutes the fundamental phenomenon of this neurosis (Breuer and Freud 1893–1895).

Janet derived his ideas of splitting from hypnosis. Much of his published work has rested upon hypnotizing patients and undertaking various manipulations both before, during, and after hypnosis in order to demonstrate the separation of functions between different parts of the mind, as he thought. He used hypnosis on behalf of Charcot to produce hysterical paralyses and other motor phenomena which Charcot was able to demonstrate corresponded to the patients' ideas rather than to organic neurological findings (Charcot 1872). This confirmed Reynolds' view that such symptoms could be due to the influence of an idea. Today, when hypnosis is best understood as the enactment of a social role, we need not linger on the issue as to what is a hypnoid state of consciousness. Few if any serious students of hypnosis now consider it to be a state or trance phenomenon.

Freud took dissociation more for granted than Janet. He used it at first, but then his attention was more taken with dynamic drives and motives. Breuer (Breuer and Freud 1893–1895) emphasized that dissociation was related to 'an excessive efficiency, the habitual coexistence of two heterogeneous trains of ideas' — which may not add very much.

Dalbiez (1941, I: p. 190) expressed the view that has been generally accepted that, according to Janet, abnormalities of physical activity are explained by 'the purely negative idea of "*deficiency*". Janet's idea was essentially one of hereditary degeneration. A deficiency of integration of the whole field of consciousness only occurred in the individuals who suffered from dissociation or splitting. His thoughts about weakness and deficiencies in development extended also to hysterical personality. The many unattractive traits that have been linked to hysterical personality owe something to his view of the disorder as a degenerative state based upon hereditary weakness.

Freud did not like the idea of deficiency and emphasized dynamic explanations and the play of mental forces, and invoked the special process of 'repression' (Breuer and Freud 1893–1895, p. 61). He also viewed hereditary degeneration as predisposing to hysteria. He typically viewed dissociation as the removal of ideas from one compartment to another, as in the *Introductory Lectures* (1917, p. 248), where he uses the metaphors of rooms with door-keepers for the unconscious and conscious minds. It seems that Freud made the link between dissociation and conversion because he was adding something (i.e. the notion of active processes) to the concept of dissociation, rather than in order to substitute conversion for dissociation. The usual understanding of Freud's position is that dissociation was part of the mechanisms powered by the psychodynamics of repression.

Meanwhile Janet, although now often credited with the recognition of post-traumatic stress disorder, made little reference to the idea of conflict until quite late in his career (Janet 1925), and then only briefly.

Probably everybody writing about Freud and his original ideas turns to the *Studies on Hysteria* (Breuer and Freud, 1893–1895) to find the theoretical origins of conversion disorder. Typically, this is seen as a process in which an emotional problem is converted into a physical disorder. For example, in one of his patients (Elisabeth von R.), Freud described her facial pain as a successful conversion phenomenon which spared her from the conviction that she loved her sister's husband: 'she repressed the erotic idea from consciousness and transformed the amount of its affect into physical pain'. This idea of quantitative conversion of 'psychic' affect into a physical disorder is not maintained in later dynamic formulations. Early on, Freud distinguished between actual neuroses, such as anxiety due to sexual repression or coitus interruptus on the one hand, and psychoneurosis on the other. In the actual neuroses, a physical symptom was produced by the conversion of physical energy due to anxiety into a bodily symptom. In the psychoneuroses, the whole mechanism was psychological.

As is well recognized, the distinction was later dropped. The theory of repression became popular and is dealt with in the chapter in this volume by Temple (p. 283). I need only make one or two comments upon it therefore for the purpose of this discussion.

Repression and dissociation

The nature of repression as described by Freud is rather fluid. Erdelyi (1985, 1990) has listed thirty-two words or phrases that Freud used to refer to repression, ranging from 'not thinking of the unbearable idea' through 'preventing . . . from becoming' and including dissociation, intentional forgetting, keeping away from consciousness, suppression, keeping something out of consciousness, and 'splitting' of the mind/ego. Erdelyi takes 'the essence of repression lies simply in turning something away and keeping it at a distance from the conscious' (Freud 1915) as the most clear formulation possible.

Erdelyi argues that the terms repression and dissociation have no formal distinction and that the essence of repression is simply 'not thinking' about a topic. The terms repression and dissociation have often been used simultaneously and, also, repression is used as an automatic accompaniment to the idea of conversion in dynamic psychiatry. Despite the fact that Freud attributed such varied meanings to repression, it usually suggests some absolute blocking of knowledge or awareness or recognition of unwanted material, so that it is not spontaneously accessible to the person unless some exceptional manouevre is performed.

The heretical alternative is to say that repression or dissociation is a graded phenomenon without hard and fast boundaries — but that is not how it has been typically seen. This alternative viewpoint however would accommodate quite well the observation by Sir Charles Symonds (1995) that typical patients with conversion hysteria seem always to have some awareness that they can do differently.

For those who want to defend repression as a powerful force there is another embarrassment. Social psychologists have failed to produce by experiment any adequate evidence of repression. After reviewing more than sixty years of research on repression, Holmes (1990) concluded that the effort to demonstrate the occurrence of repression in the human laboratory had failed. Not only that, but belief in it has led to an enormous disaster in the form of the recovered memory movement which produced so many demonstrably false allegations against innocent people. These allegations have included recovered memories from before the age of three (a biological impossibility), recollections of visits by aliens from outer space, recollections of past lives, memories of organized Satanic ritual abuse, and preposterous beliefs in dozens, scores, hundreds, and even thousands of alter personalities. They have produced an inevitable reaction of scepticism, leading professional societies to warn strongly against therapies based upon such theory (Canadian Psychiatric Association 1996, Royal College of Psychiatrists 1997, Brandon et al. 1998).

Clinical patterns of dissociation

Are there then no true examples of dissociation? Typically, psychiatrists and neurologists, but especially psychiatrists, have believed in the occurrence of dissociative amnesia — an acute short-term, psychologically induced loss of memory. Even if we reject the view that long-term dissociation can occur, does the same apply to short-term effects? There is literature on dissociative amnesia presenting as an acute loss of memory or as a 'mood state'. The former is a simple loss of memory; the latter, a loss of memory with wandering or travel and after a mood change. Looking at the clinical circumstances in which such cases appear, it turns out that the moment one asks: 'Is this really a case of lost memory with convincing repression?' the claim becomes hard to accept.

Some short-term loss of memory that might be psychogenic occurs in relation to organic brain damage whether from head injury or other physical illness affecting the brain — or so it is thought. Since symptoms of this sort are usually brief, it is reasonable to consider whether they are related in some fashion to the disturbance of consciousness that occurs organically.

In patients with acute paralysis from strokes, complete or partial remission of neurological signs is sometimes followed by an apparent hysterical motor disorder, in which the patient is able to do things on physical examination which are incompatible with an organic paralysis. Since such symptoms usually remit very quickly, it may be that there is a temporary disorganization of brain function which goes beyond damage to the pyramidal tracts and involves some cortical or other region linked with volition or the intention to act. An organic effect gains credence from imaging studies that suggest that there are cortical locations which function when an intention to act is formed by a subject and other areas (e.g. orbito-frontal and anterior cingulate cortex) are activated when movement is apparently volitionally inhibited (Marshall *et al.* 1997). Even if more evidence is needed to flesh out this latter information, it remains the case that short-term, seemingly psychogenic symptoms have a clinical link with organic paralyses and remit fairly soon after the organic injury has recovered or stabilized. Thus, they raise an obstacle to any strong psychological theory of continuing repression as an important part of mental functioning.

Another type of apparently psychogenic memory loss is found in individuals who otherwise have clear consciousness and report a sudden disappearance of their memory for personal details (who they are, where they are from, and so forth), but retain excellent memories for other events in their environment and continuing sophisticated skills like the ability to play chess, handle mathematical manipulations, or manage a computer. One of the simplest such patterns, seen in the British army in the 1950s, was of conscript soldiers facing charges for being late back from leave or absent without leave, and reporting a loss of memory. These men ordinarily recovered with a little history taking and gentle suggestion or persuasion. More persistent cases of amnesia have been claimed, but ordinarily in circumstances where their truthfulness is suspect, as in individuals facing legal proceedings.

A third type of apparent psychogenic amnesia occurs most often in elderly individuals, who are perhaps on the verge of mild cognitive decline related to age and troubled. Pseudo-dementia from depression is a well-recognized problem, even if it is not a formal diagnostic category. Treatment of the depression generally leads to recovery of memory which is ordinarily not wholly lost but rather impaired by poor attention and difficulty in concentration.

I have also seen conversion symptoms or dissociative symptoms (astasia, abasia, hysterical gaits, or brief memory impairment of a psychogenic type) arising after an overdose of sedatives, in the recovery phase, or in patients whose anticonvulsants, especially diphenyl-hydantoin, had reached levels higher than the usual desirable upper limit. These symptoms too remitted quickly on the return of the organic situation to normal. If these are, as I think, the main patterns of acute psychogenic amnesia, or other acute dissociative symptoms, we might well conclude that they can be symptoms that serve a purpose in some instances but that they may also be understood variously as pathophysiological aberrations, transitory claims to a particular social role, the effect of depression, or a factitious claim close to malingering.

Hacking (1997, 1998) has made an important historical contribution to modern understanding in this respect. Hacking argues that dissociative fugue was first treated as a distinct psychiatric illness in Bordeaux in 1887 by Tissié, and was taken up by Charcot as *automatisme ambulatoire* in 1888. The diagnosis was closely associated with vagrancy as a social problem and with the existence of conscription on the European continent. Typical patients laid claim to losses of memory or a compulsion to travel (including walking long distances), or both. By 1910, in France, this phenomenon had faded like the super-ordinate diagnosis of hysteria — although it was exported to Italy, Germany, and Russia. It did not invade the Anglo-Saxon world which lacked conscription, but I suspect it contributed to the acceptability of the idea of memory loss as a psychological (i.e. non-organic) phenomenon.

It seems that a continuing search of the medical literature and clinical experience both lead to serious doubts about the veridicality of memory loss in psychogenic amnesia. Thus, once one asks the simple question referring to absolute loss of memory 'How can this be?', the diagnosis of psychogenic amnesia begins to fade also.

As a twentieth-century example of the same issue we have multiple dissociative or conversion symptoms in the First World War. It now seems clear that shell-shock diagnosed by British doctors, but not by many others, was a convenient term which allowed patients to have symptoms resembling those of the physically injured (and often modelled upon physical symptoms that the soldier had first suffered), powered by enormous anxiety which gripped the soldiers who had been exposed to terrible stress, and who could not declare that they were anxious or frightened but could say that they had suffered a disability (Merskey 1995*a* and *b*). In other words, the shell-shock of World War I probably reflected genuine post-traumatic stress disorder to which hysterical symptoms were added because of physical injury and the modelling pattern. It also reflected the necessary convention that it was better to have a seemingly physical complaint than admit to tremendous fear, no matter how justifiable the latter. Hysterical symptoms were less frequent in the Second World War, presumably because symptoms of anxiety were more accepted and usually would be taken into account (see Palmer's chapter in this volume, p 12).

These clinical events lead to continuing doubts about the validity of the view that even acute memory loss or acute conversion symptoms reflect the occurrence of a mechanism of repression.

I still want to take into account however one other type of seemingly psychological loss of capacity. This example comes from Kretschmer, as well as other more casual observers. Kretschmer (1926) was one of the many German doctors who acquired ample knowledge of combat hysteria in the First World War, adopting what we would now call a psychobiological view. He regarded spasmodic seizures, catatonic stupors, tremors, convulsive tics, paralyses, muscular contractions, anaesthesias, and hyper-anaesthesias of psychic origin as 'hysteria', and argued that these forms of behaviour were primitive survival reactions. (Forerunners of this view included Mörchen and Kraepelin.) For Kretschmer, 'hysterical' means psychogenic patterns of reaction in which a tendency to dissimulate finds expression through instinctive, reflexive action or as a built-in survival mechanism. There were two major primitive patterns that seemed to him to be highly relevant. One was the 'instinctive flurry' and another, the 'death feint'. The instinctive flurry is like the behaviour of a bee or bird imprisoned in a room and flying frantically, until carried out by one movement through a crack in a window; death feint is, in other words, 'playing dead'. Both have survival value, and the second may also be labelled fear paralysis, at least in some instances.

Perhaps all the phenomena of dissociation or conversion can be more or less accounted for by putting together the several types of event or symptom that I have just described, and saying of them that they reflect understandable reactions, but that they involve neither repression nor dissociation as latterly understood. This fits well with the luminous discussion of hysterical symptoms by Babinski who identified the essential features of 'hysteria' as corresponding to those symptoms that could be produced by experimental suggestion, claiming that the form, intensity, and duration of those symptoms could also be determined by suggestion. He called this 'pithiatism' from the Greek words for persuading and curable (Babinski and Froment 1918). Not everyone is satisfied of course with such an approach to dissociation, and there are other issues connected with conversion, and I comment on those next.

Conversion and somatization

DSM–III, the *Diagnostic and Statistical Manual: Third Edition* of the American Psychiatric Association, was firmly based, according to its authors, on an 'atheoretical approach'. The only exceptions were those conditions where aetiology was held to be fairly well established. Ironically, somatoform and dissociative disorders were described as usually being due to conflicts. I do not mean to say that they are not now seen as due to conflicts, but that the role of conflict and the dynamic theory that underlay those views is now questioned.

The use of the word somatoform and the category of somatization disorder has led to a particular way of talking about symptoms that in the past were considered to be conversion symptoms. Individuals who now have the symptoms are often described as somatizers or subject to somatization. Lipowski (1988) provided an amended description of somatization as 'the tendency to experience and communicate somatic distress and symptoms unaccounted for by pathological findings, to attribute them to physical illness, and to seek medical help for them'. Kirmayer and Robbins (1991) made three operational definitions of somatization: (1) high levels of functional somatic distress; (2) hypochondriasis; and (3) presentations among patients with current major depression or anxiety. In an extensive survey (685 patients attending two family medicine clinics), 23.6 per cent met criteria for one or more forms of somatization, but a majority of patients met only one type of these three criteria. In clinical practice and in research reports the term somatization is used in a variety of ways which may be summarized, perhaps not completely, as follows:

(1) somatization disorder; (2) conversion symptoms; (3) hypochondriasis; (4) heightened bodily awareness resembling hypochondriasis but responding to reassurance on examination or investigations; (5) psychophysiological events associated with anxiety or depression; (6) certain types of somatic complaints in schizophrenic patients perhaps with a delusional basis; and (7) any of these combined with organic disease.

This variety of meanings almost rivals the number of meanings or subdivisions which have been offered for hysteria, although somatization is a far more recent term. It might be best not to use the term at all.

But we still have to consider those physical symptoms which appear to be due to ideas, or resemble a patient's expectation. ICD–10 (World Health Organization 1992) described such symptoms as 'dissociative (conversion)', and what I have been talking about as dissociative symptoms were also called dissociative. This approach was logical. It is fair to suppose that conversion disorders are similar to dissociative disorders in the ways in which they occur and in which they are treated by patients and physicians, and that there is no particular value in distinguishing between dissociation and conversion. Doxomorphic would be a better label for the whole range.

The expansion of dissociation

Proponents of the belief that the mind can rigidly split off the awareness of a problem from conscious operations face a serious difficulty. In response, an attempt has been made to bolster the classical idea of dissociation as splitting by adding to it the experiences of 'numbing' or 'depersonalization' or 'derealization', 'dizziness', and 'forgetfulness' about particular items in the environment at the time of stress. Thus the very common phenomenon of differential attention or preferential treatment for particular material in consciousness is emphasized. One such type of the contents of consciousness may be information that is not immediately important to a particular thought. For example, a driver ignoring house numbers while concentrating on the flow of vehicles at the next set of traffic lights gives selective attention to the most relevant sense data or thoughts about a particular task. Another type is neglecting material which is unwanted emotionally rather than unattractive. A failure to hear a request to undertake a chore such as 'take out the garbage' when one is reading an interesting book, provides the most commonplace example.

Inappropriately exploiting such effects, a test such as the Dissociative Experiences Scale (Bernstein and Putnam 1986) can be used to secure positive personal answers to questions based on statements like 'Some people have the experience of driving a car and suddenly realizing that they don't remember what has happened during all or part of the trip', or 'Some people have the experience of finding themselves dressed in clothes that they don't remember putting on', or 'Some people have the experience of being in a familiar place but finding it strange and unfamiliar', or 'Some people find that they sometimes are able to ignore pain'.

Questions based on these statements may elicit strongly positive, personal answers without the individuals involved having had anything like the experience of 'splitting' which is supposed to occur with dissociative disorders. Similarly, a structured clinical interview for DSM–IV disorders by Steinberg (1995) asks questions about 'amnesia':

'Have you ever felt as if there were large gaps in your memory?', 'How much time was missing?', 'How often has it occurred?', 'Have you ever had difficulty remembering your daily activities?', and 'Have you ever been unable to remember your name, age, address, or other important personal information?'.

Under 'depersonalization' individuals are asked 'Have you ever felt that you were watching yourself from a point outside your body?', 'Have you ever had the feeling that you were a stranger to yourself?', 'Have you ever felt that you were going through the motions of living, that the real you was far away from what was happening to you?', 'Have you ever felt that you are two different people, one person going through the motions of life, and the other observing quietly?', and 'Have you ever felt as if your emotions were not in your control?'. These questions, among others, raise grave doubts about the reliability of scales purporting to assess dissociation or depersonalization.

Traditionally, certain symptoms such as subjective vertigo ('dizziness'), depersonalization, and derealization have been considered as potentially hysterical complaints, but they may also relate to anxiety. Similarly, in the sort of questionnaire just cited, the sensation of feeling numb in the face of the catastrophe, or a lesser trouble, is now taken as evidence of a dissociative phenomenon. The symptoms or experiences just described may also have a strong relationship to anxiety, especially acute anxiety, and may easily be suggested to any susceptible individual.

Those who have wished to expand the influence of the notion of dissociation have focussed upon post-traumatic stress disorder and included symptoms like this in their evaluation of the condition. That is not legitimate. While it is true that DSM–IV does include depersonalization under the heading of 'dissociative disorders', it also says that it should not be diagnosed separately when the symptoms occur only during a panic attack i.e. as part of a panic disorder, a social or specific phobia, or post-traumatic or acute stress disorders. It adds that the loss of feeling associated with depersonalization (e.g. numbness) may mimic depression. These restrictions ought to be enough to keep most illnesses with features of depersonalization out of the rubric of dissociative disorders, but in fact such symptoms are counted in the Dissociative Experiences Scale and the Structured Interview for Dissociative Disorders as just described.

ICD–10 is stronger and places F48.1 (depersonalization–derealization syndrome) under 'other neurotic disorders'. This includes an initial state of 'daze' with some constriction of the field of consciousness and narrowing of attention, inability to comprehend stimuli, and disorientation as part of an acute stress reaction; it adds that partial or complete amnesia for the episode may be present. In the latter event, dissociative amnesia may be diagnosed. But here too one feels bound to consider the flexibility and false precision of the dissociative label.

Doxomorphic disorders

I have noted some of the features of conversion and dissociative disorders rather than reviewed them. I have sampled some of the issues relating to the concepts of dissociation and conversion, found problems with the attempt to link them with post-traumatic stress disorder, and expressed grave doubts about these diagnoses. I see most of them as fulfilling a social role, even though I have not discussed this at any length. Given my sceptical conclusions regarding these disorders, the question arises 'Can they be given another, more useful name?' We could revert to hysteria, which will be unpopular (for the reasons cited by Wessely in his chapter) and I do not think we should be obliged for much longer to continue to use the terms dissociation or conversion, since they are now bereft of their original meanings. Somatoform has led to other difficulties, just like hysteria before it.

Earlier, I mentioned the term 'doxogenic disorders'. I think that fits rather well with a condition like multiple personality disorder, now lurking under the transparent disguise of dissociative identity disorder. However, I have problems in applying the term to some 'psychogenic' amnesias and also with some of the conversion symptoms which arise against a background of substance use or misuse and other organic concomitant mechanisms. If for instance we decide that, in association with stroke, areas dealing with the intent to act or with volition may be disturbed, or if we were to find that the contingent negative variation was eliminated temporarily in individuals after stroke, then I would be uneasy calling a hysterical-like paralysis a doxogenic disorder and attributing it to the patient's thought processes or to the encouragement of the media.

Another option would be to talk of these illnesses as doxomorphic i.e. having the pattern of illnesses produced by the patient's thoughts or that reflect a social role. Thus we describe the phenomenon, identify its special feature — the similarity to thought processes — but also leave it open to be proven whether or not the condition is doxogenic. Some physical illnesses would then also come under the same heading as doxomorphic. For example, regional pain (which I have not discussed in detail but which may be due to the effects of nociception without the intervention of particular thoughts by the patient) can produce diffuse pain in an arm or leg or other part of the body, and this may seem to be hysteria — and has been taken to be so in the past — but is much more likely to be due to pathophysiological processes. Here we would have a non-doxogenic illness which was nevertheless doxomorphic.

I therefore suggest that, according to the situation, we should consider the joint use of these two terms — although we are likely to use doxomorphic more often than doxogenic.

Informed opinion is increasingly sceptical about dissociative disorders, and ultimately I think it will be the same for conversion disorders. In a recent survey of American psychiatrists, designed with notable skill, Pope *et al.* (1999) have found that only about one-quarter of respondents felt that diagnoses of dissociative amnesia and dissociative identity disorder were supported by strong evidence of scientific validity. One-third replied that dissociative amnesia and dissociative identity disorder should be included without reservations in DSM–IV. A larger proportion stated however that these categories should be included only as proposed diagnoses. I am pleased to say that Pope has remarked that a survey conducted in Canada has found an even stronger tendency to reject those diagnoses.

References

Babinski, J. and Froment, J. (1918). Hysteria or pithiatism and reflex nervous disorders. In *The Neurology of War* (ed. Buzzard, E. F.) (trans. Rolleston, J. D.), pp. 13–15. University of London Press, London.

Bernstein, E. M. and Putnam, F. W. (1986). Development, reliability and validity of a dissociation scale. *Journal of Nervous and Mental Disease*, **174**, 727–35.

Brandon, S., Boakes, J. P., Glaser, D., *et al* (1998). Recovered memories of childhood sexual abuse. *British Journal of Psychiatry*, **172**, 296–307.

Breuer, J. and Freud, S. (1895). Studies on Hysteria, The Complete Psychological Works. Vol III, (standard edn. (1955), ed. Strachey, J.) pp. 19–305. London: Hogarth.

Canadian Psychiatric Association. (1996). Position statement. Adult recovered memories of childhood sexual abuse. *Canadian Journal of Psychiatry*, **41**, 305–6.

Charcot, J. M. (1872). *Clinical Lectures on Diseases of the Nervous System, Delivered at La Salpêtrière, Vol. 3* (trans. (1889) Savill, T.). The New Sydenham Society, London.

Dalbiez, R. (1941). *Psychoanalytical Method and the Doctrine of Freud* (trans. Lindsay, T. F.). Longmans, Green & Co., London.

Dorland's *Illustrated Medical Dictionary, 25th Edition* (1974), p. 473. W. B. Saunders, Philadelphia.

Erdelyi, M. (1985). *Psychoanalysis: Freud's Cognitive Psychology*. Freeman, New York.

Erdelyi, M. (1990). Repression, reconstruction and defence: history and integration of the psychoanalytic and experimental frameworks. In *Repression and Dissociation. Implications for Personality Theory, Psychopathology, and Health* (ed. Singer, J. L.), pp. 1–31. University of Chicago Press, Chicago.

Freud, S. (1915). Repression. In *The Standard Edition of the Complete Psychological Works of Sigmund Freud, Vol. 14*. (Ed. Strachez, J.). Hogarth Press, London. (Cited in Erdelyi, M. (1990).).

Freud, S. (1917). *Introductory Lectures on Psychoanalysis* (trans. (1922) Rivire, J.). Allen & Unwin, London.

Hacking, I. (1997). Les aliénés voyageurs. How fugue became a medical entity. *History of Psychiatry*, **7**, 425–49.

Hacking, I. (1998). *Mad Travelers. Reflections on the Reality of Transient Mental Illnesses*. University of Virginia Press, Charlottesville.

Hirschmuller, A. (1989). *The Life and Work of Josef Breuer: Physiology and Psychoanalysis*. New York University Press, New York.

Holmes, D. S. (1990). The evidence for repression: an examination of sixty years of research. In *Repression and Dissociation. Implications for Personality Theory, Psychopathology, and Health* (ed. Singer, J. L.), pp. 85–102. University of Chicago Press, Chicago.

Hurst, A. F. (1920). *The Psychology of the Special Senses and their Functional Disorders*. Oxford Medical Publications, London.

Janet, P. (1889). *L'Automatisme Psychologique*. Alcan, Paris.

Janet, P. (1907). *The Major Symptoms of Hysteria*. Macmillan, New York.

Janet, P. (1925). *Psychological Healing. A Historical and Clinical Study* (trans. Paul, E. and C.). Allen & Unwin, London.

King, H. (1994). Once upon a text: the Hippocratic origins of hysteria. In *Hysteria in Western Civilization* (ed. Gilman, S. *et al.*). University of California Press, Berkeley.

Kirmayer, L. J. and Robbins, J. M. (1991). Three forms of somatization in primary care: prevalence, co-occurrence and sociodemographic characteristics. *Journal of Nervous and Mental Disease*, **179**, 647–55.

Kretschmer, E. (1926). *Hysteria: Reflex and Instinct*. Peter Owen, London.

Lipowski, Z. J. (1988) Somatization: the concept and its clinical application. *American Journal of Psychiatry*, **145**, 1358–68.

Marshall, J. C., Halligan, P. W., Fink, G. R., *et al.* (1997). The functional anatomy of a hysterical paralysis. In *Cognition*, **64**, B1–B8. Elsevier.

Merskey, H. (1994). Conversion fits, pseudo-attacks or doxogenic seizures. *General Hospital Psychiatry*, **16**, 246–7.

Merskey, H. (1995*a*). *The Analysis of Hysteria: Understanding Conversion and Dissociation* (2nd edn). Gaskell Press, London.

Merskey, H. (1995*b*). Post-traumatic stress disorder and shell shock: clinical section. In *A History of Clinical Psychiatry* (ed. Berrios, G. E. and Porter, R.), pp. 490–500. Athlone, London.

Merskey, H. and Merskey, S. J. (1993). Hysteria or the suffocation of the mother. *Canadian Medical Association Journal*, **148**, 399–405.

Merskey, H. and Potter, P. (1989). The womb lay still in Ancient Egypt. *British Journal of Psychiatry*, **154**, 751–3.

Pope, H. G. Jr., Oliva, P. S., Hudson, J. I., *et al.* (1999). Attitudes toward DSM-IV dissociative disorders diagnoses among board-certified American psychiatrists. *American Journal of Psychiatry*, **156(2)**, 321–3.

Reynolds, J. R. (1869). Remarks on paralysis and other disorders of motion and sensation, dependent on idea. *British Medical Journal*, **ii**, 483–485. (Discussion, 378–9.).

Royal College of Psychiatrists' Working Group on Reported Recovered Memories of Child Sexual Abuse. (1997). Recommendations for good practice and implications for training, continuing professional development and research. *Psychiatric Bulletin*, **21**, 663–5.

Steinberg, M. (1995). *Handbook for the Assessment of Dissociation: A Clinical Guide*. American Psychiatric Press Inc., Washington DC.

Sydenham, T. (1697). Discourse concerning hysterical and hypochondriacal distempers. In *Dr. Sydenham's compleat method of curing almost all diseases, and description of their symptoms, to which are now added five discourses of the same author concerning pleurisy, gout, hysterical passion, dropsy and rheumatism* (3rd edn). Newman and Parker, London.

Symonds, Sir C. (1995). Hysteria: an address given by Sir Charles Symonds at The National Hospital for Nervous Diseases, Queen Square, London, 27th February 1970. In *The Analysis of Hysteria: Understanding Conversion and Dissociation* (ed. Merskey, H.), pp. 407–13, Appendix C. Gaskell Press, London.

Willis, T. (1684). *An Essay of the Pathology of the Brain and Nervous Stock in which Convulsive Diseases are Treated* (trans. Pordage, S.). Dring, Leigh and Harper, London.

World Health Organization (1992). *The ICD-10 Classification of Mental and Behavioural Disorders*. WHO, Geneva.

13   Pyschodynamic theories in conversion hysteria

P. J. Shoenberg

Freud's theory of hysterical conversion represented a departure from previous nineteenth-century neurological and gynaecological models of this condition. His argument for a psychological aetiology in hysterical conversion, based on an understanding of the unconscious mind, allowed for a new psychological approach to treatment and provided an insight into the origins of this condition in childhood as well as a new way of relating to these patients. Nowadays, psychotherapists recognize that many other personality disorders and psychiatric illnesses may also underlie hysterical conversion.

This chapter considers recent developments in psychodynamic theory about the hysterical personality and its relationship to hysterical conversion. The dynamic psychopathology of hysterical conversion is discussed and compared with that of the other somatoform disorders. The psychoanalytic model, which provides an understanding both of the symbolic meaning of the hysterical conversion symptom and of the way in which the hysteric handles affects, makes us aware of the underlying distress of the patient with hysterical conversion. It also gives us a way of appreciating the significance of the hysteric's relationship with others.

Introduction

A 19-year-old girl with an alteration in the pattern of her epileptic fits was admitted to a neurology ward. Originally these had been grand mal fits in childhood; more recently she developed a new form of fit: she appeared to suddenly lose consciousness and become lifeless or else become violent. Sometimes during an attack she put her hands up to her throat as if to strangle herself. Physical examination was normal. On the ward her fits increased in frequency. We moved her into a room where she was placed beside an oxygen cylinder and given oxygen whenever she had a fit. We increased her dose of anti-convulsants. One day during a ward round she had a fit in front of the consultant neurologist, who surprised us all by speaking to her. He asked her what she wanted: she opened her eyes, and pointing to the oxygen cylinder asked for oxygen. This conversation between the consultant and patient changed our diagnosis from epilepsy to hysterical conversion, and our approach to her. Her attacks also diminished in frequency and she now began to talk to me. She told me about her fears of leaving home and getting married; she also told me about her experiences in early adolescence of being close to a male cousin who was an asthmatic. She had witnessed him dying of suffocation during an asthmatic attack when, for some reason he had deliberately not taken his broncho-dilators with him on a walk (Shoenberg, 1975).

Although Mace (1992) and Hunter and MacAlpine (1963) have pointed out that the term 'hysterical conversion' was used by the English physician, John Ferriar, as early as 1795,

Freud's contribution was to give new meaning to this term. At the time when Freud and Breuer made their discoveries, theories about hysteria were largely neurological or gynaecological, except for the psychological theories of Moebius and Oppenheim. Freud's account superceded ideas of 'physical stigmata' and theories of an inherited brain degeneracy advocated by Charcot. Instead, Freud sought the origins of the illness 'in the organisation of the fantasy with its spatio-temporal laws in the shifting, multiple and concealed identificatory positions' (Pontalis, 1981).

So the scene shifted from Charcot's stage, as depicted in Brouillet's picture 'Dr. Charcot's Clinical Lecture' (1887), to a private theatre in which the neurotic's unconscious communication could be received in a new relationship between therapist and patient. In this new 'therapeutic frame' (Khan, 1972), the 'transferences' of the patient, once described by Charcot as one of the stigmata of hysteria, were no longer merely one of the physical expressions of this condition but now had a new meaning as an essential driving force in the psychological treatment of the patient. If interpreted, these transferences could not only allow a re-enactment of the past in this new therapeutic space but also a working through of the patient's past unresolved conflicts and reminiscences with the analyst. Although Wisdom has said that there is 'much that is obscure' in psychoanalytic theory of hysterical conversion (Wisdom, 1961), there is a good deal that *is* clear and still relevant.

Freud's theory of hysterical conversion

Freud's concept of hysterical conversion was one that evolved slowly, beginning with his introduction of the term in 1894 when he described what was, in effect, a mental mechanism for rendering an incompatible idea innocuous by transforming its 'sum of excitation into something somatic' (Freud, 1894). This new concept was most fully described in his case study of Dora (Freud, 1905) and in a few further papers including 'Some general remarks on hysterical attacks' (Freud, 1909), his autobiographical study (Freud, 1925), and his commentary on the 'epileptic' attacks of Dostoevsky (Freud, 1928). In his autobiographical study he still argued that psychoneuroses were, without exception, disturbances of sexual function expressed mentally. By contrast, the actual neuroses, which included anxiety neurosis and neurasthenia, were caused by direct toxic expression of a disturbance of sexual function.

It has been argued that Freud's contribution to the understanding of hysterical conversion was primarily an aetiological one (Mace, 1992). This was Freud's own assessment of his discoveries: his argument was that a current psychologically provocative situation, with its own conflicts, might reawaken deeply unconscious memories of similar unresolved conflicts of a sexual nature from the patient's childhood. This aroused unpleasant or unwanted emotions in the patient. These emotions had to be denied and repressed and converted into a symbolically significant physical symptom that represented, as in the dream, an unconscious repressed wish (Wiseberg and Yorke, 1986). The choice of the symbolically significant physical symptom was influenced by many developmental factors (that is, it was 'over-determined') and dependent on that part of the body which was already in some way physically vulnerable (that is, 'somatically compliant'). At one stage he argued that without somatic compliance no conversion would take place (Freud, 1894).

Initially, Freud believed that the source of the conflicts in childhood lay in an actual sexual seduction by a sibling, a parent, or another adult, to which the child had been passive but aroused sexually, and about which the child felt still guilty. Later, after the discoveries of his own self-analysis, he abandoned the seduction theory. He argued instead that the causes of hysterical conversion and the other neuroses lay in childhood sexual fantasies that were exciting and guilt-provoking, belonging to, and dependent on, arrests in the emotional development of the child in the first six years of its life following conflicts in key relationships.

He had also originally believed that hysteria could be caused by childhood 'hypnoid' states of mind, in which relatively less traumatic events might become traumatic (Breuer and Freud, 1895). This he later abandoned.

With each hysterical symptom the patient received a 'primary gain' in their unconscious — the physical symptom expressed in a bodily metaphor something which could not be expressed openly otherwise. It contained, in addition, a self-inflicted punishment to deal with the original guilt aroused by the childhood conflicts. The symptom gave rise to secondary gain, (Freud, 1905) allowing the functionally disabled person to enjoy the privileged status of an invalid more than the freedom of being well.

As long as the meanings of their conversion symptoms were hidden from the patient, he or she was protected from their unconscious conflicts (Cameron, 1963). In 1912, he discussed 'the types of onset of neurosis' in some detail (Freud, 1912). There had to be a frustration of an instinctual drive resulting in a disturbance of the mental economy. Such a threat could be posed by the excess of instinctual pressure accompanying the biological reinforcements of puberty or the menopause; it might stem from the frustration of instinct, or it might derive more or less directly from arrests in emotional development during childhood never properly mastered. A crisis in these vicissitudes transformed a predisposing factor into a precipitant (Wiseberg and Yorke, 1986).

Such an aetiological approach to hysterical conversion, described as a defence neurosis, allowed Freud also to separate it from the 'actual neuroses' of anxiety neurosis and neurasthenia. Freud now became more interested in the psychopathology of the hysterical personality and less preoccupied with the psychophysiology of this hysterical conversion (Levin, 1978). In 1909 he wrote that hysterical fits could be brought about 'organically' for entirely 'internal somatic reasons' as a result of external psychological influences — that is, without conversion (Freud, 1909).

Subsequent psychodynamic views on hysterical conversion

For Freud's followers, not only did the notion of the hysterical personality undergo various developments but so too did the notion of what constituted hysterical conversion symptoms. So it is difficult to assess much of the psychoanalytic literature, especially in the light of the work by Chodoff on the range of psychiatric disorders other than the hysterical personality disorder in which conversion symptoms can occur (Chodoff and Lyons, 1958). With respect to personality, many psychoanalysts, including Nemiah, Engel, and Rangell have acknowledged these new observations on conversion, but others have not. With respect to the concept of conversion, Rangell (1959) uses the term to cover many of the other somatoform disorders; in another account, Engel (1962) includes patients with symptoms of irritable bowel, skin blushing and blanching, fainting, narcolepsy, and fatigue.

Hysterical personality

Concepts about the hysterical personality were revised with Zetzel's paper, 'The so-called good hysteric' in 1968. She differentiated between the relatively analyzable hysterical personality with oedipal and pre-oedipal conflicts and those much less analyzable, much more disturbed personalities in whom pre-oedipal oral pathology predominated. Gabbard refers to this second group as histrionic (Gabbard, 1994; Zetzel, 1968). Their reality testing is faulty and impulse control is poor. They resemble borderline personalities who are still in the throes of separation-individuation — failing to establish integrated object representations, using splitting and projection as the main defence mechanisms (Kernberg, 1975). Zetzel felt these patients had suffered a significant loss and/or a separation from key figures in childhood. It may be in this group, too, that conversion symptoms are more likely to occur. They are likely to form an early, intense transference to the therapist, with little insight; the transference is likely to be sexualized. In the less severe hysterical personalities a sexualized transference may develop gradually over a long period of time, and with preserved insight. Such a transference can be worked through.

Some psychoanalysts have tended to see these two groups of disorders as being distinct (Baumbacher and Amini, 1980–81; Sugarman 1979), whereas others like Zetzel see them as gradations of psychopathology along a continuum of severity (Blacker and Tutin, 1977; Lazare, 1971; Wallerstein, 1980–81). Glenn (1993) argues that Freud's 'Dora' would nowadays have been considered to fall more within the histrionic–borderline personality group.

Khan has argued that what the hysteric remembers from early childhood is largely somatic memories derived from maternal care, that have not lent themselves to psychic elaboration or verbalization: hence the demand by the hysteric in the clinical situation for a sensual gratification, in which the whole relationship to the therapist may be refused. He sees the hysteric as returning to 'the safety of that blankness which is a negation of the self and object'. 'It is the threat from mutuality that sets up in the hysteric a life-long battle between seeking an exciting object and refusing it through the very act of gratification' (Khan, 1975). Khan's argument is that the hysteric's experience of maternal care is one in which the mother, by responding to the id demands for sensual gratification, fails the baby in its ego needs. Winnicott argued that the 'good enough mother' in contrast would meet the ego needs of the child while at times not always responding to the child's id demands; in this way healthy emotional growth will be promoted (Winnicott, 1972).

Hysterical conversion

With regard to hysterical conversion itself, some have simplified matters further. For example, Szasz (1962) regards the symptom as a communication alone, whereas others regard it as the expression of dependency needs (Nemiah, 1967). Fairburn (1954) attempted to explain this condition using his object relations theory, which allowed psychoanalysis to move from a theory of instincts to a theory based on the intrapsychic relationships of the subject to others (that is, his or her 'objects').

> I had been seeing for once weekly psychoanalytic psychotherapy a young married nurse. She came into treatment to deal with her delayed grief reaction over the loss of her father, about whom she had ambivalent feelings. In her childhood her mother had died of an inoperable brain tumour when she was 5 years old and since that time it had been as if the patient had been allowed by her father to replace her mother in his affections. After she had been in treatment with me for four months I went away on holiday for two weeks. When I returned, I was telephoned by the husband, a doctor: he was very worried about his wife. She had been depressed during my absence. When I saw her she told me about fears of harming her baby. She added that during the week after I had gone away on my holiday, on the day and at the hour when she normally would have come to see me, she began to choke. She rushed to the hospital where her husband, the doctor, had come to hold her hand and the attack of choking had subsided. It was clear that this episode was probably caused by hysterical dysphagia. In the transformation of this patient's symptomatology from a depression, brought to me for treatment by psychotherapy, to a conversion symptom of hysterical dysphagia shown towards her husband as a physician, we can see the way in which the symptom in the same person addressed itself in different guises in different environments. Also the elements of psychodynamic theory relevant to under-standing hysterical conversion are well illustrated in this case. (Shoenberg, 1975)

While it is true that in private practice, psychoanalytic psychotherapists see very few cases of hysterical conversion, a few of these patients are referred for assessment to hospital psychotherapy services. There are far fewer however than are referred to neurologists (Crimslisk *et al.*, 1998). Perhaps there is an anthropological explanation for this mutation of hysterical conversion in its presentation to the psychoanalyst, as opposed to its presentation to the neurologist (Pouillon, 1972; Shoenberg, 1975). However, I suspect that the real reason lies in the resistance of such patients to explore the meaning of their symptoms, which protect them from facing their conflicts.

Hysterical conversion and other somatoform disorders

It is also important to differentiate hysterical conversion as a somatoform disorder from the other somatoform disorders (see Mace's chapter in this volume, p. 1). This not only gives us deeper insights into these two different psychopathologies but it allows us, with certain hysterical patients, to make more sophisticated clinical decisions, especially in emergencies. In acute hysterical conversion we risk much by ignoring the denial of the very self-destructive affects of the patient.

> In a ward where patients were admitted for observation following head injuries, one patient after a mild concussion developed a right hemiparesis with no neuro-anatomical basis from which he recovered in 24 hours. He was discharged from hospital, but was found dead on a railway line 24 hours later, having committed suicide by jumping out of a train. It seemed to me that we had missed a diagnosis of an acute hysterical conversion in this patient, which might have led us to considering the possibility of his denied depression.

We still differentiate hysterical conversion as a somatoform disorder from the other somatoform disorders by the way in which the patient deals with the affect (that is, by denial and repression). Freud himself used this to distinguish it from the actual neuroses of neurasthenia and anxiety neurosis in which there was no repression of the affect. In his chapter on somatoform disorders, in his co-authored book *Disorders of Affect Regulation*, Taylor (1997) argues that in the non-hysterical somatoform disorders the problem with affects may be similar to the problem Freud described of those patients with actual neuroses. Here, the underlying psychopathology has to do with a different developmental defect from that of the patient with hysterical conversion. This defect is in learning to regulate, process, and express affects — in particular, intolerable affects. Such a difficulty in regulating and processing affects results in adult life in what has been called the 'alexithymic personality'. It has been suggested that these personalities have a strong tendency to develop somatoform disorders or a psychosomatic illness.

In spite of these two different psychodynamic psychopathologies for hysterical conversion and the other somatoform disorders respectively, hysterical conversion symptoms may occur with other somatizations. Freud recognized this, although he neither called these conditions somatizations (a term only coined later by one of his followers, Stekel, in 1925), nor did he appreciate any difference in their psychopathologies. Neither his model nor any other psychodynamic models of hysterical conversion provide us with an adequate explanation of the underlying psychophysiology of the condition. In terms of aetiology, in some cases of hysterical conversion we should accept that more recent traumatic factors may have been the main cause of the patient's symptoms, although the symptoms will still be expressed in a symbolic bodily form. This evokes an old controversy between the psychiatrists, Rivers and Eder, and the psychoanalyst, Ernest Jones, about the true causes of shell shock in World War I.

Conclusion

The contribution of psychodynamic theory to an understanding of the psychology of hysterical conversion remains significant in allowing therapist and doctor alike to consider:

1. the importance of the underlying factors (that is, particular life events) that contribute to the circumstances that have precipitated the hysterical symptom;

2. the role of the symbolic meaning in the hysteric's physical symptom: this is often over-determined and refers to unresolved, unconscious conflicts belonging to the patient's childhood as well as their recent past;

3. the relationship of conversion as a mental mechanism for dealing with significant affects associated with these unconscious conflicts that have been aroused at the onset of the disorder; here an understanding of the defences of denial and repression is still important.

Such considerations distinguish conversion hysteria from the other somatoform disorders where there are earlier developmental defects in affect regulation.

It is in the hysteric's use of part or parts of their body to convey symbolically an unconscious conflict and in the underlying handling of the affect that hysterical conversion is different from the other somatizations. This is the most valuable contribution of psychodynamic theory, and we risk a great deal if we ignore the potential symbolic meaning of the hysteric's symptom and their handling of affect.

So I believe that it is important to consider the underlying psychodynamics of the patient in understanding and treating hysterical conversion. These are especially relevant in the treatment of acute hysterical conversion which may present as a psychiatric emergency, especially in post-traumatic stress disorder. They are also relevant to the management of cases of chronic hysteria, where an appreciation of the power of the secondary gain of the symptom and its effects on the counter-transference of the carer should not be underestimated. Furthermore, the psychodynamics of the hysteric's relationships with key others are often highly relevant, even if in many of these cases psychoanalytic psychotherapy is unlikely to play a key role in treatment.

References

Baumbacher, G. and Amimi, F. (1980–81). The hysterical personality disorder: a proposed clarification of a diagnostic dilemma. *Int. J. Psychoan. Psychother.* **8**, 501–32.

Blacker, K. H. and Tupin, J. P. (1977). Hysteria and hysterical structures: developmental and social theories. In *Hysterical Personality* (ed. Horowitz, M. J.). New York, Jason Aronson: pp. 95–141.

Breuer, J. and Freud, S. (1893). Studies in hysteria. In *The Complete Psychological Works of Sigmund Freud, Vol.2* (standard edn, 1962, ed. Strachey, J.). London, Hogarth Press.

Cameron, N. (1963). In *Personality Development and Psychopathology*. Boston, Houghton Mifflin Co.

Chodoff, P. and Lyons, H. (1958). Hysteria, the hysterical personality and 'hysterical conversion'. *Am. J. Psychiatry*, **114**, 734–40.

Crimslisk, H. L., Bhatia,K., Cope, H., Marsden, C. D. M., and Ron, M. A. (1998). Slater revisited: six year follow-up of patients with medically unexplained motor symptoms. *BMJ* **316**, 582–6.

Engel, G. L. (1962). *Psychological Development in Health and Disease*. London, W. B. Sanders & Co.

Fairburn, W. R. D. (1954). Observations on the nature of hysterical states. *Brit. J. Med. Psychol.*, **27**, 105–25.

Ferriar, J. (1795). *Medical Histories and Reflections, Vol. 2*. London, Cadell and Davies.

Freud, S. (1894). The neuro-psychoses of defence. In *The Complete Psychological Works of Sigmund Freud, Vol. 3* (standard edn, 1962, ed. Strachey, J.). London, Hogarth Press: pp. 160–72.

Freud, S. (1905). Fragment of an anlysis of a case of hysteria. In *The Complete Psychological Works of Sigmund Freud, Vol 7.* (standard edn., 1962, ed. Strachey, J.). London, Hogarth Press: pp. 3–125

Freud, S. (1909). Some general remarks on hysterical attacks. In *The Complete Psychological Works of Sigmund Freud, Vol. 9* (standard edn, 1962, ed. Strachey, J.). London, Hogarth Press: pp. 229–34.

Freud S. (1912). Types of onset of neurosis. In *The Complete Psychological Works of Sigmund Freud, Vol. 16* (standard edn, 1962, ed. Strachey, J.). London, Hogarth Press: pp. 349–87.

Freud, S. (1925). An autobiographical study. In *The Complete Psychological Works of Sigmund Freud, Vol. 20* (standard edn, 1962, ed. Strachey, J.). London, Hogarth Press: pp. 19–29.

Freud, S. (1928). Dostoevsky and parricide. In *The Complete Psychological Works of Sigmund Freud, Vol. 21* (standard edn, 1962, ed. Strachey, J.). London, Hogarth Press: pp. 177–95.

Gabbard, G. O. (1994). *Psychodynamic Psychiatry in Clinical Practice. The DSM4 Edition.* Washington, American Psychiatric Press Inc.

Glenn, J. (1993). Dora's dynamics, diagnosis and treatment: old and modern views. *Annual of Psychoanalysis*, **21**, 125–38.

Hunter, R. and MacAlpine, I. (1963). *Three Hundred Years of Psychiatry*. London, Oxford University Press.

Kernberg, O. F. (1975). Borderline Conditions and Pathological Narcissism. New York, Jason Aronson.

Khan, M. M. R. (1972). On Freud's provision of the therapeutic frame. In *The Privacy of the Self*. London, Hogarth Press: pp. 129–36.

Khan, M. M. R. (1975). Grudge and the hysteric. *Int. J. Psychoanal. Psychother.*, **4**, 349–58.

Lazare, A. (1971). The hysterical character in psychoanalytic theory: evolution and confusion. *Arch. Gen. Psychiatry*, **25**, 131–7.

Levin, K. (1978). *Freud's Early Psychology of the Neuroses*. Hassocks, Harvester Press Ltd.

Mace, C. O. J. (1992). Hysterical conversion. I: a history. *Brit. J. Psych.*, **161**, 369–78.

Nemiah, J. (1967). Conversion reaction. In *Comprehensive Textbook of Psychiatry* (2nd edn) (ed. Freedman, A. M., Kaplan, H. I. and Kaplan, H. S.). Baltimore, Williams and Wilkins: pp. 870–85.

Pontalis, J. B. (1981). In *Frontiers in Psychoanalysis*. London, Hogarth Press.

Pouillon, J. (1972). Doctor and patient: same and/or the other? (Ethnological remarks.) *Psychoanal. Study of Society*, **5**, 9–32.

Rangell, L. (1959). The nature of conversion. *J. Am. Psychoanal. Assoc.*, **7**, 632–62.

Shoenberg, P. J. (1975).The symptom as stigma or communication in hysteria. *Int. J. Psychoanal. Psychother.*, **4**, 507–17.

Stekel, N. (1925). *Peculiarities of Behaviour, Vol.I–II*. London, Williams and Norgate.

Sugarman, A. (1979). The infantile personality: orality in the hysteric revisited. *Int. J. Psychoanal.*, **60**, 501–13.

Szasz,T. (1962). *The Myth of Mental Illness*. London, Secker and Warburg.

Taylor, G. J. (1997). Somatoform disorders. In: *Disorders of Affect Regulation*. (eds Taylor, G. J., Bagby, M. and Parker, J. D.). Cambridge, Cambridge University Press: pp. 114–38.

Wallerstein, R. S. (1980–81). Diagnosis revisited (and revisited): the case of hysteria and the hysterical personality. *Int. J. Psychoanal. Psychother.*, **8**, 533–47.

Winnicott, D. W. (1972). Ego distortion in terms of the true and false self. In: *The Maturational Process and the Facilitating Environment*. London: Hogarth Press, pp. 140–53.

Wisdom, J. O. (1961). A methodological approach to the problem of hysteria. *Int. J. Psychoanal.*, **42**, 224–37.

Wiseberg, S. and Yorke, C. (1986). Physicality and conversion hysteria: developmental considerations. *Bulletin of the Anna Freud Centre*, **9(1)**, 3–18.

Zetzel, E. P. (1968). The so-called good hysteric. In *The Capacity for Emotional Growth*. London, Hogarth Press: pp. 230–45.

14 Conversion hysteria: the relevance of attentional awareness

Mauricio Sierra and German E. Berrios

Early neurophysiological models of conversion hysteria postulated cortico-fugal inhibitory mechanisms. In particular it was believed that the putative inhibitory mechanism might take place at a higher level of information processing, and that conversion hysteria resulted from a selective depression of awareness of a bodily function. Placing the locus of inhibition at such a high stage of sensory processing (that of attentive processing) also had the advantage of accounting for the lack of anatomical constraints characteristic of conversion phenomena as well as the lack of concern shown by some of the patients. Consistent with the view of a 'high level' cognitive mechanism, recent single-case studies have found altered P300 in patients with conversion disorder.

Attention will be drawn to clinical and neurophysiological similarities (for example, preserved early sensory processing in the face of altered P300 and selective loss of awareness) between patients with neglect syndromes and conversion hysteria, and it will be suggested that a deficit in attention processing might constitute a relevant mechanism in some forms of conversion hysteria.

Introduction

Often encountered in neuropsychiatric practice, so-called 'conversive symptoms' refer to sensory or motor deficits which cannot be mapped onto conventional neuroanatomical knowledge. Historically, they did not always belong to the 'hysteria' complex. The fact that they were added later has created interesting conceptual obstacles to their analysis. Conversive symptoms, however, cannot be said to be *specific* to hysteria; indeed, 50–80 per cent are reported to 'coexist' with other psychiatric disorders, most commonly depression (Guze *et al.* 1971; Lecompte 1987). In about 50 per cent of cases, some form of 'personality disorder' is also found (Binzer *et al.* 1997). But in 80 per cent, conversive symptoms are not associated with the so-called hysterical personality or Briquette's syndrome (Marsden 1986).

The concept of 'conversion' itself is not less confusing. Originally adopted as a useful *deux-ex-machina* to explain clinical exceptions to the nascent rules and categories of neurology, the concept has since forced clinicians to accept the existence of an explanatory chiaroscuro and of mechanisms that cannot be assimilated into conventional neuroscience except by facile analogy (for example, the search of a neurophysiological meaning for Freud's energy conversion model). To be fair, before the turn of the nineteenth century the level of definition and conceptual focus of neurophysiological and neuropsychological models may not have been up to the task: concepts such as higher cortical function, binding, or multimodal sensory integration (essential to any current explanation of conversive symptoms) were not yet available (Sierra and Berrios 1999).

Efforts have since been made to formulate explanations in terms of current cognitive and neurophysiological models. In this chapter, we review and integrate the results of studies, early and recent, linking neuroscience to conversive symptoms, including intriguing single-case psychophysiological reports. These findings are organized around a hypothesis connected with current views on the neuropsychology of attention and awareness. In this regard, we propose that at least some types of conversion phenomena might be an active exclusion from awareness of sensory or motor functions.

Early neurophysiological studies

An early neurophysiological model of conversive phenomena was proposed by the Mexican neurophysiologist, Hernández–Peón, based on his ideas that gating of sensory information inflow at brainstem (or lower) level was exercised by cortico-fugal inhibitory pathways. For example, he showed that there was a reduction in click-elicited cochlear nucleus-evoked potentials in a cat when a mouse was presented to its visual field (Hernández–Peón et al. 1956a). This drop in activity suggested that the attentional shift from auditory to visual modality was presided over by a powerful inhibition on auditory processing.

Hernández–Peón postulated that similar inhibitory mechanisms might be present in hysterical and hypno-anaesthesia (Hernández–Peón et al. 1956b) and proceeded to record somatosensory evoked potentials in a patient with a conversive 'glove and sleeve' type of analgesia and with thermo-anaesthesia of the left arm. As expected, no 'significant evoked activity' was detected by scalp electrodes when the anaesthetic arm was touch-stimulated. He also tested earlier findings that the gating action of the cortico-fugal inhibitory mechanism could be abolished by barbiturates or by a substantial increase in the intensity of the 'blocked out' stimulus. After the administration of intravenous barbiturate, his patient showed normal evoked responses upon stimulation of the 'anaesthetic' arm. Similar recordings were also obtained after a long-lasting, painful stimulus (intramuscular vitamin C injection) was administered to the affected arm (Hernández–Peón et al. 1963).

Hernández–Peón's findings were not replicated at the time (Bergamini and Bergamasco 1967; Halliday 1968), and contradicted those by Alajouanine et al. who had reported *normal* evoked potentials in seven patients with hysterical anaesthesia (Alajouanine et al. 1958). Levy et al. suggested that these discrepancies had resulted from methodological differences, and in two independent studies of their own (one on nine patients with unilateral conversive anaesthesia), they showed that low-intensity stimuli (à la Hernández–Peón) caused no evoked potentials but that the latter were obtained if high-intensity stimuli were delivered directly to the nerve (Levy and Mushin 1973; Levy and Behrman 1970) (That is, they replicated the 'unblocking' effect of intense stimuli reported by Hernández–Peón et al.)

This led to elaborate cognitive models of conversive hysteria. For example, Whitlock (1967) and Ludwig (Ludwig and Lexington 1972) suggested that the putative inhibitory mechanism took place at a very high level of information processing, and that conversive hysteria resulted from a 'selective depression of awareness of a bodily function'. Placing the locus of inhibition at such a high stage of sensory processing (that of attentive processing) helps to explain the absence of anatomical constraints characteristic of conversive phenomena and also the lack of concern shown by sufferers.

Reports of negative findings resulting from conventional (clinically oriented) evoked potential studies continued well into the 1970s, reinforcing the received view that conversive hysteria was entirely mediated by psychological mechanisms. Indeed, 'normal' evoked potentials in patients with unexplained sensory or motor dysfunctions became the hallmark of conversive hysteria (Behrman and Levy 1970; Moldofsky and England 1975; Kaplan *et al.* 1985; Howard and Dorfman 1986). Interpreted as evidence that in these patients early cortical processing was intact, these findings also fit in well with reports that in hysterical blindness processing of information took place in spite of the patient's claim that he or she could not see (Bryant and McConkey 1989).

P300 in conversion disorders

More recent studies, however, seem to have confirmed the view that, at least, the P300 component of event-related response is altered in conversive disorders. This is of particular interest, for the P300 and other late components seem to correlate well with high-level cognitive functions (as will be discussed) (Rugg and Coles 1995). Hence these studies support the view that in conversion disorder the inhibitory mechanism operates at a high level of cognitive processing (thought to be responsible for the conscious representation of sensory and motor events). In this regard, studies on a patient with conversive right-arm sensory loss and motor paralysis distal to the elbow by Lorenz *et al.* (1998) showed that the early sensory components of evoked potentials triggered by laser stimuli administered to the non-sentient hand were normal. However, on a modified oddball task, the P300 component failed to appear. The P300 was present in a normal volunteer instructed to simulate a right-hand anaesthesia.

In short, both subjects were given a random sequence of frequent and rare, slightly painful stimuli (laser stimuli) to left and right thumbs respectively. In contrast to traditional oddball paradigms, each stimulus had to be verbally reported by stating which side had been stimulated. The ingenuity of this design was that it required the feigning subject to consciously inhibit verbal responses to stimuli delivered to the right thumb (the feigned anaesthetic hand), thereby generating a 'no go' event, which is known to elicit a P300. As expected, and in contrast with the patient, each time the right hand of the malingerer was stimulated a distinct P300 was recorded (Lorenz *et al.* 1998).

In a female patient with left-sided 'functional hearing loss', Fukuda *et al.* (1996) found reduced amplitude of the P300 component of event-related response to left monaural stimulation, but the N1 and N2 (earlier sensory-perceptual components) were normal. According to the authors, stimuli successfully reached the auditory cortex of their patient but were then gated out from further processing.

Using visual stimuli in a standard oddball paradigm, Towle *et al.* found that the P300 of a patient with conversive blindness and two malingerers could not be differentiated, although both groups had smaller P300s than healthy controls (Towle *et al.* 1985). Lorenz *et al.* (1998) have pointed out that Towle *et al.* asked the experimental subjects *mentally to count* rare events, and thus the malingerers might have implemented private strategies to distract from the stimuli. Furthermore, the bilateral nature of the conversive blindness precluded using the other eye as a control.

Taken together, and because P300 is believed to represent a cognitive stage at which processed information is rendered conscious (Picton 1992), these findings suggest that an inhibitory mechanism may be at work in conversion hysteria, and that it operates well above the level of early sensory processing. These findings also agree with evidence that there is implicit sensory processing in conversion disorder; for example, not unlike patients with blindsight, patients with hysterical amaurosis can modify their behaviour in response to visual information they deny seeing (Bryant and McConkey 1989).

In this respect, Hilgard's 'hidden observer' model can be illuminating. In subjects with hypnotically induced anaesthesia, a dissociation can be observed between one part of the self that is aware of the intensity of the pain and the 'conscious mind' that remains totally unaware of it (Hilgard 1977). Thus, the resemblance between conversive and hypno-anaesthesia may be more than phenomenological; indeed, Spiegel et al. (1989) have reported significant decreases in the amplitude of the late components P100 and P300 in 10 subjects in whom anaesthesia was induced by hypnosis.

Conversion hysteria as a form of attention neglect

Similar dissociations have been reported in the neuropsychological literature on hemineglect related to right parietal lesions. Indeed, although patients thus affected are not aware of stimuli in the affected sensory hemifield (Vallar and Perani 1986), there is also some evidence that they may process information not registered consciously (Driver et al. 1992). Interestingly, these patients have been found to show a similar pattern of evoked responses as that reported in conversion hysteria. For example, in nine patients with non-hemianopic visual neglect due to parietal lobe lesions, L'hermitte et al. showed that stimulation of the hemispace contralateral to the lesion yielded a lengthening in latency and a decrease in amplitude of P300, specifically related to visual stimulation (L'hermitte et al. 1985). Moreover, in parietal neglect there also seems to be a dissociation between the early and late components of the evoked response. Thus, Vallar et al. found that the early components of the evoked response were normal in three right hemisphere-damaged patients with neglect (Vallar et al. 1991). Other studies, however, have reported increased latency of the early components in patients with brain damage and neglect (Spinelli et al. 1994).

Patients with parietal neglect are not only unaware of stimuli on the contralateral side of the lesion but on occasions they also have reduced contralateral movements (hypo-kinesia) to the extent that in formal neurological testing limbs may appear as paretic in spite of their preserved strength (Laplane and Degos 1983; Mattingley et al. 1998).

Recent studies seem to suggest that in addition to the 'neurological' lesion, neglect may also have a 'functional' component. For example, following trauma or infection of a limb some patients may show a reduced utilization of a limb segment in the face of physiological and anatomical recovery (segmental exclusion syndrome) and the absence of neurological or psychiatric pathology. In a controlled study of somatosensory evoked potentials in 19 patients, Beis et al. tested the hypothesis that segmental exclusion is a form of neglect related to that seen in hemineglect syndromes. Similar to results reported in hysteria and in hemineglect (already discussed), the segmental exclusion patients did not differ from controls in regards to the early components of sensory processing but showed a significant lengthening of P300 latency (Beis *et al.* 1998).

Further suggesting a relationship of conversion symptoms with right parietal networks controlling attention and awareness, Ramasubbu and Sandor (1997) have recently reported the case of a 35-year-old woman with a five-year history of multiple, unexplained physical symptoms and a three-year history of indistinct sensory symptoms confined to the left half of the body (splitting from midline). Neurological and psychiatric assessment suggested the diagnosis of conversion hysteria, but interestingly enough MRI revealed an old infarct in the right parietal lobe. Also in agreement with what has been said in earlier sections, evoked potentials were found to be normal in this patient.

To sum up, three apparently unrelated clinical phenomena — conversion hysteria, neglect syndromes, and exclusion syndromes — seem to share a dysfunction of the attentional–awareness system which expresses itself in similar neurophysiological correlates, to wit, a preserved early sensory processing in the face of altered P300 and selective loss of awareness.

The relevance of laterality

The clinical observation that neglect is predominantly observed in patients with right-sided brain damage (Stone *et al.* 1998) fits well with accumulating evidence from normal subjects (and neglect patients) that the right parietal and prefrontal cortex play a predominant role in the control of attention systems. One prediction of the hypothesis that conversion symptoms are mediated by a local inhibition of the attentional–awareness system, is that conversion symptoms should occur more frequently on the left side. That this may be the case has been observed (and debated) at least since the nineteenth century (for example, Galin 1974).

In his *Traité Clinique et Thérapeutique de L'Hystérie*, Paul Briquet (1859) documented 'hysterical' phenomena in 430 patients, observing that 'hyperaesthesia, anaesthesia, chronic convulsions and paralyses were more frequent on the left side of the body' (p. 557) — 70 cases left- versus 20 right-sided for the sensory syndromes; and a ratio of 3:1 for paralysis. Weber (quoted by Briquet) reported that 11 of his 14 patients had left-sided sensory symptoms and Landouzy (also quoted by Briquet) observed left-sided hemiplegia in 8 of 14 cases. Weber also believed that the skin on the left side of the body was more sensitive than on the right. During the first decades of the twentieth century, similar biases were noted in neurological (Purves–Stewart 1924) and psychodynamic (Ferenczi 1926) practice.

More recently, Magee (1962) observed that only 3 out of 50 cases of hysterical hemianaesthesia or hemiplegia were right-sided. In 191 subjects, Stern (1977) found that out of 74 per cent of unilateral sensory symptoms, 78 per cent and 55 per cent of motor symptoms were right-sided. Interestingly enough, the left lateralization effect cut across handedness, undermining the hypothesis that unilateral conversion symptoms occur most frequently on the most 'convenient' (non-dominant) side of the body. In 52 subjects (42 females, 10 males), Galin *et al.* (1977) found left-sided symptoms in 65 per cent of cases; female predominance was noticeable (71 per cent of females had left-sided symptoms). Axelrod *et al.* (1980) found that out of 150 cases, 50 per cent had left-sided symptoms and Keane (1989) identified, out of 13 cases with a hemiparetic gait, 9 with left-sided symptoms. Lastly, out of 31 patients with unilateral motor/sensory conversion symptoms, Pascuzzi (1994) found that 84 per cent had left-sided symptoms.

To summarize, at least for some types of 'hysterical' or 'functional' symptoms there seems to be some evidence that they are more frequent on the left side. However, there seem to be some intervening variables such as gender, handedness, and culture (for example, similar results have not been reported in non-western samples amongst which the symbolism of the left may be less marked) (see Cathébras 1993) whose true role needs to be urgently determined. In addition, there are also studies calling into question even the primary effect. For example, in 40 patients with conversion hysteria, Fallik and Sigal (1971) found that 76 per cent had *right* -side symptoms (83 per cent of subjects were lateralized). Interestingly, 90 per cent of their subjects were male. A non-significant predominance of right-sided symptoms (61 per cent) was reported by Stefansson *et al.* (1976) in a sample of subjects suffering from pain and a variety of organic or functional illness. Lastly, Reagan and LaBarbera (1984) found that in a sample of 11 *children* and adolescents with unilateral conversion symptoms, 10 showed symptoms on the right side of the body.

Further support for the lateralization hypothesis comes from reports that when sensory symptoms are successfully induced (for example by hypnosis) they tend to lateralize to the left. Fleminger *et al.* (1980) studied a sample of psychiatric patients and nurses who were given a standard, taped suggestion of altered sensation in their hands. In both groups there was a majority of left-sided responses. In a different study, hypnotic induction was administered to 80 right-handers and 6 non-right-handers; overall, right-handers were more responsive on the left side (Sackeim 1982).

Another piece of evidence suggesting abnormal right hemisphere functioning in conversion hysteria comes from a recent study of abnormal nocturnal limb movements in a patient with conversion paralysis. It has been known from earlier studies that, regardless of handedness, the non-dominant hand is about twice as active during both REM and non-REM sleep (Casagrande *et al.* 1992; Lauerma *et al.* 1992), and it is believed that this might reflect a greater activation of right hemisphere motor programs during sleep. Lauerma studied this phenomenon in a 42-year-old female with conversive paraplegia. Recordings of hand movements during seven consecutive nights revealed no inversion of the lateral distribution of hand movement (Lauerma 1993); this was interpreted as being compatible with a right-hemisphere abnormality. A functional hemispheric asymmetry has also been recently reported in two patients with left-sided conversive hemiparesis. When the motor cortex was stimulated with transcranial magnetic stimulation it was found that, at moderate stimulus intensities, the right hemisphere was less excitable than the left (Foong *et al.* 1997). Although it has been suggested that hemispheric excitability correlates with handedness (Macdonell *et al.* 1991), this might not fully account for this finding, as one of the patients was left-handed.

Neurobiological correlates of conscious experience

From what has been said so far, it would seem that knowledge about the neurobiological correlates of conscious awareness may be important to the understanding of conversion hysteria. In this regard, converging evidence suggests that, inter alia, the right inferior parietal cortex, the anterior cingulate, and the prefrontal cortex, are all components of a parallel distributed network that integrates attentional responses and generates awareness. During the last decade there has been particular interest in the neural correlates of visual awareness and a summary of these findings provides a relevant background to the present discussion on conversion hysteria.

There is enough evidence to believe that residual visual processing takes place in the absence of visual awareness. For example, the fact that blindsight patients (with lesions in primary visual cortex) saccade or point towards light spots projected onto their scotoma, while denying awareness of the stimuli, suggests that primary visual cortex may play a role in visual awareness. Now, in patients with neglect due to right parietal lesions (neglect can also arise from lesions in other locations), visual unawareness is also reported in spite of an intact visual cortex. As with blindsight, non-conscious processing also takes place in patients with neglect (Driver and Mattingley 1998), but unlike blindsight, their loss of visual awareness is not constrained by the retinotopic organization of the visual cortex. This lack of anatomical constraint is reminiscent of that observed in conversion symptoms.

Further support for the role that the inferior parietal lobe plays in visual awareness has come from studies in 'binocular rivalry'. When dissimilar images are presented to the two eyes, they compete, so that each becomes perceptual-dominant for a few seconds at a time. Neurophysiological studies of rivalry in awake monkeys have established that whilst in primary visual cortex, the firing of most neurons correlates with stimulus and not percept; neuronal activity in the infero-temporal and parietal cortex reflects the perceptual state. A recent MRI study addressing the likely mechanism of perceptual shifting in rivalry suggests that the fronto-parietal areas play a central role in conscious perception (Lumer *et al.* 1998).

Neuroimaging studies

As seen earlier in this chapter, evidence is accumulating that hysteric conversion may be related to the activity of a mechanism that inhibits processing of information at levels necessary for awareness to occur. Evidence from the neurological literature, on the other hand, suggests that the right inferior parietal cortex is a crucial component in a network controlling attention and awareness, and that the right prefrontal cortex (and anterior cingulate) may also be important structures in the regulation of an awareness 'gate keeper' (Parasuraman 1998).

Evidence that a fronto-cortical mechanism may be at play in conversion hysteria comes from two recent studies. Tiihonen *et al.* have reported the case of a 32-year-old woman with a conversive left-sided paralysis and paresthesiae, whose motor disorder had resolved spontaneously by the time she was tested but whose limbs she still reported as 'numb'. Both her somatosensory and motor evoked potentials were normal (no P300 testing was done) but a SPECT carried out whilst the numb hand was being stimulated (electric stimulation of the left median nerve) showed hyperperfusion of the right frontal lobe and hypoperfusion in the right parietal region. A follow-up SPECT, when she had clinically recovered, showed normal right frontal perfusion and the expected increase of right parietal blood flow to tactile stimulation of her left hand. These findings were interpreted as suggesting a simultaneous activation of frontal inhibitory areas and inhibition of the somatosensory cortex (Tiihonen *et al.* 1995).

A second study by Marshall *et al.* reported the case of a woman with left-sided paralysis but without somatosensory loss in whom no structural lesion had been found. A positron emission tomography (PET) study on brain activity was undertaken when the patient was preparing to move her paralysed limb and when she actually tried to move it (her right, normal leg was used as control). Preparing to move or moving her good (right) leg, and also preparing to move her paralysed leg, activated motor and/or premotor areas known to participate in the preparation and execution of movement. However, the *attempt* to move her paralysed leg failed to activate right primary motor cortex; instead, an activation appeared in the right orbito-frontal and right anterior cingulate cortex. These findings were interpreted as suggesting that when the patient attempted to move her left leg, the two frontal areas in question lit up as they inhibited prefrontal (willed) effects on the right primary motor cortex (Marshall *et al.* 1997). This is in keeping with earlier studies in both humans and animals showing the existence of 'negative' motor areas which inhibit spontaneous movement, and that these negative areas include the anterior cingulate and orbito-frontal cortex (Devinsky *et al.* 1995).

Summary and conclusions

The development of important research techniques, together with an emphasis on the single-case study, have led to important advances in the field, and for the first time, testable hypotheses can be put forward to explain conversion disorders. Thus, neuro-physiological evidence suggests that inhibitory mechanisms may be at play at high-level (cognitive) stages of sensory/motor processing, leading to an exclusion from awareness of sensory and/or motor function. Neuroimaging studies in turn suggest that prefrontal structures may be the more likely substrate for such inhibitory mechanisms.

This putative alteration of attention and awareness should be understood in terms of the current neuropsychological views that selective gaps of awareness may run together with residual unconscious cognitive processing. It is also suggested that the fact that the right inferior parietal cortex (a crucial structure mediating awareness) is not dependent on topological constraints (like the primary sensory cortices), may explain the very lack of anatomical constraint observed in conversion symptoms. Circumstantial evidence for the involvement of the brain attentional system in conversion hysteria is also provided by lateralization studies which show that, as in parietal neglect, conversion symptoms also tend to lateralize to the left side regardless of hand dominance.

However, a neurobiological understanding of conversion symptoms should not neglect the need for other aetiological mechanisms, particularly for the explanation of symptom selection (that is, the choice of networks). As discussed in the conceptual and historical section of this chapter, the advantage of the Freudian over the Breuerian model was that the former included a 'symbolism' mechanism. For various reasons this did not work well and was replaced by a modern semantic model of symptom choice. The advantage of such a model is that it may fit better into current neurobiological and neural networks theory than the old one-to-one theory of symbols that Freud was forced to use.

References

Alajouanine, T., Scherrer, J., Barbizet, J., Calvelt, J. and Verley, R. (1958). Potentiels évoqués corticaux chez de sujets atteints de troubles somesthesiques. *Revue Neurologique*, **98**, 757.

American Psychiatric Association (1994). *Diagnostic and Statistical Manual of Mental Disorder* (4th edn). Washington DC: American Psychiatric Press.

Axelrod, S., Noonan, M. and Atanacio, B. (1980). On the laterality of psychogenic somatic symptoms. *Journal of Nervous and Mental Diseases*, **168**, 517–25.

Axenfeld, A. (1883). *Traité des Nvroses* (2nd edn). Paris: Baillière.

Behrman, J. and Levy, R. J. (1970). Neurophysiological studies on patients with hysterical disturbances of vision. *Psychosomatic Research*, **14**, 187–94.

Beis, J. M., Andre, J. M., Vielh, A. and Ducrocq, X. (1998). Event-related potentials in the segmental exclusion syndrome of the upper limb. *Electromyography and Clinical Neurophysiology*, **38**, 247–52.

Bergamini, L. and Bergamasco, B. (1967). *Cortical evoked potentials in Man*. Thomas, Springfield.

Binzer, M., Andersen, P. M. and Kullgren, G. (1997). Clinical characteristics of patients with motor disability due to conversion disorder: a prospective control group study. *Journal of Neurology Neurosurgery and Psychiatry*, **63**, 83–8.

Briquet, P. (1859). *Trait Clinique et Thérapeutique de L'hystérie*. Paris: Baillière.

Bryant, R. A. and McConkey, K. M. (1989). Visual conversion disorder: a case analysis of the influence of visual information. *Journal of Abnormal Psychology*, **98**, 326–9.

Casagrande, M., Violani, C., Braibanti, P., De Gennaro, L. and Bertini, M. (1992). Performances in behavioral tasks reveal shifts in hemispheric asymmetries during the transition from wakefulness to sleep. *Journal of Sleep Research*, **1(Suppl 1)**, 37.

Cathébras, P. (1993) De la latéralisation a gauche des symptômes somatiques functionnels. *Annales Médico-Psychologiques*, **151**, 105–17.

Devinsky, O., Morrell, M. J. and Vogt, B. A. (1995). Contributions of anterior cingulate cortex to behaviour. *Brain*, **118**, 279–306.

Driver, J. and Mattingley, J. B. (1998). Parietal neglect and visual awareness. *Nature Neuroscience*, **1**, 17–22.

Driver, J., Baylis, G. C. and Rafal, R. D. (1992). Preserved figure ground segmentation and symmetry perception in visual neglect. *Nature*, **360**, 73–5.

Fallik, A. and Sigal, M. (1971). Hysteria – The Choice of Symptomsite Psychotherapy and Psychosomatics, **V19**, 310–318.

Ferenczi, S. (1926). An attempted explanation of some hysterical stigmata. In *Further Contributions to the Theory and Technique of Psychoanalysis* (ed. Ferenczi, S.). London: Hogarth Press.

Fleminger, J. J., McClure, G. M. and Dalton, R. (1980). Lateral response to suggestion in relation to handedness and the side of psychogenic symptoms. *British Journal of Psychiatry*, **136**, 562–6.

Foong, J., Ridding, M., Cope, H., Marsden, C. D. and Ron, M. A. (1997). *Journal of Neuropsychiatry and Clinical Neurosciences*, **9**, 302–3.

Fukuda, M. *et al.* (1996). Event-related potential correlates of functional hearing loss: reduced P3 amplitude preserved N1 and N2 components in a unilateral case. *Neuropsychiatry and Clinical Neurosciences*, **50**, 85–7.

Galin, D. (1974). Implications for psychiatry of left and right cerebral specialization. *Archives of General Psychiatry*, **31**, 572–83.

Galin, D., Diamon, R. and Braff, D. (1977). Lateralization of conversion symptoms: more frequent on the left. *American Journal of Psychiatry*, **134**, 578–80.

Guze, S. B., Woodruff, R. A. and Clayton, P. J. (1971). A study of conversion symptoms in psychiatric outpatients. *American Journal of Psychiatry*, **128**, 135–8.

Halliday, A. M. (1968). Computing techniques in neurological diagnosis. *British Medical Bulletin*, **24**, 253.

Hernández–Peón, R., Sherrer, H. and Velasco, M. (1956*a*). Central influences on afferent conduction in the somatic and visual pathways. *Acta Neurologica Latino Americana*, **2**, 8–12.

Hernández–Peón, R., Sherrer, H. and Jouvelt, M. (1956*b*). Modification of electrical activity in cochlear nucleus during 'attention' in unanaesthetized cats. *Science*, **123**, 331.

Hernández–Peón, R., Chávez–Ibarra, G. and Aguilar, E. (1963). Somatic evoked potentials in one case of hysterical anaesthesia. *Electroencephalography and Clinical Neurophysiology*, **15**, 889–92.

Hilgard, E. (1977). *Divided Consciousness. Multiple Controls in Human Thought and Action*. New York: Wiley.

Howard, J. E. and Dorfman, L. J. (1986). Evoked potentials in hysteria and malingering. *Journal of Clinical Neurophysiology*, **3**, 39–49.

Kaplan, B. J., Friedman, W. A. and Gravenstein, D. (1985). Somatosensory evoked potentials in hysterical paraplegia. *Surgical Neurology*, 23, 502–6.

Keane, J. R. (1989). Hysterical gait disorders: 60 cases. *Neurology*, **39**, 586–9.

Kent, D. A., Tomasson, K. and Oryell, W. (1995). Course and outcome of conversion and somatization disorders. *Psychosomatics*, **36**, 138–44.

Laplane, D. and Degos, J. D. (1983). Motor neglect. *Journal of Neurology Neurosurgery and Psychiatry*, **46**, 152–8.

Lauerma, H. J. (1993). Nocturnal limb movements in conversion paralysis. *Journal of Nervous and Mental Disease*, **181**, 707–8.

Lauerma, H. J. *et al.* (1992). Laterality of motor activity during normal and disturbed sleep. *Biological Psychiatry*, **32**, 191–4.

Lecompte, D. (1987). Associated psychopathology in conversion patients without organic disease. *Acta Psychiatr Belg*, **87**, 654–61.

Levy, R. and Behrman, J. (1970). Cortical evoked responses in hysterical hemianaesthesia. *Electroencephalography and Clinical Neurophysiology*, **29**, 400–2.

Levy, R. and Mushin, J. (1973). The somatosensory evoked response in patients with hysterical anaesthesia. *Journal of Psychosomatic Research*, **17**, 81–4.

Lhermitte, F., Turell, E., LeBrigand, D. and Chain, F. (1985). Unilateral visual neglect and wave P300. A study of nine cases with unilateral lesions of the parietal lobes. *Archives of Neurology*, **42**, 567–73.

Lorenz, J., Kunze, K. and Bromm, B. (1998). Differentiation of conversive sensory loss and malingering by P300 in a modified oddball task. *NeuroReport*, **9**, 187–91.

Ludwig, A. M. and Lexington, K. Y., (1972). Hysteria:a neurobiological theory. *Archives of General Psychiatry*, **27**, 771–7.

Lumer, E. D., Friston, K. J. and Rees, G. (1998). Neural correlates of perceptual rivalry in the human brain. *Science*, **280**, 1930–4.

Macdonell, R. A. *et al.* (1991). Hemispheric threshold differences for motor evoked potential produced by magnetic coil stimulation. *Neurology*, **41**, 1441–4.

Magee, K. (1962). Hysterical hemiplegia and hemianesthesia. *Postgraduate Medicine*, **31**, 339–45.

Marsden, C. D. (1986). Hysteria – a neurologist's view. *Psychol. Med.*, **May 16(2)**, 277–88.

Marshall, J. C., Halligan, P. W., Fink, G. R., Wade, D. T. and Frackowiak, R. S. (1997). The functional anatomy of a hysterical paralysis. *Cognition*, **64**, B1–B8.

Mattingley, J. B., Husain, M., Rorden, C., Kennard, C. and Driver, J. (1998). Motor role of human inferior parietal lobe revealed in unilateral neglect patients. *Nature*, **12**, 179–82.

Moldofsky, H. and England, R. S. (1975). Facilitation of somatosensory average-evoked potentials in hysterical anesthesia and pain. *Archives of General Psychiatry*, 32, 193–7.

Parasuraman, R. (1998). *The Attentive Brain*. Cambridge, Mass: The MIT Press.

Pascuzzi, R. M. (1994) Nonphysiological (functional) unilateral motor and sensory syndromes involve the left more often than the right body. *Journal of Nervous and Mental Disease*, **182**, 118–20.

Picton, T. W. (1992). The P300 wave of the human event-related potential. *Journal of Clinical Neurophysiology*, **9**, 456–79.

Purves–Stewart, J. (1924) *The Diagnosis of Nervous Disease*. London: Butler and Tanner.

Ramasubbu, R. and Sandor, P. (1997). Conversion symptoms in parietal lobe infarct: a case report. Report from 7th Annual Meeting of American Neuropsychiatric Association. *Journal of Neuropsychiatry and Clinical Neurosciences*, **7**, 35.

Regan, J. and LaBarbera, J. D. (1984). Lateralization of conversion symptoms in children and adolescents. *American Journal of Psychiatry*, **141**, 1279–80.

Rugg, M. D. and Coles, M. G. H. (1995). *Electrophysiology of Mind: Event-Related Brain Potentials and Cognition*. Oxford: Oxford University Press..

Sackeim, H. A. (1982). Lateral asymmetry in bodily response to hypnotic suggestions. *Biological Psychiatry*, **17**, 437–47.

Sierra, M. and Berrios, G. E. (1999) Towards a neuropsychiatry of conversive hysteria. *Cognitive Neuropsychiatry*, **4(3)**, 267–87.

Spiegel, D., Bierre, P. and Rootenberg, J. (1989). Hypnotic alteration of somatosensory perception. *American Journal of Psychiatry*, **146**, 749–54.

Spinelli, D., Burr, D. C. and Morrone, M. C. (1994). Spatial neglect is associated with increased latencies of visual evoked potentials. *Visual Neuroscience*, **11**, 909–18.

Stefansson, J. G., Messina, J. A. and Meyerowitz, S. (1976). Hysterical neurosis, conversion type: clinical and epidemiological considerations. *Acta Psychiatrica Scandinavica*, **53**, 119–38.

Stern, D. B. (1977). Handedness and the lateral distribution of conversion reactions. *Journal of Nervous and Mental Diseases*, **164**, 122–8.

Stone, S. P., Halligan, P. W., Marshall, J. C. and Greenwood, R. J. (1998). Unilateral neglect: a common but heterogeneous syndrome. *Neurology*, **50**, 1902–5.

Tiihonen, J., Kuikka, J., Viinamaki, H., Lehtonen, J. and Partanen, J. (1995). Altered cerebral blood flow during hysterical paresthesia. *Biological Psychiatry*, **15**, 134–5.

Towle, V. L., Sutcliffe, E. and Sokol, S. (1985). Diagnosing functional visual deficits with the P300 component of the visual evoked potential. *Archives of Ophthalmology*, **103**, 47–50.

Vallar, G. and Perani, D. (1986). The anatomy of unilateral neglect after right hemisphere stroke lesions. A clinical/CT-scan correlation study in man. *Neuropsychologia*, **24**, 609–22.

Vallar, G., Sandroni, P., Rusconi, M. L. and Barbieri, S. (1991). Hemianopia, hemianesthesia, and spatial neglect: a study with evoked potentials. *Neurology*, **41**, 1918–22.

Whitlock, F. A. (1967). The aetiology of hysteria. *Acta Psychiatrica Scandinavica*, **43**, 144–62.

World Health Organization (1993). *The ICD–10 Classification of Mental and Behavioural Disorders. Diagnostic Criteria for Research*. Geneva: World Health Organization.

15 Hysteria and hypnosis: cognitive and social influences

Kevin M. McConkey

Investigating hypnosis helps to understand the processes of hysteria. I consider conceptual links of hysteria and hypnosis, and empirical investigations of hypnotic blindness, anaesthesia, and identity distortion. These investigations underscore how hypnotic individuals actively respond to social factors by cognitively resolving conflict between objective information and their suggested, subjective experience. The findings provide a way of understanding hysteria, and I propose a model of hypnosis and hysteria that has the ability to account for the phenomenal experience, implicit awareness, and the influence of social factors in both conditions. Despite some inherent differences, hysteria and hypnosis share influences and interactions of similar cognitive and social processes that shape the initiation and maintenance of both conditions.

Introduction

The cognitive and social factors that influence hypnosis seem to influence hysteria as well. Thus, investigating and understanding hypnosis is one way of investigating and understanding the processes of hysteria. This has been recognized in both historical and contemporary links of hysteria and hypnosis, and I consider these links before turning to consider selected investigations of hypnotic phenomena (specifically blindness, anaesthesia, and identity distortion), to then look at some major influences and interactions, and finally to make a concluding comment.

Historical and contemporary links

The relationship of hysteria, hypnosis, and suggestion has been recognized by many in the history of psychiatry and psychology (for example, Crabtree 1993; Ellenberger 1970; Gauld 1992; Hull 1933; Merskey 1995; Macmillan 1991; Showalter 1997; Spanos 1996). This relationship is important not only historically but also for current theoretical understanding and clinical practice. The 'influence of the idea' on the behaviour and experience of individuals is perhaps the key feature of this relationship, whether that idea is from another person or from the person himself or herself.

In discussing the complaints of patients following railway accidents, Reynolds (1869) commented on the importance of 'ideas' in the clinical picture of his patients. Despite the 4000 or so years in the history of hysteria (Veith 1965), this appears to have been the first specific attribution of an hysterical symptom to an idea (Merskey 1983 and his chapter in this volume, p. 171). The influence of the idea is not only powerful but also self-renewing: it shapes the experiences of the individual, and those experiences reciprocally shape the idea and its effects.

A similar process can be seen in the phenomena of hypnosis. At the simplest level, hypnosis occurs when one individual responds to the suggestions of another with changes in his or her memory, mood, or behavior (Kihlstrom 1985). At a more complex level, hypnosis involves the interaction of an array of internal and external influences. Looking at recent considerations of hysteria (for example, Halligan and David 1999; Horowitz 1977; Merskey 1979, 1995; Micale 1990; Roy 1982; Slavney 1990) and hypnosis (for example, Fromm and Nash 1992; Lynn and Rhue 1991), and their similarities and interactions (for example, Chertok 1984; Bryant and McConkey 1999; Frankel 1994; Kihlstrom 1979, 1994; Sackeim *et al.* 1979), it is apparent that hysteria and hypnosis share much in common conceptually and clinically. Also, it needs to be said that they share much in common in terms of myth and misunderstanding. Nevertheless, there are some major aspects of hypnosis and suggestion that appear to be relevant to an understanding of the function and nature of hysteria.

Let me turn to describe hypnosis and hypnotizability briefly. Individuals differ in their capacity to experience hypnosis, and this trait of hypnotizability is relatively stable throughout adulthood (Hilgard 1965; Sheehan and McConkey 1982). Hypnotizability tends to be associated with a cognitive capacity for imagination and for the personality characteristic of absorption (Roche and McConkey 1990), and this combination of capacities allows individuals to experience a range of effects suggested by the hypnotist. These effects may be influenced also by an underlying dissociative process that is associated with hypnotizability in normal subjects and that may be a major process in various psychopathologies such as psychogenic amnesia (Hilgard 1977; Kihlstrom 1979, 1984, 1987). Suggested hypnotic effects can range from relatively simple ideomotor effects such as an arm feeling light and floating upwards (for example, McConkey *et al.* 1998) to complex ones such as an experience of changing sex (for example, Noble and McConkey 1995). Moreover, many of these suggestions can be experienced in a compelling way when given either by another person (as in a typical hypnotic interaction) or by the person to himself or herself (as in self-hypnosis) (Orne and McConkey 1981).

One of the key features of hypnosis is that the suggested experiences have a compulsive and sometimes non-volitional quality to them (Kirsch and Lynn 1995; Lynn *et al.* 1989). Moreover, hypnotized subjects invest personal meaning in those experiences and believe that they represent an actual state of affairs for a defined period of time (McConkey 1991). Orne (1959), for instance, argued that the hypnotized subject develops a transient belief that reality is as conveyed by the communications of the hypnotist rather than by objective information.

In recognition of this, Sutcliffe (1961) argued that 'the main feature of [hypnosis] is the hypnotized subject's emotional conviction that the world is as suggested by the hypnotist' (p.200). This emotional conviction persists even when hypnotized subjects are experiencing quite bizarre effects that have been suggested by the hypnotist and reinforced by themselves. It can be seen also when hysterical individuals are experiencing similarly bizarre effects that have been suggested, directly or indirectly, by themselves and reinforced by others.

Selected investigations of hysteria and hypnosis

Various empirical investigations have examined the relationship between hysteria and hypnosis. For instance, Bryant and Somerville (1995) explored hysterical seizures or epilepsy induced by hypnosis, and Kuyk *et al.* (1996) argued that hysterical seizures can be 'considered as a paroxysmal behavior pattern that mimics epilepsy and is initiated by psychological mechanisms' (p.468). Also, Moene *et al.* (1998) reported that the use of hypnosis in the treatment of eight patients with motor conversion symptoms yielded good results. Bryant and Somerville (1995) reported a case study in which they used hypnosis to precipitate a seizure in a patient who had refractory epilepsy. On two occasions they administered to the subject a hypnotic induction and a suggestion to age regress to a day when he was distressed and suffering repeated seizures; an epileptic seizure was observed during the second session. These authors argued that such seizures are mediated by emotional and cognitive factors which hypnosis can help to understand (see also Kuyk *et al.* 1995).

Similarly, Zimbardo *et al.* (1981) investigated the effects of hypnotically induced deafness and found that subjects who were made partially deaf by hypnotic suggestion, but kept unaware of the source of the deafness, became more paranoid as indicated on a variety of assessment measures. This points to the psychological consequences of hypnotic (and hysterical) effects and underscores how ideas can be bidirectional in their influence. These findings overall highlight the close relationship between hysteria and hypnosis and suggest that an understanding of hypnosis can move us toward an understanding of hysterical phenomena. To illustrate this further, I turn now to selected investigations of blindness, anaesthesia and analgesia, and identity distortion.

Blindness

Hysterical blindness involves the total or partial loss of vision in the absence of any organic cause for that disturbance. Bryant and McConkey (1989a) tested an hysterically blind subject on a task that involved pressing one of three switches on a machine to terminate a tone. Above the switches there was a display of three arrows, and the arrow that was in an orientation different from the others indicated the switch that terminated the tone. Our subject performed at chance level on the control trials (when the visual information was absent), but at above-chance level on the experimental trials (when the visual information was present). Moreover, the subject's performance improved when he was told that visual information was influencing his behaviour, and he reached near-perfect performance when he was instructed to improve his performance on the decision task. Notably, and importantly, the subject denied the presence of the visual information across all of the trials. This case analysis highlighted the impact of the idea of blindness on the experience of the individual, as well as the separation that can occur between awareness of visual material and the influence of that material on aspects of behavioural performance.

Hypnotic blindness involves a suggestion for total or partial loss of vision and Bryant and McConkey (1989b, 1989c, 1995) investigated hypnotic blindness in research that employed a range of measures of visual processing. The initial paradigm (Bryant and McConkey 1989b) used the task that involved hypnotically blind subjects looking at a small machine and turning off a tone that it emitted by pressing one of three switches on the front plate of the machine. A light on a visual display above the front plate indicated the correct switch, and the switch and the corresponding light varied across trials. Whereas hypnotized subjects reported phenomenal blindness following hypnosis, they responded on the task as if they were processing the available visual information. In a subsequent study, Bryant and McConkey (1989c) presented hypnotically blind subjects with uncommon spellings of homophones and later required them to complete a word-spelling task that included the homophones. Consistent with the other findings, hypnotically blind subjects demonstrated on the homophone-spelling task that they had processed the visual information that was presented during the hypnotic blindness (by spelling the homophones in the uncommon way, rather than the common way).

In another study, Bryant and McConkey (1995) presented words to hypnotically blind subjects and subsequently required them to complete a word-fragment task. Hypnotized subjects correctly completed more word-fragments of words that had been presented during hypnotic blindness than words that had not been presented. Overall, these findings indicate that, as in hysterical blindness, hypnotized subjects report phenomenal blindness, but that they show implicit perception by using visual information to complete various tasks.

Anaesthesia

Hysterical anaesthesia involves a total or partial loss of sensitivity in a particular area of the body, in the absence of any organic cause for that disturbance. James (1890/1981) argued that experiences such as hysterical and hypnotic anaesthesia were not sensory but psychological in nature. Of the subject experiencing anaesthesia (by which he meant the abolition of felt sensation in any modality, not just tactile), he wrote:

> He has *felt* it, but not *perceived* it . . . Paradoxical as it may seem to say so, he must distinguish it with great accuracy . . . in order to remain blind to it . . . He 'apperceives' it, as a preliminary to not seeing it at all! . . . We have, then, to deal in these cases neither with a sensorial anaesthesia, nor with a mere failure to notice, but with something much more complex; namely, an active counting out and positive exclusion of certain objects. (James 1890/1981, pp. 1206 and 1207–8, emphasis in original)

Despite their lack of awareness of sensory stimuli, hysterically anaesthetized individuals will respond in a way that is consistent with their having perceived the external stimuli; however, they will maintain that they cannot feel. For instance, Binet (1905) commented on an experiment with a hysterical individual who had an anaesthetized hand in the following way:

> Let us put a key, a piece of coin, a needle, a watch into the anaesthetic hand, and let us think of any object whatsoever; it will still happen . . . that the subject is thinking of the precise object that has been put into his insensible hand (p. 28).

Hypnotic anaesthesia involves a suggestion for total or partial loss of sensitivity in a particular area of the body. In research that drew on classic reports of hysterical anaesthesia by Binet (1905) and Janet (1924), Wilton and McConkey (1994) placed ordinary objects into the anaesthetized and non-anaesthetized hands of highly hypnotizable subjects and asked them to identify those objects. The subjects who reported experiencing complete anaesthesia identified fewer objects in the anaesthetized than in the non-anaesthetized hand. Notably, although some subjects who experienced complete anaesthesia identified none of the objects, other subjects identified some or all of the objects in the anaesthetized hand. Those subjects who did not identify any objects reported greater success in experiencing anaesthesia and greater belief in the reality of their anaesthesia than did those subjects who identified at least one object in the anaesthetized hand. The external reality of the task of identifying objects did not decrease the reported success or belief for subjects who did not identify any of the objects; in fact, their ratings of success in experiencing anaesthesia increased from before hypnosis to after the object task. These findings underscore the complexities involved when an internal, subjective experience is challenged through the presentation of an external, objective stimulus.

In a second experiment, Wilton *et al.* (1997) used the circle-touch test to explore hypnotic anaesthesia. This test involves suggesting to subjects that a circular area marked on their hand is anaesthetized and then testing their responses to touches inside and outside that defined area. We found that hypnotized individuals could experience suggested anaesthesia in a compelling way and could sustain that experience when tested by aesthesiometers, even when the external stimulus was relatively strong. In addition, we found that subjects' success in achieving anaesthesia and their belief in the genuineness of the experience were associated with hypnotizability. Once again, the findings highlight the continuing influence of an embraced idea on behaviour and experience.

Identity distortion

Hysterical identity distortion is somewhat different from the phenomena just described in that it is not so much a phenomenon of somatic or sensory experience but one of self-belief or self-deception (for a discussion of self-deception see Mele 1997); it involves delusory components, as do many hysterical phenomena. In this sense, it is somewhat closer to the dissociative phenomena, which are related to hysterical phenomena; in fact, hysteria can be thought of as a dissociative disorder of sensation and perception. Such disorders involve the exclusions of some mental processes from awareness and a change in the relationship of those processes to the individual's sense of self.

A similar change in the sense of self can be seen in hypnotically suggested identity distortion. One example of this is hypnotic sex change. This relatively under-investigated phenomenon seeks to alter something that is highly personalized and held with conviction. Sutcliffe (1961) used a suggestion for sex change to investigate the processes of hypnosis. He reported that more hypnotic than non-hypnotic subjects responded to the suggestion. Following this work, Noble and McConkey (1995) suggested a change of sex to hypnotic subjects within a real-simulating paradigm (Orne 1959). The real-simulating design involves high hypnotizable subjects who are tested normally and low hypnotizable subjects who are instructed to fake hypnosis; the hypnotist is unaware of who is faking and who is not. The simulation condition is a quasi-control one that allows inferences to be drawn about the extent to which the responses of the high hypnotizable, real subjects may be based in the nexus of cues operating in the experimental setting rather than in the subjective experience of hypnosis.

In this experiment, we used hypnotic virtuoso and high hypnotizable subjects as reals, and low hypnotizable subjects as simulators. We found that a compelling hypnotic experience could be established among virtuoso subjects in particular. In addition, we challenged subjects' experiences of hypnotic sex change through contradiction (in which a hypothetical authority figure questioned their experience) and confrontation (in which they looked at an image of themselves on a video monitor). We found that virtuosos were more likely than either highs or simulators to maintain their response when challenged. In particular, across our investigations of suggested blindness and anaesthesia these individuals appeared to reinterpret the conflicting information in a way that confirmed their suggested experience.

Burn *et al.* (in press) used hypnotic sex change to explore further the particular type of information processing shown by hypnotized individuals. We were interested in the degree to which subjects selectively interpreted information that is consistent with the suggested experience. To do this we gave subjects a hypnotic suggestion for sex change and during that experience we asked them to listen to a structured story that involved a male and female character; following hypnosis, we asked subjects to recall the story. We found that after listening to the story, virtuosos were less likely than were other subjects to identify with the character consistent with their suggested sex. However, when asked to recall the story after hypnosis, virtuosos recalled more information about the character consistent with their suggested sex than did highs or simulators. In other words, virtuosos were less likely to identify with the character consistent with their suggested sex, but they recalled significantly more information relevant to that character. Thus, selectivity in information processing occurred during the encoding stage and simple identification with the character was not the factor that influenced the enhanced recall of virtuosos. Rather, these findings suggested that hypnotic virtuosos interpreted aspects of the information as more significant to their internal belief as it was shaped by the hypnotically suggested experience of sex change.

This points to the operation of different cognitive processes in the development and maintenance of the suggested experience in hypnotic virtuoso subjects; a similar process could be occurring in hysteria. This work highlights that, like hysterical distortions of self-identity and self-belief, hypnotically suggested identity distortion can be compellingly experienced and resistant to challenge; moreover, the hypnotized subject processes and reinterprets information to support that experience.

Major influences and interactions

The strong belief that hysterical and hypnotized individuals hold in their experiences can be understood within a broader framework of theorizing about anomalous experiences. For example, Bonanno and Siddique (1999) highlighted the tension that exists in hysteria between the inward focus of attention (toward the self and private experience) and the outward focus of attention (toward other people and the external, non-self environment), and underscored how the balance of this focus can lead to emotion dissociation and self-deceptive enhancement of anomalous experiences. Reed (1988) argued that to fit anomalous experiences into an understandable framework, individuals impose cognitive structures on those experiences in a way that leads to personal clarification of their experiences. Conceptually, this is similar to the finding, for instance, that hypnotized subjects place personally appropriate interpretations on visual and tactile information in a way that leads them to a subjectively compelling experience of blindness or anaesthesia (Bryant and McConkey 1999; McConkey *et al.* 1999; Wilton *et al.* 1997; Wilton and McConkey 1994). Consistent with this view, hypnosis and hysteria can be understood best as a cognitive, rather than perceptual, process that is occurring within a social context. The essentially delusory or self-deceptive influence of the idea is highlighted, for instance, by evidence that both hysterical and hypnotized individuals strongly resist challenges to their experiences.

To return to the example of hypnotic blindness and Bryant and McConkey's (1989*c*) visual presentation to subjects of uncommon spellings of homophones during hypnotic blindness (see p. 206), post-experimentally we presented subjects with evidence that they had spelt the homophones in ways that were influenced by the uncommon spellings presented during their reported blindness. The subjects vehemently defended their experience of blindness by attributing their visual processing to factors that did not involve a contradiction of their phenomenal blindness. For example, one subject insisted that he spelt the homophone 'stake' the uncommon way because as a child he had never eaten 'steak'. Another subject claimed that she did not spell the homophone 'break' the common way because her father was a mechanic and he often worked with 'brakes'. This commitment to the experience of hypnotic blindness is similar conceptually to the commitment that hysterical patients have to their clinical experiences. Even when evidence of visual processing is provided to hysterically blind patients, they strongly maintain that they are phenomenally blind (Bryant and McConkey 1989*a* ; Miller 1968).

This commitment when challenged can be seen also in suggested distortion of identity. In hypnotic sex change, some subjects will not deviate from their suggested experience even in the face of strong challenge; they will in fact deny reality, even when it is staring them in the face. For instance, Noble and McConkey (1995) found that in response to the confrontation procedure (which involved subjects looking at their image on a video monitor) virtuosos were more likely than highs or simulators to either reinterpret the image in line with the suggestion (for example, one male subject commented 'Well, I'm not as pretty as I thought, but I have long, blond hair') or to deny that the image was them (for example, 'That's not me, I don't look like that'). In these cases, the subjects were expending effort to maintain the meaning of their experience, and that effort represents a key similarity between hypnosis and hysteria.

Effortful protection of the embraced experience can be seen also in cases of hysterical identity distortion. For example, Baddeley *et al.* (1996) reported the case of a 31-year-old man who believed that he was a rock star and a Grand Master of chess. Although he readily accepted that he could not play the guitar or chess, and could discuss this fact rationally and analytically, acknowledging the lack of evidence, he nevertheless maintained a strong conviction in their truth. When asked to provide evidence for his beliefs, he described having seen himself interviewed on television as a rock star and having a friend who is a rock star. For instance, when the interviewer asked, 'Can you remember being a rock star?' he replied 'No. I've had some flashback type things, like remembering I was in this studio with these particular people' (Baddeley *et al.* 1996, p. 389).

Various social psychological frameworks consider hypnotic and hysterical behaviour to be the outcome of individuals' interpretations of the particular social context in which they are behaving (Sarbin and Coe 1972; Spanos 1996). That is, their reported experience is understood in terms of the situational demands that are placed on them to behave in a way that is consistent with the suggested state of affairs (for example, the absence of processing of the visual percept, the absence of feeling of the tactile stimulation). In recognition of the role of motivation and social factors in functional blindness, for instance, Sackeim *et al.* (1979) proposed a two-stage model of functional blindness. In the first stage, perceptual representations are reportedly blocked from awareness; in the second stage, subconscious sensory representations influence the subject's behaviour depending on the subject's motivation to maintain blindness. For example, whereas a subject who is highly motivated by social factors to be blind, will not show behaviour that is consistent with visual processing, a subject who is not thus highly motivated will show behaviour consistent with visual processing. Although this model remains largely untested, it did underscore the importance of understanding contextual and social factors in functional blindness.

Frankel (1994) argued strongly that a full understanding of hypnosis and hysteria requires not only an appreciation of the effects of suggestion and imagination, but also an appreciation of the social and interpersonal context in which these processes are operating. He argued, in particular:

> . . . that a reasonable understanding of hysteria and hysterical behavior minus its context of interpersonal interaction is likely to be difficult if not impossible, and this refers not only to the interaction between patients and their families, but also to that between patients and their caretakers (Frankel 1994, p. 81).

Ziegler and Schlemmer (1994) examined three members of a family (a man and his two adult children) who experienced psychogenic blindness and severe headaches for periods of time ranging from days to years. Ziegler and Schlemmer pointed to the role of familial modelling and suggestion in the creation and maintenance of such a *folie en familie* (see also Bryant 1997).

In a broader sense of the interaction of cognitive and social influence, incidents of mass hysteria highlight the impact of suggestions and ideas, the preparedness of people for anomalous experiences, and the role of psychological contagion; all of these can be seen in the interaction of suggestion, imagination, absorption, and social communication. Elkins *et al.* (1988), for instance, reported an incident at a high-school football game where following the collapse of a student with what was tentatively diagnosed as food poisoning, 30 students were admitted to hospital with symptoms of abdominal pain. Food poisoning was never established as the cause of the collapse of the first student and Elkins *et al.* argued that suggestions by the paramedics that food poisoning had occurred led the other students to experience symptoms consistent with this diagnosis. Elkins *et al.* interpreted this incident in terms of active, alert hypnosis and suggestion.

MacLachlan *et al.* (1995) reported a more complex incident of mass hysteria that involved 110 students at a high school in Malawi. These students showed a syndrome that included screaming, laughing, crying, falling, rolling, speaking gibberish, noise hyper-sensitivity, and headache. These symptoms disappeared when the students were separated and sent home. MacLachlan *et al.* interpreted this epidemic psychological disturbance as reflecting a reaction to the major social changes that were occurring in

Malawi. For a related analysis of epidemic psychological disturbances in Russia, see Shchigolev and Vale (1997) who emphasized the interaction of individual characteristics and social environment.

Concluding comment

Hypnosis provides a useful model for understanding hysteria, and a useful tool for investigating it. It does need to be acknowledged, however, that conceptual and operational precision remains elusive when we are talking about hypnosis, hysteria, and many related phenomena and processes. These examples of dissociation between awareness and function indicate that hypnotic and hysterical phenomena may involve a distinctive management of awareness and a distinctive separation of the self from information.

Kihlstrom (1984, 1994) argued that both hysteria and hypnosis could be understood as dissociation between episodic and semantic representations of visual, tactile, and other events. Semantic representations are defined, for instance, as the visual percepts or tactile stimulation; episodic representations, on the other hand, refer to representations that contain contextual and self-referential features that are associated with the percept or stimulation. That is, episodic representations pertain to the notion that 'I am seeing here and now' and 'I am feeling here and now', rather than to the notion that 'visual or tactile information is being processed'. During functional blindness, deafness, numbness, and other related phenomena, the links between semantic and episodic representations are altered in a way that allows a phenomenal experience of blindness, deafness, or numbness. Nevertheless, because semantic representations are activated in the absence of awareness, some implicit perception occurs. Because this framework does not require episodic awareness to be involved in semantic processing, it accounts for the findings that functionally blind individuals are influenced by the presence of visual information and functionally anaesthetic individuals are influenced by the presence of tactile stimulation. The cognitive changes observed in such functional phenomena occur in a social context, and expectancy factors, motivation, and demand characteristics can strongly influence experience and behaviour.

The model proposed by Bryant and McConkey (1999; for other relevant models, see Oakley 1999 and his chapter in this volume (p. 312), Sackeim *et al.* 1979) suggests that rather than being passive recipients, hypnotic and hysterical individuals actively respond to social factors (for example, motivation, expectancy) by resolving the conflict between the reality of objective information and their commitment to their subjective experience. That is, through various social influences that define expected response, the hypnotic or hysteric individual is motivated to respond in a way that is appropriate. This model's recognition of the division of episodic and semantic representations permits modifications in behavioural response and simultaneous maintenance of phenomenal experience. Moreover, this model holds that the cognitive response to social requirements demands attentional resources and requires specific cognitive styles that permit reduction of the conflict between reality and self-deceptive belief. Further, the maintenance of hypnosis and hysteria requires appropriate and acceptable attributions about incongruent behaviour that may conflict with the subjective experience.

Although the existing data help to explain some of the common features of hypnosis and hysteria, I recognize that whereas the former is an experimentally elicited phenomenon observed in non-clinical individuals, the latter is a pathological condition. Accordingly, their similarities must be understood with acknowledgment of their inherent differences. Nevertheless, using hypnosis as the basis of a model can assist understanding of a complex system, provide a framework in which investigation can be conducted, and allow comparison with related phenomena. The phenomenal experience of hysteria interacts with the social and cognitive processes that underlie the initiation and maintenance of the condition. Moreover, the trilogy of mind — cognition, affection, and conation (Hilgard 1980) — needs to be more fully explored and incorporated into the model. As James (1890/1981) noted 'How to conceive of this state of mind is not easy' (p.1207).

Nevertheless, I hope that this model of hypnosis and hysteria has the ability to account for the phenomenal experience, implicit awareness, and the influence of social factors. Finally, I hope that further testing and development will not only enhance understanding of hypnosis and hysteria, but also permit a more refined understanding of consciousness and the powerful, if sometimes perverted, influence of ideas.

Acknowledgments

I am grateful to Melissa Sankey and Amanda Barnier for assistance in the preparation of this chapter. I am grateful also to the Australian Research Council which supported the empirical work by myself and my colleagues referred to in this chapter.

References

Baddeley, A., Thornton, A., Chua, S. E. and McKenna, P. (1996). Schizophrenic delusions and the construction of autobiographical memory. In *Remembering our past: studies in autobiographical memory* (ed. Rubin, D.), pp. 384–428. Cambridge University Press, Cambridge MA.

Binet, A. (1905). *On Double Consciousness*. The Open Court Publishing Co, Chicago.

Binet, A. and Féré, C. (1890). *Animal Magnetism*. D. Appleton, New York.

Bonanno, G. A. and Siddique, H. I. (1999). Emotional dissociation, self-deception, and psychotherapy. In *At Play in the Fields of Consciousness: Essays in Honor of Jerome L. Singer* (ed. Singer, J. A. and Salovey, P.), pp. 249–70. Erlbaum, Mahwah, NJ.

Bryant, R. A. (1997). Folie en familie: a cognitive study of delusional beliefs. *Psychiatry: Interpersonal and Biological Processes*, **60**, 44–50.

Bryant, R. A. and McConkey, K. M. (1989a). Visual conversion disorder: a case analysis of the influence of visual information. *Journal of Abnormal Psychology*, **98**, 326–9.

Bryant, R. A. and McConkey, K. M. (1989b). Hypnotic blindness: a behavioral and experiential analysis. *Journal of Abnormal Psychology*, **98**, 71–7.

Bryant, R. A. and McConkey, K. M. (1989c). Hypnotic blindness, awareness, and attribution. *Journal of Abnormal Psychology*, **98**, 443–7.

Bryant, R. A. and McConkey, K. M. (1995). Hypnotic blindness and the priming effect of visual information. *Contemporary Hypnosis*, **12**, 157–64.

Bryant, R. A. and McConkey, K. M. (1999). Functional blindness: a construction of cognitive and social influences. *Cognitive Neuropsychiatry*, **4**, 227–41.

Bryant, R. A. and Somerville, E. (1995). Hypnotic induction of an epileptic seizure: a brief communication. *International Journal of Clinical and Experimental Hypnosis*, **43**, 274–83.

Burn, C., Barnier, A. J. and McConkey, K. M. (in press). *Information Processing During Hypnotic Sex Change*. International Journal of Clinical and Experimental Hypnosis.

Chertok, L. (1984). Hypnosis and suggestion in a century of psychotherapy: an epistemological assessment. *Journal of the American Academy of Psychoanalysis*, **12**, 211–42.

Crabtree, A. (1993). *From Mesmer to Freud: Magnetic Sleep and the Roots of Psychological Healing*. Yale University Press, New Haven, CT.

Elkins, G. R., Gamino, L. A. and Rynearson, R. R. (1988). Mass psychogenic illness, trance states, and suggestion. *American Journal of Clinical Hypnosis*, **30**, 267–75.

Ellenberger, H. F. (1970). *The Discovery of the Unconsciousness: The History and Evolution of Dynamic Psychiatry*. Basic Books, New York.

Frankel, F. H. (1994). Dissociation in hysteria and hypnosis: a concept aggrandized. In *Dissociation: Clinical and theoretical perspectives* (ed. Lynn, S. J. and Rhue, J. W.), pp. 80–93. Guilford Press, New York.

Fromm, E. and Nash, M. R. (1992). *Contemporary Hypnosis Research*. Guilford Press, New York.

Gauld, A. (1992). *A History of Hypnotism*. Cambridge University Press, Cambridge.

Halligan, P. W. and David, A. S. (ed.) (1999). *Conversion Hysteria: Towards a Cognitive Neuropsychological Account*. Psychology Press, Hove.

Hilgard, E. R. (1965). *Hypnotic Susceptibility*. Harcourt, Brace, and World, New York.

Hilgard, E. R. (1977). *Divided Consciousness: Multiple Controls in Human Thought and Action*. Wiley–Interscience, New York.

Hilgard, E. R. (1980). The trilogy of mind: cognition, affection, and conation. *Journal of the History of the Behavioural Sciences*, **16**, 107–17.

Horowitz, M. J. (ed.) (1977). *Hysterical Personality*. Jason Aronson, New York.

Hull, C. L. (1933). *Hypnosis and Suggestibility: An Experimental Approach*. Appleton–Century–Crofts, New York.

James, W. (1890/1981). Principles of psychology (3 vols.). In *The Works of William James* (ed. Burkhardt, F.). Harvard University Press, Cambridge, MA.

Janet, P. (1924). *The Major Symptoms of Hysteria* (2nd edn). The MacMillan Company, New York.

Kihlstrom, J. F. (1979). Hypnosis and psychopathology: retrospect and prospect. *Journal of Abnormal Psychology*, **88**, 459–73.

Kihlstrom, J. F. (1984). Conscious, subconscious, unconscious: a cognitive perspective. In *The Unconscious Reconsidered* (ed. Bowers, K. S. and Meichenbaum, D.), pp. 149–211). Wiley–Interscience, New York.

Kihlstrom, J. F. (1985). Hypnosis. *Annual Review of Psychology*, **36**, 385–418.

Kihlstrom, J. F. (1987). The cognitive unconscious. *Science*, **237**, 1445–52.

Kihlstrom, J. F. (1994). One hundred years of hysteria. In *Dissociation: Clinical and Theoretical Perspectives* (ed. Lynn, S. J. and Rhue, J. W.), pp. 365–94. Guilford Press, New York.

Kirsch, I. and Lynn, S. J. (1995). The altered state of hypnosis: changes in the theoretical landscape. *American Psychologist*, **50**, 846–58.

Kuyk, J., Jacobs, L. D., Aldenkamp, A. P., Meinardi, H., Spinhoven, P. and VanDyck, R. (1995). Pseudo-epileptic seizures: hypnosis as a diagnostic-tool. *Seizure*, **4**, 123–8.

Kuyk, J., VanDyck, R. and Spinhoven, P. (1996). The case for a dissociative interpretation of pseudoepileptic seizures. *Journal of Nervous and Mental Disease*, **184**, 468–74.

Lynn, S. J. and Rhue, J. W. (1991). *Theories of Hypnosis: Current Models and Perspectives*. Guilford Press, New York.

Lynn, S. J., Rhue, J. W. and Weekes, J. R. (1989). Hypnosis and experienced nonvolition: a social-cognitive integrative model. In *Hypnosis: The Cognitive-behavioral Perspective* (ed. Spanos, N. P. and Chaves, J. F.), pp. 78–109. Prometheus Books, Buffalo, NY.

MacLachlan, M., Banda, D. M. and McAuliffe, E. (1995). Epidemic psychological disturbance in a Malawian secondary school: a case study in social change. *Psychology and Developing Societies*, **7**, 79–90.

Macmillan, M. (1991). *Freud Evaluated: The Completed Arc*. Elsevier Science, Amsterdam.

McConkey, K. M. (1991). The construction and resolution of experience and behavior in hypnosis. In *Theories of Hypnosis: Current Models and Perspectives* (ed. Lynn, S. J. and Rhue, J. W.), pp. 542–63. Guilford Press, New York.

McConkey, K. M., Gladstone, G. L. and Barnier, A. J. (1998). Experiencing and testing hypnotic anaesthesia. *Contemporary Hypnosis*, **16**, 55–67.

McConkey, K. M., Wende, V. and Barnier, A. J. (1999). Measuring change in the subjective experience of hypnosis. *International Journal of Clinical and Experimental Hypnosis*, **47**, 23–39.

Mele, A. R. (1997). Real self-deception. *Behavioral and Brain Sciences*, **20**, 91–136.

Merskey, H. (1979). *The Analysis of Hysteria*. Ballire Tindall, London.

Merskey, H. (1983). Hysteria: the history of an idea. *Canadian Journal of Psychiatry*, **28**, 428–33.

Merskey, H. (1995). *The Analysis of Hysteria: Understanding Conversion and Dissociation*. Gaskell, London.

Micale, M. S. (1990). Hysteria and its historiography: the future perspective. *History of Psychiatry*, **1**, 33–124.

Miller, E. (1968). A note on the visual performance of a subject with unilateral functional blindness. *Behaviour Research and Therapy*, **6**, 115–16.

Moene, F. C., Hoogduin, K. A. L. and VanDyck, R. (1998). The inpatient treatment of patients suffering from (motor) conversion symptoms: a description of eight cases. *International Journal of Clinical and Experimental Hypnosis*, **46**, 171–90.

Noble, J. and McConkey, K. M. (1995). Hypnotic sex change: creating and challenging a delusion in the laboratory. *Journal of Abnormal Psychology*, **104**, 69–74.

Oakley, D. A. (1999). Hypnosis and conversion hysteria: a unifying model. *Cognitive Neuropsychiatry*, **4**, 243–65.

Orne, M. T. (1959). The nature of hypnosis: artifact and essence. *Journal of Abnormal and Social Psychology*, **58**, 277–99.

Orne, M. T. and McConkey, K. M. (1981). Images: imagined and believed. *Journal of Mental Imagery*, **4**, 50–3.

Reed, G. (1988). *The Psychology of Anomalous Experience: A Cognitive Approach* (rev. edn). Prometheus Books, Buffalo, NY.

Reynolds, J. R. (1869). Remarks on paralysis and other disorders of motion and sensation dependent on idea. *British Medical Journal*, **2**, 483–5.

Roche, S. M. and McConkey, K. M. (1990). Absorption: nature, assessment, and correlates. *Journal of Personality and Social Psychology*, **59**, 91–101.

Roy, A. (ed.) (1982). *Hysteria*. John Wiley, New York.

Sackeim, H. A., Nordlie, J. W. and Gur, R. C. (1979). A model of hysterical and hypnotic blindness: cognition, motivation, and awareness. *Journal of Abnormal Psychology*, **88**, 474–89.

Sarbin, T. R. and Coe, W. C. (1972). *Hypnosis: A Social Psychological Analysis of Influence Communication*. Holt, Rinehart, and Winston, New York.

Shchigolev I. I. and Vale, M. (1997). Some aspects of mental epidemics in Russia. *International Journal of Mental Health*, **26**, 10–14.

Sheehan, P. W. and McConkey, K. M. (1982). *Hypnosis and Experience: The Exploration of Phenomena and Process*. Erlbaum, Hillsdale, NJ.

Showalter, E. (1997). *Hystories: Hysterical Epidemics and Modern Culture*. Picador, London.

Slavney, P. R. (1990). *Perspectives on Hysteria*. Johns Hopkins University Press, Baltimore.

Spanos, N. P. (1996). *Multiple Identities and False Memories: A Sociocognitive Perspective*. American Psychological Association, Washington, DC.

Sutcliffe, J. P. (1961). 'Credulous' and 'skeptical' views of hypnotic phenomena. Experiments on esthesia, hallucination, and delusion. *Journal of Abnormal and Social Psychology*, **62**, 189–200.

Veith, I. (1965). *Hysteria: The History of a Disease*. University of Chicago Press, Chicago.

Wilton, H. J. and McConkey, K. M. (1994). Hypnotic anaesthesia and the resolution of conflict. *Contemporary Hypnosis*, **11**, 1–8.

Wilton, H. J., Barnier, A. J. and McConkey, K. M. (1997). Hypnotic anaesthesia and the circle-touch test: investigating the components of the instructions. *Contemporary Hypnosis*, **14**, 9–15.

Ziegler, D. K. and Schlemmer, R. B. (1994). Familial psychogenic blindness and headache: a case study. *Journal of Clinical Psychiatry*, **55**, 114–17.

Zimbardo, P. G., Andersen, S. M. and Kabat, L. G. (1981). Induced hearing deficit generates experimental paranoia. *Science*, **212**, 1529–31.

16 Imaging hysterical paralysis

B. S. Athwal, P. W. Halligan, G. R. Fink,
J. C. Marshall, and R. S. J. Frackowiak

Although Freud's observation that hysterical paralysis behaved 'as though anatomy did not exist or as though it had no knowledge of it' has often be interpreted as implying the futility of neuropsychological accounts, hysterical paralysis must express itself through the physiological medium of brain anatomy. Placing conversion phenomena in the context of (normal) voluntary movement suggests a possible answer to Freud's dilemma. We review the first attempt to investigate a case of hysterical paralysis using PET. This case meets the full DSM–IV criteria for conversion disorder and the neurological investigation to rule out a possible 'organic' explanation has been more extensive than any previously reported. Using the patient as her own control, brain activity was measured when the patient prepared to move and /or attempted to move each of her legs. With the normal leg, the expected premotor and motor areas were duly activated. When the patient attempted to move her paralysed leg, two new areas — the right anterior cingulate and the orbito-frontal cortex — were activated. We suggest that these areas act to inhibit the intentional effects of prefrontal areas on motor outcome.

It is not the muscles which refuse to obey the will but the will itself which has ceased to work.
(Sir Benjamin Brodie 1837)

There can be little doubt that the term hysterical is applied often as a diagnosis to something that the physician does not understand. It is used as a cloak for ignorance. (C. D. Marsden 1986)

Introduction

The concept of a conversion disorder (such as 'hysterical paralysis') remains controversial, and the classification of hysterical symptoms (for example, in DSM–IV) continues to be the subject of criticism both within and outside clinical psychiatry. The main problem relates to the diagnostic imprecision of the label 'hysteria' and the lack of a coherent, theoretically motivated, neuropsychological account concerning the pathophysiology of this disorder.

Such criticisms are not, however, specific to hysteria. In a recent review, Charlton (1995) attacks psychiatry for failing to contribute significantly to either the practical or theoretical understanding of the major functional disorders. He suggests that current classifications 'should be abandoned in favour of developing a cognitive nosology . . . based upon a modern understanding of human psychological architecture'. Although many psychiatric conditions remain 'functional' in the sense that no current physical pathology can be established, it is nonetheless feasible to offer explanations for certain psychopathologies in terms of impairments to neuropsychological processes. The extent to which discrete psychopathologies can be insightfully mapped onto *neurophysiological processes* however remains to be established.

The advent of functional brain imaging has made it possible to in principle localize symptom- or task-dependent psychological processes of human cognition in the living brain. Sophisticated functional neuroimaging techniques, such as PET (positron emission tomography) and fMRI (functional magnetic resonance imaging), demonstrate task-related regionally-specific brain activity. PET in particular has formed the basis for many studies investigating cognitive and sensorimotor processes. A detailed discussion of the technique of PET is beyond the scope of this chapter but useful reviews thereof may be found in Carrson *et al.* (1998) and Frackowiak *et al.* (1997). These recent developments in brain imaging have already contributed valuable insights into the brain areas activated in established 'functional' conditions such as depression (Bench *et al.* 1992; Drevets *et al.* 1992), auditory hallucinations (McGuire *et al.* 1993), post-traumatic stress disorder (Raunch *et al.* 1996), schizophrenia (Frith 1995; Silbersweig *et al.* 1995; Liddle *et al.* 1992), and obsessive-compulsive disorder (McGuire *et al.* 1994).

Given the desire to provide a principled account of hysterical symptoms capable of linking a putative abnormal psychological state with the production of physical symptoms, there is a surprising dearth of relevant neuropsychological or anatomico-physiological reports in the literature (Flor-Henry *et al.* 1981; Ludwig 1972; Lader 1982; Miller 1991). To understand the neurophysiological mechanisms underlying symptoms such as hysterical motor paralysis or somatosensory loss, it is important to first appreciate how normal motor and sensory functioning is produced and differentially impaired after 'structural' brain damage. If 'hysterical' paralysis is found to associate reliably with a distinct pattern of brain activation, then this association may form the basis for a neurobiological explanation of the symptom, which in turn may constrain and inform a deeper neuropsychological understanding.

In this chapter, some previous attempts to understand and demonstrate objective brain correlates for hysterical symptoms are reviewed. We then provide a brief description of the functional organization of the normal motor system together with a more detailed description of an experimental paradigm used to investigate brain areas that may be involved in hysterical *paralysis*. Finally, a tentative account of hysterical paralysis, based in part on the results of this case is discussed in relation to previous neuroscience findings.

Early neuroscience accounts of hysteria

When the concept of hysterical hemiparesis was the subject of intense debate in the late nineteenth century, Charcot (1889) argued that there was 'without doubt a lesion of the nervous centres . . . in the grey matter of the cerebral hemisphere on the side opposite the paralysis, and more precisely in the motor zone of the arm'. He further maintained that it was 'one of those lesions which escape our present means of anatomical investigation, and which, for want of a better term, we designate *dynamic* or *functional* lesions'. Students who attended Charcot's clinical lectures took these functional lesions to be akin to localized oedema, anaemia, or active hyperaemia 'of which no trace is found after death'. Sigmund Freud, a student of Charcot at the time, was unconvinced by this conjecture about the locus of functional lesions. Freud (1893) pointed out that Charcot's position required a close similarity between the behavioural effects of conventional 'organic' lesions and these purported 'dynamic' lesions. Thus, although transitory, a 'hysterical' paralysis due to some local change in the 'primary motor areas' should nevertheless involve the same symptoms as paralyses originating from conventional lesions confirmed at necropsy.

By contrast, Freud (1893) argued against the concept of a local, anatomical lesion, maintaining that the clinical presentation of 'hysterical paralysis' was qualitatively different from 'organic cerebral paralysis' in several important ways. Unlike organic lesions, hysterical paralysis is 'characterised by *precise limitation* and *excessive intensity*'. On the basis of these and other clinical observations, Freud felt that 'we must not draw conclusions on the subject of cerebral anatomy . . . based on the symptomatology of those paralyses'. He concluded that 'the lesion in hysterical paralyses must be completely independent of the anatomy of the nervous system, since in its paralyses and other manifestations hysteria behaves as though anatomy did not exist or as though it had no knowledge of it'.

Rather than offer an alternative physical location, Freud preferred to consider the dynamic lesion in psychological terms, likening the paralysis to 'the abolition of the associative accessibility of the conception of the arm'. This dispute between Charcot and Freud could not be resolved with the technology then available and the issue is in many respects just as active today.

Attempts to reveal brain areas associated with hysteria

Surprisingly, over the past one hundred years, there have been comparatively few attempts to investigate the neurobiological basis of hysterical symptoms and it is only in the last 15 years that empirical studies have begun to appear. Two recent studies will serve as illustration (others are described by Sierra and Berrios in their chapter in this volume, p. 192).

In 1988, Drake and colleagues used computerized frequency analysis of EEG recordings to compare normal brain function in a group of 10 healthy control subjects with brain dysfunction in patients with hysterical and somatoform disorders (Drake *et al.* 1988). This study represents one of the first attempts to differentiate patients with hysteria or conversion disorder from each other and from healthy control subjects by the use of objective physiological measures. The 10 patients with hysteria (7 female and 3 male) reported either hemisensory loss or hemiparalysis. Another 10 patients (8 female and 2 male) fulfilled diagnostic criteria for somatoform disorder. EEG recordings were acquired over a period of 15 minutes with electrodes placed according to the standard international 10/20 system. During the recordings, three of these patients suffered non-epileptic seizures and one, a transient trance-like alteration of consciousness for which no organic explanation could be found. The recordings were analysed in four frequency bands: 0.25–4.0Hz, 4.25–8Hz, 8.25–13.0Hz, and 13.25–30Hz. From these, measures of the ratio of high (8.25–30hz) to low (0.25–8.0hz) spectral power were derived for each hemisphere, and then the ratio of left- and right-sided power calculated for both the frontal and the posterior brain regions. EEG mobility, related to the number of polarity changes per second (a measure of fast EEG activity), was also calculated for both left and right frontal regions.

In frontal regions, the power ratio between high and low frequencies was negative in the conversion disorder patients and positive in the somatoform disorder patients, each differing from the control subjects. Statistical significance was *not* needed. Conversion disorder patients showed significantly less EEG mobility in the left frontal region when compared to controls and somatoform disorder patients ($p < 0.01$). This was not seen for patients with somatoform disorder. In the right frontal regions, somatoform disorder patients showed less EEG mobility than either patients or controls ($p < 0.05$).

These results, whilst not permitting strong inferences, nonetheless highlight physiological differences, particularly in frontal lobe function, between the patient groups and controls, and also between the conversion and somatoform disorder groups. The study did not make inferences as to the precise nature of the processes underlying the neurophysiological differences found. However, the authors concluded that their results suggested that hysterical disorders may have a physiological basis, and furthermore, that the physiological abnormalities underlying conversion and somatoform disorder may be distinct.

In 1995, Tiihonen and colleagues reported a single case study of a 32-year-old female with an acute left-sided hysterical paralysis and sensory disturbance following psychological stress and an episode of depression (Tiihonen *et al.* 1995). Neurophysiological tests, including motor-evoked potentials, were normal and remained so for the duration of the symptoms. The hysterical episode lasted a few days and ^{99m}HMPAO SPECT brain images were obtained two days after the onset, when symptoms were present, and again six weeks later, following symptom resolution. The scans were taken during electrical stimulation of the left median nerve with the aim of investigating brain activity, which in normals would be predicted as an increase in blood flow in the somatosensory parietal region. During the period of left-sided weakness and sensory disturbance however, there was instead an increase in blood flow in the right frontal region and an unexpected decrease in blood flow in the right parietal region (Fig. 16.1a) despite left median nerve stimulation. Following symptom resolution, blood flow in the frontal regions equalized and blood flow in the right parietal region increased to the level expected during median nerve stimulation (Fig. 16.1b).

The authors interpreted their results in terms of an activation of inhibitory areas in the frontal lobes and a simultaneous deactivation of the sensory cortex of the parietal lobes, thus accounting for the patient's symptoms of parasthesia and paralysis. As only two scans were taken, both during sensory stimulation, it was not possible to determine whether frontal activity was increased throughout the illness or only during such stimulation. The symptoms, however, were continuous. These authors took the view that the illness related to stressful adverse events in the patient's life and therefore interpreted the observed blood flow changes to indicate that psychological events altered brain physiology to produce the symptoms experienced. They concluded that psychodynamic and biological models of hysteria are therefore not necessarily in opposition but may be complementary — psychodynamic processes produce symptoms through dysfunctions in brain physiology.

An important aspect of this study was that it showed a physiological abnormality associated with hysteria that subsequently normalized upon symptom resolution.

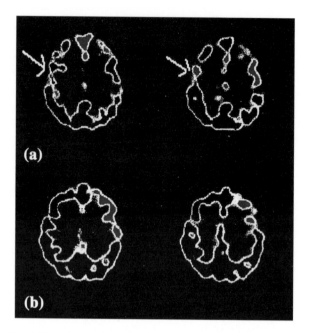

Fig. 16.1 Cerebral blood flow (CBF) during the electric stimulation of the left median nerve, (a) prior to recovery and (b) after recovery from left-sided paresthesia and paralysis. Two transaxial slices seen from below both conditions are shown. The arrows point to the right parietal cortex demonstrating hypoperfusion during paresthesia. The images are normalized to the mean slice density. (Reproduced with permission from *Biological Psychiatry*.)

Furthermore, the authors were able to relate the symptoms to neural events (albeit loosely), thus providing a bridge between mental processes underlying symptom production and regionally selective blood flow in the brain. However, the conclusions were based upon a small number of observations in a single subject, and the study was not able to control for the possible confounding influence of attentional variation upon the blood flow changes observed. In addition, whilst the approach of studying a patient before and after resolution of symptoms is valuable, it is difficult to separate the effects of other accompanying changes in mental state from the effects relating specifically to hysteria. Finally, although useful in demonstrating differential and regionally specific activations, the study highlights the difficulties inherent in applying sophisticated imaging techniques in the absence of a coherent, hypothesis-led approach to the putative neuropsychological mechanisms involved. Ultimately no unifying explanation mechanism was proposed.

Both these studies (Drake *et al.* 1988; Tiihonen *et al.* 1995) suggest that the sensory and motor symptoms of hysteria are associated with specific alterations in cerebral physiology, which in the case of sensory loss involve areas associated with higher levels of sensory processing (that is, sensory cortex and the frontal lobes). A frequent criticism of such work concerns the focus on 'representative', well worked-up single cases. As hysterical conversion is a protean disorder (Ron 1996), groups of patients who meet the diagnostic criteria are likely to be heterogeneous. The resultant inter-subject variability in any group study may obscure significant effects, and thus hinder understanding in this area. In the absence of a more precise classification well controlled case studies are still important.

Neurophysiological indications of hysterical paralysis

It is worth pointing out that both the previous studies only considered sensory abnormalities, which did not require the active involvement of the patient. Hysterical *paralysis* is, however, a more striking and incapacitating symptom which affects the patient's voluntary attempts to move specific parts of their body. Until recently, no published data using functional imaging was available. This was in spite of the fact that there are certain advantages to the study of hysterical phenomena using a model of movement-related impairments:

1. The brain areas underlying movement selection and execution in normal subjects have been well defined both with functional imaging and other methods.

2. PET is capable of demonstrating changes in brain activity during the performance of selective tasks

3. Unilateral motor paralysis allows for a ready-made internal control in a single subject (that is, comparing requests to move the affected with the unaffected side) without the confounding effects inherent in inter-subject comparisons.

Functional anatomy of human movement

Functional brain imaging has made it possible to interpret normal movement in terms of the activity within specific brain areas during the constituent parts of an action. Recent functional imaging studies indicate that voluntary movements are the result of a dynamic cerebral process that involves: (1) the formulation of a movement intention, which gives rise to (2) a motor command/preparation, that in turn results in (3) the execution of the intended movement (Jeannerod 1997).

Placing conversion phenomena in the context of (normal) voluntary movement may suggest an answer to Freud's problem of how hysterical paralysis 'behaves as though anatomy did not exist or as though it had no knowledge of it'. Freud's observation is true insofar as it relates to the effects of demonstrable, organic (that is, structural) lesions and highlights the fact that hysterical paralysis does not present clinically with the same lines of demarcation and the same patterns of association as organic paralysis (Weintraub 1985).

If, however, as Freud suggested, the source of the pathology lies within the very 'conception' or 'idea' of moving the affected limb (albeit unconsciously), such a psychological account must nevertheless express itself through the medium of brain physiology. In considering these points, and in appraising the results of functional brain imaging studies of hysterical paralysis, it is helpful to outline some of the brain areas involved in controlling the normal human voluntary motor system. A brief review of the differential organization of the motor system follows.

1. The motor system displays regionally specific functional organization

Specific brain regions appear to undertake selective roles in the planning, organization, and execution of voluntary movements. Frontal brain regions are important for the generation of the movement intention, the selection of individual movements, and the formulation of a movement plan (see Passingham 1993; Rowe and Frackowiak 1999). These functions mainly concern premotor regions such as the dorsal premotor cortex and the supplementary motor area (Jueptner *et al.* 1997). A number of less well-defined regions in the frontal lobes may also be involved in movement-related activity (Fink *et al.* 1997).

The primary motor cortex on the pre-central gyrus is thought to be involved in the subsequent generation of a movement command to the musculature and interacts with other regions in the on-going control of a specified movement. The integration of movement intention, information from the environment, and the internal state of the organism into purposeful movement is a complex process that involves the motor-associated regions of the basal ganglia, the frontal regions, and the motor areas of the medial hemispheric wall, including limbic structures such as the cingulate sulcus and gyrus (Pickard and Strick 1996). Throughout, there are interactions between these regions expressed through the multiple neuronal feedback loops passing between the different structures.

2. Areas within the motor system display somatotopic organization

It is therefore possible to assign a functional role to the significantly activated brain areas in functional imaging studies. For example, PET studies of the motor cortex during simple limb movements (Colebatch *et al.* 1991) demonstrate somatotopic organization analogous to that first shown by Penfield and Boldrey (1937). Movements of the legs are associated with dorsal regions of the motor cortex, and movements of the upper limbs and face with the more ventral motor cortex. This concept of somatotopy within regions of the motor system has now been extended with the demonstration of equivalent maps in the premotor regions of the frontal lobes (Fink *et al.* 1997; Muakassa and Strick 1979; Mitz and Wise 1987).

3. Activations related to movement are at least partly connected to the processing of reafferent sensory information

A number of movement-related brain areas seem also to be involved in sensory functions. Both the primary motor cortex and the cerebellum receive sensory information via a number of different sources (Kandel *et al.* 1991). These sensory functions are highlighted in functional imaging experiments that show how a large proportion of the brain activity elicited by limb movement is replicated by passive movement of the limbs (Weiller *et al.* 1996; Jueptner *et al.* 1997).

4. Different levels of motor performance give rise to differential motor-related functional activations

Studies in which the intensity or frequency of movement is varied parametrically show that activity within the primary motor cortex, the premotor cortices, and the cerebellum varies as a function of task demands. Thus, there are increases in activity within the motor cortex with increasing frequency of finger movements (Sadato *et al.* 1996) or with increasing muscular effort (Dettmers *et al.* 1995, 1996). These observations inform both the design of functional imaging experiments and the interpretation of results by highlighting the importance of strict control of task-related motor performance to avoid unwanted variations that may in themselves give rise to signal change.

5. Preparation to make a movement or imagining a movement produce specific patterns of brain activity

Motor preparation may be thought of as the act of 'establishing a state of readiness to make a specific planned movement' (Henry and Rogers 1960). The act of preparing to make a movement results in activation of motor areas of the brain (Deiber *et al.* 1996). Similarly, imagining self-movement or even the movement of another person produces activity within the motor structures of the premotor cortex (for a review, see Crammond 1997). This activity can be distinguished from, and may be a subset of, activity related to the actual execution of the same movement.

6. Suppression of movements gives rise to specific patterns of activity

Functional imaging studies of motor tasks, in which subjects must voluntarily inhibit the execution of intended, automatic, or learnt responses show activation in specific areas of the brain (Garavan *et al.* 1999). Examples of this type of paradigm include variations of the Stroop colour–word naming task, which activates the anterior cingulate and orbito-frontal cortex (Bench *et al.* 1993; Pardo *et al.* 1990). In functional imaging experiments where subjects suppress a pre-potent motor response, the anterior cingulate cortex is particularly active (Paus *et al.* 1993).

In summary, the control of movement by the human brain is the result of co-ordinated activity in a number of interacting areas, some of which display regional functional specialization. Experimentally, this process is capable of being decomposed into broad constituent elements that may be examined with functional brain imaging in cases of clinical interest.

In considering the possible neuropsychological hypotheses that might explain how 'pathological' mental states could be 'converted' into selective somatic symptoms, the following points are worth reflecting on:

1. Brain areas that help maintain a hysterical paralysis are likely be located within areas involved in the normal generation and execution of movement (or in areas known to be functionally related).

2. Whatever the neural basis of hysterical paralysis, it is not yet clear whether the underlying functional deficit is *continuous* or only present on occasions when the patient attempts to move. In other words, it is possible that dysfunction is selectively triggered by volitional intentions to move the affected part. This possibility is echoed in the clinical finding of patients who display a total inability to generate volitional movement yet produce some normal movement of the same limb while, for example, unconsciously maintaining posture/balance or when asleep.

In terms of hysterical conversion, functional disorder(s) could therefore occur at any one of several different levels and may indeed involve more than one level:

1. The patient is unable to move because some aspect of their motor *intentional* system has been rendered dysfunctional. This in turn could produce difficulty or loss of movement despite the patient's insistence that they genuinely intended to move. Although possible, a disorder at this level seems unlikely (assuming that the patient is

not malingering) given that (a) most patients appear aware of their ability to intend, (b) intentions are translated into normal movement for those parts of the body not affected by hysteria, and (c) for the most part, patients do not report difficulty in imagining movements and in preparing or generating intentions to move the affected side.

2. The disorder may exist further downstream, more specifically at the level of motor preparation and/or execution. In keeping with the patient's phenomenological report, this position assumes a normal intentional output. But the processes that translate this intention into actual movement may not proceed normally, and an appropriate motor command to the muscles is not generated. Thus the patient is aware of the intention to move, but upon attempting to do so is unable to produce movement.

Imaging hysterical paralysis – an illustrative case study

Hysterical paralysis was investigated in a case of chronic motor conversion and initially reported as a brief article (Marshall *et al*. 1997). The purpose of the study was to examine the specific areas of brain uniquely associated with the inability to move the affected limb. As the patient in question claimed that she was unable to move her left leg (despite the absence of clinical or structural damage), a response-dependent paradigm using that limb was used. Given the long-standing nature of the impairment it was assumed that the neural mechanisms responsible for the paralysis would be comparatively stable.

Case background

BL was a 45-year-old right-handed widow with three children. Her relevant history included intermittent depression and reports of somatic symptoms such as mutism and lower limb weakness extending over 17 years. In the three years preceding her diagnosis for conversion hysteria, at least two documented psychologically traumatic events had occurred against a more general background of familial and financial problems. The events associated with the onset of her hysterical paralysis dated from the middle of 1994 when she experienced weakness of the left arm and leg and was (by her own report) unable to talk for some time.

Neuropsychological investigations

She scored 24/28 on the Short Orientation Memory and Concentration Test. Neuropsychological testing for language functions, visuo-spatial cognition, visual recognition, and buccofacial and manual praxis (right hand and arm) yielded results within normal limits. Mild impairments were seen on verbal recall (Wechsler Logical Memory) and visual reproduction tasks (Rey Osterreith Design). Verbal IQ, estimated from the National Adult Reading Test (NART), was 115.

Neurological investigations

There was a flaccid paralysis of the left side with little movement in the fingers and no movement at all at the ankle or the toes. Reflexes were symmetrical and plantar reflexes flexor. The right arm and leg were normal in terms of power, bulk, and tone. On the Motricity Index, BL scored 27 per cent for the left arm and 0 per cent for the left leg; visual fields were normal, as were eye movements and fundi. The left arm was held flexed at the wrist and the fingers could not be extended due to fixed flexion contractures; there was no voluntary movement of the left fingers or thumb, although occasional slight involuntary movements were observed. The left arm itself moved through restricted postures when BL tried to move other parts of her body. By contrast, the left leg was always flaccid and showed no flicker of movement under any circumstances. Nonetheless, there was no evidence of muscle wasting and reflexes were equal and normal in both arms and legs. The left plantar reflex could not be obtained; the right was normal. Somatosensory testing was normal in both arms and legs; bladder control was unaffected. There was no evidence of unilateral neglect (in any modality) or any speech problems.

Stroke was initially suspected but a comprehensive range of investigations including CT brain scan, chest radiographs, a full blood count, urea electrolytes, liver function tests, blood glucose, calcium, prothrombin time, thyroid function tests, ECG, and Doppler ultrasound of the carotid arteries showed no discernible pathology. Finally, the patient underwent repeated magnetic resonance imaging (MRI) to rule out 'structural' lesions not detected on CT scan. This neuroradiological analysis of the brain and upper and lower spine was entirely normal. A central motor conduction study was undertaken: recordings from the left abductor digiti minimi showed a normal threshold for activating the motor cortex and a normal conduction time in the central motor pathways.

There was no evidence of a generalized failure of 'intention': BL could voluntarily move her right limbs, and when asked to move her left limbs she gave every impression (from facial grimaces to changes of bodily position) that she was trying hard to do so.

Clinical summary

When she underwent the experimental PET study, BL met all the DSM–IV criteria for conversion disorder. Psychological factors (conflict and stress) had been associated with the initiation and exacerbation of these symptoms from time to time. Finally, there was no evidence to suggest that her symptoms were intentionally produced or feigned. Although it is difficult to rule out conclusively the possibility of malingering, there was a revealing episode in which a small fire broke out on the patient's ward. Nursing staff on duty at this time noted that BL did not (could not?) attempt to escape like other patients — rather, she became seriously withdrawn and unresponsive.

Experimental procedure

The patient was studied using a Siemens ECAT PET scanner in 3D mode with a 15-cm axial field of view. Structural images were obtained with 2 T Magnetom VISION (Siemens). BL lay on the bed of the scanner throughout the experiment. Cerebral activity, indexed by regional cerebral blood flow (rCBF), was measured during repetitions of a total of five conditions (one control and four experimental). In all conditions, continuous electromyographic (EMG) recordings were taken from four surface electrodes on each leg. To control for the effects of the sensory feedback from the limbs, which would obviously differ between the moving and non-moving limb, the patient's legs were strapped down so that overt movement of either leg was highly restricted. The experiment is therefore best interpreted in terms of the ability to appropriately command muscular contraction rather than movement *per se*, although the former may be thought of as the prerequisite of the latter. During each scanning epoch, a metronome beat was presented every two seconds. In the four experimental conditions (three repeats each), the patient was instructed either to prepare to lift the left or the right leg, or to attempt to lift the left or right leg, on each metronome beat.

In the *preparation* conditions, the patient was told to attend to and get ready to lift the left/right leg on each metronome beat, but *not* to actually move the leg unless touched on that leg by the experimenter. To ensure that the patient 'prepared to move', touches were delivered both before and after, but not during, the active phase of the PET scan, which lasted 90 seconds.

In the *move* conditions, the patient was instructed to try to lift the left/right leg against the previously mentioned restraints on each beat. In the control condition (which involved six repeats), nothing was required of the patient, who was simply asked to lie still.

Statistical parametric mapping (SPM95) software was used for the realignment, transformation into standard stereotactic space, smoothing, and statistical analysis of the PET images. All measurements per condition were averaged. State-dependent differences in global flow were varied out using ANCOVA. The experimental effects were assessed using contrasts of the adjusted task means using the t-statistic subsequently transformed into the normally distributed Z statistic. Each resulting set of Z values constituted a statistical parametric map (SPM{z}) which was then thresholded at $P < 0.001$. Areas identified by the interaction were thresholded in the same way as the (independent) main effects ($P < 0.001$).

Moving/preparing to move the (normal) right leg

The areas differentially activated (relative to the control state) when the patient attempted to lift her right leg against restraint were consistent with previous studies of normal movement (Fink *et al.* 1997; Frackowiak *et al.* 1997). These included bilateral dorsolateral prefrontal (DLPFC) and left lateral premotor activation compatible with the intention to change position in space. There was also substantial activation of the left primary sensory motor areas (S1 and M1) and the inferior parietal cortex. Bilateral cerebellar activations were also seen and were consistent with regulation of the descending motor pathways.

A subset of these areas was also implicated when the patient prepared to lift the right leg (Stephan *et al.* 1995). Activations of the bilateral DLPFC, the lateral premotor cortex, the inferior parietal cortex, and both cerebellar hemispheres showed that preparation to move involved a substantial yet selective pattern of brain states. As expected, no significant activation was seen in the left primary sensory motor cortex.

Moving/preparing to move the (affected) left leg

Preparation to move the left leg (relative to the passive control state) likewise activated the lateral premotor cortex (Brodmann area 6) and both cerebellar hemispheres, indicating the patient's 'readiness' to move the paralysed leg when touched. This finding was considered evidence against the suspicion that the 'hemiparalysis' was intentionally produced or feigned.

The attempt to move the paralysed side (left leg) produced a qualitatively different pattern of activation from that observed for the right leg. As expected, no activation was seen in the primary sensory motor cortex; this was consistent with the absence of movement and muscle innervation shown on the EMG. Instead, there were significant activations in the left DLFPC (Brodmann area 9), the right anterior cingulate (Broadmann areas 24/32 24), and the cerebellum (bilaterally), as well as some midbrain and upper brainstem structures. Significant activations (relative to the baseline,) of the left DLPFC and cerebellum were again considered evidence against faking (and support of the patient's attempt to comply with our instructions). The anterior cingulate cortex was activated when the attempt to move the left leg was compared with the preparation condition for the same leg. This latter comparison also revealed significant activation of the right orbito-frontal cortex. These activations were found *only* in those conditions where the patient attempted to move her left leg. Left leg movement versus both passive control *and* preparation showed significant activation of the right anterior cingulate, as did left leg movement versus right leg movement.

To investigate more fully those brain regions that differentially increased their activity when the patient attempted to move the paralysed leg when compared to the non-paralysed leg, we employed an interaction analysis that controlled for the effects of side by considering only the differential activations between each respective move and prepare state. This interaction (computed as [move(paralysed) − prepare(paralysed)] − [move (non-paralysed) − prepare(non-paralysed)]) showed those increases ($p < 0.001$) in brain activity that related specifically to the inability to move the hysterically paralysed leg. Activations specific to attempted movement of the left leg relative to movement of the right leg are shown in Fig. 16.2.

Significant activations in the right anterior cingulate region (Brodmann areas 24/32) and the medial orbito-frontal cortex (Brodmann area 10) were the only two areas that were differentially involved in this comparison. Activity in these regions has not previously been reported in studies of either movement generation or attempted movement under normal circumstances. It is important to point out that the corresponding reverse interaction (involving that which was unique to movement of the good right leg) did not show this pattern of activation, even when examined using a very low statistical threshold. In contrast, movement of the normal limb activated the expected motor network of the left sensory motor cortex and temporo-parietal areas. The lateralized cingulate and orbito-frontal activations were therefore unique to the patient's attempted movement of the hysterically paralysed limb.

Towards a neuropsychological account of hysterical paralysis

Do the activations observed provide a basis for a neuropsychological account of hysterical paralysis? Candidate regions for such a role would be expected, in healthy subjects, to function in the integration of emotion, motivation, and movement. Both the anterior cingulate cortex and the orbito-frontal cortex function as part of the rostral limbic system, and are thought to be involved in mediating emotional and central

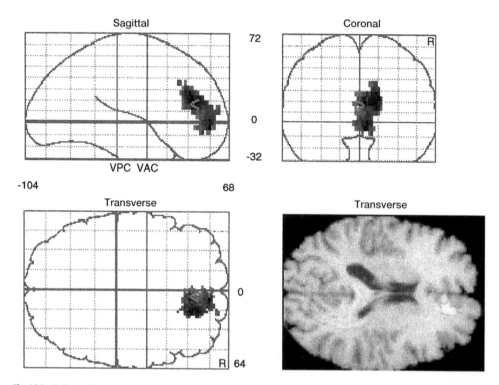

Fig. 16.2 Relative rCBF increases associated with attempted movement of the left (bad) leg. The interaction shown is derived by the following comparison of conditions: (attempt to move left leg — prepare to move left leg) (move right leg — prepare to move right leg). This interaction reveals relative rCBF increases during attempts to move the bad (left) leg that did not occur when the good (right) leg was moved. Areas of significant rCBF increases ($P < 0.001$) are shown as through-projections onto representations of standard stereotactic space. In addition, the transverse SPM{z} map has been superimposed upon the patient's MR image that had been spatially normalized into the same anatomical space. Arrows indicate the local maximum within the area of activation. There is activation in the right anterior cingulate and the right orbito-frontal cortex. (Sagittal = side view; transverse = view from above; coronal = view from the back; R = right; VAC = vertical plane through the anterior commissure; VPC = vertical plane through the posterior commissure; numbers at axes refer to co-ordinates of stereotactic space.) Reproduced with permission from Cognition.

executive functions (Devinsky 1995). This system is involved in the integration of environmental stimuli with internal motivational states, and the regulation of context-dependent behaviours. It is thus implicated in the integration of action with both internal and external emotional and motivational factors. The rostral anterior cingulate cortex is closely connected with adjacent prefrontal and premotor regions and has a more specific role in the control of movement, particularly in the initiation of movements in response to external stimuli.

Cingulate lesions after stroke result in a variety of disorders of voluntary movement including akinetic mutism, impairments of movement initiation, or motor neglect. That the anterior cingulate may have inhibitory functions is suggested by its role in the 'stroop effect'. Activation of the anterior cingulate has been reliably found when subjects must suppress competing responses when, for example, colour names are presented in incongruent colours (Bench *et al.* 1993; Carter *et al.* 1995; Pardo *et al.* 1990). Conversely, cingulate over-activity, such as that seen in cingulate epilepsy, may give rise to motor tics and motor automatisms (see Devinsky 1995 for a review).

The orbito-frontal cortex is involved in the learning and reversal of stimulus-reward associations and thus in the regulation of behaviour related to the external environment. Damage to this region may result in impairments in the performance of tasks that require adaptations in response to altering environmental cues. For example, in Wisconsin card sorting or in maze navigation, such patients may be unable to adapt their motor responses despite being able to comprehend and vocalize any new strategies required. In the context of emotional responses, this region may correct behavioural stimulus-reponse associations when they become inappropriate (see Rolls 1996 for a review of this work). A dysfunction in this region therefore provides a possible explanation for the association of an inappropriate motor response (that is, the absence of a response) to either an internal or external signal to move, and furthermore a null response that persists despite the patient's awareness of its unsuitability.

Further evidence of the involvement of a putative rostral limbic motor network in the generation of inappropriate motor responses comes from the study of Tourette's syndrome and 'negative motor areas'. Tourette's syndrome is characterized by multiple unwanted extra movements that patients find both embarrassing and difficult to suppress (Robertson and Stern 1998). In this condition a very similar pattern of combined functional abnormality in the cingulate and orbito-frontal cortex has been observed (Weeks *et al.* 1996). Conversely, electrical stimulation of these areas, including the anterior cingulate and orbito-frontal cortex, has been shown to produce inhibition of spontaneous movements (Kaada 1960).

In our study, increases in activity in the cerebellum were related to attempted movements of the hysterically paralysed limb. Our interpretation for these changes relates to the discrepancy between the patient's intention to move and the absence of any overt movement. We suggest that in our case of hysterical paralysis, there exists both the intention to move and a subsequent failure of designated regions of the motor system to implement the specified movement instruction. In these circumstances, there is a neurophysiological mismatch between the movement intention and those parts of the movement system normally involved in its execution. The cerebellum has functions relating to motor control and, in particular, sensorimotor integration and has been implicated as a likely site for a comparator that modulates movement intentions and the sensory feedback related to such intentions. Given the substantial independent connections between the DLPFC and the cerebellum, it is possible that cerebellar activation during preparation and attempted movement of the left leg represents activity signalling the mismatch between motor intention and outcome. This could be construed as evidence against the idea that the paralysis is intentionally produced or feigned in BL's case, although further study of feigned incapacity or partial disability is required (Spence *et al.* 2000).

In an attempt to determine the neuronal equivalent of the patient's intention to move we also examined activity in the premotor regions, including the DLFPC and the supplementary motor areas in the frontal lobes. These areas are all implicated in internally generated movement (Passingham 1993, 1997) and are candidate areas in which activity changes may be seen in comparisons between conditions that involve differing intentional states. It has been argued that activation of the DLPFC is uniquely associated with the 'subjective experience of deciding when to act and which action to perform' (Spence and Frith 1999). Although in BL, activity related to attempted movement of either leg is seen in these regions, no side-specific interactions were seen. We interpreted this as indicating that, in terms of motor intention, there is no difference in our subject between *attempted* movement of the paralysed limb and of the normal limb.

In summary, when movement is attempted but fails, a distinctive and abnormal brain state was observed in BL. Although certain brain structures known to be implicated in movement are activated, taken together the overall pattern of activation differs greatly from that which has been observed in studies of normal movement or attempted movement. Significant in this regard is the lack of activation in the region of the primary motor cortex upon attempting to move the paralysed leg. Instead, significant activations occur in the anterior cingulate region and in the orbito-frontal cortex.

Although we employed an activation paradigm which requires the interpretation of relative differences between brain states, we also assumed that the resting state is an appropriate control for both left- and right-sided movements. That this state is a valid rest condition is implicit in the normal activation pattern seen when it is used in the contrast for activations related to movement of the good side. Since there is no evidence of ongoing functional pathology in the resting scans for the affected side, we suggest that it is the 'intention' to move that triggers the 'hemiparalysis' via the pathological activation of the anterior cingulate and orbito-frontal cortex.

Finally, it is unlikely that activation of the anterior cingulate in our study is due to an heightened or adverse emotional state when the patient is instructed to move her affected leg. Throughout scanning, BL showed no indications of anxiety or distress. Furthermore, we did not observe any changes in activity in those lower limbic structures (for example, the amygdaloid nuclear complex) that might be concerned with emotions experienced during attempts to raise the left leg. It is also unlikely that the observed activation of the right anterior cingulate is the result of imagining, rather than executing, the required movement. Although the anterior cingulate has been implicated in functional brain imaging studies of human motor imagery, this has always been in the context of significant activation in other motor areas including, for example, the supplementary motor area (SMA) and more lateral premotor areas. Furthermore, activation of orbito-frontal cortex has not been described in previous studies of motor imagery.

A reconsideration of hysterical paralysis

Prior accounts of hysterical paralysis have been far from specific, both in terms of their psychological structure or anatomo-physiological function. Analogies have been drawn between the 'sham-death reflex' (playing possum) and hysterical paralysis (Kretschmer 1926), but claims about the associated physiology have not progressed much beyond the speculation that 'corticofugal inhibition' is involved (Ludwig 1972). Earlier, we noted that Charcot (1889) conjectured that hysterical paralysis implicated '*dynamic* or *functional* lesions' in the cortical motor zone opposite the paralysis. Such an account was rejected by Freud (1893), who did not offer an alternative account as to which brain areas were involved. In some respects, our findings provide *a* possible reconciliation of their dispute.

In partial support of Charcot's position we found a localized failure to increase rCBF in the contralateral motor cortex. But this failure only emerged when the patient tried to move her left leg. Unlike stroke or Charcot's putative 'functional lesion', BL showed no resting asymmetry of rCBF in the motor cortices as indicated by the baseline scans. Furthermore, activations seen when the patient prepared to move both the good and the paralysed leg were similar. It was only when she attempted to move the left (bad) leg that significant activations of the right anterior cingulate and right orbito-frontal cortex were observed. We suggest therefore that hysterical paralysis is associated with a malfunction in the normal interaction between regions of the brain concerned with intention and regions concerned with execution during the process of movement.

Thus it may be that the influence of, for example, the premotor regions upon the primary motor cortex is curtailed precisely when movement of the paralysed limb is attempted. Under such circumstances, normal brain areas are unable to generate the movement, despite a legitimate 'intention' to do so (in terms of a set of motor instructions). We can as yet only speculate as to the mechanism for this functional disconnection. It is perhaps embodied in the increased activity we observe in the anterior cingulate gyrus/sulcus or the inferior frontal cortex revealed in the interaction. In this regard we recall the suggestion of Tiihonen and colleagues (Tiihonen *et al.* 1995) that the excess frontal activity observed in their patient with hysterical motor and sensory loss was in some way inhibitory and responsible for a functional deactivation of the sensorimotor cortices during the period when symptoms were present. Our findings support this contention and suggest that, in the case of motor paralysis, this inhibition relates to an interruption of the interaction between brain areas that generate intentions to move and those areas responsible for the actual execution of the intended movement.

Consequently, while the PET study does not reveal *how* the loss of left-sided motor functions came about in BL, it does suggest that Freud was right (and that Charcot was wrong) about the resting status of the contralateral motor cortex. Our results leave open many other issues concerned with 'psychodynamic' accounts of hysteria, which are neither supported nor rejected by our findings. It is nonetheless not without interest that our neurophysiological findings in a case of 'hysterical' paralysis (Marshall *et al.* 1997) are, in many ways, similar to those reported in a methodologically equivalent study in which paralysis of the left leg was hypnotically induced in a normal subject (Halligan *et al.* 2000).

Acknowledgements

PWH and JCM are supported by the Medical Research Council. The Wellcome Trust supports BSA and RSJF. GRF is supported by the Deutsche Forschungsgemeinschaft.

References

Bench, C. J. *et al.* (1993). Investigations of the functional anatomy of attention using the Stroop test. *Neuropsychologia*, **31**, 907–22.

Braun, A. R. *et al.* (1993). The functional neuroanatomy of Tourette's syndrome: an FDG-PET study. I. Regional changes in cerebral glucose metabolism differentiating patients and controls. *Neuropsychopharmacology*, **9**, 277–91.

Brodie, B. C. (1837). *Lectures Illustrative of Certain Nervous Conditions*. Longman, London.

Carrson, R. E., Daube–Witherspoon, M. E. and Herscovitch, P. (ed.) (1998). *Quantitative Functional Brain Imaging with Positron Emission Tomography*. Academic Press, London.

Carter, C. S., Mintun, M. and Cohen, J. D. (1995). Interference and facilitation effects during selective attention: an H2[15}O PET study of Stroop task performance. *Neuroimage*, **2**, 264–72.

Charcot, J. M. (1889). *Clinical Lectures on Diseases of the Nervous System*. New Sydenham Society, London.

Charlton, B. G. (1995). Cognitive neuropsychiatry and the future of diagnosis: a 'PC' model of the mind. *British Journal of Psychiatry*, **167**, 149–58.

Colebatch, J. G., Deiber, M. P., Passingham, R. E., Friston, K. F. and Frackowiak, R. S. J. (1991). Regional cerebral blood flow during voluntary arm and hand movements in human subjects. *Journal of Neurophysiology*, **65**, 1392–401.

Crammond, D. J. (1997). Motor imagery: never in your wildest dream. *Trends in Neurosciences*, **20**, 54–7.

Deiber, M. P., Ibanez, V., Sadato, N. and Hallet, M. (1996). Cerebral structures participating in motor preparation in humans: a positron emission tomography study. *Journal of Neurophysiology*, **75**, 1233–47.

Dettmers, C. *et al*. (1995). The relationship between neuronal activity and force in the motor areas of the human brain. *Journal of Neurophysiology*, **74**, 802–15.

Dettmers, C., Lemon, R. N., Stephan, K. M., Fink, G. R. and Frackowiak, R. S. J. (1996). Cerebral activation during the exertion of sustained static force in man. *Neuroreport*, **7**, 2103–10.

Devinsky, O., Morrell, M. J. and Vogt, B. A. (1995). Contributions of the anterior cingulate to behaviour. *Brain*, **118**, 279–306.

Drake, M. E., Padamadan, H. and Pakalnis, A. (1988). EEG frequency analysis in conversion and somatoform disorder. *Clinical Electroencephalography*, **19**, 123–8.

Drevets, W. C., Videen, T. O., Price, J. L., Preskorn, S. H., Carmichael, S. T. and Raichle, M. E. (1992). A functional anatomical study of unipolar depression. *Journal of Neuroscience*, **12**, 3628–41.

Fink, G. R., Frackowiak, R. S. J., Pietrzyk, U. and Passingham, R. E. (1997). Multiple non primary motor areas in the human cortex. *Journal of Neurophysiology*, **77**, 2164–74.

Flor–Henry, P., Fromm–Auch, D., Tapper, M. and Schopflocher, D. (1981). A neuropsychological study of the stable syndrome of hysteria, *Biological Psychiatry*, **16**, 601–26.

Frackowiak, R. S. J., Friston, K. J., Frith, C. D., Dolan, R. J. and Mazziota, J. C. (1997). *Human Brain Function*. Academic Press, London.

Freud, S. (1893). Quelques considrations pour une étude comparative des paralysies motrices organiques et hystériques *Archives de Neurologie*, **26**, 29–43.

Frith C. D. *et al*. (1995). Regional brain activity in chronic schizophrenic patients during the performance of a verbal fluency task. *British Journal of Psychiatry*, **167**, 343–9.

Garavan, H., Ross,T. J. and Stein, E. A. (1999). Right hemisphere dominance of inhibitory control: an event-related functional MROI study. *Proceedings of the National Academy of Science:* **96**, 8301–6.

Halligan, P. W., Athwal, B. S., Oakley, D. A. and Frackowiak, R. S. J. (2000). Imaging hypnotic paralysis: implications for conversion hysteria. *The Lancet*, **355**, 986–7.

Henry, F. M. and Rogers, D. E. (1960). Increased response latency for complicated movements and a 'memory drum' theory of neuromotor reaction. *Res Q*, **31**, 448–58.

Jeannerod, M. (1997). *The Cognitive Neuroscience of Action*. Blackwell Publishers, Oxford.

Jueptner, M. *et al*. (1997). The relevance of sensory input for the cerebellar control of movements. *Neuroimage*, **5**, 41–8.

Kaada, B. R. (1960). Cingulate, posterior orbital, anterior insular and temporal pole cortex. In *Handbook of Physiology (Vol. 2)* (ed. Field, J.). Williams and Wilkins, Baltimore.

Kandel, E. R., Schwartz, J. H. and Jessel, T. M. (ed.) (1991). *Principles of Neural Science*. Appleton & Lange, Norwalk, Connecticut.

Kretschmer, E. (1926). *Hysteria: Reflex and Instinct*. Peter Owen, London.

Lader, M. (1987). The psychophysiology of hysterics. *Journal of Psychosomatic Research*, **17**, 265-9.

Liddle, P. F. (1987). The symptoms of chronic schizophrenia: a re-examination of the positive-negative dichotomy. *British Journal of Psychiatry*, **151**, 145–51.

Lorenz, J., Kunze, K. and Bromm, B. (1998). Differentiation of conversive sensory loss and malingering by P300 in a modified oddball task. *Neuroreport*, **9**, 187–91.

Ludwig, A. M. (1972). Hysteria. A neurobiological theory. *Archives of General Psychiatry*, **27**, 771–7.

Marsden, C. D. (1986). Hysteria — a neurologist's view. *Psychological Medicine*, **16**, 277–88.

Marshall, J. C., Halligan, P. W., Fink, G. R., Wade, D. T. and Frackowiak, R. S. (1997). The functional anatomy of a hysterical paralysis. *Cognition*, **64**, B1–8.

McGuire, P. K., Bench, C. J., Frith, C. D., Marks, I. M., Frackowiak, R. S. J. and Dolan, R. J. (1994). Functional anatomy of obsessive-compulsive phenomena. *British Journal of Psychiatry*, **164**, 459–68.

Mitz, A. R. and Wise, S. P. (1987). The somatotopic organisation of the supplementary motor areas: intracortical microstimulation mapping. *Journal of Neuroscience*, **7**, 1010–21.

Muakkassa, K. F. and Strick, P. L. (1979). Frontal lobe inputs to primate motor cortex: evidence for four somatotopically organised 'pre-motor areas'. *Brain Research*, **177**, 176–82.

Pardo, J. V., Pardo, P. J., Janer, K. W. and Raichle, M. E. (1990). The anterior cingulate mediates processing selection in the Stroop attentional conflict paradigm. *Proceedings of the National Academy of Science USA*, **87**, 256–9.

Passingham, R. E. (1993). *The Frontal Lobes and Voluntary Action*. Oxford University Press, Oxford.

Passingham, R. E. (1997). Functional organisation of the motor system. In *Human Brain Function* (ed.,Frackowiak, R. S. J., Friston, K., Frith, C., Dolan, R. J. and Mazziota, J. C.) Academic Press, London.

Paus, T., Petrides, M., Evans, A. C. and Meyer, E. (1993). The role of the human anterior cingulate cortex in the control of oculomotor, manual and speech response: a positron emission tomography study. *Journal of Neurophysiology*, **70**, 453–69.

Penfield, W. and Boldrey, E. (1937). Somatic motor and sensory representation in the cerebral cortex of man as studied by electrical stimulation. *Brain*, **60**, 389–443.

Picard, N. and Strick, P. L. (1996). Motor areas of the medial wall: a review of their location and functional activation. *Cereb Cortex*, **6**, 342–53.

Raunch, S. L., van der Kolk, B. A. and Fisler, R. E. (1996). A symptom provocation study of post traumatic stress disorder using positron emission tomography and script-driven imagery. *Archives of General Psychiatry*, **53**, 380–7.

Robertson, M. M. and Stern, J. S. (1998). Tic disorders: new developments in Tourette syndrome and related disorders. *Current Opinions in Neurology*, **11**, 373–80.

Rolls, E. T. (1996). The orbitofrontal cortex. *Philosophical Transactions of the Royal Society, London B*, **351**, 1433–4.

Ron, M. A. (1996). Somatisation and conversion disorders. In *Neuropsychiatry* (ed., Fogel, B. S., Schiffer, R. B. and Rao, S. M.). Williams and Willliams, Baltimore.

Rowe, J. B. and Frackowiak, R. S. (1999). The impact of brain imaging technology on our understanding of motor function and dysfunction. *Current Opinion in Neurobiology*, **9**, 728–34.

Sadato, N., Ibanez, V., Deiber, M. P., Campbell, G., Leonardo, M. and Hallet, M. (1996). Frequency-dependent changes of regional cerebral blood flow during finger movements. *Journal of Cerebral Blood Flow Metab*, **16**, 23–33.

Silbersweig, D. A. *et al.* (1995). A functional neuroanatomy of hallucinations in schizophrenia. *Nature*, **378**, 176–9.

Spence, S. A. and Frith, C. D. (1999). Towards a functional anatomy of volition. *Journal of Consciousness Studies*, **6**, 11–29.

Stephan, K. M. *et al.* (1995). Functional anatomy of the mental representation of upper extremity movements in healthy subjects. *Journal of Neurophysiology*, **73**, 373–86.

Tiihonen, J., Kuikka, J., Viinamaki, H., Lehtonen, J. and Partanen, J. (1995). Altered cerebral blood flow during hysterical parasthesia. *Biological Psychiatry*, **37**, 134–7.

Weeks, R. A., Turjanski, N. and Brooks, D. J. (1996). Tourette's syndrome: a disorder of cingulate and orbitofrontal function? *Quarterly Journal of Medicine* **89**, 401–8.

Weintraub, M. I. (1983). *Hysterical Conversion Reactions: A Clinical Guide to Diagnosis and Treatment*. Spectrum Publications, New York.

Weiller, C. *et al.* (1996). Brain representation of active and passive movements. *Neuroimage*, **4**, 105–10.

17 Disorders of willed action

Sean A. Spence

Hysterical paralysis is an unusual diagnosis, necessitating the physician's inference of the patient's intention when the latter fails to act. The physical 'signs' are those of voluntary motor inconsistency; the volitional system is the focus of abnormality but explanatory organic disorder is excluded (by definition). The distinction between 'hysteria' and 'feigning' requires validation. The 'paralysed' patient fails to perform certain acts, while performing others that utilize the same muscle groups. Therefore, hysterical paralyses are essentially disorders of action; indicating either an executive dysfunction of 'intention in action' or an 'intention to act' to deceive (the 'self' or the 'other'). Functional neuro-imaging may be used to differentiate a pathophysiology of disordered action (in hysteria) from an anatomy of intentional feigning (in deception). The pivotal role of the dorsolateral prefrontal cortex in disordered action is borne out by recent data from a study of hysterical patients and controls feigning motor dysfunction.

Introduction

Hysteria, or conversion disorder, is a curious diagnostic entity, characterized by a putative psychological mechanism rather than a specific symptom or pathognomonic finding. Indeed, it is the absence of such features which renders the diagnosis, combined with the belief (on the part of the physician) that the patient is not consciously feigning dysfunction; however, physicians can be poor judges of deception (Turner, 1999). Although the standard psychiatric diagnostic criteria no longer use the psychodynamic term 'conversion' to describe the psychopathological mechanism, a hypothetical effect of the 'mind' upon the 'body' is retained:

> Psychological factors are judged to be associated with the symptom . . . because the initiation or exacerbation of the symptom . . . is preceded by conflicts or other stressors . . . The symptom . . . cannot be fully explained by a general medical condition. (DSM–IV)

> [T]here should be no evidence of physical disorder . . . [S]ufficient must be known about the psychological and social setting and personal relationships of the patient to allow a convincing formulation to be made of the reasons for the appearance of the disorder. (ICD–10)

And yet, '[t]he symptom . . . is not *intentionally* produced or feigned' (DSM–IV; emphasis added).

This diagnosis is troublesome because, of necessity, it requires that the patient 'does not know what she is doing' — otherwise she would be feigning. In addition, the physician must 'know' that the patient does not know, and must invoke an unconscious mechanism to explain the patient's absence of (conscious) intent (Spence, 1999a).

Incidentally, although the patient is thought to lack insight into her symptom production, there is no suggestion that this is a psychotic disorder (although some have applied neuroleptic treatment: Rampello *et al.*, 1996). The dilemma for the physician is how to interpret what the patient does not do (when she fails to move a limb) in the light of what the patient does not say (when she denies intent).

Involuntary cessation of voluntary movement

Given that the concept of 'gain' has been central to the diagnosis of hysteria (the initial gain of the 'conflict' avoided; the secondary gain of the invalid role), and given that, of necessity, the voluntary musculature is affected, it is perhaps surprising that such paralyses are not routinely perceived as feigned.

The 'signs of hysteria' are those of *voluntary* motor inconsistency. The patient with hysterical aphonia may be unable to whisper but able to cough, thereby demonstrating that his or her vocal cords can function. The patient is said not to realize that there is an anatomical overlap between these superficially different procedures. Again, in the limb, hysterical paralysis is marked by the simultaneous contraction of agonistic and antagonistic muscles:

> . . . a basis for one of the favourite signs, which is to ask a patient to press a heel down on the bed while lying supine. When the patient finds that . . . she cannot do it, the hand is placed under that heel and the patient is asked to lift the opposing limb. The synergistic response of the 'paralysed' leg produces pressing down of the heel while the 'good' leg is lifted. (Merskey, 1995)

How specific are these 'signs' to hysteria, compared to feigning? The current diagnostic criteria acknowledge uncertainty:

> Conscious simulation of loss of movement . . . is often very difficult to distinguish from [hysterical conversion]; the decision will rest upon detailed observation, and upon obtaining an understanding of the personality of the patient, the circumstances surrounding the onset of the disorder, and the consequences of recovery versus continued disability. (ICD–10).

It is difficult to see how these factors might objectively distinguish hysteria from feigning. In either case patients may exhibit neurological inconsistency:

> The degree of disability resulting from . . . these types of symptoms [conversion disorder] may vary from occasion to occasion, depending upon the number and type of other people present, and upon the emotional state of the patient . . . [A] variable amount of attention-seeking behaviour may be present in addition to a central and unvarying core loss of movement . . . which is not under voluntary control. (ICD–10)

The physician is required to determine whether an inability to perform voluntary motor acts, in the absence of demonstrable pathology, is attributable to the patient's unconscious or conscious (hence 'feigning') mind. This is clearly problematic.

Having presented a rather sceptical account of hysterical paralyses, I will now consider a counter-argument — that they constitute disorders of willed action.

Willed action

'Will' is taken to mean the higher-order ability to consider choices of action. Necessarily, it will be a complex process imbued not just with strategic considerations, but also with ethics — of right and wrong. This use of the term derives from Locke:

> [t]his power that the mind has to order the consideration of any idea, or the forbearing to consider it; or to prefer the motion of any part of the body to its rest, and vice versa, in any particular instance, is that which we call the will. (in Berrios and Gili, 1995)

He goes on:

> [t]he actual exercise of that power, by directing any particular action, or its forbearance, is that which we call volition or willing.

Hence, the process of exercising the will is termed volition; it is voluntary. Following on from the philosopher, Macmurray (1991), I will use the term 'agent' to describe the one 'who chooses', the one who exercises her or his will. Their action is their chosen performance in the world; and 'action without thought is a self-contradictory conception' (Macmurray, 1991). Hence, to Macmurray, there are no 'involuntary actions', merely events; an involuntary 'movement' is just that, a movement — it is not an 'action'. An action requires a deliberate choice (in consciousness) by an agent; it requires an intention (see Table 17.1).

A number of issues emerge if we adopt a philosophical approach to action. First, it is apparent that if we consider hysteria to be a disorder of the will, then we are acknowledging that it is implemented through the voluntary motor system. This is consistent with the motor 'signs' of hysteria (already discussed) and is compatible with past descriptions of the disorder:

> It is not the muscles which refuse to obey the will, but the will itself which has ceased to work. (Brodie, 1837, quoted in Merskey, 1995)

> . . . [t]hey say, 'I cannot'; it looks like 'I will not'; but it is 'I cannot will'. (Paget, 1873, quoted in Merskey, 1995)

Table 17.1 A volitional vocabulary

Term	Meaning
Will	The capacity to deliberate over decisions, to decide, to make a choice.
Agent	The one 'who chooses'.
Intention to act	Conscious choice of the agent (subject to introspection).
Action	The chosen performance of the agent 'in the world'.
Intention in action	The motor programmes out of awareness (cognitively-unconscious) that 'enact' the agent's actions in the world (Searle, 1983; Jeannerod, 1997).
Volition	'Willing' (after Locke); the process of executing the 'willed action' or 'its forbearance'. Volitions constitute a category of voluntary movement; there may be voluntary movements which are not 'willed actions', e.g. stereotypies and utilization behaviours.

> We recognise the deep disturbance of the will, which we never fail to see in hysterical patients. (Kraepelin, 1904, quoted in Merskey, 1995)

Furthermore, if we re-examine the motor signs of hysteria, it is clear that the voluntary musculature still functions in hysteria so long as a given movement is not part of an 'action' that the patient has prohibited. Thus, although the patient 'will' not speak, she 'will' produce a voluntary cough (when asked to); the patient has a disorder of volition, precluding certain actions (speaking) but not others (voluntary coughing). In the case of the 'paralysed' leg, the voluntary musculature is contracted as part of an involuntary change in posture; the patient will not contract this set of muscles (voluntarily), but he or she will do so 'un-intentionally' when distracted.

Hence, the problem in hysterical motor disorders is not the voluntary motor system *per se*, but the way that the motor system is utilized in the performance (or non-performance) of certain chosen, 'willed' actions.

A second consequence of invoking the 'will' to describe hysteria is its moral tone. A disordered will may produce abnormal acts; it might also produce *immoral* acts. A disordered will might help 'explain' feigned disorder in the context of psychopathy. So arguments which invoke 'will' or 'conversion' might be distinguished by their moral tone: the latter being apparently neutral ('the patient didn't choose to be this way, it's unconscious'; 'she' — necessarily indicating her 'conscious' mind — is 'innocent').

Third, the 'will' and 'conversion' models may be contrasted in their implication of conscious versus unconscious mechanisms. Both views of the mind are dualistic. The philosophical ('will') model invokes a consciousness that acts upon the body and the world. The psychodynamic ('conversion') model invokes an unconscious mechanism 'acting' independently of consciousness. Are these approaches incompatible? Not necessarily; a psychoanalyst might argue that all conscious thoughts emerge from a dynamic unconscious, thereby dictating those 'actions' which we think we choose; a disordered unconscious might give rise to a disordered 'will', and hence, disordered 'action'. Indeed, recent Lacanian accounts of hysterical behaviours have talked of 'failed acts' either as an identification with the 'will' of the 'other' (Zizek, 1991) or as an 'acting in' within a fantasy (or 'erotogenic') body space (David–Menard, 1989).

Attention to action

In the 'rational' mind, actions follow on from the exercise of the will (cf. Libet, 1993; see the following text), and the chain of 'causality' implies that conscious intentions lead to actions. Indeed, philosophically, this is the case by definition (see Table 17.1). Yet, we are all aware of complex (voluntary motor) tasks that may be undertaken without conscious attention. Some level of awareness is necessary for such tasks, but we do not need to deliberate continuously. Thus, in the oft-quoted example of the car drive, where we cannot remember the journey in detail or the particular movements we made in turning the steering wheel, we may not have attended to specific details, but we can be sure that our eyes were open!

There appears to be a continuum in conscious attention to (voluntary) movements, with little attention to the movements of non-REM sleep at one extreme, and focussed concentration and precision when defusing a bomb, towards the other. But it might also be argued that some heightened degree of attention to a voluntary movement is required for that movement to be considered an action. It is difficult to imagine an 'action' that is not attended to, although it is possible to attend to movements that are not actions (for example, reflexes and tremors). This view is congruent with that of James (1910): 'Effort of attention is . . . the essential phenomenon of will'.

Attention is relevant here because patients can be 'distracted' or their level of awareness altered pharmacologically to induce temporary remission. Hence, Ellis (1990) administered intravenous diazepam to a woman with hysterical quadriplegia; examination under the drug restored voluntary flexion and extension of upper and lower limbs. A similar case responded to intravenous midazolam (Keating *et al.*, 1990). Adrian and Yealland (1917) used general anaesthetic to influence the paralyses of their 'battle-shocked' soldiers, although their intention was to show the conscious patient that he could move his limbs after all:

> [I]n the stage of excitement the patient will struggle, cry out . . . he will often regain consciousness whilst he is in the act of moving the arm which was formerly paralysed or using the voice which was formerly dumb. (Adrian and Yealland, 1917)

Hysterical paralyses are disorders of action

Thus far, we have acknowledged a psychodynamic view of hysterical paralyses which states that they are caused by an unconscious mechanism — conversion. Such a model assumes the patient is not (consciously) feigning disorder. We have shown that this view of hysteria persists in our diagnostic systems. Crucially (and of necessity), such systems require the physician to decide between dichotomous alternatives: unconscious hysteria versus conscious feigning.

Yet, from the clinical, phenomenological perspective, it seems that hysterical paralyses are reliant not upon unconscious mechanisms but on conscious processes. The disorder affects certain (consciously chosen) acts and not others (which the patient, allegedly, regards as distinct). The maintenance of these symptoms requires the patient's attention — a characteristic of higher motor acts; the paralyses break down when the subject is distracted, consciousness is obtunded, or when the 'paralyses' are circumvented by other motor routines. Thus, hysterical paralyses are quintessentially disorders of action.

Actions and intentions

Actions may be executed abnormally, despite the intentions of the agent. Hence, a patient with Parkinson's disease (PD) may formulate an intention to act (see Table 17.1), but their performance may be abnormal (their limbs rigid and bradykinetic). Action is impaired while its reflexive counterpart (a movement) may be relatively spared; sudden environmental stimuli may elicit paradoxical kineses, for example, a thrown object may be caught. By attending to their gait, the patient may improve his or her action performance (by the use of focussed attention or visual cues; Morris *et al.*, 1996). Action is affected in PD, yet the patient may achieve some modest improvement in performance by conscious means. In contrast, 'hysterical' motor dysfunction, although action-based, is improved by relative lack of attention (through distraction or sedation; Spence, 1999b). Hence, both PD and hysteria affect willed actions, but in the former the patient's attention may be used to enhance performance, while in the latter, it facilitates dysfunction. Thus, either the hysterical patient intends to deceive (and therefore is not 'hysterical' by definition), or it is the physiology of their 'intending' which is itself disturbed (that is, he or she is better when not exercising 'intentions to act').

Similarly with 'action dystonia', which may accompany certain circumscribed motor acts (such as writing) and for which there is no 'organic' diagnostic test. This diagnosis is phenomenological, but because of its consistencies, action dystonia(s) may nevertheless be distinguished from hysterical dystonia (Koller *et al.*, 1997); hysterical dystonia, like hysterical paralysis, is ameliorated by distraction (Lang, 1992). Hence the role of 'attention' in making the distinction between hysteria and 'organic' disease.

Thus, hysterical motor symptoms pose a problem: they behave like actions, yet the patient denies (conscious) intent. If they were feigned, they would result from an intention to deceive, but instead, they seem to constitute a unique disorder — a disorder of the cognitively unconscious 'intention in action', which relies for its expression upon the simultaneous (conscious) 'intention to act' (see Tables 17.1 and 17.2). Where organic disorders are somewhat ameliorated by increasing attention to action, hysterical symptoms improve with 'inattention'. The next section will consider whether there are any other indicators of cognitive dysfunction in those who exhibit these symptoms.

Table 17.2 Intentional phenomena in some neuropsychiatric disorders affecting action

Disorder	Intention to act	Intention in action
Hysterical paralysis	Reported as normal.	Abnormal in the presence of intentions to act. Attention to action impairs, but distraction and sedation improve performance.
Parkinson's disease	Present, although little empirical study of subjective intention.	Abnormal, but may be assisted by attentional strategies (Morris *et al.*, 1996; cf. hysteria). Tremor can be suppressed consciously (Lang, 1992; cf. hysterical tremor).
Tic disorders	Forced quality to intention, but perceived as voluntary; subjects report having 'urge' to act (Bliss, 1980).	Abnormal, but behaviours may be 'resisted', suppressed, through attentional strategies (Lang, 1992).
Utilization behaviour	Denied.	Behaviours 'disinhibited'; more likely to arise when motor system is not engaged by motor task (Shallice *et al.* 1989; cf. hysterical symptoms).

Abnormalities of mind

Functional decompensation is frequently implied in those who develop hysteria — the immigrant to the industrial conurbation, the intellectually impaired or immature personality experiencing stress, or the vulnerable patient with predisposing physical or psychiatric disorders. Comorbidity with depression is common (Slater and Glithero, 1965; McKegney, 1967; Bibb and Guze, 1972; Lewis, 1975; Merskey and Buhrich, 1975; Cybulska, 1998) and is seen in those with hysterical movement disorders (Koller et al., 1998). In one such study, Factor et al. (1995) elicited psychiatric comorbidity in 50 per cent of patients (mostly depression).

In studies of patients with paralyses, comorbidity has varied. Baker and Silver's (1987) 'hysterical paraplegics' lacked formal psychiatric assessment; yet, 35 per cent of the group had past psychiatric histories. Although depression was not over-represented relative to an 'organic' (control) group, these groups did differ on a number of criteria, including neurological inconsistency (in the 'hysterical' patients): 'One patient was observed skipping in the physiotherapy department. One, with an ostensible triparesis, assisted the doctor taking blood with her allegedly paralysed arm' (Baker and Silver, 1987). The extent to which these patients satisfied a diagnosis of conversion disorder is unclear: the authors acknowledged it was 'open to discussion'.

Binzer and colleagues (1997), studying patients with hysterical paralyses, found a high rate of depressive symptoms, with 33 per cent of hysterical patients satisfying a psychiatric syndromal diagnosis. In addition, 50 per cent had a personality disorder. Compared to an 'organic' disorder control group, hysterical paralysis was associated with low education and increased personality disorder and depression.

In patients with unexplained motor symptoms, Crimlisk et al. (1998) found that psychiatric disorders (75 per cent) and personality disorders (45 per cent) were common; depression affected 41 per cent of the sample.

Collectively, these data suggest that many patients presenting with motor signs of hysteria (who are formally assessed by psychiatrists) have an abnormal mental state. Depressive illness and personality disorder seem to be the most common diagnoses. These diagnoses do not prove that patients are not consciously 'feigning' motor disorder, but in contrast to the 'binary' diagnostic choice between unconscious conversion and conscious feigning, they do permit a further alternative: that disorders of action might be secondary to mental disorder. Such patients might not be 'deliberately' deceiving others any more than a psychomotor-retarded, depressed patient 'feigns' alogia.

A further alternative: the disavowal of action

The 'requirement', for the diagnosis of conversion disorder, that the physician ascribe paralysis to an unconscious mechanism of which the patient is unaware, rehearses a dilemma which is integral to the philosophical problem of 'self-deception'. The notion that one may truly deceive oneself is paradoxical. If one knows the truth, how might one simultaneously 'know' the opposite? Such a paradox has provoked a variety of philosophical responses, ranging from those arguing that self-deception is impossible to those resorting to a partitioning of the 'self' (Mele, 1987).

Part of the problem hinges on whether self-deception is modelled upon deception of the 'other' ('interpersonal deception'). For the latter, the deceiver must truly believe what he or she knows, and must set out to deceive the other (the victim) into believing the opposite. If the same model is applied to the self, then two paradoxes arise: the static paradox (that is, the simultaneous belief in opposites) and the dynamic paradox (how could one set out to successfully believe the opposite of what one already knows to be true?) Yet, self-deception remains a common notion in folk psychology. How might it be maintained?

Using the interpersonal model, the inevitable conclusion is that there is more than one compartment to the self. This argument clearly resembles the dynamic account of conversion disorder: if not feigning, there must be an unconscious mechanism, implying a divided self. Hence, the patient may unconsciously 'know' that their limb can move, but may be consciously unaware of this. The patient has 'deceived' him or herself, and is not deceiving the other (the physician). Under such circumstances the patient is regarded as 'sincere'. However, this solution of the static paradox does not resolve the dynamic one (Mele, 1987).

The interpersonal model may not generalize to self-deception. One solution, provided by Fingarette (1969), abjures the requirement that there be more than one 'self'; indeed it posits that the process of self-deception is conscious and involves the disavowal of actions which the 'self' regards as incongruent with its 'own' identity. It is a disorder of action: 'the self-deceiver is engaged in the world . . . and yet [she] refuses to identify [herself] as one who is so engaged; [she] refuses to avow the engagement as [hers]' (Fingarette, 1969). Such disavowal is 'always, inherently, purposeful self-expression rather than mere happenings suffered by the person'. So, on this reading, the hysterical paralysis is a form of engagement, which the subject will not acknowledge (avow) as intended. To do so might disturb the patient's image of herself. Notice that it is herself, and not (primarily) the other whom the deceiver is deceiving. Note also that a moral dimension emerges in view of this deception being an act of the will (unlike the morally neutral 'unconscious' deception).

Interestingly, the clinical case outlined in Fingarette's (1969) introduction is one of a bedridden patient who would not move post-operatively. This patient admitted his reasons for not doing so under sodium amytal. Fingarette equates the avowal of all one's actions with integrity of the self — authenticity. Hence, disavowal is an immature, regressive strategy, utilized '[because] to avow [such engagement] would . . . lead to such intensely, disruptive, distressing consequences as to be unmanageably destructive to the person'.

That the patient may 'know' what he or she is doing, but be unable to accept expressing it, is inherent in some of the therapeutic strategies which physicians have used. It offers their patients a credible ('face-saving') path toward symptom resolution (Merskey, 1995). Such an approach is advocated by Fingarette (1969). The goal of therapy should be the subject's avowal of their actions: '[t]he medical aim is thus in substance a spiritual aim. It is to help the individual become an agent and cease to be a patient; it is to liberate, not indoctrinate' (Fingarette, 1969).

Functional anatomy of volition

If hysteria is a disorder of the will, then we may hypothesize dysfunction of those brain regions involved in volition (Spence, 1999a; Spence et al., 2000). An anatomy of volition has been described elsewhere (Spence and Frith, 1999). A number of lines of neuro-scientific investigation converge upon the dorsolateral prefrontal cortex (DLPFC) as a key locus in volition (see Table 17.3); both through its role in response generation ('choice') and its involvement in working memory (the temporary store in which information may be manipulated and deliberated upon 'on line').

Frith and colleagues (1991*a*) studied normal subjects performing verbal fluency and finger movement tasks. In both tasks subjects were called upon to choose their responses, while in control conditions their responses were specified by an experimenter. In each task, activation of the left DLPFC was associated with the subjects' choosing ('internally generating') their responses. Subsequently, Spence and colleagues (1997) studied normal subjects making joystick movements. The cerebral regions activated by choosing a sequence of movements (in contrast to a pre-specified sequence) again included the left DLPFC.

Spence and colleagues (1998) also considered whether any brain region might be activated by choice of movement independent of the precise mode of motor output (see Table 17.3). Combining data from the joystick study with those obtained from a mouth movement protocol, we found activation within an area of the left DLPFC to occur whether subjects chose sequences of limb or mouth movements. In contrast, parietal lobe activations were confined to the limb movement task (that is, to those movements executed in space).

It is important to acknowledge the limited nature (in philosophical terms) of the 'actions' being described in such studies. Subjects are compliant with the wishes of the experimenter and perform even their 'chosen' actions within narrow constraints. Yet we may conclude that the left DLPFC plays a substantial role in generating novel action sequences.

A converse observation has been made in psychiatric patients who, as a consequence of depression or chronic schizophrenia, exhibit 'poverty of action' and a marked reduction of spontaneous speech. When scanned at rest these patients have a specific reduction of activity in the left DLPFC, which relates to poverty of speech rather than diagnosis (Dolan *et al.*, 1993; see Tables 17.3 and 17.4).

The evidence accumulated supports a specific role for this brain region (DLPFC) in the spontaneous generation of action. One suggestion is that the DLPFC formulates action 'goals', while specific motor commands are 'delegated' to premotor regions (Passingham, 1993; see Table 3). This notion is compatible with data from single-unit recording in animals revealing movement-related DLPFC activity which precedes that seen in premotor and subcortical regions (Goldman–Rakic *et al.*, 1992). By what mechanism does the prefrontal cortex select one of a number of possible actions? One possibility is that most behavioural outputs are inhibited so that one 'single appropriate act' is selected (Goldman–Rakic, 1987). This formulation is consistent with the observation that patients with damage to the prefrontal cortex are often unable to inhibit inappropriate responses to their environment. It is also congruent with the emergence of stereotypic response patterns following transcranial magnetic stimulation over the left DLPFC in 'normals' (cf. other frontal loci; Jahanshahi *et al.*, 1998).

Hence, we might hypothesize that in patients with hysterical motor phenomena, the DLPFC (especially the left DLPFC) is one brain region where abnormal 'willed' action might have a neurophysiological correlate.

Table 17.3 Putative loci of action-related functions

Author(s)	Function	Location
Baddeley and Della Sala (1996)	Central executive of working memory	Frontal lobe/ prefrontal cortex
Devinsky et al. (1995)	'Emotional will power'	ACC
Dolan et al. (1993)	Alogia (a dysfunction)	Left DLPFC (BA 9)
Frith (1987); Frith et al. (1991a, b)	'Internal generation', 'willed action'	DLPFC (& ACC)
Fuster (1980)	'The proper temporal organisation of motor action'	Prefrontal cortex
Goldman–Rakic (1987); Goldman–Rakic et al. (1992)	'Inhibitory control'	Prefrontal cortex
Goldman–Rakic (1996)	Domain-specific central executive	DLPFC (spatial), OFC (object), left BA 45 (verbal)
Ingvar (1994)	'Wilful mobilisation of inner representations of future events', action programmes	Prefrontal cortex
Jahanshahi et al. (1998)	'Controller' of random response generation network	Left DLPFC (BA 9)
Jeannerod (1997)	Prior intention to act	DLPFC
Knight et al. (1999)	Selective and parallel inhibitory and excitatory control to remote brain regions during behaviour	Prefrontal cortex
Luria (1966)	Ideational apraxia, loss of 'goal' (a dysfunction)	Prefrontal cortex
Passingham (1993)	Response generation	DLPFC (?BA 9)
Passingham (1996)	Attention to action	DLPFC & ACC
Perret (1974)	Suppression of habitual responses in verbal categorical behaviour	Left frontal lobe
Petrides (1996)	'Monitoring' of action; 'self-ordering' tasks	DLPFC
Shallice et al. (1989); Shallice & Burgess (1996)	Supervisory attentional system (SAS), 'will', 'monitoring'	Frontal/ prefrontal cortex
Spence et al. (1997, 1998)	Internal generation of action, independent of movement modality	Left DLPFC (BA 9)

References refer to papers cited in the text and bibliography.
The question mark (Passingham, 1993) denotes the speculative nature of Passingham's remarks regarding BA 9's role in response generation.
Abbreviations: ACC = anterior cingulate cortex; BA = Brodmann area; DLPFC = dorsolateral prefrontal cortex; OFC = orbito-frontal cortex. The numbers 9 and 45 refer to specific Brodmann areas.

Table 17.4 Response of left dorsolateral prefrontal cortex in some neuropsychiatric disorders studied with PET

Disorder	Left DLPFC dysfunction
Psychomotor poverty syndrome of schizophrenia	Reduced activity at rest (compared with other patients with schizophrenia; Liddle *et al*, 1992).
Alogia patients with depression or schizophrenia	Reduced activity at rest (compared to other patients with schizophrenia or depression; Dolan *et al.*, 1993).
Deluded schizophrenia patients, while acutely ill	Failure of activation during movement task (compared to controls and patients themselves, when recovering; Spence *et al.*, 1998).
Deluded schizophrenia patients, when recovering	Activation, but lacks gradation of response between stereotypic and freely-chosen motor responses (Spence *et al.*, 1998).
Patients with hysterical arm weakness	Deactivation when performing acts (cf. controls performing normally and controls feigning difficulty; Spence *et al.*, 2000).

Scanning hysteria

In the first published functional neuroimaging study concerned with hysterical paralysis, Marshall *et al.* (1997) examined a 45-year-old female with a left-sided paralysis precipitated by 'psychological stress and trauma'. There was a history of depression, sometimes accompanied by mutism and lower limb weakness, but organic investigations were normal. The patient undertook a PET scanning experiment during which she was scanned 18 times in five conditions: at rest (six times), while preparing to move her 'good' right leg (three times), while moving her 'good' leg (three times), and while preparing (three times) and attempting to move (three times) her 'bad' left leg. These conditions were paced and concurrent EMG revealed that there was no activity in the affected leg while the patient attempted to move it. In effect, the patient was required to make or prepare to make stereotypic leg movements. (Further details in Athwal *et al.* p.216 of this volume).

The activations seen when the patient moved her 'good' right leg included regions that would be expected: left sensorimotor and premotor cortices, although not the basal ganglia. Other activations included bilateral DLPFC, cerebellar, and parietal regions. When the patient attempted to move the 'bad' left leg, she activated the bilateral DLPFC and cerebellum, but not the right sensorimotor or premotor cortices. The authors construed activation of the former as 'evidence against faking' (Marshall *et al.*, 1997). There was also activation of the right anterior cingulate, an area not normally activated by stereotypic limb movement. The authors concluded that the anterior cingulate is playing a role in the genesis of hysterical paralysis; it is inhibiting movement of the left leg 'despite DLPFC activation and downstream activation in the cerebellum' (Marshall *et al.*, 1997).

The conclusion drawn resembles that of Tiihonen *et al.* (1995) in a study of hysterical paraesthesia — namely that 'higher' brain regions inhibit 'lower' regions. Explicit is the belief that the patient is not 'faking' dysfunction because the DLPFC is activated. This begs a question: what is the functional neuroanatomy of 'feigned paralysis'? We have argued that the DLPFC is activated during intentional actions, but intentional feigning is also an 'act'. It is also worth noting that Marshall *et al.*'s patient appears to activate bilateral DLPFC when moving or preparing to move either limb — a finding not necessarily within normal limits (unverifiable without a control group). Her failure to activate the right sensorimotor cortex is unsurprising if she is not moving her left leg, but such an absence of regional brain activity, compared with the resting state, begs a further question: how can we know that a patient is 'trying'?

Problems for the neuroimager

Hysterical paralyses present particular problems for the neuroimager. Structural imaging of the brain will not prove explanatory (if it were, then the diagnosis might be excluded), while functional imaging, reliant upon 'activation' during the performance of cognitive (and ideally overt) tasks, may be handicapped by the inability of the patient to perform relevant movements and the subjective nature of his or her 'intention'.

As we have seen, hysterically paralysed patients are often depressed, and it may be that an appropriate control group for such studies is not a 'normal' population but a sample of depressed patients without paralyses. The confounding effects of other symptomatology (including other hysterical symptoms) and concurrent medication need to be addressed.

Despite a careful consideration of a functional anatomy of volition, we have noted that access to the subject's 'intention to act' is ultimately limited. The study by Marshall and colleagues does not indicate (objectively) the extent to which the subject was consciously generating her symptoms. To address this problem we require a different approach. One that we have used is to ask normal subjects to feign motor symptoms, in an attempt to discover whether feigned difficulty in moving will be functionally distinguishable from that which is 'hysterical' in (presumed) aetiology. Our data indicate that the left DLPFC is specifically dysfunctional during hysterical action, while 'feigning' may implicate the right prefrontal cortex (Spence *et al.*, 2000). Whereas patients with psychomotor poverty show reduced activity in the left DLPFC at rest (Dolan *et al.*, 1993), hysterical patients appear to specifically 'deactivate' the left DLPFC during action (Fig. 17.1; see Table 17.4) — further evidence that hysterical symptoms are disorders of action.

Conclusions

The concept of hysterical paralysis (conversion) persisting in the diagnostic systems is anachronistic, even within psychodynamic theory (Mitchell, 1996; Britton, 1999). The diagnostic process it instantiates is one in which the physician makes judgements about what the patient 'knows' (unconsciously) but does not (cannot) say. Strategically, the diagnosis saves the patient from an accusation of 'feigning', although the objective criteria for this distinction require validation. The motor signs of hysteria argue for its being a disorder of action.

If the central question asked of neuroimaging is whether the patient is feigning disorder, then it is probable that the technique may provide an answer. But, given the increased prevalence of depression and personality disorder in conversion patients, such investigation may miss the point if unaccompanied by a detailed consideration of comorbidity.

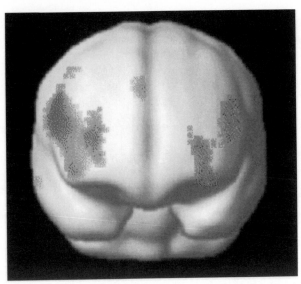

Fig. 17.1 Statistical parametric maps (SPMs) rendered onto a smooth magnetic resonance image of the anterior surface of the brain (the right prefrontal cortex is on the left of the image). These SPMs sre thresholded at P < 0.001. They show those regions where patients with hysterical motor symptoms exhibit hypofunction relative to controls (right-hand side of figure), and where subjects feigning motor symptoms exhibit hypofunction relative to controls (left-hand side of figure). Hysteria implicates left prefrontal cortex; feigning implicates right prefrontal cortex (see Table 17.4). (Adapted from Spence *et al.* 2000 and reproduced with permission from the Lancet.)

I have suggested other ways in which these symptoms may be conceptualized: as the product of the disordered will (in the abnormal mind) or the action disavowed (in those existentially challenged). A thorough (prospective) examination of these patients at the level of subjective phenomenology is required, as is a large, well-controlled study using functional neuroimaging.

Even the initiation of 'normal' actions is paradoxical, if we accept the observations of Libet and others (using electroencephalography): that the conscious intention to act is itself preceded by relatively long predictive trains of electrical activity (of the order of 300–400 ms). Our own 'intentions to act' may be merely the (late) phenomenological correlates of preceding (cognitively-unconscious) 'intentions in action' (Libet, 1993; and see Spence, 1996; Frith, 1996; Libet, 1996). If they are, then although we may subjectively distinguish those 'acts' for which we feel responsible from those 'movements' which are ours but unintended, the notion of 'choice'— a choice which is conscious and directing action — may be itself illusory. It may be neurophysiologically detectable, but nevertheless not constitutive of the 'agency' we perceive ourselves as possessing. The left DLPFC may play a key role in the generation of action, but we cannot simply say that this is where intention 'is'.

Acknowledgements

During writing, the author was supported by a De Witt–Wallace Research Fellowship at the New York Hospital (Cornell Medical Center). The author thanks members of the Functional Neuroimaging Laboratory, Cornell, for their feedback in discussion. The

PET studies described here were conducted on the MRC Cyclotron Unit, Hammersmith Hospital, London, at which time the author was supported by a Medical Research Council Training Fellowship.

References

Adrian, E. D. and Yealland, L. R. (1917). The treatment of some common war neuroses. *Lancet*, **I**, 867–72.

Baddeley, A. D. and Della Sala, S. (1996). Working memory and executive control. *Philosophical Transactions of the Royal Society of London [Series B]*, **351**, 1397–1404.

Baker, J. H. E. and Silver, J. R. (1987). Hysterical paraplegia. *Journal of Neurology, Neurosurgery, and Psychiatry*, **50**, 375–82.

Berrios, G. E. and Gili, M. (1995). Will and its disorders: a conceptual history. *History of Psychiatry*, **vi**, 87–104.

Bibb, R. C. and Guze, S. (1972). Hysteria (Briquet's syndrome) in a psychiatric hospital: the significance of secondary depression. *American Journal of Psychiatry*, **129**, 224–8.

Binzer, M., Andersen, P. M. and Kullgren, G. (1997). Clinical characteristics of patients with motor disability due to conversion disorder: a prospective control group study. *Journal of Neurology, Neurosurgery, and Psychiatry*, **63**, 83–8.

Bliss, J. (1980). Sensory experiences of Gilles de la Tourette syndrome. *Archives of General Psychiatry*, **37**, 1343–7.

Britton, R. (1999). Getting in on the act: the hysterical solution. *International Journal of Psychoanalysis*, **80**, 1–14.

Crimlisk, H. L., Bhatia, K., Cope, H., *et al.* (1998). Slater revisited: 6 year follow up study of patients with medically unexplained motor symptoms. *British Medical Journal*, **316**, 582–6.

Cybulska, E. M. (1998). Globus hystericus or depressivus? *Hospital Medicine*, **59**, 640–1.

David–Menard, M. (1989). *Hysteria from Freud to Lacan: Body and Language in Psychoanalysis* (trans. Porter, C.). Cornell University Press, Ithaca.

Devinsky, O., Morrell, M. J. and Vogt, B. A. (1995). Contributions of anterior cingulate cortex to behaviour. *Brain*, **118**, 279–306.

Dolan, R. J., Bench, C. J., Liddle, P. F., *et al.* (1993). Dorsolateral prefrontal cortex dysfunction in the major psychoses; symptom or disease specificity? *Journal of Neurology, Neurosurgery, and Psychiatry*, **56**, 1290–4.

Ellis, S. J. (1990). Diazepam as a truth drug. *Lancet*, **336**, 752–3.

Factor, S. A., Podskalny, G. D. and Molho, E. S. (1995). Psychogenic movement disorders: frequency, clinical profile, and characteristics. *Journal of Neurology, Neurosurgery, and Psychiatry*, **59**, 406–12.

Fingarette, H. (1969). *Self-Deception*. Routledge and Kegan Paul, London.

Frith, C. D. (1987). The positive and negative symptoms of schizophrenia reflect impairment in the perception and initiation of action. *Psychological Medicine*, **17**, 631–48.

Frith, C. D. (1996). Commentary on 'Free will in the light of neuropsychiatry'. *Philosophy, Psychiatry, and Psychology*, **3**, 91–4.

Frith, C. D., Friston, K., Liddle, P. F., *et al.* (1991*a*) Willed action and the prefrontal cortex in man: a study with PET. *Proceedings of the Royal Society of London B*, **244**, 241–6.

Frith, C. D., Friston, K., Liddle, P. F., *et al.* (1991*b*) A PET study of word finding. *Neuropsychologia*, **29**, 1137–48.

Fuster, J. M. (1980). *The prefrontal cortex*. Raven Press, New York.

Goldman–Rakic, P. S. (1987). Motor control function of the prefrontal cortex. In: *Motor Areas of the Cerebral Cortex*. Ciba Foundation Symposium 132. Wiley, Chichester.

Goldman–Rakic, P. S. (1996). The prefrontal landscape: implications of functional architecture for understanding human mentation and central executive. *Philosophical Transactions of the Royal Society of London [Series B]*, **351**, 1445–62.

Goldman–Rakic, P. S., Bates, J. F. and Chafee, M. V. (1992). The prefrontal cortex and internally generated motor acts. *Current Opinion in Neurobiology*, **2**, 830–5.

Ingvar, D. H. (1994). The will of the brain: cerebral correlates of wilful acts. *Journal of Theoretical Biology*, **171**, 7–12.

Jahanshahi, M., Profice, P., Brown, R. G., *et al.* (1998). The effects of transcranial magnetic stimulation over the dorsolateral prefrontal cortex on suppression of habitual counting during random number generation. *Brain*, **121**, 1533–44.

James, W. (1910). *The Principles of Psychology*. McMillan, London.

Jeannerod, M. (1997). *The Cognitive Neuroscience of Action*. Blackwell, Oxford.

Keating, J. J., Dinan, T. G., Chua, A., *et al.* (1990). Hysterical paralysis. *Lancet*, **336**, 1506–7.

Knight, R. T., Staines, W. R., Swick, D. and Chao, L. L. (1999). Prefrontal cortex regulates inhibition and excitation in distributed neural networks. *Acta Psychologica*, **101**, 159–78.

Koller, W. C., Marjama, J. and Troster, A. I. (1998). Psychogenic movement disorders. In: *Parkinson's Disease and Movement Disorders* (ed. Joseph, J. and Tolosa, E.), pp. 859–68. Williams & Wilkins, Baltimore.

Lang, A. E. (1992). Clinical phenomenology of tic disorders: selected aspects. In: *Advances in Neurology* (ed. Chase, T. N. *et al.*), **58**, 25–32. Raven Press, New York.

Lewis, A. J. (1975). The survival of hysteria. *Psychological Medicine*, **5**, 9–12.

Libet, B. (1993). The neural time factor in conscious and unconscious events. In: *Experimental and Theoretical Studies of Consciousness*, pp. 123–46. Ciba Foundation Symposium 174. Wiley, Chichester.

Libet, B. (1996). Commentary on 'Free will in the light of neuropsychiatry'. *Philosophy, Psychiatry, and Psychology*, **3**, 95–6.

Liddle, P. F., Friston, K. J., Frith, C. D., *et al.* (1992). Patterns of cerebral blood flow in schizophrenia. *British Journal of Psychiatry*, **160**, 179–86.

Luria, A. R. (1966). *Higher Cortical Functions in Man*. Tavistock, London.

Macmurray, J. (1991). *The Self as Agent*. Faber and Faber, London.

Marshall, J. C., Halligan, P. W., Fink, G. R., *et al.* (1997). The functional anatomy of hysterical paralysis. *Cognition*, **64**, B1–B8.

McKegney, F. P. (1967). The incidence and characteristics of patients with conversion reactions. I: a general hospital consultation service sample. *American Journal of Psychiatry*, **124**, 542–5.

Mele, A. (1987). Recent work on self-deception. *American Philosophical Quarterly*, **24**, 1–17.

Merskey, H. (1995). *The Analysis of Hysteria. Understanding Conversion and Dissociation*. Gaskell, London.

Merskey, H. and Buhrich, N. A. (1975). Hysteria and organic brain disease. *British Journal of Medical Psychology*, **48**, 359–66.

Mitchell, J. (1996). Sexuality and psychoanalysis: hysteria. *British Journal of Psychotherapy*, **12**, 473–9.

Morris, M. E., Iansek, R., Matyas, T. A., *et al.* (1996). Stride regulation in Parkinson's disease. Normalisation strategies and underlying mechanisms. *Brain*, **119**, 551–68.

Passingham, R. E. (1993). *The Frontal Lobes and Voluntary Action*. Oxford University Press, Oxford.

Passingham, R. E. (1996). Attention to action. *Philosophical Transactions of the Royal Society of London [Series B]*, **351**, 1473–9.

Perret, E. (1974). The left frontal lobe of man and the suppression of habitual responses in verbal categorical behaviour. *Neuropsychologia*, **12**, 323–30.

Petrides, M. (1996). Specialised systems for the procession of mnemonic information within the primate prefrontal cortex. *Philosophical Transactions of the Royal Society of London [Series B]*, **351**, 1455–62.

Rampello, L., Raffaele, R., Nicoletti, G., *et al.* (1996). Hysterical neurosis of the conversion type: therapeutic activity of neuroleptics with different hyperprolactinaemic potency. *Neuropsychobiology*, **33**, 186–8.

Searle, J. (1983). *Intentionality. An Essay in the Philosophy of Mind*. Cambridge University Press, Cambridge.

Shallice, T. and Burgess, P. W. (1996). The domain of supervisory processes and temporal organisation of behaviour. *Philosophical Transactions of the Royal Society of London [Series B]*, **351**, 1405–12.

Shallice, T., Burgess, P. W., Schon, F., *et al.* (1989). The origins of utilisation syndrome. *Brain*, **112**, 1587–98.

Slater, E. and Glithero, E. (1965). A follow-up of patients diagnosed as suffering from 'hysteria'. *Journal of Psychosomatic Research*, **9**, 9–11.

Spence, S. A. (1996). Free will in the light of neuropsychiatry. *Philosophy, Psychiatry, and Psychology*, **3**, 75–90.

Spence, S. A. (1999*a*) Hysterical paralyses as disorders of action. *Cognitive Neuropsychiatry*, **4**, 203–26.

Spence, S. A. (1999*b*) Does a 'philosophy of the brain' tell us anything new about psychomotor disorders? *Philosophy, Psychiatry and Psychology*, **6**, 227–9.

Spence, S. A. and Frith, C. D. (1999). Towards a functional anatomy of volition. *Journal of Consciousness Studies*, **6**, 11–29.

Spence, S. A., Brooks, D. J., Hirsch, S. R., *et al.* (1997). A PET study of voluntary movement in schizophrenic patients experiencing passivity phenomena (delusions of alien control). *Brain*, **120**, 1997–2011.

Spence, S. A., Hirsch, S. R., Brooks, D. J., *et al.* (1998). PET studies of prefrontal activity in people with schizophrenia and control subjects. Evidence from positron emission tomography for remission of 'hypofrontality' with recovery from acute schizophrenia. *British Journal of Psychiatry*, **172**, 316–23.

Spence, S. A., Crimlisk, H. L., Cope, H., *et al.* (2000). Evidence for discrete neurophysiological correlates in prefrontal cortex during hysterical and feigned disorder of movement. *Lancet*, **355**, 1243–4.

Tiihonen, J., Kuikka, J., Viinamaki, H., *et al.* (1995). Altered cerebral blood flow during hysterical paraesthesia. *Biological Psychiatry*, **37**, 134–5.

Turner, M. (1999). Malingering, hysteria and the factitious disorders. *Cognitive Neuropsychiatry*, **4**, 193–201.

Zizek, S. (1991). *Looking awry: An Introduction to Jacques Lacan Through Popular Culture*. October Books (MIT Press), Cambridge, Massachusetts.

18 The anthropology of hysteria

Laurence J. Kirmayer and Radhika Santhanam

This chapter reviews the cross-cultural literature on hysteria and conversion disorders. Ethnographic research suggests that conversion symptoms remain common around the world, particularly in primary care medical settings. Sociocultural processes may influence conversion disorder at several different levels: (1) the nature of illness beliefs and practices and the expression of distress; (2) the salience and availability of dissociative mechanisms; (3) the response of the family, health care system, and larger social systems to specific types of symptom. The higher prevalence of conversion symptoms in some societies can be attributed to the fit of symptoms with local ethnophysiological notions and cultural idioms of distress as well as the stigma attached to frankly psychological or psychiatric symptoms. The distinctive nature of conversion symptoms, compared to other forms of culturally patterned somatic distress, resides in the experience and ascription of agency or volition, which in turn depends on cultural knowledge and social practices that shape cognitive processes of bodily control.

While current psychiatric theory tends to view dissociation (and by extension, conversion) as a consequence of trauma, dissociation can be understood as culturally patterned or scripted and depends on specific modes of narrating the self. Contemporary anthropology approaches hysteria as a mode of self-construal in which narratives of 'not knowing' and 'not doing' fit with prevalent cultural conceptions of the person and serve to convey serious distress and disablement.

Introduction

Hysteria in its various guises has been a staple of anthropological studies of illness and healing. This is both because of the dramatic and colourful performances associated with many hysterical conditions and because of their obvious links with cultural beliefs and practices. A cross-cultural comparative perspective has much to offer researchers and clinicians approaching the problem of hysteria. A wealth of ethnographic research shows that culture influences the clinical phenomena of hysteria in three basic ways:

1. shaping the form and content of symptoms;

2. regulating underlying mechanisms of dissociation; and

3. informing psychiatric nosology and diagnostic practices and their wider social consequences.

In this chapter, we summarize some current perspectives on hysteria derived from ethnographic work. First, we acknowledge the wide prevalence and persistence of various forms of hysterical or conversion symptoms. Although epidemiological data are lacking, there are clear clinical impressions that conversion disorders remain prevalent in many developing countries (see Akagi and House's chapter in this volume, p. 73). In some cases, this may parallel a general tendency for people to make clinical presentations of somatic symptoms in place of emotional distress in order to avoid psychiatric stigmatization. More commonly, there is a close fit between hysterical symptoms and prevailing cultural beliefs about illness. Local notions of how the body works (ethnophysiology), of the nature of the person and emotion (ethnopsychology), and culturally prescribed patterns of illness behaviour and help-seeking all serve to shape bodily reactions. These processes affect all somatic symptoms and in this regard hysteria is no different from any other bodily illness.

What may be distinctive about hysteria is the use of cognitive mechanisms of dissociation which manifest as complexly organized and motivated behaviour of which the person claims no conscious intention or control. Hence, our second aim is to explore the fit between the mechanisms of dissociation, which may underlie hysteria, and specific aspects of social structure, cultural belief, and practice. This fit with culture does not imply that hysteria always has a social function or is adaptive for the individual. However, the meanings of hysterical symptoms in the family or wider social context may help account for their prevalence and persistence even where the medical response is scepticism or stigmatization.

Hysteria can be approached as a medical phenomenon and as a social process. The medical perspective seeks to describe diseases and disorders that are understood as entities with specific pathophysiology and a 'natural history', which includes its distribution, course, and prognosis. The social perspective emphasizes the fact that illness occurs to individuals with a personal biography and history, in an interactional matrix that includes families, the health care system, and larger social institutions. As such, the identification of problems and pathology emerges out of the everyday world and social context of the individual.

A social perspective does not preclude attention to neurology, biology, and psychological processes, but the social history of medicine shows how much diagnostic entities are creatures of particular cultural times, political ideologies, religious concerns, and other institutional interests. Indeed, the history of hysteria provides some of the most dramatic examples of the cultural and social shaping of psychiatric nosology. And yet, we will argue, hysteria is not simply a cultural construction or a bodily expression of local power dynamics that is misappropriated by medicine: there is something distinctive going on in the psychology and social interaction of people with conversion symptoms.

Defining hysteria

Historically, the term 'hysteria' referred to a congeries of physical symptoms and behaviours in women attributed to erratic wandering of the womb. In seventeenth-century medicine, hysteria was distinguished from hypochondriasis, with the latter found more commonly in men (Boss, 1979). By the nineteenth century, hysteria had become an affliction of the working class (Shorter, 1992). Paralyses, sensory loss, and alterations of consciousness characteristic of hysteria were common among soldiers in the First World War (see Palmer's chapter in this volume, p. 12). While enlisted men received the diagnosis of shell-shock or hysteria, officers exposed to similar traumatic events tended to be diagnosed with neurasthenia. Evidently, these nosological distinctions reflect the ways that symptomatology is interpreted on the basis of psychiatric theories and diagnostic practices that reflect cultural assumptions about gender, social class, and character (Young, 1995). To think clearly about whatever may lie behind our historically contingent constructions of hysteria, we must critically examine these assumptions.

The colloquial use of the term 'hysteria' refers to agitated and dramatic displays of strong emotion, often with the implication that these are frivolous, foolish, exaggerated, and irrational. As such, the term 'hysteria' has strongly pejorative connotations. This notion of hysteria also carries a strong gender bias, not only in its etymology which implies troubles due to a wandering womb, but also because it is closely linked to stereotypical notions of women as more emotionally expressive and less rational than men. The narrower definitions of hysteria employed in psychiatry have never completely escaped from this gender bias and moral opprobrium (Chodoff, 1982; Micale, 1995; Winstead, 1984).

The introduction of the term 'conversion disorder' reflected a psychodynamic model in which emotional conflict and distress were 'converted' into somatic symptoms. The term was retained in DSM–III, at a time when other psychoanalytic terminology like 'neurosis' was jettisoned, in the hope that this would disentangle the conceptually and empirically distinct clinical problems of discrete pseudoneurological symptoms (conversion disorder), polysymptomatic high health care utilizers (somatization disorder), and patients with a dramatic style of symptom presentation (histrionic personality) (Hyler and Spitzer, 1978). There is evidence that most patients with conversion symptoms do not have multiple medically unexplained somatic symptoms or a histrionic personality (Kirmayer *et al.*, 1994; Singh and Lee, 1997). However, the symptoms and behaviours of hysteria must challenge some deeply rooted cultural values and attitudes about human agency because any new, sanitized term quickly takes on the same negative connotations.

The narrow definition of conversion disorder in ICD or DSM refers to interference with motor or sensory function that cannot be accounted for by neurological disorder. Conversion symptoms thus are one type of medically unexplained symptom. They share with other unexplained symptoms a common social predicament — namely, that doctors are frustrated in their efforts to make a definite diagnosis, and that patients, consequently, face a crisis of legitimating their distress and finding effective treatment. Is there anything distinctive about conversion symptoms that sets them apart from other medically unexplained symptoms? Where should the boundaries be drawn between conversion disorder and other medically unexplained symptoms? To make the question more specific, should chronic idiopathic pain or fatigue be considered forms of conversion disorder? If it is simply that conversion symptoms are 'pseudoneurological', does this reflect some underlying process or only more or less arbitrary disciplinary boundaries in medicine? The answer to these questions hinges on our understanding of the mechanisms of conversion.

Purely descriptive or behavioural definitions tend to suggest that there is little other than arbitrary convention to distinguish conversion symptoms from other medically unexplained symptoms. However, there are some distinctive features of conversion symptoms that argue for the value of considering the category different from such common — and commonly unexplained —somatic complaints as pain or fatigue (see Table 18.1). Conversion symptoms involve observable behaviour, they interfere with voluntary function, they closely follow patients' idiosyncratic or cultural models for illness, and they are

Table 18.1 Some characteristics of conversion symptoms compared to other common, medically unexplained symptoms

	Conversion symptoms	Other medically unexplained symptoms
Type of symptom	Neurological	Autonomic or other functional system
Mode of expression	Behaviour	Symptom report
Control system involved in symptom	Usually voluntary	Usually involuntary
Physiological mechanisms	Higher-order neurocognitive functioning	Lower-level physiological perturbation
Cognitive mechanisms	Denial or dissociation	Somatic amplification
Suggestibility, hypnotizability	High	Variable
Cultural template	Usually present	Often incomplete

extremely malleable and responsive to suggestion. In addition to the absence of physiological explanation, these features have contributed to the assumption that conversion symptoms are psychogenic, that is, they involve specific psychological mechanisms.

The term 'psychogenic' has many potential meanings with different epistemological and pragmatic implications (Kirmayer, 1988; 1994a). These include the notion that the symptom is caused by psychological processes that may be conscious or non-unconscious[1], wilful or outside the control of the person, due to explicit plans and ideas or implicit consequences of images and metaphors, and so on. There are many more or less automatic psychological processes that could give rise to conversion symptoms, complicating the simple dichotomies of wilful/accidental, motivated/unmotivated, and conscious/unconscious. These distinctions have important cultural dimensions related to the sense of self and consequent configurations of self-awareness, self-deception, and control (Ames and Dissayanake, 1996).

However, these subtle distinctions are largely ignored in biomedical practice so that, for both professional and lay person, to call something 'psychogenic' is to imply it is somehow 'not real' or 'all in your head' or worse, that it is due to psychological weakness or moral failing on the part of the patient (Kirmayer, 1988). This stigma arises from the pervasive effects of a dualistic cultural concept of the person, in which bodily illness is fundamentally different from mental or psychological problems. Even where the same dualistic notions of the person do not prevail, the stigma attached to severe psychiatric disorders ensures that patients will struggle to have their condition defined as somatic and medical rather than psychiatric (Raguram et al., 1996).

The psychological processes that might contribute to medically unexplained symptoms can be roughly divided into two groups (Kirmayer, 1999):

1. exacerbation of symptoms by attentional focus (amplification); and
2. ignoring, suppressing, denying, and dissociating (strategies for not attending and for not attributing cause to oneself).

Hysterical symptoms usually are assumed to involve the mechanisms of denial and dissociation. Indeed, the alterations of sensory experience and motor control seen in conversion disorder commonly co-occur with alterations of consciousness characteristic of dissociative disorders.

An emphasis on mechanisms would suggest that, ultimately, the specific form of conversion symptom is less crucial for definition than the underlying cognitive process, interpersonal interaction, and social context. Conversion symptoms are directed by patients' own construal of the body as vulnerable and by social factors that make the body a credible site of affliction as well as an effective expressive medium.

The cross-cultural prevalence of conversion symptoms

Cross-cultural study of the prevalence of hysteria requires that we define it in a way that is comparable in different cultural contexts. There is a wide range of culture-specific somatic symptoms that might qualify as conversion symptoms. The compendium by Simons and Hughes (1985) lists some 150 culture-bound syndromes, idioms of distress, and folk psychiatric terms (of which about 22 involve primarily dissociative symptoms) and at least eight conversion symptoms in the narrow sense.

Simons attempted to group the better-studied conditions into major taxons character-ized by startle-matching behaviour (e.g. *latah*), sleep paralysis, genital retraction (*koro*), sudden mass assault (*amok*), and running wild. With the possible exception of sleep paralysis, all of these culture-related conditions have been viewed as types of individual or epidemic ('mass') hysteria by many authorities. The largest group of culture-related conditions, unnamed by Simons and Hughes, involves multiple somatic and dissociative complaints. Epidemiological studies of the prevalence of somatoform disorders have generally ignored this evidence for culture-specific syndromes in favour of simple counts of common somatic symptoms. Unfortunately, this does not provide sufficient informa-tion to make meaningful cross-cultural comparisons since it may leave some of the most salient symptoms and illness categories untapped.

Although it is commonly asserted that the prevalence of conversion symptoms has declined over the last hundred years (particularly in urban westernized settings), there are few clear data to support this claim (Leff, 1988; Singh and Lee, 1997). Clinicians working in developing countries share the impression that conversion symptoms remain common in general medical settings. The WHO Cross-National Study of Mental Disorders in Primary Care found a high prevalence of medically unexplained symptoms, including conversion symptoms, in all 14 countries (Simon and Gureje, 1999).

In one of the few longitudinal studies, Nandi and colleagues (1992) compared changes in the prevalence rates for hysteria and depression in two rural Indian villages near Calcutta, from 1972, when the first survey was undertaken, to follow-up surveys in 1982 and 1987. A research psychiatrist interviewed all the families of the two villages with a Bengali Case Detection Schedule, tapping a wide range of psychopathology.

Over a 10- to 15-year follow-up period, there were no significant changes in total psychiatric morbidity or in the male/female prevalence ratios, which were comparable to figures found elsewhere in India. There were, however, very significant changes in the rates of specific disorders. The prevalence of hysteria fell dramatically from 32.3 per 1000 in one village and from 16.9 to 4.6 per 1000 in the other. Although hysteria was and remained much more common in women, similar declines in its rate were seen in both genders. At the same time, rates of depression rose significantly, from 61.9 to 77.2 per 1000 in one community and from 37.7 to 53.3 per 1000 in the other.

While there was no change at follow-up in individual socioeconomic level, substantial changes in the communities had occurred with improvement in housing, educational facilities, and health care delivery. Nandi and colleagues attributed much of the decrease in rates of hysteria to improvements in the status of women. In a previous survey of villages in West Bengal, they found that hysteria was more common among women of lower social and economic status. In some cases, hysteria occurred in local clusters as a result of emotional contagion or an expression of solidarity. The authors conjectured that the improved social status of women now able to work outside their home for wages for the first time made them less dependent on their husbands and hence, less vulnerable and more self-confident. This had the effect of reducing the prevalence and frequency of conversion symptoms.

Chakraborty (1993) pointed out various methodological problems with Nandi's study[2] but, based on her research and clinical experience in Calcutta, reached the same conclusion that some types of conversion symptoms are decreasing in prevalence:

> There is no doubt that we are seeing less of dramatic conversion symptoms. Nowadays young girls complain more of somatoform symptoms . . . Education, upgrading of the status of women and changes in public credulity certainly have contributed to changes in the form of expressions of anxiety, and probably made it more 'free floating'. (Chakraborty, 1993, p. 398).

It is safe to conclude that while classic conversion symptoms of motor paralysis and sensory loss are seen more commonly in clinics in many developing countries, they have diminished in westernized health care settings. However, if disorders of pain, fatigue, dizziness, or vague malaise are understood as equivalent, then conversion disorders have not so much disappeared as changed shape to fit common health beliefs and expectations in the health care system. This transformation is striking evidence both of the malleability of conversion symptoms and of the importance of social and cultural factors in hysteria.

The cultural shaping of somatic distress

In surveys of the history of hysteria, both Shorter (1992) and Showalter (1997) have argued that prevailing cultural models of illness give shape to the inchoate suffering of people subjected to psychological disturbance and social stress. Hysteria is the outcome of a contagion of ideas, which in recent times often has its origin in the medical profession. These accounts suggest that there is a more or less direct link between medical nosology and the shaping of bodily distress in hysteria and other medically unexplained symptoms.

Many mental health professionals share a tacit assumption that people who are more psychologically aware will not express their problems in physical terms. Psychoanalytic theory posited a hierarchy of sophistication in which somatic expressions of distress are more primitive than explicit talk about psychological conflict. However, somatic symptoms remain extremely common in all cultures and are found among individuals with all levels of education and psychological-mindedness (Kirmayer and Young, 1998).

The changing nature of conversion symptoms may reflect the ability of medical authority to legitimate certain forms of distress rather than any general change in psychological sophistication. This is illustrated by the recent epidemic of chronic fatigue in the US and UK in which viral infection serves as a folk explanation for otherwise inexplicable states of enervation, weakness, dysphoria, and debilitation. While infectious agents or immunologic disorder eventually may be found in some patients, it seems likely that much chronic fatigue is related to depression, anxiety, and to wider social problems involving alienation in the workplace and what Sir William Osler called 'the habit of using the body as a machine' (Rabinbach, 1990). However, many sufferers and clinicians prefer viral explanations to psychological attributions such as depression, which are widely seen as morally stigmatizing.

In addition to the response of the health care system, conversion symptoms reflect specific ethnophysiological ideas about how the body works. In many cultures, the body is viewed as vulnerable to spirit attack or malign magic which can result in sudden losses of function including paralyses, sensory alterations, and seizures. Such bodily conditions are not viewed in psychological terms as evidence for personal conflicts or failings of the individual but as the outcome of social and spiritual forces. As a result, afflicted persons do not receive the stigma usually associated with psychiatric disorders (Piñeros *et al.*, 1998).

In most forms of 'epidemic hysteria', the line between dissociative alterations of bodily experience and the effects of anxiety is blurred. For example, *koro* is a syndrome characterized by the conviction that the penis is shrinking into the body and that this will result in death (Tseng *et al.*, 1988). Sufferers may present to the clinic holding on to the penis to prevent its retraction. Koro is associated with intense anxiety and so has often not been included with other conversion symptoms. However, the central symptom is an alteration in body perception. Koro has occurred in epidemic form in South-East Asia and China. As with other epidemics of hysteria, social stresses create widespread feelings of vulnerability in a population or ethnic group, and combine with individual vulnerabilities to anxiety to give rise to symptoms that follow culturally available symptom schemas. Those who are close to or who identify with the initial cases are more likely to be affected (Small *et al.*, 1991).

To explain the pattern of distribution of such 'epidemics' we need notions of individual psychology (e.g. temperamental predisposition to anxiety, sense of bodily vulnerability), social psychology (family dynamics, affiliation, social conflict), and specific cultural knowledge about bodily affliction and loss of awareness or control. A combination of these factors can give rise both to epidemic and sporadic cases of what Ian Hacking has termed 'transient mental illness':

> By a 'transient mental illness' I mean an illness that appears at a time, in a place, and later fades away. It may spread from place to place and reappear from time to time. It may be selective for social class or gender, preferring poor women or rich men. I do not mean that it comes and goes in this or that patient, but that this type of madness exists only at certain times and places. The most famous candidate for a transient mental illness is hysteria or any rate its florid French manifestations toward the end of the nineteenth century. Cynics would offer multiple personality today as another transient mental illness and can go on to compose a list of other disorders that will prove transient — chronic fatigue syndrome, anorexia, intermittent explosive disorder, or whatever they choose to criticize. (Hacking, 1998, p. 1)

In his engaging account of the diagnosis of fugue in France in the late 1800s, Hacking suggests that we think of the social circumstances that shape or give rise to a transient disorder in terms of the availability of a specific ecological niche for the illness. He describes these niches in terms of 'vectors' which include:

1. a medical taxonomy, which gives a place to the illness;

2. a cultural polarity of morally good and bad valuations within which the illness can be situated, that fuels public and professional interest and debate;

3. observability — that is, the illness should be visible as a form of suffering that commands attention and that can be studied;

4. the ways in which the illness offers some benefit for the individual that is not otherwise available.

This notion of ecological niche is useful, particularly if we take the ecological metaphor seriously enough to move beyond the static notion of 'vectors' to describe the dynamics of the social processes that form a self-sustaining system. This is precisely what contemporary anthropology has done in examining a range of culture-related syndromes as well as the generation of psychiatric knowledge itself.

For example, *latah*, a Malaysian syndrome of hyperstartling, involves a temporary loss of control with echolalia, echopraxia, and coprolalia. This has been viewed as dissociative or hysterical by some authors. Simons (1996) has shown the link between latah and neurological mechanisms of startle, which are exaggerated in some individuals. However, videotapes of people displaying latah behaviour (or the analogous phenomena of 'jumping' found among some Acadians in Maine) also show the filmed subjects continuing behaviour well beyond the moment of startle in ways that seem to comply with the observers' expectations or implicit suggestions.[3]

Ethnographic work too, suggests the degree to which we can understand latah not as a 'reflex' but as a role performance sensitive to social context and expectations (Winzeler, 1995). Indeed, although latah is portrayed as an affliction of the individual, it occurs because of a pattern of interpersonal interaction in which people are deliberately and repeatedly startled by others to create the condition. Latah occurs primarily among lower status and marginalized women and it allows them to transgress social codes of etiquette with their outrageous behaviour. This is a source of entertainment and amusement for others. Thus, social processes explain the causes, distribution, course, and consequences of latah behaviour — which, in any event, is not viewed as a medical condition within Malaysian society.

The wider social context has been elided in many accounts of culture-bound syndromes, leading to confusion about the fundamentally social nature of the symptoms and disorder. For example, arctic hysteria or *pibloktoq* was characterized by running wild across the tundra or ice, tearing off one's clothes, eating excrement, and raving incoherently (Foulks, 1985). It was described originally among Inuit women of Greenland on one of Admiral Peary's expeditions. A substantial anthropological literature grew up around these accounts attempting to explain the wild behaviour in terms of cultural beliefs and shamanistic practices, neurotic conflicts, nutritional deficiencies (hypocalcaemia), or toxicity (hypervitaminosis A) (cf. Simons and Hughes, 1985). The historian, Lyle Dick (1995), reviewed all published accounts of pibloktoq and found that the prototypical cases emerged from a situation of sexual exploitation and abuse of the Inuit by Peary's men. This missing social context makes the 'hysterical' behaviour intelligible as a response to interpersonal violence and social disruption and, perhaps, as the only available form of protest in this situation of intercultural encounter.

All of these examples also serve to emphasize the importance of the body as a medium of communication. We can understand the impact of culture on symptoms, not strictly through specific beliefs or illness representations, but through the various ways that people actively deal with distress, making use of whatever social and cultural resources are at hand. These include what Marcel Mauss (1979) called 'body practices' (i.e. ways of handling and transforming the body, and a wide range of discursive practices — ways of talking, idioms of distress, modes of self-depiction, constructions of self-awareness through conversation, and so on). Indigenous theories of socio-somatics that relate bodily affliction to specific social events can make conversion symptoms both an expected outcome of traumatic experiences and an effective means of social protest.

While ethnographic evidence suggests that there is some fit between symptom, illness representations, and cultural practices, this fit is never perfect. Accounts that make it seem as though conversion symptoms are simply adaptive responses to difficult social situations, based on prevalent illness conceptions, ignore the tensions and contra-dictions found on close examination of any clinical case. Thus, people with conversion symptoms face scepticism, rejection. and, at times, harsh treatment by others who doubt the reality of their condition. At the same time, most people with conversion symptoms are clearly upset and experience their problems as distressing events that just 'happen to them'. This experiencing of 'happening to' can be understood as a misattribution of fundamentally voluntary behaviour or it may reflect those deeper divisions in the sense of agency, identity, and control that are termed dissociation. This leads us to consider how social and cultural factors shape the dissociative mechanisms that may account for hysterical symptoms.

Culture and dissociation

Dissociation is a hypothetical construct presumed to underlie a broad range of expe-riences marked by ruptures in the continuity of memory, volition, and perception. As such, it is the presumptive mechanism of conversion disorder or hysteria (see Merskey's chapter in this volume, p.171, for further discussion). Phenomenologically, dissociation differs from suppression in that there is no conscious effort to avoid a thought; as a result, self-report and non-verbal cues are consistent with the view that the individual has no conscious control over behaviour that nevertheless requires complex cognitive–symbolic mediation and that continues to be shaped by significant interpersonal communication and social context.

Dissociative phenomena commonly occur in three settings:

1. in response to stress, trauma, or inescapable threat;

2. in socially sanctioned rituals under the guidance of a healer, religious leader, or artistic performer;

3. sporadically and spontaneously as part of everyday experience (although this is usually only recognized or reported when it fits a culturally shaped idiom of distress or category of religious experience).

Ethnographic accounts suggest that certain cultures have a relatively high prevalence of dissociative phenomena both in terms of number of individuals affected and frequency of episodes (Bourguignon, 1967).

In most cases, the high prevalence of dissociation is a consequence of the popularity of a healing or religious cult that engineers such dissociative experiences (e.g. *Zar*, *Umbanda*, *Candomblé*). Culturally sanctioned trance may be the outcome of affliction (illness, spontaneous possession, acute trauma), deliberate ascetic practice (sexual abstinence, social isolation, austerities, fasting), or dramatic evocation (dance, drumming, possession rites). Of course, even in settings where trance is actively sought, individuals may have non-sanctioned, unexpected, or 'negative' dissociative experiences that deviate from local norms and which will then be viewed as afflictions (Bourguignon, 1989). In other situations, dissociation occurs as part of a culture-specific idiom of distress in which lapses of consciousness, memory, or self-control are part of the common description and cultural form of illness episodes.

This underscores the need to understand conversion symptoms and other forms of dissociation in terms of cognitive and social processes. There is a rich social psychological literature on hypnosis that is relevant (Kirmayer, 1992; de Rivera and Sarbin, 1998; also McConkey's chapter in this volume, p. 203) as well as several attempts to relate specific aspects of social structure and process to dissociative phenomena.

One of the more interesting anthropological accounts of dissociation comes from Gregory Bateson's work on the social interactions that prepare Balinese for the frequent trance experiences that are part of their religious and artistic life.[4] Bateson (1973) found parallels between Balinese conceptions of the body and body practices in artistic performance and everyday life that predispose to dissociative experience. The Balinese method of teaching traditional dance has the master exert direct control over the body of the student, moving body to body, shaping arms, hands, fingers, and even the eyes in precise gestures. The student must yield to the teacher and, at the same time, make the movements his own. Yielding bodily control to another results in the ability to perform complex sequences of action 'unconsciously' or automatically.

The teacher's manipulation of different parts of the student's body combines with prevailing representations of the body as composed of finely articulated discrete components, to foster a sense of the body as capable of fragmentation or dissociation into its parts. This is reflected in fantasy:

> The Balinese cemetery is haunted not by whole ghosts but by the ghosts of separate limbs. Headless bodies, separate legs, and unattached arms that jump around and sometimes a scrotum that crawls slowly over the ground — these are the boggles of Balinese fantasy . . . From this it is a small step to perceiving the body as a puppet. (Bateson, 1973, p. 153)

For Bateson then, culture shapes dissociative experience through body practices, fantasies, and images that are facets of the same social system. Bodily experiences, beliefs, and cultural ideologies are mutually supporting elements of a way of life that encourages one to feel one's body moving on its own.

Bateson's account of the unselfconscious nature of Balinese performance has been challenged by Unni Wikan's (1990) person-centred ethnography which depicts the Balinese as involved in effortful striving to achieve the outward appearance of calm, even when the inner world of emotion is in turmoil. The culturally valued appearance of 'smoothness' in everyday life is a result of conscious effort, not reflexes. Such effort and training may, nonetheless, make trance and dissociative experience more accessible during times of threat or trauma. As well, trance dances provide a vehicle for the expression of anger, aggression, and other strong emotions that are unacceptable to Balinese in everyday life (Jensen and Suryani, 1992).

Building on her earlier work on boundaries and purity, the social anthropologist Mary Douglas (1973) argued that social factors influence the way the body is perceived and controlled. She saw two ways in which body and social structure are linked:

> First, the drive to achieve consonance in all levels of experience produces concordance among the means of expression, so that the use of the body is co-ordinated with other media. Second, controls exerted from the social system place limits on the use of the body as medium. (Douglas, 1973, p. 95).

This means:

> . . . bodily control is an expression of social control — abandonment of bodily control in ritual responds to the requirement of a social experience which is being expressed. Furthermore, there is little prospect of successfully imposing bodily control without the corresponding social forms. (Douglas, 1973, p. 99)

For Douglas, greater social structure means fewer options and choices for behaviour and hence greater control, while less structure means less social (and individual) control over behaviour. This leads her to extend the notion of the relationship of social structure to bodily control to a quantitative correlation: 'strong social control demands strong bodily control'. The corollary, that weak social control allows weak bodily control (that is, weak volitional control by consciousness) leads her to hypothesize that, 'as trance is a form of dissociation, it will be more approved and welcomed the weaker the structuring of society'.

The problem with Douglas' hypothesis, of course, is that there is no single metric to gauge the comparative degree of structuring of disparate societies. A further difficulty with Douglas' account is its static portrait of the relationship between individual experience and social structure. Individuals do not simply respond to the constraints of social structure, they are actively involved in negotiating, working with and against, or challenging boundaries.

Douglas' assumption that dissociation represents weak bodily control is true only in so far as that is exactly what some forms of dissociative behaviour are meant to convey. There is much evidence that dissociative behaviour is highly scripted or sculpted, and hence controlled by some social model or personal plan (de Rivera and Sarbin, 1998). Ethnographic accounts indicate a high degree of formulaic structure within which 'anarchic' gestures have a prescribed and covertly controlled role (Lambek, 1989). For this reason, the account of dissociation in possession cults offered by I. M. Lewis (1971) seems more plausible. Lower-class women, oppressed by family circumstances (often conflict with a mother-in-law, co-wife, or husband) are inducted into cults which allow them to assume the voice of a spirit who demands compensation. Husbands and powerful others often accede to these demands. There is thus an obvious social advantage conferred by the experience of dissociation and possession in the form of power over others and the gratification of specific desires. This scenario also fits that of conversion symptoms in many cases. A rich ethnographic literature attests to the importance of dissociative behaviour as a challenge to rigid social structures and inequities as well as a means of forging individual and collective identity (Ong, 1988; Boddy, 1994).

Guy Swanson (1978), a sociologist of religion, studied the relationship between family structure and 'openness to absorbing experiences' (a personality trait related to hypnotizability). For Swanson, openness basically reflects the ability to take on the perspective or directives of others as though they are one's own. This is acquired through participation in groups of which the most basic and formative is the family. Family structures may differ in similar ways to different societies. Swanson suggested that families can be arranged according to their style of organization along a dimension from *social system* (relatively structured, role differentiated, and hierarchical with group goals and collective interests considered most important) to *association* (diffused, undifferentiated, democratic with individual goals and special interests considered most important). He argued that individuals from families at the structured/social system end are likely to display greater tendency for dissociative experience.

Using a self-report of style of family decision making he had devised and a measure of dissociative experiences (Tellegen and Atkinson, 1974), Swanson found some evidence for his hypotheses. Of the three clusters of dissociative experiences — absorption in received imaginings, role playing, and adventure seeking — the first two showed the expected tendency to correlate especially in large families (where Swanson argued, the structuring process is likely to have a larger effect).

Applied cross-culturally, Swanson's account runs into much the same methodological trouble as Douglas' theory. Anthropologists have characterized many societies as *sociocentric* — those in which the concept of the person includes the intimate family or social circle and heteronomy is more highly valued than autonomy. It is unclear whether such societies are, as we might expect from Swanson's account, more prone to dissociative experience. Indeed, since this characterization of societies as sociocentric is something of a caricature, it is uncertain what dimensions of social structure are at stake. Finally, as with Douglas, Swanson's account is relatively static and does not indicate how dissociation might function as a dynamic process in relation to other mental mechanisms or social processes.

From social structure to praxis

Although they work at different levels, these theoretical attempts to relate culture and social structure to the prevalence of dissociation (and by extension to conversion symptoms) share common elements. Both Bateson and Swanson invoke a notion of submission to others, although in Bateson's version of the Balinese it is explicit physical yielding, while for Swanson it is a process of adopting the perspectives of others (or a collectivity) and identifying them as one's own. Bateson and Douglas also propose socially mediated experiences of bodily fragmentation or of being 'out of control'. For Douglas, these experiences are a consequence of the relatively *laissez-faire* interactional style of the cultural group compared to more rigidly structured societies that demand tighter control of body and self. What underlies all of these models are certain metaphoric connotations of the concept of dissociation, which contrast wildness versus domesticity, fragmentation versus wholeness, other-directedness versus autonomy and self-control.

Contemporary anthropological accounts of dissociative phenomena emphasize the construction of experience through narrative or discursive practices. Talk about the body and its ailments are not only attempts to interpret and organize bodily events and experiences, they can constitute experience itself. The most obvious way this happens is through the performative functions of speech. Declaring one is sick puts one in a particular social position with profound consequences for the subsequent handling of one's body. The effect of such self-labelling can be decisive, but the influence of discourse goes deeper. There is a great deal of evidence that narration and other cognitive structuring processes work top–down to reorient attention and structure memory rehearsal and retrieval, so that discourse can result in gaps in attention, memory, and awareness (Schacter, 1995; Kirmayer, 1996).

Thus, the ways in which culture may influence dissociative experience include specific forms of praxis:

1. body practices of yielding to others foster automaticity and involuntariness;

2. narrative or discursive practices of ignoring or sidestepping gaps in experience result in tolerance for lacunae;

3. causal explanations of agencies within or outside the person that allow for attributions of involuntariness.

All of these forms of praxis are situation specific — tied to social roles and contexts in which dissociative experience and behaviour is deemed appropriate or inevitable.

Older accounts of culture and psychopathology often reflect a view of culture and social worlds as closed, internally consistent, homeostatic systems. This view of culture has become increasingly difficult to defend. Historical and ethnographic work has led to the recognition that cultural worlds are constantly in flux, riven by conflict, and challenged by tensions from within and without. Cultures present individuals with resources they can use to construct, stabilize, and position a socially viable self, as well as for the collective work of creating and maintaining social institutions (Obeyesekere, 1981; 1991). This perspective would have us see the individual with a conversion symptom not simply as embodying a cultural template for illness but participating in a contested field of representations of the body and the agentic self that both reflects and re-creates cultural notions of body, self, and agency.

Cultural configurations of agency and its disorders

In the information processing metaphors of cognitive psychology, dissociation involves relinquishing higher-order ('executive') control of some facet of behaviour or experience to a stream of information processing that is not closely identified with the self (Hilgard, 1977; Kihlstrom, 1992). Dissociated mental contents, while fully activated, are not linked with either an active mental representation of the self or the active mental representation of the context, or both (Kihlstrom and Hoy, 1990). This process can lead a person to exhibit complex, motivated behaviour yet honestly disavow awareness of its origin, intention, or control. Something like this is posited for dissociation, but accepting the notion that complex behaviour can occur without conscious mediation violates some assumptions of our everyday folk psychology.

Western folk psychology exaggerates 'rationality' and univocality. We tend to see behaviour as directed by a self-conscious and rational 'I' or observing ego. This valorization of the univocal self and its agency has important moral implications that justify our unease about hysteria (Kirmayer, 1994*a* ; Radden, 1996), but there are ethical systems that allow for polyvocality and multiple, context-dependent forms of rational behaviour (Ames and Dissayanake, 1996). Indeed, these alternative models of human agency reveal important truths about the multiplicity of the self that are obscured by our tacit assumption of a monological self.

Reflection on everyday experience reveals at least four different 'states of mind' that may govern behaviour (Kirmayer, 1992; 1994*b*):

1. self-conscious or self-focussed awareness, characterized by the prominent sense of 'I' and by the critical comparison of experience with self-standards;

2. unselfconscious awareness, characterized by awareness of the perceived object;

3. automatic or 'mindless' behaviour which, in the realm of social behaviour, appears to be rule-governed or script-like but which may, on analogy with motor skills, be better understood as the application of procedural knowledge;

4. imaginative reverie — the stuff of daydreaming, artistic creation, and play.

Table 18.2 summarizes some characteristics of these states of mind and corresponding research literature.

Each of these states of mind can sustain complex, motivated behaviour. However, the individual's experience of agency, and the ascriptions others make to explain their behaviour may differ markedly in each case. Dissociation represents a shift between these states of mind away from self-conscious awareness and toward some form of reverie, absorption, or automatic behaviour. During socialization we learn the appropriate states of mind to use in specific social contexts and acquire experience in changing our states of mind to fit the situation. The tasks or roles we assume within society may in turn affect the time we get to spend in one or another state of mind. As a result of these transitions, memory and experience are full of gaps or discontinuities. We learn how to fill in these

Table 18.2   States of mind and modes of awareness

State of mind	Example of tasks	Discursive forms	References
Self-consciousness	Self-description	Narrative centred on 'I'	Wicklund and Frey, 1980
Other consciousness	Aesthetic appreciation	Narrative centred on 'it'	Tellegen, 1974
Reverie	Daydreaming	Description of imagery	Singer, 1978
Mindlessness	Procedural learning motor tasks	Non-discursive	Langer, 1989

Adapted from Kirmayer, 1992 and 1994*b*

gaps, to give an account of 'where we have been' in our mental travels with socially acceptable narratives.

Cultures differ in their tolerance of gaps in memory and awareness, for the attribution of actions and events to agencies extrinsic to the self, and for the radical shifts in voice or perspective that may accompany shifts in states of mind. Cultural variations in the concept of person determine how we construe our experiences and what sorts of bodily events we expect to be able to control and to be held to account for by others. Since the person is, in fact, constantly presented with events that cannot be unambiguously attributed to self-direction, the potential for dissociative attributions ('it just happened to me') is always present.

In many cultures, invoking a supernatural agency is a credible explanation for affliction including loss of sensory or motor function. Until recently, physical illness was a credible explanation for such loss as well, but as diagnostic technology advances, the physiological basis of bodily symptoms can be challenged, leaving some patients' symptoms delegitimated or transformed from a bodily to a psychological affliction. Since in most cultures psychological disorders are stigmatized, this is usually a highly undesirable outcome.

What is at stake in hysteria, as in other medically unexplained symptoms, is the validation of suffering and its characterization as somatic rather than social or psychological. This depends in part on demonstrating that the affliction is not due to one's own failings or actions. Often this requires proving that psychological factors do not play a role, since otherwise one's whole problem may be conveniently ascribed to some idiosyncratic conflict or characterological flaw. Thus, patients' systematic denial of the psychological dimensions of their illness usually comes about not because of psychological defensiveness but because of realistic concerns about the social consequences of emphasizing one's own emotional distress (which implies some personal deficiency) or pointing to intolerable social circumstances which are dangerous to challenge because of the threat of rejection or retaliation (Kirmayer, 1999). The recognition that one is powerless to change social circumstances is a good reason to avoid thinking about them and to focus instead on acceptable means of claiming some attention and support.

These considerations apply to all medically unexplained illness. What hysteria adds to this general picture is the deployment of specific cognitive strategies of dissociation. This involves a shift in agency such that alterations in the control of action and the interpretation of sensory experience occur outside awareness. The person thus has an internally consistent experience of affliction that reduces their own cognitive dissonance, at the same time as it presents a credible message of suffering to others.

Unfortunately, the position of the hysteric is precarious — both epistemologically (Kirmayer, 1994a) and morally (Kirmayer 1988; Radden, 1996). Medical invalidation leaves the sufferer culpable for his own symptoms and the result may be rejection by care providers and others. Understanding hysteria as the outcome of forces beyond the patients' control is a first step toward a therapeutic alliance that can move the sufferer from powerlessness to a renewed sense of self-efficacy and restored control.

Conclusion

Ethnographic research suggests that conversion symptoms and other forms of hysteria remain common around the world. While some conversion symptoms (such as paralyses and pseudoseizures) have decreased in frequency in westernized urban settings in the last hundred years, it is likely that conversion symptoms have not disappeared, only changed their form and clinical site of presentation — being seen more often in primary care than in neuropsychiatric settings and manifesting more often as pain, weakness, dizziness, fatigue, and other non-specific somatic complaints than as focal symptoms reminiscent of neurological disorders.

Social and cultural processes may influence conversion disorder at many levels including:

1. the nature of illness beliefs and practices, and the expression of distress;
2. the salience and availability of dissociative mechanisms;
3. the response of the family, health care system, and larger social systems to specific types of symptom, including the nosological concept of hysteria itself.

The higher prevalence of conversion symptoms in some societies can be attributed to several factors. Generally, conversion symptoms fit local ethnophysiological notions and cultural idioms of distress. Psychiatry has a limited presence in many parts of the world and is associated only with severe mental disorder, so that somatic symptoms are less stigmatized than frank expressions of emotional distress while at the same time commanding serious attention from family and healers.

The distinctive nature of conversion symptoms, compared to other culturally patterned forms of somatic distress, resides in the experience and ascription of lack of agency or volitional control, which in turn depends on cultural knowledge and social practices that shape cognitive processes of bodily control. These can give rise to processes of automaticity and dissociation. Many cultures sanction dissociative experiences in religious and other ritual contexts (e.g. possession cults, trance performances), making such psychological processes both more available to the individual at times of distress and more credible to others as an explanation for disorder.

Current psychiatric theory views dissociation (and by extension, conversion) as a consequence of severe trauma (Kirmayer, 1996). Far from being an automatic response to trauma, however, dissociation can be understood as culturally patterned or scripted. Dissociation may involve patterns of behaviour that are learned preconsciously as automatic or non-volitional responses. However, dissociative behaviour usually conforms to a cultural template and may be intricately scripted or orchestrated with the actions of others. Hence, contemporary anthropology suggests we approach hysteria as a mode of self-construal, in which narratives of 'not knowing' and 'not doing' fit with prevalent cultural conceptions of the person, and serve to convey serious distress, vulnerability, and disablement.

This social perspective does not mean that hysteria or dissociation can be reduced to the performance of a social role. While in some cases dissociation appears to be little more than an attribution of involuntariness or a disavowal of control over behaviour, such attributions and modes of self-narration may affect memory retrieval and attention to create real and persistent gaps in memory and the experience of control.

This perspective on hysteria as social communication, interaction, and positioning can go further to explain the clinical phenomena than purely psychological or physiological explanations that ignore the social matrix of experience. Many conversion symptoms are transient and self-limited; they may persist just long enough for others to get the message.

When conversion symptoms become chronic, it may be because symptom behaviour forms part of a cycle of interpersonal interaction or social contingencies that maintain symptoms and disability. On this view, the pathology that underlies conversion symptoms can be sought not in individual neuropsychological functioning or psycho-dynamics, but in problematic social interactions (Rabkin, 1964). This would suggest the value of a family systems approach to diagnosing and treating conversion disorder (e.g. Griffith *et al.*, 1998; Madanes, 1981; Rabkin, 1977).

A cultural perspective alerts us to the profound effects of psychiatric theory and practice on patients' illness behaviour. However, neither the longstanding medical fascination with hysteria, nor the dismissive stance taken by many physicians toward patients whose symptoms are unexplained by physiological disorder can fully account for the changing nature of conversion hysteria. Conversion hysteria reflects more pervasive cultural concepts of body, mind, and consciousness. It is precisely because hysteria contravenes commonsense notions of rational self-control and autonomy that it continues to evoke both theoretical interest and scepticism. Hysteria has much to teach us, not only about the mechanisms of attention, self-control, and awareness, but also about the social and cultural roots of our sense of self.

Notes

1 Note that the *non-conscious* is a much larger domain than the Freudian *unconscious* (equated with fantasy or a realm of thought similar to conscious conflict, but kept out of consciousness by active cognitive processes of repression). There is much that is not actively kept out of consciousness by some censor but does not have access to it (except as belated re-description or re-representation) and which nonetheless accounts for socially organized and, potentially, motivated behaviour. Acknowledging the ubiquity of non-conscious cognitive processes in behaviour does not commit us to any specific map of psychic topography, psychoanalytic or otherwise.

2 'It is common knowledge that the villages Nandi visited had gross peculiarities. For example one was all Muslim and communication with Hindu male doctors would be very suspect, another was devastated by Maoist and police killings a few months earlier and is an area where the local dialect is incomprehensible to others and out-migration of upper caste and upper class has left only the sick behind. These surely have some effect on the prevalence of dissociative states.' (Chakraborty, 1993, p. 396)

3 See: Simons, R. C. (1983). *Latah: A Culture-Specific Elaboration of the Startle Reflex.* Bloomington, Indiana: Indiana Audiovisual Center. (The Center also has archive videotape material produced by the author.)

4 Jensen and Suryani (1992) report that in one village in Bali about 25 per cent of the inhabitants experience trance states at twice-yearly ceremonies. Unfortunately, we have no way of comparing this with the 'trance' experiences of, say, North American theatre-goers.

References

Ames, R. T. and Dissayanake, W. (ed.) (1996). *Self and Deception: A Cross-Cultural Philosophical Inquiry.* Albany: State University of New York.

Bateson, G. (1973). Some components of socialization for trance. *Ethos*, **3**:143–55.

Boddy, J. (1994). Spirit possession revisited: beyond instrumentality. *Annual Review of Anthropology*, **23**:407–34.

Boss, J. M. N. (1979). The seventeenth-century transformation of the hysteric affection, and Sydenham's Baconian medicine. *Psychological Medicine*, **9**, 221–34.

Bourguignon, E. (1967). World distribution and patterns of possession states. In *Trance and Possession States* (ed. Prince, R.), pp. 3–34). Montreal: R. M. Bucke Society.

Bourguignon, E. (1989). Trance and shamanism: What's in a name? *Journal of Psychoactive Drugs*, **21**, 9–15.

Chakraborty, A. (1993). Possessions and hysterias: what do they signify? *Transcultural Psychiatric Research Review*, **30(4)**, 393–9.

Chodoff, P. (1982). Hysteria and women. *American Journal of Psychiatry*, **139**, 545–51.

de Rivera, J. and Sarbin, T. R. (ed.) (1998). *Believed-In Imaginings: The Narrative Construction of Reality*. Washington: American Psychological Association.

Dick, L. (1995). 'Pibloktoq' (Arctic hysteria): a construction of European-Inuit relations? *Arctic Anthropology*, **32(2)**, 1–42.

Douglas, M. (1973). *Natural Symbols: Explorations in Cosmology* (2nd edn). London: Barrie & Jenkins.

Foulks, E. F. (1985). The transformation of Arctic hysteria. In *The Culture Bound Syndromes* (ed. Simons, R. C. and Hughes, C.). Dordrecht: D. Reidel.

Griffith, J. L., Polles, A. and Griffith, M. E. (1998). Pseudoseizures, families, and unspeakable dilemmas. *Psychosomatics*, **39(2)**, 144–53.

Hacking, I. (1998). *Mad Travellers: Reflections on the Reality of Transient Mental Ilnesses*. Charlottesville: University Press of Virginia.

Hilgard, E. R. (1977). *Divided Consciousness: Multiple Controls in Human Thought and Action*. New York: John Wiley.

Hyler, S. E. and Spitzer, R. L. (1978). Hysteria split asunder. *American Journal of Psychiatry*, **135(12)**, 1500–3.

Jensen, G. D. and Suryani, L. K. (1992). *The Balinese People: A Reinvestigation of Character*. Singapore: Oxford University Press.

Kihlstrom, J. F. (1992). Dissociation and conversion disorders. In *Cognitive Science and Clinical Disorders* (ed. Stein, D. J., Young, J. and Orlando, F. L.), pp. 247–70. New York: Academic Press.

Kihlstrom, J. F. and Hoyt, I. P. (1990). Repression, dissociation, and hypnosis. In *Repression and Dissociation: Implications for Personality Theory, Psychopathology, and Health* (ed. Singer, J. L.), pp. 181–208. Chicago: University of Chicago Press.

Kirmayer, L. J. (1988). Mind and body as metaphors: hidden values in biomedicine. In *Biomedicine Examined* (ed. Lock, M. and Gordon, D.), pp. 57–92. Dordrecht: Kluwer.

Kirmayer, L. J. (1992). Social constructions of hypnosis. *International Journal of Clinical and Experimental Hypnosis*, **40(4)**, 276–300.

Kirmayer, L. J. (1994*a*). Improvisation and authority in illness meaning. *Culture, Medicine and Psychiatry*, **18(2)**, 183–214.

Kirmayer, L. J. (1994*b*). Pacing the void: social and cultural dimensions of dissociation. In *Dissociation: Culture, Mind and Body* (ed. Spiegel, D.), pp. 91–122. Washington: American Psychiatric Press.

Kirmayer, L. J. (1996). Landscapes of memory: trauma, narrative and dissociation. In *Tense Past: Cultural Essays on Memory and Trauma* (ed. Antze, P. and Lambek, M.), pp. 173–98. London: Routledge.

Kirmayer, L. J. (1999). Rhetorics of the body: medically unexplained symptoms in sociocultural perspective. In *Somatoform Disorders—A Worldwide Perspective* (ed. Ono, Y., Janca, A., Asai, M. and Sartorius, N.), pp. 271–86. Tokyo: Springer–Verlag.

Kirmayer, L. J., Robbins, J. M. and Paris, J. (1994). Somatoform disorders: personality and the social matrix of somatic distress. *Journal of Abnormal Psychology*, **103(1)**, 125–36.

Kirmayer, L. J. and Young, A. (1998). Culture and somatization: clinical, epidemiological and ethnographic perspectives. *Psychosomatic Medicine*, **60**, 420–30.

Lambek, M. (1989). From disease to discourse: remarks on the conceptualization of trance and spirit possession. In *Altered States of Consciousness and Mental Health: A Cross-cultural Perspective* (ed. Ward, C. A.), pp. 36–61. London: Sage.

Langer, E. J. (1989). *Mindfulness*. Reading, Mass.: Addison–Wesley.

Leff, J. (1988). *Psychiatry Around the Globe: A Transcultural View*. London: Gaskell.

Lewis, I. M. (1971). *Ecstatic Religion: An Anthropological Study of Spirit Possession and Shamanism*. London: Penguin Books.

Madanes, C. (1981). *Strategic Family Therapy*. San Francisco, CA: Jossey–Bass.

Mauss, M. (1979). *Sociology and Psychology*. London: Routledge & Kegan Paul.

Micale, M. (1995). *Approaching Hysteria: Disease and Its Interpretations*. Princeton, NJ: Princeton University Press.

Nandi, D. N., Banerjee, G., Nandi, S. and Nandi, P. (1992). Is hysteria on the wane? A Community survey in West Bengal, India. *British Journal of Psychiatry*, **160**, 87–91.

Obeyesekere, G. (1981). *Medusa's Hair: An Essay on Personal Symbols and Religious Experience*. Chicago: University of Chicago Press.

Obeyesekere, G. (1991). *The Work of Culture: Symbolic Transformation in Psychoanalysis and Anthropology*. Chicago: University of Chicago Press.

Ong, A. (1988). The production of possession: spirits and the multinational corporation in Malaysia. *American Ethnologist*, **15**, 28–52.

Piñeros, M., Roselli, D. and Calderon, C. (1998). An epidemic of collective conversion and dissociation disorder in an indigenous group in Colombia: its relation to cultural change. *Social Science and Medicine*, **46(11)**, 1425–8.

Rabinbach, A. (1990). *The Human Motor: Energy, Fatigue, and the Origins of Modernity*. New York: Basic Books, Harper Collins.

Rabkin, R. (1964). Conversion hysteria as social maladaptation. *Psychiatry*, **27**, 349–63.

Rabkin, R. (1977). *Strategic Psychotherapy: Brief and Symptomatic Treatment*. New York: Basic Books.

Radden, J. (1996). *Divided Minds and Successive Selves: Ethical Issues in Disorders of Identity and Personality*. Cambridge: MIT Press.

Raguram, R., Weiss, M., Channabasavanna, S. M. and Devins, G. M. (1996). Stigma, depression, and somatization in South India. *American Journal of Psychiatry*, **153**, 1043–9.

Schacter, D. L. (ed.) (1995). *Memory Distortion: How Minds, Brains and Societies Reconstruct the Past*. Cambridge, Mass.: Harvard University Press.

Shorter, E. (1992). From Paralysis to Fatigue: A History of Psychosomatic Illness in the Modern Era. New York: MacMillan.

Showalter, E. (1997). *Hystories: Hysterical Epidemics and Modern Culture*. New York: Columbia University Press.

Simon, G. and Gureje, O. (1999). Stability of somatization disorder and somatization symptoms among primary care patients. *Archives of General Psychiatry*, **56**, 90–5.

Simons, R. C. (1996). *Boo! Culture, Experience and the Startle Reflex*. New York: Oxford University Press.

Simons, R. C. and Hughes, C. C. (ed.) (1985). *The Culture-Bound Syndromes: Folk Illnesses of Psychiatric and Anthropological Interest*. Dordrecht: D. Reidel.

Singh, S. P. and Lee, A. S. (1997). Conversion disorders in Nottingham: alive, but not kicking. *Journal of Psychosomatic Research*, **43(4)**, 425–30.

Singer, J. L. (1978). Experimental studies of daydreaming and the stream of thought. In K. S. Pope & J. L. Singer (Eds.), *The Stream of Consciousness* (ed. Pope, K. S. and Singer, J. L.), pp. 187–225. New York: Plenum Press.

Small, G. W., Propper, M. W., Randolph, E. T. and Eth, S. (1991). Mass hysteria among performers: social relationship as a symptom predictor. *American Journal of Psychiatry*, **148**, 1200–5.

Swanson, G. E. (1978). Travels through inner space: family structure and openness to absorbing experiences. *American Journal of Sociology*, **83**, 890–919.

Tellegen, A. and Atkinson, G. (1974). Openness to absorbing and self-altering experiences ('absorption'), a trait related to hypnotic susceptibility. *Journal of Abnormal Psychology*, **83**, 268–77.

Tseng, W. S. *et al.* (1988). A sociocultural study of koro epidemics in Guangdong China. *American Journal of Psychiatry*, **145(12)**, 1538–43.

Wicklund, R. A. and Frey, D. (1980). Self-awareness theory: when the self makes a difference. In *The Self in Social Psychology* (ed. Wegner, D. M. and Vallacher, R. R.), pp. 31–54. New York: Oxford University Press.

Wikan, U. (1990). *Managing Turbulent Hearts: A Balinese Formula for Living*. Chicago: University of Chicago Press.

Winstead, B. A. (1984). Hysteria. In *Sex Roles and Psychopathology* (ed. Widom, C. S.), pp. 73–100. New York: Plenum Press.

Winzeler, R. L. (1995). *Latah in Southeast Asia: The History and Ethnography of a Culture-Bound Syndrome*. Cambridge: Cambridge University Press.

Young, A. (1995). *The Harmony of Illusions: Inventing Posttraumatic Stress Disorder*. Princeton, NJ: Princeton University Press.

19 The prognosis of hysteria/somatization disorder

Maria A. Ron

Neurological symptoms for which no adequate physiological explanation is found occur in one in five of all neurological out-patients and in nearly two-thirds of those admitted to neurological wards. It is assumed that psychological factors determine these symptoms, although in clinical practice the diagnosis is made when symptoms remain unexplained after full investigation. In this chapter, the prognosis of these unexplained neurological symptoms is reviewed, together with the factors that predict outcome. Some comments are also included about the use of health-care facilities.

Introduction

Neurological symptoms for which no adequate physiological explanation can be found are subsumed under the diagnoses of hysteria and somatization disorder. Controversy remains as to the causal mechanisms, but more is known about their clinical course and comorbidity. In this chapter, follow-up studies of unexplained neurological symptoms are reviewed, including those dealing with childhood presentations. The evidence from these studies suggests that the diagnosis of hysteria/somatization disorder is stable over time when detailed investigations are performed to exclude the presence of neurological disease. These studies also suggest that the prognosis is similar for different unexplained symptoms and that the chances of recovery are higher for young patients, with symptoms of recent onset, while those with personality disorders and chronic symptoms are likely to do worse. The aetiological implications of these findings and the use of health resources by these patients are also discussed.

Neurological symptoms for which no adequate physiological explanation can be found are common in clinical practice. One in five neurological out-patients may fall into this category (Mace and Trimble 1991), and surveys of in-patient neurological admissions suggest that in 60 per cent of patients, organic pathology may be absent or provide only a partial explanation for the symptoms (Ewald *et al.* 1994). It is then assumed that psychological factors are important in determining these symptoms and the diagnosis of hysteria or conversion disorder is often made, although positive psychiatric criteria (for example, the presence of a stressor, the lack of conscious motivation) are often missing. In many of these patients, neurological symptoms are part of a much wider range of unexplained symptoms, and the diagnosis of somatization disorder is applied to those with the more severe and chronic clinical picture.

Controversy remains as to whether the same mechanisms determine isolated, unexplained symptoms (that is, hysteria) and somatization disorder. There is no clear-cut answer to this question, but clinical experience suggests that separation between the two may in many cases be arbitrary. Finding a significant psychological stressor (required for the diagnosis of hysteria) may depend on the thoroughness of the clinical examination and is open to subjective bias. Even if such stressor is present, its relevance may be difficult to determine. On the other hand, it is far more likely that the causal mechanisms may differ between acute and chronic symptoms and between symptoms that are sporadic or continuous. For the purpose of this chapter, hysteria will be considered as a loss or distortion of function not fully explained organically, as determined by clinical examination and full investigation (Marsden 1986), regardless of whether psychological stressors are in evidence or whether other unexplained symptoms are also present. This definition places hysteria and somatization disorder in the same continuum, the main difference being one of chronicity and multiplicity of symptoms. This makes it possible to review the prognosis of these symptoms without artificial compartmentalization.

Various aspects of prognosis will be considered here: the outcome of the index symptom, the development of neurological and psychiatric disease over time, and the factors that predict prognosis. In addition, some comments will be made about the use of health care facilities by these patients.

Early follow-up studies

Briquet (1859) was one of the first to follow up patients with unexplained neurological symptoms, to acknowledge their poor prognosis, and to mention prognostic indicators. He studied 430 patients for 10 years with a variety of symptoms including sensory changes, 'spasms', seizures, and paralysis. Impressionable females with labile mood were thought to be particularly prone to the disorder. In about half of these patients the onset of symptoms had been insidious and the course one of progressive, chronic deterioration. In some cases recurrent episodes were common, while in others, recovery occurred after three to six months. Briquet considered that a favourable change in social circumstances, the development of intercurrent physical disease, 'violent moral emotions', and the presence of a strong will carried a good prognosis. Onset in early adolescence, marriage, and pregnancy, on the other hand, did not.

Systematic follow-up studies started to appear in the 1950s and sampled psychiatric and neurological populations with unexplained physical symptoms. These studies further identified prognostic factors and reported a high incidence of psychiatric or neurological morbidity depending on the provenance of the sample.

One of the lengthiest studies ever performed is that of Ljungberg (1957), who followed up 381 patients for over 15 years. Many have replicated Ljungberg's findings, but few have added substantially to them. A unique feature of this study is that it included patients from psychiatric and neurological settings, in contrast with most others which have sampled from only one type of population. Ljungberg's patients presented with a variety of symptoms, including motor and sensory abnormalities, disorders of consciousness, and amnesia, although in a given patient one set of symptoms tended to dominate the picture. Ljungberg made the observation, confirmed many times since, that when recovery occurred it tended to happen early, usually during the first year of the illness (62 per cent became symptom-free). After that, recovery was much rarer, with the percentage of symptomatic patients being very similar five and fifteen years later (25 per cent and 20 per cent respectively). The very long duration of the study made it possible to determine the rate of relapse, which during the first five years appeared to be somewhat higher in women (10 per cent) than in men (7 per cent). Women who relapsed were more likely than men to exhibit different symptoms.

Regarding the incidence of undetected neurological disease, epilepsy was more common than in the general population, but other neurological conditions (for example, multiple sclerosis, head injuries, and brain tumours) were not, and there was no increase in the overall mortality. Gender and age did not influence the outcome of the unexplained symptoms, but those with higher IQ (more than 90) and non-deviant personalities were more likely to recover. Marital status had no prognostic significance in men, but unmarried or divorced women did worse. No specific type of personality disorder was associated with a poor prognosis. The study also made the point that the incidence of psychiatric illness was higher than in the general population. Thus, by the end of the study, 3 per cent had developed schizophrenia and 2.4 per cent, bipolar disorder. Ziegler and Paul (1954) had reported even higher rates. In their 25-year follow-up study, 22 out of 66 women with the initial diagnosis of hysteria had been readmitted to hospital with other psychiatric diagnoses (for example, dementia praecox, manic depressive illness, and dementia).

In 1965, Slater published in the *British Medial Journal* one of the most influential studies, but also one that has led to important misconceptions. Slater followed up 85 patients (32 men and 53 women) seen in the early 1950s at the National Hospital for Nervous Diseases with the diagnosis of hysteria. The startling finding of the study was that 60 per cent of the patients had acquired a neurological diagnosis that in the view of Slater could have explained the original symptoms. Only 19 patients were symptom-free at follow-up, 12 had died, and 40 were totally or partly disabled. Psychiatric disease had become apparent in many others. Slater concluded that hysteria was 'a fertile source of clinical error . . . not only a delusion but also a snare'. Walshe, an eminent neurologist from the same hospital (1965), challenged his views and argued that hysteria was a disorder of behaviour and as such a valid diagnosis, even if its clinical manifestations were protean. These opposing views still prevail despite the enormous advances in diagnostic accuracy over the past 30 years.

A closer look at Slater's data suggests that a different interpretation of some of his findings may have been possible even at the time of the study. Slater (1965) failed to distinguish undetected neurological disease that accounts for the presenting symptoms from neurological disease that coexists with hysterical symptoms but is not sufficient to account for them. Thus, the diagnosis of hysteria was rejected in patients who more correctly should have received a dual diagnosis. Slater also made the assumption that the diagnosis made at follow-up, based on notes and information from general practitioners, was more accurate than the original one made while the patient was in hospital. In some of his patients the symptoms had remained unchanged, but a different explanation had been put forward (for example, patients with pseudoseizures were considered to have epilepsy and those with non-organic facial pain to have trigeminal neuralgia). Slater regarded these changes of emphasis as diagnostic errors. In other cases, isolated findings of doubtful significance (for example, 'cortical atrophy' detected by air encephalography in a young woman) were elevated to the rank of explanatory neurological diagnoses. In a small number of cases an organic disease had genuinely been missed. Most of these cases (one spinal tumour, two cases of dementia, one of Takayasu's disease, repeated strokes), would have been correctly diagnosed at an early stage if non-invasive, accurate imaging had been available.

It is of interest to note that a later study from the same hospital (Merskey and Buhrich 1975) found the prevalence of neurological disease in patients with the diagnosis of hysteria (67 per cent) to be similar to that of patients with non-hysterical psychiatric symptoms (such as depression or anxiety). The authors concluded that the presence of neurological disease was a predisposing factor in the development of hysteria and other psychiatric symptoms, rather than a mistake in the diagnosis.

A study performed close in time to that of Slater, but reported much later (Lewis 1982), exemplifies the differences between neurological and psychiatric populations seen in tertiary referral centres. Lewis collected retrospectively 98 patients seen over a period of five years at the Maudsley Hospital and traced their outcome. Of the 73 women, 61 had recovered or improved, and the same was true of 16 of the 25 men. Undetected neurological disease was rare and only three patients died of a neurological condition that may have explained the original symptoms. Lewis observed that coexisting psychiatric illness, abnormal personality, and poor social adjustment had persisted unchanged throughout the follow-up and carried a bad prognosis. In his series, only minor changes in psychiatric diagnosis were made (from example, from hysteria to depression with hypochondriasis). The presence of psychiatric illness or personality disorder was noticed to carry a bad prognosis.

More recent studies have also reported a higher prevalence of coexisting organic disorder (up to 50 per cent) in neurological patients with unexplained symptoms (Marsden 1986; Lelliott and Fenwick 1991; Factor et al. 1995) compared with that (around 3 per cent) in psychiatric populations (Roy 1979). The reasons for the high prevalence of organic disease, which in itself does not invalidate the diagnosis of hysteria, are complex. Toone (1990) has suggested that neurological illness may provide a model for the development of symptoms and an opportunity for the patients to spend time in a medical environment where illness behaviour is rewarded. It has also been suggested that cerebral dysfunction may provide a fertile soil for the development of hysterical symptoms, although the recent study by Crimlisk et al. (1998) reported that organic neurological disease in patients with unexplained symptoms was as likely to be extracerebral.

Recent follow-up studies

Advances in clinical diagnosis, in particular imaging, allow for the safe detection of neurological disease in its early stages. In addition, the pathophysiology of some neurological conditions is more clearly understood, and advances in molecular genetics have made it possible to classify as organic, conditions hitherto thought to be hysterical (for example, certain types of dystonia). The widespread use of standardized psychiatric diagnostic criteria is also likely to have had an impact in the detection of psychiatric morbidity. It is therefore to be expected that more recent studies would have an enhanced diagnostic accuracy. These studies have also investigated in greater detail the prognosis of the unexplained symptoms, the factors that predict outcome, and the subsequent incidence of psychiatric disease.

Studies of patients with acute symptoms

Studies of patients with acute unexplained symptoms have uniformly reported good outcome, regardless of the type of symptom. Most of these studies also report that the majority of those likely to recover do so before leaving hospital — spontaneously or after explanation and reassurance. Other findings common to these studies are a better prognosis for younger patients and the very low incidence of neurological disease at follow-up.

Krull and Schifferdecker (1990), in a retrospective survey of 220 patients with a variety of unexplained neurological symptoms, observed that 40 per cent had recovered at the time of discharge from the hospital, some improvement had been observed in a similar proportion, and 21 per cent were unchanged. Recovery was more likely in young men who had symptoms for shorter periods. Couprie *et al.* (1995) reported similar findings in a follow-up study of 56 patients admitted to hospital four years earlier with conversion disorder other than pseudoseizures. Two-thirds of the patients were women and the mean age of admission was 36 years. Over half the patients had been admitted to hospital within days of the onset of symptoms and only 12 patients had symptoms for more than a year. Patients with coexistent neurological disease were excluded from the study, and treatment during admission consisted of reassurance and exercise. Telephone interviews and contact with general practitioners ascertained outcome. At follow-up, 59 per cent of the patients had recovered completely and 22 were still disabled. Those with acute symptoms were two and a half times more likely to have recovered, especially if a traumatic life event had preceded the symptoms. The condition at the time of discharge was a strong predictor of outcome, indicating that those likely to improve tended to do so early. Older patients were less likely to do well. Only two patients had developed neurological conditions that could have explained the presenting symptoms and, in retrospect, the authors considered that investigations had not been sufficiently detailed to detect neurological disease in these patients.

A study of particular interest is that of Binzer and Kullgren (1998), who used a case-control design to study the features and outcome of 30 patients with non-organic motor disorders of acute onset. When the patients were reassessed two to five years later, all but three had recovered or improved, and most had done so by the time they were discharged from the hospital. No new neurological diagnoses had emerged at follow-up. Age, gender, and education had no bearing on the prognosis, but coexisting physical, non-neurological illness was associated with poor outcome.

The similarity in outcome across different cultures is exemplified by the study of Chandrasekaran *et al.* (1994) who followed up 38 women seen five years earlier with heterogeneous symptoms including pseudoseizures. At follow-up, two-thirds of the patients were symptom free and no new neurological diagnoses had been made. As in previous studies, short duration of symptoms carried a good prognosis.

Studies of patients with chronic symptoms

Two studies have recently reported the long-term outcome of patients with chronic unexplained neurological symptoms. These studies involve patients from the same hospital as those previously studied by Slater and provide some information about the impact of current diagnostic techniques in the accuracy of the diagnosis of hysteria.

The first of these studies by Mace and Trimble (1996) followed up a group of 73 patients with heterogeneous symptoms who had received a diagnosis of conversion disorder 10 years earlier. Diagnosis at follow-up was ascertained from the notes and by talking to general practitioners. Contrary to what may have been expected in a chronic population, 22 patients had recovered and a further 43 had improved. Older age, longer duration of symptoms, and the use of non-psychotropic medication were indicators of bad prognosis. In 11 patients, a neurological diagnosis was found that could have partly or completely explained the original symptoms. In most of these patients an organic diagnosis had already been suspected during the initial admission. Surprisingly, the number of unexplained symptoms present in a given patient did not seem to influence prognosis.

The second study by Crimlisk *et al.* (1998) included only patients with unexplained motor symptoms (35 with limb paralysis and 38 with abnormal movements). Patients were consecutive admissions to the National Hospital during a two-year period. The mean duration of the presenting symptoms was 18 months, but some patients had symptoms for more than 10 years. Retrospective analysis of the notes suggested that 8 per cent of the subjects had organic pathology that may have contributed, but could not have explained the symptoms. Nearly half of the patients had previously experienced unexplained neurological symptoms, a similar proportion had previously experienced unexplained medical symptoms, and 42 per cent had a history of organic neurological disorder unrelated to the presenting complaints. At follow-up, the presenting symptoms had resolved in a quarter of the patients and improved in a further 20 per cent. As in previous studies, symptoms present for less than a year had better prognosis.

Undetected neurological disease was rare. Neurological diagnoses that could have accounted for the original symptoms were made *de novo* in only three patients. In two of them, communication problems and learning disability made it difficult to obtain a reliable history. In the third patient, a rare movement disorder (paroxysmal kinesogenic dyskinesia), not well characterized at the time of the initial admission, was diagnosed at follow-up. The striking differences in diagnostic accuracy between these two studies and that of Slater can be explained by the availability of better non-invasive investigative techniques and improved neurological diagnostic skills.

The role of psychiatric morbidity and other factors in prognosis

In evaluating outcome predictors, most studies refer to the possible effect of a given factor on the recovery of the unexplained neurological symptoms, although this is only a facet of the overall picture of disability and social adaptation. It is also unlikely that the various outcome predictors (for example, personality disorder, marital status, additional psychiatric diagnosis) would act independently of each other, even if most studies deal separately with each of them.

The high prevalence of psychiatric diagnosis in this population is well documented. Crimlisk *et al.* (1998) reported the presence of personality disorder in half of their patients, affective illness in 41 per cent, anxiety and phobic symptoms in 15 per cent, and psychotic symptoms in 7 per cent. Mace and Trimble (1996) had previously reported comparable figures.

The most consistent finding across all these studies is that *personality disorder* carries a poor prognosis. But there is no clear association between prognosis and any specific type of personality disorder. In the Crimlisk *et al.* (1998) study, different personality types, including dependent, emotionally unstable, and histrionic, were equally common. These findings are similar to those of Binzer *et al.* (1997) and to those of previous studies (Ljungberg 1957; Mace and Trimble 1996) which have disputed the specific link with histrionic personality.

There is less agreement as to the prognostic significance of *other types of psychiatric comorbidity*. In the Mace and Trimble (1996) and Crimlisk *et al.* (1998) studies, the presence of depression and anxiety carried a good prognosis, suggesting that the resolution of psychiatric symptoms was linked to that of the neurological ones. Other studies (Krull and Schifferdecker 1990; Binzer and Kullgren 1998; Leibbrand *et al.* 1999) had failed to find this association. *Other prognostic indicators* were reported by Crimlisk *et al.* (1998), who found that a change in marital status, likely to signal an improvement in personal circumstances, indicated good outcome. Being the recipient of social benefits and involvement in litigation, on the other hand, were associated with poor prognosis.

Early follow-up studies tend to suggest that medically unexplained symptoms could also be an early manifestation of a yet undiagnosed psychiatric illness that will become apparent with time. Ziegler and Paul (1954) reported that 22 out of 66 women initially diagnosed as having hysteria had been admitted to hospital over the next 25 years with diagnoses of dementia praecox, manic depressive illness, and dementia. Ljungberg (1957) found that the incidence of schizophrenia and manic depressive illness in his patients was higher than in the general population, and Slater (1965) reported the development of major psychiatric illness in 10 out of 33 patients who had not acquired an organic neurological diagnosis at follow-up. Guze *et al.* (1986) in their six- to eight-year follow-up study of 422 patients with a diagnosis of 'somatization' (and therefore more pervasive and chronic symptoms) reported that 20 per cent had received an alternative psychiatric diagnosis (for example, anxiety neurosis or affective disorder).

More recent studies have contradicted these findings, suggesting that earlier diagnostic practices, less likely to be based on standardized diagnostic criteria, may account for these differences. Thus in the Crimlisk *et al.* (1998) study, only three out of sixty-four patients had developed a new psychiatric diagnosis during the six-year follow-up period. Psychiatric morbidity continued to be high, but for most patients the current psychiatric problems represented a continuation or relapse of previous ones.

As could be expected, the presence of multiple unexplained symptoms — an index of severity and chronicity — has also been associated with poor prognosis. Kent *et al.* (1995) reported that patients fulfilling the criteria for somatization disorder were more likely than those with the diagnosis of conversion disorder to have more unexplained symptoms at follow-up and higher psychiatric morbidity.

Outcome of conversion disorder in children

Unexplained neurological symptoms are very rare in children below the age of six years. Their reported prevalence is lower in those attending psychiatric clinics (less than 10 per cent) than in paediatric in-patients (17 per cent). Children and adolescents with conversion disorders tend to be younger, to be of lower socio-economic status, and to have higher parental physical and psychiatric morbidity than those with other diagnoses referred to the same clinics (Steinhausen *et al.* 1989). Girls are over-represented, and presentations are usually polysymptomatic, with gait disturbances being particularly common (Leslie 1988). Children with conversion disorder appear to have much less personal and family psychopathology than adults with the same disorder. Most of these children are well adjusted and tend to be perfectionistic and keen to do well academically (Garralda 1992). The proportion of children in whom organic neurological disease had been missed during the initial consultation is close to that in adults, and has been reported to be around 6 per cent in two follow-up studies (Steinhausen *et al.* 1989; Spierings *et al.* 1990). The outcome of the presenting symptoms has been described as favourable in those with symptoms of recent onset. Thus, Leslie (1988) reported recovery in 17 out of 20 children, three months after admission to hospital, and Grattan–Smith *et al.* (1988) gave a comparable figure for recovery in a group with heterogeneous clinical presentations.

Many of the studies in this age group have been performed on patients with pseudo-seizures and some of their findings may not apply to children with other unexplained neurological symptoms. In one of the best-documented studies using telemetry to ascertain the diagnosis (Wyllie *et al.* 1999), over 70 per cent of children were free from attacks two years later. Personality disorder and psychiatric morbidity appear to be rare in these children (Turgay 1990; Lancman *et al.* 1994), although more recently, Wyllie *et al.* (1999) have reported mood disorders in a third of such patients, together with a very high rate of stressors (a third had been sexually abused and nearly half had experienced family difficulties). The role of psychiatric morbidity in the outcome of pseudoseizures remains to be determined but seems to be less relevant than early age of onset and long duration of symptoms, both of which carry a poor prognosis.

The outcome of specific symptoms

Few studies have directly compared the outcome of different unexplained symptoms, and those that have have reached different conclusions. Ljungberg (1957) in his long follow-up study considered that astasia abasia, tremor, aphonia, and disorders of consciousness had a better prognosis than paralysis and fits. Carter (1972) believed that tremor and fits had a worse prognosis than blindness and paralysis, which were more likely to recover. Krull and Schifferdecker (1990) did not find differences in the type of symptoms exhibited by patients who recovered during their admission to hospital and those who entered a chronic course, although they observed that monoparesis and bladder dysfunction were more persistent than speech problems.

A survey of follow-up studies focussing on patients presenting with the same unexplained symptoms suggest that the outcome may be similar across the different presentations and that similar prognostic factors (for example, age, duration of symptoms, early recovery) operate in all of them. Thus, Lempert and Schmidt (1990), in a follow-up study of patients with pseudoseizures, reported a third of patients were free from attacks, 22 per cent had them less frequently, while the rest were unchanged. Psychiatric problems were present in two-thirds of the patients and many had other unexplained symptoms. Short duration of symptoms was commonly associated with improvement, while personality disorder and unemployment predicted chronicity. Another study (Betts and Boden 1992) also suggested that improvement takes place in many patients during their admission to hospital, although attacks tended to recur. These results are similar to those of Crimlisk *et al.* (1998) in patients with unexplained motor symptoms, and Binzer and Kullgren (1998) in patients with more acute symptoms.

Less common hysterical symptoms also appear to behave in the same fashion. Sletteberg *et al.* (1989) followed up 54 patients with unexplained visual disturbances for periods between 1 and 25 years. Half of the patients had recovered at follow-up, while the rest claimed to have poor vision, and a quarter were significantly handicapped. Those who were well at follow-up were more likely to be young and to have improved by the time they left hospital. These results are similar to those of Timon *et al.* (1991), who studied prospectively a group of 80 patients with globus pharyngeus over a period of two years. A quarter of the patients had recovered and a further 35 per cent had improved, while the rest were unchanged. A short history of symptoms was once again a predictor of good prognosis.

Other outcome measures

It is outside the scope of this chapter to do a detailed analysis of the cost of hysteria and somatization disorder, but a few comments seem appropriate here. From childhood, the use of medical services by children with unexplained physical symptoms is high (8–10 per cent of attenders to primary care facilities). Use of medical facilities is particularly common during elementary school years for boys and in early adolescence for girls. This pattern of high use of medical facilities continues into adulthood, by which time depression has been added to unexplained somatic symptoms (Lewis and Lewis 1989).

Studies looking at adult populations (Coryell 1981) suggest that there is no excess mortality compared to the general population and that mortality is lower than in patients with unipolar depression. On the other hand, those with unexplained symptoms are more likely to undergo hospital admissions and surgical procedures and to show reluctance to engage in psychiatric treatment. In the USA, health care expenditure was nine times higher in patients who met the criteria for somatization disorder (Smith *et al.* 1986), and these patients underwent three times more surgical procedures than those with major depression (Zocolillo and Cloninger 1986). Even for those patients with less chronic or widespread unexplained physical symptoms, the health care costs are likely to be substantially increased.

Crimlisk *et al.* (in press) investigated the pattern of medical referrals in a group of 64 patients with unexplained motor symptoms before and after admission to the National Hospital. They reported that, despite the stability of the diagnosis, a pattern of multiple hospital referrals continued for many of these patients. More than half had been referred to other neurologists, often to investigate the same symptoms; 34 per cent had been referred to other specialists (for example, rheumatologists, general physicians) or received alternative therapies; but only 10 per cent had seen psychiatrists. New referrals were often initiated after patients changed their general practitioners. As in another study (Binzer and Kullgren 1998), these patients often changed their general practitioners after being discharged from hospital, indicating dissatisfaction with their management and with the general practitioner's reluctance to initiate new referrals and investigations.

Summary and conclusions

1. Hysterical symptoms and somatization disorder are likely to share similar mechanisms and are best considered as part of the same continuum.

2. Early follow-up studies of patients with unexplained symptoms have reported a higher rate of undetected neurological disease than could retrospectively have explained the presenting symptoms. Changes in diagnostic practice, the better characterization of rare neurological syndromes, and the availability of non-invasive, accurate imaging has drastically reduced the rates of undetected organic pathology in these patients. The diagnosis of hysteria can be made safely and accurately.

3. There are also aetiological implications accruing from these follow-up studies. The stability of the diagnosis over time strongly suggests that neurological disease is not a sufficient explanation for the symptoms of these patients.

4. Psychiatric morbidity is high in those with unexplained neurological symptoms, but in most patients, psychiatric symptoms are evident at the time of presentation and psychiatric disease appearing de novo years later is rare. The aetiological implications of these findings are complex. In some patients, the parallel course and resolution of unexplained symptoms and psychiatric features suggest a causal role for the latter. For the many others in whom psychiatric symptoms are absent or appear much later, their role seems less relevant.

5. A short history and young age are held to be predictors of good outcome, while personality disorder, chronicity of symptoms, receipt of disability benefits, and involvement in litigation augur poor recovery.

6. Hysteria is uncommon in very young children. Personality disorder and psychiatric morbidity are rare in those with unexplained symptoms. The indicators of good and bad prognosis are similar to those encountered in adults.

7. There is no evidence to suggest that different hysterical symptoms have different prognoses, although few studies have made direct comparisons. Prognostic indicators also appear to operate in a similar fashion across different symptoms.

8. Patients with unexplained neurological symptoms use more health care resources and are more likely to be referred for multiple consultations, often for the same symptoms.

References

Betts, T. and Boden S. (1992). Diagnosis, management and prognosis of a group of 128 patients with non-epileptic attack disorder. Part I. *Seizure*, **1**, 19–26.

Binzer, M. and Kullgren, G. (1998). Motor conversion disorder — a prospective 2–5 year follow up study. *Psychosomatics*, **39**, 519–27.

Binzer, M., Andersen, P. M. and Kullgren G. (1997). Clinical characteristics of patients with motor disability due to conversion disorder: a prospective control group study. *Journal of Neurology, Neurosurgery and Psychiatry*, **63**, 83–8.

Briquet, P. (1859). *Traité de L'hystérie*. Baillière, Paris.

Carter, A. B. (1972). A physician's view of hysteria. *Lancet*, ii, 1241–3.

Chandrasekaran, R., Goswami, U., Sivakumar, V. and Chitralekha, V. (1994). Hysterical neurosis — a follow-up study. *Acta Psychiatrica Scandinavica*, **89**, 78–80.

Coryell, W. (1981). Diagnosis-specific mortality. Primary unipolar depression and Briquet's syndrome (somatization disorder). *Archives of General Psychiatry*, **38**, 939–42.

Couprie, W., Wijdicks, E. F. M., Rooijmans, H. G. M. and van Gijn, J. (1995). Outcome in conversion disorder: a follow up study. *Journal of Neurology, Neurosurgery, and Psychiatry*, **58**, 750–2.

Crimlisk, H. L, Bhatia, K., Cope. H., David, A., Marsden, C. D. and Ron, M. A. (1998). Slater revisited: 6 year follow up study of patients with medically unexplained motor symptoms. *British Medical Journal*, **316**, 582–6.

Crimlisk, H. L., Bhatia, K. P., Cope, H., David, A. S., Marsden, D. and Ron, M. A. (In press). Patterns of referral in patients with medically unexplained motor symptoms. *Journal of Psychosomatic Research*.

Ewald, H., Rogne, T., Ewald, K. and Fink, P. (1994). Somatisation in patients newly admitted to a neurological department. *Acta Psychiatrica Scandinavica*, **89**, 174–9.

Factor, S. A., Podskalny, G. D. and Molho, E. S. (1995). Psychogenic movement disorders: frequency, clinical profile and characteristics. *Journal of Neurology, Neurosurgery and Psychiatry*, **59**, 406–12.

Garralda, M. E. (1992). A selective review of child psychiatric syndromes with a somatic presentation. *British Journal of Psychiatry*, **161**, 759–73.

Grattan–Smith, P., Fairley, M. and Proscopis, P. (1988). Clinical features of conversion disorder. *Archives of Disease in Childhood*, **63**, 408–14.

Guze, S. B., Cloninger, C. R., Martin, R. L. and Clayton, P. J. (1986). A follow up and family study of Briquet's syndrome. *British Journal of Psychiatry*, **149**, 17–23.

Kent, D. A., Tomasson, K. and Coryell, W. (1995). Course and outcome of conversion and somatization disorders: a four-year follow-up. *Psychosomatics*, **36**, 138–44.

Krull, F. and Schifferdecker, M. (1990). Inpatient treatment of conversion disorder: a clinical investigation of outcome. *Psychotherapy and Psychosomatics*, **53**, 161–5.

Lancman, M. E., Asconap, J. J., Graves, S. and Gibson, P. A. (1994). Psychogenic seizures in children: long-term analysis of 43 cases. *Journal of Child Neurology*, **9**, 404–7.

Leibbrand, R., Hiller, W. and Fichter, M. M. (1999). Effect of comorbid anxiety, depressive, and personality disorders on treatment outcome of somatoform disorders. *Comprehensive Psychiatry*, **40**, 203–9.

Lelliott, P. T. and Fenwick, P. (1991). Cerebral pathology in pseudoseizures. *Acta Neurologica Scandinavica*, **83**, 129–32.

Lempert, T. and Schmidt, D. (1990). Natural history and outcome of psychogenic seizures: a clinical study in 50 patients. *Journal of Neurology*, **237**, 35–8.

Leslie, S. A. (1988). Diagnosis and treatment of hysterical conversion reactions. *Archives of Disease in Childhood*, **63**, 506–11.

Lewis, A. (1982). The survival of hysteria. In *Hysteria* (ed. Roy, A.), pp. 21–6. John Wiley and Sons, Chichester.

Lewis, C. E. and Lewis, M. A. (1989). Educational outcome and illness behaviors in participants in a child-initiated care system: a 12 year follow up. *Pediatrics*, **84**, 845–50.

Ljungberg, L. (1957). Hysteria: a clinical, prognostic and genetic study. *Acta Psychiatrica et Neurologica Scandinavica*, **32**, Suppl 112, 1–162.

Mace, C. J. and Trimble, M. R. (1991). 'Hysteria', 'functional' or 'psychogenic'? A survery of British neurologists' preferences. *Journal of the Royal Society of Medicine*, **84**, 471.

Mace, C. J. and Trimble, M. R. (1996). Ten-year prognosis of conversion disorder. *British Journal of Psychiatry*, **169**, 282–8.

Marsden, C. D. (1986). Hysteria — a neurologist's view. *Psychological Medicine*, **16**, 277–88.

Merskey, H. and Buhrich, N. A. (1975). Hysteria and organic brain disorder. *British Journal of Medical Psychology*, **48**, 359–66.

Roy, A. (1979). Hysteria: a case note study. *Canadian Journal of Psychiatry*, **24**, 157.

Slater, E. (1965). Diagnosis of hysteria. *BMJ*, **1**, 1395–9.

Sletteberg, O., Bertelsen T. and Hovding G. (1989). The prognosis of patients with hysterical visual impairment. *Acta Ophthalmologica*, **67**, 159–63.

Smith, G. R., Monson, R. A. and Ray, D. C. (1986). Patients with multiple unexplained symptoms: their characteristics, functional health, and health care utilization. *Archives of Internal Medicine*, **146**, 69–72.

Spierings, C., Poels, P. J., Sijben, N., Gabreels, F. J. and Renier, W. O. (1990). Conversion disorders in childhood: a retrospective follow-up study of 84 inpatients. *Developmental Medicine and Child Neurology*, **10**, 865–71.

Steinhausen, H. C., Aster, M., Pfeiffer, E. and Gobel, D. (1989). Comparative studies of conversion disorders in childhood and adolescence. *Journal of Child Psychology and Psychiatry*, **30**, 615–25.

Timon, C., O'Dwyer, T., Cagney, D. and Walsh, M. (1991). Globus pharyngeus: long term follow up and prognostic features. *Annals of Otology, Rhinology and Laryngology*, **100**, 351–4.

Toone, B. K. (1990). Disorders of hysterical conversion. In *Somatisation: Physical Symptoms and Psychological Illness* (ed. Bass, C.), pp. 207–34. Blackwell, Oxford.

Turgay, A. (1990). Treatment outcome for children and adolescents with conversion disorder. *Canadian Journal of Psychiatry*, **35**, 585–9.

Walshe, F. (1965). Diagnosis of hysteria. *BMJ*, **2**, 1451–4.

Wyllie, E., Glazer, J. P., Benbadis, S., Kotagal, P. and Wolgamuth. B. (1999). Psychiatric features of children and adolescents with pseudoseizures. *Archives of Pediatric and Adolescent Medicine*, **153**, 244–8.

Ziegler, D. K. and Paul, N. (1954). On the natural history of hysteria in women. *Diseases of the Nervous System*, **15**, 301–6.

Zoccolillo, M. S. and Cloninger, C. R. (1986). Excess medical care of women with somatization disorder. *Southern Medical Journal*, **79**, 532–5.

20 Psychodynamic psychotherapy in the treatment of conversion hysteria

Nick Temple

This chapter describes how psychoanalytic practice and theory originated from Freud's treatment of hysterical patients. It reviews the early theories which he advanced to explain the origin of hysterical symptoms. It considers a modern psychodynamic, object–relations approach to treating hysteria and discusses hypnosis as a treatment from a psychodynamic perspective. Some of the other types of displacement of psychological conflict into the body are considered, such as psychosomatic illness and hypochondriasis, and contrasted with hysteria. The recent literature on the effectiveness of psychodynamic psychotherapy is briefly reviewed. The chapter concludes that psychodynamic psychotherapy has a place in the treatment of hysteria, but the importance of careful assessment is emphasized. The complex problems encountered in treating chronic hysterical personalities are described and illustrated with some clinical examples.

Introduction

The history of hysteria is closely tied to the beginnings of psychotherapy and psychoanalysis. Patients with hysteria were the first patients Freud treated, at the outset with hypnosis and then with psychotherapy, and this work led to the development of the original principles of psychoanalysis. It is useful to examine the history to clarify the present status of psychodynamic psychotherapy in the treatment of conversion hysteria and to recognize the radical changes in the therapeutic methods employed by modern psychodynamic therapy from those of early psychoanalysis.

Freud's study of hysteria was strongly influenced by Charcot's teaching and the interest in hysteria among neurologists and psychologists in the late nineteenth century. His important contribution was to develop a psychotherapeutic method of treating hysterical patients and from this experience to advance psychodynamic hypotheses about the aetiology of the disorder. Freud developed and changed these theories as a result of his experience with patients. Psychoanalytic theory has continued to advance in a similar way.

His first published paper on psychoanalysis, *Studies in Hysteria* (1895), published jointly with Breuer, described the treatment of five cases of hysteria. In this paper Freud first introduced the term 'conversion' to describe how libidinal energy in the dynamic instinctual model is *converted* into somatic symptoms. He described this transformation taking place when an idea is repressed and is displaced into the body and continues to be represented in the physical symptom. Freud's first psychodynamic theory of neurosis was based on the hypothesis that psychic trauma, particularly sexual abuse, led to hysterical

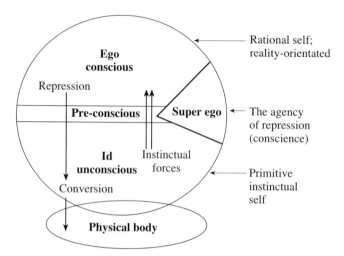

Fig. 20.1 Freud's structural model in which ideas and feelings are repressed and converted into bodily symptoms.

symptoms when painful and conflicting memories were repressed into the unconscious and then displaced into the body.

The development of Freud's ideas

In Freud's instinctual dynamic model, a transfer of libido from mind to body was seen as the underlying mechanism of hysterical symptoms. Although this model is based on nineteenth-century energy physics, it is as much a useful metaphor as scientific theory. Freud believed that it could become an established part of scientific psychology.

Freud's instinctual energy model is now little used in psychotherapy or psychoanalysis, but it is historically important. The term 'conversion' remains useful to describe a mental process by which ideas and feelings are repressed and converted into bodily symptoms to avoid an emotional conflict which is felt to be intolerable to the individual. Repression is a psychological mechanism, mediated by the superego, in which unbearable feelings are removed from consciousness. This act of repression is an unconscious mechanism and is not available to the individual's conscious mind.

The basis of Freud's treatment was to reverse the displacement into the body and to endeavour to make an unconscious conflict into a conscious one. He stated that 'hysterics suffer mainly from reminiscences' (Freud, 1895) and discovered that hysterical symptoms disappeared when he succeeded in bringing to light the traumatic memories and the feelings which he believed caused the symptoms. From the start, Freud was interested in the psychological causes of neurotic symptoms. His clinical experience confirmed that patients gained relief from knowing about the emotional conflicts which caused their difficulties. He believed that symptoms have meaning and provide a compromise solution to the emotional conflict (for example, as will be discussed below, the hysterical symptoms in shell-shock). The technique of abreaction was based on this theory. It assumes that emotional catharsis leads to a relief of hysterical or neurotic symptoms by bringing the repressed feelings to consciousness.

Freud initially employed hypnosis as the main therapeutic method to bring to light repressed feelings. However, hypnosis emphasized the patient's passivity and avoidance of reality and supported a belief in the omnipotence of the therapist. The resulting distorted view of the therapeutic task was found to be a serious obstacle to progress in the treatment: the patient expected to be cured by the physician without having to take an active part in the process. For these reasons, Freud abandoned hypnotic suggestion as the principal form of therapy.

After discarding hypnosis, the free association method was developed and became a basic technique of psychoanalytic therapy. The patient was invited to let their thoughts wander and to report whatever came to mind. It involved the patient's active and thoughtful participation in observing his or her mental life. This was an important turning point because the use of suggestion and the power of the therapist's personality to bring about change was considered unreliable. Apparent change based on maintaining an idealization of the therapist is a misleading use of the relationship with the therapist and is likely to be short-lived and to depend on the therapist's constant support and agreement. It will encourage an avoidance of the real relationship with the therapist and its inevitable limitations. This avoidance of reality is often a problem in the psychodynamic treatment of hysterical patients and is similar to the difficulties the patients have in facing painful aspects of themselves.

In a later modification of his views, Freud (1910) regarded the conflict inherent in the Oedipus complex as the underlying cause of neurosis and of hysteria. The patient with hysteria was unable to resolve the conflict experienced in the triangular relationship with the parents. As with Miss A. (to be described), this situation could respond rapidly to interpretation and discussion.

Psychodynamic mechanisms in hysteria

The central problem underlying hysteria is a conflict between opposing wishes or emotions which the patient feels cannot be resolved by discussion or thought and so are avoided by being repressed and displaced into physical symptoms. When a conflict is felt to be loaded with the expectations and requirements of others which are opposed to the individual's psychological needs, it may seem to be impossible to resolve. The conflict may assume a powerful moral dimension involving guilt. The patient may feel that the wish to break free and become independent of a parent is the same as killing the parent. In Freud's instinctual model he describes the conflict as being between the primitive instinctual forces of the id seeking gratification regardless of the consequences and the superego seeking to impose guilt and concern for others necessary in a civilized society.

In the First World War a high incidence of conversion hysteria occurred when soldiers were faced with an impossible conflict — they were required to face a high risk of death with courage, but the natural desire to run away from the danger was treated with extreme contempt, punishment, and rejection. An hysterical symptom displacing the conflict into the body could then become a necessary solution to the conflict. The false or deceptive quality of the illness could be felt to be justified in the patient's unconscious mind by the cruel and intolerable sacrifice required of the soldier by his family, his country, and his military superiors. Many patients, even if they are not in an extreme military situation, may experience a psychic conflict which is intolerable and unresolvable, for example, a wish for independence versus a desire to remain close to parents in adolescence. The conversion of this psychic conflict into a physical symptom provides an apparent compromise solution in the short term.

The dynamics of the therapeutic relationship in psychodynamic psychotherapy today are not primarily concerned with repressed traumatic memories, but with the human issues of the present relationship between the patient and the therapist. This is influenced and affected by the patient's internal world as a modified and distorted memory of the past. This has to be resolved and worked through in the psychotherapy. The patient's wish to control the psychotherapist in order to avoid the conflict from coming out into the open as a result of the therapist's enquiry will be an important part of the struggle.

The object–relations approach

The psychodynamic treatment of hysteria is now based on the object–relations approach which focusses attention on the interaction between the patient and the therapist in the here and now situation, and examines how this has been affected by past experiences. This approach was developed by Fairbairn (1952), Balint (1965), and Winnicott (1965) and differs sharply from Freud's instinctual model in that it is concerned with internal relationships and with representations of people referred to as 'internal objects'. These will be historically constructed versions of parents and others who form enduring internal figures and have a profound influence on all later relationships. Modern psychodynamic practice focusses on the way in which these internal objects appear powerfully in the transference and counter-transference relationship with the therapist. They are the main means of understanding the patient (Temple 1996) and may give important clues as to the nature of the primary relationships with parents which have been internalized.

The relationship between the past and the present is complex, and it is difficult to draw simple conclusions about the past from the patient's memories or from the transference relationship. It is always hard to assess accurately the true nature of early relationships and the patient's view of their past experiences may change a great deal during the course of treatment. Distortion will be introduced into the patient's recall of the past and its effect on the present, so that the historical truth is difficult to arrive at. The therapist's own training and knowledge of unconscious processes in himself and the patient will be important in dealing with this transference. The transference will include elements of distortion of aspects of the therapist's personality and exaggeration of his or her shortcomings. The therapist will need to use it to help the patient understand his or her own inner world. The patient's projection of internal figures onto the therapist will be an important part of the transference.

The object–relations approach had its origins in the understanding of the transference and the identification of counter-transference as a valuable source of information about the patient's inner world derived from the therapist's emotional reactions to the patient. This is a development from the early view that counter-transference was a problem derived solely from the analyst's difficulties. The therapist's capacity to enquire into the patient's inner world and draw conclusions is a necessary part of bringing what is unconscious into conscious awareness.

The object–relations approach would describe the central conflict in hysteria as being one between important figures in the patient's internal world, derived from their childhood development, and often displaced into present relationships. A patient with hysteria, in common with many patients, will tend to recreate these conflict situations in new relationships. When displacement into the body occurs, the intense anxiety is reduced and fears of catastrophe are removed, so that the conversion appears to be a solution. In addition, there is considerable secondary gain for the patient from the illness role in elucidating sympathy and 'escaping' into the neutral territory of hospital. This is not a conscious manipulation or planned advantage; it is an unconscious mechanism. Freud (1905, 1926) distinguished secondary gain from primary gain: primary gain was derived from the advantage inherent in construction of the neurotic symptom as a compromise to avoid the underlying conflict; secondary gain was derived from an already established neurotic illness which might confer advantages in self-preservation and in gratification, which follow from being ill and a patient.

There may also be a belief that medical treatment can remove the conflict by treating the physical symptoms, so that the problem could be solved in the body alone and avoided completely in the patient's mind. The psychodynamic treatment is focussed on the transference relationship. The therapist becomes directly part of the conflictful situation and is experienced as a figure who has played a part in the conflict. Transference work requires the patient to explore and discover the nature of the internal conflict through experiencing it directly in the relationship with the therapist. This involves a complex interplay between experiencing the therapist as if he or she were an internal figure and also being able to stand back from this situation sufficiently to understand it as a distortion of the relationship to the therapist and to gain insight into themselves from this knowledge. The patient's capacity to work with the therapist on these difficult feelings about the therapist in the transference will determine whether they can benefit from a psychodynamic therapy. If the patient is unable to engage in the process of exploration, or cannot move from the position of experiencing the therapist as an internal figure, then psychodynamic treatment will not succeed.

An excellent account of working through a transference relationship is given in Pat Barker's description, in her trilogy on the First World War (Barker, 1996), of Siegfried Sassoon's psychotherapeutic treatment in 1917 by W. H. Rivers. Sassoon's ambivalence in the transference relationship is clear. He regards Rivers as genuinely concerned for him, but at the same time he hates him as part of a military machine whose aim in treating him is to return him to the trenches and his likely death. This illustrates the intense attachment and idealization involved in a transference relationship, as well as the ambivalence derived from hatred and suspicion of the same figure whom he fears seeks to harm him. This shows the intense conflict in Sassoon's internal word which would be at the core of his neurotic symptoms.

Distinction of hysteria from psychosomatic disorders and hypochondriasis

In considering the psychopathology of conversion hysteria from a psychodynamic perspective, it is important to clearly differentiate it from other disorders in which there is a significant displacement of feelings and conflicts into the body, such as psychosomatic illness and hypochondriasis (see Schoenberg's chapter in this volume, p. 184). The psychopathology of these other conditions is qualitatively distinct from hysteria and the effects on the body are also distinct. It will be evident however that there is considerable overlap in psychopathology between hysteria and somatization disorder.

The displacement mechanism in conversion hysteria needs to be compared with these other forms of displacement from the mind into body which have been identified but appear to employ different psychological mechanisms of displacement. In hysteria, no neurological or pathological disease is present. In a psychosomatic disease, pathological disturbance of the body, including the immune system, occurs with consequent tissue damage. In hypochondriasis there is an intense preoccupation with a feared illness when no objective evidence for the illness can be found. These other mechanisms are seen in Sifneos' (1973, 1975) concept of Alexithymia and Marty and de Muzan's (1963) concept of Pensée Opératoire in psychosomatic illness. In these there is an absence of appropriate affect and an inability to describe feelings, with a focus on the physical illness.

In psychosomatic illness, the displacement from mind to body is accompanied by a significant pathological disruption in the body which can be detected by clinical examination and investigation. For example, a disturbance of the immune system often occurs in psychosomatic conditions which may contribute to the development of auto-immune disorders such as alopecia areata, asthma, and eczema. In hysteria there is no demonstrable physical pathology underlying the symptoms, hence the use of the term 'functional' disorder. The displacement from mind to body employs a different mechanism in hysteria from that in psychosomatic illness and hypochondriasis. As well as employing different neurological and hormonal pathways, it could also occur at a different level psychologically. In clinical experience these conditions can occur together to create a mixed and confusing picture.

In setting out to treat patients with these conditions with psychodynamic psychotherapy, the different types of psychopathology and defences need to be assessed carefully. A thorough psychodynamic assessment will help to avoid taking on patients who cannot cope with the exploration needed in a psychodynamic approach and will ascertain the patient's psychopathology in order to choose the most appropriate approach (see the case of Mrs P. that follows). The treatment approach will need to be different according to the patient's personality and psychopathology. For example, the unstable nature of severe borderline personality disorder, where hysterical symptoms are not uncommon, will present special difficulties in psychodynamic treatment because of the risk of deterioration. In some instances, psychodynamic psychotherapy will not be an effective form of treatment or may indeed be contraindicated.

It is evident that different conflicts and problems will be represented in the distinct somatic conditions. For example, there is clinical evidence to suggest that psychosomatic patients experience conflicts related to primitive guilt and their illness may relieve the persecution of the guilt by causing physical suffering and pain (Temple, 1986). The form of guilt describes a persecutory state in which an individual cannot bear to face the damage they believe they have done. Here the conflict is between love and hate and there is no capacity to bear the ambivalence felt towards a loved person. From her clinical work with young children, Klein (1952) described the paranoid schizoid position before the infant had acquired a capacity for mature guilt, when the tendency to split the world into good and bad figures leads to persecutory anxiety when the child feels attacked by the bad figure. This state of affairs persists in many disturbed adults. Klein called the state of being able to accept ambivalence and guilt and to tolerate loss the 'depressive position' and saw it as the basis of all good relationships.

Some observers have noted the frequent occurrence of psychosomatic illness in violent criminals who began to acknowledge their guilt during psychotherapy in prison (Hyatt Williams, 1999). There is often a paranoid element in hypochondria with the patients feeling persecuted by an internal superego figure who they feel is imposing the feared illness on them as a punishment. The patient is preoccupied by the thoughts of the illness as a threat and anxiously looks for signs of the onset of symptoms. This is in contrast to hysterical patients who appear not to experience guilt and whose symptoms allow them to avoid any sense of responsibility for what is occurring in their relationships. In all of these states, when psychotherapy is embarked on, the patient's psychopathology will become central to the transference relationship towards the therapist and it will also affect the therapist powerfully in the counter-transference.

An important factor in understanding hysteria is to recognize the patient's avoidance of emotional conflict. The avoidance also exists in the relationship with others, when the conversion process becomes a way of avoiding emotional honesty and displacing the issue into the body where it can be got rid of. It is no longer symbolized or communicated by words, feelings, or fantasies, nor does the patient feel responsible for it. Inevitably, the emotional truth that is displaced is likely to be experienced as frightening and painful; hence the need for displacement into the body which brings relief. This can be seen to account for 'La belle indifférence', classically described in some hysterics who appear unconcerned about their symptoms. This is in contrast to patients with psychosomatic illness where the symptoms cause distress and suffering, but the patient is apparently unconcerned about their feelings.

The return of the emotional conflict to consciousness is therefore likely to be accompanied by intense anxiety. Successful treatment will depend on the patient's capacity to give up the avoidance and to work with the therapist to allow the difficult issues to be faced. If the unconscious conflict is to become conscious, the patient's ego or conscious self must develop the capacity to cope with the conflict. The therapist's interpretative work will have brought to the patient's attention the nature of the conflict and will also provide support to the patient's ego in accepting painful truth. A capacity for mature guilt will be an important part of coping with the truth. Inevitably and appropriately in psychodynamic psychotherapy, these problems become part of the transference feelings towards the psychotherapist. In the transference, the therapist may either be experienced as being under the control of the patient or, if the therapist maintains autonomy, they may be experienced as a cruel, persecutory figure, forcing the patient to suffer mental pain. The force of these projections explains the manipulative power that hysterical patients can demonstrate over mental health workers.

Clinical example

Mrs P., a 40-year-old patient with an hysterical personality, expected that the therapist would see the world exactly as she did. A disagreement with her view caused her to become angry at this unjust treatment. Attempts to interpret her wish to control the therapist led to her becoming aggressive and threatening. She stated that she experienced the therapist's reluctance to accept her view as a catastrophic attack on her psychic equilibrium and showed signs that she would decompensate into a more overtly paranoid state if the therapist continued to press his independent observation and comment upon her. She needed to feel in control of his thinking. She demonstrated the limits of a psychodynamic approach, since she could not cope with a full exploration of her interaction with the therapist without becoming distinctly paranoid in her thinking and agitated. It was clear that she would only be able to cope with supportive therapy and not an interpretative approach.

Hypnotic suggestion

The discovery by Charcot and others that hypnotic suggestion could give rise to hysterical symptoms demonstrates that the hysterical symptoms have a histrionic, deceptive component to them (Stewart, 1963). The symptoms can be created in the highly charged atmosphere of hypnosis and are equally easily removed (see Oakley's chapter in this volume, p. 312). The symptoms avoid the psychological truth but make a drama which is itself compelling. It is important to consider the psychodynamic understanding and formulation of hypnosis and its relationship to hysteria. Clearly in hypnosis a powerful magical figure, in the form of the hypnotist, is invited to take charge of the individual's free will — involving strong regressive dependency phantasies. Hypnosis runs the risk of being a collusion by the hypnotist with the patient's wish to be dependent on the hypnotist, handing over all power and action to him or her. The view of hypnosis as a purely benign process — often put forward by medical hypnotists and hypnotherapists — does not seem to take into account the pathological side of this system. The fantasy that the powerful hypnotist figure can solve problems in a magical omnipotent manner is likely to lead to disillusionment because it is based on a false idea shared by the patient and the hypnotist.

Stewart (1963) has pointed out that, despite the appearance to the contrary, the hypnotist is also controlled by the patient and is required to fit in with the rules of the game set by the patient. He suggests that the hypnotist may, in retaliation, have a desire to control the patient and manipulate their feelings. This is demonstrated in the hypnotic setting where the patient is invited to submit their conscious ego to the hypnotist. From a psychodynamic point of view this suggests strong counter-transference feelings in the hypnotist, giving rise to a desire to control the patient's conscious mind. While a dependent relationship may have an important therapeutic function in normal regression during illness, when there is a need to depend on a safe parental figure, the regression that occurs in hysteria can be a distortion of this helpful regression.

Stewart (1966) has also pointed out that hypnosis as a therapeutic technique suffers from severe drawbacks when attempting to deal with psychological truth in the therapeutic relationship, since it relies on a falsehood which introduces distortion in the relationship between the hypnotist and the patient.

Abreaction and catharsis

The techniques of abreaction or catharsis are based on the belief that letting out the traumatic memory will result in a removal of the hysterical symptom, and there is an assumption that a trauma can be expelled from the mind by the cathartic process when the traumatic memory is recovered. This process is analagous to the surgical idea of lancing the boil, as if the traumatic memory was the pus that could be released. Abreaction was practised in cases of war neurosis with hysterical symptoms derived from battle trauma. It is still sometimes used for cases of conversion hysteria. The procedure appears to rely on an inadequate psychological understanding of the mental conse-quences of trauma and the nature of traumatic memories. Modern work with traumatized patients indicates the likelihood that abreaction exacerbates the tendency for patients suffering from post-traumatic stress disorder to suffer from disturbing flashbacks to the trauma situation. Far from having a cathartic effect, these flashbacks may be repetitive and profoundly disturbing to the patient and represent an extreme difficulty in recovering from the trauma (Garland, 1998). One of the problems that can cause an impasse in psychodynamic treatment is a compulsive preoccupation with a past trauma which may be given an intense prominence leading to the patient's wasting of developmental opportunities in their lives (Temple, 1998).

The significance of the Oedipus complex

Freud developed the Oedipal theory of neurosis when he realized that memories could be subject to a serious distortion due to unconscious phantasy, and that the development problems and anxieties of each individual in negotiating a three-person relationship from a primary two-person relationship were significant aetiological factors in all neuroses. This has led to an accusation in recent years that Freud denied the common occurrence of sexual abuse and his views on the Oedipus complex led to its being overlooked (Masson, 1984). This has not been upheld by many clinicians who observe that Oedipal difficulties do play a part in the origin of neurosis and some forms of hysteria (see Miss A below), and this can be distinguished from the effects of sexual abuse which are of a different order. Sexual abuse involves complex problems of neglect in the early mother–child relation-ship, which have allowed a child to be exposed to the perverse sexuality that has strong elements of sadism.

Clinical example

Miss A., aged 15, is a patient who demonstrates the value of a psychodynamic approach in defusing a developmental conflict which has been displaced into the body. She had been admitted to an adolescent unit with a paralysis of her legs of functional origin. No neurological findings were elucidated. She was in a state of conflict at home with her mother, while her father seemed distant and did not intervene in this conflict. The conflict clearly had to do with her sexual development and her experience that she had to battle with her mother for her autonomy as a young woman. There was immediate improvement in her state of mind as a result of her admission, although her condition deteriorated following her mother's visits. There was evidence of considerable secondary gain from the illness, since being ill and in hospital removed her from the acutely conflictful situation.

She responded well to the interpretations made by the young male psychiatrist about the conflict situation, although she was at first shocked to acknowledge consciously a fight over sexuality with her mother. The psychiatrist was a helpful transference figure in being able to intervene actively as her father had failed to do and to cope with her accusations that he, like her mother, wished to control her. This conflict and a dialogue about it enabled her to find more appropriate ways of recognizing her feelings, and the necessity for her to be paralyzed gradually reduced. Presumably an unconscious motive in the paralysis was that it made it impossible for her physically to fight with her mother. The improvement in the paralysis was reversed when she was under stress or when a discussion about her return home took place. Such an unconscious motive is distinguished from malingering by its stability and long-lasting nature and by the absence of a conscious wish to manipulate. Malingering patients are extremely reluctant to enter psychodynamic exploration. The adherence to lying and falsehood is an important part of their psychopathology and allows a triumph over those who engage with them (see Bass's chapter in this volume, p. 126).

The limitations of psychodynamic treatment for hysteria

Although hysteria proved to be such a fertile field for the development of early psychoanalytic technique and theory, in modern practice hysterics are not always the easiest patients to treat by a psychodynamic approach. Indeed, in some cases it may be contraindicated, especially when the patient demonstrates an inability to explore his or her conflicts openly in the context of the relationship with the therapist.

Follow-up studies of the psychoanalysis of hysterical patients have not been reassuring. Elizabeth Zetzel (1968) and Knapp et al. (1960) surveyed the psychoanalytic treatment of hysterics and demonstrated that while it could be successful, it was also often a failure. One problem was that there were obviously different types of hysterical patient. This led to a distinction being made between the hysteric and the hysterical personality. Zetzel, in reviewing this situation, suggested that a diagnosis of either 'hysterical character' or 'hysterical neurosis' tended to fall into one of four subgroups. These subgroups were defined according to the patient's capacity to enter into an exploratory therapeutic relationship. Zetzel's first group showed a positive capacity to use a therapeutic relationship to help them (as in the case of Miss A. already described), while at the other extreme, the fourth group had chronic hysterical symptoms and were highly intolerant of an exploratory relationship (like Mrs P. already described).

She noted that the patients in groups 3 and 4 tended to have distorted relationships with their therapist and were unable to explore their thoughts and fantasies without believing that the therapist might really be a gratifying parent figure or lover on the one hand or a critical persecutor on the other. Neither were they able to develop any insight that these perceptions might be the result of their own projections.

This situation is well illustrated by Stewart's (1977) case in which his hysterical patient, who was preoccupied with a sexual fantasy about him, became convinced that he was sexually excited by her and had an erection. On several occasions she attempted to touch him to discover whether this was so. The analyst was forced to restrain her from doing this — clearly with a less experienced, more anxious, or less physically strong therapist it would have been necessary to break off the treatment rapidly at this point. Fortunately, Stewart was able to manage the situation and to continue the treatment, with a good outcome over a long period. This kind of distorted thinking about the therapist is characteristic of some borderline patients and tends to be indicative of early disturbance in the dyadic relationship with the mother rather than the Oedipal-level neurotic disturbance which was originally thought by Freud to underlie hysteria. This sort of patient has a problem in distinguishing their own thoughts and feelings from those that they attribute to others around them. In Stewart's patient there is a concrete assumption that because she is sexually excited, he is also.

Stewart's paper graphically warns of the problems of treating severely disturbed hysterics and describes some problems which may be encountered. This is also the kind of disturbance which can be seen in somatizing patients with very concrete beliefs about their physical symptoms. This symptomatology is not in the descriptive sense psychotic, but it is developmentally primitive and is based on profound problems about the capacity to symbolize within a relationship. As Segal (1988) has pointed out, these defects in symbolization resulting in concrete thinking have their root in failures to negotiate emotional development in the first year of life. This involves the infant's developing capacity to cope with ambivalence towards its mother at the depressive position and the necessity of finding ways to verbalize these problems.

Recent work has shown that in patients with chronic hysterical symptoms there are considerable areas of overlap with borderline personality disorder. Hysterical conversion cannot therefore be seen as a simple neurotic condition, and thus therapeutic work is far from straightforward. In patients with severe and chronic conversion hysteria there may be overlap with more primitive mechanisms in which reality is disavowed, and in some cases this can lead to actual clinical psychotic episodes, when the patient is under severe stress. The most clear precursor of this kind of problem is when a patient can only experience the therapist in a concrete manner and not as a real other person who has an existence which is independent of the patient's mind.

Interpretation or elucidation of an underlying conflict may prove to be extremely difficult for the patient to accept, since it will involve a radical change in attitudes towards him or herself and family members by revealing unconscious feelings and wishes which are unacceptable. Inevitably this will become part of the transference relationship with the therapist, when the therapist will be felt to be forcing the patient to accept unpleasant aspects of themselves. This is one of the reasons for impasse in treatment, when the resistance to accepting difficult conflicts may prevent psychic development.

The decline in the prevalence of hysteria

A change in cultural attitudes towards physical symptoms as displacements of emotional states seems to have occurred in Western societies. Hysterical conversion is much less common (Leff, 1988), although it is still encountered in neurological practice and often in young adolescents, children, and in some groups of patients from ethnic minorities. In the latter, the cultural attitude towards mental conflict may be different from the prevailing Western approach, which has been significantly influenced by psychoanalytic ideas and other ideas about the value of greater emotional expression of conflict and rejection of the idea that it is better to repress feelings than to express them. It may be that adolescents who are allowed a reasonable expression of their emotional conflict with parents are likely to be protected from the development of hysterical symptoms. It is certainly the case that patients who suffer from anorexia have extreme difficulty in dealing with ambivalence and conflict in personal relationships. They attempt to deal with emotional conflict in themselves by means of intense control of their bodies.

Other somatic conditions, such as anorexia nervosa and chronic fatigue syndrome, may have taken the place of classical hysterical conversion. Certainly, they currently command much more media attention than hysteria. This is contradicted by the experience of neurologists and neuro-psychiatrists, who still see many hysterical patients (see the chapter in this volume by Akagi and House, p. 73).

In discussing the place of psychodynamic psychotherapy in the treatment of conversion hysteria, it is important to be clear that Freud's early model no longer holds as the main basis of a therapeutic approach. The continuing development of psychodynamic theory and psychoanalytic practice has led to replacement of the instinctual model by the object–relations approach which focusses on the detailed work with the patient's relationships in the past and present; both the patient's unconscious internal world and its interaction with their present-day relationships will be important in the psychotherapy. There has been a distinct tendency for psychodynamic therapies to be criticized for therapeutic methods and theories which in fact belong to an historical era of psychoanalysis and which have long since been superseded by modern theory and practice based on a more complex model of psychological development. Modern practice has enabled psychodynamic treatment to be applied to more seriously disturbed patients, particularly those with personality disorders. Recent outcome studies are beginning to demonstrate its effectiveness with such patients (Sandell *et al.*, 1997).

The evidence base for psychodynamic psychotherapy

Roth and Fonagy (1996), in their review of the evidence for clinical effectiveness of psychological treatments, pointed out the lack of randomized controlled trials for psychodynamic psychotherapy. Their review excluded studies which did not specify the psychodynamic treatment for specific diagnostic categories, which led to the exclusion of some good studies, as psychodynamic psychotherapy does not usually focus on diagnostic categories. Since then a number of controlled studies have been published which begin to show the effectiveness of psychodynamic therapies and psychoanalysis, including longer-term therapies.

Although specific outcome trials on the psychodynamic treatment of hysteria are not yet available, a number of studies have emerged since Roth and Fonagy's review which demonstrate the effectiveness of brief psychodynamic psychotherapy for anxiety and depression: for example, Piper *et al.* (1998); Sandell *et al.* (1999*a*); Guthrie *et al.* (1999). In the latter study, the treatment resulted in improved social functioning and reduced health utilization.

In the field of personality disorders (including patients with borderline personality disorders where there are often hysterical features), recent studies have shown that psychodynamic treatments are effective in comparison to controls: for example, Dolan *et al.* (1997); Bateman and Fonagy (1999); Svartberg and Stiles (1999). New outcome studies on psychodynamic and psychoanalytic treatment methods are appearing at a considerable rate, many of which involve long-term follow-up of treatment. These are reviewed by Fonagy *et al.* (1999).

These findings suggest that Andrews (1999) has not taken into account recent publications when he states that 'long term dynamic psychotherapy derived from the ideas of Freud has not in the 50 years since the first randomized controlled trial been shown to be superior to talking to a mature and kindly adviser'. The present relative lack of enough good controlled trials for psychodynamic psychotherapy places it alongside about 70 per cent of medical psychiatric practice for which there is as yet no clear evidence for its efficacy (Richardson and McPherson, 2000). Sandell *et al.*'s (1999*b*) large-scale Stockholm study has gone a considerable way to demonstrating the effectiveness of long-term psychodynamic therapy and psychoanalysis. While these large-scale studies include some cases of hysteria, specific randomised controlled trials of the psychodynamic treatment of hysteria are inevitably difficult to organize because of the small number of cases seen.

Conclusion

In conclusion, psychodynamic psychotherapy does have a place in the treatment of hysteria —particularly for patients whose condition is part of a developmental crisis rather than an established, long-standing pattern of relating to others. In the latter patients the disorder has its roots in a very early disturbance in the mother–child relationship.

For patients in a crisis, who have retreated from conflict and difficulties in their psychological development into hysterical symptoms, a psychodynamic approach is likely to be effective because it concentrates on the interaction between the patient and the therapist as a means of both understanding conflict and of finding a way of resolving it within the relationship. Hysterical symptoms of this kind may represent a short-term regression from the capacity to use language and imagination within a relationship to explain and resolve internal conflict.

It is much more uncertain what place psychodynamic treatments have for the more severely disturbed chronic hysteric characterized by a lifelong pattern of disturbance in the capacity to relate, and the hysterical symptoms represent a serious defect in the patient's capacity to make and maintain relationships. These patients have some features in common with severe borderline personality disorder. Their treatment should only be undertaken cautiously by experienced therapists who need to be aware of the dangers and the possibility of a poor outcome following difficult and challenging work. Success with this group of patients is likely to be the result of more extended treatment. A psychodynamic approach may have a special contribution to make to the informed management of hysterical patients in day hospital or in-patient settings.

If careful assessment is carried out there are many patients whose conflict situation can be assisted by psychodynamic therapy. They can be encouraged to develop ways of dealing with psychic conflict which are based on language and a capacity for symbolic fantasy rather than physical symptoms.

Overall, psychodynamic work has a valuable contribution to make to the study and treatment of hysteria because it provides a rich perspective of explanation and understanding between patient and therapist, which can engage the patient in a dialogue about human meaning rather than about physical symptoms.

References

Andrews, G. (1999). Randomized controlled trials in psychiatry: important but poorly accepted. *British Medical Journal*, **319**, 562–4.

Balint, M. (1965). *Primary Love and Psychoanalytic Technique*. London, Tavistock Publications.

Barker, P. (1996). *The Regeneration Trilogy*. Penguin Books, London.

Bateman, A. and Fonagy, P. (1999). The effectiveness of partial hospitalization in the treatment of borderline personality disorder — a randomised controlled trial. *American Journal of Psychiatry*, **156**, 1563–9.

Dolan, B., Warren, F. and Norton, K. (1997). Change in borderline symptoms one year after therapeutic community treatment for severe personality disorder. *British Journal of Psychiatry*, **171**, 274–9.

Fairbairn, W. R. D. (1952). *Psychoanalytic Studies of the Personality*. London, Tavistock Publications.

Fonagy, P., Kachele, R., Jones, E. and Perron, R. (1999). An open-door review of outcome studies in psychoanalysis: Report prepared by the Research Committee of the IPA. Available at http://www.ipa.org.uk/R-outcome.htm.

Freud, S. (1895). Studies in hysteria. *Standard Edn, Vol. II*, p. 148. London, Hogarth Press.

Freud, S. (1905). Fragment of an analysis of a case of hysteria. *Standard Edn, Vol. VII*, p 43. London, Hogarth Press.

Freud, S. (1910). A special type of object choice made by men. *Standard Edn, Vol. XI*, p. 171. London, Hogarth Press.

Freud, S. (1926). Inhibitions, symptoms and anxiety. *Standard Edn, Vol. XX*, p. 99. London, Hogarth Press.

Garland, C. (ed.) (1998). *Understanding Trauma: A Psychoanalytical Approach*. London, Duckworth, Tavistock Clinic Series.

Guthrie, E. *et al.* (1999). Cost-effectiveness of brief psychodynamic-interpersonal therapy in high utilizers of psychiatric services. *Archives of General Psychiatry*, **56**, 519–26.

Hyatt Williams, A. (1999). *Cruelty, Violence and Murder — Understanding the Criminal Mind*, p. 16. Karnac Books, London.

Klein, M. (1952). Some theoretical conclusions regarding the emotional life of the infant. In *The Writings of Melanie Klein, Vol. 3, Envy and Gratitude and Other Works* (1975). London, Hogarth Press.

Knapp, P. *et al.* (1960). Suitability for psychoanalysis: a review of one hundred supervised analytic cases. *Psycho-Analysis Quarterly*, **29**.

Leff, J. P. (1988). The history and geography of hysteria. In *Psychiatry Around the Globe*, Chapter 5. Gaskell, London.

Marty, P. and de Muzan, M. (1963). La pensée opératoire. *Revue Français Psychoanalytique*, **27** **(suppl)**, 1345–56.

Masson, J. (1984). The Assault on Truth. New York, Farrar Strauss and Giroux.

Piper, W. E., Joyce, A. S., McCallum, M. and Azim, H. A. (1998). Interpretive and supportive forms of psychotherapy and patient personality variables. *Journal of Consulting and Clinical Psychology*, **66**, 558–67.

Richardson, P. and McPherson, S. (2000). *Clinical Audit and Clinical Effectiveness Resource Pack for Clinicians*. Tavistock and Portman NHS Trust.

Roth, A. and Fonagy, P. (1996). *What Works for Whom? A Critical Review of Psychotherapy Research*. New York. Guilford.

Sandell, R., Blomberg, J. and Lazar, A. (1997). When reality doesn't fit the blueprint: doing research on psychoanalysis and long term psychotherapy in a public health service programme. *Psychotherapy Research*, **7**, 333–44.

Sandell, R., Blomberg, J., Lazar, A., Schubert, J., Carlsson, J. and Broberg, J. (1999*a*). [As time goes by: long-term outcomes of psychoanalysis and long-term psychotherapy.] *Forum der Psychoanalyse: Zeitschrift Fuer Klinische Theorie & Praxis*, **15(4)**, 327–47.

Sandell, R., Blomberg, J. and Lazar, A. (1999*b*). [Reported long-term follow-up of long-term psychotherapies and psychoanalyses. First results of the 'Stockholm Outcome of Psychotherapy (STOP) Project'.] *Zeitschrift Fuer Psychosomatische Medizin und Psychoanalyse*, **45(1)**, 43–56.

Segal, H. (1988). Notes on symbol formation. In *Melanie Klein Today, Vol. 1: Mainly Theory* (ed. Spillius, E. B.). London, Routledge.

Sifneos, P. E. (1973). The prevalence of Alexithymic characteristics in psychosomatic patients. *Psychotherapy and Psychosomatics*, **22**, 255–62.

Sifneos, P. E. (1975). Problems of psychotherapy of patients with Alexithymic characteristics and physical disease. *Psychotherapy and Psychosomatics*, **26**, 65–70.

Stewart, H. (1963). A comment on the psychodynamics of the hypnotic state. *International Journal of Psycho-Analysis*, **44**, 372.

Stewart, H. (1966). On consciousness, negative hallucinations and the hypnotic state. *International Journal of Psycho-Analysis*, **47**, 50.

Stewart, H. (1977). Problems of management in the analysis of an hallucinating hysteric. *International Journal of Psycho-Analysis*, **58**, 67.

Svartberg, M. and Stiles, T. (1999). *The Trondheim Psychotherapy Study: A Randomised Trial of Short Term Dynamic Therapy vs. Cognitive Therapy for Cluster C Personality Disorder*. Paper presented to the Thirtieth International Conference of the Society for Psychotherapy Research, Braga, Portugal, June 1999.

Temple, N. O. T. (1986). The significance of guilt in somatic reactions to change. In *Bulletin of the British Psycho-analytical Society*, **No. 9**.

Temple, N. O. T. (1996). Transference and counter-transference. In *Forensic Psychotherapy, Crime Psychodynamics and the Offender Patient, Vol. 1, Mainly Theory* (ed. Cordess, C. and Cox, M.), pp. 23–39. London, Kingsley.

Temple, N. O. T. (1998). Development injury: its effect on the inner world. In *Understanding Trauma: A Psychoanalytical Approach* (ed. Garland, C.). London, Duckworth, Tavistock Clinic Series.

Winnicott, D. (1965). *The Maturational Processes and the Facilitating Environment*. London, Hogarth Press.

Zetzel, E. (1968). The so-called good hysteric. *International Journal of Psycho-Analysis*, **49**, 256.

21 Cognitive behavioural therapy as a treatment for conversion disorders

Trudie Chalder

The purpose of this chapter is to outline a model for understanding so-called 'conversion' symptoms and to describe an approach to management based on the model. The model assumes that a number of factors contribute to the onset of symptoms but that once established, a combination of physiological, cognitive, behavioural, and social factors interact to maintain them. It also assumes that behavioural and/or cognitive changes will bring about physiological change. Pragmatic cognitive and behavioural interventions evolve from the model and vary according to the individual and the chronicity of the condition.

Clinical manifestations

Patients present with a variety of symptoms and disabilities ranging from a perceived inability to see to a perceived inability to walk. Primarily, this chapter will focus on those individuals who are unable to move a limb or who cannot walk — that is, those with hysterical paralysis.

Definition

The term 'conversion hysteria' is often used in place of 'conversion disorder'. Both are inadequate for a number of reasons, not least because they are often seen as pejorative and judgemental by the patient. However, they can also be misleading, and if used in clinical practice are apt to alienate and upset the patient (see Merskey's chapter in this volume, p. 171). In DSM–IV, the diagnostic criteria for conversion disorder include the presence of psychological conflicts and primary and secondary gain (Mayo *et al.* 1995). It is often difficult though, especially in the early stages of assessment, to ascertain a specific psychological trigger, and the concept of secondary gain is a dubious one for which there is no conclusive evidence. It is clear that the current classification system is unsatisfactory from both a descriptive and explanatory perspective (Mayou *et al.* 1995; see also Wessely's chapter in this volume, p. 63). However, given the lack of an acceptable alternative the term conversion disorder will be used in this chapter.

Mind–body dualism

Society tends to view illness and disease in a *dualistic way* — the problems are seen as being either physical or psychological. If there is an obvious physical cause then the problem is perceived as being 'real', whereas illnesses without demonstrable organic pathology are viewed as being 'all in the mind' or psychiatric and therefore potentially 'not real'. The model inherent in our society and therefore our health service is inadequate. It assumes that because we cannot find specific organic pathology to account for the symptoms that the symptom does not exist and cannot be treated. This is reflected in the attitudes and behaviour of some doctors and many others. Largely speaking, the doctor has internalized the current scientific approach to disease. That is, a linear cause–effect model in which aetiological pathogenic agents lead to bodily pathology (Singh *et al.* 1981).

This split between mind and body has been traced back to Rene Descartes' dualistic philosophy of the seventeenth century, but these ideas were not entirely new. They evolved from earlier ideas espoused by the Greeks. For example, Plato saw man as being divided between the soul (of divine origin) and the body (its fleshly prison). Clearly this presents the patient with a problem. The patients referred to in this chapter have real physical symptoms, but on the whole do not have demonstrable organic pathology to account for them. Some will have an obvious psychiatric disorder such as depression or anxiety, but many will not. The patient senses that something is wrong and tries to make sense of their experience. It is taught from childhood that a visit to the doctor seems to be a sensible course of action. There is an expectation that after an adequate assessment the doctor will reveal the cause of the symptoms and will then state clearly what needs to be done in order to get better (Singh *et al.* 1981).

In patients with a conversion disorder this does not happen for a number of reasons. First, the doctor's knowledge of the physiological and psychological processes associated with the patient's symptom and disability may be inadequate, resulting in a mismatch between patient and doctor's explanatory models. Second, it is rare for patients to be offered specific practical advice with ongoing support about how to manage their symptom or illness. Simply reassuring the patient that everything is normal does not work. Neither does providing them with a psychiatric diagnosis such as depression, anxiety, or conversion disorder. The patient will understandably feel that the doctor is refusing to acknowledge the reality of the symptoms and clinical experience suggests that they will feel misunderstood, insulted, or even abused. This is not to say that psychological problems are not real, but the patient may feel this to be the case.

Model for understanding conversion disorders

Given that it is important that the treatment approach used is based on a sound theoretical framework, a *hypothetical* model will now be described. A distinction is made between factors which predispose, precipitate, and perpetuate the condition. It seems likely that a variety of factors contribute to the onset which culminate in a physiological reaction, the precise mechanism of which is unknown, while different factors are responsible for the maintenance of the symptoms and associated disability. Pragmatic cognitive and behavioural interventions are based on the model and initially focus on perpetuating factors. Later on in treatment, factors which triggered the symptoms may be addressed in order to prevent relapse.

Predisposing factors

Little is known about what makes an individual vulnerable to developing conversion disorders, although some progress has been made in other somatoform disorders (see Craig's chapter in this volume, p. 88). However, there is good evidence that childhood experiences of illness affects expression of distress in adulthood (Craig *et al.* 1993; Hotopf 1996).

Precipitating factors

Physical illnesses

Many conversion disorders appear to begin with a specific organic or physical illness such as an infection (Vandvik and Skjeldal 1994). Probable or definite Guillain–Barre syndrome has been associated with the onset of conversion disorders (Buschbacher 1995) and the difficulties in distinguishing the two have been discussed (Wherry *et al.* 1991). Many patients with non-epileptic attacks report having had an epileptic seizure in the past related to epilepsy or rapid withdrawal from alcohol.

Life events

In a case-controlled study investigating factors associated with acute motor symptom disability due to a conversion disorder, an increased number of negative life events before the onset of the problem were associated with the symptoms (Binzer *et al.* 1997). This topic is dealt with in more detail in the chapter in this volume by Craig (p. 88).

Relationship conflicts

It is inevitable that children who develop conversion symptoms will have relationship difficulties with parents (Dittmann 1994; Kukleta *et al.* 1997). Whether this is related to the cause or effect of the symptoms is not established. However, little is known about the quality of close relationships in adults with conversion disorders.

Modelling

It is not unusual for patients with conversion symptoms to have specific knowledge or experience of a disease which presents itself in a similar way to their current complaint. For example, patients with non-epileptic attacks may have witnessed epileptic seizures in others.

Perpetuating factors

Once a particular symptom has been triggered, the problem is maintained essentially by cognitive and behavioural factors such as fear and avoidance.

Behavioural responses

In its chronic stage (that is, after six months), some patients with conversion disorders are substantially disabled. They have gradually slipped into an inconsistent approach to engaging in activities and exercise, consistent with their fear of making symptoms worse and the perception that they cannot sustain a particular action. With the passage of time problems of disuse set in. The longer the duration of immobility, the more wasted the muscles become and the harder it is for the individual to either motivate him or herself to engage in movement or to actually move even if the intention is there. This process is very similar in chronic pain and chronic fatigue syndrome (CFS), where the role of avoidance behaviour is central in sustaining the cycle of symptoms and disability (Philips 1987; Chalder *et al.* 1996; Sharpe *et al.* 1992).

In the long term, a variety of other more subtle behaviours (for example, persistent reassurance seeking) intended to check current health status, actually serves to perpetuate symptom focussing, increases the intensity of symptoms and preoccupation with the illness, and further increases levels of disability. The same process is seen in hypochondriasis (Salkovskis 1991).

Cognitive responses

Most patients with medically unexplained somatic complaints, regardless of the type, have a tendency to persistently misinterpret innocuous physical symptoms as evidence of something more serious. In CFS, patients are fearful of making the symptom of fatigue worse (Chalder *et al.* 1996); in chronic pain, patients worry about exacerbating the pain (Philips 1987); in hypochondriasis, physical symptoms are interpreted as evidence of serious disease such as AIDS. In patients with conversion disorders there is usually a worry that activity or exercise will make the condition worse in the long term or that the doctors have indeed missed something serious which may be detected on further tests. There is some evidence, in patients with CFS and in those who present in primary care with unexplained somatic symptoms, that they have a general tendency to misinterpret bodily symptoms, and that this is not necessarily peculiar to their current health status (Butler *et al.* in press; Sensky *et al.* 1996), implying that the process may be important as a primary aetological factor.

Physiological responses

Interestingly, with the advent of new technology such as PET, functional anatomy and physiological processes associated with medically unexplained somatic experiences such as hysterical paralysis are being elucidated (Marshall *et al.* 1997). Research in this area is in its early stages, but as methodologies are refined, further work of this kind may help to distinguish patients with hysterical symptoms from those who might be feigning.

Summary

A variety of complex factors such as childhood experience of illness and stressful life events are associated with the onset of symptoms. Symptoms are then maintained and perpetuated by unhelpful cognitions and avoidant or maladaptive coping strategies. Patient behaviour is also influenced by the behaviour of health professionals. Whilst the prevailing culture in the health service is dualistic, health professionals and patients will continue to misunderstand one another. A three-systems model that incorporates physiological, cognitive, and behavioural aspects of illness can be useful for both understanding and managing these difficult problems.

It is easy to become judgemental about how patients manage their symptoms, but it is important to remember that patients have striven to make sense of a poorly understood condition and will have probably received a plethora of contradictory advice from health professionals and the media about the nature of the problem and its management. Many patients report unsatisfactory communications with health professionals (Davison *et al.* 1999). Some patients will be depressed or anxious, but those who are not will undoubtedly feel very frustrated and demoralized at being stuck in an ever-increasing spiral of symptoms and disability.

Management

Acute conversion

In new onset cases it is very important to develop a therapeutic alliance and negotiate the diagnosis with the patient as soon as possible. In addition, good communication between primary, secondary, and tertiary care is essential (McCahill 1995; Davison *et al.* 1999) as patients often report considerable disagreement between doctors about diagnosis and aetiology. Irrespective of the intervention used, a clear rationale which seems to make sense to the patient and health professional should always be provided. It is sensible to avoid overly sophisticated psychodynamic explanations as patients are likely to be defensive about the nature of their difficulties and may not necessarily agree with such an explanation. If rehabilitation comprising exercise or physiotherapy is suggested, a rationale based on the three-systems model will probably facilitate compliance.

In adults, evidence suggests that behavioural treatment consisting of physiotherapy for new onset conversion disorders can provide clinically significant, long-lasting resolution of symptoms (Baker and Silver 1987; Speed 1996). A 42-year-old woman with a three-week history of left forearm weakness associated with relationship difficulties with her mother was treated with a combination of assertiveness training and practice of motor tasks to enhance movement in the forearm (Kukleta *et al.* 1997).

In children, a number of controlled single-subject designs support the use of contingent reinforcement in the treatment of conversion disorders (Scott Mizes 1985). For example, three children with hysterical blindness were asked to point out big letters which appeared on a board. Verbal praise was given to them when they answered questions correctly and gradually the letters were changed to a smaller size. This was combined with an unspecified family intervention. All three improved significantly, with two regaining full visual ability (Abe *et al.* 1987).

Chronic conversion

Cognitive behavioural treatment

A cognitive behavioural model enables a practitioner to carry out a comprehensive assessment and to make an individual formulation of the patient's problems which then lead on to effective cognitive behavioural treatment. Cognitive behaviour therapy is a pragmatic approach to managing symptoms which enables patients to change aspects of their behaviour and the way in which they think in order to bring about a change in symptoms. This model is widely used in the treatment of anxiety disorders and is referred to as Lang's three-systems model (Lang 1978; Hugdahl 1981). Physiological, behavioural, and cognitive processes operate largely in synchrony with one another. Changing one particular system, such as the person's behaviour, will bring about changes in the other two response systems.

Treatment is usually conducted on a one-to-one basis, fortnightly. Although patients who have an acute 'conversion' may respond quite quickly to support and specific rehabilitation, those with long-standing problems may need considerably more sessions over a long period of time. In order to sustain behavioural changes it may be desirable to follow up some patients for several years.

Each treatment session is structured. At the start of every session an agenda is agreed between patient and therapist. This is to ensure that all issues are addressed within the time available. Sessions usually last up to one hour. Homework, which takes the form of specific behavioural or cognitive goals which have previously been agreed, are discussed. Success with homework and problems are discussed. New homework is negotiated and agreed upon by therapist and patient. At the end of each session, key points discussed are summarized. The therapist always keeps in mind the end of treatment targets which have previously been agreed, as these are to be worked towards systematically, through the following series of phases:

Phase 1 — behavioural analysis

Phase 2 — developing a therapeutic alliance

Phase 3 — generating the willingness to change

Phase 4 — giving the patient a rationale for treatment

Phase 5 — conducting the treatment

Phase 6 — generalizing the progress and ending treatment

Phase 1 — behavioural analysis

During the first session, a behavioural analysis should be conducted using the three-system's model as guidance. As well as information about the number and severity of symptoms, it is important to establish precisely what the patient is unable to do as a consequence of the symptoms or impairment, for example, a paralysed arm. Compensatory behaviours such as carrying out all tasks with one fully functioning arm should be noted. This is similar to how patients who have had a stroke often cope. Patients should be asked to describe a couple of typical days detailing social, work, private, and home-related activities. It is important to get some idea, however vague at this stage, about whether the patient has long-term plans regarding work. Some patients will spend a lot of time talking about their symptoms and/or seeking reassurance and such like. It is essential that details regarding these behaviours are elicited, as these will be the focus of the intervention initially, regardless of what contributed to the onset.

Specific fears about the nature of symptoms and illness attributions should be enquired about. Future discussions will be directed to some extent by the patient's degree of psychological sophistication and perceptions about the illness; these will give a helpful, longitudinal view of the illness which is important in establishing what was happening in the patient's life before onset of the illness. Enquiring about family illness in childhood may be helpful later on in treatment but may serve to aggravate the patient if asked about too early. It is important to check whether the patient is depressed or anxious. Finally, it can be revealing to ask how the patient thinks his or her life might be in five years' time and whether any changes are envisaged.

Phase 2 — developing a therapeutic alliance

During the early phases of treatment, any communication that could be interpreted negatively should be avoided. There should be a value-free acceptance of the patient's world and no attempt should be made to try to dissuade the patient from his or her point of view. The patient must feel listened to. It is imperative to be explicit in conveying belief in the reality of the symptom; the patient may be hypervigilant in looking for signs that he or she is not believed and should not be given any grounds for suspicion. In keeping with the three-systems model already described, any discussion about whether the problem is psychological or physical should be avoided.

It is likely that the patient's views about what is wrong will be, and will have been, influenced by interactions with health professionals. Usually, when a broad, interactive model of the patient's symptoms is adopted, antagonistic responses are avoided. Even if the view of the health professional is markedly different from that of the patient, it is important that the patient's view is respected and not contradicted. The focus of the discussion should shift from one of cause to one of symptom management. This will inherently challenge the therapeutic nihilism and the feeling that nothing can be done, which at times clouds both the patient and health professional's view of the problem. By joining with the patient, cognitive dissonance will be minimized. The patient gradually begins to trust the health professional and to offer more information, which adds to the formulation and understanding of the problem.

In short, qualities such as warmth, patience, empathy, persistence, being supportive, hopeful, non-confrontational, but realistic, are an essential basis for change. The role of positive reinforcement and praise has been highlighted by a number of authors (Abe *et al.* 1987; Donohue *et al.* 1997; Brady and Lind 1961). The therapist should not rush the patient but should almost wait until the patient is displaying signs of frustration at the approach. It can be helpful to tell the patient that change takes a lot of time and effort but that if he or she perseveres, some change will occur. The therapist should not be tempted to stray off into other territories but should remain focussed.

Phase 3 — generating the willingness to change

The next phase involves persuading the patient that change is possible. Many patients feel demoralized when presenting for treatment and may already have seen a number of other professionals who have not offered any hope of recovery or improvement. Several studies have demonstrated that support is experienced positively by patients and helps to elicit behavioural change. It can be helpful to examine formally the advantages and disadvantages of change. Research carried out demonstrating the effectiveness of a particular intervention should be shared with the patient.

Phase 4 — giving the patient a rationale for treatment

After an assessment has been completed, a preliminary formulation of the patient's problems can be made. This should be integrated into a rationale for treatment. It is essential that the formulation and rationale for treatment is individualized, making it acceptable and plausible to the patient. It is impossible and foolish to include everything in the rationale for treatment at the beginning. At best it would confuse the patient, at worst it would antagonize him or her. It can be helpful to divide the rationale for treatment into two parts. The first will involve some discussion about factors which precipitated the problem; the second will include more detailed discussion about the factors which have maintained it and how any unhelpful patterns can be changed. The rationale will need to be repeated several times during treatment.

The rationale should be based on a coherent model which makes sense to the patient and which is honest. Lang's three-systems model that relates physiological, behavioural, and cognitive responses, should be used to illustrate the approach (Lang 1978). That is, physiological changes in the central nervous system will be perpetuated by unhelpful cognitions, possibly related to the fear of making symptoms worse, as well as unhelpful behaviour such as avoidance of activity or exercise. Undoubtedly, changes will have occurred in the central nervous system which as yet are not clearly understood. However, it is likely that these changes are reversible and that alteration in behaviour will bring about physiological changes.

Tactfully, the patient should be told that some of the things that he or she does in order to try to control the symptoms inadvertently make them worse and that effective coping is different in acute and chronic illnesses. Emphasizing the physical nature of the problem can be strategically helpful (Teasell and Shapiro 1994). Physical illness analogies can illustrate the approach, for example, physical rehabilitation is helpful after strokes. It can be helpful to explain that in the majority of illnesses, the degree of pathology does not match the degree of disability.

An example of a treatment rationale for someone with an inability to walk, diagnosed as conversion disorder, is as follows:

> It sounds as though from what you've said that the problem started about three years ago after you were diagnosed as having Guillain Barre syndrome. You mentioned that you were particularly busy at work at the time and had been feeling under pressure given your new management responsibilities. Your wife had just had a fourth baby and you had had to go away on a management course. You were rushed into hospital and, as I understand it, there was some confusion over not only the diagnosis but also the advice you were given about the prognosis and how to get better. Am I right in thinking that things have never really been right since then? . . .

> You described how the weakness in your legs improved a little at first but then, despite having two courses of physiotherapy, the symptoms of fatigue and the weakness in your

legs increased again and, in an attempt to make yourself better, you started to rest . . . rather than to persist with the rehabilitation which you were struggling with. Initially, resting worked, but when you tried to return to work the weakness got worse again. So gradually over a long period of time your ability to do things reduced and the symptoms got worse. And as I understand it, you now have difficulty standing without the aid of your wife. Does that seem like a fair description so far?

At this point there may be some discussion about the course of the illness and how resting, even though helpful in the short term, can inadvertently make the symptoms worse in the long term. This will lead automatically into the next phase of the rationale; that is, how to do things differently and what to expect.

So, even though it is understandable that you rest when you feel weak and that it probably feels impossible to move your legs, immobility in the long term can only result in one thing . . . more weakness and loss of muscle bulk and fitness. In fact, did you know that bed rest results in a 3 per cent reduction in muscle bulk per day? So, in the long term, inactivity and lack of exercise will contribute to you remaining disabled. I understand that you are worried about making the problem worse, but if you carry out specific exercises and tasks consistently, every day, you will slowly start to build up both your activity levels and your strength again. In the early stages we will ask the physiotherapist for advice about specific exercises which will help.

More detailed discussion about the precise nature of activity scheduling is required and the patient should be told that the rationale is to break the association between experiencing symptoms and stopping activity. The patient should continue with whatever he or she is doing, despite being symptomatic; symptoms will then improve gradually with time. The key to success in the beginning is consistency, starting off at a low enough level of activity or exercise to achieve success and gradually increasing activity as confidence grows. It can take many months and sometimes years for patients to reach their long-term goals.

Clearly, for those patients who have been inactive for a long time, problems of disuse may have developed and change will be more difficult. Goals should be realistic and made according to the individual needs of the patient.

Phase 5 — conducting the treatment

The interventions used will depend entirely on the assessment and the nature of the presenting problem. At the outset of treatment, the patient's relatives or significant other people should be involved in the treatment process. This is essential when treating children and adolescents, but in adults the behaviour of others may shape the patient's illness behaviour, often dramatically. It is wise when planning treatment of any kind to start with the simplest solution. The patient is more likely to comply with treatment and, if successful, will repeat the intervention more enthusiastically. This usually means focussing on perpetuating factors such as inactivity (see Table 21.1).

For patients with conversion disorders, changing the pattern of activity takes time. Noticeable improvements in symptoms or disability often do not occur for several months. What is required is persistence and patience on the part of the health professional and the patient. In short, active treatment involves negotiating weekly targets of structured, planned activity and exercise.

Table 21.1 Interventions for patients with motor conversion disorders

1. Diary of behavioural avoidance or excess such as reassurance seeking
2. Physiotherapy (i.e. exercise non-functioning limb several times daily)
3. Graded consistent approach to activity
4. Establishing a sleep routine
5. Treatment of associated problems (e.g. exposure for phobias)
6. Attention to negative reinforcements i.e. family member may be reinforcing unhelpful illness behaviour
7. Ban on reassurance seeking
8. Cessation of investigations — all involved to agree to this
9. Discuss advantages and disadvantages of changing
10. Role play new behaviours face to face in session
11. Rationalize medication
12. Discuss how patient will explain improvement to others ('face saver' important)
13. Assertiveness training
14. Anger management
15. Cognitive restructuring
16. Make links between symptoms, mood, thoughts, and behaviour

Behavioural interventions

Physiotherapists can be of assistance in the early stages of treatment in patients with a conversion paralysis of the lower limbs. Some patients have difficulty making movements on request because of agonist and antagonist muscles contracting simultaneously. The physiotherapist can suggest balance exercises, such as using an unstable support, which necessitates the patient using the power of an under-functioning limb or trunk to prevent him or herself from toppling over. By increasing the difficulty of the balance exercises, the patient uses the limbs more (Delargy *et al.* 1986). Trunk balance and limb exercises help to improve muscle weakness which has developed from disuse. Once a patient has developed good balance, sitting, and then standing, standard gait training is encouraged.

Behavioural goals such as walking should then be focussed upon, but in addition a wider repertoire of activities such as household chores, socializing, concentration development, hobbies, and so on will also be included in the schedule. The emphasis is on consistency and breaking the association between experiencing symptoms and stopping activity. The goals are gradually built up as tolerance to symptoms increases, until the longer-term targets are reached. This usually takes several months. Patients are warned that a worsening of symptoms may occur as activities are increased but are advised to persist with the programme. Increases in symptoms, if any, are usually temporary. Tasks such as reading, which require concentration, can be included, but mental functioning does seem to improve in synchrony with physical functioning. Care must be taken when setting goals to ensure that these fall within the tolerance level of the patient.

Establishing a sleep routine

Disturbed sleep is not uncommon in patients with conversion disorders. Some complain of hypersomnia (sleeping too much), while others wake intermittently throughout the night. It is often associated with lack of activity and exercise, although sometimes it is related to worry. The quality of sleep will usually improve once the patient starts to do more. However, by tackling the sleep disturbance directly, a more rapid improvement is expected.

Early on in treatment, patients are asked to keep a diary of what time they go to bed, how long they sleep, what time they wake up, and what time they get up. The total number of hours spent asleep is calculated. Bed restriction is then used to improve the quality of sleep. A routine of going to bed and getting up at a pre-planned time, whilst simultaneously cutting out daytime catnaps, helps to prevent insomnia. Change in sleep routine can be done slowly depending on the severity of the problem (Morin *et al.* 1994). For those patients who worry when they get into bed, it can be useful to teach them problem-solving techniques which can be used prior to going to bed. Used in conjunction with stimulus control, where the patient is asked to get up, rather than to lie in bed tossing and turning, and then to return to bed fifteen minutes later, the effect can be quite powerful.

Cognitive restructuring

Worry about health will involve misperceptions about the meaning of symptoms. Most patients with conversion symptoms will experience a variety of frightening symptoms which they will ascribe to the 'disease'. It is important to remember that symptoms are real, but they may not mean what the patient thinks they mean. Specific fears will include worry about the effects of increasing activities, but these diminish quite quickly once treatment starts. However, any residual unhelpful thoughts can be tackled using traditional cognitive techniques (Burns 1981).

Negative automatic thoughts are referred to as such because they tend to pop into people's heads almost unconsciously. They are difficult to control, particularly as they may be plausible. An example of a negative thought might be 'If I go for a walk today I am bound to pay for it tomorrow and will feel worse. I will then have to rest for a couple of days to get over it'. Change in symptoms however does often take considerable time. It is during this transition period that cognitive strategies can be usefully employed.

Patients are asked to write down negative thoughts (like the example just given) as precisely as possible. They are then taught to evaluate these thoughts in an objective way. Patients will usually have a bias in their thinking and will tend to ignore certain facts in favour of others which support their negative view. There are many ways of challenging unhelpful thoughts but essentially the main skill that patients neeed to master is that of a questioning solicitor. They should ask themselves questions which will discourage them from taking a purely negative or positive view of the situation; rather, they are encouraged to adopt a more balanced view based on information or evidence which has previously been ignored. A number of alternative explanations may be generated at any one time. Thus, in response to the negative thought mentioned previously, a patient might challenge it by saying 'If I go for a short walk, twice a day, then I will gradually build up my strength and confidence. It is important for me not to overdo it on a good day. Consistency is what is important'. Links can be made between somatic symptoms, affects such as low mood, cognitions, and behaviour (Greenberger and Padesky 1996). Assertiveness training can be helpful for patients who experience difficulty in acknowledging and expressing feelings such as sadness or anger.

The same technique can be used for different types of thinking such as perfectionism, self-criticism, and guilt. A good therapist will be flexible in his or her use of cognitive techniques. Some patients will find the approach useful at the start of therapy, while others will need to develop more psychological sophistication before they find it useful. The skill is in using the right technique at the right time.

Phase 6 — generalizing the progress and ending therapy

At the start of treatment, the patient should be told roughly how many sessions to expect. It can be quite motivating to know that therapy will not go on forever! It also reinforces the idea that therapy should be both enabling and goal-directed. With the passage of time, the patient should be encouraged to take on more and more responsibility for his or her own treatment. It is likely that when therapy ends there will still be much more to be achieved. It can be helpful therefore to assist the patient in setting goals which are to be worked towards after regular therapy has stopped. Minor setbacks should be predicted and a plan of action identified to manage them. Long-term follow-up appointments are often requested by patients and if possible should be offered.

Special issues

The role of attributions

It is not necessary to convert patients' attributions from the organic to the psychological. This would merely reinforce a dualism which serves no function in this treatment. Rather, it is far more therapeutic to broaden a patient's views, thereby enabling him or her to adopt more adaptive coping strategies.

The angry patient

Many patients are initially ambivalent to the idea of seeing a psychiatrist or psychologist. It is better to address such feelings immediately on seeing the patient, and to openly sympathize with their plight. 'Did you think that seeing me meant that your symptoms were not being taken seriously?' can lead directly to questions about the experience of disconfirmation and perceived stigmatization implicit in referral to a psychological service. The value of simple compassion should never be underestimated.

The insurance assessment

The issue of benefits and insurance payments is exceptionally difficult in this area, and can lead to misunderstandings unless carefully handled. It is helpful to adopt a pragmatic approach to this problem. When asked to comment on benefits or insurance claims, it is important to support the patient as much as is possible, but it is not helpful to support claims for permanent disability or medical retirement until all reasonable efforts at rehabilitation have been tried. Difficulties for the health professional arise when there are clear conflicts of interest, for example, when stress at work contributed to the development of the problem and a return to work would exacerbate the symptoms. If discussed openly, the issue of benefits can be addressed and change is possible, long term.

Role of significant others

Reinforcement of unhelpful coping responses by well-meaning family members must be addressed in treatment. Hence, if it is felt that either partners or parents are encouraging disability, albeit inadvertently, it will be as important to engage them in treatment as the individual patient. Relatives or friends often act as co-therapists in cognitive behavioural therapy.

Conclusions

A number of single-case reports and case series suggest that a combination of behavioural and strategic interventions can improve disability in patients who are unable to walk and who have attracted the label of conversion disorder (Delargy *et al.* 1986; Teasell and Shapiro 1994; Wade's chapter in this volume, p. 330) or chronic fatigue syndrome (Powell *et al.* 1999). For new onset cases, a positive diagnosis should be given early, but care should be taken over the diagnosis used. Generally, patients do not take kindly to being told that they have hysteria. A rationale which includes a physiological explanation should be given for the use of rehabilitation, which may include physiotherapy. In chronic cases, patients may benefit from long-term treatment which would involve rehabilitation, support, renegotiating disability allowances, and long-term follow up.

References

Abe, K., Nishikawa, K. and Akagi, M. (1987). Behavioural approach to hysterical blindness. *Shinshin-Igaku*, **27**, 413–19.

Baker, J. H. E. and Silver, J. R. (1987). Hysterical paraplegia. *Journal of Neurology, Neurosurgery and Psychiatry*, **50**, 375–82.

Binzer, M., Anderson, P. M. and Kullgren, G. (1997). Clinical characteristics of patients with motor disability due to conversion disorder. *Journal of Neurology, Neurosurgery and Psychiatry*, **63**, 83–8.

Brady, J. P. and Lind, D. L. (1961). Experimental analysis of hysterical blindness. *Archives of General Psychiatry*, **4**, 331–9.

Burns, D. D. (1981). *Feeling Good: The New Mood Therapy*. New York: Signet.

Buschbacher, R. (1995). Guillain–Barre syndrome leading to conversion reaction in a teenage girl. *American Journal of Physical Medical Rehabilitation*, **74**, 230–3.

Butler, J. A., Chalder, T. and Wessely, S. (In press). Causal attributions for somatic sensations in patients with chronic syndrome and their partners. *Psychological Medicine*.

Chalder, T., Power, M. and Wessely, S. (1996). Chronic fatigue in the community: 'a question of attribution'. *Psychological Medicine*, **26**, 791–800.

Craig, T., Boardman, A., Mills, K., Daly-Jones, O. and Drake, H. (1993). The South London somatisation study: longitudinal course and the influence of early life experiences. *British Journal of Psychiatry*, 579–588.

Davison, P., Sharpe, M., Wade, D. and Bass, C. (1999). Wheelchair patients with nonorganic disease: a psychological enquiry. *Journal of Psychosomatic Research*, **47**, 93–103.

Delargy, M. A., Peatfield, R. C. and Burt, A. A. (1986). Successful rehabilitaion in conversion paralysis. *British Medical Journal*, **292**, 1730–1.

Dittmann, R. W. (1994). Psychogenic thoracic pain attacks. Pathogenesis, follow up therapy. *Z Kinder Jugenpsychiatr*, **22**, 114–22.

Donohue, B., Thevenin, D. M. and Runyon M. K. (1997). Behavioural treatment of conversion disorder in adolescence: a case of globus hystericus. *Behaviour Modification*, **21**, 231–51.

Greenberger, D. and Padesky, C. (1996). *The New Mood Therapy*. Guilford.

Hotopf, M. (1996). *Psychiatric Disorder and Childhood Experience of Illness in the Development of Physical Symptoms in Adulthood: A Prospective Cohort Study*. London School of Hygiene and Tropical Medicine.

Hugdahl, K. (1981). The three-systems model of fear and emotion – a critical examination. *Behaviour Research and Therapy*, **19**, 75–85.

Kukleta, M., Dufek, J. and Rektor, I. (1997). Possible mechanism of functional dystonia of the hand induced by psychological conflict. *Studia Psychologica*, **39**, 325–7.

Lang, P. J. (1978). Anxiety: Toward a psychophysiological definition. In: Psychiatric diagnosis: Exploration of biological predictors (eds Akiskal, H. S. and Webb, W. L.), New York: Spectrum.

Marshall, J., Halligan, P., Fink, G., Wade, D. and Frackowiak, R. (1997). The functional anatomy of a hysterical paralysis. *Cognition*, **64**, B1–B8.

Mayou, R., Bass, C. and Sharpe, M. (1995). *The Treatment of Functional Somatic Symptoms*. Oxford: Oxford University Press.

McCahill, M. E. (1995). Somatoform and related disorders: delivery of diagnosis as first step. *American Family Physician*, **52**, 193–204.

Morin, C. M., Culbert, J. P. and Schwartz, S. M. (1994). Non pharmacological interventions for insomnia: a meta-analysis of treatment. *American Journal of Psychiatry*, **151**, 1172–80.

Philips, C. (1987). Avoidance behaviour and its role in sustaining chronic pain. *Behaviour Research and Therapy* **25**, 273–9.

Powell, P., Edwards, R. H. T. and Bentall, R. P. (1999). The treatment of wheelchair bound chronic fatigue syndrome patients: two case studies of a pragmatic rehabilitation approach. *Behavioural and Cognitive Psychotherapy*, **27**, 249–60.

Salkovskis, P. (1991). The importance of behaviour in the maintaince of anxiety and panic: a cognitive account. *Behavioural Psychotherapy*, **19**, 6–19.

Scott Mizes, J. (1985). The use of contingent reinforcement in the treatment of a conversion disorder: a multiple baseline study. *Journal of Behaviour Therapy and Experimental Psychiatry*, **16**, 341–5.

Sensky, T., MaCloud, A. K. and Rigby, M. F. (1996). Causal attributions about common somatic sensations among frequent general practice attenders. *Psychological Medicine*, **26**, 641–6.

Sharpe, M., Hawton, K., Seagroatt, V. and Pasvol, G. (1992). Follow up of patients with fatigue presenting to an infectious diseases clinic. *British Medical Journal*, **302**, 347–52.

Singh, B., Nunn, J., Martin, J. and Yates, J. (1981). *British Journal of Medical Psychology*, **54**, 67–73.

Speed, J. (1996). Behavioural management of conversion disorder: retrospective study. *Archives of Physical Medical Rehabilitation*, **77**, 147–54.

Teasell, R. W. and Shapiro, A. P. (1994). Strategic behavioural intervention in the treatment of chronic non organic motor disorders. *American Journal of Physical Medical Rehabilitation*, **73**, 44–50.

Vandvik, I. H. and Skjeldal, O. (1994). Conversion disorders in children and adolescents. A multidisciplinary approach. *Tiddsskr–Nor–Laegeforen*, **114**, 1405–8.

Wherry, J. N., McMillan, S. L. and Hutchison H. T. (1991). Differential diagnosis and treatment of conversion disorder and Guillain–Barre syndrome. *Clinical Pediatric Phila*, **30**, 578–82.

22 Hypnosis and suggestion in the treatment of hysteria

David A. Oakley

Similarities between conversion symptoms of hysteria and hypnotic phenomena are reviewed and a two-level model is outlined which proposes that both are produced by the same neuropsychological mechanisms. In this model, a Level 2 central executive structure can be influenced by suggestion to alter the contents of self-awareness (Level 1). This indicates the use of suggestive procedures as a means of removing conversion symptoms by providing the Level 2 executive system with a plausible rationale for ending the strategic enactment by which they are produced. To match the cognitive style of the Level 2 systems, the use of indirect suggestion, imagery, and metaphors would be expected to be particularly effective. The model also proposes that hypnotic techniques facilitate changes in Level 2 executive system processes. Suggestive therapies should therefore be particularly effective when conducted in an hypnotic context. Some relevant case studies are reviewed and these provide evidence in support of this view.

Introduction

> Hypnotized subjects are asked to experience paralysis, amnesia, anaesthesia, involuntary movements and hallucinations. In fact hypnotizability is measured as the number of conversion and dissociative symptoms that the person is able to display. (Kirsch, 1990, p. 171)

The various phenomena associated with hypnosis have been known for many centuries as relatively easily produced but powerful alterations in subjective experience. There has equally been a recognition of the close relationship between hypnotic phenomena and hysteria, as the quotation above testifies (see also Gauld, 1992; Mersky, 1995; Oakley, 1999a; Thornton, 1976). Historically, the fact that hypnotic procedures could induce symptoms similar to those seen in hysteria was discussed by Gilles de la Tourette (1887, 1891) and Babinski emphasized the link between hysteria and suggestibility (Babinski and Froment, 1918). The influential neurologist, Charcot, went further in his belief that though suggestion was important, hypnosis and hysteria were linked by a common underlying neurological condition (Charcot, 1886–90; see also Gauld, 1992; Kihlstrom, 1994).

The classic symptoms of hysteria have been separated in more recent classifications of mental disorders into two descriptive categories: conversion disorder (which is a sub-class under the more general heading of 'somatoform disorders') and dissociative disorders. In DSM–IIIR (American Psychiatric Association, 1987), the link with the older classification was retained in the alternative terms 'hysterical neurosis, conversion type' and 'hysterical neurosis, dissociative type' respectively. In the more recent DSM–IV

(American Psychiatric Association, 1994) classification, the link with hysteria has been abandoned. While this separation is defensible from a descriptive point of view — conversion disorders affect voluntary motor or sensory functions that suggest neurological or other general medical conditions, whereas dissociation disorders are manifest as disturbances in more complex cognitive/psychological processes underlying consciousness, memory, identity, or perception of the environment — it is unfortunate on theoretical grounds (see Kihlstrom, 1994). I have argued elsewhere that, as they are closely related in terms of their underlying mechanisms and are explicable within the same model of psychological functioning, conversion and dissociative disorders should be classified together as 'auto-suggestive disorders' (Oakley, 1999a). Another reason for reuniting them is their frequent coexistence in the same individual, a fact which is recognized in DSM–IV:

> Conversion Disorder shares features with Dissociative Disorders. Both disorders involve symptoms that suggest neurological dysfunction and may also have shared antecedents. If both conversion and dissociative symptoms occur in the same individual (which is common) both diagnoses should be made. (DSM–IV, 1994, p. 456)

Having said that however, this chapter will, for convenience, focus on conversion disorders as described in DSM–IV, though the case that is presented here could apply equally, both in terms of mechanism and treatment, to dissociative disorders.

Similarities of hysteria and hypnosis

Hysterical conversion features predominantly negative symptoms such as deafness, blindness, paralysis, speech inhibition, and speech distortion, all of which have parallels in hypnosis. In hypnosis, positive phenomena such as arm levitation are also easily demonstrated, and these too have some parallels in conversion disorders in the form of non-epileptic seizures and involuntary motor movements. Apart from obvious similarities in behavioural appearance there are more general parallels between the symptoms of conversion disorder and the phenomena of hypnosis. Both are experienced as 'involuntary' and do not generate the 'concern' that might be expected. Both appear 'faked' when objective tests are applied. For example, they are both 'pseudoneurological' in presentation. Losses of tactile sensation and of movement tend to be manifest as 'glove anaesthesias' and paralyses which do not correspond to any underlying neuroanatomy. Similarly, the subjects and patients display 'implicit knowledge' or awarenesses which they should not have if the symptoms are physiologically 'real'. Hysterically deaf individuals, for instance, raise their voices when white noise is played and hypnotically blind subjects show effects of priming by unseen words. Furthermore, the symptoms in both cases are influenced by motivation, social pressures, and expectancies. There are also some differences. Most importantly in hypnosis, in contrast to conversion hysteria, the individual is aware of the context within which the effects occur and is an active participant in the interaction which produces them. Such effects are very easily reversible. These similarities and differences are discussed more fully in Oakley (1999a) and more specifically, for hypnotic and hysterical blindness, in Bryant and McConkey (1999).

For the purposes of this chapter, the main conclusion I would like to draw is that overall the two sets of phenomena are very similar and may be based on similar underlying neuropsycholgical mechanisms. Secondly, they present a similar paradox: on the one hand, the relevant phenomena are experienced as involuntary, as 'real' things which happen to the subject or patient, but, on the other hand, especially to an objective observer, the whole process has the characteristics of an enactment, a role play in which expectancies and social pressure play an important part.

A model of brain processes in hypnosis and hysteria

A model of brain processing which addresses the hypnosis/hysteria paradox as well as providing a framework for describing the similarities and common mechanisms that underlie both sets of phenomena is shown in Fig. 22.1 (see also Oakley 1999a, 1999b). This model builds on ideas developed by Oakley and Eames (1985) and by Shallice (1988) and proposes two main areas, or levels, of cognitive processing. Contained within the double-lined box in Fig. 22.1 are the majority of the cognitive processes (learning, memory, planning, and so on) carried out by the brain. In previous versions of this model these have been identified as belonging to 'consciousness systems', though with hindsight a less semantically loaded term seems preferable and in Fig. 22.1 they are designated simply as Level 2 processes. Processing within Level 2 is construed as being of high capacity, holistic, intuitive, more 'experiential', and associated with 'gut feelings', creativity, imagery, and more metaphoric representations (see Brown and Oakley, 1997, 1998; Oakley, 1999b).

It is assumed that the lower-level schemata and representations within Level 2 are semi-autonomous and can handle routine activities such as driving a car without placing great demands on attention. These semi-automatic processes correspond to what Shallice (1988) calls 'contention scheduling'. Also within Level 2 is an executive structure which can influence the lower-level schemata to produce non-routine activities such as might be required in response to novel situations. This executive structure corresponds broadly to Shallice's (1988) supervisory attentional system.

The executive control system in the present model shown in Fig. 22.1 has an additional important role however — that of selecting a subset of the currently active representations for further processing in a more analytical, 'rational' manner, with a high probability of this processing resulting in action. This additional level of processing has been described before as the 'self-awareness' system to reflect the fact that it is only at this level (now labelled Level 1) that we become subjectively aware of those selected Level 2 representations which enter into it. We are also aware of some of the processing which takes place in Level 1 in the form of our apparently continuous stream of thoughts, that is, the internal dialogue we have with ourselves and can convey to others. Actions which are processed via Level 1 are experienced as 'voluntary'. Level 1 is a limited capacity system and the assumption (in line with Gazzaniga, 1998) is that as little as 5 per cent or less of all cognitive activity is processed via this system, though from the perspective of the individual, it is perceived to constitute all mental activity. As they are central to the discussion which follows, the characteristics of Level 1 and Level 2 are summarized in Table 22.1.

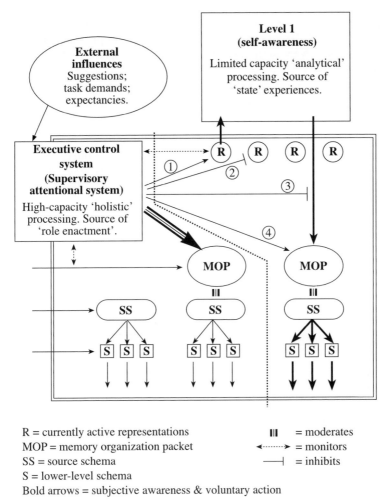

Fig. 22.1 The relationship between Level 1 ('self-awareness') and Level 2 and the effects of external influences on the executive system's control over the contents of Level 1. The double-outlined box represents the Level 2 systems, which incorporate the executive control system. The supervisory attentional system (SAS) plus the lower part of the figure to the left of the dotted line corresponds to the model described by Shallice (1988). The SAS plus the upper part of the figure corresponds to the model described by Oakley and Eames (1985). See text for further explanation.

The influences affecting Level 2 executive systems are 'suggestions' which emerge from the environment (for example, as task demands), from another person or are internally generated (for example, as beliefs, motives, and expectancies). Within the current model, this process is facilitated by the focussing of attention, by disattention to extraneous stimuli, and by absorption in inner mental processes — the essential components of hypnotic procedures (Oakley 1999*b*). If we assume that, in both hypnosis and hysteria, the relevant phenomena are produced by influences which act on the executive control system (within Level 2) to alter the contents of self-awareness (Level 1), it is easy to account for the relevant subjective experiences. In Fig. 22.1 four types of effect are identified, all based on 'normal' activities of the (Level 2) executive system:

1. The normal processing of a selection of Level 2 representations into self-awareness (Level 1), which may be influenced to produce, for example, hallucinations and the experience of age regression. Percepts and narratives passed into Level 1 are experienced as 'real'.

2. The reverse of this process, corresponding to the normal processes of selective attention, whereby some representations (for example, of the visual world) are blocked at a very late stage of Level 2 processing from entry to self-awareness (Level 1). In this example the result would be a subjectively 'real' blindness.

3. Representations of motor movement (or representations of the intention to move — Libet, 1996) are prevented from producing that movement *after* being processed by self-awareness (Level 1) and hence after the 'subjective' intention to move has been experienced. Examples here might be limb paralysis or a hypnotically induced finger lock.

4. The central executive (in Level 2) can also initiate and execute acts without involving self-awareness (Level 1). In fact it does this much of the time. These acts are experienced subjectively as being 'involuntary'. Relevant phenomena are hypnotic arm levitations and non-epileptic seizures.

Table 22.1 A summary of the characteristics of Level 1 and Level 2 systems in the proposed model. (See Brown and Oakley, 1997; Oakley, 1999a,b; and accompanying text for further explanation.)

Level 1
- Accounts for 5 per cent of all mental processing.
- Receives final-stage representations of ideas, beliefs, percepts, speech, memories, feelings, and intentions most relevant to the task in hand as selected by the executive structure in Level 2.
- Is low-capacity and its processing style is linear, analytical, literal, and 'rational'.
- Processing has a high probability of resulting in action.
- Processes and representations are reflected in subjective experience. They form the contents of consciousness, support an internal dialogue, and can be described to others.
- Experiences represented in Level 1 are attributed to the self and labelled as 'real'.
- Actions executed with the involvement of Level 1 are experienced as 'voluntary' or intentional.

Level 2
- Accounts for 95 per cent of all mental processes.
- Processes representations as ideas, percepts, speech, memories, feelings, and intentions to their final stages.
- Is high-capacity and its processing is holistic, intuitive, and 'experiential' — associated with 'gut' feelings, creativity, imagery, and metaphoric representations.
- Mediates automatic and semi-automatic processes involved in action and incorporates an executive structure which influences the activity of the semi-automatic processes in response to novelty.
- The executive structure also selects those late-stage representations most relevant to the task in hand for re-representation in Level 1.
- The process of selecting representations for re-representation in Level 1 can be influenced by suggestion, expectations, and social pressure acting on the executive structure.
- Processes and representations within Level 2 are not reflected directly in subjective experience. They do not form the contents of consciousness.
- Actions executed entirely within Level 2 are experienced (at Level 1) as 'involuntary', habitual, or reflexive.

In terms of the hypnosis/hysteria paradox it is possible to accept that a 'real' subjective state-change is felt at Level 1, as reflected by what the individuals concerned report of their experience. Hypnotic subjects and hysterics will tend to be what in the hypnosis literature are referred to as 'state theorists' (Kirsch and Lynn, 1995; Oakley, 1999*b*) — at least where their own experience is concerned. It is also possible to say, and to demonstrate, that these phenomena and the accompanying subjective experiences are the products of role enactment or social influence, which in this model operate via the central executive within Level 2. Experimenters and 'objective' observers will thus tend to be non-state or socio-cognitive theorists (Kirsch and Lynn, 1995; Oakley, 1999*b*).

Predictions from the model

Three major predictions follow from the model presented in Fig. 22.1:

1. The brain processes underlying parallel phenomena in both hypnosis and hysteria will be the same. There are some preliminary data from positron emission tomography (PET) imaging studies involving both hysterical and hypnotic paralysis to support this (Halligan *et al.*, 2000; Marshall *et al.*, 1997)

2. If the behaviour in both cases is produced by similar mechanisms (following various forms of 'suggestion'), it should be possible to classify hypnotic phenomena and hysteria symptoms meaningfully in a single schema with hysteria (conversion disorders and dissociative disorders) forming a single diagnostic category such as auto-suggestive disorder (see Fig. 22.2). A corollary to this is that suggestibility, of a form similar to that measured by hypnotizability scales, might serve as a predisposing factor to symptoms of hysteria. Both conversion disorder and dissociative disorder patients would therefore be expected to show higher levels of hypnotizability than general population groups, and the small amount of evidence available to date appears to support this (see Oakley, 1999*a*).

3. Similar procedures to those used in removing the phenomena of hypnosis should be effective in removing the symptoms of hysteria. It is this third prediction, with particular reference to conversion disorders, which is addressed in the remainder of this chapter.

Implications for the treatment of conversion disorders

On the basis of what has been said so far, and by analogy with strategies commonly employed within hypnosis, two clear predictions for the treatment of conversion disorder emerge. The first is that 'suggestive' procedures which increase expectancy and provide plausible rationales for ending the symptom/enactment should be effective. As these would be dealt with by Level 2 systems this in turn may entail a change in language with perhaps greater use of imagery, metaphors, and indirect as well as direct suggestions. It should be possible in some circumstances to remove hysterical symptoms, at least temporarily, by suggestion during hypnotic procedures, particularly where a plausible

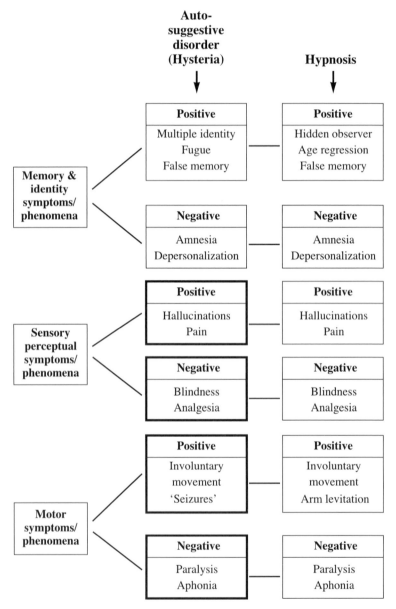

Fig. 22.2 Proposed scheme for classifying the positive and negative symptoms of hysteria (both conversion and dissociative) under the general heading of 'auto-suggestive disorder' and showing parallels with hypnotic phenomena. Examples of particular hysteria symptoms and the corresponding hypnotic phenomena in each of the sub-categories are shown in the two sets of boxes to the right of the figure. The boxes with the heavier outlines highlight those conversion disorder symptoms which form the focus of this chapter.

and appropriate context has been established, such as age regression to a time before the onset of the problem. There are a number of instances (for hysterical aphonia, for example) where this has been demonstrated (for example, McCue, 1979; McCue and McCue, 1988; Neeleman and Mann, 1993; Pelletier, 1977).

This could suggest a potential diagnostic as well as therapeutic role for hypnosis. There are in fact some precedents for this. Levbarg (1940) used the return of speech and its improvement with direct suggestion during hypnosis in three cases to demonstrate their functional status and to confirm preliminary diagnoses of hysterical aphonia. Similarly, Kuyk *et al.* (1995, 1999) have proposed that the recovery in hypnosis of memory for the events occurring during a 'seizure' may be a useful diagnosistic criterion for the identification of pseudo-epileptic seizures.

The second prediction for treatment is that the process of therapy may be facilitated by 'hypnotic' contexts and procedures which increase access to Level 2 executive systems by an emphasis on focused attention, disattention to extraneous stimuli, and the processes of absorption.

It is important here to emphasize the general point that hypnosis should not be considered to be a therapy in its own right, rather it is an adjunctive procedure which facilitates a range of established psychological approaches to treatment (Kirsch *et al.*, 1995; Oakley *et al.*, 1996, 1997). As all therapies can be construed as 'suggestive', hypnotic procedures or contexts might be assumed to facilitate a range of different therapies for that reason. The remainder of this chapter will review some of the literature pertaining to the use of suggestive and hypnotic procedures in the treatment of conversion disorders which generally supports these predictions.

An overview of studies involving the use of hypnotic procedures and strategies in the treatment of conversion disorder

Table 22.2 summarizes 13 studies which have used hypnotic techniques in the treatment of conversion disorders. The majority are single-case studies, but one of them, Moene *et al.* (1997), involves eight patients and the treatment principles it embodies derive from a much larger series. For this reason the Moene *et al.* (1997) study will be presented in more detail in the following text. The main focus of treatment in the 12 single-case studies is on motor symptoms and on speech disturbances.

It is also clear from Table 22.2 that most studies use a number of different techniques and strategies in treatment, as well as employing hypnotic procedures. This is consistent with the use of hypnosis as an adjunctive procedure. There is also a general division between those therapists who have used predominantly cognitive–behavioural, symptom-oriented approaches and those with a more psychodynamic emphasis. In the latter, hypnosis has been used as a context in which to explore the precipitating events by means of revivification (or age regression) and to uncover underlying, 'unconscious' psychological conflicts and motivations. Two of the single-case studies are described more fully to illustrate a cognitive–behavioural approach (Davies and Wagstaff, 1991) and a primarily psychodynamic approach (Pelletier, 1977). These two case studies involve a motor disturbance (ataxia) and a speech disorder (aphonia) respectively and so serve also to illustrate the two main symptom types contained within Table 22.2. Outcomes are generally said to be good, though this may well reflect a selective bias in that treatment failures are less commonly reported.

Table 22.2 A summary of 13 studies in which hypnotic procedures were used in the treatment of conversion disorders.

Study	Problem	Techniques used	Outcome
Braybrook, 1994 (Single case, male)	Dislocation of shoulders	Direct and indirect hypnotic suggestion, hypnotic uncovering**, dream analysis, metaphors, face-saving strategies	Loss of symptoms after 33 sessions
Collinson, 1972 (Single case, female)	Paralysis, anaesthesia	Spontaneous hypnotic state, indirect suggestion (story), face-saving strategy (confession)	Complete symptom removal
*Davies & Wagstaff, 1991 (Single case, female)	Ataxia	'Physical' explanation of symptoms, cognitive–behavioural techniques, face-saving strategies, creative imagery, positive suggestion	Significant symptom loss after 2 sessions
Dunnet & Williams, 1988 (Single case, female)	Aphonia	Direct hypnotic suggestion, cognitive–behavioural techniques, speech therapy	Normal voice after 6 months of treatment
Giacalone, 1981 (Single case, 10-year-old female)	Dysphonia	Direct and indirect hypnotic suggestion, face-saving strategies, imagery	Normal voice after 5 weekly sessions
Horsley, 1982 (Single case, female)	Dysphonia	Hypnotic relaxation training, self-hypnosis, personal responsibility for recovery	Normal voice after 2 sessions and at 16-month follow-up
Little, 1990 (Single case, female)	Dysphonia	Hypnotic relaxation training, direct hypnotic suggestion	Normal voice after 2 sessions and at 5-month follow-up
Mander, 1998 (Single case, male)	Dysphonia	Hypnotic relaxation training, direct hypnotic suggestion, self-hypnosis, imagery	95% normal after 5 sessions. Normal at 2-month follow-up
McCue, 1979 (Single case, female)	Aphonia	Direct hypnotic suggestion, hypnotic uncovering**, symptom loss in hypnosis	Normal voice after 1 session and at 4-month follow-up
McCue & McCue, 1988 (Single case, female)	Aphonia	Direct hypnotic suggestion, symptom loss in hypnosis, face-saving strategies	Improved voice after 5 sessions. Normal after 11 sessions and at 2.5-years follow-up
*Moene et al., 1998 (8 cases, all female)	Paralysis, gait disorder, contractures, tremor, non-epileptic seizures	A package including 'physical' explanation of symptoms, face-saving strategies, direct and indirect hypnotic suggestion, hypnotic uncovering**, physiotherapy, supportive psychological therapy	One patient dropped out, 7 completed with symptom removal, 3 relapsed

Cont

Study	Problem	Techniques used	Outcome
Neeleman & Mann, 1993 (Single case, female)	Aphonia	Direct hypnotic suggestion, challenge, symptom loss in hypnosis, face-saving strategies	Voice returned after 15 sessions. Relapse after 1 week and at 2-year follow-up
*Pelletier, 1977 (Single case, female)	Aphonia	Direct and indirect hypnotic suggestion, hypnotic uncovering**, symptom loss in hypnosis, face-saving strategies	Normal voice after 8 sessions. Relapse after 14 months

* These studies are described in more detail in the text.
** Where 'hypnotic uncovering' is included in the techniques used, this refers to exploratory procedures employing hypnotic age regression or revivification to uncover psychological factors underlying the presenting symptoms and reflects a more psychodynamic therapeutic approach. See the text for further explanation.

A multiple-case study illustrating general principles of treatment

A general treatment package based on a series of over 80 motor conversion disorder cases has been described by Moene *et al.* (1997) with the results from eight cases reported in detail. All the cases were long-standing and patients had received a variety of (mostly physical) interventions before they embarked on the treatment programme summarized here.

The major components of the treatment package, with the accompanying rationale as offered by Moene *et al.* (1998), are:-

1. **A rationale to explain the symptoms as 'physical'.** As conversion disorder patients experience symptoms as involuntary, they are disposed towards a somatic or 'state' explanation for their symptoms and treatment, rather than a psychological explanation. Two types of rationale are offered to the patients for the treatment they are to receive. One is that their physical symptoms are to be treated using rehabilitation procedures designed to strengthen muscles and so on. The other is that their symptoms are physical signs of prolonged stress. Any psychological problems, such as depression, which they manifest concurrently can be explained as responses to the physical symptoms.

2. **Preventing 'loss of face'.** That is, finding a socially acceptable way for the patient to lose symptoms without the accusation of previous malingering. To achieve this, clinicians continue to express their belief in the 'physical' reality of the patient's symptoms; the treatment is presented as demanding and difficult (that is, no 'miracle cures') and the patient's significant others are encouraged to become involved in the 'struggle' to recover.

3. **Psychotherapy.** Psychological factors (for example, depression, relationship problems) which may have precipitated, maintained, or followed from the disorder are worked on in psychotherapy sessions without being presented as the cause of the problem. The rationale for this is to prevent relapse or symptom substitution.

4. **Hypnosis.** Weekly sessions are offered in which hypnosis is used either to directly influence the expression of the symptom or to explore ('uncover') its origins. The symptom-oriented suggestions vary depending on the nature of the symptoms presented. Where these are uncontrolled movements, a catalepsy procedure is taught.

The patient then uses the catalepsy, sometimes switching it off and on, to inhibit movement and regain control. Where the problem is a paralysis, direct suggestions are given for altered sensation (for example, tingling) and small movements of muscles, building up to complete and normal movements. Exploratory procedures involve a 'revivification' (that is, an age regression) back to the presumed precipitating event. The patient is encouraged to re-experience the event and release the pent-up emotions associated with it. The patient is given the rationale that releasing the feelings can allow the symptoms to remit.

5. **Physiotherapy**. Intensive physiotherapy treatment has two aims. First, the practical one of correcting muscle wastage and other physiological consequences of a long-term conversion symptom. Second, 'physical' treatment, which entails a lot of homework, can form part of the 'face-saving' strategy; recovery can then be attributed in a socially acceptable way to intensive physiotherapy.

6. **Group therapy**. These sessions are intended to improve problem-solving capacities, social skills, and such like, as a preparation for returning to normal social interactions without the symptoms.

7. **Bed rest**. All patients are encouraged to take two hours of bed rest every day. No specific rationale is given for this but it may add to the perception that the patient is undergoing an arduous process of recovery and act as part of a face-saving strategy.

Patients and outcome

The eight patients reported in detail by Moene *et al.* (1998) were all females with motor conversion disorders (primarily paralysis) of, on average, nine years' duration. Psychiatric screening for conversion disorder followed DSM–IIIR criteria and was accompanied by neurological examination and, where appropriate, structural brain imaging. All of the patients had initially sought physical treatment. A precipitating event was reported in four of them; six had suffered incest or other abuse as a child; and all scored average to high on the Stanford Hypnotic Clinical Scale (Morgan and Hilgard, 1978).

Treatment lasted, on average, two months as an in-patient and twenty sessions as an out-patient. One patient dropped out of the programme after one week but the other seven continued and at the end of treatment were reported to be completely or almost completely relieved of their symptoms. Over a follow-up period ranging from 1.5 to 7 years, three of the seven who completed treatment relapsed, but two of these recovered again.

Single-case studies

I: a symptomatic approach using creative imagery and behavioural methods

Davies and Wagstaff (1991) reported the case of a 73-year-old female patient who had suffered hysterical ataxia for three years commencing at the time of the death of her husband. She could not stand without swaying and staggered widely to the left and right when walking. Her gait problem was sufficiently severe as to prevent her from engaging in activities outside the house. Consistent with the diagnosis, no neurological explanation could be found, though she believed that there was one and that she had been misdiagnosed. She was said to have an artistic temperament, she wrote poetry, and her premorbid personality was described as 'histrionic'. These and other indicators suggested to the authors that she was likely to be highly hypnotizable (or at least fantasy-prone), but no formal tests were reported.

The patient's interpretation that this was a physical illness was not challenged. She was told she would be treated in a 'mobility rehabilitation context' and that her own imagination and effort would be decisive in recovery. It was suggested that improvement 'could reasonably be expected' once rehabilitation commenced. As she was resistant to the idea of hypnosis, no formal induction was used, instead she was to be treated using her 'creative imagery skills'. As in a formal hypnotic procedure, she was encouraged to focus her attention and to become absorbed in imagery of her own creation.

A preliminary behavioural assessment confirmed that when walking freely she 'staggered dramatically' but when moving purposefully this was less marked and she could stand steadily at her cooker to make tea. Walking was worst in open spaces, easier in corridors. When attempting to walk she rose up on her tiptoes, looked down (or closed her eyes), raised her arms to shoulder level, and arched her back before staggering forward. It was suggested to her that her 'wobbles' were entirely understandable in the light of her 'posture' and that her task was to generate some images for herself to correct this. She offered an image of her feet being encased in concrete (to keep her heels 'stuck to the ground') and 'a rigid iron rod' to keep her back straight.

Whilst engaged in this imagery she was given 12 practical trials in a single session, progressing from standing still to walking with small steps (allowing the 'cement' to loosen and set with each step). During trials 4 to 10 she used the additional image of being in a corridor only as wide as her shoulders, and on trial 11, approximately one hour from the beginning of the session, she succeeded in walking 30 metres along a street. Significantly, this was the first time she had been outside for a year. On trial 12 she stood steadily and conversed for a period of five minutes.

In addition to the self-generated imagery, a behavioural management strategy was maintained throughout the practical trials in which she was corrected if she deviated from the 'correct posture' and was praised whenever appropriate for her self-control. As a face-saving strategy she was told that rehabilitation needed practice and that she was not to be surprised if she occasionally slipped. She was also advised to tell anyone who noticed an improvement that it was due to her progress in the new rehabilitation programme.

On a second session, three weeks later, the patient arrived showing some evidence of the former stagger, but within five minutes of having the 'rehabilitation programme' outlined to her again she was walking outside for 100 metres and could stand steady whilst talking for 15 minutes. Her grandson, and then later others, were recruited to walk with her to the shops and so on. These assignments were completed successfully and at this point, one month after the second treatment session, she said she no longer needed the images of the cement and the rod. The need for her to continue to build up her strength was emphasized and she was encouraged to practise her walking in different kinds of weather, carrying different kinds of bags, and so forth.

Davies and Wagstaff (1991) argued that although a behavioural programme was involved, progress was too rapid for that to entirely account for the improvement. As evidence for this they cited a study by Munford and Paz (1978) which required seven sessions to achieve a similar improvement with intensive behavioural techniques alone. They concluded that a suggestive approach coupled with absorbed involvement in imagery in a fantasy-prone individual served as the facilitators for a reversal of a motivated role enactment.

II: a dynamic analytical approach using formal hypnotic procedures and age regression

This case study reported by Pelletier (1977) involved a 55-year-old female patient who had suffered 'hysterical aphonia' for one year and was able to achieve only an occasional whispering voice limited to a few words. This case report is based on eight weekly, joint sessions with the author (a hypnotherapist) and the psychiatrist who had been treating her for the previous 12 months. The salient features of these eight sessions are as follows:

Session 1. No hypnosis was used but relaxation training and modelling of slow relaxed speech was given with embedded suggestions — '*try* and *see* that *you* can *speak* slowly but clearly just as I am doing' (emphasis in original).

Session 2. This session introduced an hypnotic induction (relaxation) and deepening procedure (counting down 20 steps) followed by guided imagery of a tree for ego strengthening with embedded direct and indirect suggestions for strength, control, and the ability to '*choose to speak well*'. During hypnosis the patient's speech was markedly improved and this continued after hypnosis.

Session 3. In an exploratory age regression using hypnosis the patient's speech was completely clear during both 'childhood' and 'adolescence' in both home and school settings. A post-hypnotic suggestion was given that 'her unconscious mind knew what the cause of her aphonia was and that she would prepare her mind to uncover it in the subsequent session *if she chose* to do so'. The improved voice again carried over after hypnosis (speaking clearly but softly), but this improvement was lost by the next session.

Session 4. A significant part of this session involved an hypnotic regression to an evening at home with her husband. During this the patient spoke clearly as she recounted preparations for the meal and mixing a drink, but as she described going into the room to join her husband her voice became a hoarse, laboured whisper as she said: 'He . . . doesn't . . . have . . . time . . . for . . . me . . . he won't . . . listen . . . he's . . . too . . . busy . . . and . . . tired'. Her voice remained laboured for the rest of the session and thereafter.

Session 5. In hypnosis, ego-strengthening and assertiveness exercises were introduced and the patient rehearsed speaking to her husband in a non-confrontational, confident way, which she was able to do 'without flaw, and with confidence and charm'. This fluent speech was carried over after the hypnosis but was lost on her return home.

Session 6. This was a joint session with the patient's husband in which his confrontational and unsympathetic communication style were pointed out to him and he agreed to modify this. In hypnosis, the patient was given a post-hypnotic suggestion that when any one — especially her husband — said 'and now Anna relax' she 'would *choose* to relax — speak well and carry on a conversation'. The husband was instructed to use the phrase when appropriate.

Sessions 7 and 8. These were support sessions as the patient was conversing normally with her husband and others and had resumed social engagements with her friends which had lapsed because of her voice problem.

The interpretation offered by Pelletier (1977) was that the patient had felt inferior to her prominent husband who was, by training, precise and perfectionistic. Once the children left home the patient *unconsciously* had no further need to verbalize, especially as she felt her husband had no time for her. Also she could *unconsciously* take charge and elect not to speak, thereby punishing him by awakening his concern and frustration (as well as saddling him with a year of psychiatric treatment costs). The therapy was directed towards these presumed unconscious motivations and provided an opportunity for the enactment to be discontinued and for the aphonia symptoms to be relinquished. The patient's normal voice continued until her husband died 14 months later of a heart attack, whereupon the hysterical aphonia returned.

Common features in the studies discussed in this chapter

Though the approaches adopted in the multiple-case and two single-case studies arose from different theoretical backgrounds, there are a number of common features which are worth mentioning, with some comments on their relationship to the model outlined at the beginning of this chapter.

In all cases the reality of the symptoms is accepted by the clinicians and the patient's view that this is an 'involuntary' physical problem is never directly challenged. In terms of the model presented earlier this is consistent with the subjective experience (at Level 1) of the patient. This does not of course exclude the possibility that the symptoms are part of a strategic enactment based on Level 2 systems, and the fact that a precipitating event can be identified in most cases is consistent with it being an enactment motivated by a need to deal with stressful or traumatic circumstances. In fact, Davies and Wagstaff (1991) make this suggestion explicitly and Pelletier refers frequently to 'unconscious' processes and motivations (which in terms of the model correspond to Level 2 processes).

Direct and indirect suggestions involving the symptoms themselves and attempts to manipulate the expectancy of recovery are also commonly employed. These are construed as influencing the activity of the Level 2 executive structure and the various demonstrations of the alleviation of symptoms in response to suggestion during hypnosis (or engagement in 'creative imagery') is again consistent with the predictions of the model.

If the Level 2 enactments are seen as serving a useful psychological purpose, an important prerequisite for the abandonment of these enactments is for new solutions to the precipitating problem to be found. Equally, one of the roles of Level 1 systems is to provide a coherent internal and external personal narrative: consequently, there is a strong need for recovery to have a rational explanation which preserves the integrity of the individual for themselves and for society at large. In the studies reviewed, new explanations for the symptoms are offered and new solutions to the problem or ways of dealing with the situation are suggested. The need for personal consistency (or 'saving face') is addressed by the introduction of plausible 'new' treatments such as hypnosis, creative imagery, and rehabilitation programmes. Also, the need for 'hard work' is emphasized and in some instances explicitly built into the treatment programme — particularly in the form of rehabilitation and physiotherapy in the Moene *et al.* (1997) study. In all instances, the patients themselves are given responsibility for progress, significant others are involved in the treatment programme (to witness the 'struggle' for recovery), and reasons for recovery are explicitly suggested to ensure that such recovery is socially acceptable.

All the studies reviewed involved the use of hypnotic procedures or their equivalent via engagement in creative imagery. This is of course because the use of hypnosis was one of the reviewer's selection criteria. There are no clinical trials comparing directly the same therapeutic procedures in conversion hysteria with or without an hypnotic context. The model provides a rationale however to suggest that a hypnotic context would facilitate access to Level 2 systems and hence present a heightened opportunity to influence the process of symptom removal. There are other reasons why a hypnotic context should be considered for the treatment of conversion disorders. To the extent that cognitive–behavioural approaches have any effectiveness with these disorders, it is known that the addition of hypnosis significantly improves the outcome of such treatments (Kirsch *et al.*, 1995). Hypnosis also provides a powerful means of manipulating expectancy and, in clinical contexts, of increasing the expectancy of a positive outcome (see Council, 1999; Kirsch 1990, 1994).

Similarly where imagery is part of a treatment process, hypnotic context and hypnotizability are relevant to the subjective reality of the imagined experience. In particular, when individuals are encouraged by suggestion to treat the imagined situation as a real one (that is, to hallucinate), the brain activity of high hypnotizables becomes much more like that produced by the real situation than that which occurs when they are asked simply to 'imagine' (Szechtman *et al.*, 1998). There are, as noted earlier, some indications from the literature and the studies reviewed in this chapter that individuals with conversion disorders are higher than normal in hypnotizability. If this proves to be the case, with appropriate suggestions any imaginal procedures they engage with in the course of treatment can have a more *in vivo* quality if hypnosis is used.

Finally, hypnosis itself, if it has not been used before with a particular patient, can be presented as a powerful new tool, to which any improvement can be attributed, and hence can serve as a face-saving device. The fact that symptoms can be removed in some cases during hypnotic procedures adds further plausibility of this attribution for the patient. The generality of this effect remains to be tested however.

Conclusions

The model presented at the beginning of this chapter and the predictions based on it for treatment of conversion disorders were generated independently of this review of the treatment literature. It has been found that a variety of empirically derived, and apparently successful, interventions with conversion disorder patients can be explained within the framework of the model. This provides some validation to the model itself but, more importantly, it enables the model to be used prospectively as an empirically testable framework for both understanding currently employed therapeutic approaches and also for guiding therapeutic strategies in the future.

There is a major need for well-controlled clinical trials with good outcome measures to evaluate the 'suggestive' therapies which have been identified, from both the model and from the treatment literature, as potentially clinically effective; (see the chapter by Wade in this volume, p. 330). In terms of the model, the latter of course implies not just the removal of the presenting symptom but also the resolution of the underlying psychological problem, to which the symptom represents a self-generated (Level 2) solution. A second issue is whether using a hypnotic context, and in particular formal hypnotic procedures, is a therapeutically helpful adjunct. Exploring this possibility would entail comparing the effectiveness of the same 'suggestive' therapies with and without 'hypnosis', either as a label or as a set of formal procedures.

References

American Psychiatric Association (1987). *Diagnostic and Statistical Manual of Mental Disorders.* (3rd edn, revised; DSM–IIIR). Washington, DC: APA.

American Psychiatric Association (1994). *Diagnostic and Statistical Manual of Mental Disorders* (4th edn; DSM–IV). Washington, DC: APA.

Babinski, J. and Froment, J. (1918). *Hysteria or Pithiatism* (ed. Farquhar Buzzard, E.). London: University of London Press.

Braybrook, Z. (1994). Hypnosis in the treatment of conversion hysteria. *Australian Journal of Clinical and Experimental Hypnosis*, **22**, 125–36.

Brown, R. J. and Oakley, D. A. (1997). Hypnosis and cognitive experiential self theory: a new conceptualisation for hypnosis? *Contemporary Hypnosis*, **14**, 94–9.

Brown, R. J. and Oakley, D. A. (1998). Hypnotic susceptibility and holistic/emotional styles of thinking. *Contemporary Hypnosis*, **15**, 76–83.

Bryant, R. A. and McConkey, K. M. (1999). Functional blindness: a construction of cognitive and social influences. *Cognitive Neuropsychiatry*, **4**, 227–41.

Charcot, J. M. (1886–90). *Oeuvres Completes de J. -M. Charcot.* Paris: A. Delahaye et E Lecrosnier.

Collinson, D. R. (1972). Conversion paralysis: ancient and modern. *British Journal of Clinical Hypnosis,* **3**, 43–5.

Council, J. R. (1999). Hypnosis and response expectancies. In *How Expectancies Shape Experience* (ed. Kirsch, I.), pp. 383–401. Washington, DC: American Psychological Association.

Davies, A. D. M. and Wagstaff, G. F. (1991). The use of creative imagery in the behavioural treatment of an elderly woman diagnosed as an hysterical ataxic. *Contemporary Hypnosis*, **8**, 147–52.

de la Tourette, G. (1887). *L'Hypnotisme et les États Analogues au Point de Vue Médico-légale.* Paris: Plon, Nourrit.

de la Tourette, G. (1891). *Trait Clinique de l'Hysterie d'Apres l'Enseignement de la Salpetrière. Hystérie Normale ou Interparoxystique.* Paris: Plon, Nourrit.

Dunnet, C. P. and Williams, J. E. (1988). Hypnosis in speech therapy. In *Hypnosis: Current Clinical, Experimental and Forensic Practices* (ed. Heap, M.), pp. 246–56. London: Croom Helm.

Gauld, A. (1992). *A History of Hypnotism.* Cambridge: University Press.

Giacalone, A. V. (1981). Hysterical dysphonia: hypnotic treatment of a ten-year-old female. *American Journal of Clinical Hypnosis*, **23**, 289–93.

Halligan, P. W., Athwal, B. S., Oakley, D. A. and Frackowiak, R. S. J. (2000). The functional anatomy of a hypnotic paralysis: implications for conversion hysteria. *The Lancet*, 355, 986–987.

Horsley, I. A. (1982). Hypnosis and self-hypnosis in the treatment of psychogenic dysphonia: a case report. *American Journal of Clinical Hypnosis*, **24**, 277–83.

Kihlstrom, J. F. (1994). One hundred years of hysteria. In *Dissociation: Clinical and Theoretical Perspectives* (ed. Lynn, S. J. and Rhue, J. W.), pp. 365–94. New York: Guilford Press.

Kirsch, I. (1990). *Changing Expectations: A Key to Effective Psychotherapy*. Pacific Grove, California: Brooks/Cole.

Kirsch, I. (1994). Clinical hypnosis as a nondeceptive placebo: empirically derived techniques. *American Journal of Clinical Hypnosis*, **37**, 95–106.

Kirsch, I, Montgomery, G. and Sapirstein, G. (1995). Hypnosis as an adjunct to cognitive-behavioural psychotherapy: a meta-analysis, *Journal of Consulting and Clinical Psychology*, **63**, 214–20.

Kuyk, J., Jacobs, L. D., Aldenkamp, A. P., Meinardi, H., Spinhoven, P. and Van Dyck, R. (1995). Pseudoepileptic seizures: hypnosis as a diagnostic tool. *Seizure*, **4**, 123–8.

Kuyk, J., Spinhoven, P. and Van Dyck, R. (1999). Hypnotic recall: a positive criterion in the differential diagnosis between epileptic and pseudoepileptic seizures. *Epilepsia*, **40**, 485–91.

Levbarg, J. J. (1940). Hysterical aphonia. *Eye, Ear, Nose and Throat Monthly*, **19**, 306–12.

Libet, B. (1996). Neural processes in the production of conscious experience. In *The Science of Consciousness: Psychological, Neuropsychological and Clinical Reviews* (ed. Velmans, M.), pp. 96–117. London: Routledge.

Little, M. E. (1990). Hypnosis in the treatment of a case of spastic dysphonia. *British Journal of Experimental and Clinical Hypnosis*, **7**, 181–3.

Mander, A. (1998). Hypnosis in the treatment of dysphonia. *Australian Journal of Clinical and Experimental Hypnosis*, **26**, 43–8.

Marshall, J. C., Halligan, P. W., Fink, G. R., Wade, D. T. and Frackowiak, S. J. (1997). The functional anatomy of a hysterical paralysis. *Cognition*, **64**, B1-B8.

McCue, P. A. (1979). A case of hysterical aphonia: successful treatment with brief hypnotherapy. *Bulletin of the British Society of Experimental and Clinical Hypnosis*, **2**, 18–19.

McCue, E. C. and McCue, P. A. (1988). Hypnosis in the elucidation of hysterical aphonia: a case report. *American Journal of Clinicial Hypnosis*, **30**, 178–82.

Merskey, H. (1995). *The Analysis of Hysteria: Understanding Conversion and Dissociation* (2nd edn). London: Royal College of Psychiatrists.

Moene, F. C., Hoogduin, K. A. L. and Van Dyck. R. (1998). The inpatient treatment of patients suffering from (motor) conversion symptoms: a description of eight cases. *International Journal of Clinical and Experimental Hypnosis*, **46**, 171–89.

Morgan, A. H. and Hilgard, J. R. (1978). The Stanford Hypnotic Clinical Scale for Adults. *American Journal of Clinical Hypnosis*, **21**, 134–47.

Munford, P. R. and Paz, G. (1978). Differential attention in the treatment of abasia-astasia. *Journal of Behavior Therapy and Experimental Psychiatry*, **9**, 369–71.

Neeleman, J. and Mann, A. H. (1993). Treatment of hysterical aphonia with hypnosis and prokaletic therapy. *British Journal of Psychiatry*, **163**, 816–19.

Oakley, D. A. (1999a). Hypnosis and conversion hysteria: a unifying model. *Cognitive Neuropsychiatry*, **4**, 243–65.

Oakley, D. A. (1999b). Hypnosis and consciousness: a structural model. *Contemporary Hypnosis*, **16**, 215–23.

Oakley, D. A., Alden, P. and Degun Mather, M. (1996). The use of hypnosis in therapy with adults. *The Psychologist*, **9**, 502–5.

Oakley, D. A., Alden, P. and Degun Mather, M. (1997). The use of hypnosis in therapy with adults. *Australian Journal of Clinical and Experimental Hypnosis*, **25**, 108–17.

Oakley, D. A. and Eames, L. C. (1985). The plurality of consciousness. In *Brain and Mind* (ed. Oakley, D. A.), pp. 217–521. London: Methuen.

Pelletier, A. M. (1977). Hysterical aphonia: a case report. *American Journal of Clinical Hypnosis*, **20**, 149–53.

Shallice, T. (1988). *From Neuropsychology to Mental Structure*. Cambridge: Cambridge University Press.

Szechtman, H., Woody, E., Bowers, K. S. and Nahmias, C. (1998). Where the imaginal appears real: a positron emission tomography study of auditory hallucinations. *Proceedings of the National Academy of Science*, **95**, 1956–60.

Thornton, E. M. (1976). *Hypnotism, Hysteria and Epilepsy: An Historical Synthesis*. London: Heinemann.

23 Rehabilitation for hysterical conversion states

A critical review and conceptual reconstruction

Derick T. Wade

This chapter considers the available evidence that might guide clinicians in managing patients with hysterical conversion disorder. Some quality criteria are developed, and the available evidence is judged against those criteria and found to be weak. This leads to further consideration of the nature of the phenomenon, setting it in the context of the widely used World Health Organisation's (WHO) model of disability as formulated in the International Classification of Impairments, Disabilities, and Handicaps (ICIDH), the second version of which is used. Reformulating hysterical conversion disorder in this context shows that it is only one subset of the much more common group of conditions known as functional somatic syndromes (inter alia). Evidence from research into the management of somatization disorders suggests that a rehabilitation approach based on (but not exclusively) cognitive behavioural therapy is likely to be the most effective method of managing patients with hysterical conversion disorder.

Introduction

The management of patients whose neurological symptoms, signs, and disabilities do not have a satisfactory or adequate explanation in terms of an underlying disease or diagnosis has always been difficult for doctors. Such patients challenge doctors and health care professionals in many ways: scientifically (what is the explanation of this state in terms of anatomy and physiology?); practically (how can we help? how much investigation should we undertake?); and ethically (should we simply ignore and discharge such patients? how do health care professionals cope with the irritation they may arouse in themselves?). To many people such patients abuse society's benefits, failing to follow accepted social rules that people can only exhibit illness behaviour and adopt the sick role when they have a medically legitimate disease (usually taken to mean a pathologically proven disease). Doctors are at the interface — they may deny the patient a legitimate sick role, or they may legitimize the role (and hence the illness) but attempt to change it, or they may legitimize the sick role through re-enforcing the abnormal, possibly maladaptive illness behaviour.

This chapter considers the published evidence relating specifically to the management of patients with hysterical conversion disorder over the last century. There is little, and so the nature of hysterical conversion disorder is reconsidered, using a version of the World Health Organisation's (WHO) model of illness that is published as the International Classification of Impairments, Disabilities, and Handicaps (ICIDH). This will give the reader a framework to work within. The model proposed supports evidence presented (Wessley *et al.*, 1999) in suggesting that hysterical conversion disorder is only one manifestation of a very common phenomenon variously termed 'medically unexplained symptoms' (Carson *et al.*, 2000), 'somatoform disorder', and 'non-organic functional disorder' — to give but a few names. It also suggests that there will be several factors playing an aetiological role in any one patient, and that the factors will vary between patients, so that a standard approach may not be desirable. Evidence concerning somatoform disorders shows that cognitive behavioural therapy may help some patients. Finally, the chapter proposes a standard rehabilitation approach as the most effective way of managing these patients, using cognitive behavioural therapy as one, but not the only, means of treatment.

Evaluating the evidence

When considering the evidence for treatment interventions for any disease or medical problem, the following questions need to be considered:

1. Is the clinical condition well described and defined? This is essential both for future replication of the study and to determine whether the findings apply to your patient.

2. Is the treatment intervention well described and defined? Again, this is essential both for future replication of the study and to enable you to use (or avoid) the treatment for your patient. It is not necessary for the treatment to be justified, although it would be usual to give some explanation of its rationale.

3. Does the study design control or account for the non-specific (that is, 'placebo') effects associated with any intervention? This allows the intended specific effect of the intervention to be disentangled from all the other general effects associated with any intervention, so that the central effective component of the intervention can be further investigated and hopefully improved upon. It is particularly important in hysterical conversion disorder as it may well be that the non-specific psychological effects of any intervention are especially powerful in this condition.

4. Does the study design control or account for any systematic or naturally occurring change that may be affecting the clinical state of the patient? This will ensure that one is not simply observing the natural history of the condition.

5. Is the effect attributed to the intervention statistically unlikely to arise simply from normal variation in the clinical state and measurement process? Even after controlling, through the design, for predictable chance variation, there will always be uncontrolled variation and it is important to estimate whether the change or difference is simply random chance or 'real'.

6. Is the effect attributed to the intervention clinically relevant (assuming it to be genuinely due to the intervention)? This is always the most difficult question to answer, but is of importance both to the purchaser paying the cost and to the patient taking the risks.

In relation to hysterical conversion disorder, a review of the literature suggests that there are major problems with all six questions.

The clinical condition of hysterical conversion disorder is not well defined. This is true in general, as other chapters in this book will testify. It is also true of the cases that have been studied. It is especially true when undertaking systematic searches, as the evidence in this chapter will show. One cannot know that the cases reported are comparable either with other reported cases or with those seen in the clinic. However, it is likely that most cases reported do exhibit impairments and/or disabilities that are not attributable to a pathology, and to that extent they are homogenous.

Of more concern, the treatment intervention is rarely well described or defined, although reviews do suggest principles (Silver, 1996), usually without much supporting evidence. There are exceptions (Shapiro and Teasell, 1997). This problem is almost inevitable for many reasons: it is likely that treatments are tailored to the individual; there is no easy agreed lexicon of terms available to describe most treatments; journals are reluctant to publish long descriptions of treatments; and it is likely that multiple interventions aimed at different aspects of the illness are used simultaneously.

This reviewer is unaware of any large (more than 10 patients), well-controlled studies of hysterical motor conversion disorder. As will be discussed later, an hysterical conversion state might be considered a 'placebo illness' in that it is a change in behaviour or function that arises through indirect mechanisms involving belief and expectation. It therefore seems probable that these patients will be especially susceptible to the placebo effects of any treatment.

None of the studies reviewed have controlled for spontaneous changes and fluctuation. Almost all reports are of single cases or case series, and this makes it impossible to evaluate the reports. Some have assumed that change will not occur spontaneously. The natural history of hysterical conversion disorder has not been well studied in epidemiological terms (see the chapter by Akagi and House in this volume, p. 73). However, it seems likely from clinical experience and from reported cases and on first principles that after an acute onset many patients will rapidly improve and recover (Couprie et al., 1995), which may explain the apparent benefits of early intervention (Speed, 1996). Equally, it seems likely that patients with long-standing illness will nonetheless fluctuate. Therefore it is essential that any study design controls for this natural change; no studies do.

The last two questions should only be applied once the first four conditions have been satisfied. No studies in hysterical conversion reach that standard.

The evidence — part one

On searching the Medline database 1966–99 using the term 'conversion disorder' and selecting the subsets of 'rehabilitation' and 'therapy' one finds 226 papers. They cover a range of disorders from aphonia through motor loss to camptocormia. Many papers consider hysterical conversion disorders in children. Most of the papers describe single cases or case series.

Searching the Cochrane Library (1999, issue 4) central register of controlled clinical trials showed the following. When searching for 'somatoform disorders', 124 studies were recorded; for 'hysteria', 47 studies were found (including one duplicate entry); and for 'conversion disorder', 11 studies were found. These latter 11 studies were: Pernhaupt and Quatember, 1970; Chistoni, 1971; Kelesidis et al., 1972; Uhlenhuth et al., 1972; Antonelli et al., 1973; Soskin, 1973; Cloquette, 1974; Puhakka and Kirveska, 1988; Casacchia et al., 1989; Deary and Wilson, 1994; and Moene et al., 1998. Most of these studies do not appear to relate to the generally accepted clinical syndrome being discussed here, and none are large, randomized, well-controlled studies.

Table 23.1 Some selected studies on rehabilitation of adult patients suffering hysterical conversion states

Author	Cases and design	Treatment	Outcome
Watanabe et al., 1998	Hemiparesis; 4 cases; no control	Functional and behavioural therapies and psychosocial support	Improved rapidly
Moene et al., 1998	Motor conversion disorder; 8 cases; randomized and controlled	Suggestive and behavioural techniques and eclectic treatment	Improved
Shapiro & Teasell, 1997	17 patients with apparently neurological conversion hysteria	Double-bind strategic-behavioural approach involving family	13 improved including 9 who had failed on standard behavioural approach
Silver, 1996	4 cases; no control	Multimodal intervention on principles given	Improved
Speed, 1996	Conversion disorder affecting gait; 8 cases; no control	Behavioural approach, reinforcing well behaviour	Improved; speed of recovery proportional to duration of symptoms
Deary and Wilson, 1994	Globus hystericus; 24 patients; double-blind RCT	Amitriptyline or placebo	9/12 patients on amitriptyline withdrew
Daie and Witztum, 1991	Traumatic conversion reactions; 4 cases; no control	Behavioural and paradoxi-cal techniques	Improved
Krull and Schifferdecker, 1990	Retrospective survey of 220 patients with conversion symptoms		Longer duration symptoms associated with less good recovery
Sinel and Eisenberg, 1990	Conversion gait disorder; 2 cases	Psychiatric intervention	Rapid recovery
White et al., 1988	Non-organic locomotor disorders; 11 cases of 1–10 years' duration	Intravenous thiopentone to induce drowsiness; suggestion	9 showed early recovery; 3 maintained recovery
Fishbain et al., 1988	Long-standing conversion paralysis; four cases; no control	Behavioural treatment with EMG biofeedback	Recovery
Khalil et al., 1988	Conversion paralysis; 1case	Functional electrical stimulation	Recovery
Puhakka and Kirveskari, 1988	Globus hystericus; 22 patients; double-blind RCT	True or false occlusal adjustment	True adjustment associated with resolution of syndrome
Delargy et al., 1986	Conversion paraplegia; 6 cases; 1–6 years' post-on set	In-patient functional rehabilitation	Recovery; maintained over 10 months

Cont

Author	Cases and design	Treatment	Outcome
Cardenas et al., 1986	Conversion paralysis of arms; 4 cases	Shaping behavioural programme	Recovered
Withrington & Wynn Parry, 1985	Conversion paralysis of one limb; 5 cases	In-patient rehabilitation	Recovered
Hafeiz, 1980	Hysterical conversion; 61 cases	Treatment by suggestion	Recovered
Weiser, 1976	Functional paralysis; 7 cases	Suggestion, persuasion, and therapy	5 recovered
Scallet et al., 1976	Matched group of patients with 'chronic hysteria'	Central electric stimulation and relaxation, peripheral stimulation and relaxation, relaxation alone	Stimulation offered no benefits

Table 23.1 shows a selection of papers from Medline and the Cochrane register of controlled clinical trials. They were chosen from those found as at least partially covering the rehabilitation of adult patients who probably had hysterical conversion with motor loss.

On reading these papers it is apparent that most fail on nearly all of the six criteria given, and none allow any conclusion to be drawn about the clinical effectiveness of any intervention. Although searching is known only to reveal 20–50 per cent of studies within databases, it still seems likely that no good studies exist. Consequently, any discussion on management will necessarily be based on clinical anecdote, or on arguments derived from general principles, or on evidence from elsewhere. Anecdote is not evidence, but it may be used to illustrate discussion or stimulate hypotheses.

One may conclude that, at present, no good evidence to support any specific intervention for patients with hysterical conversion disorder can be found by searching databases, and indeed there is no evidence to show that any intervention has any effect. At best, the evidence available suggests that short-term gains may follow from rehabilitation. However, the evidence is strong enough to suggest that some of the specific treatment approaches should be investigated in larger, randomized, controlled studies.

In the absence of good evidence, a possible framework for future research can be developed. This draws on the published evidence and other published ideas. I will start by describing a general model of illness, based on the WHO ICIDH–2 model (described in the following text), with one major addition — I have subdivided each level and context into an objective and a subjective half. Using this model I will suggest that observed disability is influenced as much by various subjective changes as it is by objective changes. This will lead on to a discussion of disability that is not readily explained by disease or signs (such as that seen in conversion disorder). I will suggest (as have others) that there are many different labels attached to patients whose disability is out of proportion to known disease and signs, and that hysterical conversion disorder is only one of many, but that, unless proved otherwise, they should all be considered as having more similarities than differences. I will also show the many different places within the model that one might intervene, taking as examples some of the published studies. Finally, I will draw upon evidence from the broader field of rehabilitation, including research into chronic fatigue syndrome, chronic pain, and other functional disorders, to suggest that a multidisciplinary rehabilitation approach with several simultaneous interventions may well be successful, although different patients may require different approaches.

The modified WHO ICIDH–2 model

The World Health Organisation has developed a model of illness that is codified in the International Classification of Impairments, Disabilities, and Handicaps (Badley, 1993). This has recently been revised and updated (WHO, 1999). More detailed discussion can be found elsewhere (Wade and de Jong, 2000; Wade, 1996; Wade, forthcoming).

The classification system used identifies four levels of change and three contextual domains that interact with these four levels. The model can be interpreted as a systems-analytic approach to illness: each level and each context is a separate system that is largely self-contained but may interact with each other system to a greater or lesser extent. A systems analysis would make several predictions:

1. The nature and extent of any interaction between any two or more systems will be variable and often unpredictable, such that small changes in one system may have no effect or else a major effect on other systems.
2. Interactions will occur between all systems and will be two-way, such that apparently higher systems may affect apparently lower systems, and any one system may affect any other single system alone.
3. Abnormalities may arise within any one system alone.
4. The functioning of the overall system will depend upon the interaction between all systems, and the effect of changes within one system will be determined as much by the characteristics of other systems as by the nature of the initial change.

The model is shown in more detail in Table 23.2, and Fig. 23.1 shows a possible mechanism in one patient who previously lived at home in an unhappy family with no job. She might have presented with an 'attack' of marked weakness when she felt slightly weak but became over-concerned (perhaps because someone she knew had MS). This might then have been re-enforced by the family who previously ignored her emotional needs but now provide practical and emotional support; by the state who provide financial and practical support; and by doctors who investigate her and provide sick notes for her social benefits. Furthermore, she might acquire valued new roles as the 'disabled representative' on various local organizations and committees, and within the family.

The following points should be considered. First, although traditionally it has been assumed that all illness follows from an underlying disease (that is, has a pathological basis), there is no reason for this always to be the case. One specific characteristic of any hierarchy of systems is that emergent properties can arise from within a system at one level, unrelated to any of the properties of any sub-systems. As an analogy, the letters 'E', 'L', 'O', and 'V' could be considered as four sub-systems. At the next level they could be organized as one system, 'LOVE', or another system, 'VOLE' — and the emergent

Table 23.2 Expanded model of illness (WHO ICIDH–2 with additions). A way of describing a patient's illness.

	Subjective/internal judgement made by person	Objective/external judgement made by others
Level of illness (level: *term*)		
Organ within body: *pathology*	**Disease** Label attached by person, usually on basis of belief	**Diagnosis** Label attached by others, usually on basis of investigation
Person: *impairment*	**Symptoms** Somatic sensation, experienced moods, thoughts, etc.	**Signs**Observable abnormalities (absence or change), often elicited explicitly
Person in environment: *behaviour / 'activities'*	**Perceived ability** What person feels they can do, and opinion on quality of performance	**Disability/activities** What others note person does do, quantification of that performance
Person in society: *roles / 'participation'*	**Life satisfaction** Person's judgement or valuation of their own role performance (what and how well)	**Handicap/participation** Judgement or valuation of important others (local culture) on role performance (what and how well)
Context of illness		
Personal context	**'Personality'** Person's attitudes, expectations, beliefs, goals, etc.	**'Past history'** Observed/recorded behaviour prior to and early on in this illness
Physical context	**Personal importance** Person's attitude towards specific people, locations, etc.	**Resources** Description of physical resources (buildings, equipment, etc.) and personal resources (carers, etc.) available
Social context	**Local culture** The people and organizations important to person, and their culture; especially family and people in same accommodation	**Society** The society lived in and the laws, duties, and responsibilities expected from and the rights of members of that society
Totality of illness		
Quality of life: *summation of effects*	**Contentment** Person's assessment of and reaction to achievement or failure of important goals **Or** Sense of being a worthwhile person	**Social involvement** Extent of positive interaction with society, contributing to social networks

properties are the two different meanings of the words. In this analogy 'pathology' would be exemplified by the letter 'O' changing to 'A' or 'I' or 'T'.

Consequently, this model would predict that some illnesses would not have any specific underlying pathology. The prime cause might be within the level, or might be at other

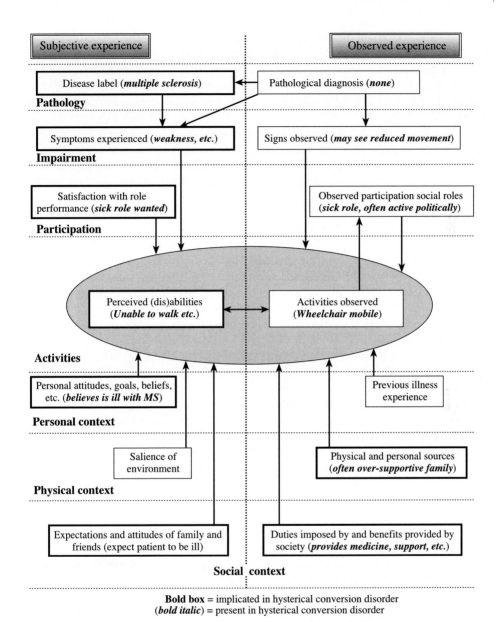

Fig. 23.1 Some of the influences on disability (alteration in activities) in conversion disorder. (Note: other arrows exist, and most are two-way.)

levels, or might arise from the contextual factors. For example, in 'apparent multiple sclerosis' hypervigilant observation of normal neurophysiological fluctuation may initiate illness.

Second, this model emphasizes that, whatever the 'prime cause' of an illness, many factors will have an influence on its manifestation (see Fig. 23.1). Furthermore, the model predicts that an abnormality at one level will not always have the same manifestation at other levels. It is a common experience both that patients with similar diseases (for example, volumes and locations of cerebral infarction) differ quite widely in their disability and also that such factors as mood can influence disability. For example, in apparent MS the family may provide emotional support that was previously absent.

In most (ill) people there is a relatively weak relationship between the nature and extent of demonstrated pathology, the nature and extent of impairment, and the quantity and quality of altered activities. It is well recognized (but poorly documented) that 'psychological factors' (such as emotional states and motivation) influence the presentation of any illness.

Thus it is possible to consider 'hysterical conversion disorder' as simply one extreme of a continuum that ranges from people with extensive disease but minimal or no problems (for example, large areas of cerebral infarction but no symptoms or disabilities) to people who have minimal disease but are severely 'disabled'. In other words, disability may follow from a mixture of pathological, structural abnormalities within cells or organs, causing functional abnormalities, and psychological abnormalities that are best considered as abnormal functioning of the whole person in the absence of any specific structural abnormality. Hysterical conversion disorder arises primarily from psychological malfunction.

Consequently, this model would predict that individuals will not fall into one of two groups with either all or none of their disability explained by their disease. Instead, the model predicts that patients will have varying proportions of their disability (or handicap) explained by their pathology.

Thirdly, the model predicts that people with similar clinical presentations may have different underlying causes and mechanisms to their disability. In patients where pathology is undoubtedly the prime cause (for example, stroke), poor gait and reduced mobility might follow from sensory loss, pain in the affected leg, motor loss, ataxia, neglect, or confusion. All these 'legitimate' impairments (that is, having a known neurophysiological explanation and basis) might culminate in a patient being in a wheelchair. A similar multitude of possible mechanisms might be available in patients where there is no underlying pathology. In patients in a wheelchair but without any pathology, important factors might include being able to fulfil a role as chairman of a local multiple sclerosis group, avoidance of the need to leave home and work, and being cared for by an important person.

Lastly, this model helps when considering treatment interventions. It allows the development of a classification for interventions, and this is discussed in more detail in the following text. The model also forces some consideration of the nature of any control intervention in research.

The placebo response is essentially the response of the person to the fact of being involved in or with an intervention and is manifested as a change in behaviour or impairment (or even pathology) without any specific cause. It is a significant factor. It is the inverse of hysterical conversion illness which is an illness (abnormality in behaviour or impairment) without any specific underlying pathology. It is quite possible that both are mediated through the medium of altered belief, although treatments will also involve other mechanisms.

In summary, this model may provide several important insights into hysterical conversion states and their rehabilitation. First, disability not explained by disease may be part of a spectrum and may manifest in many ways. Second, any particular clinical state may arise in a large number of ways. It is therefore unrealistic to anticipate either collecting a homogenous group of patients to study or to anticipate that a single intervention will be successful even in a group of apparently homogenous patients. Lastly, the placebo response to treatment may give some insight into the nature of hysterical illness in some people.

Defining the condition

The ICIDH–2 model allows for the existence and identification of illnesses where the observed (or experienced) impairments (symptoms and signs) and/or disabilities (activities, behaviour) are not caused by any (known/proven) underlying pathology (disease). These illnesses are also known by other names such as 'functional somatic syndromes' (Barsky and Borus, 1999), and it is likely that a wide variety of illnesses with many different labels fall into this category (Wesseley *et al.*, 1999). Hysterical conversion disorders fall into this group of illnesses.

Traditionally, hysterical conversion states are often defined by reference to two additional features. First, that there should be some obvious gain for the patient ('secondary gain'), usually at the level of social role or position for the patient. Quite apart from the difficulty in proving such a secondary gain, this requirement assumes that a specific causal model explains hysterical conversion disorder whereas, as has been argued in this chapter, it is probable that there are many 'causes'. Second, and less common, the speed of onset may be used to define hysterical conversion — the beginning of the illness is usually sudden and related to some identifiable stress. Again, in part this assumes a particular causal model. More generally, the speed of onset may or may not be a useful sub-classification.

Additionally, hysterical conversion disorder has been regarded as 'unconscious' in the sense that the patient is not consciously or deliberately feigning. In this chapter it is assumed that there is no method whereby this can be unequivocally proven, either in general or in a specific patient. Clinically, we have to assume that the patient is not malingering, although it seems likely that there is a mixture of 'knowing exaggeration' and 'unconsciously determined experience' in most patients. The exaggeration may be to ensure that the doctor (or other person) takes the situation seriously or, more explicitly, to achieve some desired goal.

The primary, unresolved question is whether hysterical conversion disorders form an identifiable, separate category of illness within the overall group of non-organic illness, or whether they are all essentially one illness. There is no evidence to support separation (for example, observed different prognosis, proven differential response to specific treatments). In clinical practice there is great overlap between the many supposedly different syndromes (Barsky and Borus, 1999; Wessely *et al.*, 1999). There are no theoretically sound reasons for expecting separate syndromes. Consequently, one should consider all 'medically unexplained illnesses' to be similar until proven otherwise. (In this context, medically unexplained illness is one where a positive diagnosis has been made that the illness does not have any underlying pathology, and it should not be confused with medically undiagnosed illness where no cause is yet known but there is no evidence to support a 'non-organic' cause. Patients often believe they have an undiagnosed illness.)

Defining the treatment

All patients who interact with the health care system in any setting and at any level experience many processes that could have an effect upon their illness: history taking, formal hands-on assessment, casual chatting and more formal emotional support, more or less invasive investigations, information giving, minor problem solving, interactions with several or many people, and so on. Any or all may have a beneficial effect, as the power of the so-called 'placebo response' testifies. Consequently, with the obvious exception of specific drug treatment and specific surgical operations, it is naturally difficult to define or describe in great detail the specific treatment given to patients in most health care settings.

The problem of describing non-pharmacological or non-surgical interventions is a general one, not yet well solved. This especially applies in rehabilitation (Wade, 1998). However, it is possible to give reasonable detail about some interventions (Shapiro and Teasell, 1997).

The WHO ICIDH–2 model in Fig. 23.1 allows the development of at least one way of describing interventions. They can be considered in relation to the component of the model they may alter. This is illustrated in Table 23.3 which is, at present, speculative, not least because investigators and clinicians rarely report explicitly what they expect to alter within the ICIDH–2 model.

Table 23.3 shows domains within the ICIDH–2 model that various interventions probably affect directly. Obviously any intervention may well have secondary effects (or otherwise it would not be tried), but Table 23.3 tries to identify the areas most likely to be directly affected. Even this is difficult, and any particular intervention may well have an effect on several potential areas. The use of functional electrical stimulation (FES), for example, might alter beliefs (by showing that movement is possible), might reduce perceived disability (by allowing the patient to walk), might alter family expectations, and so on. It is unlikely that FES will alter the disease label used by the patient, and in fact it could re-enforce the label if FES is usually used for patients with that disease.

The area that is targeted in any particular patient will or should be the one thought most important and most amenable to the treatments available. In nearly all patients it is likely that several areas will be targeted. The table also emphasizes the adverse effects of continuing medical investigations and treatments.

It is clear that none of the accepted treatment regimes pay much attention to the patient's satisfaction with their social role functioning associated with the illness or to the adverse effect of the benefits available from social institutions. This is a significant omission.

This scheme for considering and classifying interventions is put forward here for discussion and trial. It may or may not be useful and practical.

Table 23.3 The domains within the ICIDH–2 model that might be directly affected by some interventions. (See text for explanation.)

	Disease label	Symptoms experienced	Satisfaction with role performance	Personal beliefs and expectations	Expectations and beliefs of family	Social supports available	Perceived disabilities
Intervention							
Functional electrical stimulation	0	+/-	0	++	++	0	+/-
Biofeedback	0	+/-	0	+++	0	0	0
Functional therapy	0	0	0	0	0	0	+++
Hypnosis	+/-	++	0	+	0	0	0
Strategic-behavioural intervention	0	0	+/-	+	++	+/-	+
Further investigation	+/-	0	0	—	—	0	0
Symptomatic treatment	-	+	0	-	-	0	0
Behavioural intervention	0	0	+	0	0	0	+
Cognitive behavioural therapy	+	+	+	+	0	0	+
Continued medical treatment	—	+/-	—	—	—	—	—

Key: speculative effect on overall illness

+, ++, +++   Positive influence towards less illness
+/-   Ambivalent influence
0   No effect on illness (no effect expected or intended)
-, --, ---   Negative influence, re-enforcing abnormal illness behaviour

Table 23.4 Some studies on treatment of somatoform disorder

Author	Cases and design	Treatment	Outcome & comment
Mayou *et al.*, 1997	RCT; 37 patients with chest pain with no cause and not symptom-free after simple reassurance	CBT	More improvement in CBT group at 3 months and 6 months
Lidbeck, 1997	RCT; general practice patients with somatization disorder; RCT with no treatment control	Short cognitive behavioural group therapy focussed on patient education and stress control	Significant improvement seen in treated group
Payne & Blanchard, 1995	RCT; 34 patients with irritable bowel syndrome; individual CBT, support group, or no treatment	Individualized cognitive therapy or a self-help support group	One CBT group showed benefits
Speckens *et al.*, 1995	RCT; 79 out-patients with medically unexplained symptoms	6–16 sessions of CBT or 'optimized medical care'	CBT group improved in almost all parameters measured
Bergdahl *et al.*, 1995	RCT; 30 patients with resistant burning mouth syndrome	CBT or attention/placebo	Pain reduced in CBT group

Key:
CBT   Cognitive behavioural therapy
RCT   Randomized controlled trial

The evidence — part two

If one accepts the argument that hysterical conversion syndromes are similar to other somatization disorders, then it is reasonable to consider the evidence for treatments applicable to those disorders. Five trials were taken from the Cochrane Library 1999, issue 4. They were identified using a search on 'somatoform disorders' (all three branches of the tree) and 'cognitive behavioural therapy'. Other searches did not identify further studies, although there may be some, and this is not a systematic review.

The studies are shown in Table 23.4. In essence, all show that intervening to alter various aspects of 'personal context' such as attitudes, knowledge, perceptions of symptoms and disabilities, and beliefs and expectations was effective in reducing disability. This intervention is usually described as cognitive behavioural therapy which can be considered a structured way of altering beliefs and increasing activity. This would suggest that the best single approach towards patients with hysterical conversion is to use a cognitive behavioural approach. However, the less rigorous other research would suggest that variations on this theme may be effective.

There is one important problem to be considered in relation to the published studies in Table 23.4 — all the trials have only included patients who have agreed with the fundamental premise that psychological intervention will help. In practice, many patients with hysterical conversion disorder specifically refute any suggestion that a psychological approach may help. Consequently, other approaches will be needed, perhaps using similar principles.

The way forward

The problem may be summarized as follows. Any illness (that is, situation where a person and/or those around the person acts in a way that is associated with a state of ill health in their society) may lead to or arise from changes at the level of **pathology** (the organ), **impairment** (the person), **disability/activity** (the person's goal-directed behaviour), or **handicap/participation** (the person's social position as perceived by self and others). Important contextual factors may impact on the specific features of any illness: the person's **own context** (attitudes, expectations, past experience), the person's **physical context** (objects and people acting as carers), and the person's **social context** (people, culture, laws, and so on). There is no reason to believe that all illness is initiated by or follows from primary pathology, and a systems analytic approach would predict the opposite — that some illness would arise at other levels.

This analysis suggests that hysterical conversion states have similar aetiological mechanisms to other somatoform disorders, such as chronic fatigue syndrome, irritable bowel syndrome, non-cardiac chest pain, and chronic pain disorders, and that similar mechanisms are at play in many illnesses. The primary initiating factor may be at any level, and the initiation and maintenance of the illness will often depend upon or be potentiated by other characteristics. Treatments need to be directed at either the initiating item (if that can be identified) or at one or more of the other facilitating or maintaining factors. It is unlikely that any one specific treatment will be effective in all cases. However, an analytic approach based on the model described in this chapter, followed by targeted interventions, may help.

This treatment approach or philosophy is the essence of any standard rehabilitation approach (Wade and de Jong, 2000). Rehabilitation is a problem-solving process with multiple interventions at different levels and in different places, as shown in Fig. 23.2, and it is based on an analysis of a person's illness using the ICIDH–2 model or some other model of illness. In hysterical illness, the treatments will need to be focussed more on the subjective aspects of the illness and less on the external aspects. However, treatments aimed at altering beliefs are already part of rehabilitation interventions for patients disabled secondary to definite pathology (Wade, 2000).

Conclusions

The question that now needs to be answered is as follows: 'Do patients who present with impairment and/or disability that is grossly inconsistent with known pathology, or where disability is grossly variable and/or inconsistent with apparent impairments, become consistently less dependent on support if managed pragmatically by a multidisciplinary team using a combination of behavioural, cognitive, and other rehabilitation approaches when compared with patients who are managed by current services?'

This will need a full-scale, randomized, controlled trial to be answered fully, but given the size of the problem it is well worth undertaking.

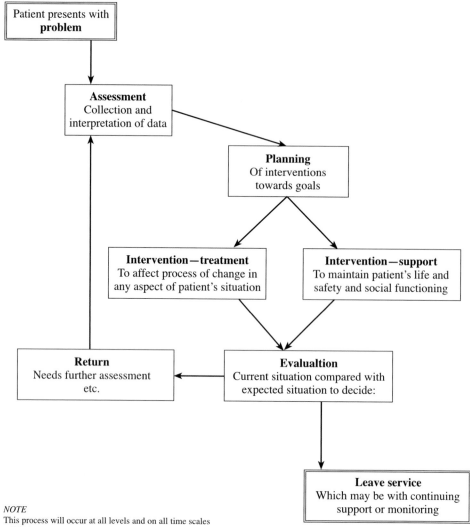

Fig. 23.2 The process of rehabilitation — the 'rehabilitation cycle'.

References

Antonelli, F., De Gregorio, M. and Dionisio, A. (1973). Trazodone in the treatment of psychoneuroses: a double-blind study. *Current Therapeutic Research and Clinical Experience*, **15**, 799–804.

Badley, E. M. (1993). An introduction to the concepts and classifications of the 'International Classification of Impairments, Disabilities, and Handicaps'. *Disability and Rehabilitation*, **15**, 161–78.

Barsky, A. J. and Borus, J. F. (1999). Functional somatic syndromes. *Annals of Internal Medicine*, **130**, 910–21.

Bergdahl, J., Anneroth, G. and Perris, H. (1995). Cognitive therapy in the treatment of patients with resistant burning mouth syndrome: a controlled study. *Journal of Oral Pathology and Medicine*, **24**, 213–15.

Cardenas, D. D., Larson, J. and Egan, K. J. (1986). Hysterical paralysis in the upper extremity of chronic pain patients. *Archives of Physical Medicine and Rehabilitation*, **67**, 190–3.

Carson, A. J., Ringbauer, B., Stone, J., McKenzie, L., Warlow, C. and Sharpe, M. (2000). Do medically unexplained symptoms matter? A prospective cohort study of 300 new referrals to neurology outpatient clinics. *Journal of Neurology, Neurosurgery, and Psychiatry*, **68**, 207–10.

Casacchia, M. *et al.* (1989). A double-blind placebo-controlled study of alpiderm, a novel anxiolytic of imidazopyridine structure in chronically anxious patients. *Acta Psychiatrica Scandinavica*, **80**, 137–41.

Chistoni, G. C. (1971). Some problems posed by double-blind investigation of psychotropic drugs: clinical trial of Nobrium Roche. *Schweiz Arch Neurol Neurochir Psychiatr*, **108**, 309–15.

Cloquette, R. (1974). Double-blind trial treatment of anxiety with b 5833. *Acta Psychiatrica Belgica*, **74**, 317–26.

Couprie, W., Wijdicks E. F. M., Rooijmans, H. G. M. and van Gijn, J. (1995). Outcome in conversion disorder: a follow-up study. *Journal of Neurology, Neurosurgery, and Psychiatry*, **58**, 750–2.

Daie, N. and Witztum, E. (1991). Short-term strategic treatment in traumatic conversion reactions. *American Journal of Psychotherapy*, **45**, 335–47.

Deary, I. J. and Wilson, J. A. (1994). Problems in treating globus pharyngis. *Clinical Otolaryngology*, **19**, 55–60.

Delargy, M. A., Peatfield, R. C. and Burt, A. A. (1986). Successful rehabilitation in conversion paralysis. *British Medical Journal*, **292**, 1730–1.

Fishbain, D. A. *et al.* (1988). The utility of electromyographic biofeedback in the treatment of conversion paralysis. *American Journal of Psychiatry*, **145**, 1572–5.

Hafeiz, H. B. (1980). Hysterical conversion: a prognostic study. British Journal of Psychiatry, **136**, 548–51.

Kelesidis, G., Hagis, P. and Samaras, C. (1972). Treatment of psychoneurotic conversion reactions with pindolol. (Effect on cardio-vasculaar response to exercise). *Indian Heart Journal*, **Suppl 1**, 238–43.

Khalil, T. M., Addel-Moty, E., Asfour, S. S., Fishbain, D. A., Rosomoff, R. S. and Rosomoff, H. L. (1988). Functional electrical stimulation in the reversal of conversion disorder paralysis. *Archives of Physical Medicine and Rehabilitation*, **69**, 545–7.

Krull, F. and Schifferdecker, M. (1990). Inpatient treatment of conversion disorder: a clinical investigation of outcome. *Psychotherapy and Psychosomatics*, **53**, 161–5.

Lidbeck, J. (1997). Group therapy for somatisation disorders in general practice: effectiveness of a short cognitive-behavioural treatment model. *Acta Psychiatrica Scandinavica*, **96**, 14–24.

Mayou, R. A., Bryant, B. M., Sanders, D., Bass, C., Klimes, I. and Forfar, C. (1997). A controlled trial of cognitive behavioural therapy for non-cardiac chest pain. *Psychological Medicine*, **27**, 1021–31.

Moene, F. C., Hoogduin, K. A. and Van Dyck, R. (1998). The inpatient treatment of patients suffering from (motor) conversion symptoms: a description of eight cases. *International Journal of Clinical and Experimental Hypnosis*, **46**, 171–90.

Payne, A. and Blanchard, E. B. (1995). A controlled comparison of cognitive therapy and self-help support groups in the treatment of irritable bowel syndrome. *Journal of Consulting and Clinical Psychology*, **63**, 779–86.

Pernhaupt, G. and Quatember, R. (1970). Psychopharmacologic contribution to the clinical use of a psychosedative. *Wien Med Wochenschr*, **120**, 737–40.

Puhakka, H. J. and Kirveskari, P. (1988). Globus hystericus: globus syndrome? *Journal of Laryngology and Otology*, **102**, 231–4.

Scallet, A., Clininger, C. R. and Othmer, E. (1976). The management of chronic hysteria: a review and double-blind trial of electrosleep and other relaxation methods. *Diseases of the Nervous System*, **37**, 347–53.

Shapiro, A. P. and Teasell, R. W. (1997). Strategic-behavioural intervention in the inpatient rehabilitation of non-organic (factitious/conversion) motor disorders. *Neurological Rehabilitation*, **8**, 183–92.

Silver, F. W. (1996). Management of conversion disorder. *American Journal of Physical Medicine and Rehabilitation*, **75**, 134–40.

Sinel, M. and Eisenberg, M. S. (1990). Two unusual gait disturbances: astasia abasia and camptocormia. *Archives of Physical Medicine and Rehabilitation*, **71**, 1078–80.

Soskin, R. A. (1973). The use of LSD in time-limited psychotherapy. *Journal of Nervous and Mental Disease*, **157**, 410–19.

Speed, J. (1996). Behavioural management of conversion disorder: a retrospective study. *Archives of Physical Medicine and Rehabilitation*, **77**, 147–54.

Speckens, A. E., van Hemert, A. M., Spinhoven, P., Hawton, K. E., Bolk, J. H. and Rooijmans, H. G. (1995). Cognitive behavioural therapy for medically unexplained symptoms: a randomised controlled trial. *British Medical Journal*, **311**, 1328–32.

Uhlenhuth, E. H., Stephens, J. H., Dim, B. H. and Covi, L. (1972). Diphenylhydantoin and phenobarbital in the relief of psychoneurotic symptoms. A controlled comparison. *Psychopharmacologia*, **27**, 67–84.

Wade, D. T. (1996). Epidemiology of disabling neurological disease: how and why does disability occur? *Journal of Neurology, Neurosurgery, and Psychiatry*, **61**, 242–9.

Wade, D. T. (1998). A framework for considering rehabilitation interventions. *Clinical Rehabilitation*, **12**, 363–8.

Wade, D. T. (2000). Personal context as a focus for rehabilitation. *Clinical Rehabilitation*, **14**, 115–18.

Wade, D. T. (Forthcoming). Disability, rehabilitation, and spinal injury. In: *Brain's Diseases of the Nervous System* (11th edn) (ed. Donaghy M), Chapter 6. Oxford University Press, Oxford.

Wade, D. T. and De Jong, B. A. (2000). Recent advances in rehabilitation. *British Medical Journal*, **320**, 1385–1358.

Watanabe, T. K., O'Dell, M. W. and Togliatti, T. J. (1998). Diagnosis and rehabilitation strategies for patients with hysterical hemiparesis: a report of four cases. *Archives of Physical Medicine and Rehabilitation*, **79**, 709–14.

Weiser, H. I. (1976). Motor and sensory dysfunction of upper limb due to conversion syndrome. *Archives of Physical Medicine and Rehabilitation*, **57**, 17–19.

Wessely, S., Nimnuan, C. and Sharpe, M. (1999). Functional somatic syndromes: one or many? *Lancet*, **354**, 936–9.

White, A., Corbin, D. O. C. and Coope, B. (1988). The use of thiopentone in the treatment of non-organic locomotor disorders. *Journal of Psychosomatic Research*, **32**, 249–53.

Withrington, R. H. and Wynn Parry, C. B. (1985). Rehabilitation of conversion paralysis. *Journal of Bone and Joint Surgery*, **67**, 635–7.

World Health Organisation (1999). *ICIDH–2: International Classification of Functioning and Disability. Beta-2 Draft.* WHO, Geneva. (Also on internet web page: < http://www.who.int/msa/mnh/ems/icidh/ >).

Index

abreaction 30, 291
'abreactive attacks' 144–5
'action dystonia' 240
actions
    attention to 238–9
    disavowal of 241–2
    hysterical paralyses as disorders of 239
    and intentions 239–40
        neuroimaging 223–4, 245–6, 247
    see also motor system, functional anatomy;
        movement disorders
acute stage
    outcomes 275–6
    psychological management 302
adoption studies, somatization 52–3
age regression 319, *320–1*
    case study 324–5
agency and its disorders 263–5
alcohol withdrawal 300
alcoholism 52–3
American Psychiatric Association 8
    see also DSM
amnesia
    and cognitive dysfunction 116–17
    dissociative 175–6, 179–80
    fugue states 152, 177, 258
    non-epileptic seizures 147, 151–2
anaesthesia, *see* sensory disturbance
anger 308
anorexia nervosa 294
anterior cingulate cortex 198, 199, 227–8, 230,
    245
    'stroop effect' 223, 228
    Tourette's syndrome 229
anticonvulsant drugs 150, 151
antidepressant drugs 58–9
anxiety disorders
    and non-epileptic seizures 150
    and somatization 52–3
    war-related 21
aphonia, *see* dysphonia
arc en cercle 144–5
arctic hysteria 258–9
attention
    hysteria as, neglect 195–6
    neurobiological correlates 197–8
    neuroimaging studies 198–9
    neurophysiological studies
        early 193–4
        P330 194–5
    relevance of laterality 195–7
    selective 179

shifts 193–4
    to action 238–9
attributions, role of 309
'auto-suggestive disorders' 313

Balinese trance experiences 260–3
behavioural analysis 303–4
behavioural interventions 307
    in hypnosis 322–4
behavioural responses, chronic stage 300–1
'belle indifference' 7, 289
    critiques 64, 108–9
blindness
    hypnotic 205–6, 209
    neurophysiological studies 194–5, 198
    outcomes 279, 302
    social factors 210
    war-related
        Epizelos 38–40, 42–4, 46
        First World War 38–9
body
    conceptions and practices 260–3
    ethnophysiological ideas 257
    as medium of communication 259, 266–7
    pathological disruption 288
    and social structure 261
borderline personality disorder 293, 295
Breuer, J. and Freud, S. 173, 174, 283
Briquet's syndrome 8, 9
    see also somatization disorder (SD)
*Burke v Royal Infirmary of Edinburgh NHS
    Trust* 163

cardiac disorders 22–3
case ascertainment 75
case definition 73–5
catharsis, *see* abreaction
cerebellum 221, 226, 227, 229
CFS, *see* chronic fatigue syndrome
'challenge', as contextual measure 94–5, 99
Charcot, J.M. 143, 177
    and Freud 4, 5, 185, 217–18, 231
    hypnotism 174, 290
    'ovarian hyperaesthesia' 108
childhood aetiology 99, 300
    factitious disorders 131
    see also Freud, S.; object relations approach
children
    acute conversion 302
    outcome 278, 279
chronic fatigue syndrome (CFS) 257, 301

chronic stage 300–1
  outcomes 276
  psychological management 302–9
classification systems 6–7, 62–3, 76, 253
  and clinical practice 64–8
  early military 15, 16–22
  proposed revision 68–9
  unsatisfactory 69
  validity of criteria 63–4
  see also DSM; ICD-10; ICIDH–2 modified
     model; Temperament and Character
     Inventory (TCI)
cognitive behavioural model 299–302
cognitive behavioural therapy 302–10
  acute stages 302
  chronic stage 302–9
    treatment phases 303–9
  and hypnosis 319, 320
  self-directedness 59
  somatoform disorders 342
  special issues 309–10
cognitive dysfunction
  and amnesia 116–17
  malingered 137–8
    assessment strategies 138
cognitive processing 193–4
  P300 195
  see also hypnosis, cognitive processing model
comorbidity
  physical disease 106–7, 130, 273–4
  psychiatric 106, 150–1, 241
    prognosis 276–8
confabulation 129
'conflict over speaking out' (CSO) 94–5
confrontational approaches 133–4
conscious experience, neurobiological
    correlates 197–8
conversion
  and dissociation 172–5
  and malingering 135–6, 138–9
  and somatization 178–9
    and hypochondriasis 287–9
    personality factors 54–6
  symptomatic groups 8
  terminology 1–2, 6–7, 73–5
  see also doxomorphic disorder; Ferriar, J.;
    Freud, S.; medically unexplained
    symptoms
cortico-fugal inhibitory pathways 193–4
cowardice and fear 15–16
  execution for desertion 19
creative imagery 322–4
criminality 52, 53
Cross-National Study of Mental Disorders in
    Primary Care (WHO) 255
CSO, see 'conflict over speaking out'
culture
  cross-cultural prevalence 255–6, 293–4
  influences 209–11, 251–2
    agency and its disorders 263–5
    and dissociation 259–62

    shaping of somatic distress 256–9
    tolerance of memory and awareness
      gaps 264–5
  social structure 261, 262–3
  -specific sick-role behaviour 53–4

DAH (disordered action of the heart) 22–3
deafness 115–16, 194
'death feint' 178
deception 129, 235–6
  see also self-deception
'depersonalization–derealization' 152, 180
  and military bravery 20–1
depression 150
  and hysteria 83, 255–6
  and life events 91, 93, 94
  and memory loss 176
descriptive–syndromal approach 74–5
developing countries 82–3, 255–6, 257, 258–9
  epidemic hysteria 210–11, 257–8
diagnosis 73–5
  clinical practice 64–8
  factitious disorders 126–8
  non-epileptic seizures 146, 147
  psychiatric 7, 8
  see also classification systems
Diagnostic and Statistical Manual, see DSM
differential diagnosis 50–2
  hysteria, factitious disorder and
    malingering 138–9
  neurology 119
  non-epileptic seizures 147–53
  somatization and anxiety disorders 52–3
disordered action of the heart (DAH) 22–3
dissociation
  clinical patterns of 175–8
  and culture 259–62
  expansion of 179–80
  information processing metaphors 263–4
  and military bravery 20–1
  non-epileptic seizures 151–2
  phenomena
    clusters 262
    settings of 259–60
  and repression 174, **175**, 176, 177
  see also doxomorphic disorders
Dissociative Experiences Scale 179, 180
dissociative vs. somatoform disorders 62, 63, 65, 74
DLPFC, see dorsolateral prefrontal cortex
doctor–patient relationship 65, 67–8
  factitious disorders 131, 132–4
dorsolateral prefrontal cortex (DLPFC)
  dysfunction 245
  'feigned paralysis' 245–6, 247
  role in volition 226, 227, 229–30, 243, 244
doxomorphic disorders 171–2, 180–1
drug(s)
  -induced symptoms 176–7
  movement disorders 239
  sensory disorders 193
  treatment of war-related hysteria 30, 31

'truth drugs' in diagnosis 117
DSM-III 52, 178, 253
DSM-III-R 65, 312
DSM-IV 8, *63*, 68, 179–80, 298, 312–13
    development of criteria 53–4
    dissociative and somatoform disorders 62, 65, 74
    factitious disorders 127
    inconsistency of symptoms 167
    malingering 135
    psychological factors 235
    somatization disorder 53, 56, 59
duty of care 162, 164–5
dysphonia 94–5, 116
    case study 324–5
dystonia 111–12

ecological niche for illness 258
'effort after meaning' 89
'effort syndrome' 23
electroencephalography (EEG) 218–19
    Bereitschaftpotential 112
    non-epileptic seizures 148–9, 149, 151
electrotherapy (ECT) 30, 31, 45
emotions, inadmissible 4–5
    see also repression
epidemic hysteria 210–11, 257–8
epidemiology 73–87
    case ascertainment 75
    case definition 73–5
    defining target population 75–6
    ethnicity 82–3
    factitious disorders 130–1
    sex ratios 81–2
    systematic review 76–83
        method 76
        results 77–83
        summary and conclusions 83–5
    see also incidence; prevalence
ethical issues 132–3
ethnicity 82–3, 293–4
evacuation syndromes 18
evoked potential studies 193–4
    P300 194–6
    transcranial magnetic stimulation 118
exaggeration of symptoms 135, 136, 155

face-saving 242, 321, 322
factitious disorders (FD) 126–34
    aetiology 131–2
        neurological abnormalities 131–2
    clinical features 130
        physical comorbidity 130
    course and prognosis 132
    diagnostic issues 126–8
    epidemiology 130–1
    ethical and legal issues 132–3
    and malingering 138–9
    management 133–4, 139–40
    pathological lying (pseudologia fantastica)
        128–30, 132

Falklands War 25–6
family
    influences 99, 150, 210, 262
    information from 107
    role in therapy 310, 324–5
FD, *see* factitious disorders
fear paralysis 178
    see also cowardice and fear
feigning 236, 245–6, *247*
        see also factitious disorders; malingering
Ferriar, J. 2, 184–5
First World War
    cowardice and fear 15–16
    diagnosis of officers/enlisted men 19, 20, 21, 37
    disorders of vision 39
    execution for desertion 19
    psychodynamic perspective 285–6, 287
    syndromes 18–19, 21, 22–3
    treatments 30
    see also shell-shock; war-related hysteria
Freud, S.
    and Breuer 173, 174, 283
    conversion theory 3, 185–6, 284–5, 294
        background 3–5
        legacy 6–8
        and neuroscientific accounts 217–18, 221,
            231
    Oedipal theory 291
    on repression 174, 175, 284–5
    on somatoform disorders 189
    therapeutic methods 285
frontal cortex 198–9, 219–20, 221, 222
see also orbito-frontal cortex; prefrontal cortex
fugue states 152, 177, 258
'functional' disorder concept 4
    and threat 91–8

gait disorders 112–13
    children 278
gastrointestinal disorders, LEDS study 91–2, 99
gender
    factitious disorders 130
    hypnotic sex change 207–8, 209
    rates of relapse 273
    ratios 81–2
    social protest 43, 258–9
    somatization disorder 51, 52–3
    see also war-related hysteria; women
globus pharyngis 116
    LEDS study 92–3
    outcomes 279
group psychotherapy 30–1, 322
guilt 288–9
Gulf War 26
Gulf War syndrome 23, 26

head injuries 149–50, 176
hemineglect syndromes 195–7
hemiparesis 109, 110
hemisensory disturbance 114, 115

Herodotus 38, 39–40, 41, 46
historical background 1–2
  ancient Greece
    medical tradition 36–7, 172
    war neurosis 38–44, 46
  and contemporary concepts 9
  conversion and dissociation 172–5
  hypnosis 203–4
  non-epileptic seizures 143
  psychodynamic theories 184–5
  treatments 43–5
  see also Ferrier, J.; First World War; Freud, S.;
    Second World War
Hoover's sign 109
hypnosis
  cognitive processing model 314–17, 325–6
    treatment implications 317–19
  and hysteria
    comparisons 173–4, 205–8, 290, 313–14
    models 211–12, 314–17, 325–6
  -induced anaesthesia 195, 197
  influences and interactions 203–4, 208–11
  psychodynamic therapy 285, 290, 319, *320–1*
    case study 324–5
  treatment outcomes 322
  treatment studies 319–27
    common features 325–6
    multi-case 321–2
    single-case 322–5
  war-related hysteria 30, 31
hypnotizability 204, 207–8
hypochondriasis
  cognitive responses 301
  psychosomatic disorders and hysteria 287–9
hysterical personality
  clinical example 289–90, 292
  psychodynamic view 186–7, 292–3

ICD-10 179, 180
  feigning vs. hysteria 236
  life events 106
  malingering 135
  psychosocial factors 235
ICIDH–2 modified model 330–1, 335–9
  defining condition 339–40
  defining treatment 340–2
identity distortion 207–8, 209
illness beliefs 107
imaging, *see* neuroimaging
impostership 129
incidence 82–4
  clinical population 79–80
  general population 77
  non-epileptic seizures 146
India 82–3, 255–6
'instinctive flurry' 178
insurance assessment 309
intentions
  and actions 239–40
    neuroimaging 223–4, 245–6, 247
  factitious disorders 126–8

pseudologica fantastica 128–30
International Classification of Disease, *see* ICD-10
International Classification of Impairments,
    Disabilities, and Handicaps, *see* ICIDH–2
    modified model

Janet, P. 173–4

Korean War 25
koro 257

latah 258
laterality 104
  attentional–awareness system 195–7
  see also hemineglect syndromes; hemiparesis;
    hemisensory disturbance
LEDS, *see* Life Events and Difficulties Schedule
legal conception of hysteria 156–61
legal framework 161–8
  consequential vs. pure psychiatric harm 162–3,
    165
  defendant 161–2
  potential causal disparity 166–8
  primary vs. secondary victim 164–5
  sudden vs. gradual 163–4
  underlying considerations 158–61
legal issues
  attitudes to medical science developments
    159–60
  'blame' agenda 160–1
  exaggeration of symptoms 135, 136, 155
  factitious disorder 132–3
  malingering **136**, 150, 155
  policy and 'floodgates' fears 158–9
life events 106, 300
  methodological considerations 88–93
    measurement of meaning 90–1
    outcome and putative causes 88–90
    threat and 'functional illness' 91–8
Life Events and Difficulties Schedule (LEDS) 90
  studies 91, 92–6, 98
'loss of consciousness' 147
loss events 93, 94

McLoughlin v O'Brian 159
McWhinnie v British Coal Corporation 163, 167
Malawi 210–11
malingering 134–9
  cognitive deficits 137–8
    assessment strategies 138
  definition 135
  differential diagnosis 138–9
  legal issues 136, 150, 155
  military psychiatry 13, 26–7
  physical disease 135–6
    clinical assessment 137
  vs. factitious disorders 126, 127
masculine values 41–2, 46
mass hysteria 210–11, 257–8
medically unexplained symptoms

anthropological perspective 253–4, 255
neurological perspective 103–4
outcomes 275–6
war-related 22–3
memory loss, *see* amnesia; repression
military psychiatry, *see* war-related hysteria
mind–body dualism 45–6, **298–9**
mind–body relationship 235
modelling 300
symptom 106–7
modified insulin treatment 31
monoparesis 110
motor system
disorders, *see* movement disorders
functional anatomy 221–4
'signs' of hysteria 236, 237–8
movement disorders
neurological examination 109–10
neurophysiology 221
case study 224–7
and neuropsychology 223–4, 227–30
nocturnal limb movements 197
and psychiatric comorbidity 241
reconsideration of 230–1
treatment
case study 322–4
cognitive behavioural interventions *307*
see also actions
Munchausen's syndrome 131–2
'sub-type' 130
myoclonus 112

narrative practices 263
negligence claims 161–2
neurasthenia 21
diagnosis of officers 19, 21, 37
electrotherapy 30
neuroimaging
attention 198–9
intentions and actions 223–4, 245–6, 247
movement 221–4
case study 225–6
MRI 117
PET 199, 217, 221, 222
SPECT 198–9, 219–20
neurological disease 106–7, 131–2, 176, 273–4
neurology 102–25
clinical approach 104–18
differential diagnosis 119
examination 107–17
history 105–7
illustrative cases 118–19
investigations 117–18
diagnostic practices 65, 68
early accounts 3–4, 7, 9, 217–18
explanations offered to patients 120
incident rates among patients *80*
outcomes 278–9
prevalence of unexplained symptoms 103–4
and psychiatry 1–2, 66
treatment role 120–1

see also non-epileptic seizures
neuroscientific accounts
associated brain areas 218–19
volition 242–5
see also specific areas
early 217–18
and personality 57, *58*
see also attention; movement disorders,
neurophysiology
non-confrontational strategies 134
non-epileptic seizures 143–54
associated psychiatric conditions 150–1
children 278
clinical features 144–5
differential diagnosis 147–53
incidence 146
investigations 152–3
medical disorders mistaken for epilepsy *148*
placebos 117
precipitating factors 300
seizure phenomenology 147
terminology 145–6
nostalgia 16–18

object relations approach 187–8
'depressive position' 288–9, 293
therapy 286–7, 294
occupational stress 164
Oedipal theory of neurosis 291
clinical example 291–2
'openness to absorbing experiences' 262
orbito-frontal cortex 223, 227–8, 229, 230
see also frontal cortex; prefrontal cortex
outcomes, *see* prognosis; rehabilitation

P300 194–5
Page v Smith 159–60
pain
abdominal 91–2, 99
back injuries 163, 167
chronic 301
and malingering 136
regional 172
paralysis, *see* actions; movement disorders
parietal cortex 198–9, 219, 220, 226
parietal neglect 195–6
Parkinson's disease (PD) 112, 239–40
pathological lying (pseudologia fantastica, PF)
128–30, 132
patients
anger 308
expectations 179
of cure 44–5
'influence of the idea' 203–4
whiplash injuries 136
explanations offered to 120, 321
medical history 105–7, 147–9, 150
neurological *80*, 103, 272–3
psychiatric *80*, 82–3, 272–3
stigmatization 252, 254, 257, 309

PD (Parkinson's disease) 112, 239–40
personal relationships 92, 99
   see also childhood aetiology; family
personality disorder 277, 294, 295
   borderline 293, 295
personality factors, *see* Temperament and Character
   Inventory (TCI)
PET, *see* positron emission tomography
PF, *see* pseudologia fantastica
physical disease
   comorbidity 106–7, 130, 273–4
   and diagnostic criteria for hysteria 63–4
   and malingering 135–6
      clinical assessment 137
   neurological 106–7, 131–2, 176, 273–4
   as precipitating factor 300
physiological responses 301
physiotherapy 307, 322
pibloktoq (arctic hysteria) 258–9
Pickford v Imperial Chemical Industries plc 166–7
placebos 45, 117, 338
positron emission tomography (PET) 199, 217, 221,
   222
post-conflict/war syndromes 23
post-traumatic stress disorder (PTSD) 180
   and non-epileptic seizures 152
   personal injury claims 159, 160, 161, 162,
      163–4
prefrontal cortex 132, 196, *247*
   see also dorsolateral prefrontal cortex
      (DLPFC)
prevalence 82–3, 293–4
   cross-cultural 255–6
   cultural factors 260–1, 266
   general population rates 77–8
primary gain 186, 287
prognosis 271–82
   acute symptoms 275–6
   children 278, 279
   chronic symptoms 276
   factitious disorders 132
   follow-up studies
      early 272–4
      recent 274–8
   health care costs 279
   psychiatric comorbidity 276–8
   referral patterns 280
   specific symptoms 278–9
   summary and conclusions 280
projection 292–3
pseudologia fantastica (PF) 128–30, 132
'pseudoseizures' 145
psychiatric comorbidity 106, 150–1, 241
   prognosis 276–8
psychiatric diagnosis, *see* classification
   systems
psychiatric harm 156–61
   see also legal framework; legal issues
psychiatric patients *80*, 82–3, 272–3
psychiatric referrals 79, *81*, 280
psychiatry and neurology 1–2, 66

psychodynamic theories 186–9
   clinical example 253–90
   contribution of 189–90
   conversion model 253, 285–6
      and neuroscience 219, 238, 239
   psychosomatic disorders and
      hypochondriasis 287–9
   see also Freud, S.
psychodynamic therapy
   abreaction 30, 291
   evidence base for 294–5
   hypnosis in 285, 290, 319, *320–1*
      case study 324–5
   limitations of 292–3
   psychoanalysis 6–8
   'uncovering' 30–1, *320–1*
   see also object relations approach
psychological accounts 4–5, 7
   critique 63–4
   legal view 157–8
   war-related hysteria 177–8
psychosomatic disorders, *see* somatization disorder
   (SD); somatoform disorders
PTSD, *see* post-traumatic stress disorder

recovery 273
reflex responses 109–10
rehabilitation 331–5, 343
   cognitive behavioural therapy 342
   process *344*
   see also ICIDH–2 modified model
relapse rates 273
religious/ritual contexts 260, 261–2, 266
repression 284–5
   and dissociation 174, **175**, 176, 177
   inadmissible emotions 4–5
running wild 258–9

Schofield v National Coal Board 165–6
SD *see* somatization disorder
Second World War
   diagnosis 21–2, 23, 27, 28
   treatments 30–1
secondary gain
   critiques 7, 64, 298
   ethnographic perspective 261–2
   Freudian concept of 5, 186, 287
   LEDS study 96–8
   and litigation 106
   and prognosis 45
segmental exclusion syndromes 195–6
seizures, *see* non-epileptic seizures
self-deception 138–9, 140, 208–9
   and deception 241–2
   see also identity distortion
self-directedness, *see* Temperament and Character
   Inventory (TCI)
sensory disturbance 113–14
   hypnotically-induced 195, 197, **206–7**
   laterality 114, 115

neurophysiological studies 193–4, 195
sensory function of movement-related brain
    areas 219–20, 222
sex change, hypnotic 207–8, 209
sex ratios 81–2
sexual aetiology 3, 4, 42, 174
shell-shock 15, 19–20, 37, 44, 177–8
    and cowardice 16
    as disguised male protest 43
sleep
    continuous sleep treatment 31
    establishing routine 307–8
    nocturnal limb movements 197
sleep disorders
    mistaken for epilepsy *148*
    somnabulism 152
social perspective, *see* culture
social protest 43, 258–9
social role performance 258, 266
socioeconomic status 80
    diagnosis of officers/enlisted men 19, 20, 21, 37
    women 256, 258–9, 261–2
somatization disorder (SD) 8, 9
    adoption studies 52–3
    and conversion 178–9
        and hypochondriasis 287–9
        personality factors 54–6
    differential diagnosis 50–2, 66–7, 68
    and non-epileptic seizures 150–1
somatoform disorders
    cognitive behavioural therapy 342
    psychodynamic approach 188–9
    treatments *342*
    vs. dissociative disorders 62, 63, 65, 74
SPECT studies 198–9, 219–20
startle mechanism 152, 158
'states of mind' 264–5
stigmatization 252, 254, 257, 309
stress
    of military combat 13–15
    occupational 164
    see also life events; threat
Structured Interview for Dissociative
    Disorders 179–80
suggestion 7, 29, 178
    hypnotic 205–8, 290
    see also hypnosis
symptom modelling 106–7

Temperament and Character Inventory (TCI)
    54–6
    implications for treatment 57–9
    and neurobiology 57, *58*
terminology 1–2, 6–7, 73–5
    colloquial use 253
    neurological 102–3
    non-epileptic seizures 145–6
    willed action 237
therapeutic relationship 286, 292–3
    cognitive behavioural therapy 302, 304
    in hypnotism 290

see also transference
threat 91–8
    deconstructing 93–4
    and other contextual measures 94–8
Tourette's syndrome 229
trance experiences, Balinese 261–3
transcranial magnetic stimulation 118
transference 287, 293
    and counter-transference 286, 289
        in hypnotism 290
'transient mental illness' 257–8
treatments
    historical background 43–5
    ICIDH–2 modified model 340–2
    TCI model 57–9
    war-related hysteria 28–31, 32
    see also cognitive behavioural therapy; hypnosis;
        psychodynamic therapy
tremor 111

Victorian Railway Commissioners v Coultas 158
videotelemetry 137, 144, 148
Vietnam War 25, 30
violence 151
    'tantrums' 144
visual disturbances 114–15
    illustrative cases 118–19
    see also blindness

war-related hysteria 12–35
    blinding of Epizelos 38–40, 42–4, 46
    comparison *24*
    conflicts from 1945 25–6
    cowardice and fear 15–16
    medically unexplained syndromes 22–3
    military psychiatry 13
    post-conflict syndromes 23
    prevention 27–8, 31–2
    psychological syndromes 16–22
    soldiers' dilemmas 13–15
    treatment 28–31, 32
        at the front 28
        behind the front 28–9
        of causes ('uncoverers') 30–1
        current practice 31
        of symptoms ('coverers') 29–30
weakness 109–10
    see also movement disorders
westernized countries 156, 157, 265–6, 293–4
    legal processes 136
whiplash injuries 136, 137–8
White v Chief Constable of South Yorkshire 159,
    161
willed action 237–8
    disorders 236, 239
    neurological investigations 242–7
    see also actions
Williams v Department of the Environment 165
willingness to change 304–5
women 81–2, 253

depression and life events 94
dysphonia 94–5
gynaecological accounts 4
of low socioeconomic status 256, 258–9, 261–2
menstrual abnormalities 195
World Health Organization (WHO)

Cross-National Study of Mental Disorders in
  Primary Care 255
see also ICD-10; ICIDH

Yom Kippur War 25